Rule of Replacement

Commutation (Comm)
$(p \cdot q) \equiv (q \cdot p)$
$(p \lor q) \equiv (q \lor p)$

Double Negation (DN)
$p \equiv \sim\sim p$

DeMorgan's Law (DM)
$\sim(p \cdot q) \equiv (\sim p \lor \sim q)$
$\sim(p \lor q) \equiv (\sim p \cdot \sim q)$

Contraposition (Contra)
$(p \supset q) \equiv (\sim q \supset \sim p)$

Implication (Imp)
$(p \supset q) \equiv (\sim p \lor q)$

Repetition (Rep)
$p \equiv (p \lor p)$
$p \equiv (p \cdot p)$

Association (Assoc)
$(p \cdot (q \cdot r)) \equiv ((p \cdot q) \cdot r)$
$(p \lor (q \lor r)) \equiv ((p \lor q) \lor r)$

Distribution (Dist)
$(p \cdot (q \lor r)) \equiv ((p \cdot q) \lor (p \cdot r))$
$(p \lor (q \cdot r)) \equiv ((p \lor q) \cdot (p \lor r))$

Exportation (Exp)
$((p \cdot q) \supset r) \equiv (p \supset (q \supset r))$

Equivalency (Eq)
$(p \equiv q) \equiv ((p \supset q) \cdot (q \supset p))$

Quantifier Rules

Quantifier Exchange (QE):
$(x)\phi x \equiv \sim(\exists x)\sim\phi x \qquad \sim(x)\phi x \equiv (\exists x)\sim\phi x$
$(\exists x)\phi x \equiv \sim(x)\sim\phi x \qquad \sim(\exists x)\phi x \equiv (x)\sim\phi x$

Universal Instantiation (UI):
$(x)\phi x$ [Where the expression represented by 'ϕx' falls entirely within
$\therefore \phi\alpha$ the scope of '(x)']

Existential Generalization (EG):
$\phi\alpha$ [Where 'x' does not occur in 'α']
$\therefore (\exists x)\phi x$

Existential Instantiation (EI):
$(\exists x)\phi x$ [Where 'α' does not occur in '$(\exists x)\phi x$' nor in any statement
$\therefore \phi\alpha$ occurring earlier in a proof in which '$(\exists x)\phi x$' occurs]

Universal Generalization (UG):
$\phi\alpha$ [Where 'α' represents an individual which has been arbitrarily
$\therefore (x)\phi x$ chosen, and 'x' does not occur in '$\phi\alpha$']

INTRODUCTION
TO LOGIC

INTRODUCTION
TO LOGIC

Michael T. Carlsen-Jones
Eastern Michigan University

McGraw-Hill Book Company
New York St. Louis San Francisco Auckland Bogotá Hamburg
Johannesburg London Madrid Mexico Montreal New Delhi
Panama Paris São Paulo Singapore Sydney Tokyo Toronto

INTRODUCTION TO LOGIC

1234567890 HALHAL 89876543

ISBN 0-07-032890-0

This book was set in Palatino by Monotype Composition Company, Inc.
The editors were Rhona Robbin and James R. Belser;
the designer was Robin Hessel;
the production supervisor was Leroy A. Young.
The drawings were done by Danmark & Michaels, Inc.
Halliday Lithograph Corporation was printer and binder.

Library of Congress Cataloging in Publication Data

Carlsen-Jones, Michael T.
    Introduction to logic.

    Includes index.
    1. Logic. I. Title.
BC71.C36 1983   160   82-13980
ISBN 0-07-032890-0

For Christine,
David, and Karen

CONTENTS

To the Student   xi
To the Instructor   xiii

CHAPTER 1
LOGIC AND LANGUAGE   1
    1:1 The Subject Matter of Logic   1
    1:2 Recognizing Arguments   5
    1:3 Language   26
    Student Study Guide   43

CHAPTER 2
INDUCTION AND DEDUCTION   48
    2:1 Good and Bad Arguments   48
    2:2 Inductive Support and Deductive Support   53
    2:3 Symbolizing Arguments   64
    2:4 Validity and Soundness   73
    2:5 Counterexamples   80
    2:6 Analyzing Arguments   83
    Student Study Guide   84

CHAPTER 3
CONDITIONAL ARGUMENTS   89
    3:1 Conditional Statements   89
    3:2 The Connective 'Not'   91
    3:3 Various Ways of Writing Conditional Statements   93
    3:4 Four Forms of Conditional Arguments   98
    3:5 Complex Arguments   106
    3:6 Conditional Proofs   113
    3:7 *Reductio ad Absurdum* Proofs (Indirect Proofs)   121
    Student Study Guide   129

CHAPTER 4
TRUTH TABLES   134
    4:1 Logical Connectives   134
    4:2 Compound Statements with More Than One Connective   141
    4:3 Determining the Truth Values of Compound Statements   146
    4:4 Truth Tables   150
    4:5 The Truth-Table Test for Validity   163
    4:6 The Short Truth-Table Method   167
    Student Study Guide   174

CHAPTER 5
STATEMENT LOGIC   178
    5:1 Rules of Inference   179
    5:2 Proofs Using the Rules of Inference   188
    5:3 The Rule of Replacement   198
    5:4 Conditional Proof   222
    5:5 Indirect Proof   230
    5:6 Deriving Tautologies   237
    Student Study Guide   242

CHAPTER 6
CATEGORICAL ARGUMENTS   246
    6:1 Categorical Statements   247
    6:2 Categorical Statements in Ordinary Language   253
    6:3 Some Relationships among Categorical Statements   261
    6:4 Categorical Syllogisms   270
    6:5 Venn Diagrams   278
    6:6 Using Rules to Determine the Validity of Categorical Syllogisms   297
    Student Study Guide   307

CHAPTER 7
PREDICATE LOGIC   313
    7:1 Some Basic Concepts   314
    7:2 Symbolizing Quantified Statements   331
    7:3 Some Additional Rules   339
    7:4 Showing Invalidity   354
    7:5 Constructing Proofs   360
    Student Study Guide   369

CHAPTER 8
INDUCTIVE ARGUMENTS   374
    8:1 The Nature of Induction   374
    8:2 Inductive Argument Forms   375
    8:3 Some Thoughts on 'Probably' as a Relational Expression   385
    8:4 When Not to Accept the Conclusion of an Inductive Argument   387

8:5 Argument from Authority   398
8:6 Argument from Analogy   407
Student Study Guide   414

CHAPTER 9
HYPOTHESES AND MILL'S METHODS   418
9:1 Inductive Arguments and Hypotheses   418
9:2 The Hypothetico-Deductive Method   420
9:3 Causality   427
9:4 Complex Characteristics   434
9:5 Testing for Necessary Conditions   437
9:6 Testing for Sufficient Conditions   443
9:7 Testing for a Particular Sufficient Condition   449
9:8 Testing for Necessary and Sufficient Conditions   454
Student Study Guide   459

CHAPTER 10
INFORMAL FALLACIES   464
10:1 An Overview   464
10:2 Analyzing Arguments   465
10:3 Arguing against People, Not Positions   466
10:4 Arguing for (or against) the Wrong Position   476
10:5 Trying to Have It Both Ways   479
10:6 Making Things Easy—Making Things Hard   484
10:7 Causality   487
10:8 Playing on Emotions   494
Student Study Guide   499

Solutions Appendix   504
Index   565

TO THE STUDENT

This text has been organized and written for you. To get the most out of your course in logic, and out of this book, you should keep the following things in mind:

1. Logic is fun, but it does involve some work. In the text, that work is broken down into "bite-size" pieces, each of which is understandable. If you have questions about the material, bring them up in class. Also consider asking someone else who may understand what you are confused about—perhaps a friend who is in your class, your instructor, a teaching assistant, or a tutor.

2. Whenever you are given a reading assignment, do it as soon as possible. Each section of the text covers a small part of the whole of logic theory and its applications. Read that small part and do the exercises, and you should have no major difficulties with the course.

3. The text includes a great many exercises. When the time for examinations rolls around, you are going to be asked to work problems which are very much like those contained in the exercises. As a result, one of the most important ways to ensure your success in the course is to do the exercises and be sure that you understand why each problem is solved in the way that it is. The solutions to many of the problems are provided at the back of the text. If you do not understand what you are to do, check there to see what the answers look like, and then attack the problem.

4. All the kinds of arguments which are discussed in the text are worked out in step-by-step detail. If you are having difficulty with any exercise, turn back to the worked-out examples to see how those problems were solved. On the other hand, if you understand the basic concepts and how the exercises are worked, you need not read through all the sample arguments and problems discussed in the text. Instead, turn to the exercises, do them, check your answers in the back of the book, and, if you have done them correctly, celebrate.

5. There is a Student Study Guide at the end of each chapter. Included in this study guide is a Chapter Summary which lists all the important points raised in the chapter, along with references to the sections in which these points are discussed. If you do not understand any of the summary remarks, reread the full discussions in the text.

6. Also included in the study guide is a list of key terms—important concepts which you should understand. I suggest that you first provide, in your own words, an explanation of each of these terms. Then check the Chapter Summary to see if you do understand the terms. If not, reread the sections in which the terms are explained. You may also find it helpful to check the index; the page number given in boldface indicates where the term or expression is defined or explained in detail.

7. Each study guide also contains a Self-Test/Exercise section whose questions and problems cover much of the material discussed in the chapter. It is unlikely that any examination will cover all the problems in this section, but if you can do those problems and understand what you are doing you should have no difficulty with exams. The answers to all the self-test problems are included in the back of the text. If you make a mistake in any of these problems, check the section of the text where its subject is discussed. To help you refer back, section numbers are included with the problems and questions.

Use the text to get the most that you can out of your introduction to logic. Keep up with the course by doing the reading and the exercises, ask questions when you are confused or do not understand what is going on, and, most of all, enjoy!

Michael T. Carlsen-Jones

TO THE INSTRUCTOR

This text is designed to be used in a one-semester terminal course in logic, although it will serve very well in any course which is a prerequisite for advanced work in logic. Additionally, if all the chapters are covered in detail, the text may be used in a two-semester sequence of courses; however, in that case you may wish to supplement the material with additional readings on logic theory and induction.

Most introductory logic texts available today tend to fall into either of two groups: those which emphasize formal logic and symbolism and those which emphasize "good reasoning." Those in the former group tend toward a more systematic approach, with an emphasis on proof and rigor. With such an approach the text often does not contain sufficient explanations of key concepts, students are often unable to apply the material and techniques discussed to new and different situations, and students often leave the course feeling that the material discussed was somewhat interesting but not of much value. Texts in the latter group tend to miss in the other direction: At the conclusion of the course most students have gained very little understanding of logical systems or appreciation for the power and usefulness of such systems. They may come away with the feeling that logic is a "shotgun" approach to the analysis of arguments, retaining little knowledge of logic theory or organizational principles which might be used to analyze other arguments.

This text is aimed between these two approaches, although admittedly with more of a traditional emphasis on theory, the development of logical techniques, and the recognition and evaluation of the structure, or form, of arguments. An effort has been made throughout the text to show that the theories and techniques are applicable to a wide range of arguments and to develop the student's ability to recognize arguments and determine which techniques are appropriate for their analysis. The rationale for this approach, and the steps which have been taken to achieve it, are as follows:

1. Almost no students come to a logic course with any background at all in logic, and many come with rather weak quantitative skills. Moreover, a large percentage of such students identify logic with mathematics and, as a result, are initially inclined to be intimidated by logic.

I have attempted to write a text which is easy to read and not intimidating, a major portion of which is devoted to explanations of the basic concepts in logic, followed first by examples of the concepts and then by exercises that allow students to work with the concepts. Moreover, reference is continually made to these concepts so that they become second nature to the students. Because concepts are introduced in this way, and not in a barrage, students quickly see that logic need not be intimidating, is comprehensible, and does have application to at least some of their concerns.

> 2. Logic is a rigorous discipline, and any text which gives the contrary impression has not succeeded in providing an introduction to *logic*, whatever other virtues the text might have.

As a result, this text does emphasize formal concepts and procedures. It does so, however, by introducing new concepts and techniques only when they are needed, and typically by introducing new problems or arguments which cannot be handled with the concepts already discussed. Logical notation is not treated as an end in itself, but as a means of simplifying the task of analyzing arguments. This approach has the advantage of treating both theory and technique as a natural and easily understood extension of problems and arguments already discussed.

> 3. "Doing logic" ultimately reduces to a form of problem-solving, and, given the goal of improving the analytical skills of students, a good text should help students to "do logic."

To meet this need, more than 250 examples and arguments are discussed in detail throughout the text. More than one-third of these are presented in step-by-step fashion, with explanations of both how and why the steps are performed. This approach provides something not found in any other text: guidelines and suggestions, along with specific examples, of how to analyze arguments. In using portions of the text in my own course, I have found that I no longer hear comments like, "I understand the problems when you do them in class, but when I try to do them myself, I don't know what to do."

> 4. Logic should be, and is, fun. But it is fun for students only when they feel they are on the right path every step of the way.

The step-by-step discussions mentioned above provide a means of ensuring that students are on this path. Moreover, the text contains numerous references to previously discussed material, so that students are reminded that they are on the right path, and each new topic or procedure is seen as a natural, small step along that path. To help students keep to this path and to reinforce their understanding of the material, nearly 2000 problems are interspersed throughout the text. The problems deal with such topics as politics, science, campus life, ethics, personal relations, and philosophy. They test students' mastery of the key concepts and the techniques for analyzing arguments, as well as their ability to apply these concepts and techniques to new and sometimes different arguments. Each chapter also ends with a self-test/study guide section with exercises covering all the material discussed in the chapter. In addition, the text includes solutions to more than 35 percent of the exercises so that students know when they are on the path and when they may have gotten lost.

The points raised above might well be summed up by saying that this is a text designed with the student in mind. The readability of the text, the problems worked out in detail, the frequent summaries, the gradual building to new concepts and techniques, and the frequent exercises and their solutions all serve to ensure students that logic is worth studying, that they can understand and apply the material, and that doing so is fun.

The organization of this text, like the organization of any text, reflects the author's pedagogical biases. Of the two basic organizational approaches—less rigorous to more rigorous and more rigorous to less rigorous—I have chosen the latter. My own classroom experience has shown that most students are more comfortable with deductive logic than with induction or informal logic (perhaps this is a part of the "right-answer syndrome"). Instead of fighting this comfort, I have chosen to treat deduction first, then induction, and finally to show that informal fallacies fail to meet the criteria for acceptability of either of these two kinds of support. I have found that by the time students have mastered deductive techniques and have become accustomed to the distinction between the form and content of an argument, they are prepared to deal with the relatively inconclusive nature of inductive arguments. Having explored these two kinds of arguments, they are then better able to handle the traditional informal fallacies.

As a result, the text is organized into four main sections. Chapters 1 and 2 contain introductory material on what logic is (and is not), the use of language, and the differences between inductive and deductive support. These chapters serve as the groundwork for following chapters, though portions of these chapters may be skipped, depending on the emphasis the instructor wishes to give to the course. Chapters 3 through 7 are devoted to deductive logic, including a rather informal introduction to proof procedures (including conditional and indirect proofs), truth tables, natural deduction, categorical syllogisms, and predicate logic. Chapters 8 and 9 discuss induction, including the criteria for acceptable inductive arguments, hypotheses and their role in induction, and Mill's methods. Chapter 10 is a treatment of informal fallacies. The approach in this last chapter is to build on the earlier discussion of deductive and inductive support and emphasize the fact that every acceptable argument has both an acceptable structure and all true premises. Informal fallacies are shown to fail to meet one or both of these criteria.

This organization allows the text to be used successfully in a variety of course structures with varying emphases. Among these structures are the following:

Option 1: A standard introductory course without natural deduction or predictive logic: Chapters 1 to 4, 6, and 8 to 10. Chapter 3 may be omitted if one does not wish to cover basic proof procedure and conditional and indirect proofs.

Option 2:   An introduction to deductive logic through predicate logic: Chapters 1 to 7. Here, most of Chapter 3 may be eliminated (with the exception of the discussion on conditional and indirect proofs).

Option 3:   An introduction to language, induction, and informal logic: Chapters 1, 2, and 8 to 10. This option may be augmented by including either or both of Chapters 4 and 5 if some introduction to deductive support is desired.

Other options are available, and all are discussed in more detail in the Instructor's Manual. It is worth mentioning, however, that the student-oriented features of this text have enabled me to cover more material in a semester than I could with any other text. Ordinarily I must spend a great deal of class time working problems and explaining how certain problems are solved. Since much of this is done in the examples discussed in this text, the amount of time which I could devote to explaining concepts and logical theory was greatly increased, with a concomitant increase in the amount of material I could cover.

In addition to detailed explanations of the course options, the Instructor's Manual includes course outlines and syllabi and suggestions for constructing quizzes and exams. Also included are section-by-section comments regarding teaching strategy, and those solutions which do not appear in the text.

A project of this scope would never have been completed without the help of many people. Although it is impossible to enumerate all of them here, the following have been especially helpful: The students in my classes who have willingly used handouts, parts of chapters, and whole chapters and who have so kindly told me when it was good and when it was bad; perhaps to them I owe the greatest debt, since they were the ones who ultimately gave form to this final product. The people who read the manuscript in whole or in part during the course of its development: Dr. Scott Arnold, North Carolina State University; Prof. Christopher Boorse, University of Delaware; Prof. Sidney Chapman, Richland College; Prof. James J. Fletcher, George Mason University; Prof. Edward A. Hacker, Northeastern University; Prof. Alan Hausman, Ohio State University; Prof. Walter E. Lockhart, Schoolcraft College; Dean J. M. Orenduff, Weber State College; Prof. John E. Parks-Clifford, University of Missouri–St. Louis; Prof. Philip A. Pecorino, Queensborough Community College; Prof. David H. Richards, Cayuga Community College; Prof. Stephen E. Rosenbaum, Illinois State University; Prof. Eileen Z. Silbermann, Essex Community College; Dr. K. Sundaram, Lake Michigan College; Prof. Ron G. Williams, Colorado State University; and Prof. Gerald K. Wuori, Wilkes College. I also wish to thank my colleagues, Sidney Gendin and William Miller, who generously used earlier drafts of the text in their own courses and made several valuable suggestions for its improvement, with a special thanks to Bill for providing some of the exercises and for being an outstanding colleague and friend for these many years.

Thanks also to Merri McClure, who typed many pages during the early development of this project, and to Christine Carlsen, who typed the final manuscript and the Instructor's Manual. Last, but most important, I wish to thank my family and friends who, between excitement for what I was doing and sadness because I was not always there with them, nonetheless saw the value in what I was doing, supported it, and were available to help me when things went badly and celebrated with me when things went well.

Michael T. Carlsen-Jones

INTRODUCTION
TO LOGIC

CHAPTER I

LOGIC AND LANGUAGE

While browsing in a bookstore some time ago, I came across a book entitled *Love Is a Special Way of Feeling*.[1] Well, I thought, that's certainly true; but if I didn't already know what love is, it wouldn't help very much to be told it's a special way of feeling. After all, having a headache is a special way of feeling too, and that's not love. There was some reason to suppose, however, that the author was going to write about love, and that she had some things to say about this special feeling. Of course, to find out what she meant by love, I was going to have to read the book.

It has since occurred to me that if someone does not already know what logic is, it's not very helpful merely to tell him or her that **logic** is the study of the relationships between the premises and the conclusions of arguments. This characterization of logic, like Anglund's characterization of love, is certainly true. But to really know what logic is, you have to do with this book what I had to do with Anglund's: read it. When you are done, you should have a very good understanding of the topics discussed by logicians; you should be aware of the uses and limitations of logic theory as applied to everyday reasoning; and you should have developed a variety of skills which will enable you both to determine when a good or a bad argument has been offered for some position and to present your own good arguments. We shall begin to address these issues in the present chapter, and in subsequent chapters you will learn more and more about this thing called logic.

1:1 THE SUBJECT MATTER OF LOGIC

One way to distinguish one discipline from another is to ask, "What do the practitioners of this discipline study and write about that those in other disciplines do not?" In the case of logic the answer is that logicians study and write about *arguments*. As a result, the essential topic we shall be discussing in this text is arguments. Viewed broadly, our task is one of developing skills in recognizing

---

[1] Joan Walsh Anglund, *Love Is a Special Way of Feeling*, Harcourt Brace Jovanovich, Inc., New York (1960).

and analyzing arguments, along with developing an assortment of methods which will aid us in our analysis. Since arguments are given in a language, we shall also have occasion to examine some of the features of language which have a bearing on the acceptability of arguments. Before turning to these topics, let's look at what logic is and what it can and cannot do for us.

Although the study of logic and language is interesting and rewarding in its own right (as well as being fun), other benefits are derivable from such study. One of the more obvious ones is that an understanding of logic helps us with decision making and problem solving. Daily, each of us confronts a diversity of situations in which we must choose from two or more available options. Such situations range from relatively inconsequential ones ("Shall I have a piece of toast or an English muffin with my breakfast?"), to interpersonal ones ("Should I spend Christmas vacation with my family or should I accept the invitation to spend that time with my best friend?"), to situations involving decisions about our own life or those of others ("Should I spend four years in the armed forces before I go to college?" or "Should groups of people who have been discriminated against in the past be given preferential treatment now?"). Of course, there are many more kinds of cases than those mentioned.

To make decisions or to solve problems, we have to do at least two things: First, we must try to gather as much relevant information as we can, both for and against each of the several options, and, second, we must consider this information and see which of the options is best supported by it. Studying logic will not provide too much help with the first task, but it is of great benefit in the second task. In particular, the skills you will develop will enable you to determine, for a great many cases, whether what is offered as reasons for doing something or for accepting some particular position really supports the position. Additionally, the skills will enable you to determine how strong the support is.

The process of giving reasons in support of a position (or of determining whether the reasons that have been given are good ones) involves the difference between reasoning well and reasoning badly. And what does logic have to do with this difference? A great deal. Insofar as possible, we all want to make the best decisions we can and to do so in a rational manner. This is true whether the decision is made in the course of our chosen profession, in the course of exercising our rights and responsibilities as citizens, or in adopting or living a certain "life-style." In all these cases, and in a great many others as well, the decisions we make or the solutions we propose can be arrived at by reasoning well or by reasoning badly. By studying logic and by understanding a few basic procedures and principles, we can increase the number of good decisions we make, and decrease the number of bad ones.

Like so many other things we learn, however, logic will be of no real lasting benefit unless we are able to apply outside the classroom what is learned in the classroom—apply it to situations in which we are making *our* decisions or solving *our* problems. For this reason, the examples discussed in the text and those included in the exercises are not, in themselves, of primary importance.

What is primary is understanding the techniques discussed and the principles behind them, so that these might be applied first to the exercises and then, more importantly, to the new and different situations you will encounter.

In this regard, the procedures employed and the benefits derived from studying logic are a bit like those involved in learning how to play a musical instrument. For most of us, playing an instrument means first learning some basic music theory and learning to read music notation. We must then learn some basic techniques which enable us to apply the theory to our particular instrument; for example, learning which piano keys must be depressed to play a particular chord. The theory, combined with the basic techniques, then enables us to play pieces of music. Of course, to play well we must practice, and this often requires that we spend a lot of time playing the same or similar pieces. Ultimately—and this is the benefit of all the work we have done—our knowledge and the techniques we have developed will enable us to play musical scores we have never seen before, and to do so with the reasonable expectation that we will play well.

Similarly, in learning logic we must first learn some basic logic theory, learn logic notation, and develop some basic techniques. The examples discussed in the text show you how these techniques are applied, and the exercises will give you the opportunity to refine your own skills by practicing. With a bit of work on your part, you should soon be able to apply the knowledge you have gained and the techniques you have developed to situations not specifically discussed in the text. Moreover, you will be able to do this with the reasonable expectation that the decisions you make or the solutions you propose are good ones.

In the rest of this chapter we shall discuss in more detail our primary topic—arguments—and the context in which arguments are given—language. In subsequent chapters we shall discuss some basic logic theory and notation, and we shall develop various techniques that are used in analyzing arguments.

1:1.1 Arguments Since we shall be dealing with arguments throughout the text, it is important that we agree on what an argument is and what it is not. Let's begin by discussing what we do *not* mean by an argument.

Each of us has, no doubt, been involved in arguments at one time or another: with parents, spouses, roommates, friends, neighbors, and so on. Some of your arguments probably proceeded in a reasonable and quiet manner. Others may well have involved shouting, name calling, sulking, or other means by which you tried to get you opponent to agree with your point of view. Now notice that, in this sense, 'argument' means a form of *activity*. In this text, when we discuss an argument, we shall *not* mean the activity of arguing.

While engaged in arguing, you may have *used arguments* in an attempt to make your point. On the occasions in which you did this, you were offering reasons why you were correct, or why your opponent was wrong, or both, and you were offering these reasons in an attempt to show your opponent that your position was the correct one. In short, you were offering arguments in support of your position. We can characterize your position and the reasons you gave for holding it in the following way:

DEFINITION 1: **Argument**

*An **argument** is a group of at least two statements, one of which is the conclusion and the others of which are the premises, which are offered as support for the conclusion.*

In terms of the above discussion, *the position you were arguing for* would be the **conclusion** of the argument, and *the reasons you offered* would be the **premises.**

There are several things to note about our definition. The first is that, in an argument, we can distinguish two elements: the position or point of view that one is maintaining (the conclusion), and what is offered in support of the position (the premises). In section 1:2 we shall examine these two elements in detail, developing some general principles which will assist us in identifying each of them.

The second thing to note is that we say the premises are offered in *support* of the conclusion. In a very real sense, this whole text is directed toward explaining what is meant by this claim and developing procedures for determining, in each argument, whether the premises actually do support the conclusion. In the next chapter we shall examine the notion of support in detail and see what role it plays in our analysis of arguments.

The third thing to note is that an argument is composed of a group of **statements.** Asserting that something is or is not the case, or making a statement, is just one of the many things that one can do in using language. As you will see, we want the sentences that are used in giving an argument to be sentences which make a statement. In section 1:3 we shall examine this and other uses of language.

EXERCISE 1-1

1. What is an argument?

2. What are the two elements of an argument?

3. Logic is primarily concerned with determining whether the reasons which have been given in support of some position do or do not support the position. If this is so, what reasons might be given in support of the claim that logic does not provide much help in *gathering* information for or against a particular position? What reasons might be given in support of the claim that it does provide some help?

EXERCISE 1-2 (For discussion)

1. Are there any instances in which you have been engaged in the activity or arguing but have not given an argument? If so, what are they?

2. Are there ways to get people to agree with your position without your giving them reasons for doing so? What are some of these ways?

3. What makes a decision a good one or a bad one? Are all decisions either good or bad?

4. Can you think of any decisions you have made to which the terms 'good' and 'bad' do not seem to apply? If so, what were they and why aren't the terms applicable?

1:2 RECOGNIZING ARGUMENTS

Our goals in this section are to develop the ability to recognize arguments when they are presented and to learn a way to represent them which makes the premises and the conclusion explicit. Once you are able to recognize arguments and identify their premises and conclusions, we will be ready to address the issue of whether the premises of any given argument support its conclusion. We shall begin our discussion of this issue in the next chapter, where we examine the relationships between the premises and the conclusions of good arguments.

In this section we shall first review briefly the definition of 'argument'. We shall then use the definition to determine whether or not a group of sentences is being used to present an argument. Next, we shall discuss some guidelines which are helpful in identifying the premises and the conclusions of arguments, and then present a standard format to follow when rewriting arguments for analysis. Finally, we shall apply this new material to some examples.

1:2.1 Some General Considerations   Let's begin by recalling the definition of 'argument':

An **argument** is a group of at least two statements, one of which is the conclusion and the others of which are the premises, which are offered as support for the conclusion.

Each of the following passages, then, contains an argument.

(1) I will not be able to attend my high school reunion this year, since I will be out of town on a business trip on October 24 and that's when the reunion is going to be held.

(2) Your Honor, I realize that my client is guilty of driving while intoxicated, but if you suspend his license he will not be able to drive. But, he needs his car in order to get to work, and if he can't get to work he will have no source of income. Therefore, if you suspend his license, you will deprive him of his source of income.

(3) Every Memorial Day I look forward to being able to go on a picnic. I guess it will rain again this year, though, and I won't be able to do it. After all, for the last five years it has rained on Memorial Day.

If we were to separate the statement which has been put forth as the conclusion from the premises which have been offered in support of that conclusion in each of the above cases, we would have the following:

(1) PREMISES

I will be out of town on a business trip on October 24.

My high school reunion is going to be held on October 24.

CONCLUSION

I will not be able to attend my high school reunion.

(2) PREMISES

If you suspend my client's license, he will not be able to drive.

My client needs his car in order to get to work, and if he can't get to work he will have no source of income.

CONCLUSION

If you suspend my client's license, you will deprive him of his source of income.

(3) PREMISES

Every Memorial Day I look forward to being able to go on a picnic.

For the past five years it has rained on Memorial Day.

CONCLUSION

It will rain this Memorial Day and I won't be able to go on a picnic.

Among the things we should notice here is that, in offering each argument, the speaker has asserted something in the conclusion which is either true or false; this has also been done in each of the premises. When we say that an argument is a group of *statements,* what we mean is that the speaker (or writer) has said things which are *either true or false.* Of course, saying something true or false is not the only thing that we do when we use language. In section 1:3 we shall examine some of the other things people do with language.

Another thing we should notice about the above arguments is that the conclusion occurs in different places. In the argument in (1) the conclusion occurs *first;* in the argument in (2) the conclusion occurs *last;* and the conclusion occurs somewhere in the *middle* of the argument in (3). This means that we need some guidelines for recognizing the premises and conclusion of arguments, since *the order in which one gives an argument does not determine which statement is the conclusion and which are the premises.* We shall discuss the identification of premises and conclusions of arguments later in this section.

Yet another thing to notice about the above arguments is that each contains words or phrases which are neither a part of some premise nor a part of the conclusion. For example, in the argument in (2) we have the expression 'I realize that' followed by a statement. Phrases like 'I realize that,' or 'we all know that,' or 'I found it surprising, but nonetheless' often occur when we are talking with one another. Such phrases help the people to whom we are talking to understand our attitude toward certain things or let them know that we are aware of certain things. Such phrases, however, are usually not part of what logicians mean by an argument. Similarly, we often find that when someone is presenting an argument, he or she often includes one or more sentences which are neither a premise nor a conclusion to the argument. For example, in the argument in (1) above, the sentence 'I realize that my client is guilty of driving while intoxicated' is not a premise in the argument; instead, it serves to impart some information about the context in which the argument is being given. When discussing arguments, we shall therefore focus on what the speaker is trying to establish, and on his or her reasons for the conclusion. We shall not be concerned with phrases which serve merely to introduce some statement or with sentences which are irrelevant to the argument.

A final thing to note about the above arguments is that when we rewrote each of them in terms of the premises and the conclusion we made each statement explicit in terms of what the speaker meant. For example, in the argument in (1) we had the sentence 'That's when the reunion is going to be held.' When rewriting this sentence we made it explicit that the date of the reunion was going to be October 24. In ordinary conversation we would have no difficulty in recognizing that this was the date of the reunion. For the purposes of logic, however, making each statement explicit will help greatly in the analysis of arguments. In many cases we can do this by merely relying on the grammatical structure of the sentences the speaker uttered (as in the present case); in others we have to do this on the basis of general knowledge or shared background information. An example of this latter kind follows.

When we talk to someone we ordinarily assume that we and the person to whom we're talking share a relatively large body of experience and knowledge. Without always realizing it, we rely on this shared background knowledge to communicate with one another. Such is the case in the following dialogue.

Sharon: Did you go to class this morning?

Ken: Yes. Where were you?

Sharon: I had an appointment with my allergist so I couldn't make it. Is the exam still going to be on Friday?

Ken: No. It's been changed to Monday and we're also going to be responsible for the material from Chapter 8. By the way, is this allergist any better than the last one you saw?

Sharon: Well, the prescription he gave me seems to be working. At least I no longer walk around looking like I've been up all night crying.

Ken: That's a big improvement.

Sharon: You know, I wish the instructor would stop changing exam dates all the time. It makes it awfully hard to plan my study time around my work schedule.

Ken: Yeah. And this is the second time he's told us right before an exam that there's gonna be additional material we're responsible for. I haven't even looked at Chapter 8.

Sharon: Cindy was thinking of taking the course next semester. I think I'll spare her some of the suffering and tell her what we've had to put up with.

Ken: It's a nice thought, but you'll be wasting your time. She never listens to your advice, especially now that you're going out with Reggie.

Sharon: I guess you're right. But what a stupid attitude. She hadn't gone out with him in over six months when I asked him to the party.

In this dialogue it is clear that Sharon and Ken share enough of a common background so that they both know which class they're talking about (even if Sharon missed more than one class that morning); Sharon assumes that Ken knows enough about allergies so that her remark about no longer looking like she's been crying will enable him to determine that she's better; they both share a sense of fairness about what should be on an exam and when it should be scheduled so that they agree that Cindy should not take the course with their instructor; and they are both talking about the same Cindy, even though they may both know someone else named 'Cindy.' All of this shared knowledge and experience, and more as well, constitutes information which is part of the *context* of their conversation and, as such, does not need to be made explicit for them to understand one another.

It is in this way that the context of a conversation provides information that the speaker and audience can rely on to understand one another. The important point here is that *context provides information that is not always made explicit in an argument.* Recall that we have said that every argument consists of two elements: the premises and the conclusion. Depending on the context, one or more of the premises or the conclusion of an argument sometimes is not stated explicitly. An argument in which this occurs is an **enthymeme,** and we say of such arguments that they have either one or more *missing premises* or an *unstated conclusion.*[2]

In the dialogue between Sharon and Ken, Ken presents an argument whose conclusion is that Sharon will be wasting her time if she tells Cindy about the course. Since all the premises have not been stated explicitly, Ken's argument is an *enthymeme.* Before reading on, try to construct the whole argument by providing the missing premise.

---

[2] In the definition of 'argument' we stated, in part, that an argument consists of at least two statements, one of which is the conclusion. However, it is possible to have an argument with only one premise and a conclusion which is not stated (making the argument an enthymeme); then it would appear that the single statement does not constitute an argument. For this reason, we shall consider enthymemes as *incomplete arguments,* and when we speak of "the argument the speaker presented," we shall mean the argument that results from supplying any missing premises or the unstated conclusion.

The premise which is missing in Ken's argument is 'If Cindy never listens to Sharon's advice, then Sharon will waste her time talking to Cindy about the course.' Making this premise explicit, we have the following argument:

PREMISES

If Cindy never listens to Sharon's advice, then Sharon will waste her time talking to Cindy about the course.

Cindy never listens to Sharon's advice.

CONCLUSION

Sharon will waste her time talking to Cindy about the course

A natural question at this point is, "How do we know which premise or conclusion to add to an argument when one or the other is not stated explicitly?" A partial answer to this question is that, by relying on the context and general knowledge, we add whatever will make the argument as good as possible. When we do this, we are using the **principle of charity** to construct the argument. The idea behind the principle is, roughly, that, since we want to accept that which is true and to reject that which is false, we should construct the strongest possible arguments for and against the position we're considering. (Recall our earlier discussion about decision making and problem solving.)

The answer to the question is only a partial one because we have not as yet discussed the recognition of the premises and the conclusions of arguments; nor have we talked about what makes an argument a good one. We shall take up the first of these issues later on in this chapter, and the second in the following chapter, when we discuss the two types of support relationships, inductive and deductive, which hold between the premises and the conclusions of arguments. Before we turn to a discussion of these matters, however, one more general consideration about recognizing arguments must be mentioned.

In the opening remarks of this chapter we noted that by the time you have completed the book you will be aware of the use and limitations of logic theory as it applies to everyday reasoning. We are about to confront the first limitation. To see what this is, suppose that the person you live with says the following to you:

Bring in the plants. After all, we agreed that the next time it got cold at night you would bring them in, and the weather forecaster just said it's going to be in the low 30s tonight.

It should be clear that the major point the speaker is making here concerns your bringing in the plants. If we tried to represent the speaker's remarks in terms of the premises and conclusion of an argument, we would have the following:

PREMISES

We agreed that the next time it got cold at night you would bring in the plants.

It's going to be cold tonight. (The weather forecaster said that it's going to be in the low 30s.)

CONCLUSION

Bring in the plants.

In one sense of the word the speaker has clearly offered an argument, since she or he has offered some reasons why you should bring in the plants. Notice, however, that what we have here called the conclusion of an argument is not something which is either true or false; that is, it is *not a statement*. In particular, the sentence 'Bring in the plants' is in this context probably being used to give an order or make a request, not to say something which is either true or false.

This example raises a difficulty for us, since logicians typically are concerned with the reasons why some given statement is either true or false. Since 'Bring in the plants' is not, in this context, used to say something either true or false, the question (from a logician's point of view) of whether the reasons offered in support of this "conclusion" are good or bad simply does not arise. That means, then, that what the person you live with has said does not constitute an argument from our point of view, even though reasons have been given to support the order or request.

And herein we find one of the limitations of the methods and procedures we shall be discussing. We shall be limiting ourselves to cases where someone puts forward a claim which is *either true or false,* and then offers reasons (which are themselves either true or false) in support of the claim. When the claim that is advanced as the conclusion is not true or false (does not have a **truth value**), or when the premises are not true or false, we do *not* have an argument in the sense that we are using that word.

We can summarize this discussion by proposing a general guideline to follow when trying to recognize arguments.

GUIDELINE 1

Make sure that the person who is offering a potential argument is using language in such a way that he or she is asserting things which are either true or false. That is, make sure the language is being used to make statements.

In the next section we shall discuss some further guidelines which will assist you in recognizing arguments.

EXERCISE 1-3

1. Present three different arguments of your own, such that the conclusion occurs first in one of them, at the end in another, and in the middle in the last.

2. What does it mean to say that in presenting an argument the speaker offers a *statement* as the conclusion and other *statements* in support of the conclusion?

3. What is the principle of charity?

4. What is an enthymeme? Give two examples of arguments which are enthymemes, one in which the conclusion is unstated and one in which there is an unstated premise.

1:2.2 Some Specific Considerations   In this section we shall develop some further guidelines which will assist you in recognizing arguments. The first of these rests on the fact that every argument consists of two elements: the premises and the conclusion. This gives us the following:

GUIDELINE 2

Make sure that something is put forward as a conclusion and that something is offered as support for the conclusion.

Guideline 2 is of importance when the speaker may have done something other than offer an argument or may have offered an incomplete argument. Some of the ways in which this might occur are the following:

(1) The speaker may have made an unsupported claim.

(2) The speaker may have offered a group of statements as an argument, but with one or more missing premises.

(3) The speaker may have offered a group of statements as an argument, but with an unstated conclusion.

(4) The speaker may have offered a group of statements, but as a narrative rather than an argument.

Consider (1). A great amount of the communication which takes place between people is simply statement-making discourse in which neither person offers arguments and neither person takes the other to be offering arguments. Sharon's telling Ken that she missed class because she had an appointment with her allergist is one such example. In these cases it is easy to recognize that no argument has been given.

Sometimes, however, a person will assert something which he or she believes is supported by evidence but will not have asserted anything in support of the claim. Suppose, for example, that in the course of discussing the past hockey season of the Philadelphia Flyers, someone says, "Montreal will win the Stanley Cup next year." Here, the speaker may have very good reasons to suppose that what was said is true, but so long as *none of these reasons has been offered,* the speaker has made only an **unsupported claim** and *has not offered an argument.*

Of course, the speaker could go on and present the available evidence, in which case an argument will have been given. But until that evidence is presented we have no argument, and, therefore, the question of whether the "premises" support the "conclusion" does not arise.

Before considering our next cases, it is worthwhile to note a kind of statement which is sometimes mistaken for an argument. Such statements are **conditional statements,** which will be discussed in detail in Chapter 3. These statements can be recognized by their 'if-then' form; one example is, 'If Montreal does well in this year's draft, then they will win the Stanley Cup next year.'[3]

There is a temptation to break conditional statements apart, taking the first part as a premise and the second part as the conclusion to an argument. In the example just cited, the result of doing this would be:

PREMISE

Montreal will do well in this year's draft. .

CONCLUSION

Montreal will win the Stanley Cup next year.

There are two significant points here: First, when someone asserts a conditional statement, we should not assume that the speaker knows or believes that the two parts of the conditional statement are true, and, second, *a conditional statement is not an argument.*

Perhaps the best way of seeing that conditional statements are not arguments is to return to our example and point out that the speaker *did not* assert that Montreal would do well in this year's draft and *did not* assert that Montreal would win the Stanley Cup next year. What the speaker did assert was that *if* certain circumstances obtained (doing well in the draft), *then* something else would happen (winning the Stanley Cup).

To reinforce the point about conditional statements not being arguments, let's consider one more example. Suppose someone asserts the following:

If Abraham Lincoln had not been assassinated, then the Civil War would have ended earlier than it did.

In asserting this conditional statement the speaker surely would *not* be asserting the following two statements and would not, therefore, have been presenting an argument in which the first of these is a premise and the second the conclusion.

Lincoln was not assassinated.

The Civil War ended earlier than it did.

That the speaker would not be asserting these two statements should be obvious

---

[3] Strictly speaking, 'If Montreal does well in this year's draft, then they will win the Stanley Cup next year' is not a statement but is, rather, a *sentence.* We shall adopt the convention of using the shorter expression 'The statement 'so and so' ' for the longer but more accurate 'The statement expressed by uttering the sentence 'so and so'.' In a similar fashion, we shall assume that declarative sentences are being used to make statements unless noted otherwise.

from two facts: First, someone who asserts the original conditional statement implies that Lincoln *was* assassinated and, hence, would not then also say that he *was not* assassinated, and, second, the claim "The Civil War ended earlier than it did" makes no sense in isolation.

As noted above, we shall discuss conditional statements in much more detail later, but the important point for now is to understand that conditional statements are just that—statements; they are not arguments.

Consider now (2) and (3), groups of statements offered as arguments but with one or more missing premises or with an unstated conclusion. As we saw earlier, such arguments are *enthymemes*. Recognizing that a group of statements is an enthymeme requires that one recognize first that the speaker has offered an argument, and second that the argument is incomplete in either of two ways. We mention enthymemes again in this section primarily to remind you that they form a subclass of all arguments and, therefore, that something which at first sight may not seem to be an argument may upon careful examination be seen to be an enthymeme and, hence, an argument.

Since not every group of statements is an argument, not even an incomplete one, enthymemes are sometimes difficult to identify. To aid in their identification, you can ask yourself the following two series of questions:

Has something been put forward as a conclusion with reasons offered in support of it?

If so, are the reasons complete?

If not, can additional reasons be provided by using the principle of charity to extract information from the context?

If the answer to the first question is yes, and to the second no, then what has been presented is an enthymeme with one or more missing premises, and you should attempt to fill out the argument in the way suggested by the third question.

Have reasons been put forward for some position without the position's being stated explicitly?

If so, can the conclusion be provided from the context by using the principle of charity?

If the answer to the first question is yes, then there is a good chance that what has been presented is an enthymeme with an unstated conclusion. You should then attempt to fill out the argument in the way suggested by the second question.

Before we turn to our last case, it should be noted that after we have discussed the material in the next two sections, ways to identify the premises and conclusions of arguments, you will find it much easier to determine whether something has been put forward as a conclusion and much easier to identify when reasons have been given. Hence, you will also find it easier to recognize enthymemes.

Now consider (4), which offers a **narrative,** not an argument. An example follows:

> Biltmore is one of the oldest and largest summer homes in Newport, Rhode Island. It was built for the Vanderbilts and contains several rooms which were formerly rooms in European palaces. Among its many charms are the option of taking fresh- or salt-water baths (hence, the four faucets for every bathtub), the exquisite view of the ocean, and the stately staircase lighted from above by a magnificent stained-glass skylight and adorned by a tapestry larger than the living rooms in most homes built today.

Each of the sentences in the above example is used to make a statement. Hence, we have a group of statements. Nonetheless, no argument has been put forward.

No argument has been given because of the part of the definition of 'argument' that says that, in an argument, the premises are offered *as support for the conclusion.* In the case under discussion no conclusion has been offered— not even implicitly. Moreover, that which has been offered does not constitute reasons given in support for some position. For these reasons, we conclude that we do not have an argument.

In this section we have discussed some general guidelines which will help you to recognize when an argument has or has not been given. These guidelines result from the definition of 'argument'; they require that, when an argument is given, language must be used to make statements, and both a conclusion and premises must be offered, either explicitly or, in the case of enthymemes, implicitly. In the following two sections we shall discuss some additional guidelines that help in recognizing arguments—in particular, how to identify the conclusions and premises of arguments.

1:2.3 Identifying the Conclusion of an Argument   Our goal in this section is to develop some skills which will be of help in identifying the conclusion of an argument; in the next section we shall do the same thing for the premises of an argument. We begin our discussion with the conclusion, since in every argument there is but one conclusion. Then, with the exception of phrases like 'we all know that' (which serve to introduce statements) and whole sentences (which help set the context in which the argument is being given), once the conclusion has been identified, the remainder of what has been asserted in the argument will be the premises.

I have found through experience that one of the best ways to identify the conclusion of an argument is to ask, ''What point is the speaker trying to make?'' or ''What is this person trying to show?'' Asking either of these questions is helpful since, as speakers of English, we already possess a highly developed ability to recognize that someone is attempting to make some point and to identify what that point is. Moreover, in the vocabulary of logic, either of these questions is the same as asking, ''What is the conclusion of this person's argument?''

Before turning to another guideline for identifying conclusions, we should recall a point made earlier: *The conclusion of an argument may occur anywhere among the group of statements asserted by the speaker.* As we saw, any of the following may occur:

The conclusion is stated first, followed by the premises.

One or more of the premises is stated, then the conclusion is stated, and then one or more additional premises is stated.

All the premises are stated, followed by the conclusion.

In short, we can say that the conclusion may come first, in the middle, or at the end of an argument. The following are examples of these three cases, in order:

The present inflationary spiral is bound to continue for another year. This is so since the major labor unions are demanding an average yearly salary increase of more than 15 percent. Moreover, management will meet their demands.

In almost all cases where unemployment has been high at the time of an election, the incumbent has been defeated. As a result, it is likely that the mayor will lose the coming election, since the unemployment level is the highest in the history of the city.

No one who owns a small business can afford to have a large inventory of slow-moving stock. Additionally, only those who have a warehouse can maintain large inventories. Consequently, no one who owns a small business also has a warehouse.

Having been told where the conclusions were located in each of the above arguments, you should have had no difficulty in identifying them. They are, of course, the following:

The present inflationary spiral is bound to continue for another year.

The mayor will lose the coming election.

No one who owns a small business also has a warehouse.

But what are you to do when you have not been told the location of the conclusion? The answer is that certain expressions often occur in arguments, and these serve to point out the conclusion. For example, in the first argument above, the expression 'this is so' indicates that what has just been asserted is the conclusion of the argument; in the second example, the expression 'as a result' indicates that what follows is the conclusion of the argument; and in the third example, the expression 'consequently' does the same thing. Words or expressions which point out the conclusion or the premises of an argument are **indicator words.**

We use many words or expressions as *conclusion indicators,* in addition to 'as a result,' 'consequently,' and 'this is so.' The following list includes some that are commonly used for this purpose. You should familiarize yourself with these expressions, for one or the other of them in the context of an argument is a highly reliable sign that what follows is the conclusion.

CONCLUSION INDICATORS

Therefore	It can be inferred that
Hence	So
Accordingly	Consequently
Thus	It follows that
So you can see that	As a result
It must be the case that	This is so

1:2.4 Identifying the Premises of an Argument   Our goal in this section is to learn how to identify the premises of an argument. For each of the points made in the previous section concerning the identification of the conclusion of an argument, there is an analogous point which can be made for identifying the premises.

The first such point is that there is a general question we can ask about the speaker's argument. In particular, since we know that the premises of an argument are put forward in support of the conclusion, we can often identify the premises by first identifying the conclusion and then asking, "What reasons has the speaker offered for his or her position?" When we have identified the *reasons*, we will have identified the *premises.*

The second point is simply a reminder. Since the conclusion may come first, in the middle, or at the end of an argument, *there is no particular order in which the premises might be given.* As a result, we cannot rely on the order of the speaker's assertions to help us identify the premises but must, instead, use other cues.

The third point concerns these cues. As is the case for conclusions, there are indicator words which serve to point out the premises of an argument. Such expressions are *premise indicators,* and the following list includes some which are typically used for this purpose. Again, you should familiarize yourself with these expressions:

PREMISE INDICATORS

Since	Assuming that
As shown by	Insofar as
Given that	Inasmuch as
In view of	For
Because	Due to
As a result of	Owing to

Two additional points about indicator words need to be emphasized. First, in some arguments all the premises and the conclusion may be marked by indicator words, but in other arguments one or more of the premises, or the conclusion, may be stated without using such words. For example, in the above argument about small businesses, both premises are stated without indicator words. In cases such as these, we should use the indicator words which are given, if there are any, to identify the conclusion and as many premises as we can. Then, by relying on the context of the speaker's assertions, we should use the answers to our general questions about the point the speaker is making and the reasons offered in support of it to fill out the remainder of the argument.

The second thing to note is that although the expressions listed as indicator words typically are used to indicate conclusions or premises of arguments, they are not always used in these ways. Exceptions occur most often with 'since' and 'because.'

Instead of being used to indicate that something is a reason for something else, 'since' is often used to indicate a *temporal relationship.* For example, in the sentence 'The governor has not held a press conference since last fall,' 'since' is used in this way. Here the word serves to indicate *how long it has been* since the governor's last press conference. In contrast, in the sentence 'We will not be able to cook the hot dogs since Dave forgot the charcoal,' 'since' is used to indicate the reason for something else: in this case, the reason for not being able to cook the hot dogs.

In a great many instances it is easy to tell which way 'since' is being used, simply by considering the sentence in which it occurs. In other cases, however, this cannot be done. For example, in 'Marty has been much happier since he decided to take a semester off from school,' it is not clear how the word is being used. In such cases we have to rely on the context to determine the use.

Similar remarks hold in the case of 'because'. Instead of being used to indicate a premise or to express a relationship between statements, this word is sometimes used to indicate a *causal relationship between events.* 'Because' is used this way in the sentence 'He died because of a heart attack,' where the word serves to point out that the heart attack was the cause of death.

In this section we have looked at some of the things which help us to identify the premises of an argument, particularly indicator words. In the next section we shall combine what we have done here with our discussion on identifying conclusions and so deal with arguments in their entirety.

EXERCISE 1-4

1. What two things should one do to determine whether an argument has been given through the use of language in a particular situation?

2. Why must language be used to make statements when giving an argument?

3. Give two examples of conditional statements, and explain why conditional statements are not arguments.

4. In section 1:2.2 we used a narrative about Biltmore as an example. If we

added 'Go see it' to the end of the narrative, would the whole thing be an argument? Explain your answer.

5. What general question can one ask to help identify the conclusion of an argument?

6. What general question can one ask to help identify the premises of an argument?

7. What is an indicator word?

8. In addition to being used as indicator words, 'since' and 'because' each have other uses. State what these uses are, and give an example of each.

9. Each of the following words or expressions is often used as an indicator word. State which ones are typically premise indicators and which ones are typically conclusion indicators.

a. Accordingly   b. As a result
c. As shown by   d. Thus
e. In view of   f. For
g. Hence   h. Insofar as
i. As a result of   j. It can be inferred that
k. So   l. Consequently
m. Due to   n. Assuming

EXERCISE 1-5

1. Assuming ordinary contexts, state which of the following are arguments and which are not. In the case of those which are *not* arguments, explain why they are not.

a. Since Slippery Soap costs 23 cents a bar and Grime Remover costs 28 cents a bar, Slippery Soap is the better buy.

b. Only vegetarians are consumers of large quantities of cheese or eggs. Consequently, no one who consumes large quantities of cheese or eggs ever orders fish at a restaurant. Why? Because people who eat fish are not vegetarians.

c. Since the new coach was hired, we have had a winning team.

d. The first time they heard that the alchemists spent a great amount of time trying to turn base metals into gold, a lot of chemistry students laughed. Recent developments in nuclear physics have shown, however, that the alchemists were not so crazy after all. As a result of recent developments in the field, it is now possible to change one element into another. Of course, it would be economically feasible to do this in the case of gold only if the gold produced was worth more than the cost of producing it. It's not.

e. You, like everyone else, no doubt enjoy a good movie. Since every classic movie is a good movie, and since *Psycho* is a classic, go see the movie.

f. Anyone who has studied anything about the solar system has either read or been told that Pluto is the planet most distant from the sun. From now until 1999, however, Neptune will be farther from the sun than Pluto. This is a result of their different orbits and where each of the planets is presently located in its orbit. Consequently, this all goes to show that you can't always trust what you have read or what you have been told.

g. A person cannot practice medicine unless he or she both has the ability and is not squeamish. That rules out Bradley, for he's the most squeamish person I've ever met.

h. At one time or another, almost everyone gets bored with what he or she is doing. Moreover, there is a high correlation between boredom and depression. As a result, to avoid depression don't get bored.

i. Because of the high incidence of crime in the Forty-eighth Precinct, more police should be assigned to that precinct.

j. The situation in the Middle East is much more serious than it looks. Consequently, only a fool would consider going to Jerusalem for a Christmas vacation.

k. If the leader of another country has suppressed the rights of the people, then our government has the obligation to cut off all foreign aid to that regime.

l. Because of his age, Trotter can no longer be depended upon when an emergency arises. We can't fire him, though, because his record is a good one, and we can't retire him, owing to the recently passed legislation. Does anyone have any suggestions about what we can do in this situation?

m. The only way to win a libel suit is to show that what the defendant wrote was both false and malicious. Since Donovan did not win his suit, then either the *News* printed the truth when they wrote that he was doing drugs at a fancy restaurant or the jury did not think the article was malicious.

n. There is no chip like a Crinkle Chip. Thinly sliced wafers of fresh Idaho potatoes, deep fried to a golden color and a crispy texture, with just the right amount of salt. Buy Crinkle Chips the next time you want a real chip.

o. Obviously it didn't snow up north last night, since, if it had, the Nortons would have gone skiing this weekend. Just as obviously, they didn't go, for I just saw Alice at the grocery store.

2. For each of the examples in problem 1 which is an argument, identify the premises and the conclusion. Remember that indicator words and other phrases which serve to introduce statements are not part of the premises or the conclusion of an argument.

EXERCISE 1-6

Each of the following arguments is an enthymeme. By using the principle of charity, add missing premises or supply a conclusion as necessary.

a. Looking for a place to get your tape deck fixed? At George's we service what we sell, and we sell every brand of tape deck on the market.

b. Marty Madlove's first feature-length film was released last week. In spite of the bad sound track, miserable editing, and lousy acting by the lead actor and actress, Metromedia insists the film will make money. With people like that running the company, I predict Metromedia will be bankrupt within the year.

c. We've got more than twenty years of experience under the car. You should let us install your next muffler.

d. Those who want the best burger eat at Better Burger. We're sure that you want the best burger too.

e. All persons ought to be allowed to seek pleasure and relaxation in their own home in any way they choose. Just as clearly, smoking marijuana at home is a wonderful source of relaxation and pleasure.

f. I recently read in the *News* that an unemployed auto worker makes more money than 75 percent of the workers who are employed in other fields. If that doesn't show you how powerful labor unions have become, nothing will.

g. We should be extremely careful when selecting our nominee for president of the school board, especially in light of all the recent backlash toward women's rights by the people in our community. Keep this in mind as we discuss the qualifications of Amy Armister and Brian Burmeister. (Assume that Amy supports women's rights.)

h. My fellow citizens: Surely you want to elect a candidate who will be responsive to your needs, work to enrich the lives of everyone in the community, and reduce the rising crime rate in our city. Let me tell you, I will do all this and more.

i. Ever since the civil rights legislation was passed in this country, blacks have had as much opportunity for advancement in the work force as anyone else. As a result, it should be perfectly clear that those who have not advanced should take the blame themselves, and stop pleading to us for special favors.

j. There is enough grain stored in this country to feed everyone in the world. It's time to stop subsidizing farmers and to take care of the hungry people of this world.

1:2.5 Putting Arguments into Standard Form   We shall say that an argument is in **standard form** when it has been written with all the premises listed first, followed by the conclusion. In addition, we shall use the symbol '∴' to indicate the conclusion. The symbol '∴' will be read as 'therefore' and will be used regardless of which, if any, conclusion indicator might have been used in giving the argument. The major reason for putting arguments into standard form is to simplify the task of determining whether the premises of an argument support its conclusion.

   It should be clear from our discussion in the previous sections that not all arguments are given with the premises and the conclusion arranged in standard form. The procedure presented below should be followed to arrange all arguments in standard form.

Since we are discussing the standard form of *arguments,* our first task always is to make sure that an argument has actually been presented. We can do this by using the material to be discussed in section 1:3.2 to accomplish the following:

(1) Make sure that language is being used to make statements.

(2) Make sure that something is put forward as a conclusion and that something is offered as support for the conclusion.

Having satisfied ourselves that an argument has been given, we are ready to put it into standard form. To do this, we must, of course, identify the premises and the conclusion. Since this has already been discussed in detail, only a summary is provided here. In general, we do the following:

(3) Identify the conclusion by asking "What point is the speaker trying to make?" and by using conclusion indicators.

(4) Identify the premises by asking "What reasons has the speaker offered for his or her position?" and by using premise indicators.

Since some arguments are incomplete (are enthymemes), we should use the material discussed in section 1:2.2 to do the following:

(5) If necessary, supply any missing premises.

(6) If necessary, supply the unstated conclusion.

Having done all the above, we are ready to put the argument into standard form. This we do as follows:

(7) List all the premises.

(8) Write the conclusion after the premises, and place the symbol '∴' in front of it.

When the above steps are completed, the result is an argument written in standard form. The results of applying this procedure to the arguments used as examples in section 1:2.3 are given below. Notice that the symbol '∴' is used to indicate the conclusion regardless of which conclusion indicator, if any, was used in giving the argument. Also notice that none of the premise indicators is used in the standard form of the argument. There are two reasons for this: First, they are not part of the sentences needed to express the statements that make up the premises of the argument; and, second, since the argument is written in standard form, it is clear that everything which is not the conclusion of the argument is a premise. In the next section we shall apply the procedure to some additional examples.

The major labor unions are demanding an average yearly salary increase of more than 15 percent.

Management will meet the labor unions' demands.

∴ The present inflationary spiral is bound to continue for another year.

In almost all cases where unemployment has been high at the time of an election, the incumbent has been defeated.

The unemployment level is the highest in the history of the city.

∴ The mayor will lose the coming election.

No one who owns a small business can afford to have a large inventory of slow-moving stock.

Only those who have a warehouse can maintain a large inventory.

∴ No one who owns a small business also has a warehouse.

1:2.6 Some Examples   In this section we shall apply the material discussed above to some examples. Since you are primarily concerned with learning how to put arguments into standard form, all the examples are arguments. Hence, we can dispense with the steps that are followed to identify arguments.

EXAMPLE 1

Unless the strike is settled, there will be no good games on television this fall. Since there will be some good games on, it follows that the strike will be settled.

Step 1: Our first step is to pick out the conclusion of the argument. Asking what the speaker's point is and noting the indicator word 'it follows that', we see that the conclusion is:

The strike will be settled.

Step 2: We must now identify the premises. One of the premises is marked by the indicator word 'since'. The other premise has no indicator word, but it can be recognized as a premise because we have already identified the conclusion, and only one statement remains; it must obviously be part of the reason for asserting the conclusion. Our two premises are:

Unless the strike is settled, there will be no good games on television this fall.

There will be some good games on television this fall.

Notice that we have rewritten the sentence 'There will be some good games on' to state explicitly that what is intended is that the games will be on television. We shall find many arguments in which we must rewrite some of the sentences so that the argument is clearly expressed when it has been put into standard form.

Step 3: Put the argument into standard form by listing all the premises followed by the conclusion, the latter indicated with '∴'. Our result is:

> Unless the strike is settled, there will be no good games on television this fall.
>
> There will be some good games on television this fall.
>
> ∴ The strike will be settled.

EXAMPLE 2

As we're all aware, the three major banks in the city have not approved any loans for the renovation of buildings included in the waterfront redevelopment project. One result of this is that it is unlikely that Samualson will be able to get the money he needs to renovate Tiffany Towers.

Step 1: Identify the conclusion. Asking our general question and noting the conclusion indicator 'one result of this is that', we see that the conclusion is:

> It is unlikely that Samualson will be able to get the money he needs to renovate Tiffany Towers.

Step 2: Identify the premises. With the conclusion identified, it is clear that the premises are included in the remainder of what the speaker asserted. After asking what reasons have been offered as support for the conclusion, we should see that the answer is that the three major banks have not approved any loans for the redevelopment project. In this argument the expression 'as we're all aware' is used only to introduce the statement about the banks; it is *not* itself part of the premise. Hence, the premise in this argument is:

> The three major banks in the city have not approved any loans for the renovation of buildings included in the waterfront redevelopment project.

Putting the results of Steps 1 and 2 together, we have the following:

> The three major banks in the city have not approved any loans for the renovation of the buildings included in the waterfront redevelopment project.
>
> ∴ It is unlikely that Samualson will be able to get the money he needs to renovate Tiffany Towers.

Step 3: In this example, unlike the earlier case, some additional information must be provided so that the conclusion follows from the premises. (In other words, example 2 is an enthymeme.) Before reading on, attempt to determine what this information is. For the given premise to provide support for the conclusion, we need the additional information that Samualson will attempt to borrow money from one or more of the major banks and that Tiffany Towers is one of the buildings included in the waterfront redevelopment project. Given the context of the argument, and by the principle of charity, it is reasonable to suppose that these are missing premises which the speaker takes to be more or less obvious. Having made these premises explicit, we are ready to put the argument into standard form.

Step 4: Put the argument into standard form. The result is:

> The three major banks in the city have not approved any loans for the renovation of buildings included in the waterfront redevelopment project.
>
> Samualson will attempt to borrow money from one or more of the three major banks in the city, to renovate Tiffany Towers.
>
> Tiffany Towers is one of the buildings included in the waterfront redevelopment project.
>
> ∴ It is unlikely that Samualson will be able to get the money he needs to renovate Tiffany Towers.

This concludes our discussion in this section. Having learned how to recognize arguments, how to identify their premises and their conclusions, and how to put them into standard form, you are now ready to look at some of the features of the medium in which we find arguments being given: language. Then, in the next chapter, we shall turn our attention to the issue of what makes an argument a good one or a bad one.

EXERCISE 1-7

1. Underline the conclusion of each of the following arguments, and put parentheses around each of the premises. Remember that indicator words are not part of the conclusion or the premises.
   a. Most people in middle-management positions feel that their chances for advancement will be jeopardized by supporting their subordinates in controversial situations. As a result, middle-level managers are natural allies of their superiors, regardless of how insane some of their decisions may be.
   b. Since political philosophy is a branch of philosophy, even the most provisional explanation of what political philosophy is cannot dispense with an explanation, however provisional, of what philosophy is.
   c. Surely it's obvious that all the planets revolve around the sun. If they didn't, we wouldn't see them first on this, side of the sun and then on the other.
   d. Since mathematics is one of the few disciplines which fosters intellectual

rigor, it can, when taught correctly, lead to startling improvements in any student's ability to comprehend other disciplines.

e. It's just not true that I took the last handful of Crinkle Chips. If I had, I wouldn't be sitting here eating this crummy carrot. But, as any fool can clearly see, that's exactly what I'm doing.

f. Mr. Scrooge, I can hardly manage to feed the children on what you've been paying my husband. Accordingly, my husband deserves a raise in pay, especially since our youngest son, Tim, also needs an operation if he is ever to walk without crutches.

g. Only members and their guests are allowed to swim here. Since every member has a membership card and every guest has a guest pass, I cannot admit you, for you obviously have neither.

h. It is extremely unlikely that there will be a Triple Crown winner this year. After all, there have not been very many such winners in the past 100 years. Moreover, to win the Triple Crown, a horse has to be both fast and able to go distances. None of this year's horses seems to have both these characteristics.

i. When it comes to the question of how severe the punishment, one thing stands clear: The younger should not be punished as severely for their faults as those who are older. After all, everyone should have a chance to mend his or her ways before being severely punished, and, as everyone knows, the older have had more time to do this than the younger.

j. It's very likely that no day this year will be a day on which the temperature reaches over 70 degrees, owing to the fact that the year is already one-quarter gone and we have yet to have a day in the 70s.

k. It takes a great deal of money to keep a prisoner incarcerated for a year. Consequently, every prisoner who has been sentenced to life and who has no chance of being paroled should be executed. For, as I am sure you will agree, it is better to spend our money on the needy and the deserving than to spend it on those who will never make a contribution to society.

l. A recent survey has shown that 2 percent of the people born in Detroit will eventually be murdered. My good friend Armadillo was born in Detroit, but with that low figure he shouldn't have to worry much.

m. If all would treat their neighbor as they themselves wish to be treated, then there would be no need for laws. As, however, it is our fate that some think so little of themselves that we too be thought as worthless, so then is it necessary that laws be made.

n. Given that some laws passed by the legislature benefit only special-interest groups, it follows that some of the laws passed are not in the interest of the general population. This is because some of the laws which are beneficial to special-interest groups are actually harmful to most people.

o. The zoo will get a new aardvark only if it increases its supply of ants. But, it will increase the supply of ants only if the ants are especially careless. Consequently, in view of the fact that ants aren't careless, the zoo won't get a new aardvark.

p. I've had all I can stand 'cause I can't stand no more.

q. To be really useful, Christmas catalogues should arrive in the mail no later than the first of December. Furthermore, anything which arrives in December, but before Christmas, is welcome. Consequently, if something isn't welcome, then it's not a Christmas catalogue.

r. No good photographer would ever print a bad picture. But to print good pictures, one needs a good enlarger, and they're awfully expensive. Accordingly, every good photographer makes good money, for only those who make good money can afford things which are expensive.

s. If the sky is falling and Foxy Loxy doesn't catch her, then Chicken Little will run to see the king. But the sky is not falling. Consequently, Chicken Little won't be running to see the king, for Foxy Loxy broke his leg playing kick-the-can, and he can't catch anyone, not even a plump chicken.

2. Put each of the arguments in problem 1 into standard form, supplying missing premises or unstated conclusions where necessary.

1:3. LANGUAGE

As mentioned earlier, one of our primary goals is to develop the ability to determine whether the premises of an argument provide support for the conclusion. But, since arguments are given in a language, it is helpful to examine some of the features of language which have a bearing on the question of whether an argument has actually been given and, if so, whether or not the argument is acceptable. It should be noted that the topics we shall discuss in this section are but a few of the many considered by logicians, philosophers of language, and linguists. Moreover, our discussion of each of them will be brief, reflecting but one of many viewpoints about language and language use.

1:3.1 Use, Mention, and Quotation Marks   Before beginning our discussion of language, we should distinguish between *using* a word or an expression and talking about, or *mentioning*, a word or an expression. In the course of drawing this distinction, we shall also discuss the use of quotation marks in this text.

Perhaps the easiest way to see the difference between use and mention is by looking at some examples. In Table 1-1 one word has been italicized in each sentence. In the sentences on the left the italicized word has been *used*, and in those on the right it has been *mentioned*.[4]

Notice that in the sentences in which the italicized word has been *used*, it has been used in one of its ordinary ways. For example, the word 'centipede' is used to pick out a kind of object, to say of that object that it is of a particular

---

[4] In some cases more than one word has been mentioned, but only the example word has been italicized.

TABLE 1-1

Use	Mention
A *centipede* is an insect.	*Centipede* comes after centimeter in the dictionary.
Stop what you are doing.	Each of those slides on the organ is called a *stop*.
The cow *jumped* over the moon.	*Jumped* is a verb.
Massachusetts is in New England.	*Massachusetts* has more letters than Connecticut.
Sabrina has a very good *memory*.	If you want to see what's there, push the button labeled *memory*.

kind, namely an insect; 'jumped' is used to describe what the cow did; 'memory' is used to say what Sabrina has; and so on.

In contrast to these ordinary ways of using the italicized words, the sentences in which the words have been *mentioned* are ones in which we are discussing *the words themselves:* We discuss the relative location of the word 'centipede' in the dictionary; we say what kind of word 'jumped' is; we discuss the word 'memory' being used as a label; and so on.

Generally, it is fairly easy to determine, on the basis of context, whether a word is being used or is being mentioned. For example, in

Pitch has more than one meaning.

it is clear that 'pitch' is being *mentioned* and that we are asserting something about the word. In contrast, in the sentence

Pitch me the ball.

it is clear that we are not talking about the word 'pitch' but are, instead, *using* the word—as we might in making a request.

Sometimes, however, it is not so easy to say whether a word is being used or is being mentioned. For example, in

Sue has three letters.

we may be *mentioning* the word 'Sue' and saying of the word that it has three letters. On the other hand, we may be *using* the word 'Sue' to pick out someone and to say something about her—for example, that she received three pieces of mail today or, perhaps, that she has earned three letters for participating in sports.

Different people have used various methods to indicate whether a word is being used or mentioned. Two of these are to use italics and to put double quotation marks around a word or an expression when it is being mentioned. The following are examples of these:

The generally implies uniqueness.

The correct term is "soluble."

Since there is no one commonly accepted convention for indicating that a word or an expression is being mentioned, I have chosen to indicate this in either of two ways. The first is by using *single* quotation marks, as in our discussion of the word 'Sue.' The second is by setting a sentence off on a line by itself, as was done above for the sentence 'Pitch me the ball.' Notice that when we set the sentence off on a line by itself, we eliminate the single quotation marks that we would ordinarily place around the sentence being mentioned.

Given our convention, the above two sentences would be written as follows:

'The' generally implies uniqueness.

The correct term is 'soluble.'

In setting these two sentences off on a line by themselves, we are, of course, mentioning them. As a result, if they were *not* set off we would have to place single quotation marks around them. For example, we would do this if we were to note that the sentence ' 'The' generally implies uniqueness' has been used as an example.

In addition to using single quotation marks, we shall also have occasion to use double quotation marks. Two standard uses of double quotation marks are to indicate that material has been taken from another source and to report direct speech; we shall adhere to these two uses. We shall also follow this latter usage in those examples where there is a dialogue going on between two people.

There is also one other case where we shall use double quotation marks: in those instances where we want to indicate that a word or an expression is being used in an atypical way. Let's briefly look at one such example.

Frederick's performance last night was nothing short of "brilliant." Who else could have walked three batters and given up four hits in just one-third of an inning?

Here the double quotation marks around 'brilliant' serve to indicate that the author is using the word in an atypical way. The author does not really mean that the performance was brilliant at all and, instead of complimenting Frederick, he is actually criticizing him. The double quotation marks used to indicate that a word or an expression is being used in an atypical way are called 'scare quotes.'

EXERCISE 1-8

1. In each of the following sentences, state whether the words or expressions in italics are being used or mentioned.
   a. *Money* is no object at all.
   b. The root of *unkind* is *kind*.
   c. Patience is the *mark* of a tolerant person.
   d. In case of an emergency, push the button labeled *alert*.
   e. Not every *word* begins with a capital *letter*.

f. The tenth letter of the alphabet is *j*.

g. Instead of writing *ploy* he wrote *play*.

h. *Sodom and Gomorra* are two ancient cities.

i. *Sodom and Gomorra* occur as part of the lyrics of a song.

j. *Heliotrope* is not an easy color to describe.

k. Give me a definition of *heliotrope*.

l. *To be or not to be;* that is the question.

m. It is not always easy to say what *human* means.

n. Is *Sam* in *Samantha* a word?

o. The *word word* occurs in the sentence *I gave him the word*.

2. Using the convention discussed above for this text, add single or double quotation marks, where necessary, to the following sentences to punctuate them correctly.

a. If I've told you once, I've told you a thousand times: don't shout wolf when you're not in trouble.

b. Tomorrow I'm going in to work and I'm going to say to my boss, I quit.

c. That 98-pound weakling has a real body.

d. A lot of people misspell misspell.

e. "Don't come near me," he shouted with a frenzied look, or I'll jump.

f. If sage is an herb, how can sage mean is wise?

g. The numeral for the word 'eight' is 8.

h. Being a millionaire is a burden I could handle.

i. Did you actually hear the defendant say, I'll get even with him, or did you just think he said that?

j. More words in the English language begin with e than with j.

k. Some scholar he is; failing four courses and getting a D in the other is hardly anything to write home about.

l. She thought he said Sunday but what he actually said was I'll see you someday.

m. One generally can change an adjective into an adverb by adding ly to the end of the word. For example, if one adds ly to the adjective slow, the result is the adverb slowly.

n. Don't use a big word like pretentious when a shorter one will do as well; if you do, people will think you're pretentious.

1:3.2 Sentences and Statements   In our definition of 'argument' we said that an argument is composed of at least two *statements*. In general, we can say that one of the many things that people use language to do is to make statements—that is, to assert something which is either true or false—and that they typically do this by uttering a sentence. Our two major points here are, first, that sentences are not statements and, second, that it is statements which are either true or false.

Grammarians typically distinguish four major types of sentences. The first of these is the *declarative* sentence, which is used to express a fact, impart information, and so on, and which is typically followed by a period. The second is the *interrogative* sentence, which is used to ask a question and which is typically followed by a question mark. The third is the *imperative* sentence, which is used to issue a command, make a request, and so on, and which is typically ended with a period. The fourth is the *exclamatory* sentence, which is used to make an interjection and which is typically punctuated with an exclamation point.

Now it is clear that not every use of a sentence is a statement-making use, since some sentences are used to ask questions, some are used to give orders, some are used to express emotions, and so on; nonetheless, there may be a temptation to say that every declarative sentence is a statement. In this section we shall discuss why it is a mistake to do this.

There are three main reasons for not identifying declarative sentences with statements:

(1) Sometimes a nondeclarative sentence is used to make a statement.

(2) The same statement can be expressed with different declarative sentences.

(3) A given declarative sentence can be used to express different statements.

With regard to (1) there are many instances in which nondeclarative sentences are used to make a statement. One such instance is the following: Suppose that Tanya asks Mark to go to the basketball game with her, and he responds by telling her that he would like to go but has to study for an exam. While at the game Tanya sees Mark with Joyce, and when Tanya sees him the next day she says to him, "Didn't I see you at the game last night?" Here the sentence uttered is clearly interrogative in form. Nonetheless, given the context, it is reasonable to take Tanya as having asserted the statement that she saw Mark at the game.[5]

As for (2), there are many ways in which any given statement might be expressed. Suppose, for example, that someone wants to assert that Janet gave Murray a necklace for his birthday. This can be done by asserting any of the following, and others as well:

Murray received a necklace from Janet for his birthday.

Janet's birthday present to Murray was a necklace.

A necklace is what Janet gave Murray for his birthday.

For his birthday, Janet gave Murray a necklace.

Here we have four *different* declarative sentences, yet each could be used to say that Janet gave Murray a necklace for his birthday.

Finally, consider (3) and the declarative sentence 'The previous President died while in office.' This sentence can be used for many purposes and on many different occasions. Two such uses might be in response to the question

---

[5] Sentences of this kind, interrogative in form but used to make a statement, are called 'rhetorical questions.'

"How did Lyndon Johnson become President?" and to the question "How did Gerald Ford become President?" Although the same sentence was used in response to both questions, the statement made in using the sentence was different in the two cases. Moreover, in the first case the statement made was true, and in the second it was false.

Among the points to be derived from the above discussion is that different kinds of sentences, or different sentences of the same kind, can be used to make statements. Further, not every use of a sentence is a statement-making use. Hence, sentences are not statements. As a result, to determine whether a statement was made when some sentence was uttered, we should ask ourselves whether the speaker, in using the sentence on that occasion, did something which can appropriately be described as having made an assertion which is either true or false. If so, then a statement was made; if not, then no statement was made.

Since arguments are given in a language, and since they are composed of statements, it follows that in presenting an argument the speaker must use language to say things which are either true or false. To put this another way, we can say that if, on some particular occasion, the speaker does *not* do this, then whatever else he or she may have done, the speaker will not have presented an argument.[6] Since no argument will have been presented, the question of whether or not the speaker's "argument" is acceptable simply does not arise.[7]

The foregoing remark underscores the need for determining whether or not language has been used to make statements when we are analyzing arguments. It is not always easy to do this, however. One reason is that different kinds of sentences can be used to make statements. In these cases we must rely primarily on the context of the utterance to determine whether a statement was made and, if so, to determine which statement it was. A second, and more complex, reason is that sometimes a speaker uses a sentence to say something that is true or false *and* to do other things as well. As an example of this latter situation, suppose that we are on a picnic and you have wandered off a little ways to take some photographs of the wildflowers. All of a sudden, I notice that there is a bull charging across the field directly toward you, and I shout out, "There a bull coming!" Here it is appropriate to say that I have asserted something which is true, namely that there is a bull coming, and so I have used

---

[6] In light of our remarks earlier in the chapter, this statement needs to be qualified. Since logicians are primarily concerned with the question of whether the *truth* of the premises provides support for the *truth* of the conclusion, uses of language in which questions of truth do not arise fall outside the scope of logic. In ordinary language, by way of contrast, we often find reasons being given in support of orders, requests, and so on; these are not, of course, either true or false.

[7] Of course, the speaker may (incorrectly) believe that he or she has presented an argument in support of some position, even though language was not used to make statements. Here the appropriate response to the speaker is to point out that no argument was presented. Similarly, in a heated disagreement between two people, neither may be presenting an argument even though both people believe they are.

a sentence to make a statement. But I have also used the sentence to *warn* you about the bull, and in giving a warning I have done something in addition to making a statement.

Another thing that may have happened is that my sentence may have frightened you. This aspect of language use—that it often arouses emotions—is an important one to keep in mind whenever we are analyzing arguments. The primary reason for keeping it in mind is this: The emotions which are aroused by a speaker's words have nothing to do with the truth or falsity of what the speaker said. As a result, they have nothing to do with the question of whether or not the reasons the speaker offers for his or her position support that position. In the above case, for example, whether you are frightened, have some different feeling, or have no feeling at all on hearing that there's a bull coming is irrelevant to the truth or falsity of the claim that there is a bull coming. Similarly, a lawyer's pointing out that her client will no longer be able to support his old, sick mother if his license is suspended for driving while intoxicated in no way affects the issue of whether the client is guilty or not; it may well arouse emotions on the part of the judge and jury, however.

The other reason for keeping in mind that language often arouses emotions is that when emotions are aroused we often tend to be less careful in our evaluation of what someone is saying. In particular, many of us are more likely to accept as true that which we have a positive feeling toward, and more likely to reject as false that which we have a negative feeling toward. If we remember that the emotions aroused by language use are irrelevant to the truth or falsity of what the speaker said, then we will be less likely to accept or reject positions only because of our attitude toward them.

In this section we have noted that one of the uses of language is to assert something which is either true or false (that is, to make a statement), and that there are many other uses of language. We have also noted that sometimes a sentence has more than one use. As a result, it is not always easy to say when a particular use is a statement-making use, or to separate out mixed uses of language—particularly when one of the uses involves arousing emotions. Given this diversity, the context in which a sentence is used is an important determinant in deciding whether it was used to make a statement, had some other use, or had elements of both. In the next section we shall briefly examine some of the difficulties this leads to in our attempt to recognize and analyze arguments.

EXERCISE 1-9

Assuming that each of the following sentences is being used in an ordinary context, state whether it is being used to make a statement, is being used in some other way, or has elements of both types of uses. Explain your answers.

a. June 6 is the last day of classes this year.

b. Parent to college student: What are you going to do to make money this summer?

c. Fifth grader to fifth grader: It takes one to know one.

d. Please pass the relish.

e. Wow! A hole in one!

f. Muhammad Ali: I am the greatest!

g. Fairy Godmother to Cinderella: Make sure you're home by midnight.

h. *The Ten Commandments* is one of the greatest film extravaganzas of all times.

i. Professor to student: If you want to be a doctor, then you had better study a lot of science.

j. Poster: Uncle Sam needs you.

k. Why ever would you go out with him?

l. Damn!

m. 'Sodium chloride' is the chemical name for common table salt.

n. Athlete to coach: If you don't stop shouting at me every time I make a mistake, I'll quit.

o. Teacher to student: Are you sure that's the right answer?

p. Physiologist to class: Vegetarians need a source of protein other than red meat.

q. Freudians and behaviorists disagree in their analysis of human motivation.

r. Student to student: Studying logic is more fun than going to a movie?

s. Advertisement: People who do not get enough vitamins in their diet need Vitafix.

t. Police officer to driver: Didn't you see that stop sign back there?

u. Parent to child: If you know what's good for you, you'll get back in bed.

v. Doctor to patient: You haven't been taking your medicine lately, have you?

w. The highest mountain in North America has snow on it all year long.

x. Advertisement: For a healthier complexion, use Beautymist.

y. Political candidate to audience: I think it's only fair to point out that my opponent was acquitted of those embezzlement charges brought against him.

1:3.3 Disagreements and Arguments People often disagree with one another, and they disagree about a great many things. Each of the following is an example of a disagreement between two people.

(1) Ken tells Sharon that their logic instructor has changed the exam date from Friday to Monday. Sharon responds by telling Ken that the exam is still going to be on Friday.

(2) While discussing her latest economic policies during a news conference,

the President says that the country is suffering from a mild recession. One of the reporters in the audience responds, "This is not a recession; it's a depression."

(3) In discussing which hockey team was the best American team during the 1970s, Brad claims that it was the Philadelphia Flyers and Martin claims that it was the 1976 U.S. Olympic team.

(4) While staying up late at night to study for exams, Anne tells Bev that she is going to go make one of her favorite sandwiches: peanut butter and bacon. Bev replies, "That tastes awful."

It should be clear that there is a disagreement of some kind or other between each pair of people mentioned in the above examples. It should be just as clear that no one in any of the examples has offered an argument in support of his or her position; each person has merely stated what his or her position is. Since no arguments have been given, we are not in a position to assess whether the reasons (if any) that these people have for their positions support them.

Now, although no arguments have been given, it's easy to imagine each person going on and attempting to convince, or persuade, the other person of the correctness or incorrectness of his or her position. In logic, as in life, it's good advice to try to locate the source of a disagreement before attempting to resolve it. Our primary purpose in this section will be to examine some of the sources of disagreements among people. Once we have done that, we will be in a position to see whether or not arguments are relevant to resolving the disagreement and, if so, what kinds of arguments.

Let's begin with the example of Ken and Sharon. What is in dispute here is whether the exam is going to be given on Friday or on Monday. Clearly they cannot both be right (assuming that only one exam is going to be given), though they could both be wrong—as would be the case if the exam were going to be on Wednesday. Moreover, it's reasonable to suppose here that they both understand each other in that they are using words in their ordinary way, and so on. What we have here, then, is a disagreement over some matter of fact; we shall say that such disagreements are **factual disagreements.**

To resolve this disagreement, Ken and Sharon are going to have to appeal to some other facts. We can imagine the following discussion taking place:

Sharon: Well, last Friday the instructor clearly announced in class that the next exam will be given on Friday.

Ken: That's true. But on Monday, when you missed class to see your allergist, he announced that the exam had been changed to the following Monday.

Once Sharon is aware of the additional fact that the instructor changed the exam date, the disagreement between Sharon and Ken is resolved.

This does not mean, of course, that the dispute *had* to be resolved. We can easily recall, from our own experiences, situations in which people steadfastly held on to their position regardless of what factual evidence was presented to them. And this brings up an important point: It is always possible for someone to continue to maintain a position regardless of what factual information is brought forward to show that the position is false. For example, Sharon could continue to hold to her position if she were to respond to Ken that the instructor was lying on Monday when he said he was going to change the exam date. What we must be aware of, then, when engaged in or discussing factual disagreements, is whether or not it is *reasonable* for someone to continue to maintain a position in light of the facts which have been brought forward. It is sad, but true, that there is no way we can make people *be* reasonable; the best we can do is engage in rational discourse with the expectation that they will be reasonable.

Not surprisingly, not all factual disagreements are as easily resolved as the one between Sharon and Ken. Among the reasons for this is that sometimes the factual evidence which is available simply is inadequate to support one position over another.[8] For example, suppose that two doctors are trying to determine which disease a patient has, to initiate an appropriate cure. It often happens that the patient will exhibit some symptoms of two different diseases but will not exhibit all the symptoms of one of them. In this case the two doctors may well end up in a factual dispute, one saying the patient has disease A and the other saying the patient has disease B. Moreover, the doctors may agree on all the facts regarding the patient's symptoms and about what diseases A and B are.

People often think that they are engaged in a factual disagreement when the source of their disagreement is something other than facts. One such disagreement follows:

Brenda: Pluto is the planet furthest from the sun.

Donna: No it's not; Neptune is.

In the course of resolving this disagreement, suppose Donna says the following:

I recently read that from now until 1999 Neptune will be further away from the sun than any of the other planets.

And suppose Brenda says:

I learned in my astronomy class that Pluto's orbit takes it further from the sun than any of the other planets.

Given these remarks, it is easy to resolve the disagreement between Brenda and Donna. What Donna means by the expression 'planet furthest from the sun' is the planet which is furthest away *now*. What Brenda means by the same

---

[8] One of the reasons why factual evidence is sometimes inadequate to support one position over another is that *facts are subject to interpretation*. This frequently happens in the sciences, where the question of what the facts are is often dependent upon what theory one holds. We shall discuss these matters in more detail in Chapter 9.

expression is the planet which is furthest away from the sun when we consider its *entire orbit*.

Here we see that Brenda and Donna are using the word 'furthest' in two different ways. This is a case in which the two disputants have used a word that each takes to have a different meaning, and neither of them realizes that they are doing this. When this occurs, we shall say that what is taking place is a **verbal disagreement**.

Once Donna and Brenda realize the source of their disagreement, it can be easily resolved. In particular, they may both agree that Neptune is further from the sun than Pluto *now*, but Pluto travels further from the sun on its orbit than Neptune does on its orbit. In short, they agree on the facts, but the way they were using the word 'furthest' made them think they were disagreeing.

It is not always easy to tell whether a disagreement is a verbal one or some other kind. The second example with which we opened this section is one such case. There, recall, the President was maintaining that the country was undergoing a mild recession, and a reporter responded that it was not a recession but a depression.

It is likely that both the President and the reporter would agree on at least some of the facts regarding the present economic situation; for example, a recent falloff in business activity. If they were to agree on *all* the facts, then the President's calling the situation a recession and the reporter's calling it a depression would be just a verbal disagreement *between the two of them*. Economists, however, do distinguish between recessions and depressions, and insofar as the economic conditions are satisfied, the economy is in a recession, or a depression, or neither; it could not be in both.

In such cases, one has to be very careful when attempting to identify the kind of disagreement that exists between the two disputants. It is a verbal disagreement if they agree on all the relevant facts but just label the situation differently. If they disagree on some of the relevant facts, it likely is a factual disagreement. We must always allow the possibility, however, that the facts are insufficient to support one position to the exclusion of others, with the result that it is unclear which position is correct. (The dispute between two economists over whether the economy is in a recession or a depression is a bit like the case of two doctors who disagree regarding the disease that some patient has. Different symptoms may support each hypothesis, without all the symptoms being present which would support one hypothesis to the exclusion of the other.)

Before leaving this example to discuss other kinds of disagreements, let us recall the earlier remark that language can be used to arouse feelings or emotions. Some words and expressions in language typically have positive or negative feelings associated with them. For example, 'beautiful', 'good', 'right', and 'winning' typically are associated with, and arouse, positive feelings. In contrast, 'ugly', 'bad', 'wrong', and 'losing' typically are associated with, and arouse, negative feelings. In our society the word 'depression' arouses negative feelings in several generations of people. Someone like the President, who is concerned with how people feel about the state of the economy, is going to be very careful about what labels he or she puts on the economy. Calling the present situation a recession has nowhere near the negative force of calling it a depression. Also notice that in our example the President even went so far as to call it a *mild* recession. As noted earlier, the feelings aroused by what someone says do not affect the truth or falsity of what was said. Nonetheless, when a word or an expression arouses positive feelings, we often tend to agree with what was said; and when negative feelings are aroused, we tend to disagree with what was said. If we keep in mind the power that words have to influence our feelings, we shall be less likely to make the mistake of supposing that when we feel good the speaker is saying something true, and when we feel bad the speaker is saying something false. We shall return to a discussion of this matter in Chapter 10.

So far we have seen that people may disagree over some fact, in which case we have a factual disagreement; or, they may agree on the facts but be using words in such a way that they don't realize that they agree on the facts, in which case we have a verbal disagreement. We have also seen that it is not always easy to tell whether a disagreement is factual or verbal; nor is it always easy to tell who is right, even when people agree on the facts. At this point it has probably occurred to you that deciding what kind of disagreement two people have may sometimes be a difficult task. If you have felt this way, take heart; you're right. When we begin to consider the complexity of language, the feelings it often arouses, and the complexity of people, it's hardly surprising that trying to identify *how* people disagree, let alone who is right, *is* a hard task. The third example we used to introduce this section shows yet another dimension in the kinds of disagreement that people can have. For convenience, this example is reproduced below:

> In discussing which hockey team was the best American team during the 1970s, Brad claims that it was the Philadelphia Flyers and Martin claims that it was the 1976 U.S. Olympic team.

To focus on why this disagreement is different from those we have so far discussed, let's suppose that Brad and Martin are both aware of all the facts about the Flyers during the 1970s, and both are aware of all the facts about the U.S. Olympic team. In short, let us suppose that, other than differing about which of the two teams was the best, they agree on all the background facts. Another way of saying this is that they have no factual disagreement about the two teams; they disagree, however, about which one was best.

Let us further suppose that both Martin and Brad agree about the meaning of the word 'best'. We add this just to prevent their being engaged in a purely verbal disagreement over the meaning of 'best'. What we have, then, is two people who are using the word 'best' in the same way, and who agree on all the background facts.

Brad and Martin are not engaged in a purely verbal disagreement, and they are not engaged in a purely factual one. What we have here is two people who agree on the facts and are using language in the same way; yet they disagree. What is the source of their disagreement?

The likely source is that they disagree over the criteria, or grounds, for one hockey team's being the best team. Brad likely holds the position that the facts which are true of the Flyers are just the things which make a hockey team best, whereas Martin likely holds the position that the facts about the Olympic team are the things which make them best. We shall say that situations like this one are **disagreements in appraisal.** The basic source of such disagreements is that people often appeal to different facts to justify their decisions about the value or worth of some thing. Moreover, this can occur even when the disputants agree on all the facts, as Brad and Martin do concerning the two hockey teams.

Disagreement in appraisal often occur in aesthetics and in situations where moral judgments are made. For example, suppose that there are two judges for an art show and they are trying to decide which work will receive the Best of Show prize. Both judges have seen all the works, and we can further suppose that they are in agreement concerning the facts about the media used by the artists, the subjects, and so on. Nonetheless, it is easy to imagine that the two judges can disagree in deciding which work is the best in the show.

This example points toward one of the difficulties in resolving disagreements in appraisal, and it points to a way in which such disagreements can sometimes be resolved. The difficulty is that since both disputants agree on the facts, neither is going to be able to appeal to the facts to support his or her position. (Recall that, in the factual disagreement between Ken and Sharon, an appeal to other facts could be used to resolve the disagreement, since these other facts clearly showed that one person was correct and the other incorrect.)

Since neither person can simply appeal to the facts, each must do something else. What they can do is try to get the other person to *see the facts in a different way.* Each person can try to get the other to focus on some feature or fact which he or she might have overlooked, or to see the facts in the context of some larger scheme. For example, suppose someone says that a particular movie was very bad because there was no continuity in the plot. He or she might change that appraisal if it were pointed out that this was a device used by the director to emphasize the disoriented feelings of the main character.

What we need to be aware of when we are confronted with a disagreement in appraisal is that sometimes such disagreements cannot be resolved; this does not mean, however, that someone has made a factual mistake or is using language in an atypical way. Most such disagreements rest on how each person sees the situation, and sometimes there is just no way to get the other person to see the situation differently.

This last point should *not* be taken to mean that both disputants are always right in disagreements of appraisal. Someone who has never developed a sensitivity for, or appreciation of, literature may hold the position that *Hamlet* is a terrible literary work, and that all of Shakespeare's work is terrible. Moreover, it may be impossible to get this person to see the works in a different way. In this case we may not be able to resolve the disagreement, but nonetheless the person's appraisal of the literary worth of Shakespeare's works is wrong.

Another group of situations, although different from disagreements in appraisal, is similar enough to sometimes be confused with them. The last example with which we began this section is one of these situations. It is the following:

> While staying up late at night to study for exams, Anne tells Bev that she is going to go make one of her favorite sandwiches: peanut butter and bacon. Bev replies, "That tastes awful."

Here Bev and Anne disagree over how a peanut butter and bacon sandwich tastes. For Bev it's awful; it's one of Anne's favorites. As in some earlier cases, we can imagine that Bev and Anne agree on the facts and are using language in the same way. As a result, the disagreement may be *mistaken* for one of appraisal. There is an important difference, however: In disagreements of appraisal the disputants are talking about the value or worth of something; in the present situation Bev and Anne are talking about *themselves*. In particular, we can well imagine the example's having involved the following exchange:

Anne: I like peanut butter and bacon sandwiches.

Bev: I don't.

When the disagreement is viewed in this way, we can see that Bev and Anne have expressed their respective positions, each understands the other's position, and each can agree that what the other says is true. That is, Bev can agree that Anne likes peanut butter and bacon sandwiches, and Anne can agree that Bev does not. In a situation like this, we shall say that we have a **disagreement in taste.**

An essential feature of such disagreements is that the disputants each say what they like, but they do not like the same thing. Additionally, it is pointless for one disputant to try to convince the other that he or she is wrong; this amounts to trying to convince one that one does like what one doesn't like.

The explanation of why disagreements in taste seem like real disagreements probably rests on the fact that people sometimes confuse what people *do* like with what they *should* like. For example, if Anne and Bev were to get into a dispute over peanut butter and bacon sandwiches, the disagreement would likely be over Anne's trying to convince Bev that she should like such sandwiches and Bev's trying to convince Anne that she shouldn't. That is, the disagreement would likely turn into one of appraisal.

Of course, arguing over whether one should or should not like a certain kind of sandwich is not particularly important. In many other areas, however, we do think it important to engage in such arguments: politics, art, morals, and literature are a few of these. What we must guard against is confusing taste with appraisal, for regarding the latter it makes sense to try to get someone to see things in a different way; regarding the former, the things that people like are the things that they like, and this is much different from the issue of what they should like.

One way to focus on the difference between appraisal and taste is to consider statements like 'That was not a very good book but I enjoyed reading it.' The first part of this claim is a matter of appraisal; the second, a matter of taste. When engaged in a disagreement, we must be careful to focus on just what is at issue, for when appraisal and taste are concerned, people can agree or disagree over both areas.

This completes our discussion of some of the kinds of disagreements people often have. In the next section we shall look at some ways of determining what kind of disagreement people are engaged in and, briefly, how one might resolve the disagreement.

1:3.4 Resolving Disagreements   In the previous section we examined four of the kinds of disagreements in which people become involved: factual, verbal, appraisal, and taste. When people disagree, they sometimes offer arguments in support of their positions. Since our central purpose in this book is to develop various skills in analyzing arguments, we should keep in mind that one of the features of a good argument is that the truth of the premises is relevant to the truth of the conclusion. As a result, it is important when people disagree that they identify the source of their disagreement, for without doing so they cannot determine whether they are offering good arguments in support of their positions.

The following procedure can be used to identify the type of disagreement and, thereby, its source:

(1) Determine whether the disputants are using language in the same way. That is, make sure the disagreement is not a verbal one.

(2) If the disagreement is not a verbal one, determine whether the disputants agree or disagree about the facts. If they disagree, the disagreement is a factual one, and an appeal to additional facts may resolve it.

(3) If the disputants are using language in the same way and they agree on the facts, the disagreement is likely one of appraisal or taste. A helpful way to determine which of these is occurring is to ask whether the disputants are each making a judgment about the value or worth of something, or whether they are reporting their likes or dislikes. In the former case it is a disagreement of appraisal, and in the latter case one of taste.

The above procedure makes it appear that locating the source of a disagreement is an easy, mechanical process. As we have seen in the examples discussed above, this is not always so. Think of the above procedure as a guideline, not a strict way to find easy answers to sometimes difficult situations, and keep in mind our discussion of the various kinds of disagreements in the previous section.

Once we have determined what kind of disagreement a disagreement is, we are ready to try to resolve it. The following are some of the things that can be done to try to resolve a disagreement, along with some of the relevant features to consider when attempting to evaluate the arguments given in support of each position in the disagreement:

(1) If the disagreement is verbal, attempt to get each disputant to agree on one common definition of the key terms in the dispute. When this is done, the disagreement is often resolved. Keep in mind, however, that many words have more than one meaning, and words which are similar in meaning often have different emotions associated with them. When the disputants agree on a common definition of key terms and yet still seem to disagree, it is often because of the emotions each of them associates with the key terms.

(2) If the disagreement is factual, attempt to resolve it be appealing to other facts. Keep in mind that facts are sometimes open to interpretation and that not all factual disagreements can be resolved easily. If someone does offer an argument in support of his or her side in a factual disagreement, look for an argument in which other facts are cited and in which it is shown how these facts, if true, support the fact in dispute. If the facts cited in the argument have nothing to do with the disputed fact, then the argument can justifiably be rejected.

(3) If the disagreement is one of appraisal, then the primary way to resolve it is to attempt to get the other person to see the facts in another way. (Remember, this cannot always be done.) Relevant strategies and arguments here involve appealing to additional facts and showing how the present ones can be seen in light of these other facts; showing how other views held by one of the disputants would, for the sake of consistency, support his or her seeing the disputed facts in another way; and showing how the disputed situation is similar enough to others which are not in dispute, and thereby using these other situations as a means of settling the present dispute.

(4) If the disagreement is one of taste, there really is no way to resolve it other than to have the tastes of one of the disputants change. If you like football and I don't, the only way we will ever agree is if our likes or dislikes change—if I come to like football or you come to dislike it. As noted in the previous section, disagreements in taste are often mistaken for disagreements in appraisal. As a result, it is a good idea, when two people agree on the facts but seem to disagree, to attempt to find out whether it is appraisal or taste which is at issue.

In this chapter we have discussed how to recognize arguments and identify their premises and conclusions. Since arguments are given in a language and are often given when people disagree with one another, we have also examined some of the uses of language and some kinds of disagreements which occur frequently. We are now ready to consider various kinds of arguments and what makes one argument a good one and another a bad one. This is our central task in the next chapter.

EXERCISE 1-10

Identify the kind of disagreement, if any, which occurs in each of the following examples. Remember that sometimes there can be more than one kind of disagreement.

a. Gerry: You're drunk again, aren't you?

   Nora: I am not. I just went out and had a few drinks with some friends after work.

b. Audrey: I'm going to apply for a job as an accountant at FGSI.

   Vernon: You won't get it. Being an accountant is a job for a man. You're obviously not that.

c. Audrey: I'm going to apply for a job as an accountant at FGSI.

   Rachel: You won't get it. They're one of the most conservative firms in the country, and they still haven't realized that a woman can do any job that a man can do.

d. Reporter: Why did you send combat troops into Central America?

   President: We did not send combat troops; those we did send are just military advisers.

e. Allen: People who major in philosophy never get jobs which enable them to use their skills.

   Patti: That's not true. Paula got a job in marketing at Dayton's, and she uses the critical skills she developed in her philosophy courses to help make important decisions in their marketing department.

f. Ron: *The Beach is a Paradise* is one of the best movies I've seen in a long time.

   Vera: Either you don't go to the movies very often or you like macho, sexist films. It's the worst picture I've ever seen.

g. Freda: There's nothing I like better than to sit in a sauna and then go jump into a snowbank.

   Glen: How awful!

h. Cathy: I just got promoted to assistant manager at Braywick's. What a great step forward in my career!

   Walt: Selling clothes to silly old women is no career; it's just a job.

i. Parent: Will you turn off that damn noise; I'm trying to read the paper.

   Child: It's not noise. It's the new record by the Unholy Five.

j. Defense attorney: It's clear that my client is a psychopath and should be found innocent by virtue of insanity.

   Prosecuting attorney: Your client may be neurotic, but he's no psychopath and he surely is not insane.

STUDENT STUDY GUIDE

Chapter Summary

1. **Logic** is the study of the relationship between the premises and the conclusions of arguments. (Introduction)

2. An **argument** is a group of at least two statements, one of which is the conclusion and the others of which are the premises, which are offered as support for the conclusion. The **conclusion** of an argument is the point or position the speaker wants to establish, and the **premises** of an argument are the reasons offered in support of the position. (section 1:1.1)

3. When we say that an argument is a group of **statements,** we mean that the speaker (or writer) has said things which are either true or false (have the **truth value** true or the truth value false). (section 1:2.1)

4. The order of the sentences one uses in giving an argument does not determine which statement is the conclusion and which are the premises. The conclusion may occur at the beginning, in the middle, or at the end of an argument. (section 1:2.1)

5. Arguments which are not explicitly stated in their entirety are **enthymemes.** Such arguments have either one or more **missing premises** or an **unstated conclusion.** (section 1:2.1

6. We add a missing premise or an unstated conclusion to an argument by using the **principle of charity.** In using this principle, we attempt to make the argument as good as possible by extracting information which may be implicit in the context of the argument and by appealing to general knowledge. (section 1:2.1)

7. In an argument, something is offered as a conclusion (either explicitly or implicitly) and something is offered as support for the conclusion (either explicitly or implicitly). An assertion fails to be an argument when the speaker simply makes an **unsupported claim** or when the speaker gives a **narrative.** (section 1:2.2)

8. Statements having the form "if–then" are **conditional statements.** Conditional statements are not arguments and should not be broken apart. (section 1:2.2)

9. Since the conclusion of an argument may occur anywhere among the group of statements asserted by the speaker, one of the best ways to identify the conclusion of an argument is to ask the question, "What point is the speaker trying to make?" In addition, some words or expressions are often used to point out the conclusion or the premises of an argument; these are **indicator words. Conclusion indicators** are helpful cues for identifying the conclusion of an argument. (section 1:2.3)

10. One of the best methods of identifying the premises of an argument is to ask the question "What reasons has the speaker offered for his or her position?" One can also make use of **premise indicators,** words or expressions often used to point out the premises of an argument. (section 1:2.4)

11. Some words which function as indicator words also have other typical uses.

Two of these are 'since', which is often used to indicate a **temporal relationship,** and 'because', which is often used to indicate a **causal relationship.** In many cases we can tell in which way these words are being used by considering the sentences in which they occur. In other cases we must rely on the context of the speaker's remarks. (section 1:2.4)

12. An argument is in **standard form** when it has been written with all the premises listed first, followed by the conclusion. The symbol '∴' is used to indicate the conclusion regardless of which, if any, conclusion indicator might have been used in giving the argument. (section 1:2.5)

13. Throughout the text we shall have occasion to distinguish between the **use** and the **mention** of a word or an expression. To do this, we shall use the convention of placing *single quotation marks* around a word or an expression which is being mentioned. (section 1:3.1)

14. One of the many things for which people use language is to make **statements.** On any particular occasion of the use of language, a statement has been made when the speaker has asserted something which is either true or false. (section 1:3.2)

15. No sentence is a statement, and, in particular, declarative sentences are not statements. Among the reasons for this are: sometimes a declarative sentence is used to do something in addition to making a statement; sometimes a nondeclarative sentence is used to make a statement; the same statement can be expressed with different declarative sentences; and a given declarative sentence can be used to express different statements. (section 1:3.2)

16. When people disagree about what is or is not the case, they typically are engaged in a **factual disagreement.** In such a disagreement, both disputants may be wrong, but they cannot both be right. Some factual disagreements are difficult to resolve because it is unclear what other facts are relevant to the disagreement; sometimes the available facts are insufficient to support one position over another; and sometimes the facts are subject to interpretation. (section 1:3.3)

17. When two disputants use a word or an expression which each takes to have a different meaning, and neither of them realizes they are doing this, the disputants are engaged in a **verbal disagreement.** Verbal disagreements are sometimes mistaken for factual disagreements and are sometimes difficult to resolve. One of the major reasons for this difficulty is the fact that some words or expressions are associated with and arouse positive feelings, and some negative feelings. (section 1:3.3)

18. One kind of disagreement which often occurs when the disputants agree on the facts and are using language in the same way is a **disagreement in appraisal.** Such disagreements are about the value or worth of something, and they often arise when people use different facts to justify their decisions or see the facts in different, inconsistent ways. (section 1:3.3)

19. Another kind of disagreement which occurs when the disputants agree on the facts and are using language in the same way is a **disagreement in taste.** Disagreements in taste are often mistaken for disagreements in appraisal; they can be distinguished by noting that the latter have to do with the value or

worth of something, and in the former the disputants are talking about their own likes and dislikes. (section 1:3.3).

20. Not all disagreements are easy to resolve, and some simply can't be resolved. The first step toward resolution is to determine what kind of disagreement the disputants are engaged in. Then, depending on the kind of disagreement, one can appeal to other facts (factual disagreement); appeal to language use (verbal disagreement); attempt to get one or the other disputant to see the facts in a different way (disagreement in appraisal); or realize that different people have different likes and dislikes (disagreement in taste). (section 1:3.4).

Key Terms

Logic	Indicator Word
Argument	Standard Form of an Argument
Premise	Use and Mention
Conclusion	Scare Quotes
Statement	Statement-Making Use of Language
Truth Value	Non-Statement-Making Use of Language
Enthymeme	Factual Disagreement
Principle of Charity	Verbal Disagreement
Unsupported Claim	Disagreement in Appraisal
Narrative	Disagreement in Taste
Conditional Statement	

Self-Test/Exercises

1. Indicate which of the following are true and which are false. For those which are false, explain why they are false.
   a. Logicians are primarily concerned with the truth and falsity of the premises and conclusions of an argument.
   b. Studying logic can help one to make better decisions and to solve problems.
   c. When people argue with one another, the one who has gotten his or her opponent to give in has presented an argument.
   d. Every argument must have at least one premise.
   e. Some arguments are incomplete in that they may have one or more missing premises or an unstated conclusion.
   f. In an enthymeme, if the conclusion is unstated then the conclusion is always obvious from the context of the argument.
   g. A speaker who believes that what he or she is saying is true and then makes a conditional statement has given an argument.
   h. Any argument with an unstated conclusion is an enthymeme.
   i. 'As a result' is often used as a premise indicator.
   j. 'As a result of' is often used as a conclusion indicator.
   k. Unsupported claims are sometimes arguments. This happens when the speaker has evidence in support of the claim but just hasn't offered the evidence.

l. Single quotation marks are used to indicate that a word is being used in an atypical way.

m. The principle of charity tells us that before we give at the office we should contribute money to our logic instructor.

n. To put an argument into standard form, one lists all the premises, followed by the conclusion, and indicates the conclusion with '∴'.

o. Declarative sentences are always used to make statements.

p. It is sometimes possible to make a statement by using a sentence which is interrogative in form.

q. No matter what the context, the speaker always either makes a statement or does something else by using language; the speaker never does both.

r. Every factual disagreement can be resolved by gathering all the relevant information bearing on the issue.

s. Sometimes what looks like a factual disagreement is actually some other kind of disagreement.

t. When there is a genuine factual disagreement, both people cannot be right, although they can both be wrong.

u. Disagreements in appraisal can never be resolved.

v. Some disagreements in taste can never be resolved.

w. Every disagreement can be resolved by defining one's terms.

x. Every verbal disagreement can be turned into a factual disagreement.

y. Nobody really likes to disagree with another person.

2. Identify the premises and the conclusions of the following arguments, and put the arguments into standard form. In some cases it may be necessary to supply missing premises or to supply a missing conclusion. (sections 1:2.3 to 1:2.5)

a. There's no fool like an old fool. My grandfather is an old fool, so he's no fool.

b. Every abortion results in the taking of a human life. Whenever one takes a human life, one does something immoral. Therefore, if the federal government continues to provide funds for abortions, it will be doing something immoral.

c. Everyone wants to be able to relax. Lay-z-chair is the chair that redefined 'relaxation'.

d. The price of gold continues to go down, and the cost of living continues to go up. Of course, a wise investment is one which keeps up with, or moves ahead of, the cost of living. It's obvious, then, that I didn't make a wise investment when I decided to buy gold.

e. Look, we all know that to play baseball, and to be good at it, you need at least four months of warm, dry weather. Is it any wonder, then, that most of the schools which have won the College World Series in the past two decades have come from the deep south or the southwest?

f. It's a rare occasion when I meet someone and then develop a lasting friendship. Indeed, as I think of the last ten parties I've gone to and all the people I've met, Sharon was the only one whom I'm now friends with. If I'm honest with myself, I may as well admit that it's unlikely that I'll meet anyone at tonight's party with whom I shall form a lasting friendship.

3. Describe situations in which each of the following sentences would have a statement-making use. Then describe situations in which each would have a non-statement-making use or a mixed use. (section 1:3.3)

a. Are you going home this weekend?
b. It's very cold in here.
c. Some people really like to suffer.
d. If you leave now, I'll never see you again.
e. You're kidding!
f. As He gave His peace unto them, so I give my peace unto you.
g. This is the beer that made Milwaukee famous.
h. No one likes a loser.

4. Identify the kind of disagreement that is going on between the two people in the following examples. Of course, more than one disagreement may be possible. (section 1:3.4)

a. Marta: Christopher Columbus was the first European to set foot on what is now America.

   Bergit: That's silly. The Vikings from the Scandinavian countries were here long before the Spaniards even thought about sailing here.

b. Janice: I thought we agreed before we went away to different colleges that we wouldn't run around on one another.

   Tim: We did. But I wasn't running around on you. I just took Theresa to a movie.

c. Reporter: Why does the present government insist upon policies that keep a great proportion of American citizens below the poverty level?

   Spokesperson: Whereas I agree with you that there is a segment of the American population which does not have very much income, no one in this country is below the poverty level. If you will just look at our recent analysis, you will see that every American family is making, or getting from the federal government, enough money to at least live at a subsistence level.

d. Herman: I've been to this restaurant before, and the best thing on the menu is the roast duck.

   Lenore: I've been here too. And the best thing on the menu is the pheasant.

e. Becky: I like the way this school keeps track of how you're doing academically, suggests ways to do better, and informs us about services they have that will help.

   Don: Well, I don't like it. Why are they always sticking their noses in where it doesn't belong?

f. Fred: When I get home after a long day during the summer, I really like to just lie down in the sun.

   Duane: I don't.

CHAPTER 2

INDUCTION AND DEDUCTION

Now that you know what arguments are and are able to recognize them when they have been given, we are ready to consider what makes some arguments good and others bad. This is one of our main goals in this chapter. Not surprisingly, we shall find that all good arguments have certain characteristics and that one or more of these characteristics is missing in every bad argument. We shall discuss these characteristics here; then, in subsequent chapters, we shall develop various ways to determine whether several classes of arguments have these characteristics.

Our procedure here will be as follows: We begin with the assumption that everyone is able to recognize at least some instances of good and bad arguments. The question then is, "What is it about the arguments which makes them either good or bad?" To answer this question, we shall consider the ways in which arguments can go wrong. This consideration will suggest two characteristics that a good argument must have: premises which are relevant to, or support, the conclusion and premises which are true. Finally, we shall provide a rigorous characterization of the two ways in which the premises of good arguments can support their conclusions.

Since the task of determining whether an argument is good or bad requires that we analyze the structure of arguments, we shall also develop some logic notation which will enable us to display these structures. We shall then conclude our discussion in this chapter by discussing a procedure which can often be used to show that the premises of an argument do not support the conclusion; the procedure is that of presenting a counterexample.

2:1 GOOD AND BAD ARGUMENTS

We saw in the previous chapter that when someone presents an argument he or she asserts some position—the conclusion of the argument—and asserts the premises as support for the conclusion. The premises, then, constitute the evidence for the truth of the conclusion. For the moment, let's consider in an informal way the conditions under which we would ordinarily say that someone had presented a good argument for some position. We shall later provide a rigorous characterization of these informal results.

The first thing that may come to your mind is that we require only that the conclusion of the argument be true. A little reflection will show, however, that this is *not* the case. That a true conclusion is not sufficient for an argument's being good is brought out by such remarks as these:

> What you say may be true, but the reasons you gave don't support your position.

> I agree with your point of view, but what you said in support of it is simply false.

> Nobody denies what you're saying; it's just that the reasons you've offered aren't any good.

> In spite of the truth of what you claim, your argument isn't any good.

We've all heard and made remarks like these—remarks which in any ordinary context clearly indicate that, even though we may agree that the conclusion of the speaker's argument is true, we nonetheless judge that the argument is not a good one.

If a true conclusion is not what we are looking for in a good argument, what do we require? The remarks already made suggest an answer to this question. In particular, anyone who asserts that "What you say may be true, but the reasons you gave don't support your position," expects that in giving a good argument the speaker will provide evidence which is somehow relevant to the position he or she is maintaining. Other remarks which indicate the same thing are:

> That has nothing to do with what you're trying to show.

> What you have just said is irrelevant to your position.

> Even granting that what you say is true, that's not a good reason for your point of view.

> Your position doesn't follow from what you've said.

Each of these remarks, and others as well, serves to say that the evidence (the premises) the speaker has offered as support for his or her position (the conclusion) are irrelevant to that position.

The above comments should make it clear that one of the things we require of all good arguments is that the premises, if true, guarantee or at least make likely the truth of the conclusion. That is, we require that the premises be related to the conclusion in such a way that, if true, they support the conclusion. In section 2:2 we shall have a more definitive account of the **support relationship** between the premises and conclusions of good arguments.

While we expect of a good argument that the premises be relevant to, or support, the conclusion, that is not all we expect. This is brought out by such ordinary remarks as these:

What you call 'reasons' aren't reasons at all since they're false.

Your conclusion would be true only if your premises were; but they're not.

That doesn't prove your point at all, since your premise is false.

Each of these remarks, and others like them, serves to say that the speaker's argument is unacceptable because one or more of the premises is false. As a result, it is clear that in a good argument we also require that all the premises be true.

When logicians talk about the truth or falsity of the premises or conclusion of an argument or, more generally, the truth or falsity of any statement, they use the expression **'truth value'**. Every statement—and, hence, each premise and the conclusion of an argument—has one and only one truth value; it has the truth value *true* if it is true, and *false* if it is false. Accordingly, we say that in an argument each premise and the conclusion has *a* truth value, but it need not have the *particular* truth value *true*.

2:1.1 Support and Truth

As we saw in the previous section, two conditions must be satisfied for an argument to be good: The premises of the argument must support the conclusion, and the premises must be true. If either of these conditions is not satisfied, then the argument is a bad one. It remains to be shown, of course, what it means to say that the premises of an argument support the conclusion. We shall take up this issue shortly, but first there are several important points to be noted about the two conditions every good argument must meet.

The first, and most important, point is that the two conditions are *independent* of each other. What we mean by this is that some arguments in which the premises support the conclusion have all true premises and some don't. Similarly, some arguments in which the premises *do not* support the conclusion have all true premises and some don't. The four possible cases are:

Support; all true premises

Support; at least one false premise

No support; all true premises

No support; at least one false premise

Because of the independence of the support relationship and the truth value of the premises in an argument, the evaluation of any argument is a two-step procedure. The first step is to determine whether the premises do support the conclusion, and the second step is to determine whether or not the premises are true. We shall see below why logicians are primarily concerned with the first step of the procedure. Before we turn to that, however, there is an additional point to note about the independence of the support relation and the truth value of the premises.

As noted above, the premises of an argument can support the conclusion even if one or all of the premises are false. This occurs because, in any language, it is possible to investigate the relationships among certain statements by asking such questions as "*If* these statements are true, which other statements would have to be true (and which false)?" or "*If* these statements are true, which other statements are likely to be true (and which are likely to be false)?" Questions like these can be answered without ever raising more concrete questions of the form "Is this particular statement *actually* true?"[1] An example should help to clarify this point.

ARGUMENT 1

Martin Van Buren was the first President of the United States.

The first President of the United States was married to Martha Washington.

∴ Martin Van Buren was married to Martha Washington.

In argument 1 we have a situation in which one of the premises, the first, has the truth value *false* and the other premise has the truth value *true*. In addition, the conclusion has the truth value *false*. In spite of the actual falsity of one of the premises and the falsity of the conclusion, we *can* ask (and answer) the question, "*If* the premises of this argument were true, would the conclusion have to be true?" The answer here is yes, for *if* it were true that Van Buren was the first President of the United States, and *if* it were true that the first President was married to Martha Washington, then it would also be true that Van Buren was married to Martha Washington. In this case, then, the premises *support* the conclusion even though one of the premises is actually false.

There are two important points that you should understand from this example: First, given the relationships which hold among some statements, it is possible to determine which other statements would be true, or which would likely be true, *if* those in a given set were true; second, since the support relationship between the premises and the conclusion of an argument depends on the relationship between them, the premises of an argument can support the conclusion even though one or all of the premises is actually false.

In saying of argument 1 that the premises support the conclusion, we are not, of course, thereby saying that the argument is a good one. We have already seen that there is an additional characteristic of all good arguments, namely that they have all true premises, which is missing in the case of argument 1.[2] Of the two characteristics of every good argument (all true premises and the premises providing support for the conclusion), we, like other logicians, shall confine our study to the support relationship. In particular, we shall investigate the general conditions which have to be satisfied so that the premises of an argument support the conclusion, and we shall develop ways to determine, for a great many arguments, whether the support relationship is satisfied.

At this point you may be feeling a bit of discomfort in hearing that, when

---

[1] In section 2:2 we shall see why this is so.
[2] Recall that determining the truth value of the premises of an argument is the second step in evaluating arguments.

it comes to arguments, we shall be concerned with the support relationship between the premises and the conclusion, and not with the actual truth value of the statements which compose the argument. What good is studying logic, you may be thinking, if that study is independent of the actual truth value of the premises and the conclusion?

A part of the answer to this question has already been given: *Even if* all the premises of a given argument are true, they do not establish the truth of the conclusion or constitute good reasons for accepting it, unless the truth of the premises is relevant to the truth of the conclusion; that is, unless the premises provide support for the conclusion. Hence, by studying logic, and in particular the support relationship between the premises and the conclusion, you will be able to determine whether this crucial requirement for good arguments has been met.

A second part of the answer is that whereas the truth value of the premises of an argument is one of the things which determines whether an argument is good or bad, determining this truth value is not something which ordinarily falls within the domain of logic. Depending on the subject matter of the argument, many others, by virtue of their own experience and knowledge, are likely better qualified to determine the truth value of some statements than are logicians. As a somewhat simple example, suppose we did not know whether or not the premises of argument 1 were true; we would not seek their truth value by studying logic, but rather by consulting a history book.

With these points in mind, we can say that the truth value of the premises of an argument does matter, but we shall focus our attention on the support relationship between the premises and the conclusions of arguments because this aspect of arguments is the one which properly falls within the domain of logic; determining whether the premises of an argument are true or false is an issue which properly falls within the domain of many different fields, depending on the content of the argument.

It is, then, possible to examine relationships among statements without knowing whether the statements are actually true or actually false (that is, without knowing their truth value). However, the question of truth value is not totally irrelevant in assessing the relationships among statements, for we do ask ourselves what would follow *if* the statements *were true*. From a logician's point of view, being able to answer this question is a result of the fact that if a given statement is true, then there are other statements which must also be true; this relationship can hold even if the given statement and the ones which follow are actually false. For example, the three statements 'Boston is in New England,' 'I live in Boston,' and 'I live in New England' are logically related such that if the first and second are true, then the third is also true—even though the second and third statements may actually be false.

In this section we have expanded our earlier remark that every good argument is one in which the premises support the conclusion and all the premises are true. We have also seen that the primary concern of logic is the study of the support relationship between the premises and conclusions of arguments. Since the support relationship depends on the logical relationships which hold or fail to hold among statements, we can determine whether or not the premises of an argument support the conclusion without having to consider the actual truth value of the statements which compose the argument; this point was illustrated by some examples. What remains to be seen is the nature of the logical relationships which hold between the premises and conclusions of good arguments; we shall take up this issue in the next section.

EXERCISE 2-1

1. What two characteristics does every good argument have?

2. Use premises and conclusions with each of the following combinations of truth and falsity to construct arguments in which the premises support the conclusion:
   a. All premises true and a true conclusion
   b. Some premises true, some false, and a true conclusion
   c. Some premises true, some false, and a false conclusion
   d. All premises false and a true conclusion
   e. All premises false and a false conclusion

3. Why is having a true conclusion not a sufficient condition for an argument's being good?

4. Give an example of a bad argument in which all the premises and the conclusion are true.

5. What does the expression 'truth value' mean?

6. What are the two possible truth values that a statement can have?

7. Why is it possible to investigate the support relationship between the premises and the conclusion of an argument without considering the actual truth values of the premises and the conclusion?

8. Of the two characteristics of every good argument, which one is primarily studied by logicians?

9. What responses might you make to someone who told you that studying logic is pointless because logicians aren't concerned with what is actually true or actually false?

10. Give an example of two false statements which are logically related such that if the first were true, the second would be true as well.

2:2 INDUCTIVE SUPPORT AND DEDUCTIVE SUPPORT

In the previous section we saw that every good argument is such that the premises, if true, support the conclusion. We saw further that if the premises *do not* provide support for the conclusion, then, even if they are true, the argument is a bad one. Now, if we confine our discussion to those cases where we do have support, the support will be of either of two kinds: The premises, if true, will provide *conclusive* support for the conclusion, or the premises, if true, will provide *probabilistic*, though not conclusive, support for the conclusion.

These two kinds of support are the primary topics investigated by logicians. The study of the relationship which holds between the premises and the conclusion of an argument, such that the premises conclusively support the conclusion, is the subject matter of **deductive logic;** the relationship which holds between the premises and the conclusion of an argument, such that the premises provide probabilistic, though not conclusive, support for the conclusion, is the subject matter of **inductive logic.** The arguments studied are called, respectively, **deductive arguments** and **inductive arguments.**

Each deductive argument whose premises support its conclusion has certain characteristics, and similarly for inductive arguments. In this section we shall discuss these two sets of characteristics.

2:2.1 Inductive Support The following characteristic is the one that is satisfied in every case in which the premises of an argument *inductively* support the conclusion:

(C1) Given that all the premises of the argument are true, then the conclusion is *probably* true, though it might be false.

To see what we mean by (C1), consider the following argument:

ARGUMENT 2

(1) Most of the animals on exhibit at the Watinki Zoo are shy.

(2) Annie Aardvark is an animal on exhibit at the Watinki Zoo.

∴ Annie Aardvark is shy.

Before proceeding with an explanation of (C1), we should note that two things are asserted in this statement of inductive support: Given that the premises are true, first, the conclusion is probably true, and second, the conclusion might nonetheless be false. In saying that the conclusion is probably true, we mean that it is more probable than not, *given the evidence presented in the premises.* In saying that the conclusion might nonetheless be false, we mean that it is possible for all the premises to be true while the conclusion is false; that is, the truth of the premises in an inductive argument does not guarantee the truth of the conclusion.

For a fuller understanding of (C1), consider Figure 2-1. This figure is read in the following way: The bigger circle represents all the animals on exhibit at the Watinki Zoo, and the circle inside the bigger circle represents all the shy animals. Any shy animal on exhibit would be located within the smaller circle (and, hence, the bigger circle), and those animals on exhibit which are not shy would be located within the bigger circle but outside the smaller circle. We shall further assume that, since the "shy" circle takes up most of the area of the bigger circle, more of the animals on exhibit are shy than not shy. Figure 2-1, then, is a pictorial representation of premise (1) of argument 2.

Figure 2-1

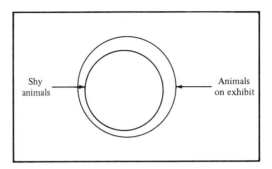

What about premise (2)? Premise (2) tells us only that Annie is an animal on exhibit at the Watinki Zoo. In other words, premise (2) is about only one of the many animals on exhibit, and all we can say is that Annie will be somewhere inside the larger circle of Figure 2.1. In particular, we don't know, on the basis of premise (2), whether Annie is also inside the smaller circle; we don't know whether she's shy or not. We can see this by considering Figures 2-2 and 2-3.

Figure 2-2

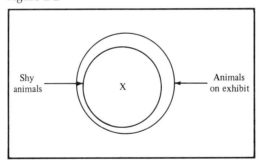

In Figures 2-2 and 2-3 the X represents Annie. The important thing to note about the two figures is that both are consistent with premise (2) of argument 2. That is, putting the X either inside or outside the smaller circle results in a

Figure 2-3

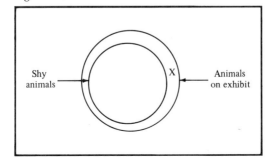

diagram of the claim that Annie is an animal on exhibit. This is so because in both cases the X is within the larger circle—the circle which represents the animals that are on exhibit.

We can now give a full explanation of (C1). Since most of the animals on exhibit at the Watinki Zoo are shy, it is more likely than not that Annie is also shy. That is, it is *probable* that Figure 2-2 represents the actual situation at the zoo; but it is *possible* that Figure 2-3 represents the actual situation at the zoo. Thus, it is probable, though not necessary, that if both premises of argument 2 are true, then the conclusion is also true. In short, given the premises, the conclusion of argument 2 is probably true, though it might be false. (The conclusion is false if Figure 2-3 represents the actual situation at the zoo, and true if Figure 2-2 does. You shold satisfy yourself that this is so.)

The following characteristic of all inductive arguments accounts for the fact that the conclusions of good inductive arguments are, given the premises, probably true and not conclusively true:[3]

> (C2) The conclusion contains information which is not contained in the premises.

To explain what is meant by (C2), we can again make use of Figures 2-1 through 2-3. Recall that Figure 2-1 is a diagram of premise (1) of argument 2. Now, to diagram premise (2), we have put the X inside the larger circle, since that premise tells us that Annie is on exhibit at the zoo. But should we put the X inside the smaller circle as well? We've already seen in our discussion of (C1) that it can go either inside or outside this circle. If we put the X inside the smaller circle, we are, in addition to saying that Annie is on exhibit at the Watinki Zoo, also saying that she is shy. Similarly, if we put the X outside the smaller circle, we are saying that Annie is not shy.

Now—and this is the important point—our conclusion to argument 2 is that Annie *is* shy. This is characterized by the location of the X in Figure 2-2. But since our two premises only allow us to say that *either* Figure 2-2 *or* Figure 2-3 is the case, but not to say which one is the case, our conclusion tells us more, or gives us more information than we have in the premises. In other words, there is only one place we can put the X such that it is consistent with the conclusion, but there are two places we can put the X such that it is consistent with the premises. The additional information we have in the conclusion of argument 2 that we do not have in the premises is that Annie is a shy animal.

Characteristic (C1) specifies the support relationship between the premises and the conclusions of all good inductive arguments, and (C2) explains why,

---

[3] This characteristic may account for the widespread, though erroneous, belief that "inductive arguments go from specific premises to general conclusions," for in arguments where this does happen, something is asserted in the conclusion about more individuals than are mentioned in the premises. Of course, these are cases to which (C2) applies, but these are not the only cases it applies to. If this is the explanation for the wrong belief, then the error probably can be explained as a hasty generalization—one of the errors discussed in Chapter 10.

given the premises, the conclusions of inductive arguments are probable though not conclusive. In addition, there is another characteristic which applies to all inductive arguments as a group:

(C3) The conclusions of different inductive arguments follow from their premises with different degrees of probability.

Characteristic (C3) is actually a consequence of (C1)—that the conclusions of good inductive arguments are, given the premises, *probable*. Accordingly, the conclusions of some inductive arguments are more probable than the conclusions of others; the difference depends on the relationship between what is asserted in the premises of the arguments and what is asserted in the conclusions. As a result, some inductive arguments are stronger than others, with strength measured as the probability of a conclusion's being true, given the premises of its argument. As an example of this, consider these two arguments:

ARGUMENT 3

98 percent of those persons stung by a scorpion survive.

Harry was stung by a scorpion.

∴ Harry will survive.

ARGUMENT 4

72 percent of those persons bitten by a cobra do not survive.

Sammy was bitten by a cobra.

∴ Sammy will not survive.

Notice, in arguments 3 and 4, that the conclusions follow from the respective premises with different degrees of probability. Also notice that the conclusion of argument 3 is more likely to be true, given the evidence presented in the premises, than is the conclusion of argument 4, given the evidence presented in the premises. As a result, argument 3 is stronger than argument 4. These different probabilities and strengths are the features of inductive arguments which (C3) describes.

In this discussion of (C3), we have considered only the probability of the conclusion's being true *given the evidence presented in the premises*. It must be emphasized that whenever we say that some statement is probable, we mean that the statement is probable *relative to the truth of some other statement or group of statements*. For example, every night across the country, local weather forecasters say things like, "The probability of precipitation tomorrow is 20 percent." Statements such as these have to be understood as a shorthand version of something like, "Given the present atmospheric conditions, the weather in other parts of the country, and what has happened in the past under these circumstances, the probability of precipitation tomorrow is 20 percent."

Since we measure the strength of inductive arguments by the probability of the conclusion's being true, given the premises, and since this probability depends on the relationship between what is asserted in the premises and in the conclusion, we often find that in the case of inductive arguments *different premises confer different probabilities on the same conclusion.* As an example, consider this argument:

ARGUMENT 5

99 percent of those persons under six months of age who are bitten by a cobra do not survive.

Sammy, who is four months old, was bitten by a cobra.

∴ Sammy will not survive.

Argument 5, like argument 4, has as its conclusion 'Sammy will not survive'. Though the conclusion is the same in both arguments, argument 5 is stronger than argument 4 in the sense that the premises of the former confer a greater probability on the conclusion than do the premises of the latter.

This means that, when we are dealing with inductive arguments, as we gain additional knowledge or information we must be prepared to reassess the likelihood of the conclusion's being true—even to the point of rejecting that which we formerly accepted. For example, the premises of argument 3 confer a high probability on the conclusion 'Harry will survive'; however, if we were to find out that *no one* under the age of three months had ever survived a scorpion sting and that Harry was two months old when he got stung, then it would be reasonable to reject the conclusion of the argument on the grounds that other information which was relevant to the truth of the conclusion was not included in the argument.

At this point you may be thinking that there is something wrong in saying that the conclusions of inductive arguments *follow from* their premises; after all, the conclusion can be false even if the premises are true. The reply to this objection is as follows: We already know that in an inductive argument the conclusion can be false even if the premises are true; (C1) tells us that. Hence, it is no criticism of inductive arguments to say simply that the conclusion might be false; that's true of *all* inductive arguments. When we say of inductive arguments that the conclusion follows from the premises, all we mean, and all we are committed to, is that given the evidence presented in the premises, the conclusion is more likely true than not. This condition is satisfied in the case of all good inductive arguments. In the next section we shall examine a stronger sense of 'follows from' than that discussed so far.

2:2.2 Deductive Support   The following characteristic is the one which is satisfied in every case where the premises of an argument *deductively* support the conclusion. All arguments having this characteristic are **valid** arguments.

(DC1) If all the premises are true, then the conclusion must be true.

To see what is meant by (DC1), consider the following deductive argument:

ARGUMENT 6

(1) All philosophy professors are kind to their students.

(2) Jones is a philosophy professor.

∴ Jones is kind to his students.

Another way of reading (DC1) is to say that every time the premises of a valid argument are true, the conclusion will also be true; or, *there can never be a valid argument in which all the premises are true and the conclusion is false.* You can get some idea of what this means by examining Figures 2-4 through 2-6. (A fuller account of validity is presented in section 2:4.1)

Figure 2-4

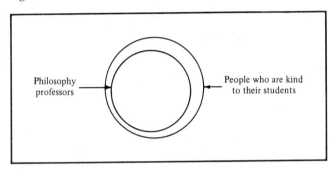

The large circle in Figure 2-4 represents all those people who are kind to their students. Premise (1) of argument 6 tells us that all philosophy professors are kind to their students; as a result, we know that all philosophy professors are within the large circle. Letting the small circle represent all philosophy professors, we have Figure 2-4; this is a diagram of premise (1) of argument 6.

Figure 2-5

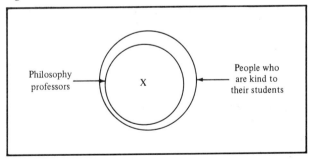

Now premise (2) of argument 6 tells us that Jones is a philosophy professor; since this is so, we know that Jones is one of those people inside the small circle of philosophy professors. If we let X represent Jones and show that he is a philosophy professor, we end up with Figure 2-5. Let us suppose it is true that all philosophy professors are kind to their students and that Jones is a philosophy professor. Could it be that Jones is *not* kind to his students? The answer is no.

If Jones is not kind to his students, then Jones cannot be included in the

Figure 2-6

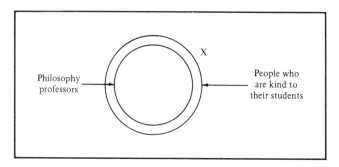

circle designating all those who are kind to their students (this is shown in Figure 2-6). Note, however, that if Figure 2-6 is a correct characterization of Jones on the "kindness-to-students" scale and a correct characterization of philosophy professors on the same scale, then Jones cannot be a philosophy professor. He cannot be a philosophy professor because he is outside the circle in Figure 2-5 which represents philosophy professors. In summary, if premises (1) and (2) of argument 6 are true, then Figure 2-5 is an accurate representation of those premises. But if Figure 2-5 is an accurate representation of those premises, then Jones must be kind to his students, for if he weren't in the big circle then he wouldn't be in the little circle. Finally, if he weren't in the little circle, then he wouldn't be a philosophy professor—but we have assumed all along that the premises were true, and premise (2) tells us that Jones *is* a philosophy professor.

I'll now try to alleviate any confusion you might be feeling about the above discussion of (DC1). The important thing to keep in mind is that Jones either is or is not kind to his students; hence, we will locate him either inside or outside the big circle in Figures 2-5 and 2-6. One way of understanding (DC1) through our example is to note that true premises and a *false* conclusion would have us locate Jones in two places (and even philosophy professors can't be in two places at the same time). Since we can't do that, the conclusion can't be false if the premises are true.

The second thing which is likely to bother some of you is the fact that not all philosophy professors are kind to their students—that is, you're going to want to say that premise (1) of argument 6 is false. You are, of course, correct. However, recall that, in our earlier comments about evaluating arguments, we said that it is a two-step procedure. The truth value of the premises comprises just one of the two steps; the support relationship can be evaluated independently. If the premises of argument 6 were true, then the conclusion would have to be true, as represented in Figure 2-5.

In our discussion of inductive support we noted that, in inductive arguments, there is information in the conclusion which is not in the premises; this is among the reasons why the conclusions of inductive arguments are at best probable, given the premises. There is a corresponding characteristic which is among the reasons why the conclusion of a valid argument must be true if the premises are true:[4]

(DC2) All the information in the conclusion is contained in the premises.

As in the case of good inductive arguments, we can understand the second characteristic of good deductive arguments by appealing to a diagram. Recall that in our discussion of inductive arguments, and in argument 2 in particular, we found that we could diagram the premises in either of two ways (Figure 2-2 or Figure 2-3), whereas we could diagram the conclusion in only one way. This gave us a way to see that there was information in the conclusion of argument 2 which was not in the premises. When we diagram a deductive argument, however, we find that *once the premises of the argument have been drawn, the conclusion also will have been drawn.* In other words, once we know all there is to know from the premises, the conclusion doesn't tell us anything additional.[5]

Figure 2-5 is perhaps the best way to see this. Figure 2-5 is the diagram of the premises of argument 6; the conclusion of that argument is that Jones is kind to his students. Is this additional information that we didn't already have once we had the premises of argument 6? No, for when we attempt to diagram the information in the conclusion, we have to put an X somewhere inside the larger circle; but we already have an X there, namely the X inside the smaller circle, denoting that Jones is a philosophy professor. In other words, once we see all the information that is contained in the premises, we see that the information in the conclusion is already contained in, or is a part of, the premises.

We also said in our discussion of inductive arguments that some of these arguments are stronger than others, and that this strength is measured in terms of the probability of the conclusion's being true, given the evidence presented in the premises. There is a corresponding characteristic which holds for all valid arguments as a group:

(DC3) The conclusions of different valid arguments always follow from their premises with the same degree of strength.

When we say of valid deductive arguments that the conclusion always follows from the premises with the same degree of strength, what we are really saying is that the conclusion's following from the premises does not involve the idea of probability at all; the conclusion follows from the premises, period. Further, to say of deductive arguments that the conclusion *follows from* the premises is

---

[4] We assume here that the arguments in question have neither a conclusion which is logically true nor contradictory premises. Valid arguments having either or both of these characteristics are discussed in Chapter 4.

[5] What is implicit in the premises may be completely surprising, however, when it is expressed as a conclusion of an argument. One reason for this is that we do not always see the relationships among the assertions of the premises; nor do we always see what follows from the premises. One of the benefits of logic is that it enables us to show explicitly what may be only implicit in the premises of an argument.

just to say that (DC1) has been satisfied; that is, if all the premises are true, then the conclusion must also be true.

To see this, consider again argument 6 and Figure 2-5. Here there is no question, given the premises, of the *probability* of Jones being kind to his students. If the premises are true, then he is kind to them; if he's not kind to them, then at least one premise is false [if this loses you, reread the discussion of (DC1)]. In other words, when we're speaking about deductive arguments, it's an "all-or-nothing" proposition. Either the premises show, in accord with (DC1), that the conclusion is true if the premises are, in which case we have a valid deductive argument, or they don't show this, in which case we do not have an argument whose premises deductively support its conclusion.

This concludes our discussion of the two ways in which the premises of an argument can support its conclusion: inductively and deductively. In the case of inductive support, if all the premises of the argument are true, then the conclusion is probably true, although it might be false. In the case of deductive support, if all the premises of the argument are true, then the conclusion must be true. Our next task is to develop some logical notation which will assist us in determining whether the premises of an argument do or do not support its conclusion. After that, we shall return to the issue of valid arguments and see in more detail what it means to say that an argument is valid.

EXERCISE 2-2

1. In what two ways can the premises of an argument support the conclusion?

2. What is the primary subject matter of deductive logic? Of inductive logic?

3. What is wrong with characterizing inductive arguments as those which proceed from specific premises to a general conclusion?

4. What is wrong with characterizing deductive arguments as those which proceed from general premises to a specific conclusion?

5. Explain the condition which is satisfied in every case in which the premises of an argument inductively support the conclusion.

6. Give an example of an inductive argument in which the support relationship is satisfied. Show that it is satisfied by diagramming the premises and the conclusion of the argument as is done in section 2:2.1.

7. In general, why is it possible for the conclusion of an inductive argument to be false even when the premises are all true?

8. What does it mean to say that the conclusions of different inductive arguments follow from their premises with varying degrees of probability?

9. Give two inductive arguments, one of which is stronger than the other, and explain why the one is stronger.

10. Give two inductive arguments having the same conclusion but different premises. State which one is stronger, and explain your answer.

11. What response might you give to someone who asserted the following: "The conclusions of inductive arguments never follow from their premises, since even if the premises are true, the conclusion might still be false."

12. What condition must be satisfied for the premises of an argument to deductively support the conclusion?

13. What is a valid argument?

14. Give an example of a valid argument. Show that it is valid by diagramming the premises and the conclusion of the argument as is done in section 2:2.2.

15. What general characteristic of good deductive arguments accounts for the fact that if all the premises are true, then the conclusion must be true?

16. What does it mean to say that all good deductive arguments are equally strong?

EXERCISE 2-3.

1. Determine which of the following are arguments. For those which are not, write "no argument." For those which are arguments, state whether the premises deductively or inductively support the conclusion. If neither situation obtains, write "no support."

a. I really expect to do well this semester since I've already had each of my professors for other courses, and I got good grades from all of them the last time I took one of their courses.

b. Sandy must like horror movies. After all, anyone who likes horror movies would go to see *The Night Creature Stalks*, and I saw her and Tom at the movie on Friday.

c. The National League is bound to win this year's All Star game; the American League has won only once in the last twenty years.

d. Motown Motors must make nothing but lemons. I bought one of their cars two months ago, and I've had it in the shop more than on the road.

e. Fred must have gone home for the weekend, since the last time I saw him he said that if he didn't go home he would be at the party. I was there all evening, and he never showed up.

f. That cold of yours sounds awful. You ought to hang a clove of garlic around your neck; I do that when I have a cold and within a week my cold's gone.

g. Given the results of the recent polls, the President is likely not to be reelected. His performance rating is the lowest since he's been in office, and people favor his opponent by a margin of almost two to one.

h. Merv must want to be happy for the rest of his life. After all, he just made an ugly woman his wife, and you know how the song goes.

i. Don't leave the window open. That last time you did that it rained while we were out, and everything got soaked.

j. I think we've just about had it in this game. We're behind 35–0, and our offense didn't do anything in the first three quarters.

k. Somebody must have it in for me. My alarm went off almost an hour late owing to last night's power failure, and when I went out to leave for class there was a flat tire waiting for me.

l. If there's one thing this business doesn't do, it's keep incompetent employees. As I see it, Johnson won't be around here much longer.

m. Since I started meditating I've found that life is much more peaceful. If you want to get rid of some of the tension in your life, take up meditation.

n. Almost all the performers on last night's television special were past their prime. I guess the producer didn't have much money to put the show together.

o. What do you mean I shouldn't swear? You do it all the time!

2. From your other reading, find two examples of good inductive arguments and two examples of good deductive arguments.

2.3 SYMBOLIZING ARGUMENTS

In the remainder of this chapter, our concern will be mostly with deductive arguments. The information in this section is also applicable to inductive arguments but will be expanded in Chapter 8. The material in the remaining sections of this chapter applies exclusively to deductive arguments; parallel material for induction is developed in Chapters 8 and 9.

In this section we shall discuss some logical notation that can be used to symbolize arguments. As you will see, this symbolism greatly simplifies the task of determining, for a great number of arguments, whether or not the support relationship between the premises and the conclusion has been satisfied. We shall first discuss two kinds of symbols; then we shall see how to represent the form of an argument by using symbols. We shall conclude the section by symbolizing some example arguments.

2:3.1 Statement Constants and Statement Variables   The best way to understand the various symbols used to represent arguments is to see how the symbols are used. Consider, therefore, the following argument:

ARGUMENT 7

If the jury found the defendant guilty, then justice was served.

The jury found the defendant guilty.

∴ Justice was served.

A quick look at argument 7 shows that, whereas there are two premises and a conclusion, the sentences used to express the second premise and that used to express the conclusion also occur in the first premise. In other words, the sentences 'The jury found the defendant guilty' and 'Justice was served' each occur twice in the argument: once in isolation and once as part of a more complex sentence.

We can readily show this feature of the argument by abbreviating each of the sentences with a symbol and rewriting the argument by using the symbols. The symbols are called **statement constants** and are written as uppercase letters. Letting 'F' represent the sentence 'The jury found the defendant guilty' and 'J' represent the sentence 'Justice was served', we can rewrite argument 7 in its abbreviated version as follows:[6]

> If F then J
>
> F
>
> $\therefore J$

Notice that the first premise of argument 7 contains an 'if' and a 'then' in addition to the two sentences we have abbreviated. Since the 'if' and the 'then' were not abbreviated when we assigned statement constants to the argument, we must write these two words in our abbreviated argument. Also notice that in the abbreviated argument, as in argument 7, the 'if' precedes the sentence 'The jury found the defendant guilty' and the 'then' comes between this sentence and the sentence 'Justice was served'.

In general, when symbolizing arguments by using statement constants, it is a good idea to first pick out the sentences being symbolized; then rewrite the argument by writing down any *unsymbolized* words or expressions in the places where they occur in the argument, along with the statement constants. One way of doing this is to put parentheses around the sentences in the original argument, assign constants to them, and then rewrite the argument in symbolized form. If we were to do this with argument 7, we would have the following:

$$F \qquad\qquad\qquad\qquad\qquad\qquad J$$
If (the jury found the defendant guilty) then (justice was served)

$$F$$
(The jury found the defendant guilty)

$$J$$
$\therefore$ (Justice was served)

The important point about statement constants is that they are used to represent *particular statements;* when they are used in a given context (an argument), they express exactly the same thing as is expressed by the statements they symbolize. As a result, once a constant has been assigned to a statement in an argument, the same constant must be assigned to every other occurrence of that statement in that argument.

We are now ready to consider another kind of symbol. To see its role, let's look at another argument and symbolize it with statement constants.

---

[6] The choice of 'F' and 'J' as statement constants is arbitrary. It does not matter which letters are used as constants, although it is helpful in longer arguments to pick out the first letter of some key word in the symbolized sentence and use that letter, uppercased, as the constant.

ARGUMENT 8

If the U.S. can put a man on the moon, then you would think they would be able to build safe airplanes.

The U.S. can put a man on the moon.

∴ You would think the U.S. would be able to build safe airplanes.

Letting 'M' represent 'The U.S. can put a man on the moon' and 'S' represent 'You would think the U.S. would be able to build safe airplanes', we have the following as the symbolization of argument 8:

If M then S

M

∴ S

If we compare the symbolization of argument 7 to that above, we see that they are similar in that every place where there is an 'F' in the former, there is an 'M' in the latter, and so too for 'J' and 'S'. Arguments 7 and 8 are, of course, different arguments, but they nonetheless have the same structure in that their constituent statements are related in the same way. The structure of an argument is its **logical form.**

For reasons that we shall discuss shortly, logicians are primarily concerned with the logical form of an argument as opposed to its particular content and have, therefore, developed a symbolism which can be used to represent the form of an argument. The symbols are **statement variables** and are written as lowercase letters. We shall use the letters 'p', 'q', 'r', 's', and so on to the end of the alphabet as statement variables.[7]

The important point about statement variables is that they are *placeholders* for statements and *do not* represent particular statements. Another way of putting this is to say that statement variables are used to represent *any statement whatsoever*, whereas statement constants are used to represent particular statements.

Let's return now to argument 8. Having symbolized the argument by using statement *constants*, we see that there are two places where 'M' occurs and two places where 'S' occurs. If we let 'p' represent the place occupied by 'M', and 'q' represent the place occupied by 'S', we have the following:

FORM 1

If p then q

p

∴ q

Note that the above is *not* an argument nor an abbreviation for an argument; we have an abbreviated argument when we use statement *constants*, for constants

---

[7] This is an arbitrary decision in the sense that any symbols could be used as statement variables. In using the variables that we do, we follow a traditional, historical procedure.

are symbols for particular statements, and arguments are composed of statements. Form 1 above is, rather, the *form* (or structure or skeleton) of argument 8. It is related to argument 8 only in the sense that the statements which compose the argument are related to one another in the way represented by the statement variables.

We have already noted that arguments 7 and 8 have the same form. This can readily be seen by putting 'The jury found the defendent guilty' in the place occupied by 'p' above and by putting 'Justice was served' in the place occupied by 'q'. The importance attached to arguments which have the same form is that if an argument is valid, every other argument having the same form is also valid; we shall see why this is so in section 2:4.1.

In summary, we have the following: Statement constants are used to represent particular statements, and statement variables are placeholders for any statement whatsoever. When an argument has been symbolized by using statement constants, the result is itself an argument whose premises and conclusion express exactly the same thing as was expressed by the original argument. When an argument has been symbolized by using statement variables, the result is not an argument but is, rather, the form of the argument, a form which many other arguments can also have.

2:3.2 Determining the Form of an Argument   In the previous section we saw that statement variables are used as placeholders for statements and are therefore used to represent the form of an argument.[8] In this section we shall expand on this point and develop a procedure for determining the forms of arguments. Before we do this, however, it will be helpful to distinguish between **simple statements** and **compound statements.**

A simple statement is one in which no other statement occurs as a component. Examples of such statements are 'Dan likes beer better than wine', 'December is warmer than June', and 'Most practicing attorneys make a good salary'. A compound statement, on the other hand, is one in which one or more other statements do occur as a component. For example, 'Dan likes beer better than wine and Tim likes wine better than beer' is a compound statement because the two simple statements 'Dan likes beer better than wine' and 'Tim likes wine better than beer' occur as components in the statement.

We distinguish between simple and compound statements because statement variables are placeholders for *any* statement; as a result, we can replace a variable with either a simple statement or a compound statement. For example, one instance of the form of arguments 7 and 8 is the following, where both 'p' and 'q' have been replaced by compound statements:[9]

---

[8] Statement variables are not the only symbols used to represent the form of an argument; there are some arguments whose form is better represented by other symbols. We shall look at such cases in detail in Chapter 6.

[9] When we substitute statements for statement variables in an argument form, the result is a *substitution instance* of the argument form. Hence, arguments 7 to 9 are all substitution instances of form 1.

ARGUMENT 9

If Sandra marries Herb and Sarah marries Henry, then Sandra will have a new brother-in-law and Henry will have a new sister-in-law.

Sandra married Herb and Sarah married Henry.

∴ Sandra has a new brother-in-law and Henry has a new sister-in-law.

The statements which replaced 'p' and 'q' in the above argument are compound statements because other statements occur in them as components. (Take a moment here to pick out the component statements in each of the compound statements.)

Just as we can replace a variable with either a simple statement or a compound statement, we can symbolize a compound statement either by assigning *different* variables to each of the component statements or by assigning *one* variable to the compound statement. For example, the statement 'If you like penguins then you'll love the new building at the zoo' can be symbolized by assigning one variable, say 'p', to 'You like penguins', and another, say 'q', to 'You'll love the new building at the zoo'. The result is a statement of the form 'If p then q'. On the other hand, we could also symbolize the compound statement by assigning one variable, say 'r', to the whole statement, giving us a statement of the form 'r'.

It should be obvious that whenever a compound statement occurs in an argument, different logical forms of the argument will result from different assignments of variables to the compound statement. For example, consider the following argument:

ARGUMENT 10

If you like penguins then you'll love the new building at the zoo.

You like penguins.

∴ You'll love the new building at the zoo.

If we symbolize the first premise of argument 10 as 'If p then q', we have the following form for the argument:

FORM 2

If p then q

p

∴ q

If, on the other hand, we were to use a single variable, say 'r', to symbolize the first premise of the argument, then we would have to use another variable for the second premise and still another for the conclusion, for neither of these statements is the same as the first premise. Using 's' to symbolize the second premise and 't' to symbolize the conclusion, we have:

FORM 3

r

s

$\therefore t$

One might reasonably ask at this point whether form 2 or form 3 is *the* form of argument 10. The answer is that neither is *the* form of the argument if *'the* form' is taken to mean that the argument has but one form. To put it another way, forms 2 and 3 are *both* forms of argument 10.

In a sense, there is no limit to the number of ways in which the form of an argument might be represented. One could, for example, use a variable to represent the words or phrases of an argument, or even the letters which occur in the argument. Each type of variable would provide a different form of the argument; however, such variables and the resultant forms would not be particularly useful, since they wouldn't help to determine whether the support relationship between the premises and the conclusion of the argument was satisfied.

In providing a form for an argument, our goal is to capture a structure of the argument which best exhibits the relationship between the premises and the conclusion. Since many arguments have more than one form, we can err in either of two ways when symbolizing an argument: We can say too little about the structure, or we can say too much. What we should try to do is say just the right amount.

For example, in symbolizing the structure of argument 10, form 3 says too little; it does not show the relationship between the compound statement and the other statements in the argument. On the other hand, if we were, say, to provide a variable for each word which occurs in the argument, we would have said too much; even though we would end up with a form, we again would not capture the relationship between the premises and the conclusion.

How, then, can we be sure that we say just the right amount when we are symbolizing an argument; that is, how can we be sure that the form we provide is the one which best exhibits the relationship between the premises and the conclusion? For the arguments we shall be considering through Chapter 5, we shall say just the right amount about their form if we adhere to the following procedure:

(1) Rewrite the argument in standard form, providing missing premises or a missing conclusion as necessary.

(2) Beginning with the first premise, determine whether the statement is a simple one or a compound one. (Remember, a compound statement is one which has at least one other simple statement as a component.)

(3) If the first premise is a simple statement, assign the variable *'p'* to the place occupied by the statement. If the first premise is a compound

statement, assign '*p*' to the first component statement, '*q*' to the second, and so on until a variable has been assigned to each statement.[10]

(4) Apply the procedure in (3) to the remaining premises and to the conclusion, using a new variable each time you encounter a new statement, and using previously assigned variables each time you encounter a statement from an earlier premise.

Note that if we apply the above procedure to argument 10, our result is form 1. In the remainder of this chapter and in the next three, when we discuss 'the form of an argument' we will be talking about the form which results from applying this procedure.

2:3.3 Some Examples   Our purpose here is to apply what we have learned about statement variables and logical form to some examples. Since we have already discussed the procedure for putting arguments into standard form, we shall dispense with that step and begin by assigning variables to the statements in the argument.

ARGUMENT 11

If the thruway is built through the north side of the city, then the historic district will be ruined.

If the thruway is built through the south side of the city, then many small businesses will have to relocate.

The thruway will be built through the north side or the south side of the city.

∴ Either the historic district will be ruined or many small businesses will have to relocate.

Step 1: We see that the first premise is a compound statement whose component statements are 'The thruway is built through the north side of the city' and 'The historic district will be ruined'. Assigning '*p*' to the first of these statements and '*q*' to the second, we have:

If *p* then *q*

Step 2: The second premise is also a compound statement. Here the component statements are 'The thruway is built through the south side of the city', and 'Many small businesses will have to relocate'. Since neither of these statements occurs previously in the argument, we must assign new variables to each of them. Assigning '*r*' to the former statement and '*s*' to the latter, we have:

If *r* then *s*

---

[10] It is, of course, arbitrary which variable is assigned to which statement. We shall adopt the convention of assigning '*p*' to the first statement in an argument, '*q*' to the second, '*r*' to the third, and so on.

Step 3: The third premise is a compound statement whose component statements are 'The thruway will be built through the north side of the city' and 'The thruway will be built through the south side of the city'. (Note that this second statement is not explicitly expressed this way in the grammatical structure of the original argument.) Both these statements occurred previously in the argument, so we must use the variables we assigned earlier: 'p' for the first statement and 'r' for the second. Having assigned variables to the component statements, we see that there is an 'or' which connects the two. Our result is:

p or r

Step 4: The conclusion of the argument is also a compound statement; the component statements are 'The historic district will be ruined' and 'Many small businesses will have to relocate'. Once again, these are statements which occurred previously in the argument, so we must use the variables we have already assigned to them: 'q' for the former and 's' for the latter. We also see that there is an 'either' before 'q' and an 'or' between 'q' and 's'. Adding this result to those obtained earlier, we have the following as the form of argument 11:

If p then q

If r then s

p or r

∴ either q or s

This concludes our discussion of the symbolizing of arguments. In the next section we shall make use of the idea of logical form to provide a more detailed account of validity. In particular, we shall show how the validity of an argument is a function of the *form* of the argument.

EXERCISE 2-4

1. What is a statement constant used for? How are statement constants represented in symbolic notation?

2. What is a statement variable? How are statement variables represented in symbolic notation?

3. What is the logical form of an argument?

4. Why is the form of an argument not itself an argument?

5. What is a simple statement? What is a compound statement?

6. Give an example of a simple statement; then give an example of a compound statement in which the simple statement is a component.

7. What is a substitution instance of an argument form?

8. Give a substitution instance of the form of argument 11 discussed above.

9. Can an argument have more than one form? Explain your answer.

10. Explain the procedure used to determine the logical form of an argument.

EXERCISE 2-5

1. Symbolize each of the following statements using the given symbols as statement constants.
   a. If the *infection* is brought under control within the next 24 hours, the patient has a good chance of *recovering*. (*I, R*)
   b. The price of *gold* continues to go up, and the price of *silver* is going down. (*G, S*)
   c. Either we *join* together to achieve our goals or we will have to settle for what the others *decide*. (*J, D*)
   d. If I *remember* correctly, chablis is the best-*selling* wine in the world. (*R, S*)
   e. Either the *East* team or the *West* team will play the pros at the end of the season. (*E, W*)
   f. You should *eat* foods that contain a lot of vitamin E if you *smoke*. (*E, S*)
   g. Nan is going to buy a new *stereo* or a color *television* with the money she earned during the summer. (*S, T*)
   h. If the Metronomes really make *money* on their recordings, then they do it by *writing* their own music. (*M, W*)
   i. People are *eligible* for workmen's compensation if, and only if, they are *injured* on the job. (*E, I*)
   j. The evidence indicates that South America and Africa were once a single *body* of land and that they *separated* millions of years ago. (*B, S*)

2. Symbolize each of the following arguments using the given symbols as statement constants.
   a. If the *infection* is brought under control within the next 24 hours, the patient has a good chance of *recovering*. Hence, the patient's chances are good, since we just administered a new drug to increase the production of *white* blood cells. Moreover, if there is an increase in white blood cells, the infection will be brought under control. (*I, R, W*)
   b. If you're thinking about *buying* any gold jewelry, then now is the *time* to do it, because the price of *gold* continues to go up and the price of *silver* is going down. (*B, T, G, S*)
   c. Either we *join* together to achieve our goals or we will have to settle for what the others *decide*. Hence, if we are to *achieve* our goals, then we had better join together, for the others will *choose* something other than what we want. (*J, D, A, C*)
   d. Research has shown that vitamin E apparently has some effect in *minimizing* the development of lung cancer. Hence, you should *eat* foods that contain a lot of vitamin E if you *smoke*. (*M, E, S*)
   e. Songwriters receive *royalty* payments every time one of their songs is

recorded. Hence, if the Metronomes make *money* on their recordings, then they do it by *writing* their own music. (R, M, W)

f. Quinton is *eligible* for workmen's compensation if, and only if, he *broke* his leg while on the job. Hence, since he's receiving workmen's compensation, that must be where he broke his leg. (Assume that one receives compensation only if eligible.) (E, B)

g. If we take the *train* to the convention, then we'll *save* money. On the other hand, if we *fly* there we'll get there more *quickly*. Since we'll go either by train or by plane, it follows that we'll either save money or get there more quickly. (T, S, F, Q)

h. Peggy will take a job either with *Hatcher* Biomedics or with *Compuware* Data Processing. But, if she takes the job with Hatcher, she will earn more *money* than with Compuware. Accordingly, she will take the Hatcher job since she will earn more money. (H, C, M)

i. If Ralph gets a good *job* this summer, then he will be able to afford to *buy* a car, and if he can afford a car then he will *commute* to school next fall. Hence, if Ralph commutes to school in the fall, then he will have had a good job this summer. (J, B, C)

j. If Jan *passes* her bar exam, then she will *move* to Rochester. Moreover, if her sister *gets* a residency at the Mayo Clinic, then the sister will also move to *Rochester*. Hence, since Jan will pass her exam and her sister will get a residency at Mayo, it follows that Jan and her sister will both move to Rochester. (P, M, G, R)

2:4 VALIDITY AND SOUNDNESS

We have so far seen that the support relation between the premises and the conclusion of an argument has to be understood in terms of what would be the case *if* the premises of the argument happened to be true. As pointed out earlier, we are also concerned with the actual truth or falsity of the premises of an argument (with their truth values) when we try to decide whether to accept the conclusion of a particular argument on the basis of the evidence offered in the premises. In the case of deductive arguments, logicians have terms for distinguishing between the support relationship and the truth of the premises of the argument. In this section we shall examine these two features further.

2:4.1 Validity We shall begin this section by examining in more detail the support relation in the case of deductive arguments.

DEFINITION 1: **Valid**

*An argument is **valid** if the following holds:*

If all the premises are true, then the conclusion must be true.

Notice that the definition of 'valid' is just characteristic (DC1) of deductive arguments. Also recall that another way of putting this is to say that, in a valid argument, it is not possible for all the premises to be true and the conclusion false. Since any argument which satisfies (DC1) of deductive arguments also satifies (DC2) and (DC3), it follows that *all valid arguments are deductive.*

One of the most, if not the most, important things we shall discover about validity is that *we can determine the validity of an argument without knowing the truth values of the premises and the conclusion.* Additionally, an argument can be valid even if the premises are (known to be) false. Why is this so? The answer to this question goes back to the definition of 'valid'; the definition specifies only that *if* the premises are true, *then* the conclusion must be true. For every argument that we examine for validity, the question that we must ask, then, is, "Does the conclusion of this argument have to be true if all the premises are true?" If the answer is yes, then the argument is valid; if the answer is no, then the argument is invalid. Chapters 3 to 7 will, in large measure, be devoted to developing methods of answering this question.

So far we have been discussing 'valid arguments.' Although this is a reasonable expression that is used by logicians and found in texts and articles, it is not precise enough. The expression 'valid argument' is actually a shorter version of the more appropriate expression 'instance of a valid argument form', for when we discuss the validity of an argument, we are actually discussing a feature of the structure of the argument. This structure is the **logical form** of the argument, and in the previous section we saw how to derive this form.

In every argument we can distinguish between the content of the argument and its form. Indeed, the use of statement constants and statement variables does just this; the former are used to abbreviate the content of the argument, and the latter the form. Since validity is a function of the form of the argument, we need not be concerned with the content of the argument; we can, instead, symbolize the argument using variables, and then consider the relationship which holds between the premises and the conclusion. Given this distinction, we can now discuss what is meant by saying a valid argument is one which is an instance of a valid argument form. Our discussion will take place within the context of statement variables, though the remarks about validity are appropriate to arguments symbolized with other variables as well.

Consider again arguments 7 and 8 and form 1, discussed in the previous section. For convenience, these are reproduced below.

ARGUMENT 7

If the jury found the defendant guilty, then justice was served.

The jury found the defendant guilty.

∴ Justice was served.

ARGUMENT 8

If the U.S. can put a man on the moon, then you would think they would be able to build safe airplanes.

The U.S. can put a man on the moon.

∴ You would think the U.S. would be able to build safe airplanes.

FORM 1

If p then q

p

∴ q

Since 'p' and 'q' are statement *variables,* there are a great many instances of arguments having form 1; arguments 7 and 8 are just two such instances. Note that each instance of form 1 is a particular argument having the form of form 1, but with the variables replaced by particular statements. Which instance we end up with will depend, of course, on which statements replace the variables.

Now, form 1 is a valid argument form. To say that the form is valid is to say that *there are no instances of this form which have all true premises and a false conclusion.* To put this in terms of our earlier discussion, every instance of form 1 is such that if all its premises are true then its conclusion must be true. Note that we have just characterized the notion of a valid argument form in a "negative" sort of way—by specifying a situation which does *not* happen in a valid argument form: namely, an instance of that form which has all true premises and a false conclusion.

Now, since no instance of a valid argument form can have all true premises and a false conclusion, it will turn out that every instance of that argument form which does have all true premises must have a true conclusion; hence, our definition of a valid argument.

Being valid or being invalid is characteristic of the support relationship in arguments. We earlier noted that the support relationship is independent of the truth value of the premises and has to be evaluated separately. At this point it is appropriate to consider the issue of what we can and cannot tell about the validity of an argument on the basis of the truth values of its premises, its conclusion, or both.

The one thing to keep in mind is that, in a valid argument, it is not possible to have all true premises and a false conclusion. Every other combination of truth values for the premises and conclusion of valid arguments is possible. Of course, in invalid arguments, every combination is possible. Table 2-1 summarizes the relationship between validity and invalidity and the truth values of the premises and the conclusion. What the table shows is that we cannot tell whether an argument is valid or invalid from the truth values of its premises and conclusion, except in one case: all true premises and a false conclusion. In this case, we know that the argument is *invalid.*

It may have occurred to you that showing the validity of a given argument form is no easy matter, and in this you are absolutely correct. Since an argument form is valid only if every instance of the form which has all true premises also has a true conclusion, the only way we could, at present, show that a form is

TABLE 2-1

Premises	Conclusion	Valid/Invalid
All true	True	Some valid and some invalid
All true	False	All invalid
Some true and some false	True	Some valid and some invalid
Some true and some false	False	Some valid and some invalid
All false	True	Some valid and some invalid
All false	False	Some valid and some invalid

valid would be to show that *all* instances of the form satisfy this condition. That would mean examining the form in terms of all the statements which could be substituted for the variables; in a language such as English, where there are potentially an infinite number of statements, this is impossible. Showing that an argument form is invalid, however, depends only on coming up with one instance of all true premises and a false conclusion, so demonstrating invalidity is something we can do now. We shall discuss this further in section 2:5; at this point, however, we can discuss what it means for an argument form to be valid. Then, in Chapter 4, we shall develop the tools for *showing* validity.

One additional point needs to be made before concluding this discussion of validity. We saw in section 2:3.2 that many arguments have more than one form. Argument 10 was one example; by assigning variables to the component statements in the first premise we got form 2, and by assigning a single variable to the compound statement we got form 3. These forms are reproduced below:

FORM 2   FORM 3

If p then q r

p s

$\therefore q$ $\therefore t$

Since an argument is valid when it is an instance of some valid argument form, argument 10 is valid because form 2 is valid. The fact that argument 10 is also an instance of the invalid form 3 in no way affects the validity of the argument. It is for this reason that it is important, in determining the logical form of an argument, to strive to say just the right amount and, in particular, to try to symbolize the argument in such a way that the result is a valid argument form if the argument is an instance of such a form.

We can summarize the above discussion in the following way:

(1) Arguments are valid or invalid by virtue of their form.

(2) Since the form of an argument can be represented in more than one way, we must work to avoid saying too little or too much, and strive to say just the right amount about the structure of the argument.

(3) Since we can sometimes assign both a valid and an invalid form to an

argument, and since an argument is valid when it is an instance of *some* valid argument form, we must be careful in labeling an argument invalid on the basis of the form assigned to it; it may also be an instance of another, valid form.

This concludes our discussion of deductive support—validity. In the next section we shall consider the truth values of the premises in deductive arguments.

2:4.2 Soundness Consideration of the truth of the premises of a valid argument gives rise to the characterization **sound,** which may be applied to arguments. Here we go beyond the consideration solely of argument form.

DEFINITION 2: **Sound**

*An argument is **sound** if, and only if, it meets both the following conditions:*

(1) The argument is valid.
(2) All the premises of the argument are true.

What is of importance in the case of a sound argument is that *the conclusion of a sound argument is always true.* This is so because any argument which satisfies condition (1) for soundness is such that its conclusion is true when it premises are true. Since condition (2) states that the premises are as a matter of fact true, it follows that the conclusion of the argument must be true.

2:4.3 A Comparison of Soundness and Validity To sharpen the distinction between valid and sound arguments, let's look at five different arguments with differing instances of the truth and/or falsity of their premises; all five have a valid argument form.[11] The first three arguments have the following form:

FORM 4

If p then q

p

$\therefore q$

The 'p' and 'q' above can be replaced with any two statements, so that each time 'p' occurs one statement replaces it, and each time 'q' occurs one statement replaces it. The statements need not be different, but once we have put a statement in the place marked with 'p', we must put that statement in every other placed marked by 'p'; and similarly for the place marked by 'q'. As yet, we cannot show that form 4 is valid, but you can probably see that it is;

---

[11] That the forms of the following arguments are valid is something which we should be able to see by looking at the arguments. So far, the only way in which we can show that the forms are valid is to show that there is no instance of those forms having all true premises and a false conclusion. For reasons pointed out above in the section on validity, this must wait until Chapter 4.

moreover, can see this even though we have no particular statements to examine. Form 4 thus provides an illustration of the fact that the actual truth values of the premises of an argument do not have anything to do with the validity of the argument, since here we don't even have any premises for which to determine truth values.

The first argument of the above form that we shall look at is a *sound* argument as well as a valid one; that is, it is both valid and has all true premises. In this and the other arguments discussed in this section, 'Bugs' refers to Bugs Bunny.

ARGUMENT 12:   **All true premises and a true conclusion**

(1) If Bugs is a rabbit, then Bugs has long ears. (T)

(2) Bugs is a rabbit. (T)

∴ Bugs has long ears. (T)

The next two arguments are of the same form as argument 12, but neither of them is sound (they are **unsound**) since each of them has at least one false premise. These two arguments will show you two of the possible combinations of truth and falsity for the premises and conclusion of a valid argument.

ARGUMENT 13:   **Some premises true, some premises false, and a true conclusion**

(1) If Bugs is a basset hound, then Bugs has long ears. (T)

(2) Bugs is a basset hound. (F)

∴ Bugs has long ears. (T)

ARGUMENT 14:   **Some premises true, some premises false, and a false conclusion**

(1) If Bugs is a rabbit, then Bugs has a long tail. (F)

(2) Bugs is a rabbit. (T)

∴ Bugs has a long tail. (F)

Notice that premise (1) of argument 13 is true even though Bugs is not a basset hound. What is claimed in premise (1) is that *if* Bugs is a basset hound (even though he isn't) he would have long ears, and this is true because anything which is a basset hound has long ears. Similarly, premise (1) of argument 14 is false, for even though Bugs is a rabbit, he does not have a long tail.

The next two arguments show the other possible combinations of truth and falsity for the premises and conclusion of a valid argument. We are here dealing with arguments whose form is different from those we have just discussed and whose form would best be represented with variables other than statement variables.

ARGUMENT 15: **All premises false and a true conclusion**

(1) All alligators are rabbits. (F)

(2) Bugs is an alligator. (F)

∴ Bugs is a rabbit. (T)

ARGUMENT 16: **All premises false and a false conclusion**

(1) All alligators are elephants. (F)

(2) Bugs is an alligator. (F)

∴ Bugs is an elephant. (F)

Argument 15 is of special interest since it does have a true conclusion although its premises are false. It is important because it is an instance in which a particular claim (here the claim that Bugs is a rabbit) is true, but the evidence given for the claim does not establish the truth of the claim. Were someone to argue that Bugs is a rabbit on the basis of the premises of argument 15, we would be justified in not accepting the conclusion *on the basis of the evidence offered*—for although the argument is valid (is an instance of a valid argument form), it has false premises. However, while we are justified in not accepting the conclusion on the basis of the evidence offered, we have *not* shown that the conclusion is false. Our complaint, then, is not with the form of the argument or the truth of the conclusion, but with the falsity of the premises. Argument 15 is one of the many instances in which one might come to hold a true opinion for the wrong reasons.

The best that we can say for argument 16 is that it is valid. It is provided just to show that even in the worst possible case of truth and falsity (everything false), we can still sometimes say something positive about an argument, namely that it is valid or satisfies the support relation.

This concludes our discussion on validity and soundness. In the next section we shall develop a procedure which is often useful for showing that a given argument is an instance of an invalid argument form and is, therefore, an invalid argument.

EXERCISE 2.6

1. Explain what it means to say that an argument is valid or invalid. Give an example of a valid argument and an example of an invalid argument.

2. What is a valid argument form? What is an invalid argument form? Give an example of each.

3. Can an argument with all false premises be valid? Why or why not?

4. Can an argument with a false conclusion be valid? Why or why not?

5. Can an argument with a false conclusion and all true premises be valid? Why or why not?

6. Is an argument invalid if it is an instance of some invalid form? Is it valid if it is an instance of some valid form? Explain your answers.

7. What is a sound argument? Give an example of each of the following:
   (a) A sound argument
   (b) An argument which is unsound but is valid

8. If one shows either that an argument's form is invalid or that its premises are false, does one thereby show that the argument's conclusion is false? If so, why? If not, what is shown thereby?

9. If one shows that the conclusion of an argument is true, does one establish that the argument is a good one? If so, why? If not, why not?

10. Construct example arguments illustrating each of the categories listed in Table 2-1.

2:5 COUNTEREXAMPLES

In this section we shall discuss a procedure for showing that an argument or an argument form is invalid. To do this we shall make use of some of the material from section 2:4.1. Consider the following argument:

ARGUMENT 17

(1) If Reginald is a duck, then Reginald has webbed feet.

(2) Reginald has webbed feet.

∴ Reginald is a duck.

Let us suppose that both premises and the conclusion are true. The temptation here might be to say on this basis that the argument is a good one. Such a move is, however, premature, since the argument is invalid. It is invalid because the premises do not provide the kind of support needed for the conclusion. In particular, there are other arguments which have the same form as argument 19, but *whose premises are true and whose conclusion is false.* You know from our earlier discussion that if there is just one instance of an argument form which has all true premises and a false conclusion, then that argument form is invalid. As a result, any other argument whose form is best expressed by this form will also be invalid.[12] It is this feature that we use in constructing **counterexamples.**

The idea behind counterexamples is to show that the conclusion of an argument need not be true, even if the premises are. This would mean, then, that it would be possible for the premises to be true and the conclusion false,

---

[12] We say "best expressed" here because, as we have seen, arguments can be instances of more than one form, and an argument is valid if it is an instance of *any* valid argument form. The symbolization procedure discussed in section 2:3.2 results in a form that best expresses the form of the argument; if this form is invalid, all arguments which are instances of this form are also invalid. (We assume here that the argument does not have a conclusion which is logically true, or any logically false premises, or premises which are inconsistent.)

even if the premises and the conclusion happened to be true in the original argument. To see how counterexamples work, let's return to argument 17. Suppose you knew that the premises of this argument were true. Could you, on this basis alone, be certain that the conclusion is true? Obviously not, for Reginald might be a goose, and, if that were so, both premises would be true but the conclusion would be false. [Premise (1) of argument 17 would be true because anything which is a duck has webbed feet; premise (2) would be true because geese have webbed feet.] Since in a valid argument we cannot have all true premises and a false conclusion, argument 17 is invalid. This is so even though the conclusion is true. The important point here is that the truth of the conclusion of argument 17 is not *guaranteed* by the premises.

In constructing counterexamples we focus on the form of the given argument rather than its content, since it is the form which determines validity. To focus on the form, we construct a new argument having the same form as the original argument, but with all true premises and a false conclusion. The content of the premises and the conclusion is, however, different from that of the original. The following argument is a counterexample to argument 17.

ARGUMENT 18

(1) If Bugs Bunny is a duck, then Bugs Bunny is an animal.

(2) Bugs Bunny is an animal.

∴ Bugs Bunny is a duck.

Arguments 17 and 18 have the same form, which is:

FORM 5

If p then q

q

∴ p

You should satisfy yourself that the forms of the two arguments in question are the same. Since it is the form (and not the argument) which determines validity, and since both arguments have the same form, they are either both valid or both invalid. But we can show that form 5 is invalid through argument 18, in which all the premises are *true* whereas the conclusion is *false*. Argument 17 is therefore invalid.

Just how does argument 18 show that the form of argument 17 is invalid? It does so in the following way: If argument 18 had a valid logical form, then its conclusion would have to be true if its premises were true; this is just what it means for an argument to be valid. Since argument 18 does have all true premises, if it were valid its conclusion would be true; but we know that the conclusion of argument 18 is false. Since the conclusion is false and the premises are true, the argument must be invalid—we can never have a valid argument with all true premises and a false conclusion. Furthermore, since argument 18 and argument 17 have the same form, and since argument 18 is invalid, argument 17 must be invalid as well. If you don't see this, reread the discussion of characteristic (DC1) of deductive arguments in section 2:2.2 and the discussion of validity in section 2:4.1.

Our comparison of argument 18 with argument 17 is known as the **method of giving counterexamples.** A summary of this method follows:

(1) Determine the form of the given argument.

(2) Try to construct a second argument which satisfies the following conditions:

   (*a*) The second argument has the same form as the original argument.

   (*b*) All the premises of the second argument are true.

   (*c*) The conclusion of the second argument is false.

(3) If a second argument can be constructed which satisfies conditions (*a*) through (*c*) of (2) above, then the original argument is an instance of an invalid form and is, as such, invalid.

What if we carry out this procedure and do not find an argument which satisfies conditions (*a*) to (*c*) of (2)? The temptation may be to say that the argument form is valid, but this claim is not warranted. Recall that, to show that an argument form is valid, we have to show that *no* instance of it has all true premises and a false conclusion. Our failure to find a counterexample may well be a result of not picking the right instances. So keep in mind that *failure to find a counterexample does not show that the argument in question is valid.*

EXERCISE 2-7

1. What is a counterexample used to show?

2. Why does giving a counterexample show an argument, or argument form, to be invalid? Explain your answer.

3. What three conditions does a counterexample have to satisfy to show that the original argument is invalid?

4. Suppose that each of the following argument forms was derived from a particular argument by using the procedure discussed in section 2:3.2. Show that these arguments are invalid by providing a counterexample for each form.

   a. If p then q
      q
      $\therefore p$

   b. If p then q
      p or r
      $\therefore q$

   c. If p then q
      If p then r
      $\therefore$ If r then p

   d. If p then q
      If r then s
      q or s
      $\therefore p$ or r

   e. If p then q
      $\therefore$ If q then p

   f. If p then q
      If r then s
      $\therefore$ If q then s

g. If p then q
   If r then s
   q and s
   $\therefore$ p and r

2:6 ANALYZING ARGUMENTS

We shall conclude this chapter with a brief discussion of the procedure one should follow in the analysis of arguments. When we raise the question of whether one is justified in accepting the conclusion of an argument on the basis of the evidence offered in the premises, two main issues arise. First, whether the form of the argument is such that the truth of the premises would provide *support* for the conclusion and, second, whether the premises are *true*. If the form of the argument is such that the truth of the premises would not provide support for the conclusion, then we are justified in rejecting the conclusion on the basis of the premises (argument 17 is such an argument). And when at least one premise is false, we are justified in rejecting the conclusion on the basis of the premises (argument 13 is such an argument).[13] Moreover, we sometimes find that the form of an argument does not support the conclusion *and* at least one premise is false. The following is one such argument:

ARGUMENT 19

(1) If Bugs is a rabbit, then Bugs is an alligator.

(2) Bugs is an alligator.

$\therefore$ Bugs is a rabbit.

These two issues, the support relation and the truth of the premises, are the two aspects of each argument that must be examined to determine the acceptability of the conclusion on the basis of the premises. The procedure we follow is outlined below; in the following chapters we shall use it in the analysis of various arguments.

PROCEDURE FOR ANALYZING ARGUMENTS

(1) Put the argument into standard form.

(2) Determine the form of the argument.

(3) If the argument is neither deductive nor inductive, then the argument does not have a form which satisfies the support relation. At this point we are justified in rejecting the conclusion of the argument on the basis of the evidence offered. This is not to say, however, that there is no

---

[13] Strictly speaking, this claim must be qualified. It sometimes happens that an argument contains premises which are irrelevant to the conclusion. In such a case, it is possible that the relevant premises, if true, would provide conclusive or probabilistic support for the conclusion. Here, the fact that some of the (irrelevant) premises are false would not provide grounds for rejecting the argument. We shall discuss this matter further in Chapters 4 and 8.

good argument which might be offered for the conclusion; it is just that the argument we are examining is not such an argument.

(4) If the argument is deductive or inductive, examine the premises to determine their truth values.

(5) If there is at least one false premise, reject the conclusion on the basis of the evidence offered in the premises. As in the case of the support relationship, this is not to say that there is no evidence—no set of true premises—which might be offered for the conclusion; but such evidence has not been offered in the argument we have been examining.

(6) If all the premises are true and the argument is deductive, the argument is sound and, moreover, has a true conclusion. We are justified in accepting the concluusion on the basis of the evidence offered.

(7) If the premises are true and the argument is inductive, certain other conditions must be satisfied. If they are, then we are justifed in accepting the conclusion on the basis of the evidence offered; if they are not, then we are justifed in rejecting the conclusion on the basis of the evidence. In Chapter 8 we shall see what these conditions are.

STUDENT STUDY GUIDE

Chapter Summary

1. Two conditions must be satisfied for an argument to be good: the premises of the argument must support the conclusion, and the premises must be true. If either or both of these conditions is not satisfied, then the argument is a bad one. (section 2:1)

2. Every statement and, hence, each premise and the conclusion of an argument has one, and only one **truth value.** It has the truth value *true* if it is true, and *false* if it is false. (section 2:1)

3. Given the logical relationships which hold among some statements, it is possible to determine which other statements would be true *if* those in a given set were true. Since the **support relationship** between the premises and the conclusion of an argument depends on the logical relationship between them, the premises of an argument can support the conclusion even though one, or even all, of the premises is *actually false.* (section 2:1.1)

4. The study of the relationship which holds between the premises and the conclusion of an argument such that the premises *conclusively* support the conclusion is the subject matter of **deductive logic,** and such arguments are **deductive arguments.** (section 2:2)

5. The study of the relationship which holds between the premises and the conclusion of an argument such that the premises provide *probabilistic,* though not conclusive, support for the conclusion is the subject matter of **inductive logic,** and such arguments are **inductive arguments.** (section 2:2)

6. The premises of an argument **inductively support** the conclusion if the argument is such that if all the premises are true then the conclusion is probably true, though it might nonetheless be false. In saying that the conclusion is probably true, we mean that it is more probable than not, given the evidence presented in the premises. (section 2:2.1)

7. The conclusions of inductive arguments contain information which is not contained in their premises. Moreover, for inductive arguments as a group, the conclusions of different inductive arguments follow from their premises with different degrees of probability. As a result, we often find that in the case of inductive arguments, different premises can confer different probabilities on the same conclusion. (section 2:2.1)

8. The premises of an argument **deductively support** the conclusion of the argument if the argument is such that if all the premises are true then the conclusion must be true. All arguments having this characteristic are **valid** arguments. In a valid argument it is impossible for all the premises to be true and the conclusion false. (section 2:2.2)

9. All the information in the conclusion of a valid argument is already contained in the premises. Moreover, for valid arguments as a group, the conclusions of different valid arguments always follow from their premises with the same degree of strength. (section 2:2.2)

10. **Statement constants** (written as uppercase letters) are used to represent particular statements; when they are used in a given context (an argument), they express exactly the same thing as is expressed by the statements they represent. (section 2:3.1)

11. **Statement variables** (written as lowercase letters) are placeholders for statements and do not represent particular statements; they are used to represent any statement whatsoever. When an argument has been symbolized by using statement variables, the result is not an argument but the **form** of the argument symbolized, a form which many other arguments can also have. (section 2:3.1)

12. A **simple statement** is one in which no other statement occurs as a component. A **compound statement** is one in which one or more additional simple statements occur as components. (section 2:3.2)

13. When we provide a form for an argument, we should strive to "capture" the structure of the argument which best exhibits the relationship between the premises and the conclusion. In general, we succeed in this if we assign individual variables to each of the component statements in a compound statement. (section 2:3.2)

14. An argument is **valid** if, and only if, it is such that if all the premises are true, then the conclusion must be true. Any argument which does not satisfy this condition is **invalid.** Since validity is a logical relationship between the premises and the conclusion, we can determine the validity of an argument without knowing the actual truth values of the premises and the conclusion. (section 2:4.1)

15. To say that an argument is valid is to say that it is an instance of a **valid argument form.** To say that a form is valid is to say that there are no instances of that form which have all true premises and a false conclusion. (section 2:4.1)

16. Invalid arguments can have any combination of truth values for their premises and conclusions. Valid arguments can have any combination *except* all true premises and a false conclusion. As a result, the only combination of truth values for the premises and the conclusion of an argument which will tell us anything about the validity of the argument is the case which shows the argument to be *invalid:* all true premises and a false conclusion. (section 2:4.1)

17. A **sound** argument is one which is valid and has all true premises. As a result, the conclusions of sound arguments are always true. (section 2:4.2)

18. A **counterexample** is used to show that a given argument or argument form is invalid. One gives a counterexample by giving an argument having the same form as the original argument, but with all true premises and a false conclusion. (section 2:5)

19. The failure to find a counterexample does *not* show that an argument is valid; the failure may be a result of not having picked the right instance with which to show invalidity. (section 2:5)

20. In analyzing an argument, we look for two things: whether the premises support the conclusion and whether the premises are true. If either or both of these conditions are not satisfied, then we are justified in rejecting the conclusion of the argument on the basis of the evidence offered in the premises. This does not mean, however, that the conclusion is false; there may be another set of true premises which do support the conclusion. (section 2:6)

Key Terms

Truth Value	Simple Statement
Support Relationship	Compound Statement
Deductive Logic	Valid Argument
Inductive Logic	Valid Argument Form
Deductive Support	Invalid Argument
Inductive Support	Invalid Argument Form
Statement Constants	Sound Argument
Statement Variables	Counterexample

Self-Test/Exercises

1. Indicate which of the following are true and which are false. For those which are false, explain why they are false.
   a.   Some statements have no truth value.
   b.   The premises of an argument can support the conclusion even if the premises are false.
   c.   The premises of an argument can support the conclusion even if the conclusion is false.
   d.   The premises of an argument always support the conclusion if the conclusion is true.
   e.   The premises of an argument do not support the conclusion if the conclusion is false.

    f.   If there is more information in the conclusion of an argument than in the premises, then the premises inductively support the conclusion.

    g.   If the premises of an argument contain more information than the conclusion, the premises deductively support the conclusion.

    h.   If all the information or factual content of the conclusion of an argument is contained in the premises, then the premises deductively support the conclusion.

    i.   Lowercase letters are used to indicate the content of an argument.

    j.   Uppercase letters are used to represent the content of particular statements.

    k.   Lowercase letters are placeholders for statements.

    l.   A statement which contains a simple statement as a component is a compound statement.

    m.   Every valid argument has a valid argument form.

    n.   Some valid arguments can be represented as having invalid argument forms.

    o.   Every argument with a true conclusion and all true premises is valid.

    p.   Every argument with a true conclusion is valid.

    q.   Every argument with at least one false premise is invalid.

    r.   Every argument with a false conclusion is invalid.

    s.   A valid argument with a true conclusion must have all true premises.

    t.   A valid argument with all true premises must have a true conclusion.

    u.   A valid argument with a false conclusion must have all false premises.

    v.   A valid argument with all false premises must have a false conclusion.

    w.   A valid argument with a false conclusion must have at least one false premise.

    x.   A valid argument with at least one false premise must have a false conclusion.

    y.   Any argument with all false premises and a false conclusion is invalid, even if it is an instance of a valid argument form.

    z.   Any argument with all true premises and a true conclusion is valid, even if it is an instance of an invalid argument form.

    aa. A valid argument with all true premises is a sound argument.

    bb. A valid argument with a true conclusion is a sound argument.

    cc. Counterexamples are used to show that a given argument is invalid.

    dd. If someone fails to construct a counterexample to a given argument, that shows that the argument is valid.

2. Determine which of the following are arguments. For those which are not, write "no argument." For those which are arguments, state whether the premises deductively or inductively support the conclusion. If neither situation occurs, write "no support." (section 2:2)

    a.   I just don't know what to do. When I was home for Christmas vacation my parents told me they would pay my expenses for the winter semester if I passed all my fall courses. I just received my grades and I failed one of my courses. It's clear what my parents will do.

    b.   I really enjoyed *The Midnight Horizon*. Moreover, everyone else I've talked with has also enjoyed reading it. On the basis of my experience, and that of my friends, you'll enjoy it too.

    c.   You may find this surprising (I know I did), but I just found out that central Europe is smaller than Texas. Moreover, both the U.S. and the Soviet Union are attempting to develop ways to use nuclear weapons to fight a war there. Can you imagine what would happen to the people in Texas if those in Louisiana and New Mexico started dropping nuclear weapons on them?

d. A great many people have become concerned about animal rights lately. Moreover, I really appreciate what they're doing. I especially like their point that if there is no relevant difference between animals and humans, then it's immoral to kill animals. After all, everyone agrees that it's immoral to kill humans.

e. Every time a storm has been coming, my cat goes and hides in the dirty laundry in the basement. I just found her down there again. What more proof do you need that there's a storm coming?

f. God simply doesn't exist. You may wonder how I know this, but just consider the following: If everyone had what he or she wanted, then God would clearly exist. Just as clearly, some of us don't have what we want.

3. Symbolize each of the following arguments using the given symbols as constants. In some cases it may be necessary to first supply missing premises or an unstated conclusion. Give the form of the argument. (section 2:3)

a. If you *really* loved me, then you would *leave*. Since you haven't left, it's clear that you don't really love me. (R, L)

b. If you *stay* with me, then you don't *really* love me. On the other hand, if you *leave* I'll be without the only person I've ever really *cared* about. Sad to say, I guess I'm in a real bind; either you don't love me or I'll be without the only person I've ever cared for. (S, R, L, C)

c. If a book is *worth* reading, then it ought at least to be *entertaining*. The one thing this book was not, was entertaining. (W, E)

d. If people *expect* government services to continue, then they ought to be *willing* to pay for them. If people *turn* down a millage request, then it's clear that they are not willing to pay for government services. Hence, if the next millage request is turned down, then people do not expect government services to continue. (E, W, T)

e. Jane is going to go to the party with either *Len* or *Conrad*. If she goes with Conrad, they'll go out for *dinner* before the party. If she goes with Len, they'll go out for an early morning *breakfast* after the party. Hence, Jane won't be *hungry*, since if she has dinner or an early breakfast she's never hungry. (L, C, D, B, H)

4. Show that each of the following argument forms is invalid by constructing a counterexample. (section 2:6)

a. If *p* then *q*
   p or *r*
   ∴ *q*

b. *p* or *q*
   If *r* then *q*
   ∴ *q*

c. If *p* then *q*
   If *q* then *r*
   q or *r*
   ∴ *p*

d. *p* or *q*
   If *q* then *r*
   ∴ *r*

e. If *p* then *q*
   If *q* then *r*
   ∴ If *r* then *p*

CHAPTER 3

CONDITIONAL

ARGUMENTS

In the previous chapter we looked at the definitions of 'argument', 'valid', and 'sound' and at some of the differences between inductive and deductive arguments. In this chapter and the next four we shall be concerned solely with deductive arguments. Each of the statements which occur in the arguments discussed in this chapter and in the next two is a **truth-functional** statement. Such statements will be discussed in detail in Chapter 4, but we should note here that a truth-functional statement is such that its truth value is determined by the truth value of its component statement or statements, along with the meanings of the logical connectives which occur in it. Among the truth-functional statements, conditional statements are especially important and will be discussed in detail in this chapter.

The purpose of this chapter, then, is to introduce you to conditional statements and to the arguments in which they occur—conditional arguments. We shall examine two valid forms of such arguments and two related, but invalid, forms. In the latter sections of the chapter we shall examine two powerful forms of conditional arguments, the *reductio ad absurdum* (indirect proof) and conditional proofs.

3:1 CONDITIONAL STATEMENTS

We discussed several conditional statements in the previous chapter; the most notable was the definition of 'valid'. As a first, rough approximation, a **conditional statement** is one which specifies what was, is, or would be the case under certain circumstances, the circumstances being specified in the statement. *All* conditional statements have the following form:

FORM OF CONDITIONAL STATEMENTS

If p then q

'p' and 'q' above are *statement variables* and are used to indicate that different statements can be substituted in the place marked by the variable.[1]

---

[1] As pointed out in the previous chapters, whereas it is *sentences* which are used in giving an argument, our concern is with the *statements* which are made in using these sentences; hence the expression 'statement variables'.

There are two parts to a conditional statement—one governed by the 'if' and the other governed by the 'then'. The part governed by the 'if' ('p' in the above example) is the **antecedent** of the statement. The part governed by the 'then' is the **consequent** of the statement. Note that we have defined the antecedent and consequent in terms of being *governed* by the 'if' and the 'then'. For example, in the statement form 'If q then p', 'q' is the antecedent and 'p' is the consequent.

We have characterized the consequent of a conditional statement as that part of the statement which is governed by 'then'. It often happens in English that the 'then' is omitted, as it is in the sentence 'If it rains, I won't go to the ball game'. Here the consequent is 'I won't go to the ball game', even though there is no 'then' in the original sentence.

Conditional statements are often expressed with the consequent grammatically preceding the antecedent; we shall say that such statements are in **inverted form.** The following are examples of such English sentences:

(1) I'll stay home if it rains.

(2) I won't go if you won't go.

(3) Tom will go to graduate school next year if he gets a fellowship.

(4) Higher education and social services will take a beating next year if the people approve the proposed tax amendment.

Notice that all the above are of the form 'p, if q'. To convert a sentence which is in inverted form to one which is in standard conditional-statement form, all we need to do is reverse the grammatical structure of the sentence. Hence, (1) to (4) above can be rewritten as follows:

(1)′ If it rains, then I'll stay home.

(2)′ If you won't go, then I won't go.

(3)′ If he gets a fellowship, then Tom will go to graduate school next year.

(4)′ If the people approve the proposed tax amendment, then higher education and social services will take a beating next year.

In rewriting (1) to (4) as (1)′ to (4)′, we have in each case merely moved the 'if' phrase to the beginning of the sentence and added 'then' between the antecedent and consequent. Of course, if each of (1) to (4) is true, then the respective rewritings are also true; similarly, if any of (1) to (4) is false, then its rewriting is also false.

EXERCISE 3-1

1. What is a conditional statement?

2. Explain which part of a conditional statement is the antecedent and which part is the consequent.

3. Underline the antecedent of each of the following statements.
   a. If the price of oil goes up, then the price of food will come down.
   b. Linda will go to Sweden if June goes to France.
   c. Mary will go to Germany if either June goes to France or Linda goes to Sweden.
   d. The price of oil will come down if either more people use less oil or they stop buying plastic toys.
   e. If it hadn't been for the Dutch elm disease, this would still be a beautiful neighborhood.
4. Underline the consequent of each of the following statements.
   a. Either the price of oil will come down or the federal government will subsidize its cost if either more people use less oil or if new sources of domestic oil are found.
   b. The tree must be cut down if you want the ivy to live.
   c. John will make more money and be happier if he either finishes school and gets a job or Aunt Matilda leaves him money instead of leaving it to the cat.
   d. There's no hope of beating the Diamonds if Murdock can't pitch by next Saturday.
   e. If you prefer asparagus and broccoli to green beans and peas, then you have a sophisticated taste in vegetables.

3:2 THE CONNECTIVE 'NOT'

In addition to saying what is the case, we often say that something is not the case. For example, we say that dictatorships are not a good form of government, that a diet high in cholesterol is not good for one's health, and so on. Although we have not yet looked in any detail at conditional statements which contain 'not', it is indispensable for our purposes that we now introduce this connective.[2]

The connective 'not' has the effect of *changing the truth value of a statement to the opposite truth value:* if some given statement is true, then appending 'not' will change the truth value of the statement to false; if some given statement is false, then appending 'not' will change the truth value of the statement to true.

When we append 'not' to a statement, we say that we have **negated** the statement, and we call the result the **negation** of the original statement. We will use the symbol '~' (called a *tilde*) to symbolize 'not'. For example, if we are using the constant 'P' to represent the statement 'Dawdlin is a murderer',

---

[2] The word 'connective' is used by logicians to denote a class of expressions which one uses to form more complex statements from simpler ones. 'If–then' is a paradigm case of a connective, since it "connects" the antecedent and the consequent. 'Not' is a connective in a secondary sense, for though it is not used to connect statements, it is used to form a more complex statement from a simpler one.

we symbolize 'Dawdlin is not a murderer' as '~*P*'. The expression '~*P*' is the negation of '*P*' and is read, 'It is not the case that *P*'. Similarly, '~~*P*' is read, 'It is not the case that it is not the case that *P*'.[3]

It is easy to generalize this to the case in which we use statement *variables* instead of constants. Since a statement variable represents any statement whatsoever (remember that statement variables are *placeholders* for statements), replacing the variable with a statement can result in something which is true or something which is false. Nonetheless, a statement of the form '~~*p*' has the same truth value as a statement of the form '*p*', for no matter which statement uniformly replaces '*p*', negating that statement and then negating the result gives us a statement with the same truth value as the original statement.

When two statement *forms* always have the same truth value no matter which statements are uniformly substituted for the variables in both forms, the two statement forms are **logically equivalent.** Since this condition holds between '~~*p*' and '*p*', these two statement forms are logically equivalent. This particular equivalency has been given the name **double negation;** it will prove to be extremely useful later on in this chapter, when we show the validity and invalidity of arguments. The usefulness of double negation results from the fact that *logically equivalent statements can be substituted for each other in an argument without changing the validity or invalidity of the argument.*[4]

Whereas 'not' has the function of changing the truth value of a statement to the opposite truth value, some English sentences which contain 'not' are ambiguous. One result is that it is sometimes difficult to determine which affirmative statement the speaker is negating. An example is

(1) Everyone who was invited to the party is not coming.

One interpretation of (1) is that *some* people who were invited to the party are not coming (and some who were invited are coming); another interpretation is that *no one* who was invited is coming.

In some cases we have to rely on the context of the speaker's utterance to determine what the speaker meant. In other cases, shared background knowledge can often be relied upon. For example, if someone asserts that all dogs are not brown, it is reasonable to take the speaker as asserting that some dogs are not brown, and *not* as asserting that *no dogs* are brown. We shall discuss this issue in much more detail in Chapter 6; our main purpose here is to point out that whereas 'not' changes the truth value of a statement, it is not always clear which statement is being negated.

Having seen how to symbolize statements containing the word 'not', and having been introduced to double negation as a logical equivalency, you are

---

[3] Although we could use a constant such as '*P*' to represent a negative statement, logicians follow the procedure of using constants to represent affirmative statements and using '~' to represent negations. This more accurately reflects the logical structure of statements which contain 'not' and is, therefore, the procedure we shall follow.

[4] This point will be developed in much more detail in the next two chapters.

almost ready to consider some arguments composed, at least in part, of conditional statements; this you shall do in section 3:4. First, in the next section, we shall examine some of the ways in which conditional statements are expressed in English, and we shall look at an important relationship which holds among some conditional statements.

EXERCISE 3-2

1. What does it mean to say that a statement is in inverted form? How are such statements converted to standard conditional-statement form?

2. Give an example of a statement in inverted form, and then convert your statement to standard conditional-statement form.

3. What is the function of the connective 'not'?

4. The negations of the following can be formed by writing 'It is not the case that' in front of them. Write the negations of these in more natural, idiomatic English. Where a given statement or its negation is ambiguous, explain the ambiguity. Note that we are not supposing that any of these statements is actually true.
   a. Henry left this morning on flight 342.
   b. Protective tariffs are the only way to stabilize the American automobile industry.
   c. People should never interfere in the affairs of others.
   d. Socialism and Marxism are not the same form of government.
   e. Some plants prefer bright sunlight.
   f. Grant was a better general then Lee.
   g. It's not safe to walk down Broad Street after dark.
   h. The Battle of Hastings is one of the most significant military encounters of all time.
   i. To determine how far a projectile will travel, one needs to know only its initial velocity.
   j. There is a high correlation between family income level and health.

3:3 VARIOUS WAYS OF WRITING CONDITIONAL STATEMENTS

Some sentence structures in the English language can be rewritten as conditional statements having the form 'If p then q', although they are not initially written in this form. In this section we shall examine some of these sentence structures and show how to rewrite them in **standard conditional-statement form**, that is, in the form 'If p then q'. The benefit derived from knowing how to rewrite such sentences is that whenever any of them occurs in an argument, we can rewrite it in standard conditional-statement form and then analyze the resultant statement by using the techniques we shall develop in subsequent sections.

3:3.1 Unless For our purposes the English word 'unless' can be translated as 'if not'. For example, the sentence 'Unless I eat, I will be hungry' can be translated into the sentence 'If I don't eat, then I will be hungry'. Whenever we replace 'unless' with 'if not', the result is a statement which is equivalent to the original statement in that both statements have the same truth value. Not surprisingly, some sentences containing 'unless' will, after the translation, be in inverted form. For example, translating 'unless' as 'if not' in the sentence 'The bank will not approve her new-car loan unless she is employed' results in 'The bank will not approve her new-car loan if she is not employed.' The statement this sentence is ordinarily used to express is equivalent to that ordinarily expressed by 'If she is not employed, then the bank will not approve her new-car loan.'

Before we conclude this section, it should be noted that, on some occasions, simply replacing 'unless' with 'if not' does not seem to be the best way of treating what the speaker said. For example, if someone says, "We won't be at the party unless we can get off work early," there are contexts in which it is reasonable to take the speaker as believing *both* that if they do not get off early then they will not be at the party *and* that if they do get off early then they will be at the party.

Because of cases like this, we shall adopt the procedure of translating what was actually written or stated in a sentence containing 'unless' by just replacing the 'unless' with 'if not'. If it is reasonable to suppose that the speaker also believes more than was stated, this can be treated as a suppressed premise in the manner discussed in Chapter 1.

3:3.2 Only If   Sentences in which the expression 'only if' occurs are such that what *looks* like the antecedent of a conditional statement is actually the consequent of a conditional statement. Before discussing this further, let's look at some examples of sentences in which 'only if' occurs, along with the equivalent sentences rewritten in standard conditional-statement form.

   (1) John is a biologist only if he is a scientist.
   (1)' If John is a biologist, then he is a scientist.

   (2) You will get good grades only if you study.
   (2)' If you get good grades, then you study.

   (3) You will be happy only if you are successful.
   (3)' If you are happy, then you are successful.

   (4) You will be successful only if you are happy.
   (4)' If you are successful, then you are happy.

   (5) Annie is an aardvark only if she is a mammal.
   (5)' If Annie is an aardvark, then she is a mammal.

The first thing you should do now is satisfy yourself that all the primed statements above have the same truth value as their unprimed counterparts. That is, if an unprimed statement is true, then so too is the related primed statement; and if an unprimed statement is false, then so too is the primed statement.

A little reflection on sentences (1) to (5) will show that what is stated following the 'only if' is a condition which must be satisfied for the remainder of the sentence to be true.[5] For example, in (1), John's being a scientist is a condition which must be satisfied for him to be a biologist. Of course, even if John is a scientist, it does not follow that he is a biologist. Hence, it would be *wrong* to translate (1) as 'If John is a scientist then he is a biologist'. On the other hand, since John couldn't be a biologist unless he were a scientist [this is one of the things entailed by (1)], it follows that if he is a biologist, then he is a scientist. Note that this is just what is asserted in (1)' above.

Similar remarks can be made for (2) to (5). In each case, the 'only if' clause specifies a condition which must be satisfied for what is asserted in the other clause to be true. This means, then, that if what is asserted in the other clause is true, this necessary condition will also be satisfied. As a result, any statement of the form 'p, only if q' is translated as a statement of the form 'if p then q'.

It should also be noted that some 'only if' statements are written grammatically with the 'only if' clause occurring first. 'Only if Fred passes logic this summer will he graduate with the rest of his class' is one such example. This statement has the form 'only if p, q' and is translated as 'if q then p'. Notice that here, as in (1) to (5), the necessary condition occurs as the *consequent* of the conditional statement.

3:3.3 Contraposition
The **contrapositive** of a conditional statement is obtained by performing the following two operations:

(1) Negate both the antecedent and the consequent of the original statement.

(2) Write a new statement in which the negated antecedent of the original statement is the consequent of the new statement and the negated consequent of the original statement is the antecedent of the new statement.

Contraposition is like double negation in that the contrapositive of a conditional statement is *logically equivalent* to the original statement. This means that any statement of the form 'If $\sim q$ then $\sim p$' will have the same truth value as a statement of the form 'If p then q', regardless of which statements uniformly replace 'p' and 'q' in both these statement forms. Thus, whenever we come across a conditional statement in an argument, we can replace it with its contrapositive and be assured that if the original argument is valid, then the resultant argument will be valid, similarly for the case of invalidity.

Let's now look at an example in which contraposition is applied to a conditional statement.

EXAMPLE 1

Give the contrapositive of 'If Annie is a mammal, then she's warm-blooded.'

---

[5] Such conditions are called *necessary conditions*; they will be discussed in detail in Chapter 9.

Step 1: Negate both the antecedent and the consequent of the original statement. Our result is:[6]

If Annie is not a mammal, then she's not warm-blooded.

Step 2: Write a new statement in which the negated antecedent of the original statement is now the consequent and the negated consequent of the original statement is now the antecedent. This gives us:

If Annie is not warm-blooded, then she's not a mammal.

We can generalize this discussion of example 1 as follows: The contrapositive of a conditional statement is logically equivalent to the original conditional statement, since, if the latter is true and the consequent isn't the case, then the antecedent could not be the case either. For this reason we have the following:

Any statement of the form 'If p then q' is logically equivalent to a statement of the form 'If $\sim q$ then $\sim p$'.

3:3.4 Converse   Although the converse of a conditional statement is not logically equivalent to the conditional statement, I mention converses here so that you will not make the mistake of thinking that they are logically equivalent. The **converse** of a conditional statement is formed simply by interchanging the antecedent and the consequent of the conditional statement. In logical form, then, the converse of 'If p then q' is 'If q then p'. We can show that the converse of a conditional statement is not logically equivalent to the original statement with the following example:

(1) If Boston is in Maine, then it's in New England.

The converse of (1) is:

(2) If Boston is in New England, then it's in Maine.

Assigning 'p' to the place occupied by 'Boston is in Maine' and 'q' to the place occupied by 'Boston is in New England', we have the following as the respective forms of (1) and (2):

(1)' If p then q

(2)' If q then p

Now, it's clear that (1) is true since any city in Maine is a city in New England (since Maine is in New England); therefore, if Boston is in Maine, then it's in New England. It's equally clear, however, that (2) is false, for whereas it's *true*

---

[6] In forming the contrapositive of a conditional statement, the result we get after applying step 1 is *not* equivalent to the original statement. Since there are two steps involved in forming the contrapositive of a conditional statement, *the result will be equivalent to the original statement only after both steps have been performed.*

that Boston is in New England (since it's in Massachusetts and Massachusetts is in New England), it's *false* that Boston is in Maine.

As a result, replacing the '*p*' in (1)' and (2)' with 'Boston is in Maine' and the '*q*' with 'Boston is in New England' results in one statement, statement (1), which is true and another, statement (2), which is false. Since two statement forms are logically equivalent only if they have the same truth value no matter which statements uniformly replace the variables occurring in them, forms (1)' and (2)' are not logically equivalent. Consequently, converses are not logically equivalent, since we have given a clear instance in which a statement is true and its converse is false.

At this point it is worth emphasizing what we did when we showed that (2) was false. What we found in the case of (2) was that the *antecedent* of the conditional statement ('Boston is in New England') was true, whereas the *consequent* ('Boston is in Maine') was false. To show that a conditional statement is false, we must show that it has a true antecedent and a false consequent, since this is the *only* set of conditions under which a conditional statement is false. We shall discuss this point further in Chapter 4.

Now that you know how to handle sentences in inverted form, and those containing the expressions 'unless' and 'only if', we are ready to consider some arguments composed, at least in part, of conditional statements. It is to this that we now turn.

EXERCISE 3-3

1. How does the word 'unless' function logically?

2. How is a sentence containing 'unless' converted into standard conditional-statement form?

3. Give an example of a statement containing 'unless', and then convert your statement into standard conditional-statement form.

4. How are statements containing 'only if' converted into standard conditional-statement form?

5. Give an example of a statement containing 'only if', and then convert your statement into standard conditional-statement form.

6. How is the contrapositive of a conditional statement formed?

7. Give an example of a conditional statement, and give its contrapositive.

8. Under what circumstances is a conditional statement false? Give an example of a false conditional statement.

EXERCISE 3-4

1. Rewrite the following statements in standard conditional-statement form.
   a. Only if we curb the flow of illegal drugs into this country can we stem the tide of inner-city crime.
   b. We can get the job done only if we all work together.
   c. We won't get the job done unless we all work together.

d. We can't win the war on poverty unless we spend money.

e. Only if capital punishment deterred crimes would it be justified.

f. Unless capital punishment deters crimes, it isn't justified.

g. Many people will starve unless the U.S. contributes to the world food program.

h. Cities can carry out good service programs only if they receive enough federal funds.

i. Unless national security is at stake, it is unjustified to tap the phones of private citizens.

j. Unless the President appeals to executive privilege, the truth will be made public.

k. Unless you put batteries in it, your portable mushroom won't work.

l. Happiness will come your way, but only if you pay attention to the words of the sorcerer.

m. Unless the day is sunny, we won't frolic in the park.

n. The car will start only if you depress the clutch pedal.

o. Paper plates are okay, but only if you're not eating something soupy.

p. Unless I get busted, I'll have the stuff at your place tomorrow morning.

q. Only if Alladin can call forth the genie will we get out of this awful mess.

r. You can see forever only if it's a clear day.

s. The Green Hornet will come to the rescue, unless he gets caught in Spiderman's web.

t. Unless Bugs is awfully stupid, Elmer is never going to get close enough to get off a good shot.

2. Give the contrapositives of the conditional statements you provided as answers to problem 1.

3:4 FOUR FORMS OF CONDITIONAL ARGUMENTS

In this section we shall examine four forms of conditional arguments, two of which are valid and two of which, though closely related to the valid forms, are invalid. A conditional argument is an argument which contains nothing but conditional statements or, in addition to conditional statements, contains nothing but statements which are the antecedents or the consequents of these conditional statements or the negations of the antecedents or consequents of these statements. We shall begin our discussion with the two valid forms.

3:4.1 Affirming the Antecedent   Consider the following argument:

ARGUMENT 2

(1) If he is a socialist, then he's for a national health plan.

(2) He's a socialist.

∴ He's for a national health plan.

The form of argument 2 is as follows:

FORM OF ARGUMENT 2

(1) If p then q

(2) p

$\therefore q$

In the form of argument 2, 'p' is used to represent 'He is a socialist' and 'q' is used to represent 'He's for a national health plan'. You should satisfy yourself that argument 2 does have the above form.

Argument 2 has the form **affirming the antecedent,** and the form is *valid.* We do not, as yet, have a way to show that the form is valid—we won't be able to do this until the next chapter. For now, if you just appeal to your intuition, you will see that whatever statements are substituted for the variables in this argument form, when the resultant premises are both true the conclusion of the argument must also be true. This is, of course, just what it means for an argument to be valid.

The argument form affirming the antecedent has the following features:

(1) The argument consists of two premises and a conclusion.

(2) One of the premises is a conditional statement.

(3) The other premise is the antecedent of the conditional statement (hence the name 'affirming the antecedent').

(4) The conclusion is the consequent of the conditional statement.

Any argument which has all these features is an instance of affirming the antecedent; any argument which lacks one or more of the features is not an instance of this form.

3:4.2 Denying the Consequent   Consider the following argument:

ARGUMENT 3

(1) If he is a socialist, then he's for a national health plan.

(2) He's not for a national health plan.

$\therefore$ He's not a socialist.

The form of argument 3 is as follows:

FORM OF ARGUMENT 3

(1) If p then q

(2) $\sim q$

$\therefore \sim p$

Argument 3 has the form **denying the consequent** and it too is *valid.*[7] As in the

---

[7] We earlier remarked that contrapositives are logically equivalent. Notice that if we replace (1) in the form of argument 3 with its contrapositive, 'If $\sim q$ then $\sim p$', the result, along with (2) and the conclusion, is an instance of the valid argument form affirming the antecedent.

case of affirming the antecedent, we cannot yet show that the form is valid, but you should attempt to satisfy yourself that it is.

The argument form denying the consequent has the following features:

(1) The argument consists of two premises and a conclusion.

(2) One of the premises is a conditional statement.

(3) The other premise is the *negation* of the consequent of the conditional statement (hence the name 'denying the consequent').

(4) The conclusion is the *negation* of the antecedent of the conditional statement.

Any argument which has all these features is an instance of denying the consequent; any argument which lacks one or more of the features is not an instance of this form.

3:4.3 Affirming the Consequent   Consider the following argument:

ARGUMENT 4

(1) If he is a socialist, then he's for a national health plan.

(2) He's for a national health plan.

∴ He's a socialist.

The form of argument 4 is as follows:

FORM OF ARGUMENT 4

(1) If p then q

(2) q

∴ p

In the form of argument 4, 'p' is used to represent 'He is a socialist' and 'q' is used to represent 'He's for a national health plan.'

Argument 4 has the form **affirming the consequent** and, though closely resembling the form affirming the antecedent, it is *invalid*. We can show that the form affirming the consequent is invalid by the method of giving counterexamples. The following argument is one such counterexample.

ARGUMENT 5

(1) If Boston is in Maine, then Boston is in New England.

(2) Boston is in New England.

∴ Boston is in Maine.

Since argument 5 has all true premises and a false conclusion, it does not have a valid logical form (recall the definition of 'valid'). Additionally, since argument 4 has the very same form as argument 5, the form of argument 4 is also invalid.

The argument form affirming the consequent has the following features:

(1) The argument consists of two premises and a conclusion.

(2) One of the premises is a conditional statement.

(3) The other premise is the consequent of the conditional statement (hence the name 'affirming the consequent').

(4) The conclusion is the antecedent of the conditional statement.

Any argument which has all these features is an instance of affirming the consequent; any argument which lacks one or more of the features is not an instance of this form.

3:4.4 Denying the Antecedent Consider the following argument:

ARGUMENT 6

(1) If he is a socialist, then he's for a national health plan.

(2) He's not a socialist.

∴ He's not for a national health plan.

The form of argument 6 is as follows:

FORM OF ARGUMENT 6

(1) If p then q

(2) $\sim p$

∴ $\sim q$

In the form of argument 6, 'p' is used to represent 'He is a socialist' and 'q' is used to represent 'He's for a national health plan'. As a result, '$\sim p$' is used to represent 'He is not a socialist' and '$\sim q$' is used to represent 'He is not for a national health plan'.

Argument 6 has the form **denying the antecedent.** Although it closely resembles the argument form denying the consequent, it is *invalid*. Again we can rely on the method of giving counterexamples to show this. The following argument will do:

ARGUMENT 7

(1) If UCLA is in the state of Washington, then UCLA is on the west coast.

(2) UCLA is not in the state of Washington.

∴ UCLA is not on the west coast.

The premises of argument 7 are true, but the conclusion is false. Hence, the logical form of argument 7 is invalid. Since argument 7 has the same logical form as argument 6, the logical form of argument 6 is also invalid.

The argument form denying the antecedent has the following features:

(1) The argument consists of two premises and a conclusion.

(2) One of the premises is a conditional statement.

(3) The other premise is the *negation* of the antecedent of the conditional statement (hence the name 'denying the antecedent').

(4) The conclusion is the *negation* of the consequent of the conditional statement.

Any argument which has all these features is an instance of denying the antecedent; any argument which lacks one or more of the features is not an instance of this form.

EXERCISE 3-5

1. What features does the argument form affirming the antecedent have? Give two arguments having this form—one sound and the other unsound.

2. What features does the argument form denying the consequent have? Give two arguments having this form—one sound and the other unsound.

3. What features does the argument form affirming the consequent have? Give an instance of this form which shows that the form is invalid.

4. What features does the argument form denying the antecedent have? Give an instance of this form which shows that the form is invalid.

3:4.5 Some Examples In this section we shall use the ideas discussed above to determine the validity or invalidity of some arguments. In each case we shall put the argument into standard form, give the logical form of the argument, and then determine whether the argument is valid or invalid.

ARGUMENT 8

Unless Sally wants more children, it is reasonable for her to get an abortion. Hence, since an abortion for Sally is reasonable, she doesn't want any more children.

Step 1: The first step here is to pick out the conclusion of the argument. We do this by asking what point the speaker is making and by looking for indicator words. We see in the above argument the indicator word 'hence'. Our conclusion, then, is:

Sally doesn't want any more children.

Step 2: Now we want to find the premises of the argument. Following the general rule that all that is left after the conclusion has been identified are the premises of the argument, and again looking for indicator words, we find that the premises are:

(1) Unless Sally wants more children, it is reasonable for her to get an abortion.

(2) An abortion for Sally is reasonable.

Note that premise (2) was marked with the indicator word 'since', whereas there was no indicator word marking premise (1).

Step 3: We are ready to put our argument into standard form, separating the premises and the conclusion and marking the latter with '∴'.

(1) Unless Sally wants more children, it is reasonable for her to get an abortion.

(2) An abortion for Sally is reasonable.

∴ Sally doesn't want any more children.

Step 4: We are now ready to provide the logical form of the argument. To do this, we let '*p*' represent 'Sally wants more children' and let '*q*' represent 'It is reasonable for Sally to get an abortion'. This gives us:

(1) unless *p, q*

(2) *q*

∴ ~*p*

Step 5: Premise (1) of our argument is not in standard conditional-statement form. Applying the procedure presented in section 3:3.1 above to premise (1), we obtain the argument form:

(1) If ~*p* then *q*

(2) *q*

∴ ~*p*

The argument form we have derived in step 5 is that of *affirming the consequent;* hence, the form of argument 8, and argument 8 itself, are invalid. Also note that, whereas the conclusion of the argument and the antecedent of the conditional premise are both negated statement forms, they are so related to each other as to satisfy condition (4) of the defining characteristics of affirming the consequent.

ARGUMENT 9:

The voters will approve the proposed tax amendment only if they don't mind spending their money on things like social services. Hence, the voters will not approve the tax amendment since they do mind spending their money on social services.

Step 1: Again our first step is to pick out the conclusion of the argument. Asking what the person's point is and noting the indicator word 'hence', we see that the conclusion is:

The voters will not approve the tax amendment.

Step 2: We now look for the premises. One of the premises is marked by the indicator word 'since'; the other premise has no indicator word but can be recognized as a premise since we have already established the conclusion. Our two premises are:

(1) The voters will approve the proposed tax amendment only if

they don't mind spending their money on things like social services.

(2) The voters do mind spending their money on social services.

Step 3: Now we put the argument into standard form:

(1) The voters will approve the proposed tax amendment only if they don't mind spending their money on things like social services.

(2) The voters do mind spending their money on social services.

∴ The voters will not approve the tax amendment.

Step 4: To provide the logical form of the argument, we let '*p*' represent 'The voters will approve the proposed tax amendment' and let '*q*' represent 'The voters do mind spending their money on social services'. This gives us:

(1) *p*, only if ~*q*

(2) *q*

∴ ~*p*

Step 5: We note that, in step 4, premise (1) is not in standard conditional-statement form. Applying the procedure discussed in section 3:3.2, we get:

(1) If *p* then ~*q*

(2) *q*

∴ ~*p*

We are now ready to determine whether the argument is valid or invalid. Noting the characteristics of the four conditional arguments discussed above, we see that this argument satisfies three of the four conditions for being an instance of *denying the consequent;* the condition that it does not satisfy is that in the argument form denying the consequent, the nonconditional premise is the *negation* of the consequent of the conditional premise. What we have, however, is a case in which the consequent of the conditional premise is the negation of the nonconditional premise. What are we to do in situations like this?

The answer to this question lies in noting that, whereas the structure of the argument isn't that of denying the consequent, the two statement forms in question, '~*q*' and '*q*', would have opposite truth values if '*q*' were replaced by any statement. Then, by using *double negation* on the second premise of the argument (thereby obtaining '~~*q*'), we will end up with an argument form which *is* denying the consequent. Since this result is a valid argument form, and since we can derive this result by a logical equivalency from the original argument, argument 9 is valid. The resulting argument is:

(1) If *p* then ~*q*

(2) ~~*q*

∴ ~*p*

The above discussion can be summarized in a very simple way by presenting a *proof* of the validity of argument 9. (Proofs will be discussed in more detail in the next section and in Chapter 5. For now, it is sufficient to note that in giving a proof of the validity of an argument, we list the premises and then show how the conclusion can be derived from them by using only valid argument forms.) The proof of the validity of argument 9 follows: the right-hand column simply specifies where each line of the proof comes from.

(1) If p then $\sim q$ Premise

(2) q Premise

(3) $\sim\sim q$ (2), double negation

$\therefore \sim p$ (1), (3), denying the consequent

The notation '(2), double negation' for line (3) of the proof tells us that we derived line (3) from line (2) by using double negation. The notation for the last line tells us that we derived the conclusion by using the statement forms on lines (1) and (3) as premises in the argument form denying the consequent.

As a general guide in assessing the validity of conditional arguments such as those discussed in this section, first check whether the argument form is one of the four discussed above. If the form is affirming the antecedent or denying the consequent, then the argument is valid; if the form is affirming the consequent or denying the antecedent, then the argument is invalid. If, on the other hand, the form is not one of the four discussed, then ask whether the two premises, or the conclusion and the conditional premise, are so related that they satisfy *some* of the criteria for being either affirming the antecedent or denying the consequent. If so, then ask whether double negation can be used on the argument in such a way as to satisfy the remaining criteria. If this can be done, then the original argument is valid.

EXERCISE 3-6

Put each of the following arguments into standard form. Symbolize the argument by using the given symbols, derive the logical form of the argument, and state the name of the form if it has a name. State whether the argument is valid or invalid and explain your answer, giving a proof where appropriate.

a. The economy will *decline* unless there is a *rise* in wages. The economy will decline, so there must not have been a rise in wages. (D, R)

b. Only if we *curb* the flow of illegal drugs into this country can we *stem* the tide of inner-city crime. But we have not stemmed the tide of inner-city crime; hence, as anyone can see, we have not curbed the flow of illegal drugs into this country. (C, S)

c. Only if we all *work* together can we get the *job* done. Hence, unless we work together we won't get the job done. (W, J)

d. If capital punishment *deterred* crime, then it would be *justified*, but we all know that it does not deter crime. Hence, capital punishment is not justified. (D, J)

e. Only if the police *spend* less time on victimless crimes will they be able to *reduce* the number of violent crimes. Hence, the number of violent crimes will be reduced because the police will spend less time on victimless crimes. (S, R)

f. If *John* were to go to the movies and Sally were to go to the basketball game, then two people would be *entertained*. Two people are entertained, for John went to the movies and Sally to the basketball game. (J, E)

g. Cities don't *receive* enough federal funds because only if cities recieve enough federal funds can they carry out *good* service programs; and they aren't carrying out good service programs. (R, G)

h. It is certainly the case that wire taps on the phones of private citizens are *justified*, since *national* security is at stake; but only when national security is at stake is it justified to tap the phones of private citizens. (J, N)

i. Unless something *drastic* happens, this country will find itself in the *throes* of a depression in a few short months. But something drastic will happen, so the country will not be in the throes of a depression. (D, T)

j. Once upon a time there was a beautiful princess who *lived* in a magnificent castle. But only if the castle was in the *deep* woods would a beautiful princess live in it, so the castle had to be in the deep woods. (L, D)

k. Why, that *masked* man must be the Lone Ranger. If he weren't, after all, he wouldn't have *left* this silver bullet. (M, L)

l. I just saw Stan, and he was trying to crawl under the *garage* to get the cat. He must be *crazy*. (G, C)

m. You wonder whether that stuff growing over there is edible. Well, it's *edible* only if it's *asparagus*, and I'm told it's actually locoweed. (E, A)

n. Jeremy is able to go to the *bathroom* only if he raises his hand to ask *permission*. Even though he does not like to ask permission to do anything, he must have done it this time, since he went to the bathroom. (B, P)

o. If an inexpensive *process* could be developed to remove oil from shale, then the energy situation would be *improved* immediately. Of course, no one has even an idea about how to develop an inexpensive process, so the energy situation isn't going to change any time soon. (P, I)

3:5 COMPLEX ARGUMENTS

The arguments one typically encounters are not neatly laid out in standard form, and they are often more complex than those we have thus far dealt with. In this section we shall examine several arguments of a more complex variety. There is no reason to be panic-stricken by the idea of complex arguments—you will quickly see that they are merely arguments which contain more than one of the argument forms we have already discussed and, as such, require that you identify various argument forms within a single argument.

Before we start, a general comment on procedure is in order: Whenever two statements in an argument entail some third statement, this latter statement can be treated as an additional premise for the purpose of deriving the conclusion from the premises. In this regard our procedure is analogous to the derivations in geometry in which one shows, through a set of intermediate steps, that the conclusion can be derived from the set of premises.

3:5.1 Some Examples

ARGUMENT 10

Marilyn Monroe was the greatest film queen Hollywood ever had. This is so because only if she were the greatest film queen would she have been so popular, and if she drew a large crowd at the box office she was very popular. We know, of course, that she always drew a large crowd at the box office.

Step 1: As in the case of simpler arguments, our first task is to identify the conclusion of the argument. Note that in this argument the conclusion is written first, marked by the indicator word 'this is so'. Our conclusion, then, is:

Marilyn Monroe was the greatest film queen Hollywood ever had.

Step 2: Now we look for the premises. Two of them are marked by the indicator word 'because':

(1) Only if Marilyn Monroe were the greatest film queen would she have been so popular.

(2) If she drew a large crowd at the box office she was very popular.

Notice that the 'because' applies to *both* the conditionals conjoined by 'and'. How about the statement 'She always drew a large crowd at the box office'? This too is a premise. Even though there is no typical indicator word marking it as a premise, we have already picked out our conclusion—so all it can be is a premise. Also note the expression 'We know, of course, that'. This should indicate to you that what follows it is more or less general information (or the arguer takes it as such), not needing an argument for support. As such, what follows is serving as support for some other claim. Our third premise, then, is:

(3) Marilyn Monroe always drew a large crowd at the box office.

Step 3: We now put the argument into standard form:

(1) Only if Marilyn Monroe were the greatest film queen would she have been so popular.

(2) If she drew a large crowd at the box office she was very popular.

(3) Marilyn Monroe always drew a large crowd at the box office.

∴ Marilyn Monroe was the greatest film queen Hollywood ever had.

Step 4: To provide the logical form of the argument, let's assign variables in the following way:

p: Marilyn Monroe was the greatest film queen Hollywood ever had.

q: Marilyn Monroe was very popular.

r: Marilyn Monroe drew a large crowd at the box office.

Notice that in assigning variables we have taken some license with the sentence structure, mood, and tense of the argument as originally given. Using the above variables, we see that the logical form of the argument is:

(1) Only if p, q

(2) If r, q

(3) r

∴ p

Step 5: Since premise (1) is not in standard conditional-statement form, we need to convert it by applying the procedure from section 3:3.2; we also need to add 'then' to premise (2):

(1) If q then p

(2) If r then q

(3) r

∴ p

We have now provided the logical form of argument 10. Suppose, however, that we raise the issue of the argument's validity. The best way, at this point, to determine the validity of the argument is to see what simpler conditional arguments the argument is composed of. We know already that simple conditional arguments consist of a conditional statement and a simple statement. Let's begin, then, with premise (3), 'r', and see if it is a part of one of the four types of simple conditional arguments.

The only other premise in which 'r' occurs is premise (2); hence our first simple conditional argument will consist of premises (2) and (3). This gives us:

(2) If r then q

(3) r

These two premises are of the same form as those in the argument form affirming the antecedent. Hence, premises (2) and (3) give us:

(4) q

Let's apply the above procedure again. We see that premise (1), thus far not used, contains '*q*'. Premise (1) and interim conclusion (4) give us:

(1) If q then p

(4) q

Note that (1) and (4) are also in the same form as the premises of the argument form affirming the antecedent. Hence, from (1) and (4) we can derive '*p*'.

Now '*p*' is, of course, the conclusion of our argument. *Since '*p*' can be derived from the premises by two instances of the valid argument form affirming the antecedent, the whole argument form in step 5 is valid.* We can summarize what we have done above as follows, where the numbers in parentheses indicate our initial assignment of numbers to premises, and the numbers in brackets indicate the steps in the proof:

[1]	(2) If r then q	Premise
[2]	(3) r	Premise
[3]	(4) q	[1], [2], affirming the antecedent
[4]	(1) If q then p	Premise
	$\therefore p$	[3], [4], affirming the antecedent

ARGUMENT 11

Since we'll save the environment only if "big business" stops polluting the air and water, and since "big business" will stop polluting the air and water, it follows that we will all live healthier lives; after all, unless we save the environment we won't live healthier lives.

Step 1: Identify the conclusion. This is done by noting the indicator word 'it follows that'. Our result is:

We will all live healthier lives.

Step 2: Identify the premises. All three premises are marked by indicator words—two by 'since' and one by 'for':

(1) We'll save the environment only if "big business" stops polluting the air and water.

(2) "Big business" will stop polluting the air and water.

(3) Unless we save the environment, we won't live healthier lives.

Step 3: Put the argument into standard form:

(1) We'll save the environment only if "big business" stops polluting the air and water.

(2) "Big business" will stop polluting the air and water.

(3) Unless we save the environment, we won't live healthier lives.

∴ We will all live healthier lives.

Step 4: Provide the logical form of the argument. To do this, we assign variables in the following way:

p: We'll save the environment.

q: "Big business" stops polluting the air and water.

r: We live healthier lives.

With this assignment of variables, the logical form of our argument is:

(1) *p*, only if *q*

(2) *q*

(3) Unless *p*, $\sim r$

∴ *r*

Step 5: Premises (1) and (3) must be put into standard conditional-statement form by applying the procedures of sections 3:3.2 and 3:3.1. The result is:

(1) If *p* then *q*

(2) *q*

(3) If $\sim p$ then $\sim r$

∴ *r*

To determine the validity of the argument form represented in step 5, we go through the procedure we used in the preceding argument. Beginning with our simple statement and the conditional statement in which it appears, we have:

(1) If *p* then *q*

(2) *q*

These are the premises which occur in the *invalid* logical form affirming the consequent. The conclusion of such an argument is:

(4) *p*

Since '*p*' cannot be validly derived from the premises we were given, the whole of argument 11 is invalid. Although we do not know what the person who offered argument 11 had in mind, we might suppose that he or she thought that from '*p*' and the third premise, 'If $\sim p$ then $\sim r$', we could derive '*r*' by double negation and the argument form denying the antecedent (another invalid argument form). Regardless of what the person who offered the argument thought, however, it is clear that since the whole argument contains *at least one invalid form*, the argument as a whole is invalid.

One way to show that argument 11 is invalid is to give a counterexample. One such counterexample is this:

(1) If I visited a friend who lives in New England, then I visited a friend who lives in the east.

(2) I visited a friend who lives in the east.

(3) If I didn't visit a friend who lives in the east, then I didn't visit a friend who lives in Boston.

∴ I did visit a friend who lives in Boston.

Now suppose that I visited a friend who lives in New York City. Here, all the premises of the argument are true, but the conclusion is false. Hence, the form of argument 11 is invalid, as is argument 11 itself.

There are two major points to derive from this example. First, *if any part of the complex argument is invalid, the whole argument is invalid.* For example, even if we had been able to derive '*p*' by a valid argument form, the whole argument would be invalid because there is no valid way to derive '*r*' from this result and (3). Second, there is sometimes more than one way to derive a statement from a set of premises. As a result, when considering a complex argument, you should make sure that there is *no* valid way to reach the conclusion of the argument before you judge that the argument form of the complex argument is invalid. Sometimes you will find that there is an invalid reconstruction of an argument but there is also a valid reconstruction. Such would have been the case in the above argument, for example, if we had also had a premise of the form 'If *q* then *r*'. With this premise and premise (2), '*r*' could have been derived from just one instance of the valid argument form affirming the antecedent; the remaining premises just wouldn't have been used to show the validity of the argument.

You can quickly check to see if there is a valid reconstruction of argument 11 in the following way: Since the conclusion is '*r*', it can only be derived from premise (3), the only premise in which '*r*' occurs, and some other premise (or a statement derivable from other premises). Since there is no valid way to derive '*r*' from premise (3), the argument must be invalid. [What follows validly from premise (3) is '∼*r*', but this is the negation of the desired conclusion.] As a result, there is no valid reconstruction of argument 11.

EXERCISE 3-7

1. What is a complex argument?

2. Under what conditions is a complex argument valid?

3. Construct an example of a valid and an invalid complex argument. Explain why the one argument is valid and the other is invalid.

4. Put each of the following arguments into standard form. Symbolize the argument using the given symbols, and then give the logical form of the

argument. State whether the argument is valid or invalid, and explain your answer by providing a summary in proof form for those arguments which are valid and giving a counterexample for those which are invalid.

a. Unless something drastic *happens,* this country will find itself in the throes of a *depression* in a few short months. Moreover, unless Congress acts to *limit* government spending, you can be sure that something drastic will happen. Therefore, this country will find itself in the throes of a depression because Congress will not act to limit government spending. (*H, D, L*)

b. Unless I *miss* my guess, you will find this problem easier than the *first.* But I'll miss my guess only if you do *worse* on this problem than on the first. Therefore, you'll find that this problem is easier than the first, since you will do better on this problem. (*M, F, W*)

c. If the Middle East is to cease being a *potential* crisis area, many western nations must *find* another source of energy. Only if the western nations *spend* much money on research, however, will they find another source of energy. It follows, then, that the Middle East will remain a potential crisis area because western nations will not spend much money on research. (*P, F, S*)

d. Unless the Soviet Union is to be in the *dark* ages of the twentieth century, they must stop *exiling* their dissidents. But, only if they *retain* their present policies will they be in the dark ages. Since they won't retain their policies, it must be the case that they will stop exiling dissidents. (*D, E, R*)

e. We won't *win* the game unless we have the *support* of the fans, but we won't have the support of the fans unless we *improve* our image. We will improve our image, then, with the result that we will win the game. (*W, S, I*)

f. This must be the *best* of all possible worlds since its creator wouldn't be all *good* if this weren't the best. Moreover, if God *created* the world, then the world's creator is all good, for, as anyone knows, God created the world. (*B, G, C*)

g. If the *price* of cars is reduced then more cars will be *sold,* and, further, if the price of cars is reduced the economy will *improve.* Hence, since more cars will not be sold, the economy will not improve. (*P, S, I*)

h. Since we'll *save* the environment only if "big business' stops *polluting* the air and water, and since "big business" will stop polluting the air and water only if made to do so by federal *regulations,* it follows that we will not *live* healthier lives. This because we will live healthier lives only if the environment is saved; and you can be sure there will be no federal regulations to stop polluting. (*S, P, R, L*)

i. Only if the major airlines do not go *bankrupt* will American travelers be able to *reach* their destinations. Since travelers will be able to reach their destinations, it must be the case that the airlines will be subsidized by the federal government. For unless they are *subsidized,* the airlines will go bankrupt. (*B, R, S*)

j. There will never be a *gas* tax to conserve energy. For, unless *Congress* approves the President's energy proposals, no *action* on energy will be taken; and if no action on energy is taken, then there will never be a gas tax. Furthermore, Congress simply will not approve the President's proposals. (*G, C, A*)

k. Unless the *blackberries* are picked, the bushes will *stop* bearing. The berries will get picked, though, only if it doesn't *rain*. Accordingly, the bushes won't stop bearing, since it's not going to rain. (*B, S, R*)

l. Unless the *driveway* is paved, we can't put up the *basket;* but the driveway isn't paved. Moreover, if we don't get the basket up, then we won't be able to *play* ball on Saturday nights. Accordingly, we won't get in *shape* since we'll do that only if we play ball on Saturday nights. (*D, B, P, S*)

m. If the Steelers *win* the AFC playoff, then they'll *go* to the Super Bowl. Additionally, if they win the AFC playoff, they'll *make* a lot of extra cash. Of course, if the Steelers do go to the Super Bowl, then the *Raiders* won't; and if the Raiders don't go, their fans will be *unhappy*. Consequently, the Raider fans will be unhappy because the Steelers will win the AFC playoff. (*W, G, M, R, U*)

n. Unless the Supreme Court had *upheld* the California Supreme Court, Burte would not have been *admitted* to medical school. Also, unless Burte had been admitted to medical school, those who *oppose* reverse discrimination would have been unhappy. Consequently, those who oppose reverse discrimination were unhappy, for the Supreme Court did not uphold the California Supreme Court. (*U, A, O*)

o. The United Nations will never come to any *agreement* about the Middle East problem, because they will come to agreement only if Israel agrees to *talk* to the PLO. But Israel will do this only if the PLO agrees to *recognize* Israel's right to exist. This, however, the PLO will never do. (*A, T, R*)

3:6 CONDITIONAL PROOFS

All the arguments we have thus far considered have had as their conclusions a simple statement of the form '*p*'. Not all arguments, however, have conclusions of this form, as the following argument shows.

ARGUMENT 12

If the President doesn't veto the bill it will become a federal law, and if it becomes a federal law many states will have to change their own laws. Hence, if the President doesn't veto the bill, many states will have to change their own laws.

Assigning the variables '*p*' to 'The President vetoes the bill', '*q*' to 'It will become a federal law', and '*r*' to 'Many states will have to change their own laws', we see that argument 12 has the following form:

FORM OF ARGUMENT 12

(1) If $\sim p$ then q

(2) If q then r

∴ If $\sim p$ then r

One of the methods for handling such arguments is the method of **conditional proof.** The idea behind such a proof is this: The conclusion of our argument is a conditional statement, stating that *if* '$\sim p$' were the case, then 'r' would also be the case. To see if this conclusion does follow from the premises of the argument, we consider what would be derivable from these premises if '$\sim p$' were the case. If we can derive 'r', the consequent of our conclusion, on the *assumption* that '$\sim p$' is the case, then we will have shown that the conclusion does follow from the premises. In other words, we will have shown that the argument is valid.

Let's first work through argument 12; then we shall look at the general structure of conditional proofs and provide further explanation of how they work.

Step 1: We begin by writing down our premises:

　　(1) If $\sim p$ then q

　　(2) If q then r

Step 2: Now we make the *assumption* that '$\sim p$' is the case. To show that it is an assumption, we mark it with an asterisk:

　　*(3) $\sim p$

Step 3: At this point we want to see if anything follows from our premises and our assumption. The answer here is yes. In particular,

　　(1) If $\sim p$ then q

　　*(3) $\sim p$

∴ *(4) q

What follows is 'q' by the valid argument form affirming the antecedent. The conclusion (4) is "starred" to show that it was derived in part from our assumption.

Step 4: We now repeat step 3; that is, we want to see if anything else follows from our premises, our assumption, and the result we got in step 3:

　　(2) If q then r

　　*(4) q

∴ *(5) r

Having derived 'q' in step 3, by using premise (2), we were able to derive 'r' by the valid argument form affirming the antecedent. Conclusion (5) is starred to show that it was derived in part from our assumption; in particular, we needed (4) to get (5), and (4) was derived in part from our assumption—so (5) was, too.

Step 5: In steps 1 to 4 we have shown that *if '~p'* were the case, then *'r'* would also be the case. We did this by assuming *'~p'* and using the argument form affirming the antecedent twice. Another way of saying this is:

(6) If ~p then r

Notice that (6) is not starred. The reason is that a statement having the form 'If ~p then r' would have to be true if statements having the forms 'If ~p then q' and 'If q then r' were true. This condition holds *whether or not the statement represented by '~p' is actually true or actually false.* In other words, the conclusion of the argument follows validity from the two given premises alone; '~p' is not needed for the argument to be valid.

But, you are probably thinking, we had to use '~p' to derive 'If ~p then r'. Doesn't that mean that in order for argument 12 to be valid, '~p' is required as a premise? The answer to this objection has two parts. First, we did not *use* '~p' to derive 'If ~p then r'; rather, we used '*~p'. That is, we did *not* assert in our proof that '~p' was the case, but instead showed what would follow from the premises *if* '~p' were the case. This point is related to the second part of the answer to the objection. In *assuming* '~p', we were able to show that *if* '~p' were the case, then 'r' would also have to be the case, because we could derive 'r' from the two premises of the argument. Having shown that we could derive 'r' *if* we had '~p', we are entitled to claim, as we did in (6), that 'If ~p then r' follows from the two different premises alone. One other way of looking at these points is to realize that 'r' *cannot* be validly derived from the two given premises, whereas it could be so derived *if '~p' were* a premise of the argument.

We shall examine the structure of conditional proofs in more detail in the next section. A summary of our analysis of argument 12 follows, where the notation 'CP' in the justification for line (6) of the proof represents 'conditional proof':

(1) If ~p then q   Premise
(2) If q then r   Premise
*(3) ~p   Assumption for CP
*(4) q   (1), (3), affirming the antecedent
*(5) r   (2), (4), affirming the antecedent
∴ (6) If ~p then r   CP

The form of argument 12 is *valid* since we are able to derive the conclusion from the premises by two applications of the valid logical form affirming the antecedent; this is shown in (1) to (6) above.

3:6.1 General Form of Conditional Proofs

All conditional proofs have the following form:

SCHEMA 1: **Form of conditional proof**

P_1 ⎫
... ⎬ Premises of the argument
P_n ⎭

*A   The assumption for the conditional proof (the antecedent of the conditional statement we wish to prove)

$*S_1$ ⎫
... ⎬ Statements derived from the premises and the assumption
$*S_n$ ⎭

*B   The consequent of the conditional statement we want to prove

∴. If A then B

Notice that in the above schema all the statements that depend on the assumption 'A' are starred. Also note that the assumption made for a conditional proof is the *antecedent* of the conditional statement we wish to prove, and that what we want to derive from this assumption and the premises is the *consequent* of the conditional statement we wish to prove. The strategy, then, in doing conditional proofs is to use the assumption along with the premises to derive the consequent of the conclusion of the argument.

A natural question at this point is to ask how our being able to derive 'B' from the premises of the argument and the assumption 'A' shows that 'If A then B' follows validity from these premises alone. To answer this question, let's simplify schema 1.

SCHEMA 2

(1) P   Premises

*(2) A   Assumption (antecedent of the conditional statement we wish to prove)

*(3) S   Statements derived from P and A

*(4) B   Consequent of the conditional statement we wish to prove

∴. (5) If A then B

Note that schema 2 is the result of trying to show that the following is valid, where 'P' represents *all* the premises of the argument under discussion.

SCHEMA 3

P

∴. If A then B

If the above argument is valid, it follows that if 'P' is the case, then so too is 'If A then B'. We can write this as follows:

(1) If P then (If A then B)

Among the statements which are logically equivalent to (1) is the following:[8]

(2) If (P and A) then B

As a result, if we show that (2) is the case, then we also show that (1) is the case. However, (1) is just another way of saying that schema 3 is valid. Consequently, showing that (2) is the case also shows that schema 3 is valid.

Notice that what is expressed by (2) is the condition which is satisfied in steps (1) to (4) of schema 2 when that schema represents an argument in which 'B' has been validly derived from 'P' and 'A'. Consequently, the validity of schema 2 justifies (2), but since (2) and (1) are logically equivalent, it also justifies (1). Since (1) is just another way of saying that schema 3 is valid, it also follows that schema 2 shows that schema 3 is valid. In the terms with which we began this discussion, being able to derive 'B' from the premises of the argument along with the assumption 'A' shows that 'If A then B' follows validly from these premises alone.

3:6.2 An Example In this section we shall go through an example showing how to construct conditional proofs and provide the justification for each step of the proof.

ARGUMENT 13

If something is not done about the present inflationary trend, then the U.S. economy will end up in shambles. On the other hand, if something is done about the inflationary trend, then wages and prices will stabilize. Hence, if the U.S. economy is not to end up in shambles, wages and prices will stabilize.

> *Step 1:* We first put the argument into standard form, separating the premises and the conclusion:
>
> > (1) If something is not done about the present inflationary trend, then the U.S. economy will end up in shambles.
> >
> > (2) If something is done about the inflationary trend, then wages and prices will stabilize.
> >
> > ∴ If the U.S. economy is not to end up in shambles, wages and prices will stabilize.
>
> *Step 2:* We next give the logical form of the argument. To do this, we assign variables in the following way:
>
> > p: Something is done about the present inflationary trend.
> >
> > q: The U.S. economy will end up in shambles.
> >
> > r: Wages and prices will stabilize.

---

[8] That (1) and (2) are logically equivalent can be shown by using the procedures we shall develop in the next chapter. Even without those procedures, you can probably see that (1) and (2) are logically equivalent.

(1) If $\sim p$ then q

(2) If p then r

$\therefore$ If $\sim q$ then r

Step 3: We are now ready to give the conditional proof. We do this by first listing the premises:

(1) If $\sim p$ then q

(2) If p then r

Step 4: We now make our assumption for the conditional proof. Recall that the assumption is the antecedent of the conditional statement we want to prove and that it is starred to show that it is an assumption.

*(3) $\sim q$

Step 5: We now want to see what follows from our assumption and our premises. Keep in mind that what we ultimately want to derive is the consequent 'r' of the conditional statement we want to prove. One of the things that follows from our assumption and the premises is:

(1) If $\sim p$ then q

*(3) $\sim q$

$\therefore$ *(4) $\sim\sim p$

Step (4) follows from (1) and (3) by the valid logical form denying the consequent. Note that (4) is starred to indicate that it was derived in part from the assumption.

Step 6: Realizing that we are going to have to derive 'r' from 'If p then r', and that to do this we need 'p', we now use double negation on (4) to derive 'p'. Our result is

(2) If p then r

*(5) p

$\therefore$ *(6) r

Step (6) follows from (2) and (5) by the valid argument form affirming the antecedent. Steps (5) and (6) are starred to show that they were derived in part from the assumption.

Step 7: We have now derived the consequent of the conditional statement we wished to prove by using the premises and the assumption. Hence, we can write

(7) If $\sim q$ then r

The above steps can be summarized as follows:

(1) If $\sim p$ then q Premise

(2) If p then r Premise

*(3)	~q	Assumption for CP
*(4)	~~p	(1), (3), denying the consequent
*(5)	p	(4), double negation
*(6)	r	(2), (5), affirming the antecedent
∴ (7)	If ~q then r	CP

This completes our discussion of conditional proofs. In the next section we shall expand the points made here so that we will be able to work with even more kinds of arguments.

EXERCISE 3-8

1. Suppose that someone says to you, "It's not surprising that you can prove anything that you want with a conditional proof; after all, you just go ahead and assume anything you want. None of these proofs, then, is any good." What reply can be made to show this person that conditional proofs are a perfectly good form of deductive argument?

2. What is a conditional proof?

3. Explain why an argument of the form

    If p then q

    If q then r

    ∴ If p then r

    can be shown to be valid by showing that the argument with the following form is valid:

    If p then q

    If q then r

    *p

    ∴ *r

4. Put each of the following arguments into standard form, and symbolize them using the given symbols. Derive the logical form of each argument and show that it is valid by giving a conditional proof.

    a. If the *Middle* East is to cease being a potential crisis area, many western nations must *find* another source of energy. However, only if the western nations *spend* much money on research will they find another source of energy. It follows, then, that unless the western nations spend much money on research, the Middle East will remain a potential crisis area. (M, F, S)

    b. If something is not *done* about the present inflationary trend, then the U.S. *economy* will be in shambles; but if something is done about the trend, *wages* and prices will stabilize. Hence, if wages and prices don't stabilize, the U.S. economy will be in shambles. (D, E, W)

    c. If the nations of the Middle East *reduce* the price of oil, then gasoline prices will not go *higher,* and if they don't reduce the price of oil, auto sales will *continue* to decline. Moreover, if the government *provides* tax relief, then auto sales will not continue to decline. Consequently, only if the government does not provide tax relief will gasoline prices go higher. (*R, H, C, P*)

d. Only if the public will *spend* tax-rebate money on new purchases, as opposed to debts, should a tax rebate be *offered.* But, since the economic situation will *improve* if the public does spend tax-rebate money on new purchases, it follows that a tax rebate should be offered only if the economic situation will improve. (*S, O, I*)

e. If the NCAA drastically *reduces* the number of grants-in-aid a university can offer, then many otherwise qualified people will not be able to *attend* universities. It follows, then, that if these people are to receive the *education* they are entitled to, the NCAA should not reduce the number of grants-in-aid. For unless these people are able to attend a university, they will not receive the education they are entitled to. (*R, A, E*)

f. The new marketing *strategy* will succeed only if the survey of customer desires was *accurate.* Moreover, unless we *implement* a new marketing approach, we shall *lose* money in a new venture. Accordingly, the new marketing strategy will succeed only if we implement a new approach, for we shall not lose money if the survey was accurate. (*S, A, I, L*)

g. Unless we continue to have *bad* weather, the air conditioner will be *installed* this week. Moreover, it will be installed only if the new building *opens* on time. Consequently, if there is no more bad weather, the building will open on time. (*B, I, O*)

h. Unless he is able to *catch* a standby flight, Brad will not be able to get home for the *funeral.* Therefore, if he makes it to the funeral he'll be *lucky,* for unless he's lucky, he will not get a flight. (*C, F, L*)

i. If Jenson and Leonard are both at the *meet,* it should be a classic *confrontation* between two great athletes. But, if Jenson doesn't *enter,* it will be because his injury has not *healed.* Therefore, if there's not a confrontation, it will be because Jenson is still injured, for if Jenson enters, then both he and Leonard will be at the meet. (*M, C, E, H*)

j. A Raydac television is *worth* buying only if it *performs* better than a Landon. Hence, unless it does perform better, you should not *spend* your money on a Raydac. After all, you should spend your money on one only if a Raydac is worth buying. (*W, P, S*)

k. If you must *listen* to that horrible music, I don't want to be in the same *room;* but unless I *stay,* you'll be able to listen to it. Since I won't be able to read my book in *peace* if I stay, it follows that if I want to be in the room, I won't be able to read. (*L, R, S, P*)

l. If this year's crop is going to be *worth* what it cost to plant it, then it had better *rain* soon. The reasons for this are threefold: First, the crop will be worth what it cost to plant it only if we can afford to pay a pilot to seed the clouds; second, we can *afford* to pay a pilot only if we make a profit; and third, we'll make a *profit* only if it rains. (*W, R, A, P*)

3:7 *REDUCTIO AD ABSURDUM* PROOFS (INDIRECT PROOFS)

In this section we shall examine another method of giving proofs: proof by *reductio ad absurdum*, or **indirect proof.** Such proofs are typically used when it is difficult or impossible to derive a desired conclusion in a direct way.[9] In an indirect proof we show that the conclusion of an argument follows from the premises by showing that the premises and the assumption that the conclusion is *false* lead to a contradiction.

The general idea behind indirect proofs is the following: In every valid argument there is a logical relationship between the premises and the conclusion such that, if all the premises are true, then the conclusion *must* also be true. We noted in Chapter 2 that this relationship is to be understood in terms of the logical *form* of the argument. In particular, we saw that no matter which statements uniformly replace the variables in a valid argument form, whenever the premises are all true, the conclusion is also true. We also noted, in our discussion of validity, that another way of characterizing the logical relationship between the premises and conclusion of a valid argument is to say that it is not possible for all the premises to be true and the conclusion to be false.

Now, if we could find a way to show that this condition is satisfied for a given argument form, then we would have a way to show that the form in question is valid. Obviously, we can do exactly that. We use indirect proofs to show that this condition is satisfied in the case of valid arguments by showing that if we take the premises of the argument to be true, and *assume that the conclusion is false,* we are able to derive a statement which is *logically false.* A logically false statement is one which is false no matter which statements are substituted for the variables which occur in the statement.[10] Most of us are familiar with at least one such statement form—contradictions, or statements of the form 'p and $\sim p$'.

An important feature of logically false statements is that they can be derived only from a set of statements that includes at least one false statement. The reason for this can be seen in a somewhat informal way by considering the case of contradictions. To derive a contradiction from a set of statements, one must be able to derive both 'p' and '$\sim p$' as conclusions. Of course, one of these statements *must* be false. Suppose it is 'p' which is false. Since 'p' is false and is the conclusion of whatever valid argument was used to derive it, at least one premise of that argument must be false. (Recall from our discussion of validity in Chapter 2 that a valid argument with a false conclusion must have at least one false premise.) Similar reasoning will show that if it is '$\sim p$' which is false, then at least one of the premises in the argument from which it was derived

---

[9] In this chapter we shall examine only arguments which can also easily be shown to be valid by a direct proof. In Chapter 5, the discussion will be expanded to show the full power of indirect proofs, particularly their role in deriving statements which are logically true and the simplification which often results from using indirect proofs.

[10] In the next chapter we shall develop, for a certain class of statements, a method which can be used to show which members of this class are logically false.

must be false. Since both '*p*' and '~*p*' are derivable from the set of statements, it therefore follows that at least one statement in the set must be false.

Since a logically false statement can be derived only from a set of statements that includes at least one false statement, it follows that if the premises of an argument are all true, then it must be the assumption which is false. But the assumption in an indirect proof is that the conclusion of the argument is *false*. Therefore, if all the premises are true, the *the conclusion must be true*; this, of course, is just what it is for an argument to be valid.

In the next section we shall fill out this general outline in more detail. Before going on to that section, you should reread the above to be sure you have a general understanding of both what we try to show in giving an indirect proof and the way in which we do so.

3:7.1 The Structure of Indirect Proofs

Any valid argument with a false conclusion must have at least one false premise (for if all the premises of a valid argument were true, then the conclusion also would be true). With this in mind, consider the following:

SCHEMA 4

$$
\left.
\begin{array}{l}
\left.
\begin{array}{l}
P_1 \\
\cdots \\
P_n
\end{array}
\right\} \text{All true} \\
P_{n+1} \\
\therefore \ C \ \text{False}
\end{array}
\right\} \text{Valid}
$$

If the argument represented in schema 4 is valid, then, since '*C*' is false, at least one of the premises must be false. And, since 'P_1' through 'P_n' are true, it must be 'P_{n+1}' which is false. Now, if 'P_{n+1}' is false, then *its negation* '~P_{n+1}' *must be true*.

In an indirect proof, our goal is to bring about a situation like that characterized in schema 4. In particular, given a valid argument form, we want to show that if we were to *assume the negation of the conclusion of the argument as a premise*, we would be able to derive, via a valid argument, a statement form which is *logically false*. This is represented in schemata 5 and 6, which follow.

SCHEMA 5

P_1

$\cdots$

P_n

$\therefore C$

Schema 5 represents our original argument, an argument consisting of *n* premises and the conclusion '*C*'.

SCHEMA 6

$$
\left.\begin{array}{l}
P_1 \\
\quad \cdots \\
P_n \\
\sim C
\end{array}\right\} \text{Valid}
$$

$\therefore R$ Logically false

In schema 6, 'R' represents any logically false statement form derived from the premises and the assumption '$\sim C$' by a valid argument. To say that 'R' is a logically false statement form is to say that no matter which statements replace the variables in 'R', the resultant compound statement will always be false.

If we are able to show that we can validly derive a logically false statement 'R' from our premises and the assumption '$\sim C$', then at least one of the premises or our assumption must be false. Now—and this is the important point—*if all the premises are true, then the assumption must be false.* As a result, if all the premises are true, then *the negation of the assumption must be true.* The negation of our assumption is '$\sim\sim C$', which is logically equivalent of 'C'. Therefore, if all of 'P_1' to 'P_n' are true, then 'C' must be true.

Notice, however, that what we have in schema 5 is an argument in which we assert that 'C' is the case because 'P_1' to 'P_n' are the case. By bringing about the situation characterized in schema 6, then, we show that the argument form represented by schema 5 is valid because we show that if 'P_1' to 'P_n' are the case, then 'C' must also be the case; this is, of course, just what it means to say that an argument is valid.

Since our strategy in indirect proofs is to show that an assumption leads to a statement which is logically false, we need some method for doing so. Fortunately, we already have such a method—that of conditional proof discussed in the preceding section. Recall that conditional proofs enable us to show that a particular conditional statement is the case. We do this by assuming the antecedent of the conditional statement we want to prove and then deriving the consequent. In the case of indirect proofs, we want to show that if the negation of the conclusion of the argument is true, then we would be led to accept a logically false statement. Hence, in constructing indirect proofs, *our assumption is the negation of the conclusion of the argument,* and we attempt to *derive a contradiction.*

The actual contradiction that is derived will vary from proof to proof. Sometimes we are able to derive the negation of one of the premises, sometimes the negation of one of the lines in the proof, and sometimes even the conclusion itself. There is no rule which can serve as a guide in the search for the contradiction in an indirect proof. Instead, one must keep in mind the three possible sources of contradiction noted above, see what is derivable from the premises and the assumption, and attempt to derive a contradiction.

We are now ready to fill out schema 6 in more detail, making explicit the various parts of an indirect proof; this we do in schema 7:

SCHEMA 7

p_1

... } Premises

P_n

~C   Assumption (the negation of the desired conclusion)

S_1

... } Statements derived from the premises and the assumption

S_n

∴ R   A logically false statement derived from the premises and the assumption (a contradiction)

Once we have derived 'R', we are justified in concluding, by conditional proof,

If ~C then R

Since 'R' is a logically false statement, it's negation '~R' is logically true. Hence, we have the following schema, in which 'C' is derived by the valid logical form denying the consequent along with double negation (for simplicity, this latter step is not shown):

SCHEMA 8

(1) If ~C then R

(2) ~R

∴ C

We have shown in schema 7 that (1) above is the case; what remains to be justified is the addition of (2) in schema 8. We earlier remarked that in an indirect proof we must derive a logically false statement—in our case 'R'. Since 'R' is logically false, its negation '~R' must be logically true. As a result, '~R' can be added as a premise without changing the essential structure of our original argument. Since (1) and (2) are true, and since the argument form of schema 8 is valid, it follows that the conclusion 'C' must also be true.

It is the argument represented in schema 8 which entitles us to conclude 'C' in our indirect proof on the basis of having derived 'R' from our assumption. We can now fill out schema 7 in its entirety.

SCHEMA 9:   **Form of indirect proof**

P_1

... } Premises

P_n

~C   Assumption (the negation of the desired conclusion)

$$\left.\begin{array}{l} S_1 \\ \ldots \\ S_n \end{array}\right\} \quad \text{Statements derived from the premises and the assumption}$$

R A logically false statement derived from the premises and the assumption (a contradiction)

$\therefore C$

The justification for concluding 'C' in schema 9 is provided in schema 8. In doing indirect proofs the justification for 'C' is simply written as 'RAA' (*reductio ad absurdum*). Schema 8 is not included in the proof itself.

Having gone through the above, rather long, explanation of the structure of indirect proofs, we can provide a very quick summary of that structure. All indirect proofs are composed of two parts: a *conditional proof* whose conclusion is of the form 'If $\sim C$ then R' and an argument of the logical form *denying the consequent*. Hence, nothing really new has been introduced in this section; rather, we have made explicit certain relationships between two forms of argument with which we are already acquainted. If you understand conditional proofs and the argument form denying the consequent, you should have no trouble understanding indirect proofs.

3:7.2 An Example   In this section we shall apply the ideas of the previous section to an example. Work through it carefully, making sure that you understand each step.

ARGUMENT 14

Unless John does something about his weight, he won't be able to wrestle in the next meet; and we'll lose the meet if he isn't able to wrestle. Furthermore, since we'll win the conference title only if we don't lose the meet, it follows that we won't win the conference title; for John won't do something about his weight.

> *Step 1:* As usual, we first put the argument into standard form:
>
> > (1) Unless John does something about his weight, he won't be able to wrestle in the next meet.
> >
> > (2) We'll lose the meet if he isn't able to wrestle.
> >
> > (3) We'll win the conference title only if we don't lose the meet.
> >
> > (4) John won't do something about his weight.
> >
> > $\therefore$ We won't win the conference title.
>
> *Step 2:* Next we determine the logical form of the argument. To do this, we shall assign variables in the following way:
>
> > p: John does something about his weight.
> >
> > q: John will be able to wrestle in the next meet.

r: We'll lose the meet.

s: We'll win the conference title.

(1) Unless p, ~q

(2) r, if ~q

(3) s, only if ~r

(4) ~p

∴ ~s

Step 3: We are now ready to begin the proof. We do this by listing the premises, at the same time converting them all to standard conditional-statement form:

(1) If ~p then ~q

(2) If ~q then r

(3) If s then ~r

(4) ~p

Step 4: We now add our assumption, starring it as in the case of conditional proofs to show that it is an assumption. Our assumption, remember, is the *negation of the desired conclusion:*

*(5) ~~s

Step 5: At this point the question of strategy arises. Since it is not apparent what contradiction we shall derive, it is best to see what, if anything, follows from the assumption and the premises. To begin, we see that we can get (7) if we first use double negation on our assumption to get 's':

*(6) s

*(7) ~r

Line (7) follows from (6) and (3) by the valid argument form affirming the antecedent.

Step 6: Here we continue the process begun in step 5, keeping in mind that we want, ultimately, to derive a contradiction:

*(8) ~~q

Line (8) is derived from (2) and (7) by the valid argument form denying the consequent.

Step 7: Continuing the process, we see that we can derive

*(9) '~~p'

Line (9) is derived from (1) and (8) by the valid argument form denying the consequent.

Step 8: Having derived '~~p', we are but a short step from a contradiction, since we were given '~p' as one of the premises. Since we have both '~~p' and '~p', we can get:

(10) ~p and ~~p

The justification for (10) is a rule of inference called *conjunction*. This rule, along with others, is discussed in Chapter 5. In its stated form, it simply tells us that from a statement of the form 'p' and another statement of the form 'q', one may infer a statement of the form 'p and q'.

Step 9: Having derived a contradiction in (10), we can now assert our conclusion:

(11) ~s

We are justified in asserting (11) on the basis of the argument form denying the consequent exhibited in schema 8. The particular instance of that argument form in our case is the following (where we have again not shown the double-negation step):

(1) If ~~s then (~p and ~~p)

(2) ~(~p and ~~p)

∴ ~s

A summary of lines (1) to (11) in proof form, with the justification for each step is as follows:

(1) If ~p then ~q	Premise
(2) If ~q then r	Premise
(3) If s then ~r	Premise
(4) ~p	Premise
*(5) ~~s	Assumption
*(6) s	(5), double negation
*(7) ~r	(3), (6), affirming the antecedent
*(8) ~~q	(2), (7), denying the consequent
*(9) ~~p	(1), (8), denying the consequent
*(10) ~p and ~~p	(4), (9), conjunction
∴ (11) ~s	RAA

Notice that we do not star line (11). The reason is that this line is like the final line in a conditional proof; it does not depend on the assumption. This is brought out by the notation 'RAA' as the justification for line (11). This notation represents the argument form of schema 8, which says that on the basis of a conditional proof we can show that our assumption leads to a contradiction and, therefore, that if all the premises of the original argument are true, then the conclusion of the argument must be true as well.

EXERCISE 3-9

1. In indirect proofs, we prove that the negation of the conclusion of an argument leads to a statement which is necessarily false, if the premises are true. Why does this prove that the argument is valid?

2. Explain the relationship between an indirect proof and a conditional proof.

3. What is a contradiction? Explain the role that contradictions play in indirect proofs.

4. All indirect proofs are composed of two parts. Explain what these parts are, and explain the relationship between them.

5. Suppose someone says to you, "One is never justified in accepting the conclusion of an indirect proof, even if it is valid, since one ought never to accept the conclusion of an argument which has false premises, and every indirect proof has at least one false premise—the assumption." What reply can be made here to show this person that one is justified in accepting the conclusion of an indirect proof?

EXERCISE 3-10

1. Provide indirect proofs for all the valid arguments in problem 4 of Exercise 3-7.

2. Put each of the following arguments into standard form, and symbolize it using the given symbols. Provide the logical form of the argument, and show that it is valid by giving an indirect proof.
   a. We won't *win* the game unless we have the *support* of the fans, and only if we *improve* our image will we have their support. Consequently, we shall improve our image because we shall win. (*W, S, I*)
   b. If the *rights* of private citizens are to be protected, then the CIA must no longer *engage* in domestic work. Furthermore, unless Congress acts to *limit* its power, the CIA will continue to engage in domestic work. Hence, the rights of private citizens will not be protected, for Congress will not limit the power of the CIA. (*R, E, L*)
   c. Monroe will *enlist* in the Army only if they guarantee to *train* him as a computer programmer. But, the Army will guarantee this only if Monroe shows that he has the ability to *understand* the training. Since he will understand the training only if he has a good background in *mathematics*, it follows that Monroe will not enlist. This is because his background in math is terrible. (*E, T, U, M*)
   d. If the mideast nations *reduce* the price of oil, then gasoline prices will not go *higher*, and if they don't reduce the price of oil, sales of large automobiles will *continue* to decline. Moreover, sales of large cars will not continue to decline unless the federal government does not *provide* tax relief to the automakers. Consequently, the price of gasoline will not go higher. After all, the government will ultimately provide tax relief. (*R, H, C, P*)
   e. Munchie-Crunchies are *worth* buying only if they are on a *huge* sale. We know, however, that Munchie-Crunchies are not a *slow*-moving item,

and if this is so then they will not be on a huge sale. Consequently, Munchie-Crunchies are not worth buying. (*W, H, S*)

f. The new marketing *strategy* will succeed only if the survey of customer desires was *accurate*. In addition, unless we *implement* a new marketing approach, we shall *lose* money in a new venture. Accordingly, the new strategy will not succeed. There are two reasons for this: First, we will not lose money if the survey was accurate and, second, we will not implement a new marketing approach. (*S, A, I, L*)

g. If Alexandra has a *history* of high blood pressure, she should not *take* the new vaccine. However, if she does not have such a history, then the vaccine will *protect* her from the flu that is going around. Therefore, since Alexandra should take the vaccine, it follows that it will protect her from the flu. (*H, T, P*)

h. If Jenson and Leonard are both at the *meet*, it should be a classic *confrontation* between two great athletes. But, if Jenson doesn't *enter*, it will be because her injury has not *healed*. Hence, it should be a classic confrontation, for Jenson's injury has healed, and if Jenson enters, both she and Leonard will be at the meet. (*M, C, E, H*)

i. If *reincarnation* does not occur, then people who testify about former lives while under hypnosis are *frauds*. Hence, these people are frauds, for unless people *survive* bodily death, reincarnation does not occur; and all the evidence indicates that they don't so survive. (*R, F, S*)

j. Since we'll make a *profit* only if it *rains,* and since we can *afford* to pay a pilot to seed the clouds only if we make a profit, it follows that this year's crop is not going to be *worth* what it cost to plant it. This is so because it would be worth what it cost to plant it only if we can afford a pilot and, what is worse, it is not going to rain soon. (*P, R, A, W*)

k. Only if it can be shown that *energy* will be saved, should a state *remain* on daylight time when the rest of the nation is on standard time. But, since energy will be saved only if people work at *cutting* back on their use of electricity, it follows that states should not remain on daylight time; for people will not cut back their use of electricity. (*E, R, C*)

l. A Raydac is *worth* buying only if it *performs* better than a Landon. Therefore, you should not *spend* your money on a Raydac, for if you do, that shows that it is worth buying. I just read, however, that Raydacs do not perform better than Landons. (*W, P, S*)

STUDENT STUDY GUIDE

Chapter Summary

1. A **conditional statement** is one which specifies what was, is, or would be the case under certain circumstances, the circumstances being specified in the statement. All conditional statements have the form 'If *p* then *q*'. (section 3:1)

2. All conditional statements have two parts: The part governed by the 'if' is the **antecedent,** and the part governed by the 'then' is the **consequent.** (section 3:1)

3. The connective 'not' changes the truth value of a statement to the opposite truth value. When we append 'not' to a statement, we **negate** the statement; the result is the **negation** of the original statement. (section 3:2)

4. When two statement forms always have the same truth value no matter which statements are uniformly substituted for the variables in both forms, the two statements are **logically equivalent.** One such logical equivalency is **double negation.** The important point about logically equivalent statements is that they can be substituted for each other in an argument form without changing the validity or invalidity of the form. (section 3:2)

5. Some sentence structures in English are not initially in **standard conditional-statement form,** though they can be rewritten in this form. A statement is in standard conditional-statement form when it has the form 'If p then q'. Among the sentence structures which can be rewritten in this form are those in **inverted form** and those containing the expressions **'only if'** and **'unless'.** (section 3:3)

6. The **contrapositive** of a conditional statement is obtained by negating the antecedent and consequent of the conditional statement and then writing a new conditional statement in which the negated consequent is the antecedent and the negated antecedent is the consequent. (section 3:3.3)

7. The **converse** of a conditional statement is formed by interchanging the antecedent and consequent of the conditional statement. Converses are *not* logically equivalent. (section 3:3.4)

8. The two valid forms of simple conditional arguments are **affirming the antecedent** and **denying the consequent.** Though closely resembling these two valid forms, the argument forms **affirming the consequent** and **denying the antecedent** are *invalid.* (section 3:4)

9. **Complex arguments** are arguments which contain more than one of the simple conditional argument forms affirming the antecedent, denying the consequent, affirming the consequent, and denying the antecedent. A complex argument is valid if all the constituent arguments are valid, and invalid if at least one of the constituent arguments is invalid. (section 3:5)

10. **Conditional proofs** are often used to show the validity of arguments which have conditional statements as their conclusions. In a conditional proof, we assume the antecedent of the conclusion as a premise and then validly derive the consequent of the conclusion from the premises. Since this shows that if the antecedent is the case then the consequent is also the case, we are justified in concluding that if all the premises of the argument are true then the conclusion must be true. As a result, we can use conditional proofs to show that arguments are valid. (section 3:6)

11. **Indirect proofs** are used to show that an argument is valid by showing that the *assumption* that the conclusion is false leads, via a valid argument, to a statement which is logically false. Since a logically false statement can be derived only from a set of statements that includes at least one false statement, it follows that if all the premises of the original argument are true, then the assumption

must be false. Consequently, if all the premises are true, the negation of the assumption (the conclusion of the original argument) must be true. (section 3:7)

12. A **contradiction** is any statement of the form 'p and $\sim p$'. Statements of this form are **logically false**; that is, no matter which statement replaces 'p', the resultant compound statement is *always false*. (section 3:7)

Key Terms

Conditional Statement	Affirming the Antecedent
Antecedent	Denying the Consequent
Consequent	Affirming the Consequent
Negation	Denying the Antecedent
Logically Equivalent Statements	Complex Argument
Double Negation	Conditional Proof
Standard Conditional-Statement Form	Indirect Proof
Inverted Form	Contradiction
Contrapositive	Logically False Statement
Converse	

Self-Test/Exercises

1. Put each of the following statements into standard conditional-statement form, and then give the contrapositive of the resultant statement. (section 3:3.3)
   a. Linda will go to Sweden only if June goes to France.
   b. Unless some action is taken, there will never be a gas tax.
   c. This would still be a beautiful neighborhood if it hadn't been for the Dutch elm disease.
   d. We will be conference champs unless we lose next Saturday's game.
   e. Only if the Phon-a-thon is successful will we have enough money to support our projects in the coming year.

2. Put each of the following arguments into standard form. Symbolize the argument by using the given symbols as constants, and then give the logical form of the argument and the name of the form if it has one. State whether the argument is valid or invalid. (section 3:4)
   a. Unless the U.S. *contributed* to the world food program many people would have *starved*. Hence, the U.S. did contribute to the world food program because many people didn't starve. (C, S)
   b. Books are *worth* reading only if they're either *educational* or entertaining. It's clear that this book was not worth reading, for it was neither. (W, E)
   c. If you don't know the *difference* between socialism and Marxism, then I *recommend* that you take a course in political science. Hence, I recommend that you not take the course only if you do know the difference. (D, R)
   d. You must have forgotten to put the *batteries* in your portable mushroom since it's clear that it's not *working*, and everyone knows that unless they have batteries they don't work. (B, W)

    e. The Green Hornet must not have gotten *caught* in Spiderman's web because he came to the *rescue*, and he would have done that only if he did not get caught. (C, R)

3. Put each of the following arguments into standard form. Symbolize the argument by using the given symbols as constants, and then give the logical form of the argument. State whether the argument is valid or invalid; explain your answer by providing a summary in proof form for those arguments which are valid and giving a counterexample for those which are invalid. (section 3:5)

    a. There is reason to think that UFOs are *spaceships* only if there is reason to think that there is *life* on other planets. It follows that there is no reason to think that UFOs are spaceships, since the Air Force has been unable to *prove* that there is life on other planets. After all, if there were life on other planets, surely the Air Force would have been able to prove it. (S, L, P)

    b. Unless the governor *decides* to run for the Senate, he will again *run* for governor. But, he will decide to run for the Senate only if he has been seriously *harmed* by the PDQ controversy. Hence, since he has not been harmed by this controversy, the governor will again run for governor. (D, R, H)

    c. Only if the stores are open *late* will I get my Christmas shopping *done*; and only if I get my Christmas shopping done will I *remain* out of the doghouse on Christmas day. Furthermore, unless I remain out on Christmas day, I won't be *out* by New Year's day. Consequently, I won't be in the doghouse on New Year's day, for the stores will be open late. (L, D, R, O)

4. Put each of the following arguments into standard form. Symbolize the arguments by using the given symbols as constants, and then give the logical form of the argument. Show that each argument is valid by giving a conditional proof. (section 3:6)

    a. Unless we *play* better this half, we're going to *lose* the game. Hence, since the alumni will *continue* to support us only if we win, it follows that unless we play better, the alumni will no longer support us. (P, L, C)

    b. Unless the *property* tax is lowered, many people on fixed incomes will be forced to sell their *homes*. Additionally, if the present city council *remains* in office, the property taxes will not be lowered. Accordingly, if the citizens *unite*, the city council will not remain in office, for if they do unite, people on fixed incomes will not have to sell their homes. (P, H, R, U)

    c. *Plato* can be understood only if one has read *Aristotle*. Hence, unless one has read Aristotle, one will not understand *neo-Platonism*; for if one understands neo-Platonism, then one understands Plato. (P, A, N)

5. Put each of the following arguments into standard form. Symbolize the arguments by using the given symbols as constants, and give the logical form of the argument. Show that each argument is valid by giving an indirect proof. (section 3:7)

    a. If Dierdre *votes* in favor of proposal A, then she must believe the *passage* of the proposal will help alleviate the problem of can and bottle litter on the highway. She would believe this, however, only if she had good *evidence* that it was true. But, unless such proposals *worked* in other states, she would not have good evidence that it would work here. Consequently, since such proposals did not work in other states, Dierdre will vote against proposal A. (V, P, E, W)

b. Unless the *property* tax is lowered, many people on fixed incomes will be forced to sell their *homes,* and if the present city council *remains* in office, property taxes will not by lowered. Consequently, since the citizens will *unite,* the present city council will not remain in office, for if they do unite, people on fixed incomes will not have to sell their homes. (*P, H, R, U*)

c. Unless he is able to *catch* a standby flight, Brad will not be able to get home for the *funeral.* Consequently, he will not make the funeral, for unless he's *lucky,* he will not get a flight; and everyone knows that Brad is about the unluckiest person around. (*C, F, L*)

CHAPTER 4

TRUTH

TABLES

So far our analysis has been limited to arguments consisting only of conditional statements, simple statements, and negated statements. However, other kinds of sentences often occur in arguments—in particular, statements of the form '*p* and *q*', '*p* or *q*', and '*p* if, and only if, *q*'. The purpose of this chapter is to develop the tools and skills needed to enable you to analyze arguments containing statements of these forms.

To this end we shall discuss a method which is useful in analyzing arguments consisting of statements of the above forms: that of constructing **truth tables.** We shall also use truth tables to illustrate the important connection between validity and logical truth and to further explain the concept of logical equivalency. Because the truth-table method is rather cumbersome, we shall also develop a shorter truth-table method.

4:1 LOGICAL CONNECTIVES

In the preceding two chapters we discussed two of the five logical connectives: 'if-then' and 'not'. In this section we shall provide a further characterization of these two connectives and characterize the connectives 'and', 'or', and 'if, and only if'.

4:1.1 Truth Functionality   In Chapter 2 we distinguished between simple and compound statements and noted that the latter contain one or more simple statements as components. In the previous chapter we discussed the connective 'not' and saw that appending '~' to a statement had the effect of changing the truth value of the statement to the opposite truth value. Now, any statement of the form '~p' is a compound statement, since such a statement contains a statement of the form 'p' as a component. In addition, since the truth value of a statement of the form '~p' is a function of the truth value of the statement which replaces 'p', statements of the form '~p' are also truth-functional compound statements.

As you will see shortly, there are other compound statements whose truth values are a function of the truth values of their component statements. Such statements are **truth-functional statements.** In addition, each of the five logical connectives that we shall discuss in this chapter is a **truth-functional connective** in that the truth value of a compound statement in which they occur is determined by the meaning of each of the connectives. For example, to determine the truth of a statement of the form *'p* and *q'*, we must know the truth values of the two component statements which replace *'p'* and *'q'* and we must know what 'and' means; and this is all we need to know. Similar remarks apply in the case of the other four connectives.

It is the fact that these connectives are truth-functional that gives rise to the method of constructing truth tables. The truth table for a particular compound-statement form is nothing more than a list of all the possible combinations of truth values that might be assigned to the statements which replace the variables, along with an assignment of a truth value to the complex statement form; this latter assignment results from the particular assignment of truth values to the statements which replace the variables.

For each of the logical connectives there is a rule stating the conditions under which the compound statements in which they occur are either true or false. By using the appropriate rule for each of the connectives, we can construct a truth table *for the connective*. In one sense of the word 'meaning', the truth table for each of the logical connectives provides us with the meaning of the connective. Knowing the meaning of the connective and the truth values of the simple statements which occur in the compound statement, we can determine the truth value of the compound statement. Later, we shall use the truth tables for the logical connectives to determine the validity of arguments.

We turn now to the development of the truth tables for the five logical connectives. Each of these connectives, when used in the way defined by its truth table, is a truth-functional connective, and the statements in which it occurs are truth-functional compound statements.

4:1.2 The Truth Table for 'Not'   We have already used the connective 'not'. In this section we shall merely make more explicit what you already know about the way in which this connective functions. The rule for determining the truth value of a statement in which the connective 'not' occurs is the following:

R1: RULE FOR 'NOT' (~)

A statement of the form '~p' is opposite in truth value to the statement of the form *'p'*.

We already know that any statement is either true or false. R1 tells us that a statement of the form '~p' is opposite in truth value to the statement which replaces *'p'*. Since the statement which replaces *'p'* might be either true or false, there are two cases which have to be considered in constructing the truth table for 'not': the case in which *'p'* is true and the case in which *'p'* is false.[1] Applying

---

[1] Strictly speaking, variables do not have a truth value since they're just placeholders for statements. As a result, when we say things like ' *'p'* is true,' this should be understood as meaning 'the statement which replaces *'p'* is true.' We shall hereafter use the shorter expression; no confusion should result from this.

R1 to each of these possibilities, we have the result that if 'p' is true then '$\sim p$' is false, and if 'p' is false then '$\sim p$' is true. Table T1 summarizes these results.[2]

T1: TRUTH TABLE FOR 'NOT'

p	$\sim p$
T	F
F	T

4:1.3 The Truth Table for 'And'   The rule which is appropriate for determining the truth or falsity of compound statements of the form 'p and q' is the following:

R2: RULE FOR 'AND' ($\cdot$)

A statement of the form '$p \cdot q$' is true when, and only when, both 'p' is true and 'q' is true.

In R2, '$p \cdot q$' is read "p and q"; the symbol '$\cdot$' is called "dot." Statements of this form are **conjunctions,** and 'p' is the *left conjunct* and 'q' is the *right conjunct*. As is the case for all the logical connectives, the truth value of '$p \cdot q$' is determined from the truth values of its component parts, 'p' and 'q'. Since 'p' can be either true or false and 'q' can be either true or false, we must consider four possible cases of the assignment of truth values to the variables 'p' and 'q' and the resultant effect on the truth value of '$p \cdot q$':

Case 1: 'p' is true and 'q' is true. R2 tells us that when 'p' is true and 'q' is true, then '$p \cdot q$' is true; hence, in this case, '$p \cdot q$' takes the value T.

Case 2: 'p' is true and 'q' is false. Again appealing to R2, we see that '$p \cdot q$' is true only when both 'p' is true and 'q' is true. Since 'q' is false in this case, '$p \cdot q$' takes the value F.

Case 3: 'p' is false and 'q' is true. Again appealing to R2 and noting that '$p \cdot q$' is true only when both 'p' is true and 'q' is true, we here assign the value F to '$p \cdot q$' since, although 'q' is true, 'p' is false.

Case 4: 'p' is false and 'q' is false. Here '$p \cdot q$', by R2, takes the value F since both 'p' and 'q' are false.

Summarizing the results of cases 1 to 4, we have T2 as the truth table for the connective 'and':

T2: TRUTH TABLE FOR 'AND'

p	q	$p \cdot q$
T	T	T
T	F	F
F	T	F
F	F	F

---

[2] In section 4:4.1 we shall discuss the general procedure for constructing truth tables for truth-functional compound statements, including the number of lines in the truth table and the assignments of truth values to the variables.

4:1.4 The Truth Table for 'Or'   The rule which is applicable in determining the truth values of statements of the form '*p* or *q*' is the following:

R3: RULE FOR 'OR' ($\lor$)

A statement of the form '*p* $\lor$ *q*' is false when, and only when, *both* '*p*' is false and '*q*' is false.

In R3, '*p* $\lor$ *q*' is read "*p* or *q*"; the symbol '$\lor$' is called "wedge." Statements of this form are **disjunctions**; '*p*' is the *left disjunct*, and '*q*' is the *right disjunct*. As for the connective 'and', we need to consider four possible cases of the assignment of truth values to '*p*' and '*q*'. These four cases give us the following truth table for the connective 'or':

T3: TRUTH TABLE FOR 'OR'

p	*q*	*p* $\lor$ *q*
T	T	T
T	F	T
F	T	T
F	F	F

R3 and the resultant truth table T3 give the truth conditions for what is called the *inclusive* sense of 'or'. Notice that under the above interpretation of 'or', '*p* $\lor$ *q*' is true in the case where *both* '*p*' and '*q*' are true, as well as when either is true. This is the interpretation logicians usually give to the connective 'or'. There is another sense of 'or' in English, however, which is roughly equivalent to 'one or the other, *but not both*'. This is the sense which is usually intended, for example, on a restaurant menu where there is an entry 'soup or salad'. The idea in this case is that the customer can choose to have either soup or salad with a meal, *but not both.* This sense of 'or' is called the *exclusive* sense of 'or'. Notice that the exclusive sense of 'or' can easily be characterized by the use of the inclusive sense of 'or' and the use of 'and' and 'not'. The symbolization is

$$(p \lor q) \cdot \sim(p \cdot q)$$

This expression tells us that either '*p*' or '*q*' is the case, but not both; this latter phrase is expressed by '$\sim(p \cdot q)$', read as "it is not the case that both *p* and *q*."

4:1.5 The Truth Table for 'If-Then'   The following rule is applicable for determining the truth values of statements of the form 'If *p* then *q*':

R4: RULE FOR 'IF-THEN' ($\supset$)

A statement of the form '*p* $\supset$ *q*' is false when, and only when, '*p*' is true and '*q*' is false.

'*p* $\supset$ *q*' is read "If *p* then *q*," and the symbol '$\supset$' is called "horseshoe." Once again we must consider four possible cases of the assignment of truth values to '*p*' and to '*q*' to determine the resultant truth value of '*p* $\supset$ *q*'. These four cases give us the following truth table for the connective 'if-then':

T4: TRUTH TABLE FOR 'IF-THEN'

p	q	$p \supset q$
T	T	T
T	F	F
F	T	T
F	F	T

Before we look at the final logical connective, a few comments are in order concerning the somewhat counterintuitive assignment of truth values to the third and fourth lines of T4. Let's begin with the third line. It may strike one as odd that when a conditional statement has a false antecedent and a true consequent the whole conditional statement is true. As a result, the following statement, for example, is true: 'If there are thirteen months in the year, then Washington, D.C., is the capital of the U.S.' Notice that the statement 'There are thirteen months in the year' is false, and the statement 'Washington, D.C., is the capital of the U.S.' is true (in accord with line 3 of T4).

What is counterintuitive here is that one knows that the number of months in the year has nothing to do with what city is the capital of the U.S.; as a result, it is hard to see what bearing the falsity of 'There are thirteen months in the year' has at all on the truth of the above conditional statement. Nonetheless, there are some things which favor this assignment of truth value.

Although we have seen one example of a conditional statement which seems counterintuitive to the assignment of truth values in T4, other conditional statements which have false antecedents and true consequents do not have this character. One such example is 'If Bugs is a cow, then Bugs is a mammal'. In this conditional statement 'Bugs is a cow' is false, whereas 'Bugs is a mammal' is true. Nonetheless, even with the antecedent's being false we do say (correctly) that it is true that *if* Bugs is a cow then he's also a mammal; he couldn't be a cow and not be a mammal.

Of course, in the statement about Bugs, unlike the statement about the number of months in the year, there is a relationship which holds between being a cow and being a mammal—namely, that all cows are mammals. What this shows us is that our assignment of truth values to the conditional statement in T4 is, in part, independent of any relationship holding between the antecedent and consequent other than the truth values of these statements.

The relationship between the antecedent and the consequent of a conditional statement expressed by using '$\supset$' is called **material implication.** In material implication the only relationship which is said to hold between the antecedent and the consequent of the conditional statement is that which depends on the truth values of the component statements. In particular, in asserting a statement of the form '$p \supset q$', we are saying only that it is *not* the case that 'p' is true and 'q' is false; we are saying nothing else about the relationship between 'p' and 'q'.

There are, of course, other senses of 'if-then' in English. In these other senses (for example, the causal sense exemplified by the statement 'If you hit your thumb with a hammer, then your thumb will hurt') *more* is being asserted about the relationship of antecedent and consequent than is being claimed in the truth table for material implication. Nonetheless, even in these other cases of conditional statements, if the antecedent is true and the consequent is false, then the conditional statement is false. What we have done in the truth table for material implication is, in effect, to characterize the minimal condition we expect of all conditional statements: that they be false if the antecedent is true and the consequent false.

Now it should be fairly easy to deal with the fourth line of T4. As in the case of the third line, some counterintuitive cases come to mind. One such case is 'If there are thirteen months in the year, then Moscow is the capital of the U.S.' Note that in this conditional statement the antecedent and the consequent are both false. This case is like the one discussed earlier in the following way: Since the number of months in the year has nothing to do with what city is the capital of the U.S., it has nothing to do with the claim that Moscow is the capital.

As previously, however, we can find some cases in which a conditional statement has both a false antecedent and a false consequent but is nonetheless true. For example, 'If UCLA is in Providence, Rhode Island, then it is in New England' is true, even though UCLA is neither in Providence nor in New England. Another such example is 'If Daffy is a reptile, then he is cold-blooded'. These two cases are similar to the Bugs case we examined while discussing the third line of T4 in that there is a relationship which holds between being in Providence and being in New England, and another relationship which holds between being a reptile and being cold-blooded. No such relationship seems to hold in the Moscow case. The reply here is the same as that given earlier: In specifying the minimal conditions we expect of conditional statements, we shall adopt T4 as the truth table for 'if-then', even the fourth line, keeping in mind that the relationship which holds between the antecedent and the consequent is based merely on the truth values of the antecedent and consequent.

4:1.6 The Truth Table for 'If, and Only If' The rule which is applicable in determining the truth values of statements of the form 'p, if, and only if, q' is the following:

R5: RULE FOR 'IF, AND ONLY IF' ($\equiv$)

A statement of the form '$p \equiv q$' is true when, and only when, 'p' and 'q' have the same truth value.

In R5, '$p \equiv q$' is read "p, if, and only if, q," and the symbol '$\equiv$' is called 'triple bar'. Sometimes '$\equiv$' is referred to as **material equivalency** or as a biconditional. The term 'biconditional' comes from the fact the '$p \equiv q$' has the same truth value as the conjunction of two conditional statements: 'If q then p' (from the 'p, if q' part) and 'If p then q' (from the 'p, only if q' part). Since '$p \equiv q$' is the same as the conjunction of '$q \supset p$' and '$p \supset q$', the truth table for '$p \equiv q$' is the same as the truth table for the conjunction of the two conditional statements.[3]

Before we look at the truth table for '$\equiv$', a few comments are in order

---

[3] We shall discuss a way of showing this, as well as the logical equivalence of other statement forms, in section 4:4.4.

regarding this connective. As in the case of material implication, the only relationship which is said to hold between the two statements in a statement of the form '$p \equiv q$' is that which depends on the truth values of the component statements. In the case of the triple bar, we say that the statement is true only when both component statements have the *same* truth value. As a result, the two statements 'Charlie is a tuna' and 'Charlie is a fish' are *materially* equivalent since they have the same truth value: true. Similarly, the statements 'Bugs is an alligator' and 'Daffy is a dragonfly' are also *materially* equivalent since they are both false.

In the preceding chapter we considered another form of equivalency: *logical* equivalency. There, recall, we noted that two statement forms are logically equivalent only when they have the same truth value no matter which statements uniformly replace the variables occurring in the statement forms. Obviously, then, not all statements of the form '$p \equiv q$' are *logically* equivalent, since we could replace 'p' with a true statement (say, 'Daffy is a duck') and 'q' with a false one (say, 'Bugs is an aardvark'). After we have discussed truth tables in more detail, we shall contrast the difference between material equivalency and logical equivalency by showing that the truth values for logically equivalent statements are the same regardless of which statements replace their variables.

As for most of the connectives we have discussed, there are four possible assignments of truth values to the variables in '$p \equiv q$'. These four cases give us the following truth table for the connective 'if, and only if':

T5: TRUTH TABLE FOR 'IF, AND ONLY IF'

p	q	$p \equiv q$
T	T	T
T	F	F
F	T	F
F	F	T

This concludes our discussion of the five logical connectives. In following sections we shall see how to apply the truth tables for the connectives to compound statements and, ultimately, how to determine the validity of arguments by using truth tables.

EXERCISE 4-1

1. What does it mean to say that a statement is truth-functional?

2. What does it mean to say that a logical connective is a truth-functional connective?

3. What is the rule for determining the truth values of statements containing 'not'? Give the truth table constructed in accordance with this rule.

4. What is the rule for determining the truth values of statements containing 'and'? Give the truth table constructed in accordance with this rule.

5. What is the rule for determining the truth values of statements containing 'or'? Give the truth table constructed in accordance with this rule.

6. What is the difference between the inclusive and exclusive senses of 'or'? Which is the sense used by logicians?

7. Give an example of a statement in which 'or' is used in the inclusive sense. Give another example in which it is used in the exclusive sense.

8. Explain how the exclusive sense of 'or' can be defined by using 'not', 'and', and the inclusive sense of 'or'. Rewrite your example of the exclusive sense of 'or' from problem 7 in accordance with this definition.

9. What is the rule for determining the truth values of statements containing 'if-then'? Give the truth table constructed in accordance with this rule.

10. Explain the relationship between the antecedent and consequent of a conditional statement in which the antecedent materially implies the consequent.

11. What is the rule for determining the truth values of statements containing 'if, and only if'? Give the truth table constructed in accordance with this rule.

12. What does it mean to say that two statements are materially equivalent? What does it mean to say that two statement forms are logically equivalent?

4:2 COMPOUND STATEMENTS WITH MORE THAN ONE CONNECTIVE

Most of the compound statements we have so far discussed have contained only one logical connective. There are, however, many statements which contain more than one connective; in this section we shall see how to symbolize such statements.

4:2.1 Avoiding Ambiguities
Let's begin by considering the following statement:

(1) I will go sailing this afternoon and play tennis this evening or go to the concert.

If we let 'S' represent 'I will go sailing this afternoon', 'T' represent 'I will play tennis this evening', and 'C' represent 'I will go to the concert', then we may rewrite (1) using these constants and the symbols for the connectives 'and' and 'or':

(2) $S \cdot T \lor C$

Now, the problem with (2) is that it is *ambiguous* in that it could be understood as either of the following:

(3) *Either* I will go sailing this afternoon and play tennis this evening *or* go to the concert.

(4) I will go sailing this afternoon *and* either play tennis this evening or go to the concert.

In (3) two options are being considered: *either* going sailing and playing tennis *or* going to the concert. In (4), on the other hand, it is asserted that I will go sailing *and* that I will in addition do one (or both) of two things: either play tennis or go to the concert. In (3), then, the statement is a disjunction, whereas in (4) it is a conjunction.

In English we can make clear what is meant by (1) by using the words 'either' and 'or' in the appropriate places to obtain (3) and (4), neither of which is ambiguous. In logical notation, we use *parentheses* to avoid this kind of ambiguity. In particular, (3) is symbolized as

(5) $(S \cdot T) \vee C$

and (4) is symbolized as

(6) $S \cdot (T \vee C)$

The use of parentheses makes it clear that (5) is a disjunction and (6) is a conjunction. In (5) the wedge is the **main connective** in the statement, and in (6) the dot is the main connective.

Instead of using 'either' in the appropriate place to remove the ambiguity in (1), we could make use of punctuation. In English, commas (as well as other punctuation marks) can sometimes be used to avoid ambiguities. Punctuating (1) with commas so as to correspond with (3) and (4) gives us the following:

(3)′ I will go sailing this afternoon and play tennis this evening, or go to the concert.

(4)′ I will go sailing this afternoon, and play tennis this evening or go to the concert.

Thus far, then, we see that we can use punctuation or word order as a way to avoid ambiguity in what is asserted. It should be noted, moreover, that *without* the use of 'either' or a comma in (1), there is no way to tell whether (1) should be symbolized as (5) or as (6); there is no way of telling whether it is a disjunction or a conjunction.

In the same way that 'either' is used to indicate which statements are the disjuncts in a disjunctive statement form, the word 'both' is often used to indicate which statements are the conjuncts in a conjunctive statement form.[4] For example, the ambiguity in statement (7) below can be cleared up by the

---

[4] In (3), the placement of 'either' serves to show that the disjuncts of the 'or' statement are the conjunction 'I will go sailing this afternoon and play tennis this evening' and the statement 'I will go to the concert'. In (4), the placement of 'either' indicates that the disjuncts of the 'or' statement are 'I will play tennis this evening' and 'I will go to the concert'.

placement of 'both' in (8) and (9) and by the use of a comma in the appropriate place:

(7) If I go sailing then I will play tennis and I will go to the concert.

(8) If I go sailing, then I will both play tennis and go to the concert.

(9) Both if I go sailing then I will play tennis, and I will go to the concert.

The placement of 'both' in (8) shows that the conjuncts of the conjunction are 'I will play tennis' and 'I will go to the concert'. Using the same constants we assigned earlier, we see, then, that the main connective in (8) is 'if-then' and that the consequent is the conjunction '$T \cdot C$'. Hence, (8) is symbolized as

(8)' $S \supset (T \cdot C)$

In (9) the placement of 'both' shows that the conjuncts of the conjunction are the conditional statement 'If I go sailing then I will play tennis' and the statement 'I will go to the concert'. Here the main connective is the dot, and (9) is symbolized as

(9)' $(S \supset T) \cdot C$

Ambiguities similar to those discussed above also occur with 'not'. For example, in (10) below it is not clear whether the statement should be understood as (11) or as (12):

(10) It's not the case that I will play tennis in the evening and I will go to the concert.

(11) Both it's not the case that I will play tennis in the evening and I will go to the concert.

(12) It's not the case that I will both play tennis in the evening and go to the concert.

The use of 'both' once again makes clear which connective is the main connective in (11) and (12), which are symbolized as follows:

(11)' $\sim T \cdot C$

(12)' $\sim (T \cdot C)$

In (11)' the main connective is the dot, whereas in (12)' it is the tilde.

One more general case needs to be considered. Let's take as our example '$(S \cdot T \cdot C)$'. As this statement stands, we cannot use our truth table for 'and' to determine its truth value. This is so since the truth tables are defined *only in terms of two variables*. What we must do, then, is rewrite the statement so that we can apply the truth table to it. To do this, we merely add parentheses to the statement, making a conjunction of two statements out of it. We obviously have two choices: '$(S \cdot T) \cdot C$' and '$S \cdot (T \cdot C)$'. However, the truth values of these two statements are the same, so the truth value of the original will be the same regardless of how the simple statements are grouped. Exactly analogous remarks apply in the case of the disjunctive statement '$(S \vee T \vee C)$'.

4:2.2 Symbolizing Compound Statements   In the previous section we saw that word order and punctuation are used in English to avoid ambiguity in expressing compound statements and to make clear which connective is the main connective. The ideas of that section provide a relatively easy procedure for symbolizing compound statements which contain more than one connective. The statements to be symbolized must, however, be written in English in such a way that they are not ambiguous. If a statement is ambiguous, the best we can do is consider all possible senses of the statement and, using the principle of charity, attempt to construct the best argument for the position in question. The procedure is this:

(1) Assign constants to each of the simple statements occurring in the compound statment.

(2) Identify all the connectives.

(3) On the basis of word placement or order and punctuation, identify the main connective.

(4) Write the statement in symbolized form, using parentheses to group the simple statements in the appropriate way, based on which connective is the main connective.

EXERCISE 4-2

1. Symbolize each of the following compound statements, using the constants 'S', 'T', and 'C'. Place an asterisk above the main connective in each statement.
   a. It's not the case that if I go sailing then I will play tennis.
   b. If I don't go sailing, then I will play tennis.
   c. If it is not the case that I will go sailing, then I will play tennis.
   d. If I go sailing, then I will not play tennis.
   e. Either I will go sailing and play tennis, or I will go to the concert.
   f. I will not go sailing and it's not the case that either I will not play tennis or not go to the concert.
   g. I will go sailing and either play tennis or go to the concert.
   h. I will not go sailing and either I will play tennis or go to the concert.
   i. Either I will go sailing or play tennis and go to the concert.
   j. Either I will go sailing or it's not the case that I will both play tennis and go to the concert.
   k. I will go sailing and it's not the case that either I will play tennis or go to the concert.
   l. If I go sailing, then it's not the case that I will both play tennis and go to the concert.
   m. It's not the case that either I will go sailing or both play tennis and go to the concert.
   n. It's not the case both that I will go sailing and that either I will play tennis or go to the concert.

o. It's not the case that either I will go sailing and play tennis, or that I will go to the concert.

p. If I go sailing and play tennis, then I will go to the concert.

2. Symbolize each of the following compound statements using the given symbols as constants. Place an asterisk over the main connective of each statement.

a. Either we will *win* the game if we make the two-point *conversion*, or if we miss the conversion then we will have to *score* on our next possession. (*W, C, S*)

b. We will *win* the game if, and only if, both the other team *punts* and we make a *touchdown* on the runback. (*W, P, T*)

c. If either the federal government *subsidizes* Wing Air or Wing Air *merges* with Flybynight, then either Wing Air will show a *profit* next year or both airlines will be *bankrupt*. (*S, M, P, B*)

d. If the *rights* of private citizens are to be protected, then either the CIA must no longer *engage* in domestic work or the agency should be *abolished*. (*R, E, A*)

e. If I both *water* the plants and see that they get plenty of *sunshine*, then they will *thrive*, and if either I don't water them or they don't get plenty of sunshine, then they will not thrive. (*W, S, T*)

f. Jeremy will *enlist* in the Army if, and only if, either he is sent to *Germany* or he is trained to be a *computer* programmer. (*E, G, C*)

g. If Deirdre is *like* most poeople and *votes* on proposal A, then either she believes that the *passage* of the proposal will go a long way toward getting rid of the litter problem or she believes that the price of *bottled* beverages will go up too much to justify the proposal. (*L, V, P, B*)

h. Munchie-Crunchies are *worth* buying only if either they are on a huge *sale* or one both *buys* the large economy size and sends for the *picture* of Fantastic Freddy. (*W, S, B, P*)

i. If Alexandra either has a *history* of heart problems or has high *blood* pressure, then she should *take* the vaccine only if it is more likely that she will *die* of the disease without the vaccine than it is that she will die of a heart attack with it. (*H, B, T, D*)

j. The American public will be *convinced* that we should spend money to develop a new bomber only if either it is *explained* to them why a new bomber is necessary for national defense, or they can be shown both that the money spent will not *increase* taxes and that there is sufficient money to continue *domestic* programs along with the new bomber. (*C, E, I, D*)

k. A state should *remain* on daylight time when the rest of the nation is on standard time only if it can be shown that either *lives* will be saved or *energy* will be saved. (*R, L, E*)

l. Either *reincarnation* is something which does occur, or both the people who testify about former lives while under *hypnosis* are frauds and a lot of people are being *taken* in by the testimony. (*R, H, T*)

m. The legislature will *approve* the governor's budget request if, and only if, either the expenses incurred by the governor's assistants can be *justified*, or the assistants both are *friends* of the legislators and get *preferential* treatment. (*A, J, F, P*)

4:3 DETERMINING THE TRUTH VALUES OF COMPOUND STATEMENTS

In this section you will see how to determine the truth values of compound statements when you know the truth values of the constants which occur in the statements. We begin by discussing how to determine truth values in general from truth tables.

4:3.1 Generalizing the Truth Tables

You know from our discussions in earlier chapters that a variable can be used to represent any sentence or statement whatsoever. In particular, the variables '*p*' and '*q*' in the truth tables for the logical connectives may represent compound statements whose truth values are themselves functions of some logical connective. For example, the compound statement 'Either Matt will go to *Bebo's* or he will go to *Neptune's* and either Matt will have a *pizza* for dinner or some *shrimp*', symbolized as '(*B* ∨ *N*) · (*P* ∨ *S*)', is itself a *conjunction*. In this statement, '(*B* ∨ *N*)' is the left conjunct, '(*P* ∨ *S*)' is the right conjunct, and the dot is the main connective. To determine the truth value of '(*B* ∨ *N*) · (*P* ∨ *S*)', we first have to determine the truth values of '(*B* ∨ *N*)' and '(*P* ∨ *S*)' by using T3 (the truth table for 'or'). Having done this, we can then use T2 (the truth table for 'and') to determine the truth value for '(*B* ∨ *N*) · (*P* ∨ *S*)'. Hence, we have to go through the following steps to determine the truth value of this statement:

Step 1: Determine the truth values for '*B*', '*N*', '*P*', and '*S*'.

Step 2: Determine the truth value for '(*B* ∨ *N*)' from the appropriate line of T3, and do the same for '(*P* ∨ *S*)'.

Step 3: Using the results of step 2, find the lines in T2 corresponding to the truth values for '(*B* ∨ *N*)' and '(*P* ∨ *S*)', and thereby derive the truth value for '(*B* ∨ *N*) · (*P* ∨ *S*)'.

This is typical of the procedure one must follow to determine the truth value of any compound statement. The actual steps will, of course, differ, depending on the particular compound statement in question and the connectives which occur in it.

Before moving on to some examples, we shall schematize the above case and then use the schematic method to make another general point.

SCHEMA 1: (*B* ∨ *N*) · (*P* ∨ *S*)

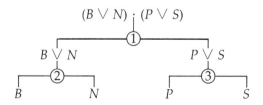

Schema 1 represents, *in reverse,* the three steps that we just examined. In particular, to determine the truth value of the conjunction '$(B \vee N) \cdot (P \vee S)$', we must first break it down into its component parts—the left conjunct '$B \vee N$' and the right conjunct '$P \vee S$'; this is indicated by the lines marked ①. Next, we must break the two disjunctions '$B \vee N$' and '$P \vee S$' into their component parts (the *left disjunct* and the *right disjunct*); this is indicated by the lines marked ② and ③. At ② and ③ we would use T3 to determine the values of the disjunctions, and at ① we would use T2 to determine the value of the conjunction.

4:3.2 Some Examples Since we shall be making reference to the truth tables for the five logical connectives, those tables are reproduced here for convenience.

T1:

p	$\sim p$
T	F
F	T

T2:

p	q	$(p \cdot q)$
T	T	T
T	F	F
F	T	F
F	F	F

T3:

p	q	$(p \vee q)$
T	T	T
T	F	T
F	T	T
F	F	F

T4:

p	q	$(p \supset q)$
T	T	T
T	F	F
F	T	T
F	F	T

T5:

p	q	$(p \equiv q)$
T	T	T
T	F	F
F	T	F
F	F	T

PROBLEM 1

Determine the truth value of 'Either if Sandy makes the dean's list then she will feel all her efforts have been worthwhile, or she will be depressed.'

Assign constants in the following way, and suppose that 'P' = T, 'Q' = F, and 'R' = T:

P = Sandy makes the dean's list.

Q = Sandy will feel all her efforts have been worthwhile.

R = Sandy will be depressed.

Step 1: This is a disjunctive statement whose left disjunct is a conditional statement, symbolized as '$P \supset Q$', and whose right disjunct is a simple statement, symbolized as 'R'.

Step 2: Schematize the compound statement. Later, when you are more familiar with the order in which to determine values, we shall eliminate the writing of this step.

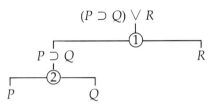

Our compound statement is a disjunction whose left disjunct is a conditional statement and whose right disjunct is a simple statement.

Step 3: Determine the truth value of '$P \supset Q$'. This we do by looking at T4. We find that when 'P' = T and 'Q' = F (second line), '$P \supset Q$' takes the value F. This gives us the truth value of the left disjunct of '($P \supset Q$) $\vee$ R'.

Step 4: Determine the truth value of 'R'. This we assumed is T. This gives us the truth value of the right disjunct.

Step 5: Determine the truth value of the disjunction. This we do by using T3. Our left disjunct '$P \supset Q$' has the value F, and our right disjunct 'R' has the value T. We see from T3 that this corresponds to the third line of the table. On that line the disjunction takes the value T, so when 'P' = T, 'Q' = F, and 'R' = T, '($P \supset Q$) $\vee$ R' takes the value T.

T F F T T

PROBLEM 2

Determine the truth value of 'If all the following conditions hold, then either Bruce will go to the party or Darlene will not: Art is going and Cindy is not; either Bruce or Darlene is going; and if Andy does not go, then Darlene will'.

Assign constants in the following way, and suppose that 'A' = T, 'B' = F, 'C' = T, and 'D' = F:

A = Art is going to the party.

B = Bruce is going to the party.

C = Cindy is going to the party.

D = Darlene is going to the party.

Step 1: Rewrite the statement so that it is divided into groups of two statements for the purposes of using the truth tables. Our result is:

$$(((A \cdot \sim C) \cdot (B \vee D)) \cdot (\sim C \supset D)) \supset (B \vee \sim D)$$

Step 2: Assign the given truth values to the variables as they occur in the statement:

$(((A \cdot \sim C) \cdot (B \lor D)) \cdot (\sim C \supset D)) \supset (B \lor \sim D)$

T B F T F F B F   F F T F   T   F T T F

Step 3: Determine the truth value of the antecedent. To do this, we must first determine the truth value of '$\sim C$', and then determine the truth value of each of '$A \cdot \sim C$', '$B \lor D$', and '$\sim C \supset D$'. We must next determine the truth value of '$(A \cdot \sim C) \cdot (B \lor D)$', and then finally determine the truth value of the whole conjunction. Our compound statement will look as follows as we do each of these things:

(a) $(((A \cdot \sim C) \cdot (B \lor D)) \cdot (\sim C \supset D)) \supset (B \lor \sim D)$
 T F F T F F F F   F F T T F   T F T T F

(b) $(((A \cdot \sim C) \cdot (B \lor D)) \cdot (\sim C \supset D)) \supset (B \lor \sim D)$
 T F F T   F F F   F T T F   F   F

(c) $(((A \cdot \sim C) \cdot (B \lor D)) \cdot (\sim C \supset D)) \supset (B \lor \sim D)$
 T F F T F F F F   F T T F   F   F

(d) $(((A \cdot \sim C) \cdot (B \lor D)) \cdot (\sim C \supset D)) \supset (B \lor \sim D)$
 T F F T F F F F   F F T T F   F   F

Step 4: Determine the truth value of the consequent. To do this we must first determine the truth value of '$\sim D$' and then the truth value of '$B \lor \sim D$'. Our results are given below, where, for clarity, the antecedent is not written out.

(a) (antecedent) $\supset (B \lor \sim D)$
 F   T F

(b) (antecedent) $\supset (B \lor \sim D)$
 F   T T F

Step 5: Determine the truth value of the compound statement. We write this value under the main connective '$\supset$'. Since our antecedent took the value F and our consequent took the value T, T4 (third line) tells us that the conditional statement is true. Our final result is

$(((A \cdot \sim C) \cdot (B \lor D)) \cdot (\sim C \supset D)) \supset (B \lor \sim D)$
 T F F T F F F F   F F T T F   T F T T F

Note that the truth value for the compound statement has been written under the '$\supset$' preceding the expression '$(B \lor \sim D)$' and, moreover, that this '$\supset$' is the *main connective* of the compound statement. This is the usual practice: When the truth value of a compound statement is determined in the manner discussed above, the truth value of the compound statement is always written under the main connective of the statement.

Having seen how to determine the truth value of a compound statement, given a particular assignment of truth values to the constants, we are now ready to develop the truth-table method fully. This we shall do in the next section.

EXERCISE 4-3

1. Determine the truth value of each of the compound statements in problem 1 of Exercise 4-2 given that 'I will go sailing' and 'I will play tennis' are true and 'I will go to the concert' is false.

2. Determine the truth values of the following compound statements, assuming that 'A', 'B', and 'C' are true and that 'X', 'Y', and 'Z' are false. Place an asterisk over the main connective.

a. $(A \cdot \sim X) \equiv (Y \vee B)$ b. $((\sim B \cdot A) \vee Y) \supset (C \cdot Z)$
c. $(C \cdot Z) \supset ((\sim B \cdot A) \vee Y)$ d. $(Y \vee \sim X) \supset (B \cdot \sim A)$
e. $((A \cdot \sim B) \supset X) \vee \sim (B \cdot \sim X)$ f. $(C \vee B) \vee (\sim A \cdot Y)$
g. $(A \equiv \sim B) \cdot \sim (Y \cdot Z)$ h. $((X \vee \sim Y) \cdot \sim C) \vee (B \cdot Z)$
i. $((X \equiv \sim C) \vee (B \equiv \sim Y)) \supset (A \equiv Z)$
j. $((A \supset B) \cdot Y) \vee (((C \supset X) \cdot Z) \vee A)$
k. $((A \supset B) \cdot (B \supset X)) \equiv ((C \supset Y) \vee (Z \cdot A))$
l. $(((A \cdot B) \vee Z) \vee ((B \vee C) \cdot Y)) \supset ((C \supset B) \vee (X \cdot A))$
m. $((A \supset Z) \cdot (X \supset C)) \supset (A \supset C)$
n. $(((A \vee B) \vee X) \cdot C) \cdot ((B \supset A) \cdot (A \vee B))$
o. $(A \vee (B \supset X)) \equiv ((A \vee B) \supset X)$

4:4 TRUTH TABLES

We remarked above that a truth table is just a list of all the possible assignments of truth values to the variables which occur in a compound statement, along with the truth value that the compound statement takes for each assignment; T1 to T5 provide instances of this. In section 4:3 we saw how to determine the truth value of a compound statement when we were given a particular assignment of truth values to its variables. In the case of truth tables, we shall be doing exactly the same thing we did in section 4:3, only this time we shall be determining the truth value of the compound statement for *each possible assignment of truth values to the variables* which occur in the statement form. To do this, we must first develop a method of determining the possible assignments of truth values to the variables of a given compound statement. This we do in the next section.

4:4.1 Determining Assignments of Truth Values to Variables
In the truth tables for the five connectives, when there is one variable involved, as in T1, the truth table has two lines; when there are two variables involved, as in T2 to T5, the truth table has four lines. In all truth tables, the number of lines depends on the number of variables occurring in the statement for which the table is being constructed. In particular:

Number of lines $= 2^n$

where n is the number of variables occurring in the statement.[5]

To see how this formula works, consider the truth table for negation. Here there is only one variable involved, so there are 2^1, or 2, lines in the table. In the case of T2 through T5, where there are two variables, there are 2^2, or 4, lines. If there were three variables in the compound statement, there would be 2^3, or 8, lines to the truth table, and so on. Note that with each additional variable the truth table *doubles* in length.

Once we know how many lines a given truth table must have, we need to assign truth values to the variables in each of these lines. We do this with the following procedure, which is presented along with an example that involves three variables, as in '$p \supset (q \lor r)$':

ASSIGNING TRUTH VALUES TO THE VARIABLES

Step 1: Write down each of the variables.

> p q r

Step 2: Determine the number of lines that the truth table will have. Here, since there are three variables, there will be 2^3, or 8, lines.

Step 3: Assign truth values to each of the lines under the left-most variable—in this case 'p'. To do this, divide the number of lines by 2, and assign the value T to the first half of the lines and the value F to the second half. In our case, dividing 8 by 2 gives us 4, so the first four lines under 'p' are given the value T and the last four are given the value F. (See the table in step 5.)

Step 4: Assign truth values to the variable to the right of the left-most variable—in this case 'q'. To do this, divide by 2 the number of lines *in which the first string of T's occurs.* Assign the value T to the number of lines corresponding to this result, and the value F to the next similar number of lines. When a truth value has been assigned to the new variable opposite each T in the first string of T's for the variable to the left, repeat the pattern.

> In our example, the variable to the left, 'p' was assigned a string of four T's. Dividing by 2 tells us that the first four lines for 'q' will consist of 2 T's and 2 F's. We then repeat the pattern. (See the table in step 5.)

Step 5: Repeat step 4 for the next variable to the right. Continue until a truth value has been assigned to all the lines for each variable. In

---

[5] In this formula, the exponent 'n' indicates how many times 2 is to be multiplied by itself. For example, 2^5 means $2 \times 2 \times 2 \times 2 \times 2$.

our case 'q', the variable to the left of 'r', has a string of two T's. Hence, the first two lines under 'r' will be a T and an F. Since we have assigned a value to 'r' for each of the lines opposite the first string of T's in 'q', we now repeat the pattern. Our result, after these five steps, is

p	q	r
T	T	T
T	T	F
T	F	T
T	F	F
F	T	T
F	T	F
F	F	T
F	F	F

This procedure can be used to assign truth values regardless of how many variables there are in a truth table. For example, if there were five variables there would be 32 lines (2^5). The left-most variable would have 16 T's under it, then 16 F's; the next variable to the right would have 8 T's followed by 8 F's, followed by 8 T's followed by 8 F's; and so on for the remaining variables until the last one, which would have a string of alternating T's and F's. When this procedure is followed, the left-most variable in the truth table *always* has the value T assigned to the first half of the lines and the value F assigned to the second half. The right-most variable is *always* a string of alternating T's and F's. If your assignment of truth values to the variables does not show this pattern, then you've made an error in using the procedure.

4:4.2 Some Examples   In this section we shall apply the material of sections 4:3 and 4:4.1 to some problems. Before we do so, it should be noted that so far we have determined the truth values for compound statements *given a particular assignment of truth values to the constants which occur in the statement.* When we construct a truth table, however, we do so for a statement form; so here we shall be working with compound-statement forms which are symbolized by using statement variables.

What we shall do in this section, then, is determine the truth value that a compound statement would have for each possible assignment of truth values to the statements which could replace the variables in the statement form. We begin by using the procedure discussed in the previous section to obtain a truth table in which each line represents *one* of the possible combinations of truth values that the statements which replace the variables might have.

PROBLEM 3

Construct a truth table for the statement form of 'Either Mark will be guided by the prospect of money and take a job with the ad agency, or he will try to open his own art studio.'

Step 1: Assign *variables* to the statement and determine its form. To do this, we make the following assignment:

p = Mark will be guided by the prospect of money.

q = Mark will take a job with the ad agency.

r = Mark will try to open his own art studio

This is an 'either-or' statement, and hence a disjunction, whose left disjunct is the conjunction '$p \cdot q$' and whose right disjunct is 'r'. We shall construct a truth table, then, for '$(p \cdot q) \vee r$'.

Step 2: Determine the number of lines in the truth table. Since we have three variables, there will be eight lines in the truth table.

Step 3: Assign truth values to the variables. This we do according to the procedure outlined above.

Step 4: For each line of the truth table, assign truth values to the variables as they occur in the compound statement. Doing this, we get:

p	q	r	$(p \cdot q)$	$\vee$	r
T	T	T	T T		T
T	T	F	T T		F
T	F	T	T F		T
T	F	F	T F		F
F	T	T	F T		T
F	T	F	F T		F
F	F	T	F F		T
F	F	F	F F		F

Step 5: For each of the lines of the truth table, determine the truth value of the compound statement for that particular assignment of truth values to the variables. In our example we would first determine the truth value for the left disjunct, '$(p \cdot q)$', for each of the lines, then the truth value of the right disjunct 'r', and then the truth value of the compound statement by using T3. Our result is

p	q	r	$(p \cdot q)$	$\vee$	r
T	T	T	TTT	T	T
T	T	F	TTT	T	F
T	F	T	TFF	T	T
T	F	F	TFF	F	F
F	T	T	FFT	T	T
F	T	F	FFT	F	F
F	F	T	FFF	T	T
F	F	F	FFF	F	F

We can now read the truth value of our compound statement for any assignment of truth values to the variables. For example, if we want to know the truth value of '$(p \cdot q) \vee r$' when 'p' = F, 'q' = F, and $'r' = $ T, we look at the seventh line. There, under the main connective '$\vee$' we see that the compound statement takes the value T.

PROBLEM 4

Construct a truth table for the statement form of (If it's the case that Adrienne will not enter the freestyle and Beth will enter the medley relay, and it's also the case that either Beth will not enter the medley or Connie will,)then it's also the case that Adrienne will not enter the freestyle and Connie will enter the medley relay.

Step 1: Assign variables to the statement and determine its form. Assigning variables in the following way,

$p = $ Adrienne will enter the freestyle.

$q = $ Beth will enter the medley relay.

$r = $ Connie will enter the medley relay.

we obtain, as the form of the statement,

$$((\sim p \cdot q) \cdot (\sim q \vee r)) \supset (\sim p \cdot r)$$

Note that this is a conditional statement whose antecedent is a conjunction; the left conjunct is also a conjunction, whereas the right conjunct is a disjunction.

Step 2: Determine the number of lines in the truth table. Again there are eight, because we have three variables.

Step 3: Assign truth values to the variables.

Step 4: Assign truth values to the variables in the compound statement.

p	q	r	$((\sim p \cdot q) \cdot (\sim q \vee r)) \supset (\sim p \cdot r)$					
T	T	T	T	T	T	T	T	T
T	T	F	T	T	T	F	T	F
T	F	T	T	F	F	T	T	T
T	F	F	T	F	F	F	T	F
F	T	T	F	T	T	T	F	T
F	T	F	F	T	T	F	F	F
F	F	T	F	F	F	T	F	T
F	F	F	F	F	F	F	F	F

Step 5: Determine the truth value of the compound statement for each line of the truth table. Since our compound statement is a conditional statement, we must determine the truth value of the antecedent '$((\sim p \cdot q) \cdot (\sim q \vee r))$' and the consequent '$(\sim p \cdot r)$', so that we can use T4. The antecedent is a conjunction, so we must determine the truth value of each of its conjuncts before we can determine the truth value of the complex statement. The steps involved in determining the truth value of the compound statement are:

(a) Determine the truth value of '~p' and '~q' by using T1.

(b) Determine the truth value of the conjunctions '~p · q' and '~p · r' by using T2.

(c) Determine the value of the disjunction '~q ∨ r' by using T3.

(d) Determine the value of the antecedent by using T2.

(e) Determine the truth value of the compound statement by using T4 with the truth value of the antecedent [found in (d)] and the truth value of the consequent [found in (b)].

The results are

p	q	r	((~p · q) · (~q ∨ r)) ⊃ (~p · r)
T	T	T	F TF T F F T T T T T F T F T
T	T	F	F T F T F F T F F T F T F F
T	F	T	F T F F F T F T T T F T F T
T	F	F	F T F F F T F T F T F T F F
F	T	T	T F T T T F T T T T F T T
F	T	F	T F T T F F T F F T T F F F
F	F	T	T F F F F T F T T T F T T
F	F	F	T F F F T F T F T F F F

EXERCISE 4-4

1. What is a truth table?

2. What formula does one use to determine the number of lines in a truth table? Explain the formula.

3. What effect does adding an additional variable have on the number of lines required in a truth table?

4. Explain the method used to assign truth values to the variables in each line of a truth table.

5. Explain the difference between determining the truth value of a compound statement, given an assignment of truth value to each constant, and constructing a truth table for a compound-statement form.

EXERCISE 4-5

Construct a truth table for each of the following statement forms.

a. $(p \supset q) \cdot \sim r$ b. $p \supset (q \supset p)$

c. $(\sim p \lor r) \cdot q$ d. $(\sim p \equiv q) \lor r$

e. $((p \supset q) \cdot p) \supset q$ f. $(p \supset q) \equiv (\sim q \supset \sim p)$

g. $(((p \supset q) \cdot (r \supset s)) \cdot (\sim s \lor \sim q)) \supset (\sim p \lor \sim r)$

h. $(p \cdot q) \supset \sim(\sim p \lor \sim q)$

i. $(p \lor q) \supset (\sim p \cdot \sim r)$

j. $(((p \cdot q) \cdot (r \cdot s)) \cdot (p \cdot r)) \supset (q \cdot s)$

4:4.3 Tautologies, Contradictions, and Contingent Statements   In problem 3 the truth value of the compound statement is T for some assignments of truth values to the variables and F for other assignments. In other statement forms, the truth value of the compound statement will be T for all possible assignments of truth values to the variables, and in still others the compound statement will take the value F for all possible assignments of truth values to the variables. These various kinds of statement form have been given names by logicians:

CONTINGENT STATEMENT

A statement form which sometimes takes the value T and sometimes takes the value F, depending upon the assignment of truth values to its variables

TAUTOLOGY

A statement form which takes the value T for all possible assignments of truth values to its variables

CONTRADICTION

A statement form which takes the value F for all possible assignments of truth values to its variables

The following are all statements which are tautologies.[6]

EXAMPLES OF TAUTOLOGIES

(1) If it is raining, then it is raining.

(2) I'll either pass this course or I won't.

(3) If it is true that if today is Monday, tomorrow is Tuesday, and if it's true that today is Monday, then it's also true that tomorrow is Tuesday.

(4) If it's true that if I study then I will get an 'A', then it's true that if I didn't get an 'A' then I didn't study.

The following are all contradictory.

EXAMPLES OF CONTRADICTIONS

(1) It's raining and it's not raining.

(2) It's not the case that I'll either pass this course or I won't.

(3) It's not the case that if a plane figure is a triangle then a plane figure is a triangle.

(4) If I don't eat then I'll be hungry and I'll neither eat nor be hungry.

---

[6] Each of the examples which follows is a *particular statement* and not a statement form. Such statements are called 'tautologies', since each is an instance of a statement form which is a tautology. A similar remark holds for the examples of contradictions and contingent statements.

The following are all contingent statements.

EXAMPI FS OF CONTINGENT STATEMENTS

(1) It's raining.

(2) It's Monday.

(3) I'll pass the course or commit suicide.

(4) There are only two species of single-called organisms.

Of these three kinds of statements, tautologies are of particular interest to logicians since *every valid argument is associated with some tautological statement.* In section 4:4.5 we shall discuss why this is so, and in section 4:5 we shall make use of this feature to determine the validity of arguments by using the truth-table method. Before turning to that discussion, however, we shall expand on our earlier remarks about logical equivalency.

4:4.4 Logical Equivalency   We earlier noted that two statement forms are logically equivalent if they always have the same truth value regardless of which statements uniformly replace the variables in the statement forms. We contrasted this with material equivalency, noting that two statements are materially equivalent if they have the same truth value.

Although this is an important difference between logically equivalent statements and materially equivalent statements, there is a relationship between the two, a relationship that is easily seen when we consider the truth table for material equivalency and the notion of a tautology. In particular:

> Two statement forms are *logically equivalent* if, and only if, the statement of their *material equivalency* is a *tautology.*

We know from our discussion of the truth table for material equivalency that two statements are materially equivalent if, and only if, they have the same truth value—either both true or both false. Now consider any two statements which are logically equivalent—statements which have the same truth value regardless of the truth values assigned to the variables occurring in them. It is clear that regardless of how many variables occur in each of these statements, the statements will both have the value T or the value F on corresponding lines of their respective truth tables. As a result, if we assert the material equivalence of these two statements, then the resultant truth table will take the value T under the main connective for each line of the truth table; that is, the resultant truth table will show that the statement of material equivalence is a tautology.

Let's look at a particular example of the general situation characterized above. We earlier claimed that the contrapositive of a conditional statement is logically equivalent to the conditional statement. We can easily show that this is so by showing that the statement that '$p \supset q$' is materially equivalent to '$\sim q \supset \sim p$' is a tautology. This we do in the following truth table:

p	q	$(p \supset q) \equiv (\sim q \supset \sim p)$
T	T	T T t T F T F
T	F	T F F T T F F
F	T	F T T T F T T
F	F	F T F T T T T

Another logical equivalency we discussed earlier is double negation. The truth table that shows this equivalency is

p	$p \equiv \sim\sim p$
T	T T T F T
F	F T F T F

When we discussed the truth table for material implication we pointed out that, in assigning truth values to the statement form in each line of the truth table, we want to rule out as true the case in which the antecedent of the conditional statement is true and the consequent false. As a result, we would expect that whenever a statement of the form '$p \supset q$' is true, the statement of the form '$\sim(p \cdot \sim q)$' is also true; similarly, if the former is false, the latter is also false. In short, we would expect these two statement forms to be logically equivalent. The following truth table shows that they are:

p	q	$(p \supset q) \equiv \sim(p \cdot \sim q)$
T	T	T T T F F
T	F	F T F T T
F	T	T T T F F
F	F	T T T F T

There is yet another way of looking at the truth table for material implication: Whenever the antecedent of a conditional statement is false or the consequent is true, the conditional statement is true. As a result, whenever a statement of the form '$p \supset q$' is true, '$(\sim p \lor q)$' should be true; and whenever the former is false, the latter should also be false. The following truth table shows that this is indeed the case:

p	q	$(p \supset q) \equiv (\sim p \lor q)$
T	T	T T F T
T	F	F T F F
F	T	T T T T
F	F	T T T T

Since '$p \supset q$' is logically equivalent to both '$\sim(p \cdot \sim q)$' and '$\sim p \lor q$', it follows that '$\sim(p \cdot \sim q)$' is logically equivalent to '$\sim p \lor q$'. This is shown below:

p	q	$\sim(p \cdot \sim q) \equiv (\sim p \lor q)$
T	T	T F F T F T
T	F	F T T T F F
F	T	T F F T T T
F	F	T F T T T T

We are now able to expand on another remark made earlier in the text. In discussing the support relationship between the premises and the conclusion of a good argument and, in particular, in discussing validity, we noted that the validity of an argument does not depend on the actual truth or falsity of the premises and the conclusion; rather, validity is a function of the *logical* relationship which holds between the premises and the conclusion such that if the former are all true then the latter must also be true.

Each of the above truth tables provides us with an example of this kind of relationship and shows that the relationship is independent of actual truth or falsity. To see this, consider the left-hand member of each statement of material equivalency. What you should find is that each of these statements is itself *contingent*, sometimes having the value true and sometimes the value false. As a result, the *actual* value of any statement having any of these forms will sometimes be true and sometimes false, depending upon which statements replace the variables. Nonetheless, the truth tables show that these statement forms are logically related to other statement forms (in these cases the right-hand member of each equivalency statement) in such a way that *if* they are true, then other statements *must* be true as well. This is readily seen by noting that whenever the left-hand member of the equivalency statement is true, the right-hand member is also true.

In the next section we shall further expand on these remarks and show the relationship between valid argument forms and tautologies.

EXERCISE 4-6

1. What is a contingent statement? Give an example statement, and give the logical form of the statement.

2. What is a tautology? Give an example statement, and give the logical form of the statement.

3. What is a contradiction? Give an example statement, and give the logical form of the statement.

4. For the statement forms you provided in problems 1 to 3, construct truth tables showing that the forms are contingent, tautological, and contradictory, respectively.

5. Explain what it means to say that two statement forms are logically equivalent.

6. Give an example of two statements which are materially equivalent but not logically equivalent.

EXERCISE 4-7

1. Using truth tables, determine whether the following statement forms are contingent, tautologous, or contradictory.
   a. $((p \supset q) \cdot q) \supset p$
   b. $((r \cdot s) \vee (p \cdot q)) \supset (s \vee q)$
   c. $((p \supset q) \cdot \sim p) \supset \sim q$
   d. $((\sim p \vee q) \cdot p) \supset q$

e. $(p \lor \sim q) \equiv \sim (\sim p \supset \sim q)$ f. $\sim (r \cdot s) \supset \sim (\sim r \cdot s)$
g. $\sim (p \lor q) \supset (\sim p \cdot \sim q)$ h. $((p \cdot q) \lor (s \cdot r)) \equiv ((p \lor s) \cdot (q \lor r))$
i. $((\sim r \supset s) \cdot \sim s) \supset \sim r$ j. $((p \cdot q) \lor (p \cdot \sim q)) \equiv q$

2. Which of the following pairs of statements are logically equivalent?
   a. $(p \supset q)$ and $(\sim p \lor q)$ b. $(\sim p \cdot \sim q)$ and $(p \cdot q)$
   c. $(r \cdot s)$ and $\sim (\sim r \lor \sim s)$ d. $(\sim p \supset q)$ and $(\sim q \supset p)$
   e. $(\sim p \supset q)$ and $(q \supset \sim p)$ f. $(\sim p \lor q)$ and $\sim (p \cdot \sim q)$
   g. $((p \lor \sim q) \cdot \sim p)$ and $(p \lor \sim p)$ h. $((p \supset q) \cdot \sim q)$ and $((p \supset q) \cdot p)$
   i. $((p \supset q) \cdot \sim q)$ and $((p \supset q) \cdot \sim p)$ j. $((p \supset p) \cdot p)$ and p

4:4.5 Valid Arguments and Tautologies

In Chapters 2 and 3 we characterized a valid argument as one whose conclusion must be true if all the premises are true. An invalid argument is one which does not satisfy this condition; in other words, an invalid argument is one in which it is possible for all the premises to be true and the conclusion false.

Let the following schema represent any argument whatsoever, where 'P_1', 'P_2', etc., are the premises, and 'C' is the conclusion.

SCHEMA 2

P_1

P_2

. . .

P_n

$\therefore C$

Now, if one claims that some particular instance of schema 2 is valid, then he or she is claiming that if 'P_1' is true, and 'P_2' is true, and so on through 'P_n', then 'C' must also be true. We can write this fact as *a conditional statement whose antecedent is a conjunction of all the premises and whose consequent is the conclusion* of the arbitrary argument represented in schema 2. Our result is:

SCHEMA 3

$(P_1 \cdot P_2 \cdot \ldots \cdot P_n) \supset C$

The important thing to note about schema 2 and schema 3 is that they represent any argument whatsoever; as a result, every argument written as schema 2 can be rewritten as a conditional statement of the form exhibited in schema 3. That is, *a conditional statement having the form of schema 3 is associated with every argument.*

The relationship of schema 3 to the question of an argument's being valid and to the truth-table method examined above is the following: The conditional statement associated with an argument (schema 3) is a compound statement whose truth value for any assignment of truth values to its variables can be determined by the truth-table method. If schema 3 represents a valid argument, then for every line of the truth table wherein *all* the premises are true, the conclusion will also be true. On the other hand, if there is at least one line of the truth table wherein all the premises are true and the conclusion is false, then the argument represented by schema 3 is invalid. The argument is invalid simply because a valid argument cannot have all true premises and a false conclusion.

Let's look at two examples which make these ideas explicit.

EXAMPLE 1

$p \supset q$

p

$\therefore q$

Example 1 is an instance of the argument form affirming the antecedent, which is valid. The conditional statement associated with this argument is

(1) $((p \supset q) \cdot p) \supset q$

Notice that the antecedent of (1) is the conjunction of the two premises of our argument, and the consequent of (1) is the conclusion of the argument. Let's now do the truth table for (1). There will be four lines, since (1) has two variables:

p	q	$((p \supset q)$	$\cdot p)$	$\supset q$
T	T	T	T	T
T	F	F	F	T
F	T	T	F	T
F	F	T	F	T

The lines of the truth table which are of interest relative to the validity of example 1 are those in which all the premises are true—in this case the first line. On that line we see that the conclusion 'q' is also true. Hence, example 1 is valid, for we have considered all the possible assignments of truth values to the variables in (1), and in every case in which the premises '$p \supset q$' and 'p' are true, the conclusion is also true.

How about the remaining lines; what effect do they have on the validity of example 1? The answer is that they are irrelevant in the determination of validity, other than to show that we have considered all possible assignments of truth values to the variables in the argument. As we discussed in Chapter 2, the falsity of any or all of the premises of the argument has no bearing whatsoever on the issue of the argument's being valid.

We also noted in the preceding section that every valid argument is equivalent to some tautological statement. Notice that the truth table for (1) has the value T under the main connective '$\supset$' for each line of the truth table. This shows that (1) is true for every possible assignment of truth values to its variables and is, therefore, a tautology. Also notice in the truth table that (1) takes the value T in the last three lines because of the falsity of the antecedent in each of these lines, and the antecedent is false because at least one of the premises in these lines is false.

These results are not unique to example 1. *Every valid argument rewritten as a conditional statement takes the truth value T under the main connective on each line of the truth table.*

Now we are in a position to reinforce a point that has been made repeatedly throughout the text: The validity of an argument depends on its form, and not on the actual truth values of its premises and conclusion. This is brought out in the truth table for (1) above, where we see that, regardless of the content of any argument having this form (regardless of the actual truth and falsity of the premises and the conclusion), there can be no case in which an argument of this form has all true premises and a false conclusion. It is because of this that validity is not a factual matter but depends, instead, on the form of an argument. And because of this, we can determine whether the deductive support relationship is satisfied, independently of knowing the truth values of the premises and conclusion of an argument. Because the support relationship and the actual truth or falsity of the premises and conclusion are independent—as we have repeatedly emphasized—the analysis of every argument has two independent components: the support relationship and the truth value of the premises.

Consider now an example of an invalid argument:

EXAMPLE 2

$p \supset q$

q

$\therefore p$

Example 2 is an instance of the invalid argument form affirming the consequent. We have already used the method of giving counterexamples to show that this argument form is invalid; here we shall show the invalidity with the truth-table method.

We must first convert example 2 to the conditional statement associated with it, a conditional statement whose antecedent is a conjunction of the two premises and whose consequent is the conclusion. Our result is

(2) $((p \supset q) \cdot q) \supset p$

Since (2) contains two variables, there will be four lines to the truth table. The truth table for (2) is

p	q	$((p \supset q)$	$\cdot q)$	$\supset p$
T	T	T	T	T
T	F	F	F	T
F	T	T	T	F
F	F	T	F	T

Notice that under the main connective there is a line of the truth table which takes the value F: the third line. Since a conditional statement takes the value F only when its antecedent is true and its consequent is false, and since the antecedent of (2) is the conjunction of the premises of example 2, the third line is a case in which all the premises of example 2 are true and the conclusion is false. Hence, the argument form of example 2 is invalid.

We can read directly from the truth table the conditions which show that example 2 is invalid. In the third line, the truth value for '$p \supset q$' is found under the connective '$\supset$', and it is T; the truth value for 'q' is found under 'q', and it is T; and finally the truth value of 'p' is read under 'p', and it is F. The assignment of truth values to the variables which shows that the form of example 2 is invalid can be read under the left-most 'p' and 'q' columns in the third line, namely, 'p' = F and 'q' = T.

Having looked at the relationship between arguments and tautologies, we are now ready to apply the truth-table method to the determination of the validity of arguments. This we shall do in the next section.

4:5 THE TRUTH-TABLE TEST FOR VALIDITY

In previous sections of this chapter we have developed all the apparatus necessary to determine the validity of arguments by the truth-table method. Hence, we shall move right on to some problems, showing how to apply the method in particular cases.

PROBLEM 5

(This chemical will burn with a yellow flame and not a blue one. Moreover, it will either burn with a blue flame or it contains sodium.) Hence, either it does not contain sodium or the chemical will not burn with a yellow flame (because this chemical contains sodium if, and only if, it burns with a yellow flame.)

> *Step 1:* Assign variables to the statements occurring in the argument, and determine the logical form of the argument. To do this, we assign variables in the following way:
>
> > p = This chemical burns with a yellow flame.
> >
> > q = This chemical burns with a blue flame.
> >
> > r = This chemical contains sodium.
>
> With this assignment of variables, our argument has the form
>
> > $p \cdot \sim q$
> >
> > $q \vee r$
> >
> > $r \equiv p$
> >
> > $\therefore \sim r \vee \sim p$
>
> *Step 2:* Rewrite the argument as a conditional statement:
>
> > $((p \cdot \sim q) \cdot (q \vee r) \cdot (r \equiv p)) \supset (\sim r \vee \sim p)$

Step 3: Group the statements occurring in the premises of the argument into groups of two:

$$(((p \cdot \sim q) \cdot (q \vee r)) \cdot (r \equiv p)) \supset (\sim r \vee \sim p)$$

Step 4: Determine the number of lines in the truth table, and assign truth values to the variables.

Step 5: Determine the truth values of the antecedent, consequent, and compound statement.

p	q	r	$(((p$	$\cdot$	$\sim q)$	$\cdot$	$(q$	$\vee$	$r))$	$\cdot$	$(r$	$\equiv$	$p))$	$\supset$	$(\sim r$	$\vee$	$\sim p)$
T	T	T		F	F	F		T		F		T		T	F	F	F
T	T	F		F	F	F		T		F	F			T	T	T	F
T	F	T		T	T	T		T		T		T		F	F	F	F
T	F	F		T	T	F		F		F	F			T	T	T	F
F	T	T		F	F	F		T		F	F			T	F	T	T
F	T	F		F	F	F		T		F		T		T	T	T	T
F	F	T		F	T	F		T		F	F			T	F	T	T
F	F	F		F	T	F		F		F		T		T	T	T	T

Step 6: Check for validity. Under the main connective, the compound statement takes the value F in the third line. Since this F indicates an assignment of truth values to the variables such that all the premises are true and the conclusion is false, the argument is invalid. The particular assignment of truth values to the variables which does make the premises true and the conclusion false is *'p'* = T, *'q'* = F, and *'r'* = T.

PROBLEM 6

Freudian psychology is wrong, and behaviorist psychology is correct. This is so, because if Freudian psychology is correct, then people's behavior would not be changed by positive reinforcement of desired behavior. Moreover, the evidence for subconscious motivation is very slim, whereas it has been clearly shown that people's behavior is changed by positive reinforcement. Additionally, either there is a lot of evidence in support of subconscious motivation or behaviorist psychology is wrong.

Step 1: Assign variables to the statements occurring in the argument, and determine the logical form of the argument. This we do by assigning variables as follows:

p = Freudian psychology is correct.

q = People's behavior is changed by positive reinforcement of desired behavior.

r = There is a lot of evidence in support of subconscious motivation.

s = Behaviorist psychology is correct.

The only difficulty with this argument is the occurrence of 'whereas' in the second premise. 'Whereas' functions here just like 'and' and indicates a conjunction. With this understanding, we see that the argument has the following form:

$$p \supset \sim q$$
$$\sim r \cdot q$$
$$r \vee \sim s$$
$$\therefore \sim p \cdot s$$

Step 2: Rewrite the argument as a conditional statement:

$$((p \supset \sim q) \cdot (\sim r \cdot q) \cdot (r \vee \sim s)) \supset (\sim p \cdot s)$$

Step 3: Group the statements occurring in the argument into groups of two so that the truth tables for the connectives can be used:

$$(((p \supset \sim q) \cdot (\sim r \cdot q)) \cdot (r \vee \sim s)) \supset (\sim p \cdot s)$$

Step 4: Determine the number of lines in the truth table, and assign truth values to the variables. Since there are four variables, there will be sixteen lines in the table.

Step 5: Determine the truth values of the antecedent, consequent, and compound statement. Our results are:

p	q	r	s	(((p ⊃~q)	· (~r	· q))	·	(r ∨ ~s))	⊃ (~p	· s)
T	T	T	T	F F	F F	F	F	T F	T F	F
T	T	T	F	F F	F F	F	F	T T	T F	F
T	T	F	T	F F	F T	T	F	F F	T F	F
T	T	F	F	F F	F T	T	F	T T	T F	F
T	F	T	T	T T	F F	F	F	T F	T F	F
T	F	T	F	T T	F F	F	F	T T	T F	F
T	F	F	T	T T	F T	F	F	F F	T F	F
T	F	F	F	T T	F T	F	F	T T	T F	F
F	T	T	T	T F	F F	F	F	T F	T T	T
F	T	T	F	T F	F F	F	F	T T	T T	F
F	T	F	T	T F	T T	T	F	F F	T T	T
F	T	F	F	T F	T T	T	T	T T	F T	F
F	F	T	T	T T	F F	F	F	T F	T T	T
F	F	T	F	T T	F F	F	F	T T	T T	F
F	F	F	T	T T	F T	F	F	F F	T T	T
F	F	F	F	T T	F T	F	F	T T	T T	F

Step 6: Check for validity. Under the main connective, there is an F in the twelfth line. This shows us that when 'p' = F, 'q' = T, 'r' = F, and 's' = F the premises of our argument are true and the conclusion is false. Hence, the argument form of problem 6 is invalid.

Having seen in this section how to apply truth tables to the determination of the validity of arguments, we shall, in the next section, examine a related but shorter method of determining validity.

EXERCISE 4-8

1. Explain the relationship between arguments and their associated conditional statements.

2. Explain the relationship between valid argument forms and tautologies.

3. What is the relationship between the method of showing an argument to be invalid with a truth table and constructing a counterexample to that argument?

4. Determine the validity of the following arguments by constructing a truth table for the conditional statement associated with each argument.

   a. If the Democrats *gain* a large majority in the House this November, then either the government will be essentially a *one*-party system or the cause of peace will be *threatened*. We know, however, that the cause of peace will not be threatened. Hence, the Democrats will gain a large majority in the House, since the government will be essentially a one-party system. (*G, O, T*)

   b. Bacon *wrote* "Macbeth" only if either *Bacon* was Shakespeare or both there was no *Shakespeare* and the whole thing was a *hoax*. Since Bacon was not Shakespeare and there was a Shakespeare, it follows that Bacon did not write "Macbeth." (*W, B, S, H*)

   c. Unless the world is *round* or *elliptical*, *Copernican* astronomy is false. So if the world is not elliptical, but the Copernican theory is true, it follows that the world is round. (*R, E, C*)

   d. If tickets are still *available* for the rock concert, I will *go* on Saturday night. Moreover, since either tickets are available for the concert or I will be able to *work* as an usher, it follows that I will go to the concert; for if I work as an usher, I will also go to the concert. (*A, G, W*)

   e. If the subject wasn't a *plant* in the audience, then the hypnotist really put on a terrific *show*, but if the subject was a plant, then a lot of people were *taken in*. Hence, since the hypnotist did not put on a terrific show, a lot of people were taken in. (*P, S, T*)

   f. Either the U.S. should *spend* more money on the defense of western Europe or it should *close* some of the bases which are useless for defense. Moreover, since it will not spend more money and it will not agree to *limiting* the number of troops in Europe, it follows that it will *increase* the number of nuclear warheads in Europe. This is so since if it should close some of the bases, then either it will agree to limit the number of troops in Europe or increase nuclear warheads. (*S, C, L, I*)

   g. The *boycott* will succeed if, and only if, everyone *refrains* from buying the products. Additionally, *pressure* will be put on the manufacturers only if both everyone refrains from buying the products and the boycott succeeds. Consequently, pressure will not be put on the manufacturers, for it's not the case that everyone will refrain from buying the products. (B, R, P)

h. Either the inflation rate will go *down* or the unemployment rate is bound to *rise*. If, however, the unemployment rate is bound to rise, many people will have a hard time *maintaining* their present standard of living. As a result, either the inflation rate will go down, or many people will have a hard time maintaining their living standard. (D, R, M)

i. If the *truck* gets here on time, then we'll either *unload* it tonight or *wait* until tomorrow morning. But, if we don't wait until tomorrow morning, then we'll both have time for *dinner* and the truck will get here on time. Since we won't have time for dinner, though, it follows that either the truck will get here on time only if we unload it tonight, or we'll wait until tomorrow morning. (T, U, W, D)

j. It's not the case that either *Ann* will win the butterfly or *Beth* will lose the freestyle. Since Beth will lose the freestyle or *Carol* will not win the backstroke, and since Beth will win only if Ann wins, it follows that Carol will win if, and only if, Ann wins. (A, B, C)

5. Determine the validity of each of the following argument forms by constructing a truth table for the conditional statement associated with each argument.

a. $\sim p \vee q$
$\therefore p \supset q$

b. $\sim(p \vee q)$
$\therefore \sim p \cdot \sim q$

c. $\sim p \vee q$
$\therefore \sim p \cdot \sim q$

d. $p \supset q$
p
$\therefore q$

e. $p \supset q$
$\sim q$
$\therefore \sim p$

f. $p \supset q$
q
$\therefore p$

g. $p \supset q$
$\sim p$
$\therefore \sim q$

h. $p \supset q$
$q \supset r$
$\therefore p \supset r$

i. $\sim(p \cdot q)$
$\therefore \sim p \vee \sim q$

j. $p \supset q$
$\therefore \sim q \supset \sim p$

k. $p \supset q$
$r \supset q$
$p \vee r$
$\therefore q$

l. $p \supset q$
$q \supset r$
$\therefore r \supset p$

m. $p \supset q$
$\sim p \supset r$
$\sim r$
$\therefore q$

n. $p \cdot q$
$p \supset r$
$q \supset \sim p$
$\therefore \sim r$

o. $\sim p \supset r$
$q \supset \sim r$
$\therefore \sim p \supset q$

p. $p \vee q$
$q \supset r$
$\therefore r$

q. $p \vee q$
$q \supset r$
$\therefore p \vee r$

4:6 THE SHORT TRUTH-TABLE METHOD

Problem 6 in the previous section is ideal for pointing out a shortcoming of the truth-table method: For any problem of even moderate complexity, the truth table becomes unwieldly owing to its length. This raises two related problems:

First, the time needed to construct the truth table is fairly long when there are very many variables, and second, the longer the table is, the greater the chance that an error will be made in the evaluation of an argument. Because of this shortcoming of the truth-table method, an easier, shorter method of determining the validity of arguments has been devised. This is the method of constructing short truth tables, the topic of this section.

4:6.1 How the Short Truth-Table Method Works   To determine the validity of an argument using the truth-table method, we first constructed a table listing all the possible assignments of truth values to the variables occurring in the argument. We then computed the truth value of the conditional statement associated with the argument and checked to see if any assignment of truth values to the variables resulted in all the premises being true and the conclusion false. Although this method will work for arguments with any number of variables and any degree of complexity, a good bit of effort is wasted— particularly in those cases in which an argument is invalid but the conditional statement associated with it takes the value F on only one or two lines (for example, problem 6), or where there is at least one false premise. Effort is wasted in this latter case because lines with at least one false premise are irrelevant in the determination of validity.

We can, however, characterize the truth-table method as follows: What we are really doing is trying to find at least one line of the truth table in which the premises are all true and the conclusion is false. If we find such a line, the argument is invalid; if there is no such line, the argument is valid. Now, we could save ourselves a lot of trouble if, instead of constructing all the lines of the truth table and looking for such a line, we could show in some other way either that there is no such line or that there is such a line. It is this idea that is exploited in the short truth-table method.

✳ In general, the method works like this: We attempt to *construct* a line of the table in which the conclusion is false and the premises are all true. To do this, we begin by assigning truth values to the variables in such a way as to *make the conclusion false*. Since the whole compound statement is truth-functional, the truth values we assign to the variables in the conclusion must also be assigned to the same variables as they occur in the premises. If we make this assignment to the premises and all the premises then can be made true, we have an instance of our argument in which all the premises are true and the conclusion is false; hence, the argument is invalid. On the other hand, *if we make the assignment but cannot make all the premises true* (at least one of them has to be false, given the assignment), *then the argument is valid*. Let's look at an example of this.

EXAMPLE 3

$p \supset q$

q

$\therefore p$

Example 3 is the logical form affirming the consequent and is, as you know, invalid. Let's begin by rewriting example 3 as its associated conditional statement:

(1) $((p \supset q) \cdot q) \supset p$

As pointed out above, we want to try to find a way to make all the premises true and the conclusion false. Assigning the value F to the conclusion 'p', we have

(2) $((p \supset q) \cdot q) \supset p$
F

Having assigned F to 'p' in the conclusion, we must also assign F to 'p' in the premises. This gives us

(3) $((p \supset q) \cdot q) \supset p$
F$$F

Since we want to make all the premises true, let's assign the value T to 'q'; the result is

(4) $((p \supset q) \cdot q) \supset p$
F   T   T   F

So far our conclusion 'p' is false, one premise 'q' is true, and the other premise '$p \supset q$' has a false antecedent and a true consequent. We know from T4, however, that a conditional statement with a false antecedent and a true consequent is true; hence, '$p \supset q$' is true. Filling out the remainder of (4), we have

(5) $((p \supset q) \cdot q) \supset p$
F T   T   T   T   F   F

Hence, by assigning the value F to 'p' and the value T to 'q', we can make the premises of (1) true and the conclusion false, thereby showing that the argument form of example 3 is *invalid*. Notice that (5) corresponds exactly with the third line of the truth table we constructed earlier for example 2, which is also an example of the argument form affirming the consequent. What we have done by the short method here is to construct only the third line of that truth table, instead of constructing the whole table and picking out the third line.

Now consider an example of a valid argument form.

EXAMPLE 4

$p \supset q$

p

$\therefore q$

Rewriting example 4 as its associated conditional statement, we have

(1) $((p \supset q) \cdot p) \supset q$

Attempting to make all the premises true and the conclusion false, we begin by assigning the value F to 'q'. Our result is

(2) $((p \supset q) \cdot p) \supset q$
         F   F

We now try to make all the premises true. Suppose we begin by assigning T to the second premise, 'p'. This gives us

(3) $((p \supset q) \cdot p) \supset q$
         F   T   F

Having assigned T to 'p' in the second premise, we must also assign T to 'p' in the first premise, '$p \supset q$'. Notice, however, that if we do this, the first premise will have a *true antecedent* and a *false consequent* and will, therefore, be *false*; that is,

(4) $((p \supset q) \cdot p) \supset q$
       T FF   T   F

The only way to avoid the result we got with the first premise in (4) would be to assign the value F to 'p'. Then '$p \supset q$' would be true due to a false antecedent:

(5) $((p \supset q) \cdot p) \supset q$
       F TF   F

Having made the first premise true by assigning the value F to 'p', we must now assign the same value to the second premise. The result is that when '$p \supset q$' is true, 'p' is false:

(6) $((p \supset q) \cdot p) \supset q$
       F TF   F   F

Lines (4) and (6) together show that there is no way of assigning truth values to 'p' and 'q' with the result that the premises will all be true and the conclusion false. Hence, the argument is *valid*.

The general procedure outlined in examples 3 and 4 is used for all arguments when validity is determined by the short truth-table method.

4:6.2 Some Examples In this section we shall determine the validity of several more complex arguments by using the short truth-table method.

PROBLEM 7

Determine the validity of the following argument form:

$p \supset q$

$q \supset r$

$\therefore p \supset r$

Step 1: Rewrite the argument as a conditional statement:

$$((p \supset q) \cdot (q \supset r)) \supset (p \supset r)$$

Step 2: Assign truth values to the variables of the conclusion of the argument (the consequent of the conditional statement) in such a way as to make the conclusion *false.* Since the conclusion is a conditional statement and conditional statements are false only when the antecedent is true and the consequent is false, we must assign the values T to 'p' and F to 'r'. Our result is

$$((p \supset q) \cdot (q \supset r)) \supset (p \supset r)$$
$$ \text{TF F}$$

Step 3: Make the corresponding assignments to the variables in the premises of the argument. This gives us

$$((p \supset q) \cdot (q \supset r)) \supset (p \supset r)$$
$$\text{T} \text{F} \text{TF F}$$

Step 4: Try to make all the premises true. It does not matter which premise one begins with, so we shall begin with the premise '$p \supset q$'. Since '$p \supset q$' is a conditional statement with a true antecedent, we must assign the value T to the consequent 'q'. Were we to assign the value F to 'q', then '$p \supset q$' would be false. Making the appropriate assignment, we have

$$((p \supset q) \cdot (q \supset r)) \supset (p \supset r)$$
$$\text{TT T} \text{F} \text{TF F}$$

Now for the second premise. We had to assign 'q' the value T in the first premise; as a result we must also assign it the value T in the second premise. This gives us

$$((p \supset q) \cdot (q \supset r)) \supset (p \supset r)$$
$$\text{TT T} \text{T F} \text{TF F}$$

Notice that the assignment of the value T to 'q' in the second premise makes the second premise false. This is so since it is a conditional statement with a true antecedent and a false consequent. Our result then is

$$((p \supset q) \cdot (q \supset r)) \supset (p \supset r)$$
$$\text{T T T} \text{T F F} \text{T T F F}$$

This completes problem 7. *Since there is no way to make all the premises true and the conclusion false, the argument is valid.*

PROBLEM 8

Unless those doing research on recombinant DNA are extremely careful, a serious accident could occur. A serious accident will occur, however, if, and only if, others working in the lab are careless. Since those working in the lab are not careless, or they would not have been selected for the job, it follows that those doing DNA research are extremely careful and have the highest professional credentials. After all, those others working in the lab have been selected for the job and those doing DNA research have the highest credentials.

Step 1: Assign variables to the statements occurring in the argument. This we do as follows:

> p = Those doing research on recombinant DNA are extremely careful.
>
> q = Those doing research on recombinant DNA have the highest professional credentials.
>
> r = A serious accident could occur.
>
> s = Others working in the lab are careless.
>
> t = Those working in the lab have been selected for the job.

Step 2: Determine the logical form of the argument. We have an 'unless' statement to convert to standard conditional-statement form. Our conclusion is indicated by 'it follows that'. As a result, the form of the argument is

> $\sim p \supset r$
>
> $r \equiv s$
>
> $\sim s \lor \sim t$
>
> $t \cdot q$
>
> $\therefore p \cdot q$

Step 3: Rewrite the argument as its associated conditional statement:

$$((\sim p \supset r) \cdot (r \equiv s) \cdot (s \lor \sim t) \cdot (t \cdot q)) \supset (p \cdot q)$$

Step 4: Assign truth values to the variables in the conclusion in such a way as to make the conclusion false. This problem is more complex than earlier ones in that the conclusion, since it is a conjunction, can be false in *three* different ways. *We must, therefore, consider all three ways of making the conclusion false,* for each of them represents a way in which all the premises could be true and the conclusion false. The three ways in which the conclusion could be false are that one conjunct is false, or the other is false, or both are false. These three ways are given below.

$$((\sim p \supset r) \cdot (r \equiv s) \cdot (\sim s \lor \sim t) \cdot (t \cdot q)) \supset (p \cdot q)$$

$$\text{T F F}$$
$$\text{F F T}$$
$$\text{F F F}$$

Step 5: Make the corresponding assignments to the premises of the argument. Here we shall be working three lines as opposed to one, but the procedure followed in each line is the same as that discussed in earlier problems.

$$((\sim p \supset r) \cdot (r \equiv s) \cdot (\sim s \vee \sim t) \cdot (t \cdot q)) \supset (p \cdot q)$$

F T	F T FF
T F	T F FT
T F	F F FF

Notice that, in the first and third lines, the last premise must have F assigned to 'q'. As a result, we need no longer consider these lines, for there is no way to make '$t \cdot q$' true in them and, hence, there is no way to make all the premises true and the conclusion false in these lines. We will therefore be concerned only with the second line for the remainder of this problem.

Step 6: Try to make all the premises true. Let's begin with the first premise, which is a conditional statement with a true antecedent. To make '$\sim p \supset r$' true, we must assign the value T to 'r'. This gives us

$$((\sim p \supset r) \cdot (r \equiv s) \cdot (\sim s \vee \sim t) \cdot (t \cdot q)) \supset (p \cdot q)$$
T T T   T   FFT

Having assigned T to 'r' in the first premise, we must also assign T to 'r' in the second premise. Since the second premise is an equivalency, it will take the value T only when both parts have the same truth value. Since we are going to assign T to 'r', we must also assign T to 's'. Our result is

$$((\sim p \supset r) \cdot (r \equiv s) \cdot (\sim s \vee \sim t) \cdot (t \cdot q)) \supset (p \cdot q)$$
TFT T   TT T   T   FFT

Having assigned T to 's' in the second premise, we must also assign T to 's' in the third premise, which gives us

$$((\sim p \supset r) \cdot (r \equiv s) \cdot (\sim s \vee \sim t) \cdot (t \cdot q)) \supset (p \cdot q)$$
TFT T   TTT   FT   T   FFT

The assignment of T to 's' in the disjunctive third premise makes the left disjunct '$\sim s$' false; hence, to make the third premise true we must assign the value F to 't', thereby making the right disjunct '$\sim t$' true. Our result is

$$((\sim p \supset r) \cdot (r \equiv s) \cdot (\sim s \vee \sim t) \cdot (t \cdot q)) \supset (p \cdot q)$$
TFT T   TT T   FTT TF   T   FFT

Having assigned F to 't' in the third premise, we must also assign F to 't' in the last premise. This gives us

$$((\sim p \supset r) \cdot (r \equiv s) \cdot (\sim s \vee \sim t) \cdot (t \cdot q)) \supset (p \cdot q)$$
TFT T   TT T   FTT TF   F T   FFT

Note, however, that the assignment of F to 't' in the last premise makes that premise *false*. Our result, then, is that there is no way to make all the premises true and the conclusion false, so the argument is valid.

Once again the simplicity of the short truth-table method is apparent in this problem. Instead of constructing thirty-two lines for the five variables, we had to deal with only one line.

EXERCISE 4-9

1. Explain the short truth-table method. How does it enable one to show that an argument is valid or invalid?

2. Determine the validity of the arguments in problem 4 of Exercise 4-8 by using the short truth-table method.

3. Determine the validity of the argument forms in problem 5 of Exercise 4-8 by using the short truth-table method.

4. Determine the validity of the following argument forms by using the short truth-table method.

a. $p \equiv q$
   $r \supset (q \cdot p)$
   $\sim q$
   $\therefore \sim r$

b. $p \equiv q$
   $r \supset (q \cdot p)$
   $\sim r$
   $\therefore \sim p$

c. $p \supset (q \vee r)$
   $\sim r \supset (s \cdot p)$
   $\sim s$
   $\therefore (p \supset q) \vee r$

d. $r \supset \sim(\sim p \cdot \sim q)$
   $\sim r \vee s$
   $\sim s$
   $\therefore p \vee q$

e. $\sim(\sim t \supset \sim r)$
   $p \supset (q \vee \sim r)$
   $(q \vee s) \equiv t$
   $\therefore \sim p$

f. $p \supset ((q \cdot r) \vee s)$
   $s \supset \sim(\sim q \vee \sim r)$
   $\sim(\sim s \cdot \sim r)$
   $\therefore p$

g. $(p \cdot q) \vee (\sim r \cdot s)$
   $\sim(\sim p \vee \sim q)$
   $s \supset (\sim(\sim r \cdot q))$
   $\therefore r \vee \sim q$

h. $\sim(p \supset (q \vee \sim r))$
   $(q \cdot r) \vee \sim(s \cdot p)$
   $(p \supset r) \equiv (q \supset \sim s)$
   $\therefore \sim r \vee s$

i. $\sim(p \vee \sim q)$
   $q \cdot \sim r$
   $q \supset p$
   $\therefore r \equiv p$

j. $(t \cdot q) \supset (r \vee s)$
   $(r \supset t) \equiv \sim(s \supset q)$
   $\therefore t \supset s$

STUDENT STUDY GUIDE

Chapter Summary

1. **Truth-functional statements** are statements whose truth values are a function of the truth values of their component statements. The logical connectives 'not',

'and', 'or', 'if-then', and 'if, and only if' are all **truth-functional connectives.** (section 4:1.1)

2. **A truth table** for a compound-statement form is a list of all the possible combinations of truth values that the statements which replace the variables might have, along with an assignment of a truth value to the compound-statement form. This assignment results from the particular assignment of truth values to the statements which replace the variables. (section 4:1.1)

3. A statement of the form '$\sim p$' is opposite in truth value to the statement of the form 'p'. (section 4:1.2)

4. A statement of the form '$p \cdot q$' is true when, and only when, both 'p' is true and 'q' is true. Such statements are **conjunctions,** the statement which replaces 'p' is the **left conjunct,** and the statement which replaces 'p' is the **right conjunct.** (section 4:1.3).

5. A statement of the form '$p \vee q$' is false when, and only when, both 'p' is false and 'q' is false. Such statements are **disjunctions,** the statement which replaces 'p' is the **left disjunct,** and the statement which replaces 'q' is the **right disjunct.** (section 4:1.4)

6. A statement of the form '$p \supset q$' is false when, and only when, 'p' is true and 'q' is false. Such statements are **conditional statements,** the statement which replaces 'p' is the **antecedent,** and the statement which replaces 'q' is the **consequent.** (section 4:1.5)

7. The relationship between the antecedent and the consequent of a conditional statement expressed by using '$\supset$' is called **material implication.** In material implication, the only relationship which is said to hold between the antecedent and the consequent is that which depends on the truth value of the component statements. In particular, to say that a statement of the form '$p \supset q$' is true is the same as saying that it is not the case that both 'p' is true and 'q' is false. (section 4:1.5)

8. A statement of the form '$p \equiv q$' is true when, and only when, 'p' and 'q' have the same truth value. Such statements are often referred to as **biconditionals,** and they express the **material equivalency** of 'p' and 'q'. In contrast to material equivalency, two statement forms are **logically equivalent** if they have the same truth value regardless of which statements uniformly replace the variables occurring in them. (section 4:1.6)

9. Word order and punctuation are used in English to indicate the **main connective** in compound statements containing more than one logical connective. In logical notation, parentheses are used to group statements and to avoid ambiguity by clearly indicating the main connective. (section 4:2.1)

10. To determine the truth value of a truth-functional compound statement, we identify the main connective, determine the truth values of the component statements, and then use the rule for the connective (section 4:2.2)

11. The number of lines in a truth table for a statement form depends on the number of variables occurring in the statement form. In particular, there are 2^n lines, where 'n' represents the number of variables. (section 4:4.1)

12. A statement form which sometimes takes the value true and sometimes takes

the value false, depending upon the assignment of truth values to its variables, is a **contingent statement.** (section 4:4.3)

13. A statement form which takes the value true for all possible assignments of truth value to its variables is a **tautology.** (section 4:4.3)

14. A statement form which takes the value false for all possible assignments of truth values to its variables is a **contradiction.** (section 4:4.3)

15. Two statement forms are logically equivalent if, and only if, the statement of their material equivalency is a tautology. (section 4:4.4)

16. For every deductive argument there is an associated conditional statement such that the antecedent is a conjunction of the premises of the argument and the consequent is the conclusion of the argument. In the case of a valid argument, the associated conditional statement is a tautology. As a result, one can use truth tables to determine the validity of an argument by first writing the conditional statement associated with the argument and then determining whether this statement is a tautology. (section 4:4.5)

17. To determine the validity of an argument by using the **short truth-table method,** we attempt to construct a line of the truth table in which all the premises are true and the conclusion false. To do this, we assign values to the variables in such a way as to make the conclusion false. If can then assign truth values to the variables in such a way as to make all the premises true, then the argument is invalid; if we cannot do this, then the argument is valid. (section 4:6.1)

Key Terms

Truth-Functional Statement	Material Equivalency
Truth-Functional Connective	Biconditional
Truth Table	Logically Equivalent Statements
Conjunction	Main Connective
Disjunction	Contingent Statement
Conditional Statement	Tautology
Material Implication	Contradiction

Self-Test/Exercises

1. Symbolize each of the following compound statements, using the symbols 'S', 'T', and 'C' as constants. Put an asterisk over the main connective in each statement. (section 4:2.2)
   a. If I go sailing or play tennis, then I will not go to the concent.
   b. If I go sailing, then I will both play tennis and go to the concert.
   c. If I go sailing, then either I will play tennis or go to the concert.
   d. If I go sailing, then if I play tennis then I will not go to the concert.
   e. If it's the case that if we go sailing then we won't go to the concert, then I'll play tennis.

2. Determine the truth values of the compound statements in problem 2 given that

'I will go sailing' and 'I will play tennis' are true and 'I will go to the concert' is false. (section 4:3.2)

3. Determine the truth values of the following compound statements assuming that 'A', 'B', and 'C' are true and 'X', 'Y', and 'Z' are false. Place an asterisk over the main connective in each statement. (section 4:3.2)
   a. $((A \lor \sim B) \cdot (X \cdot \sim C)) \supset ((X \lor \sim B) \lor (\sim A \cdot C))$
   b. $(\sim(A \lor \sim Z) \cdot ((B \cdot C) \lor Y)) \supset \sim((\sim Z \cdot \sim A) \supset \sim(B \lor C))$
   c. $(((A \cdot \sim X) \lor \sim(B \lor \sim Z)) \cdot ((\sim A \supset C) \cdot (\sim Y \lor B))) \supset (A \cdot \sim C)$

4. Using truth tables, determine whether the following statement forms are contingent, tautologous, or contradictory. (section 4:4.3)
   a. $((\sim p \lor q) \cdot \sim q) \supset \sim p$
   b. $\sim(p \cdot q) \equiv (\sim p \lor \sim q)$
   c. $((p \supset q) \cdot q) \supset p$
   d. $((\sim p \cdot q) \lor (p \cdot q)) \equiv p$
   e. $((p \supset q) \cdot (q \supset r)) \supset (r \supset q)$

5. Determine the validity of the following argument forms by constructing a truth table for the conditional statement associated with each argument. (section 4:5)

   a. $p \supset q$
   $r \supset s$
   $p \lor r$
   $\therefore p \lor s$
   d. $p \lor (q \cdot r)$
   $\therefore (p \lor q) \cdot (p \lor r)$

   b. $p \supset q$
   $r \supset \sim q$
   $\therefore p \supset \sim r$
   e. $p \cdot (q \lor r)$
   $\sim q$
   $\therefore p \cdot r$

   c. $p \lor q$
   $\sim p \cdot \sim r$
   $q \supset (r \lor s)$
   $\therefore s$

6. Determine the validity of the argument forms in problem 6 by using the short truth-table method. (section 4:6)

CHAPTER 5

STATEMENT

LOGIC

In Chapter 4 we developed two methods for determining the validity of argument forms: long truth tables and short truth tables. The latter method was developed, in part, because of the very long truth tables which must be constructed for argument forms with many variables. One of the most important features of these methods is that they can be used to show the validity or invalidity of any argument composed of statements whose form can be expressed by using statement variables and the five logical connectives. Moreover, each of the methods is purely mechanical, so that within a finite number of steps we are able to answer the question, "Is this a valid argument (form)?" for any such argument. These methods are said to provide us with a **decision procedure,** a step-by-step procedure for deciding, in each and every case, whether such an argument is valid or invalid.

There is another, related, approach to demonstrating that an argument form is valid, one which does not rely on an examination of all the possible ways in which all the premises might be true and the conclusion false. Although it was not specifically mentioned at the time, our discussion of conditional arguments in Chapter 3 was a small part of this other approach.

Recall, from our discussion of complex arguments, that any argument whose conclusion can be derived from the set of premises by repeated applications of affirming the antecedent (AA) and/or denying the consequent (DC) is a valid argument. In effect, what we did in the case of complex arguments was to set up a "chain" which tied the premises to the conclusion by means of two or more instances of valid argument forms. The essential feature of this procedure is that, in the case of a valid argument, if the premises are all true then the conclusion must be true as well. As a result, any intermediate "conclusions" derived by using AA or DC are true if the premises are true. If we use an intermediate "conclusion" as a premise in an additional instance of AA or DC, and if the other premise in this new instance is true, then the "second conclusion" is also true. We simply carried on this procedure until we reached the conclusion of the complex argument with which we began.

The only shortcoming of our discussion of complex arguments is that the procedure we developed there can be used only in the case of arguments whose premises are composed of statements having the form of conditional statements, since the only instances of valid argument forms we had available to us were AA and DC. Since that time we have introduced additional logical connectives, and we have seen that there are valid argument forms whose premises and conclusions are not limited in form to conditional statements.

The issue before us is whether the valid arguments which contain the additional logical connectives introduced in the preceding chapter can be shown to be valid in the same way that we showed the validity of some of the complex arguments in Chapter 3; in this chapter we shall find that this can be done. Our procedure will be to introduce additional basic logical forms whose validity can be established by the methods of Chapter 4. We shall then use these logical forms, in the way we used AA and DC in Chapter 3, to set up "chains" of valid argument forms leading from the premises of an argument to the conclusion.

Although we shall not prove it in this text, a small mumber of argument forms, along with some logical equivalencies, can be used to show the validity of any valid argument whose validity depends on the roles of the logical connectives contained in it. A system composed of a limited number of logical forms and equivalencies which is used to derive the conclusion of an argument from its premises in a step-by-step manner is called a system of **natural deduction.** Such systems are called 'natural' because the manner in which one ultimately derives the conclusion of the argument follows natural or ordinary patterns of reasoning.

Before we begin the development of these basic valid argument forms, an important remark is in order: Whereas it is true that we have a decision procedure for the kinds of arguments we have been discussing (namely, the truth-table method), the system of natural deduction we shall develop is *not* a decision procedure. It is not a decision procedure because it does not provide us with a method of *determining,* in a finite number of steps, whether an argument is valid or invalid. The only claim we are making about our system is that, for each valid argument expressible in it, there is a *way of showing* that the argument is valid by showing that its conclusion can be derived from its premises by using instances of basic argument forms and some logical equivalencies. There is no mechanical procedure within the system, however, for determining how this is to be done.

5:1   RULES OF INFERENCE

In this section we shall discuss six new valid argument forms. These argument forms, along with affirming the antecedent and denying the consequent, correspond to **rules of inference.** These rules will later be used in constructing proofs to show the validity of arguments.

The procedure we will follow in developing the rules of inference is built on a relationship discussed in the preceding chapter. There, recall, we saw that every argument can be rewritten as a conditional statement whose antecedent is the conjunction of the premises and whose consequent is the conclusion. We then saw that if, and only if, the argument is valid, the associated conditional statement is true for every possible assignment of truth values to the variables occurring in the argument; that is, it is a tautology.

What we shall do in this section is rewrite some argument forms in terms of their associated conditional statements, show that the argument forms are valid, and then take the conditional statements as the basis of our rules of inference.

5:1.1 Affirming the Antecedent   We already know that the following argument form is valid:

$p \supset q$

p

$\therefore q$

We showed the validity of this form by showing that its associated conditional statement '$((p \supset q) \cdot p) \supset q$' takes the value T for every assignment of truth values to the variables. We can, therefore, rewrite the conditional-statement equivalent of the argument form affirming the antecedent as a rule of inference:[1]

AFFIRMING THE ANTECEDENT (AA)

From the two statements of the forms '$p \supset q$' and 'p', one can infer 'q'.

5:1.2 Denying the Consequent   As in the case of affirming the antecedent, we can rewrite the conditional-statement equivalent of denying the consequent, '$((p \supset q) \cdot \sim q) \supset \sim p$', as a rule of inference:

DENYING THE CONSEQUENT (DC)

From two statements of the forms '$p \supset q$' and '$\sim q$', one can infer '$\sim p$'.

5:1.3 Disjunctive Syllogism   Consider the following argument:

ARGUMENT 1

The governor will either use the surplus funds to provide additional support to higher education or he will use it to provide tax relief for the elderly. But, since he will not use it for higher education, he will provide tax relief for the elderly.

Argument 1 is an instance of reasoning which runs along the following lines: "If one or the other of two things is the case, and if the first is not the case, then the second must be." We can represent this in argument form by letting 'p' represent the place occupied by 'The governor will use the surplus funds to provide additional support to higher education' and 'q' represent the

---

[1] In the rules which follow, it is understood that whenever a variable is replaced by a statement, every other occurrence of that variable will be replaced by the same statement.

place occupied by 'The governor will use the additional funds to provide tax relief for the elderly'. We see, then, that argument 1 has the following form:

FORM OF ARGUMENT 1

$p \lor q$

$\sim p$

$\therefore q$

If we rewrote argument 1 as its associated conditional statement and constructed a truth table, we could easily show that the form is valid. We shall, therefore, use the associated conditional statement of that form as the basis of another rule of inference:

DISJUNCTIVE SYLLOGISM (DS)

From two statements of the forms '$p \lor q$' and '$\sim p$', one can infer 'q'.

Consider now a slightly different argument:

ARGUMENT 2

The new intramural facilities will be built because the Board said that either those facilities would be built or a new biology building would be built. It was just announced that there will be no new biology building.

Letting 'p' represent the place occupied by 'New intramural facilities will be built' and letting 'q' represent the place occupied by 'A new biology building will be built', we have the following:

FORM OF ARGUMENT 2

$p \lor q$

$\sim q$

$\therefore p$

Two things should now be noted: First, argument 2 clearly exhibits the same kind of reasoning as we discussed for argument 1, and second, were we to construct a truth table for the form of argument 2, we would find that it is a valid form. Nonetheless, given our statement of the rule of inference disjunctive syllogism, the inference to 'p' from the premises '$p \lor q$' and '$\sim q$' *cannot be justified by appealing to the rule disjunctive syllogism.*

Perhaps the best way to see this is to characterize the rule DS in a slightly different manner, in much the same way as we gave a structural description of the argument forms AA and DC in Chapter 2.

STRUCTURE OF DS

From a disjunction and the negation of the *left* disjunct, one can infer the *right* disjunct.

A look at the structure of argument 2, on the other hand, shows that from a disjunction and the negation of the *right* disjunct we have inferred the *left* disjunct.

We have two options available to us at this point. The first, and perhaps most obvious, is to expand our rule of inference DS so as to include the kind of case exhibited in argument 2. The second option is to introduce an additional rule which would enable us to convert the structure of argument 2 so that the present statement of DS is applicable. The first option presents no difficulties, since we can clearly demonstrate the validity of argument 2 and, hence, adopt its conditional-statement equivalent as a rule of inference. Nonetheless, we shall choose the second option, since the rule of inference which is needed to convert the structure of argument 2, so that we can use DS, is useful in other contexts as well. For the same reason, we shall postpone the introduction of the rule until a later section. You might consider, however, what kind of rule would be necessary to justify the inference in argument 2 by using, in part, DS.

5:1.4 Simplification   Consider the following argument:

ARGUMENT 3

Since the inflation rate continues to go up and social security taxes are rising, it follows that the inflation rate continues to go up.

The line of reasoning here is that since both of two things are the case, the first must be the case. Were we to assign variables to the above argument, rewrite it in terms of its associated conditional statement, and test its validity by the truth-table method, we would find that argument 3 is an instance of a valid argument form. Using the conditional-statement equivalent of the form of argument 3 as the basis for a rule of inference, we get the following:

SIMPLIFICATION (Simp)

From a statement of the form '$p \cdot q$' one can infer 'p'.

It probably will have occurred to you that, given the reasonableness of the line of reasoning in argument 3, one could also have inferred that social security taxes are rising and, indeed, the resultant argument can be shown to be valid. The situation here, however, is like the situation we encountered in discussing DS. A structural description of Simp is that from a conjunction one can infer the *left* conjunct; to take the statement that social security taxes are rising as the conclusion would be to infer the *right* conjunct from the premise.

As in the case of DS, we can handle this situation by expanding Simp to include both conjuncts or we can introduce an additional rule of inference. We shall adopt the procedure of introducing a new rule of inference, but again shall postpone the discussion of this rule.

5:1.5 Conjunction   Consider the following argument:

ARGUMENT 4

Since Martha has decided to major in chemistry, it must be the case that she has decided to major in chemistry and to try to get a job with Dow, since she has already decided to get a job with Dow.

The line of reasoning which justifies the conclusion of this argument is simply this: Given that each of two things is the case, they both are the case. We can readily display this by assigning 'p' to the place occupied by 'Martha has decided to major in chemistry' and 'q' to the place occupied by 'Martha has decided to get a job with Dow'.

If we were to construct a truth table for the conditional statement associated with argument 4, we would find that the form is valid, so we can use the conditional statement as the basis for the following rule of inference:

CONJUNCTION (Conj)

From statements of the forms 'p' and 'q', one can infer a statement of the form '$p \cdot q$'.

5:1.6 Hypothetical Syllogism

We encountered the argument form which gives rise to this rule of inference in our discussion of conditional proofs in Chapter 3. Argument 5, below, is another instance of such an argument.

ARGUMENT 5

If Louise receives a Danforth Fellowship, then she will enroll at Menosa State University. This is so because if she receives the fellowship she will have enough money to go to graduate school, and she said last week that if she had enough money for graduate school, she would go to Menosa State.

Letting 'p' represent the place occupied by 'Louise receives a Danforth Fellowship', 'q' represent the place occupied by 'Louise has enough money for graduate school', and 'r' represent the place occupied by 'Louise will enroll at Menosa State', we get the following as the form of argument 5:

FORM OF ARGUMENT 5

$p \supset q$

$q \supset r$

$\therefore p \supset r$

The conditional statement associated with argument 5, '$((p \supset q) \cdot (q \supset p)) \supset (p \supset r)$' can be shown to be valid and, hence, is the basis for the following rule of inference:

HYPOTHETICAL SYLLOGISM (HS)

From two statements of the forms '$p \supset q$' and '$q \supset r$', one can infer a statement of the form '$p \supset r$'.

5:1.7 Constructive Dilemma

Consider the following argument:

ARGUMENT 6

Tom is responsible for the accident only if he was negligent in not having the brakes inspected. But if the service station didn't tell him about the worn brake linings, then they were responsible. Hence, either Tom was negligent or the service station was responsible, for either Tom was responsible or he wasn't told about the brake linings.

Letting 'p' represent the place occupied by 'Tom is responsible for the accident', 'q' represent the place occupied by 'Tom was negligent in not having the brakes inspected', 'r' represent the place occupied by 'The service station didn't tell him about the worn brake linings', and 's' represent the place occupied by 'The service station was responsible', we have the following as the form of argument 6:

FORM OF ARGUMENT 6

$p \supset q$

$r \supset s$

$p \lor r$

$\therefore q \lor s$

The conditional statement associated with the argument form of which argument 6 is an instance serves as the basis for the following rule of inference:

CONSTRUCTIVE DILEMMA (CD)

From statements of the form '$p \supset q$', the form '$r \supset s$', and the form '$p \lor r$', respectively, one can infer a statement of the form '$q \lor s$'.

Another variation of the rule of inference CD is exhibited in the following argument:

ARGUMENT 7

If Tom stays home tonight he will study for the physics midterm, and if he does not stay home he will go see the latest science-fiction movie. Hence, he will either study for the midterm or go see the latest science-fiction movie.

There is, of course, a missing premise to this argument, namely, that Tom will either stay home or not stay home. With the addition of this premise, we see that argument 7 has the following form:

FORM OF ARGUMENT 7

$p \supset q$

$\sim p \supset r$

$p \lor \sim p$

$\therefore q \lor r$

Argument 7, then, is also an instance of CD. If you don't see why this is so, consider giving a structural description of CD, and then see how the form of argument 7 fits that description.

5:1.8 Addition   The final rule of inference to be introduced in this section is exhibited in the following argument:

ARGUMENT 8

Donna is going to be a physicist or a ballerina since she is going to be a physicist.

Letting '*p*' represent the place occupied by 'Donna is going to be a physicist' and '*q*' represent the place occupied by 'Donna is going to be a ballerina', we have:

FORM OF ARGUMENT 8

p

$\therefore p \lor q$

The line of reasoning here is that if something is the case, then it or something else is also the case. We can easily show, using truth tables, that the form of argument 8 is valid; it gives rise, therefore, to the following rule of inference:

ADDITION (Add)

From a statement of the form '*p*', one can infer a statement of the form '*p* $\lor$ *q*'.

It may seem to you now that Add is a pretty trivial rule of inference. However, when we begin to construct some proofs using the rules of inference, you will see that Add is a very useful rule, for it is the only one which enables us to introduce a new variable into our proofs.

5:1.9 Applying the Rules of Inference Each of the rules of inference we have so far introduced is given in terms of statement variables. As a result, the rules are applicable to any argument which has the structure of the rules, no matter how complex the statements composing the argument may be. For example, the following argument can be justified as valid by the rule AA, even though the antecedent of the conditional premise and the nonconditional premise are themselves compound statements:

EXAMPLE 1

$(S \lor T) \supset R$

$(S \lor T)$

$\therefore R$

The above form fits the structure of AA; the compound statement '*S* $\lor$ *T*' occupies the place indicated by '*p*' in our rule, and the simple statement '*R*' occupies the place indicated by '*q*'.

Similarly, the following can be justified as valid by appealing to the rule Simp:

EXAMPLE 2

$(S \lor (T \cdot V)) \cdot R$

$\therefore S \lor (T \cdot V)$

Simp tells us that, given a *conjunction,* we can infer the left conjunct. '$(S \vee (T \cdot V)) \cdot R'$ is a conjunction whose left conjunct is '$S \vee (T \cdot V)'$, so this is an acceptable application of the rule.

Consider now the following argument:

EXAMPLE 3

$(S \cdot T) \supset R$

$\therefore S$

This is *not* an inference which can be justified by appealing to Simp. In this case 'S' has been inferred wrongly, presumably from the conjunction '$S \cdot T'$. However, the form of the original statement is *not* that of a conjunction but rather that of a *conditonal statement;* Simp is applicable only in the case of conjunction.

The following argument is one which can be justified as valid by the rule CD:

EXAMPLE 4

$(R \vee S) \supset T$

$(P \cdot Q) \supset V$

$(R \vee S) \vee (P \cdot Q)$

$\therefore T \vee V$

This is a correct use of CD since we have conditional statements as the first two premises, the disjunction of the antecedents of the two conditional statements as the third premise, and the disjunction of the two consequents as our conclusion.

A general principle can be gleaned from these few examples concerning the applicability of the eight inference rules so far introduced: *The eight rules must be applied to a complete statement, and not to a statement which is itself part of a statement.* In example 1, for instance, our use of AA was justified since we applied it to the complete statement '$(S \vee T) \supset R'$, first affirming the antecedent as a nonconditional premise and then inferring the consequent as conclusion. In example 2, we applied Simp to the complete statement '$(S \vee (T \cdot V)) \cdot R'$, inferring the left conjunct from it. In example 3, on the other hand, we applied Simp to just the antecedent of '$(S \cdot T) \supset R'$; as a result, since we applied the rule to only part of the statement, the rule was used incorrectly.

EXERCISE 5-1

1. What is a decision procedure? Explain why the method of constructing truth tables is a decision procedure.

2. What is a system of natural deduction?

3. Why doesn't a system of natural deduction provide a decision procedure for the arguments of statement logic?

4. State the rule of inference AA. Give an example of a conclusion inferred from premises in accordance with this rule.

5. State the rule of inference DC. Give an example of a conclusion inferred from premises in accordance with this rule.

6. State the rule of inference DS. Give an example of a conclusion inferred from premises in accordance with this rule.

7. State the rule of inference Simp. Use truth tables to show that the conditional statement associated with this rule is a tautology. Give an example of a conclusion inferred from premises in accordance with this rule.

8. State the rule of inference Conj. Use truth tables to show that the conditional statement associated with this rule is a tautology. Give an example of a conclusion inferred from premises in accordance with this rule.

9. State the rule of inference HS. Use truth tables to show that the conditional statement associated with this rule is a tautology. Give an example of a conclusion inferred from premises in accordance with this rule.

10. State the rule of inference CD. Give an example of a conclusion inferred from premises in accordance with this rule.

11. State the rule of inference Add. Use truth tables to show that the conditional statement associated with this rule is a tautology. Give an example of a conclusion inferred from premises in accordance with this rule.

12. Explain the general principle which must be followed in applying the eight rules of inference discussed in the last section.

EXERCISE 5-2

1. Indicate which of the following symbolized arguments are instances of the eight rules of inference. If a rule applies, give its name; if no rule applies, write "none."

a. $R \supset S$
R
$\therefore S$

b. $(L \cdot M) \supset S$
$\sim S$
$\therefore \sim(L \cdot M)$

c. $(R \supset S) \supset T$
R
$\therefore T$

d. $(A \lor B) \supset C$
$C \supset (D \cdot E)$
$\therefore (D \cdot E) \supset (A \lor B)$

e. $P \lor (Q \lor R)$
$\sim(Q \lor R)$
$\therefore P$

f. $L \supset M$
$R \supset T$
$R \lor L$
$\therefore T \lor M$

g. $(A \lor B) \cdot C$
$\therefore B \cdot C$

h. $(R \supset S) \supset (T \supset V)$
$\sim(T \supset V)$
$\therefore \sim(R \supset S)$

i. $P \cdot Q$
$R \lor S$
$\therefore (P \cdot Q) \cdot (R \lor S)$

j. $R \supset T$
$L \supset M$
$T \lor M$
$\therefore R \lor L$

k. $(A \cdot B) \supset D$
$\sim(A \cdot B)$
$\therefore \sim D$

l. $P \lor \sim Q$
Q
$\therefore P$

m. $(A \lor C) \supset B$
$\sim B$
$\therefore \sim A \lor C$

n. $P \cdot Q$
$\therefore (P \cdot Q) \lor R$

o. $R \lor S$
$\therefore S$

2. Which conclusion follows from a set of premises having each of the following forms? Which rule justifies each inference?

a. $p \supset q$
   $r \supset s$
   $p \lor r$

b. $(p \lor q) \lor r$
   $\sim(p \lor q)$

c. $(p \cdot q) \supset (r \lor s)$
   $\sim(r \lor s)$

d. $(p \lor q) \cdot \sim(r \cdot q)$

e. $(\sim r \cdot s) \supset (p \lor \sim q)$
   $\sim r \cdot s$

f. $(\sim p \lor q) \supset (r \lor s)$
   $(r \lor s) \supset \sim(t \supset s)$

g. $\sim(p \supset q)$
   $r \supset s$

h. $p \supset (r \cdot \sim s)$
   $\sim p \supset (r \lor \sim q)$
   $p \lor \sim p$

i. $p \lor (\sim q \supset \sim r)$
   $\sim p$

j. $(p \supset \sim q) \supset (r \supset \sim q)$
   $\sim(r \supset \sim q)$

5:2 PROOFS USING THE RULES OF INFERENCE

We introduced—rather informally—the idea of a proof in our discussion of complex arguments and conditional and indirect proofs in Chapter 3. In this section we shall be more explicit as to what constitutes a proof, and discuss one way of writing down proofs. We shall take the following as our definition of 'proof':

DEFINITION: **Proof**

*A **proof** is a sequence of statements in which the premises occur first and the conclusion occurs as the last line, and in which every statement is either a premise or is inferred from previous statements in the sequence by one of the given rules of inference.*

The general structure of any proof is, then, the following:

P_1
P_2 } Premises
. . .
P_n

S_1
S_2 } Statements derived from the premises using the rules of infer-
. . .   ence
S_n

$\therefore C$ Conclusion

We shall additionally stipulate that a *justification* must be given for every line of a proof. The justification is simply an explanation of how each line of the proof was derived, and it is written next to the line. Example 5 is a proof of the validity of the following argument form, along with the justifications:

$p \lor (q \cdot r)$

$\sim p$

$\therefore q$

EXAMPLE 5

(1) $p \lor (q \cdot r)$ Premise

(2) $\sim p$ Premise

(3) $q \cdot r$ (1), (2), DS

$\therefore$ (4) q (3), Simp

Notice in example 5 that the two premises were written first, and the conclusion is the last line. Line (3), '$q \cdot r$', corresponds to the statements S in the general structure for proofs presented above. In the justification column there is an entry for each line of the proof, indicating how we derived that line. The justification for line (3), '(1), (2), DS', is to be read as follows: Line (3) was derived from lines (1) and (2) by the rule of inference disjunctive syllogism. Similarly, the justification for line 4 is to be read: Line (4) was derived from line (3) by the rule of inference simplification.

One additional point must be made concerning proofs: In a proof, *only one rule of inference can be used in each step*. As a result, the following "proof" is erroneous.

EXAMPLE 6

(1) $p \supset (q \cdot r)$ Premise

(2) p Premise

$\therefore$ (3) q (1), (2), AA, Simp (*error*)

Line (3) of example 6 violates the requirement that just one rule of inference be used in each step of the proof, for there 'q' was derived from the premises by using the rules AA *and* Simp. We can, of course, provide a proof of 'q' from '$p \supset (q \cdot r)$' and 'p' which does not violate this requirement; this is done as follows:

EXAMPLE 7

(1) $p \supset (q \cdot r)$ Premise

(2) p Premise

(3) $q \cdot r$ (1), (2), AA

$\therefore$ (4) q (3), Simp

5:2.1 Some Examples   In this section we shall look at some arguments, present proofs of their validity, and develop some rules of thumb for the construction of proofs.

ARGUMENT 9

If a national health-insurance plan is approved, then many private insurance companies will go out of business. Moreover, either a national insurance plan will be approved or many people will no longer be able to afford adequate medical care. Hence, since if many private companies go out of business, the insurance industry will become monopolistic, it follows that many will no longer be able to afford medical care; for the insurance industry will not be allowed to become monopolistic.

Step 1: Assign variables to the statements occurring in the argument, and determine the logical form of the argument. To do this, we assign variables in the following way:

p = A national health-insurance plan is approved.

q = Many private insurance companies will go out of business.

r = People will be able to afford adequate medical care.

s = The insurance industry will become monopolistic.

Argument 9 can now be seen to have the following form:

$p \supset q$

$p \lor \sim r$

$q \supset s$

$\sim s$

$\therefore \sim r$

Step 2: Determine how the conclusion can be derived from the premises. We want to derive '$\sim r$', and the only premise in which this variable occurs is the second one. We ask, then, what rule of inference, if any, could be used to derive '$\sim r$' from the second premise; we note that DS would work if we had '$\sim p$'.

Step 3: We check the premises to see if '$\sim p$' has been given as a premise. Since it has not, we check to see if it can be derived from the premises we have been given. We find that the first premise '$p \supset q$' could be used to derive '$\sim p$' by DC if we had '$\sim q$'. (Also note that this is the only premise which we could use with our rules of inference to derive '$\sim p$'.)

Step 4: We see that '$\sim q$' has not been given as a premise and, hence, that we must derive it if we are to use the first premise to derive '$\sim p$'. Checking our set of premises, we see that we could derive '$\sim q$' from the third premise '$q \supset s$' and the rule DC if we had '$\sim s$'. We also see that '$\sim s$' has been given as a premise.

Step 5: We have now seen how we can derive the conclusion from the premises. We shall use DC with the third and fourth premises to derive '~q'. We shall then use '~q' with the first premise to derive '~p', which can then be used with DS and the second premise to derive '~r'.

Step 6: We begin the proof by writing down the premises of the argument, along with the justification 'Premise'.

(1) $p \supset q$	Premise
(2) $p \lor \sim r$	Premise
(3) $q \supset s$	Premise
(4) $\sim s$	Premise

Step 7: Now all we have to do is summarize, in proof form, the strategy we developed in step 5; the complete proof is as follows:

(1) $p \supset q$	Premise
(2) $p \lor \sim r$	Premise
(3) $q \supset s$	Premise
(4) $\sim s$	Premise
(5) $\sim q$	(3), (4), DC
(6) $\sim p$	(1), (5), DC
∴ (7) $\sim r$	(2), (6), DS

This proof of the validity of argument 9 is not the only one that we could have given. We might instead have started by using HS with premises (1) and (3). We could then have used DC to derive '~p', and then used DS to derive the conclusion. Either of these is a satisfactory proof of the validity of argument 9. In general, there is no *one* correct proof of the validity of an argument; any is correct so long as it follows the general structure of a proof and the rules of inference have been applied correctly in deriving the conclusion. Which proof one gives for a particular argument often depends on whether the argument has been approached backward, as in our first, detailed, proof of argument 9, or frontward, as in the outlined proof. It also depends on one's ability to pick out premises with which the rules of inference can be used; this is a developed ability that improves with practice.

ARGUMENT 10

If Cathy wins the tournament, then she will collect the prize money and pay off the debts she owes. Additionally, if she either collects the prize money or decides to sell her car to raise some cash, she will not have to worry about her debts anymore. Hence, since Cathy will either worry or find a way to get out of her debts, it follows that she will find a way out; for she will win the tournament and change her buying habits.

Step 1: Assign variables to the statements occurring in the argument, and determine the logical form of the argument. To do this, we assign variables in the following way:

p = Cathy wins the tournament.

q = Cathy collects the prize money.

r = Cathy pays off her debts.

s = Cathy decides to sell her car to raise some cash.

t = Cathy has to worry about her debts.

u = Cathy finds a way to get out of debt.

v = Cathy changes her buying habits.

Argument 11 then has the following form:

$p \supset (q \cdot r)$

$(q \lor s) \supset {\sim}t$

$t \lor u$

$p \cdot v$

$\therefore u$

Step 2: Determine how the conclusion can be derived from the premises. We want to derive 'u', and the only premise in which this variable occurs is the third one. We ask, then, what rule of inference could be used to derive 'u' from the third premise. We see that DS would work if we had '${\sim}t$'.

Step 3: We check the premises to see if we have '${\sim}t$'. Since we don't, we check to see if it can be derived from the premises that we do have. The only premise from which we could derive '${\sim}t$' is the second premise '$(q \lor s) \supset {\sim}t$', and for that we need '$q \lor s$' to use with AA.

Step 4: Since we do not have '$q \lor s$', we once again have to try to derive what we need from the set of premises. At this point, a word concerning strategy is in order. If we want to derive a statement having the form of a disjunction, then two inference rules should immediately come to mind, CD and Add. This is not to say that these are the only rules which can be used to derive a disjunction (AA would work, for example, if the disjunction we wanted was the consequent of a conditional statement and we either had or could derive the antecedent of that conditional statement); but, as a rule of thumb, they are the obvious ones to consider. To derive a disjunction by using CD, we need two conditional statements, each of which has as its consequent one of the disjuncts of the disjunction we want to derive. However, the set of premises does *not* include a conditional statement with 'q' as consequent and one with 's' as consequent. As a result, we shall try to derive 'q ∨ s' by using Add.

Step 5: To derive 'q ∨ s' by Add, we must first derive 'q'. The only premise with which we could do this is the first, 'p ⊃ (q · r)'; with 'p' and the rule AA we could derive 'q · r', and then we could use Simp to get 'q'. Our task now is to derive 'p'.

Step 6: Once again checking our premises, we see that we can derive 'p' from the last premise 'p · v' by using Simp. This completes our strategy.

Step 7: The strategy developed in steps 2 to 6 is the following: We shall derive 'p' from the last premise by Simp, and use it with the first premise to derive 'q · r' by AA. We shall then use Simp on 'q · r' to derive 'q', and then derive 'q ∨ s' by Add. We shall then use 'q ∨ s' and the second premise with AA to derive '~t'. Finally, using '~t' and DS with the third premise 't ∨ u', we shall derive 'u'. (Notice that this procedure is merely a restatement of steps 2 to 6 in *reverse* order.)

Step 8: Now all we have to do is to summarize the procedure detailed in step 7. The proof follows:

(1) $p \supset (q \cdot r)$		Premise
(2) $(q \lor s) \supset {\sim}t$		Premise
(3) $t \lor u$		Premise
(4) $p \cdot v$		Premise
(5) p		(4), Simp
(6) $q \cdot r$		(1), (5), AA
(7) q		(6), Simp
(8) $q \lor s$		(7), Add
(9) ${\sim}t$		(2), (8), AA
∴ (10) u		(3), (9), DS

Although our eight rules of inference enable us to show the validity of a great many arguments, they are inadequate by themselves for showing the validity of all valid arguments which can be symbolized by using statement variables and the logical connectives. An argument which demonstrates this is the following:

ARGUMENT 11

The flight is going to arrive late, and the passengers are going to be bitter. But the flight will arrive late only if the flight controllers are on strike. Hence, we shouldn't go to the airport early, for if either the weather is bad or the flight controllers are on strike, we shouldn't go early.

After variables are assigned to the argument, we get the following as its form:

$p \cdot q$

$p \supset r$

$(t \lor r) \supset {\sim}s$

$\therefore {\sim}s$

Although this argument can be shown to be valid by the truth-table method, we cannot show its validity using the eight rules of inference (we need '$t \lor r$', and there is no way to derive this). One of our goals in this chapter is to develop a system of rules which will enable us to demonstrate the validity of those arguments which can be shown to be valid by truth tables; for this, we are going to have to add to the eight rules already introduced, and we shall do so in section 5:3.

In this section we have characterized *proofs* and have used the eight rules of inference introduced in section 5:1 to construct proofs of some valid arguments. We have also noted that more than one proof can be given for the validity of some arguments (argument 9 is one such case). As we constructed proofs for the arguments of this section, some points about the strategy for constructing proofs were also mentioned. They are worth emphasizing once again.

(1) It is often helpful to work backward from the conclusion of an argument, by seeing which premises contain the variables that occur in the conclusion and which rule of inference could be used to derive the conclusion. This process is continued to the point where the required statements are either given as premises in the argument or derivable from the premises by using the rules of inference.

(2) If the conclusion is a disjunction, one should check to see if CD or Add can be used. To use CD, we need two conditional statements, one of which has as its consequent one of the disjuncts of the conclusion, and the other of which has as its consequent the other disjunct of the conclusion. To use Add, we add a *right* disjunct to a statement which already occurs on one of the lines of the proof.

(3) To derive a statement from a compound statement, consider using either AA or DC if the compound statement is a conditional statement; Simp if the compound statement is a conjunction; and DS if the compound statement is a disjunction.

(4) If you encounter difficulty in seeing how the proof will go, apply as many rules of inference to the premises as you can. This will often indicate to you how some of the results can be combined to reach the desired conclusion. This process does not always result in the shortest possible proof; but if it results in a correct proof, you will have shown the validity of the argument in question.

EXERCISE 5-3

1. What is a proof?

2. What is a justification of a line of a proof?

3. Which two rules of inference should you consider when you are trying to derive a disjunctive statement form?

4. Which two rules of inference should you consider when you are trying to derive a simpler statement from a conditional statement?

5. Which rule of inference should you consider when you are trying to derive a simpler statement from a conjunctive statement form?

6. Which rule of inference should you consider when you are trying to derive a simpler statement from a disjunctive statement form?

EXERCISE 5-4

1. Provide a justification for each line in the following proofs.

a. (1) $p \lor q$ Premise
   (2) $q \supset r$ Premise
   (3) $\sim p$ Premise
   (4) q
   ∴ (5) r

b. (1) $(p \supset q) \cdot (r \supset s)$ Premise
   (2) p Premise
   (3) $p \supset q$
   (4) q
   ∴ (5) $q \lor r$

c. (1) $(t \cdot u) \lor (p \lor q)$ Premise
   (2) $(t \cdot u) \supset (r \lor s)$ Premise
   (3) $\sim(r \lor s)$ Premise
   (4) $\sim(t \cdot u)$
   ∴ (5) $p \lor q$

d. (1) $(p \supset q) \lor s$ Premise
   (2) $(p \supset q) \supset r$ Premise
   (3) $\sim r \cdot \sim t$ Premise
   (4) $s \supset (r \lor q)$ Premise
   (5) $\sim r$
   (6) $\sim(p \supset q)$
   (7) s
   (8) $r \lor q$
   ∴ (9) q

e. (1) $p \cdot q$ Premise
   (2) $(p \lor r) \supset (p \supset s)$ Premise
   (3) $p \supset t$ Premise
   (4) p
   (5) $p \lor r$
   (6) $p \supset s$
   (7) s
   ∴ (8) $p \cdot s$

f. (1) $((p \lor q) \cdot (r \lor s)) \supset ((p \cdot r) \supset (r \supset s))$ Premise
   (2) p Premise
   (3) $(s \lor q) \supset t$ Premise
   (4) r Premise
   (5) $p \lor q$
   (6) $r \lor s$
   (7) $(p \lor q) \cdot (r \lor s)$
   (8) $(p \cdot r) \supset (r \supset s)$
   (9) $p \cdot r$

(10) $r \supset s$
(11) s
(12) $s \lor q$
(13) t
∴ (14) $t \lor q$

g. (1) $r \supset q$ Premise
   (2) $(s \lor r) \supset (p \supset t)$ Premise
   (3) $\sim p \cdot s$ Premise
   (4) $r \lor s$ Premise
   (5) $q \supset p$ Premise
   (6) $\sim p$
   (7) $r \supset p$
   (8) $\sim r$
   (9) s
   (10) $s \lor r$
   (11) $p \supset t$
∴ (12) $r \supset t$

h. (1) $p \supset q$ Premise
   (2) $q \supset r$ Premise
   (3) $q \supset s$ Premise
   (4) $\sim s$ Premise
   (5) $q \lor p$ Premise
   (6) $\sim q$
   (7) p
   (8) q
   ∴ (9) r

i. (1) p Premise
   (2) $(p \lor q) \supset r$ Premise
   (3) $p \lor q$
   (4) r
   ∴ (5) $p \cdot r$

j. (1) $(t \supset (r \lor s)) \supset (u \cdot v)$ Premise
   (2) $p \supset q$ Premise
   (3) $(t \supset (r \lor s)) \lor p$ Premise
   (4) $\sim(u \cdot v)$ Premise
   (5) $(u \cdot v) \lor q$
   (6) q
   ∴ (7) $q \lor (\sim r \cdot \sim s)$

2. Using the eight rules of inference, construct proofs to show the validity of the following arguments.

a. $\sim C \supset (D \supset E)$
   $A \supset B$
   $\sim C$
   $C \lor (A \lor D)$
   ∴ $B \lor E$

b. $\sim A \supset (B \supset C)$
   $A \supset B$
   $C \supset D$
   $\sim B$
   ∴ $B \supset D$

c. $E \supset \sim D$
   E
   $D \lor C$
   ∴ C

d. $(R \lor C) \supset (P \supset (S \equiv T))$
   $P \cdot S$
   $(P \lor Q) \supset R$
   ∴ $S \equiv T$

e. $\sim P \supset (R \supset \sim Q)$
   $P \supset \sim Q$
   $(\sim S \lor \sim R) \supset \sim\sim Q$
   $\sim S$
   ∴ $\sim R$

f. $(\sim A \lor \sim B) \supset \sim(C \supset D)$
   $\sim A$
   $(C \supset D) \lor (E \supset D)$
   $\sim D$
   ∴ $\sim E$

g. $\sim A \supset E$
   $A \supset \sim C$
   $\sim\sim C \cdot B$
   ∴ E

h. A
   ∴ $(((A \lor C) \lor (\sim B \cdot D)) \lor C) \lor (\sim B \supset C)$

i. $P \supset (R \cdot Q)$
   $P \cdot U$
   $S \lor T$
   $(R \lor V) \supset \sim S$
   ∴ T

j. $\sim\sim R$
   $((P \lor Q) \lor (\sim R \lor \sim S)) \cdot T$
   $\sim(P \lor Q)$
   ∴ $\sim S$

EXERCISE 5-5

Symbolize the following arguments using the indicated constants, and show that each argument is valid by constructing a proof.

a. Either if Sally is *elected* president then there will be significant *changes* made in student government or student *indifference* will continue. Moreover, if it's the case that if she is elected, changes will be made, then there will be a *renewed* interest on the part of students. But, if student indifference continues, then either there will be renewed interest or significant changes will be made. As a result, changes will be made, for there will not be a renewed interest on the part of students. (E, C, I, R)

b. Either *price* controls will be initiated or *inflation* will continue; and if inflation continues, then *unemployment* will rise. Hence, since price controls will not be initiated, it follows that unemployment will rise. (P, I, U)

c. If either *Ohio* State wins or *Alabama* loses, then if Ohio State wins, they will be *national* champions. Moreover, if Ohio State wins, their coach will be *chosen* Coach of the Year. Hence, since Ohio State will win, and win big, they will win and be national champions. (O, A, N, C)

d. Both if the number of *police* is increased *crime* will go down and if the Mayor has his *way* the City Council will *approve* his decision. Hence, either crime will go down or the Mayor will have his way; for the number of police will be increased. (P, C, W, A)

e. Either *Matt* and *Sam* will both pitch in the game, or *Brad* will go the distance himself. If Matt and Sam both pitch, then *Tom* will do the catching. If Brad goes the distance, *Keith* will catch. Hence, Tom or Keith will catch. (M, S, B, T, K)

f. If *Arlene* runs the hurdles, then *Beth* will enter the 100 meters. But if it's the case that if *Ellen* runs the relay either *Connie* or *Darlene* will run the 100 meters, then both *Fran* and *Gloria* will run the hurdles. Additionally, if Beth enters the 100 meters, then if Ellen runs the relay then Connie or Darlene will also run the 100 meters. Since it's not the case that both Fran and Gloria will run the hurdles, it follows that Arlene will not run the hurdles. (A, B, C, D, E, F, G)

g. If the proceeds from the sale are put into a *trust*, then they will not be *available* for reinvestment for at least ten years. Either the proceeds will be put into a trust, or they will both be put into *savings* and be available for reinvestment. Since it's not the case that they will not be available for reinvestment, it follows that the proceeds will be put into savings. (T, A, S)

h. If the doctor is dispensing *tranquilizers* to all his patients, then if his patients *drink*, they are taking a serious *risk*. Moreover, if he is dispensing tranquilizers, then, if his patients are taking a serious risk, the doctor is not doing his *job*. Since the doctor is dispensing tranquilizers to all his patients, it follows that if his patients drink, then the doctor is not doing his job. (T, D, R, J)

i. If a fetus is a *person* and *killing* people is wrong, then *abortion* is wrong.

Moreover, either it's the case that a fetus is a person and killing people is wrong, or those who approve of abortions hold a *reasonable* position. Hence, those who approve of abortions are reasonable, since abortion is not wrong. (*P, K, A, R*)

j. If either the prisoner was arrested as the result of *entrapment* or was not *read* his rights, then his civil rights were *violated*. Moreover, if he was *held* without charges, his rights were violated. However, if he was not read his rights, then if he was not arrested as the result of entrapment, the arresting officer did not do his *job* correctly. Everyone admits that the prisoner was not read his rights. As a result, either the arresting officer did not do his job correctly or the prisoner's rights were violated. This, because either he was not arrested as the result of entrapment, or he was held without charges. (*E, R, V, H, J*)

5:3 THE RULE OF REPLACEMENT

In our discussion of the rules of inference disjunctive syllogism and simplification and in our discussion of argument 11, we noted that some arguments can be shown to be valid by the truth-table method but cannot be shown to be valid by using only the eight rules of inference so far introduced. A careful look at the three cases just mentioned points out the difficulty with the present rules and at the same time suggests what is needed to augment our system. We shall examine only the case of disjunctive syllogism, but the kinds of remarks we make here apply as well to the other cases.

Recall that the argument

$S \lor T$

$\sim S$

$\therefore T$

can be justified by appealing to DS, but the following argument cannot:

$S \lor T$

$\sim T$

$\therefore S$

We cannot use DS in the second case because DS tells us that, given a disjunction and the negation of the *left* disjunct, we can infer the right disjunct. In this second case we have a disjunction and the negation of the *right* disjunct.

The difficulty, then, is that the structure of this second case is not correct for DS. This suggests that if the structure could somehow be changed to that needed for DS, and if this could be done while maintaining essentially the same argument form with which we began, our problem would be solved. It has probably occurred to you that all that is needed is to replace '$S \lor T$' with '$T \lor S$'. Moreover, since these two statement forms are *logically equivalent,* as can be shown by a truth table for '$(S \lor T) \equiv (T \lor S)$', we still have essentially the same argument with which we began, and we are able to show that it is valid.

It is important to note here that we are suggesting the replacement of one statement form with another which is *logically equivalent* to it. Any two statement forms that are logically equivalent *always* have the same truth value regardless of which statements uniformly replace the variables occurring in the statement forms; thus, if the original argument is valid, then the result of using this **Rule of Replacement** also is a valid argument.

By adding the Rule of Replacement to our system of natural deduction, we are able to expand the range of arguments whose validity can be shown within the system. The next section contains an explicit characterization of this rule, along with an explanation of why it is acceptable for use in showing the validity of the kinds of arguments we are presently considering.

5:3.1 Statement of the Rule of Replacement
The following general rule is the *Rule of Replacement:*

> *Given any statement form, or a part of a statement form which is itself a statement form, one can replace the statement form with another which is logically equivalent to it.*

We can show this graphically in the following way:

Figure 5-1

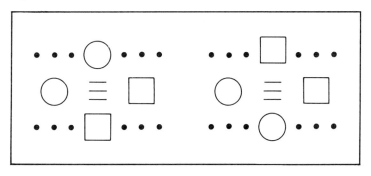

In Figure 5-1, the second line in each diagram is a statement of the *logical* equivalency of the two statement forms represented by '○' and '□'. That is, given the same assignment of truth values to the variables occurring in '○' and in '□', '○' and '□' will always have the same truth value. The three dots on either side of the '○' and '□' in the first and third lines indicate that '○' and '□' might themselves be parts of a more complex statement form. Now, what the Rule of Replacement tells us, and what is pictured in the left-hand diagram of Figure 5-1, is that if we are given a statement form '○', and if '○' is logically equivalent to '□', then we can replace '○' with '□'; similar remarks hold for '□' and '○' in the right-hand diagram of Figure 5-1.

To show why the Rule of Replacement is a permissible addition to our rules of inference, we shall consider two cases; in the first, 'O' (or '□') is a statement form which is *not* part of a statement form, and in the second, 'O' (or '□') is a statement form which *is* part of a statement form.

Case 1: 'O' is a statement form which is not part of a statement form. This is schematized in Figure 5-2. You know from our discussion of the truth table for equivalency (in Chapter 4) that 'O ≡ □' is equivalent to the conjunction of 'O ⊃ □' and '□ ⊃ O'. As a result, one of the logical consequences of 'O ≡ □' is 'O ⊃ □'. This latter, along with 'O' and the rule of inference AA, gives us '□', the conclusion in Figure 5-2. The right-hand diagram of Figure 5-1, where we replace '□' with 'O' given that 'O ≡ □', can be handled in the same way by using '□', the logical consequence '□ ⊃ O' derivable from 'O ≡ □', and AA to derive 'O'.

Figure 5-2

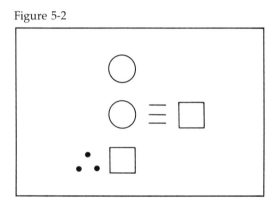

Case 2: 'O' is a statement form which is itself part of a statement form. To see how the Rule of Replacement works in this case, let us suppose that 'Δ' is the statement form of which 'O' is a part. Now, 'Δ' will consist of some finite number of variables n, including those variables which occur in the statement form represented by 'O'. By constructing a truth table containing 2^n lines, we would be able to assign a truth value to the statement form represented by 'Δ' for all the possible assignments of truth values to the variables which occur in 'Δ'; these would include an assignment of a truth value to 'O' on each line of the truth table. Now, 'O ≡ □' means that 'O' and '□' take the same truth value for every assignment of truth values to the variables which occur in these two statement forms; so if we replace 'O' with '□' in the statement form represented by 'Δ', every line of the truth table for 'Δ' will have the same truth value as it had when 'O' was a part of 'Δ'.

We can summarize these two cases as follows: Since logically equivalent statement forms have the same truth value given the same assignment of truth values to the variables which occur in the statement forms, truth values are not changed by replacing a statement form with one which is logically equivalent to it. Because the Rule of Replacement will never take us from a statement which is true to one which is false, it is truth-preserving in the same way as all the other valid rules of inference.

5:3.2 Limiting the Rule of Replacement Strictly speaking, the addition of the Rule of Replacement to our system allows us to replace any statement form by any other which is logically equivalent to it. In other words, the 'O' and '□' which occur in Figure 5-1 could be any statement forms whatsoever, so long as 'O ≡ □'. We do not, however, need such wide latitude with the Rule of Replacement to show, with our system of natural deduction, the validity of those arguments which can be shown to be valid by the truth-table method. We shall be concerned with just ten instances of logically equivalent statements, to serve as the 'O ≡ □' in Figure 5-1. Moreover, some redundancy is associated with these ten instances since some of them can be derived from others.

5:3.3 Commutation Our first instance of the Rule of Replacement is that used to handle valid arguments from section 5:1.3 and argument 11, whose validity could not be shown with the original eight rules. The rule we need is the following:

COMMUTATION (Comm)

$$(p \cdot q) \equiv (q \cdot p) \qquad (p \lor q) \equiv (q \lor p)$$

Notice that Comm has two uses: one for changing the order of the two conjuncts in a conjunction, and the other for changing the order of the two disjuncts in a disjunction.

Consider the following argument:

ARGUMENT 12

Either God is both benevolent and omnipotent or traditional theism is wrong. Hence, God is omnipotent because traditional theism is correct.

Step 1: Assigning variables to the statements in argument 12 as follows:

p = God is benevolent.

q = God is omnipotent.

r = Traditional theism is wrong.

We obtain, as the form of the argument,

$(p \cdot q) \lor r$

$\sim r$

$\therefore q$

Step 2: We see that 'q' could be derived by Simp if we could somehow derive '$q \cdot p$'. Moreover, we could derive '$q \cdot p$' by Comm if we could first derive '$p \cdot q$'.

Step 3. Considering the derivation of '$p \cdot q$', we see that since we are given '$\sim r$' as a premise, we could derive '$p \cdot q$' from the first premise if the order of the disjuncts in that premise were changed; this we can do by Comm.

Step 4: Our strategy, then, is to use Comm on the first premise so that we can then use the second premise and DS to derive '$q \cdot p$' and, finally, use Simp to derive 'q'.

Step 5: Summarizing the strategy outlined in step 4, we have the following as our proof:

(1) $(p \cdot q) \vee r$	Premise	
(2) $\sim r$	Premise	
(3) $r \vee (p \cdot q)$	(1), Comm	
(4) $p \cdot q$	(2), (3), DS	
(5) $q \cdot p$	(4), Comm	
$\therefore$ (6) q	(5), Simp	

In our proof of the validity of argument 12 we have used Comm in both of its versions, conjunction and disjunction.

5:3.4 Double Negation   We have already made use of this equivalency in some of the material discussed earlier. The equivalency is given in the following rule:

DOUBLE NEGATION (DN)

$p \equiv (\sim\sim p)$

As is shown in the two diagrams of Figure 5-1, we can either replace a statement of the form 'p' with another of the form '$\sim\sim p$', or replace a statement of the form '$\sim\sim p$' with another of the form 'p'. For each of the ten equivalencies to be discussed, the Rule of Replacement allows us to make the replacement in both directions of the equivalency.

Examples 8 to 11 below are all correct applications of DN.

EXAMPLE 8

$r \vee (s \cdot t)$

$\therefore \sim\sim r \vee (s \cdot t)$

EXAMPLE 9

$s \equiv (\sim\sim t \vee r)$

$\therefore s \equiv (t \vee r)$

EXAMPLE 10

$s \cdot (r \vee \sim t)$

$\therefore \sim\sim(s \cdot (r \vee \sim t))$

EXAMPLE 11

$\sim\sim(t \equiv (s \cdot \sim r))$

$\therefore t \equiv (s \cdot \sim r)$

In the first two examples, we applied DN to a statement form which is *part of* a statement form; in the second two we applied DN to a complete statement form. In examples 8 and 10 we used DN in one direction, and in examples 9 and 11 we used it in the other direction.

5:3.5 DeMorgan's Law

This application of the Rule of Replacement becomes useful when we must deal with the expressions 'not both' and 'neither-nor' in ordinary language.

For example, consider the statement that the two applicants for the scholarship, Beth and Marie, will *not both* be accepted. This means that it is not the case that both Beth will be accepted *and* Marie will be accepted. If we use 'B' to represent the statement 'Beth will be accepted' and 'M' to represent the statement 'Marie will be accepted', our original statement has the form '$\sim(B \cdot M)$'. Notice that the expression 'not both' does *not* mean that Beth will not be accepted and that Marie will not be accepted. That is, '$\sim B \cdot \sim M$' is a wrong symbolization of the original statement.

The first application of DeMorgan's law that we shall consider enables us to eliminate the outside negation sign before a conjunction. It should be clear that '$\sim(B \cdot M)$' takes the value true whenever the conjunction '$B \cdot M$' takes the value false; and '$B \cdot M$' takes the value false when one or the other or both conjuncts are false. In the case under discussion, then, the statement that Beth and Marie will not both be accepted for the scholarship is equivalent to the statement that Beth will not be accepted for the scholarship, *or* Marie will not be accepted for the scholarship, *or* neither will be accepted for the scholarship. This sense of 'or' is the *inclusive* sense symbolized in the preceeding chapter by '$\lor$'. Hence, we can rewrite '$\sim(B \cdot M)$' as '$\sim B \lor \sim M$'.

Now consider the statement that *neither* Harry *nor* Martin will be accepted for the scholarship. If we use 'H' to represent the statement 'Harry will be accepted for the scholarship' and 'M' to represent the statement 'Martin will be accepted', we see that our original statement has the form '$\sim(H \lor M)$'. Notice that the expression 'neither-nor' does *not* mean that Harry will *not* be accepted *or* that Martin will *not* be accepted, for that leaves open the possibility that one of them might be accepted; we have been told that *neither* will. In other words, '$\sim H \lor \sim M$' is a wrong symbolization of the original statement.

The second application of DeMorgan's law enables us to eliminate the outside negation sign before a disjunction. The conditions under which '$\sim(H \lor M)$' would take the value true are, of course, those conditions under which '$H \lor M$' takes the value false. A disjunction is false in only one case—when *both* disjuncts are false—so we can rewrite '$\sim(H \lor M)$' as '$\sim H \cdot \sim M$'. In other words, if *neither* Harry *nor* Martin will be accepted for the scholarship, then Harry will not be accepted *and* Martin will not be accepted.

Our consideration of the above cases provides us with the following instance of the Rule of Replacement:

DEMORGAN'S LAW (DM)

$$\sim(p \cdot q) \equiv (\sim p \lor \sim q) \qquad \sim(p \lor q) \equiv (\sim p \cdot \sim q)$$

The examples discussed above were presented in terms of *eliminating* outside negation signs on conjunctive and disjunctive statement forms; however, the equivalency holds in *both* directions, so that we may also replace a disjunction with a negated conjunction, or a conjunction with a negated disjunction.

DeMorgan's law is used in the next example to both add and eliminate an outside negation sign.

EXAMPLE 12

Show that the following argument is valid:

$(S \cdot T) \supset (M \lor N)$

$\sim M \cdot \sim N$

$\therefore \sim S \lor \sim T$

The proof of the validity of example 12 is:

(1)	$(S \cdot T) \supset (M \lor N)$	Premise
(2)	$\sim M \cdot \sim N$	Premise
(3)	$\sim(M \lor N)$	(2), DM
(4)	$\sim(S \cdot T)$	(1), (3), DC
$\therefore$ (5)	$\sim S \lor \sim T$	(4), DM

On line (3) we used DM with line (2) to add an outside negation sign, and on line (5) we used DM with line (4) to eliminate an outside negation sign.

Let's now look at another argument whose proof of validity requires the use of DM.

ARGUMENT 13

Neither the U.S. nor the Soviet Union wants to be behind in the arms race. But, since not both China and France want to be behind in the arms race, it follows that neither the Soviet Union nor China wants to be behind. This is so because France wants to be behind.

Step 1: Put the argument into standard form. Our conclusion is indicated by 'it follows that'; the remainder of the statements are premises.

Neither the U.S. nor the Soviet Union wants to be behind in the arms race.

Not both China and France want to be behind in the arms race.

France wants to be behind in the arms race.

$\therefore$ Neither the Soviet Union nor China wants to be behind in the arms race.

Step 2: Assign constants to the statements occurring in the argument.

U = The U.S. wants to be behind in the arms race.

S = The Soviet Union wants to be behind in the arms race.

C = China wants to be behind in the arms race.

F = France wants to be behind in the arms race.

Step 3: Symbolize the argument. We know from our earlier discussion that 'neither-nor' is symbolized as the negation of a disjunction, so the first premise has the form '$\sim(U \lor S)$'. The second premise is a 'not both' statement, which is the negation of a conjunction, so it has the form '$\sim(C \cdot F)$'. The conclusion is another 'neither-nor' statement, so it too is symbolized as the negation of a disjunction: '$\sim(S \lor C)$'. Our argument then has the form

$\sim(U \lor S)$

$\sim(C \cdot F)$

F

$\therefore \sim(S \lor C)$

Step 4: We have to derive the negation of a disjunction as the conclusion of the argument. A quick look at the premises shows that we cannot derive '$\sim(S \lor C)$' by either AA or DC (since we do not have the appropriate conditional statements). At this point, then, it would be a good idea to use DM on the conclusion, obtaining '$\sim S \cdot \sim C$'. It is often convenient to use DM on negated conjunctions and negated disjunctions, since this typically makes it easier to apply the original eight rules of inference.

Step 5: Having used DM on the conclusion, we see that we must derive a conjunction. It should occur to you at this point to try to use Conj. For this, we would need to derive '$\sim S$' and then derive '$\sim C$'.

Step 6: Asking how we might derive '$\sim S$' from the set of premises, we note that the use of DM on the first premise would give us a conjunction with '$\sim S$' as one of the conjuncts. Comm and Simp would enable us to get '$\sim S$'.

Step 7: The second premise is the most likely one from which to derive '$\sim C$'. If we use DM on this premise, we will have a disjunction with '$\sim C$' as one of the disjuncts and '$\sim F$' as the other. By using Comm, we could then use the third premise 'F' with DS to derive '$\sim C$'.

Step 8: We now have determined how the derivation will go; the proof follows:

(1)	$\sim(U \lor S)$	Premise
(2)	$\sim(C \cdot F)$	Premise
(3)	F	Premise
(4)	$\sim U \cdot \sim S$	(1), DM
(5)	$\sim S \cdot \sim U$	(4), Comm

$$(6) \quad \sim S \qquad\qquad (5), \text{Simp}$$
$$(7) \quad \sim C \vee \sim F \qquad (2), \text{DM}$$
$$(8) \quad \sim F \vee \sim C \qquad (7), \text{Comm}$$
$$(9) \quad \sim\sim F \qquad\qquad (3), \text{DN}$$
$$(10) \quad \sim C \qquad\qquad (3), (9), \text{DS}$$
$$(11) \quad \sim S \cdot \sim C \qquad (6), (10), \text{Conj}$$
$$\therefore (12) \quad \sim(S \vee C) \qquad (11), \text{DM}$$

Another type of situation in which DM is useful is that of the next example.

EXAMPLE 13

$(R \vee S) \supset (T \cdot V)$

$\sim T$

$\therefore \sim R$

Notice that in this example the premise '$\sim T$' and the conclusion each consist of a variable which occurs elsewhere as part of a more complex statement. It should be clear to you that we are somehow going to have to derive '$\sim R$' from '$R \vee S$'; the two ways that suggest themselves are DS and Simp (recall that we earlier suggested these two rules as a way of deriving part of a compound statement). DS does not look promising, since there is no occurrence of 'S' anywhere in the premises except as it occurs in '$R \vee S$'. How, then, might we use Simp? Our strategy follows:

Step 1: To get '$\sim R$' from a statement by Simp we need a conjunction, one of whose conjuncts is '$\sim R$'. That is, we need a statement of the form '$\sim R \cdot$ —' or '— $\cdot \sim R$'. Our first premise is a conditional statement whose antecedent is '$R \vee S$'. If we had the negation of this statement, '$\sim(R \vee S)$', DM could be used to derive the statement form we need to get '$\sim R$' by Simp.

Step 2: Now, how might we get '$\sim(R \vee S)$' from our premises? Given that the first premise is a conditional statement, we could get it only by DC, and for this we would have to have the negation of the consequent of the first premise; that is, we need '$\sim(T \cdot V)$'.

Step 3: We now consider how we might derive '$\sim(T \cdot V)$'. It should occur to you, as you look at the form of this statement, that it is equivalent to the disjunction '$\sim T \vee \sim V$', so that if we could derive '$\sim T \vee \sim V$' we would have what we need.

Step 4: According to our discussion of the first eight rules of inference, we can derive a disjunction by Add if we have one of the disjuncts. We have '$\sim T$' as a premise, so we can use Add to get what we need.

Step 5: Our overall strategy, then, is to use Add with '$\sim T$' to derive

'~T ∨ ~V'. By using DM on this statement form, we will be able to derive the statement needed along with the first premise to derive '~(R ∨ S)' by DC. One more application of DM will give us a conjunction from which we can then derive '~R' by Simp.

Step 6: The proof is as follows:

(1)	(R ∨ S) ⊃ (T · V)	Premise
(2)	~T	Premise
(3)	~T ∨ ~V	(2), Add
(4)	~(T · V)	(3), DM
(5)	~(R ∨ S)	(1), (4), DC
(6)	~R · ~S	(5), DM
∴ (7)	~R	(6), Simp

5:3.6 Contraposition   This equivalency was introduced in Chapter 3 when we were discussing conditional arguments. The rule is:

CONTRAPOSITION (Contra)

$(p \supset q) \equiv (\sim q \supset \sim p)$

The application of the rule is a two-step process:

(1) Negate both the antecedent and the consequent of the original statement.

(2) Write a new statement in which the negated antecedent of the original statement is the consequent of the new statement, and the negated consequent of the original statement is the antecedent of the new statement.

5:3.7 Implication   This instance of the Rule of Replacement enables us to convert a statement whose form is that of a conditional statement into one whose form is that of a disjunction and vice versa. Cases in which conversion of the first kind might be useful are those where we want to be able to use either DS or CD; cases in which conversion of the second kind might be useful are those where we want to use AA, DC, or HS. The statement of the equivalency is:

IMPLICATION (Imp)

$(p \supset q) \equiv (\sim p \vee q)$

Applying Imp is basically a two-step process in either direction:

Converting a conditional statement to a disjunction:

(1) Add a negation sign to the antecedent.

(2) Change '⊃' to '∨'.

Converting a disjunction to a conditional statement:

(1) Remove a negation sign from the left disjunct.[2]

(2) Change '$\lor$' to '$\supset$'.

EXAMPLE 14

Apply Imp to '$(\sim R \lor S)$'.

> *Step 1:* We first remove the negation sign, obtaining
>
> $\qquad R \lor S$
>
> *Step 2:* Now we change '$\lor$' to '$\supset$', obtaining
>
> $\qquad R \supset S$

EXAMPLE 15

Apply Imp to '$(T \supset \sim S)$'.

> *Step 1:* We first add a negation sign to the antecedent:
>
> $\qquad \sim T \supset \sim S$
>
> *Step 2:* Now we change '$\supset$' to '$\lor$'. Our result is
>
> $\qquad \sim T \lor \sim S$

Imp, like all the equivalencies discussed here, can be applied to part of a line as well. For example, we could apply Imp to just the antecedent of '$(T \lor \sim R) \supset (\sim S \equiv Q)$'. To do this, however, we must have a negation sign preceding the left disjunct so that it can be removed. As a result, we first use DN on the left disjunct of the antecedent, obtaining '$(\sim\sim T \lor \sim R) \supset (\sim S \equiv Q)$', and then apply Imp to this result. This gives us

$\qquad (\sim T \supset \sim R) \supset (\sim S \equiv Q)$

Since the above has the form of a conditional statement, we could apply Imp again to the whole statement. Were we to do that, we would have

$\qquad \sim(\sim T \supset \sim R) \lor (\sim S \equiv Q)$

5:3.8 Repetition   Our next instance of the Rule of Replacement is the following:

> REPETITION (Rep)
>
> $p \equiv (p \lor p) \qquad\qquad p \equiv (p \cdot p)$

The usefulness of Rep is brought out in the proof of the validity of the following argument.

ARGUMENT 14

If the Wilsons move to Miami, then their children will no longer be able to go skiing every weekend, and if they move to Denver, the children will be able to

---

[2] Sometimes there is no negation sign to eliminate, as in '$R \lor S$'. In this case we first use DN to replace 'R' with '$\sim\sim R$', and then eliminate a negation sign. Applying Imp to '$R \lor S$' after first using DN gives us '$\sim R \supset S$'.

ski. Moreover, if the Wilsons don't move to Miami, they won't move to Denver either. Since they will either go to Miami or they won't, they won't move to Denver.

Step 1: Symbolize the argument. To do this, we assign constants in the following way:

M = The Wilsons move to Miami.

S = The Wilson children ski every weekend.

D = The Wilsons move to Denver.

Then we have

$(M \supset {\sim}S) \cdot (D \supset S)$

${\sim}M \supset {\sim}D$

$M \lor {\sim}M$

$\therefore {\sim}D$

Step 2: Checking the premises to see how we might derive '${\sim}D$', we see that if we had '${\sim}M$' we could get '${\sim}D$' from the second premise by AA; we have not been given '${\sim}M$', however. Considering the first premise, we see that with Comm and Simp we could derive '$D \supset S$' and then, if we had '${\sim}S$', we could use DC to get '${\sim}D$'.

Step 3: Since we do not have '${\sim}S$' as a premise, we now check to see if it can be derived from the premises. We could get it from the left conjunct of the first premise, after using Simp, if we had 'M'. We have not been given 'M', however.

Step 4: In step 2 we saw that we could derive '${\sim}D$' if we have '${\sim}M$', and in step 3 we saw that we could derive '${\sim}D$' if we had 'M'. Whereas we did not have either of these as a premise, we do have '$M \lor {\sim}M$'. As a result, we can use CD to derive '${\sim}D \lor {\sim}D$'. We could then use Rep to get our desired conclusion. The proof follows:

(1)	$(M \supset {\sim}S) \cdot (D \supset S)$	Premise
(2)	${\sim}M \supset {\sim}D$	Premise
(3)	$M \lor {\sim}M$	Premise
(4)	$M \supset {\sim}S$	(1), Simp
(5)	$(D \supset S) \cdot (M \supset {\sim}S)$	(1), Comm
(6)	$D \supset S$	(5), Simp
(7)	${\sim}S \supset {\sim}D$	(6), Contra
(8)	$M \supset {\sim}D$	(4), (7), HS
(9)	${\sim}D \lor {\sim}D$	(2), (8), (3), CD
$\therefore$ (10)	${\sim}D$	(9), Rep

5:3.9 Association This instance of the Rule of Replacement enables us to reorder the conjuncts in a conjunction which contains more than two conjuncts and to reorder the disjuncts in a disjunction which contains more than two disjuncts; in cases where a conjunction contains only two conjuncts or a disjunction contains only two disjuncts, we can use Comm to change their order.

In Chapter 4, it was claimed that the truth tables for the connectives 'or' and 'and', have to be used with statement forms with just two parts; where there are more than two parts, as in '$(P \cdot Q \cdot S)$', for example, it does not matter how we place the parentheses: That is, either '$(P \cdot Q) \cdot S$' or '$P \cdot (Q \cdot S)$' is acceptable. This was brought out in the discussion in section 4:2.1.

Now, we have not yet justified the claim that it does not matter how the parentheses are placed in such instances. Association enables us to do this. The rule follows:

ASSOCIATION (Assoc)

$$(p \cdot (q \cdot r)) \equiv ((p \cdot q) \cdot r) \qquad (p \vee (q \vee r)) \equiv ((p \vee q) \vee r)$$

In the remarks which follow we shall consider only the conjunctive form of Assoc, though the same kinds of remarks are applicable to the disjunctive case.

The first thing you should notice is that both the left part and the right part of the equivalency are conjunctions, and each conjunction consists of just two parts—'p' and '$q \cdot r$' in the left conjunction, and '$p \cdot q$' and 'r' in the right conjunction. The second thing to notice is the structural relationship between the left and right parts of the equivalency. In particular, in replacing the left part with the right part on the basis of the equivalency, we merely move the innermost parentheses to the left so that the middle "conjunct" is now associated with the left conjunct instead of the right conjunct. In replacing the right part with the left part on the basis of the equivalency, we move the innermost parentheses to the right. The effect of either of these "shifts" is to take the statement form which occurs in the middle of the conjunction out of its original part of the conjunction and "associate" it with the other part. An example will clarify this.

EXAMPLE 16

Show, using Assoc, that '$((S \cdot (T \vee M)) \cdot R)$' is equivalent to '$(S \cdot ((T \vee M) \cdot R))$'.

In this case we use Assoc to replace the right part of the equivalency with the left part.

(1) Our first step is to make '$T \vee M$' the left conjunct of a new conjunction whose right part is 'R'. This gives us '$(T \vee M) \cdot R$'.

(2) We now take the result from (1) as the right conjunct of a conjunction whose left conjunct is 'S'. This gives us '$(S \cdot ((T \vee M) \cdot R))$', the desired result.

Notice in example 16 that '$T \vee M$' is a *disjunction*, but it occurs as one of the *conjuncts* in the overall statement form. It is, in fact, the statement form which occupies the place indicated by 'q' in the statement of Assoc. As in all our instances of the Rule of Replacement, the actual statement forms which replace the variables in the rules can be any statement forms which can be written correctly by using statement variables and the five logical connectives.

5:3.10 Distribution   In the previous section we discussed the use of Assoc to change the conjuncts and disjuncts of statements whose forms are either conjunctive or disjunctive. In some cases, however, we might want to reorder the variables in statements whose statement forms are composed of both conjunction *and* disjunction. One such statement form is '$p \cdot (q \lor r)$'; a statement having this form is 'Pete will go get the keg of beer and either Larry or Jim will go with him'. If this statement is true, then it follows that either Pete and Larry will go get the keg or Pete and Jim will go. Another statement form of interest in this regard is '$p \lor (q \cdot r)$'.

The following instance of the rule of replacement enables us to work with these kinds of equivalency:

DISTRIBUTION (Dist)

$$(p \cdot (q \lor r)) \equiv ((p \cdot q) \lor (p \cdot r))$$

$$(p \lor (q \cdot r)) \equiv ((p \lor q) \cdot (p \lor r))$$

Notice that Dist also enables us to change the main connective of the statement forms from conjunction to disjunction, or from disjunction to conjunction.

We make use of Dist in both directions in the following example:

EXAMPLE 17

Show that the following argument is valid:

$(P \cdot Q) \supset (R \cdot S)$

$P \cdot (Q \lor R)$

$(P \cdot R) \supset (R \cdot T)$

$\therefore R \cdot (S \lor T)$

Step 1: The form of the statement that we must derive is conjunctive. It should occur to you, then, to consider using Conj to do this. To use Conj, we must independently derive 'R' and '$S \lor T$'. From the premises, it does not appear that there is any obvious way of deriving either of these statements by itself. Before reading on, you should consider the premises to see that this is so.

Step 2: Since Conj does not look like it will work, we now consider rewriting the conclusion in some other form. Dist enables us to replace the conclusion with '$(R \cdot S) \lor (R \cdot T)$'. This statement has a disjunctive form, so we should consider trying to derive either disjunct and then getting the result we want by Add, or we should consider using CD.

Step 3: To derive '$R \cdot S$' by itself, we would need '$P \cdot Q$' to use with the first premise and AA; we could get 'P' from the second premise, but there is no obvious way to get 'Q'. To derive '$R \cdot T$' by itself, we need '$P \cdot R$' to use with the third premise and AA. As before, we can get 'P', but there is no obvious way to get 'R'.

Step 4: Since Add does not look as though it will work, let's consider using CD. The disjuncts of the disjunction we would like to derive, '$(R \cdot S) \vee (R \cdot T)$', each occur as the consequent of a conditional statement. If, then, we were able to derive a disjunction whose disjuncts were the antecedents of the two conditional statements, we would be able to use CD to derive what we want. What we need, then, is to derive '$(P \cdot Q) \vee (P \cdot R)$'.

Step 5: We do not have this disjunction as a premise, but we can get it easily enough from the second premise by Dist.

Step 6: Our strategy, therefore, is to use Dist on the second premise and then use CD to derive '$(R \cdot S) \vee (R \cdot T)$'. One more use of Dist on this result will give us the desired conclusion. The proof follows:

(1) $(P \cdot Q) \supset (R \cdot S)$	Premise	
(2) $P \cdot (Q \vee R)$	Premise	
(3) $(P \cdot R) \supset (R \cdot T)$	Premise	
(4) $(P \cdot Q) \vee (P \cdot R)$	(2), Dist	
(5) $(R \cdot S) \vee (R \cdot T)$	(1), (3), (4), CD	
∴ (6) $R \cdot (S \vee T)$	(5), Dist	

Notice that in line (4) we used Dist in one direction and in line (6) we used it in the other direction.

5:3.11 Exportation Suppose that the following is true: If Ron vacations in Ft. Lauderdale and Don vacations in Miami, then Jeff's two roommates will not help paint the living room. Given the truth of this statement, something else is true as well; namely, if Ron vacations in Ft. Lauderdale, then if Don vacations in Miami then Jeff's two roommates will not help paint. In this case, a conditional statement whose antecedent is a conjunction is seen to be equivalent to a conditional statement whose consequent is a conditional statement whose antecedent is just the right conjunct of the original antecedent. This relationship is made explicit in the following instance of the Rule of Replacement.

EXPORTATION (Exp)[3]

$$((p \cdot q \supset r) \equiv (p \supset (q \supset r)))$$

The usefulness of Exp is brought out in the following example:

---

[3] Read from right to left, Exp is the justification for rewriting (1) as (2) in section 3:6.1 when we earlier discussed conditional proofs.

ARGUMENT 15

If Ron goes to Ft. Lauderdale and Don goes to Miami, then Jeff will have to do the painting all by himself. Hence, if Don goes to Miami, Jeff will have to paint by himself, because Ron is going to Ft. Lauderdale.

Step 1: We assign constants to the statements which occur in the argument:

R = Ron goes to Ft. Lauderdale.

D = Don goes to Miami.

J = Jeff paints by himself.

and obtain the following:

$(R \cdot D) \supset J$

R

$\therefore D \supset J$

Step 2: If we use Exp to replace '$(R \cdot D) \supset J$' with '$R \supset (D \supset J)$', and then use AA with 'R' and this result, we shall have the desired conclusion. The proof follows:

(1) $(R \cdot D) \supset J$	Premise	
(2) R	Premise	
(3) $R \supset (D \supset J)$	(1), Exp	
$\therefore$ (4) $D \supset J$	(2), (3), AA	

We could have derived the conclusion of argument 15 from the premises *without* using Exp, as is shown below. But, as you can see, Exp saves quite a few steps in the proof.

(1) $(R \cdot D) \supset J$	Premise
(2) R	Premise
(3) $\sim(R \cdot D) \vee J$	(1), Imp
(4) $(\sim R \vee \sim D) \vee J$	(3), DM
(5) $\sim R \vee (\sim D \vee J)$	(4), Assoc
(6) $\sim\sim R$	(2), DN
(7) $\sim D \vee J$	(5), (6), DS
$\therefore$ (8) $D \supset J$	(7), Imp

The fact that we are able to show the validity of argument 15 without using Exp should suggest to you that we may not need exportation as an instance of the Rule of Replacement. As a matter of fact, this is correct; Exp provides one instance of the redundancy of our rules. Below we derive Exp from some of the other rules, and other similar derivations are left as an exercise. However, whereas some of the rules are redundant, having them in our system of natural deduction simplifies our proofs; the two proofs of the validity of argument 15 shows this vividly.

To show that Exp can be derived from our other rules, we must show, first, that from a statement of the form '$(p \cdot q) \supset r$' we can derive a statement of the form '$p \supset (q \supset r)$'; second, we must show that from a statement of the form '$(p \supset (q \supset r)$' we can derive a statement of the form '$(p \cdot q) \supset r$'. This is done in two separate parts.

PART I

Show that the following is a valid argument form:

$(p \cdot q) \supset r$

$\therefore p \supset (q \supset r)$

(1)	$(p \cdot q) \supset r$	Premise
(2)	$\sim(p \cdot q) \lor r$	(1), Imp
(3)	$(\sim p \lor \sim q) \lor r$	(2), DM
(4)	$\sim p \lor (\sim q \lor r)$	(3), Assoc
(5)	$p \supset (\sim q \lor r)$	(4), Imp
$\therefore$ (6)	$p \supset (q \supset r)$	(5), Imp

PART II

Show that the following is a valid argument form:

$p \supset (q \supset r)$

$\therefore (p \cdot q) \supset r$

(1)	$p \supset (q \supset r)$	Premise
(2)	$p \supset (\sim q \lor r)$	(1), Imp
(3)	$\sim p \lor (\sim q \lor r)$	(2), Imp
(4)	$(\sim p \lor \sim q) \lor r$	(3), Assoc
(5)	$\sim(p \cdot q) \lor r$	(4), DM
$\therefore$ (6)	$(p \cdot q) \supset r$	(5), Imp

Parts I and II establish both parts of the biconditional of exportation and show, therefore, that the statement forms derivable by using Exp can be derived without Exp.

5:3.12 Equivalency We have referred to this instance of the Rule of Replacement throughout the text. Recall that in discussing the truth table for '$\equiv$' in Chapter 4, we read the symbol as 'if, and only if'. As a result, a statement of the form '$p \equiv q$' is the same as 'p, if and only if, q', where this latter is the same as a conjunction of 'p, if q' and 'p, only if q'. Making this explicit, we have:

EQUIVALENCY (Eq)

$(p \equiv q) \equiv ((p \supset q) \cdot (q \supset p))$

Of course, one could replace either or both of the conditional statements with other statement forms equivalent to them by using the Rule of Replacement. For example, by using Imp on both conditional statements, we obtain

$$(p \equiv q) \equiv ((\sim p \lor q) \cdot (\sim q \lor p))$$

One obvious use for Eq is when an 'if, and only if' statement is part of an argument, and we need to break that statement down into its conjunctive form to show the validity of an argument. The following is one such case:

EXAMPLE 18

Show that the following argument is valid:

$(Q \lor R) \equiv (\sim P \cdot S)$

$(\sim P \cdot S) \supset (T \lor M)$

$\sim(\sim T \supset M)$

$\therefore \sim Q \cdot \sim R$

Step 1: The conjunctive conclusion that we have to derive contains the same variables as the left part of the equivalency in the first premise. Moreover, by DM we know that the conclusion is equivalent to '$\sim(Q \lor R)$', the negation of the left part of the equivalency.

Step 2: We could derive '$\sim(Q \lor R)$' from the first premise by considering just the conditional statement '$(Q \lor R) \supset (\sim P \cdot S)$' if we had '$\sim(\sim P \cdot S)$'.

Step 3: We could derive '$\sim(\sim P \cdot S)$' from the second premise by DC, if we also had '$\sim(T \lor M)$'. This latter we can get by Imp from the third premise.

Step 4: Our strategy, then, is to use Imp to derive '$\sim(T \lor M)$', which we shall use with the second premise to get '$\sim(\sim P \cdot S)$'. By using Eq to replace the first premise with its conjunctive form, we shall then be able to derive '$\sim(Q \lor R)$', which, by DM, will give us the conclusion. The proof follows:

(1) $(Q \lor R) \equiv (\sim P \cdot S)$		Premise
(2) $(\sim P \cdot S) \supset (T \lor M)$		Premise
(3) $\sim(\sim T \supset M)$		Premise
(4) $\sim(\sim\sim T \lor M)$		(3), Imp
(5) $\sim(T \lor M)$		(4), DN
(6) $\sim(\sim P \cdot S)$		(2), (5), DC
(7) $((Q \lor R) \supset (\sim P \cdot S)) \cdot ((\sim P \cdot S) \supset (Q \lor R))$		(1), Eq
(8) $(Q \lor R) \supset (\sim P \cdot S)$		(7), Simp
(9) $\sim(Q \lor R)$		(6), (8), DC
$\therefore$ (10) $(\sim Q \cdot \sim R)$		(9), DM

We could have shortened the proof by using HS on what are now lines (2) and (8) and then using the present line (5) and DC to get '~$(Q \lor R)$'.

Another use of Eq is in deriving statements whose form is an 'if, and only if' statement. This we do by considering Eq in its right-to-left form. Notice that this form of the rule may be taken to mean that if we can establish both '$p \supset q$' and '$q \supset p$', then we will have shown the '$p \equiv q$'. We do this in the next example.

EXAMPLE 19

Show that $(R \equiv S)$, given that

$(M \cdot T) \cdot L$

$L \supset (M \supset S)$

$(L \cdot M) \supset R$

Step 1: To derive '$R \equiv S$', we must derive both '$R \supset S$' and '$S \supset R$'. Consider the '$R \supset S$' case first. The first thing to notice is that none of the premises contains both 'R' and 'S'; we are not, then, going to be able to derive '$R \supset S$' from just one premise. We might consider using HS, but for that we need a conditional statement with 'R' as antecedent, and we don't have such a statement form. The other option open to us is to rewrite '$R \supset S$' in some equivalent form with which we can work.

Step 2: The most obvious equivalent form to work with is '~$R \lor S$'. Once again, since we want to derive a disjunction, we should consider using either Add or CD. To use Add, all we have to do is derive either '~R' or 'S'.

Step 3: Checking the premises, we see there is no obvious way of deriving '~R', so we consider deriving 'S'. We have an occurrence of 'S' in the second premise, so if we had 'L' we could derive '$M \supset S$', and then if we had 'M' we could get 'S' by two uses of AA. On the other hand, we could use Exp on the second premise and then use AA to get 'S'. In either case, we can derive 'S' and, hence, '$S \lor$ ~R', which, by Comm and Imp, would give us '$R \supset S$'.

Step 4: Now for '$S \supset R$'. As in the case of '$R \supset S$', we have no premise in which both 'S' and 'R' occur, and HS will not work; so we will rewrite '$S \supset R$' as '~$S \lor R$'.

Step 5: Now all we have to consider is whether we can derive either '~S' or 'R' and get the disjunction by Add. If we cannot do this, we'll consider using CD. There is no obvious way of deriving '~S', so we consider 'R'. We could get 'R' from the third premise if we had '$L \cdot M$'.

Step 6: We can get '$L \cdot M$' from the first premise by Assoc and Comm, so we can do the proof.

Step 7: Our overall strategy is to derive '$R \supset S$' from Imp after we have derived '$\sim R \vee S$' by Add and Comm from 'S', and then to derive '$S \supset R$' from Imp after we have derived '$\sim S \vee R$' by Add and Comm from 'R'. The proof follows:

(1)	$(M \cdot T) \cdot L$	Premise
(2)	$L \supset (M \supset S)$	Premise
(3)	$(L \cdot M) \supset R$	Premise
(4)	$(L \cdot M) \supset S$	(2), Exp
(5)	$L \cdot (M \cdot T)$	(1), Comm
(6)	$(L \cdot M) \cdot T$	(5), Assoc.
(7)	$(L \cdot M)$	(6), Simp
(8)	S	(4), (7), AA
(9)	$S \vee \sim R$	(8), Add
(10)	$\sim R \vee S$	(9), Comm
(11)	$R \supset S$	(10), Imp
(12)	R	(3), (7), AA
(13)	$R \vee \sim S$	(12), Add
(14)	$\sim S \vee R$	(13), Comm
(15)	$S \supset R$	(14), Imp
(16)	$(R \supset S) \cdot (S \supset R)$	(11), (15), Conj
$\therefore$ (17)	$R \equiv S$	(16), Eq

This concludes our discussion of the Rule of Replacement. For convenience, all ten instances of the rule are listed below.

COMMUTATION (Comm)

$(p \cdot q) \equiv (q \cdot p)$
$(p \vee q) \equiv (q \vee p)$

DOUBLE NEGATION (DN)

$p \equiv \sim\sim p$

DeMORGAN'S LAW (DM)

$\sim(p \cdot q) \equiv (\sim p \vee \sim q)$
$\sim(p \vee q) \equiv (\sim p \cdot \sim q)$

CONTRAPOSITION (Contra)

$(p \supset q) \equiv (\sim q \supset \sim p)$

IMPLICATION (Imp)

$(p \supset q) \equiv (\sim p \vee q)$

REPETITION (Rep)

$p \equiv (p \vee p)$
$p \equiv (p \cdot p)$

ASSOCIATION (Assoc)

$(p \cdot (q \cdot r)) \equiv ((p \cdot q) \cdot r)$
$(p \vee (q \vee r)) \equiv ((p \vee q) \vee r)$

DISTRIBUTION (Dist)

$(p \cdot (q \vee r)) \equiv ((p \cdot q) \vee (p \cdot r))$
$(p \vee (q \cdot r)) \equiv ((p \vee q) \cdot (p \vee r))$

EXPORTATION (Exp)

$((p \cdot q) \supset r) \equiv (p \supset (q \supset r))$

EQUIVALENCY (Eq)

$(p \equiv q) \equiv ((p \supset q) \cdot (q \supset p))$

EXERCISE 5-6

1. State the Rule of Replacement. What problem is the rule designed to solve?

2. Explain why the Rule of Replacement can legitimately be added to the list of rules of inference.

3. State each of the ten instances of the Rule of Replacement, and give an example of an argument in which it is used.

EXERCISE 5-7

1. State which instance of the Rule of Replacement is used in each of the following arguments. If no inference applies, write "none."

a. $(A \cdot B) \vee C$
   $\therefore (A \cdot B) \vee {\sim}{\sim}C$

b. $(S \supset T) \cdot {\sim}(L \vee M)$
   $\therefore {\sim}(L \vee M) \cdot (S \supset T)$

c. ${\sim}(({\sim}A \cdot B) \vee ({\sim}C \supset D))$
   $\therefore {\sim}({\sim}A \cdot B) \vee {\sim}({\sim}C \supset D)$

d. $(R \cdot M) \supset ({\sim}S \vee T)$
   $\therefore {\sim}({\sim}S \vee T) \supset {\sim}(R \cdot M)$

e. $((S \cdot {\sim}T) \vee R) \supset ({\sim}M \vee L)$
   $\therefore ((S \cdot {\sim}T) \vee {\sim}{\sim}R) \supset ({\sim}M \vee L)$

f. $A \supset {\sim}B$
   $\therefore {\sim}A \vee {\sim}B$

g. ${\sim}S \vee (L \cdot M)$
   $\therefore ({\sim}S \cdot L) \vee ({\sim}S \cdot M)$

h. ${\sim}S \cdot (L \vee M)$
   $\therefore ({\sim}S \vee L) \cdot ({\sim}S \vee M)$

i. $(A \vee B) \supset {\sim}C$
   $\therefore A \supset (B \supset {\sim}C)$

j. ${\sim}((L \vee M) \cdot (L \vee M))$
   $\therefore {\sim}(L \vee M)$

k. $(S \cdot (L \vee T)) \supset {\sim}M$
   $\therefore S \supset ((L \vee T) \supset {\sim}T)$

l. $(R \cdot S) \supset (P \cdot L)$
   $\therefore (S \cdot R) \supset (P \cdot L)$

m. $(A \supset {\sim}B) \cdot ({\sim}B \supset A)$
   $\therefore A \equiv B$

n. $({\sim}M \cdot N) \supset (S \supset {\sim}T)$
   $\therefore (({\sim}M \cdot N) \cdot S) \supset {\sim}T$

o. $({\sim}P \vee Q) \vee (R \vee S)$
   $\therefore (({\sim}P \vee Q) \vee R) \vee S$

p. $S \vee ({\sim}T \cdot L)$
   $\therefore (S \vee {\sim}T) \cdot (S \cdot L)$

q. $A \cdot {\sim}({\sim}M \vee L)$
   $\therefore A \cdot (M \cdot {\sim}L)$

r. $R \cdot (S \cdot {\sim}T)$
   $\therefore (R \cdot S) \cdot {\sim}T$

s. $(S \supset T) \cdot (M \supset {\sim}L)$
   $\therefore ({\sim}S \vee T) \cdot (M \supset {\sim}L)$

t. $(A \supset {\sim}(B \vee C)) \supset (D \vee E)$
   $\therefore ((A \supset {\sim}(B \vee C)) \cdot (A \supset {\sim}(B \vee C)) \supset (D \vee E)$

u. $(S \cdot (T \vee U)) \vee (S \cdot ({\sim}M \supset Q))$
   $\therefore S \cdot ((T \vee U) \vee ({\sim}M \supset Q))$

v. $({\sim}M \vee {\sim}T) \supset (R \supset {\sim}{\sim}S)$
   $\therefore {\sim}({\sim}M \vee {\sim}T) \vee (R \supset {\sim}{\sim}S)$

w. $(A \vee B) \cdot ({\sim}A \vee {\sim}B)$
   $\therefore ((A \vee B) \cdot {\sim}A) \vee ((A \cdot B) \cdot {\sim}B)$

x. $(S \supset (T \vee M)) \vee (S \supset (T \vee M))$
   $\therefore S \supset (T \vee M)$

y. $({\sim}A \supset B) \supset ({\sim}C \vee {\sim}D)$
   $\therefore {\sim}(A \supset B) \supset {\sim}(C \cdot D)$

2. Provide the justification for each line in the following proofs.

a. (1) $(A \vee {\sim}B) \vee C$ Premise
   (2) ${\sim}A \vee (B \cdot {\sim}A)$ Premise
   (3) $({\sim}A \vee B) \cdot ({\sim}A \vee {\sim}A)$

   (4) $(\sim A \vee \sim A) \cdot (\sim A \vee B)$
   (5) $\sim A \vee \sim A$
   (6) $\sim A$
   (7) $A \vee (\sim B \vee C)$
   (8) $\sim B \vee C$
∴ (9) $B \supset C$

b. (1) $R \supset (S \cdot T)$ Premise   c. (1) $(A \cdot B) \supset C$ Premise
   (2) $\sim S$ Premise   (2) $(A \supset C) \supset D$ Premise
   (3) $R \equiv U$ Premise   (3) $(B \cdot A) \supset C$
   (4) $(R \supset U) \cdot (U \supset R)$ (4) $B \supset (A \supset C)$
   (5) $\sim S \vee \sim T$ ∴ (5) $B \supset D$
   (6) $\sim(S \cdot T)$
   (7) $\sim R$
   (8) $(U \supset R) \cdot (R \supset U)$
   (9) $U \supset R$
∴ (10) $\sim U$

d. (1) $R \vee (S \cdot T)$ Premise   e. (1) $A \cdot (B \vee C)$ Premise
   (2) $U \supset \sim R$ Premise   (2) $A \supset (B \supset (D \cdot E))$ Premise
   (3) $U \vee T$ Premise   (3) $(A \cdot C) \supset \sim(D \vee E)$ Premise
   (4) $\sim\sim U \vee T$ (4) $(A \cdot B) \supset (D \cdot E)$
   (5) $\sim U \supset T$ (5) $(A \cdot C) \supset (\sim D \cdot \sim E)$
   (6) $\sim\sim R \supset \sim U$ (6) $(A \cdot B) \vee (A \cdot C)$
   (7) $R \supset \sim U$ ∴ (7) $(D \cdot E) \vee (\sim D \cdot \sim E)$
   (8) $R \supset T$
   (9) $(R \vee S) \cdot (R \vee T)$
   (10) $(R \vee T) \cdot (R \vee S)$
   (11) $R \vee T$
   (12) $T \vee R$
   (13) $\sim\sim T \vee R$
   (14) $\sim T \supset R$
   (15) $\sim T \supset T$
   (16) $\sim\sim T \vee T$
   (17) $T \vee T$
∴ (18) T

f. (1) $P \vee Q$ Premise   g. (1) $(A \vee B) \supset (C \cdot D)$ Premise
   (2) $\sim Q \vee R$ Premise   (2) $\sim C$ Premise
   (3) $\sim P \cdot (R \supset S)$ Premise   (3) $\sim C \vee \sim D$
   (4) $\sim P$ (4) $\sim(C \cdot D)$
   (5) Q (5) $\sim(A \vee B)$
   (6) $\sim\sim Q$ (6) $\sim A \cdot \sim B$
   (7) R ∴ (7) $\sim A$
   (8) $(R \supset S) \cdot \sim P$
   (9) $R \supset S$
∴ (10) S

h. (1) $((M \cdot N) \cdot O) \supset P$ Premise
   (2) $Q \supset ((O \cdot M) \cdot N)$ Premise
   (3) $Q \supset (O \cdot (M \cdot N))$

(4) $Q \supset ((M \cdot N) \cdot O)$
(5) $Q \supset P$
∴ (6) $\sim Q \vee P$

i. (1) $P \equiv (Q \cdot R)$ Premise
(2) $(P \supset (Q \cdot R)) \cdot ((Q \cdot R) \supset P)$
(3) $(\sim(Q \cdot R) \supset \sim P) \cdot ((Q \cdot R) \supset P)$
(4) $(\sim(Q \cdot R) \supset \sim P) \cdot (\sim P \supset \sim(Q \cdot R))$
(5) $\sim\sim((\sim(Q \cdot R) \supset \sim P) \cdot (\sim P \supset \sim(Q \cdot R)))$
(6) $\sim(\sim(\sim(Q \cdot R) \supset \sim P) \vee \sim(\sim P \supset \sim(Q \cdot R)))$
(7) $\sim(\sim(Q \cdot R) \supset \sim P) \supset \sim(\sim P \supset \sim(Q \cdot R))$
(8) $\sim((\sim(Q \cdot R) \supset \sim P) \supset \sim((Q \cdot R) \supset P)$
∴ (9) $\sim((\sim Q \vee \sim R) \supset \sim P) \supset \sim((Q \cdot R) \supset P)$

j. (1) $A \supset ((B \cdot D) \supset (E \vee C))$ Premise
(2) $\sim E$ Premise
(3) $(D \cdot B) \cdot A$ Premise
(4) $(A \cdot (B \cdot D)) \supset (E \vee C)$
(5) $A \cdot (D \cdot B)$
(6) $A \cdot (B \cdot D)$
(7) $E \vee C$
(8) $\sim\sim E \vee C$
(9) $\sim E \supset C$
∴ (10) C

EXERCISE 5-8

1. Show that each of the following arguments is valid by giving a proof.

a. $P \supset (Q \cdot R)$
 $P \cdot S$
∴ R

b. $(A \vee B) \supset S$
 $\sim C$
 $S \supset C$
∴ $\sim A$

c. $(L \vee M) \supset \sim S$
 S
∴ $\sim L$

d. $\sim O$
 $(L \vee M) \supset N$
 $\sim(N \cdot \sim O)$
 $\sim L \supset P$
∴ P

e. $A \supset (B \supset C)$
 $D \supset \sim C$
 D
∴ $A \supset \sim B$

f. $A \supset (\sim B \cdot C)$
 $C \vee (A \cdot \sim B)$
∴ C

g. $\sim A$
 $\sim B$
 $(A \vee B) \equiv C$
∴ $\sim(C \cdot D)$

h. $\sim(T \vee S) \supset R$
 $T \supset M$
 $\sim S$
∴ $M \vee R$

i. $(A \cdot B) \cdot (A \vee C)$
 $(C \cdot D) \cdot (C \vee A)$
∴ $B \vee D$

j. $\sim C \vee ((B \supset D) \cdot (E \supset D))$
 $C \cdot (B \vee E)$
∴ D

k. $(\sim M \supset W) \cdot (L \supset W)$
 $\sim(\sim L \cdot M)$
∴ W

l. $E \supset (B \vee (C \vee A))$
 $(A \vee (B \vee C)) \supset (D \supset C)$
∴ $(E \cdot D) \supset C$

2. Symbolize each of the following arguments using the given symbols as constants, and give a proof of the validity of each argument.

   a. If either her grandmother comes to the *birthday* party or takes Sandy to the *movies,* Sandy will be *happy.* Hence, if Sandy isn't happy, her grandmother didn't come to the birthday party. (*B, M, H*)

   b. Since the party will be a *success* (no matter who attends), it will be a success if Martin *attends.* (*S, A*)

   c. If the thief *entered* through the side window, then both the *alarm* did not work and the *lights* did not go on. But, if either the alarm did not work or the lights did not go on, the security *system* we just installed is not reliable. Hence, if the thief entered through the side window, the security system is not reliable. (*E, A, L, S*)

   d. The hostages should be put on *trial* if they are foreign *agents.* Either they are *representatives* of the government or they are agents. Since they are not representatives of the government, they should be put on trial. (*T, A, R*)

   e. Loni will be *accepted* by the group only if she learns to be more *open* about her feelings. But if she learns this, then she must realize that her feelings are sometimes going to be *hurt.* Consequently, she must realize that her feelings are going to be hurt, for she has been accepted by the group. (*A, O, H*)

   f. If the *regulations* have been carefully drawn up and are *enforced,* there will be far fewer consumer *complaints* than there are now. If enforcing the regulations results in fewer complaints, then we can reduce the size of our office *staff.* Since the regulations were carefully drawn up, the staff can be reduced. (*R, E, C, S*)

   g. If we give the needs of the *organization* the highest priority, then we must *sacrifice* some of our individual needs; and if we make *decisions* with the organization in mind, we shall all be *happier* in the long run. Either we should give organizational needs the highest priority or at least make decisions with the organization in mind. Moreover if we do give organizational needs the highest priority, we will not all be happier; and if we make decisions with the organization in mind, we will not sacrifice some individual needs. Consequently, we must sacrifice some individual needs if, and only if, we will not all be happier in the long run. (*O, S, D, H*)

   h. If the court-appointed lawyer does not do a *good* job on the case and the defendant is *convicted,* then the lawyer will have acted *irresponsibly* and the defendant will have *suffered.* Assuming that the lawyer neither does a good job nor that the defendant is acquitted, we can conclude that the defendant will have suffered. (*G, C, I, S*)

   i. It is not the case that both a *settlement* was reached and the teachers are back at *work,* since had a settlement been reached, the *children* would be back in school and last night's *violence* could have been avoided. Moreover, if the violence could have been avoided, the teachers would not be back to work. (*S, W, C, V*)

   j. If there is *evil* in the world, then either God is not *willing* to prevent that evil or God is not *able* to prevent it. However, if God is all-*powerful,* He is able to prevent evil, and if He is *beneficient* he is willing to prevent evil. Of course, if *God* exists, then he is both all-powerful and beneficient. We know, however, that there is evil in the world. Consequently, God does not exist. (*E, W, A, P, B, G*)

k. If people have *free* will, then their actions are not *caused*. If people have free will, then if their actions are not caused their actions cannot be *predicted*. Moreover, if their actions are not caused, then if their actions cannot be predicted then the *results* of their actions cannot be predicted either. Since utilitarianism is a *viable* ethical theory only if the results of peoples' actions can be predicted, it follows that if people have free will, utilitarianism is not viable. (*F, C, P, R, V*)

l. Candy cannot both have a full-time *job* and go to *school* full time. But if she doesn't go to school full time, she will not be able to *graduate* in June; and if she doesn't graduate in June, she will not have a full-time job. If Candy has not been *careful* with her money, then she will have to get a full-time job if she is going to be able to pay her *tuition* next semester. If she doesn't pay her tuition, she won't be able to graduate. Consequently, if Candy pays her tuition, she must have been careful with her money. (*J, S, G, C, T*)

3. Show that the following rules are redundant by deriving each of them from other rules.
   a. Contraposition
   b. Denying the Consequent
   c. Disjunctive Syllogism

5:4 CONDITIONAL PROOF

We discussed conditional proof in Chapter 3, but because the only rules of inference introduced in that chapter were AA and DC, we were able to construct proofs only for arguments composed of statement forms with the main connective '⊃'. Now that we have additional rules of inference, we can expand our discussion of conditional proofs to include other statement forms. Before reading on, you may wish to review the earlier discussion of conditional proof; as a reminder, however, recall that we use CP to derive conclusions whose form is a conditional statement, and we do this by *assuming the antecedent of the conditional statement and then deriving the consequent.*

One benefit of adding conditional proof to our system of natural deduction is that CP often simplifies the demonstration of the validity of an argument. Of more importance, however, is the fact that without the addition of CP to our system, there would be some arguments whose validity could be shown by using truth tables but not by using the rules so far introduced. The following is one example:

EXAMPLE 20

$\sim p \lor q$

$\therefore p \supset (p \cdot q)$

It is an easy task to show, by using CP, that the argument form in example 20 is valid. The proof follows:

  (1) $\sim p \lor q$ Premise

*(2) p Assumption

*(3) $\sim\sim p$ (2), DN

*(4) q (1), (3), DS

*(5) $p \cdot q$ (2), (4), Conj

$\therefore$ (6) $p \supset (p \cdot q)$ (2) to (5), CP

We have used the notation from Chapter 3 in giving the above proof. In particular, a statement form occurring on a "starred" line is either an assumption or was derived, at least in part, on the basis of the assumption. The justification for line (6) is read "Line 6 was derived by conditional proof from lines (2) through (5)."

For reasons that will become obvious shortly, we are going to begin using a different notation to keep track of our assumptions. In the new notation, we shall simply replace the row of asterisks with a straight line, beginning with the step in which the assumption was made and ending with the step in which we have derived the consequent of the conclusion of the argument; then we shall underline this last step. With our new notation, the above proof is as follows:

  (1) $\sim p \lor q$ Premise

(2) p Assumption

(3) $\sim\sim p$ (2), DN

(4) q (1), (3), DS

(5) $p \cdot q$ (2), (4), Conj

$\therefore$ (6) $p \supset (p \cdot q)$ (2) to (5), CP

The line which runs from line (2) to line (5) indicates the **scope** of our assumption. That is, the line shows that every step to the right of the line is either an assumption or depends on an assumption. By drawing the horizontal line under line (5), we show that we have **discharged the assumption.** Wherever an assumption is discharged, the line immediately following will be a conditional statement whose antecedent is the statement form which occurs at the top of the vertical line [in the above case, 'p' on line (2)] and whose consequent is the line of the proof under which the horizontal line is drawn [in the above case, '$p \cdot q$' on line (5)].

5:4.1 Some Examples In this section we shall look at a few arguments in which CP is used to show validity. Proofs using CP are no different from other proofs constructed within our system, except that we are working with an assumption (which is like an additional premise) that must be discharged.

ARGUMENT 16

If the governor decides to seek reelection, then if he is smart he will choose a well-known running mate. But, only if he does not choose a well-known running mate will his opponent carry the urban vote. Hence, if the governor seeks reelection, he is not smart, because his opponent will carry the urban vote.

Step 1: Symbolize the argument. To do this, we assign constants in the following way:

R = The governor decides to seek reelection.

S = The governor is smart.

C = The governor will choose a well-known running mate.

V = The governor's opponent will carry the urban vote.

With this assignment of variables, argument 16 has the form

$R \supset (S \supset C)$

$U \supset {\sim}C$

U

$\therefore R \supset {\sim}S$

Step 2: Since we shall be using CP for the proof of the validity of argument 16, let's rewrite the form of the argument to make our task explicit:

$R \supset (S \supset C)$	Premise
$U \supset {\sim}C$	Premise
U	Premise
R	Assumption
$\therefore {\sim}S$	

Step 3: By assuming the antecedent of the conclusion, we see that we have to derive '${\sim}S$'. Our premises indicate that we could get '${\sim}S$' by DC if we could get '$S \supset C$' from the first premise and if we could get '${\sim}C$'.

Step 4: We could get '$S \supset C$' by using our assumption and AA. And '${\sim}C$' can be derived with another instance of AA by using the second and third premises. This completes our strategy; the proof follows:

(1) $R \supset (S \supset C)$	Premise
(2) $U \supset {\sim}C$	Premise
(3) U	Premise
(4) R	Assumption
(5) $S \supset C$	(1), (4), AA
(6) ${\sim}C$	(2), (3), AA
(7) ${\sim}S$	(5), (6), DC
$\therefore$ (8) $R \supset {\sim}S$	(4) to (7), CP

Notice that, starting at line (4), where we made our assumption, a vertical line is drawn down to line (7) to indicate the scope of the assumption. Also notice that line (7) is the line where we derived the consequent of the conditional statement we wished to prove. The horizontal line under line (7) indicates that we are going to discharge our assumption. This we do at line (8); we indicate that this has been done with the notation '(4) to (7), CP' in the justification column.

So far, we have used CP only to derive the conclusion of an argument which had the form of a conditional statement. We can, however, use CP any time we wish to derive a conditional statement, *even if the derived conditional statement is not the conclusion of an argument*. This is shown in the next proof.

ARGUMENT 17

The defendant will be convicted if it's the case that if his victim testifies then the jury believes the testimony. But either the jury will believe the testimony or the judge will allow the victim to be intimidated by the defendant's attorney. Hence, the defendant will be convicted, for if his victim testifies, the judge will not allow the defendant's attorney to intimidate her.

Step 1: Symbolize the argument. Constants are assigned as follows:

C = The defendant will be convicted.

T = The defendant's victim testifies.

B = The jury believes the victim's testimony.

A = The judge allows the victim to be intimidated.

With this assignment of variables, argument 17 has the following form:

$(T \supset B) \supset C$

$B \lor A$

$T \supset {\sim}A$

$\therefore C$

Step 2: We must derive 'C', and the obvious premise from which to get it is the first. Moreover, if we had '$T \supset B$', we could get 'C' from this premise by using AA.

Step 3: Checking our premises, we see that we do not have '$T \supset B$'. But, since '$T \supset B$' is a conditional statement, we can consider deriving it with CP by assuming 'T'. In this case, we would use 'T' to derive 'B'.

Step 4: We could get 'B' from the second premise by Comm and DS if we had '${\sim}A$'. We can get '${\sim}A$' from the third premise by using AA and our assumption.

Step 5: Our strategy, then, is to use CP to derive '$T \supset B$' and then use '$T \supset B$' to derive 'C'. The proof follows:

(1) $(T \supset B) \supset C$ Premise

(2) $B \lor A$ Premise

(3) $T \supset {\sim}A$ Premise

⎡(4) T Assumption

| (5) ${\sim}A$ (3), (4), AA

| (6) $A \lor B$ (2), Comm

⎣(7) B (5), (6), DS

(8) $T \supset B$ (4) to (7), CP

∴ (9) C (1), (8), AA

In the above proof we discharged our assumption 'T' at line (8) by the rule CP. Once we have done so, the result (in this case, '$T \supset B$') can be used with the rules of inference just like any other line in the proof, for when the assumption has been discharged the result is outside the scope of the assumption. That '$T \supset B$' in the above proof is outside the scope of the assumption is shown by the absence of a vertical line to the left of line (8).

The fact that we can use CP anywhere in a proof so long as we discharge the assumption can be further generalized in that we can use more than one instance of CP in a given proof. Two cases may arise; in the first, there are two independent occurences of CP in a proof, and in the second, the scope of one instance of CP falls within the scope of another instance. Both are treated below. The first case is discussed in example 21; the second is shown in the proof of the validity of argument 18.

EXAMPLE 21

Show that the following argument is valid:

$A \supset (B \supset C)$

${\sim}C$

$B \lor A$

∴ $A \equiv {\sim}B$

Step 1: Since the conclusion is a statement of equivalency, we could use Eq to derive it, if we could derive '$A \supset {\sim}B$' and '${\sim}B \supset A$'. Both are, of course, conditional statements, so we shall consider using CP to derive them.

Step 2: To derive '$A \supset {\sim}B$', we assume the antecedent 'A', and try to derive '${\sim}B$'. With this assumption we can derive '$B \supset C$' from the first premise; '${\sim}C$' and DC would then enable us to derive '${\sim}B$'.

Step 3: To derive '${\sim}B \supset A$', we assume '${\sim}B$' and try to derive 'A'. This we can get easily by DS with the third premise.

Step 4: Having derived both conditional statements, we can conjoin them with Conj and then get '$A \equiv {\sim}B$' by Eq. The proof follows:

(1) $A \supset (B \supset C)$ Premise

(2) $\sim C$ Premise

(3) $B \lor A$ Premise

(4) A Assumption

(5) $B \supset C$ (4), (1), AA

(6) $\sim B$ (2), (5), DC

(7) $A \supset \sim B$ (4) to (6), CP

(8) $\sim B$ Assumption

(9) A (3), (8), DS

(10) $\sim B \supset A$ (8), (9), CP

(11) $(A \supset \sim B) \cdot (\sim B \supset A)$ (7), (10), Conj

(12) $A \equiv \sim B$ (11), Eq

ARGUMENT 18

If either the House passes the bill or the President supports it, then if the Senate is concerned about public pressure, they will both have a short debate and pass the bill. But, if the Senate passes the bill or the President supports it, it is likely that the President will have trouble in the next election. As a result, if the House passes the bill, then if the Senate cares about public pressure, the President will have trouble in the next election.

Step 1: Symbolize the argument. To do this, constants are assigned as follows:

     P = The House passes the bill.

     S = The President supports the bill.

     C = The Senate is concerned about public pressure.

     D = The Senate will have a short debate.

     B = The Senate will pass the bill.

     T = The President will have trouble in the next election.

Then we have

     $(P \lor S) \supset (C \supset (D \cdot B))$

     $(B \lor S) \supset T$

     $\therefore P \supset (C \supset T)$

Step 2: The conclusion of the argument has the form of a conditional statement, so we should consider trying to derive it by using CP. In this case, we would assume 'P' and then attempt to derive '$C \supset T$'. The structure we would then be working with is

$(P \lor S) \supset (C \supset (D \cdot B))$ Premise

$(B \lor S) \supset T$ Premise

P Assumption

$\therefore C \supset T$

Step 3: Now consider how we might derive '$C \supset T$'. In checking our premises we do not find any one premise in which both 'C' and 'T' occur, so there is no obvious rule we could apply to get '$C \supset T$'.

Step 4: We could, instead, attempt to derive '$C \supset T$' by CP. To do this, we would make an *additional assumption* 'C' and then try to derive 'T'. The structure we would now be working with is

$(P \lor S) \supset (C \supset (D \cdot B))$ Premise

$(B \lor S) \supset T$ Premise

P Assumption

C Assumption

$\therefore T$

Step 5: We could get 'T' from the second premise if we could first derive either 'B' or 'S'. There is no obvious way to get 'S', so we consider 'B'.

Step 6: We could get 'B' from the first premise if we could first derive '$D \cdot B$'. We could get '$D \cdot B$' from '$C \supset (D \cdot B)$' by AA and our assumption 'C' if we could get '$C \supset (D \cdot B)$'.

Step 7: Our task now is to derive '$C \supset (D \cdot B)$'. This we could do with the first premise and AA if we had '$P \lor S$'. But, since we have assumed 'P', we can get '$P \lor S$' easily enough by Add.

Step 8: Our overall strategy, then, is to assume 'P' and assume 'C' · 'P' and Add will enable us to derive '$C \supset (D \cdot B)$', and 'C' will enable us to derive '$D \cdot B$'. By using Comm, Simp, and Add, we shall then be able to get '$B \lor S$' so we can derive 'T'. We shall then have to discharge our two assumptions. The proof follows:

(1) $(P \lor S) \supset (C \supset (D \cdot B))$ Premise

(2) $(B \lor S) \supset T$ Premise

(3) P Assumption

(4) C Assumption

(5) $P \lor S$ (3), Add

(6) $C \supset (D \cdot B)$ (1), (5), AA

(7) $D \cdot B$ (4), (6), AA

(8) $B \cdot D$ (7), Comm

(9) B	(8), Simp
(10) $B \lor S$	(9), Add
(11) T	(2), (10), AA
(12) $C \supset T$	(4) to (11), CP
∴ (13) $P \supset (C \supset T)$	(3) to (12), CP

There are several things to note about the above proof. First, unlike the case of example 21, the scope of our second assumption 'C' falls within the scope of our first assumption 'P'. This is shown by the fact that the vertical line from line (3) through line (12) includes within its scope the vertical line (4) through line (11). The second thing to note is that we discharged both our assumptions. 'C' was discharged on line (12), and 'P' was discharged on line (13). As required, the line where each assumption was discharged is a conditional statement whose antecedent is the assumption and whose consequent is the entry on the line of the proof where the vertical line indicating the scope of the assumption ends.

The final, and perhaps most important, thing to note is the order in which we made our assumptions. In particular, we had to assume 'P' before we assumed 'C'. Before reading on, you should consider why this is so.

If we had assumed 'C' and then assumed 'P', the scope of the assumption 'P' would have fallen within the scope of the assumption 'C'. As a result, when we were ready to discharge our assumptions, we would have had to discharge 'P' first and then 'C'. (The principle here is that we have to discharge our assumptions in order, from the right-most vertical line to the left-most vertical line.) The result of this would have been a conditional statement with 'C', rather than 'P', as the antecedent, whereas the conclusion of the argument is a conditional statement with 'P' as antecedent. As a procedural rule, when trying to derive a conditional statement by CP which is itself composed of conditional statements, make your assumptions from left to right.

In this section we extended the discussion of conditional proof in Chapter 3 to include additional kinds of arguments. We also determined that more than one assumption may be made in a proof—a particularly useful feature for deriving statements of equivalency. Additionally, we changed our method of indicating which steps in a proof result from an assumption so as to make clear how, and in which order, our assumptions are discharged.

EXERCISE 5-9

1. What is a conditional proof?

2. Why is it necessary to have conditional proof as a procedure in our system of natural deduction?

3. What is the scope of an assumption? What does it mean to discharge an assumption? How is each of these indicated in proofs?

4. What procedure should be followed in making assumptions for a conditional proof when some assumptions are within the scope of one or more other assumptions?

5. Explain the procedure used for constructing conditional proofs. Under what circumstances should such proofs be used?

EXERCISE 5-10

1. Show the validity of each of the following arguments by providing a conditional proof.

a. $P \lor \sim Q$
   $\sim R \supset \sim P$
   $\therefore Q \supset R$

b. $P \supset Q$
   $\therefore P \supset (P \supset Q)$

c. $A \supset C$
   $(\sim A \lor C) \supset (D \supset B)$
   $\therefore A \supset (D \supset B)$

d. $(P \lor Q) \supset (R \cdot S)$
   $\therefore \sim P \lor R$

e. $(A \supset B) \cdot (\sim A \supset C)$
   $C \supset D$
   $\therefore \sim B \supset D$

f. $P \supset (Q \lor R)$
   $\sim (S \supset R)$
   $S \supset P$
   $\therefore P \supset Q$

g. $(A \lor B) \supset C$
   $\therefore ((C \lor D) \supset E) \supset (A \supset E)$

h. $(A \supset B)$
   $\therefore (A \cdot C) \supset B$

i. $\sim A \lor \sim (B \cdot C)$
   $\therefore B \supset (C \supset \sim A)$

j. $(P \lor Q) \supset R$
   $\therefore P \supset R$

2. Show the validity of the following arguments from problem 2 of Exercise 5-8 by constructing a conditional proof.

a. Argument a
b. Argument c
c. Argument g
d. Argument k
e. Argument l

5:5 INDIRECT PROOF

In this section, as in the previous one, we are going to expand on some material discussed earlier in the text. In Chapter 3 we introduced indirect proofs; you may wish to review that discussion prior to reading on in this section.

Recall that indirect proof is just a special case of conditional proof. As a result, adding indirect proof to our system will not allow us to prove as valid any arguments which could not also be proved valid with our rules of inference, the Rule of Replacement, and conditional proof. In an important respect, then, indirect proof need not be added to our system to make it complete. However, it will facilitate proofs in our system—making our work just a little easier in some cases.

Before looking at some examples, let's briefly review the essential features of indirect proof. Recall that the idea is to derive a *contradiction* on the assumption that the conclusion of our argument is false. Since all contradictions are necessarily false (as can easily be shown by constructing a truth table for '$p \cdot {\sim}p$'), we are then justified in asserting that our assumption is false.

With the rules of inference developed in this chapter, we can make the structure of indirect proofs more explicit. To do this, suppose we have some arbitrary argument with n premises, which we symbolize as follows:

P_1

P_2

. . .

P_n

$\therefore C$

In showing the validity of such an argument by indirect proof, we *assume the negation of the conclusion* and then attempt to derive a contradiction. Let us suppose that we have been able to do this, and let the contradiction be represented by '$Q \cdot {\sim}Q$'. Our proof would contain at least the following lines [the lines indicated as missing by the ellipses (dots) would depend on what the particular premises of our argument were]:

(1) P_1 Premise

(2) P_2 Premise

. . .

(n) P_n Premise

(a) ${\sim}C$ Assumption

. . .

(b) Q However Q was derived

. . .

(c) ${\sim}Q$ However ${\sim}Q$ was derived

(d) $Q \cdot {\sim}Q$ (b), (c), Conj

Having derived '$Q \cdot {\sim}Q$', we could then discharge our assumption by using CP. This would give us

(e) ${\sim}C \supset (Q \cdot {\sim}Q)$

This result, along with the earlier steps, is what was referred to in Chapter 3 as the conditional-proof component of every indirect proof. We also noted that every indirect proof has a DC component. This is brought out in the following steps, which could be added to the above schema:

(f) ${\sim}Q \lor Q$ (c), Add

(g) ${\sim}(Q \cdot {\sim}Q)$ (f), DM

(h) ${\sim}{\sim}C$ (e), (g), DC

$\therefore$ (i) C (h), DN

Lines (e) through (h) make explicit the DC component of an indirect proof. Since we can always produce lines (e) through (i) in a proof, once we have derived a contradiction on the assumption that the conclusion of the argument is not the case, we instead simply discharge our assumption by writing 'C' on the line following the one where we derived our contradiction. We then note in the justification column the lines falling under the scope of the assumption and 'RAA'. In the justification column, RAA stands for the lines corresponding to (e) through (i) in the schema above, which we could have included in the proof. The actual structure of indirect proofs is then as follows:

(1)	P_1	Premise
(2)	P_2	Premise
	. . .	
(n)	P_n	Premise
(a)	~C	Assumption
	. . .	
(b)	Q	However Q was derived
	. . .	
(c)	~Q	However ~Q was derived
(d)	$Q \cdot \sim Q$	(b), (c), Conj
∴ (e)	C	(a) to (d), RAA

A word concerning the strategy for constructing indirect proofs is in order before we turn to some examples. In conditional proofs we always know what has to be derived from the assumption (namely the consequent of the conditional statement we want to prove), but the only thing we know in the case of indirect proofs is that we have to derive a contradiction; *there is no particular contradiction that has to be derived.* On the positive side, this means that any contradiction we can derive will do; on the negative side, this means that we have no specific "direction" to follow in the structure of our proof.

To have at least some direction as you consider how to prove a result, remember that the contradiction will concern one of the following three pairs of statements:

(1) The assumption and its negation

(2) One of the premises and its negation

(3) Some statement and its negation derived from the premises and the assumption

As a rule of thumb, it is generally best to consider (1) or (2) before (3), since in the former two cases you have some idea of just which statements you want to derive. It is also sometimes helpful, once the assumption is made, to use the assumption with an appropriate premise to derive some statement, and then to see if the negation of this statement can be derived. As is the case for all types of proofs within our system, the more practice you have, the easier it becomes to use indirect proof.

5:5.1 Some Examples   In this section we shall look at two indirect proofs. It should be clear to you that indirect proofs are just like any of the other proofs within our system, with the addition of an assumption that we can use as an additional premise. Since you have no doubt developed a certain expertise by doing the exercises accompanying the earlier material, our purpose here is primarily to provide familiarity with the strategy, structure, and notation for indirect proofs.

ARGUMENT 19

If either Descartes' solution to the mind-body problem is correct or there is mental substance, materialism is false. Moreover, since materialism is false only if Hobbes was fundamentally wrong in his analysis of the problem, it follows that Descartes' solution is incorrect. This is so because Hobbes' analysis is fundamentally sound.

Step 1: Symbolize the argument. Constants are assigned as follows:

D = Descartes' solution to the mind-body problem is correct.

S = There is mental substance.

M = Materialism is false.

H = Hobbes was fundamentally right in his analysis of the mind-body problem.

With this assignment of constants, the argument has the following form:

$(D \lor S) \supset M$

$M \supset {\sim}H$

H

$\therefore {\sim}D$

Step 2: Once again we begin by assuming the negation of the conclusion, in this case 'D'. (The actual negation is '${\sim}{\sim}D$' but, by DN, it is equivalent to 'D'.) Now we must consider how to derive a contradiction.

Step 3: Having assumed 'D', and considering how it might then be used, we see that by using Add with 'D' we could derive '$D \lor S$' and, hence, 'M'.

Step 4: If we could derive '${\sim}M$', we would have our contradiction. Checking our premises, we see that we can get '${\sim}M$' from the second and third premises. That will give us our contradiction, '$M \cdot {\sim}M$', so we can proceed with our proof. The proof follows:

(1) $(D \lor S) \supset M$ Premise

(2) $M \supset \sim H$ Premise

(3) H Premise

(4) D Assumption

(5) $D \lor S$ (4), Add

(6) M (1), (5), AA

(7) $\sim\sim H$ (3), DN

(8) $\sim M$ (2), (7), DC

(9) $M \cdot \sim M$ (6), (8), Conj

∴(10) $\sim D$ (4) to (9), RAA

In this proof of the validity of argument 19, the contradiction is formed by deriving a statement and its negation from the premises and the assumption. This is not, however, the only proof that can be given. It is also possible to derive '$H \cdot \sim H$', and you may wish to try constructing that proof yourself.

ARGUMENT 20

If it's the case that only if we are not directly aware of the contents of our mental states is phenomenalism false, then neither Hume's nor Berkeley's empiricist position is correct. But, if Berkeley's position is not correct, then both Hume's is and representative realism is false. Moreover, if either phenomenalism is true or we are directly aware of the contents of our mental states, then representative realism is false; so it is false.

Step 1: Symbolize the argument by assigning constants in the following way:

D = We are directly aware of the contents of our mental states.

P = Phenomenalism is true.

H = Hume's empiricist position is correct.

B = Berkeley's empiricist position is correct.

R = Representative realism is false.

The argument has the following form:

$(\sim P \supset \sim D) \supset \sim(H \lor B)$

$\sim B \supset (H \cdot R)$

$(P \lor D) \supset R$

∴ R

Step 2: Our assumption for RAA is '$\sim R$'. Since there is no obvious way of working with the premises alone to see what contradiction might be derived, we consider how '$\sim R$' might be used with the premises.

Step 3: '$\sim R$' and the third premise can be used with DC to derive '$\sim(P \lor$

D)'. This, as it stands, does not appear useful, but if we use DM, we shall be able to get '~P · ~D'; with Simp we can get either '~P' or '~D' by itself.

Step 4: Considering how we might use '~P · ~D' or '~P' or '~D', we see that the first premise is the only likely one with which to work. Since we can get '~D', we can also get, by Add, Comm, and Imp, '~P ⊃ ~D', the antecedent of the first premise. This would enable us to derive '~(H ∨ B)' by AA.

Step 5: Following the rule of thumb of eliminating outside negation signs, we see that from '~(H ∨ B)' we shall be able to derive '~H · ~B'. This result can be used with the second premise to derive 'H · ~H', so our strategy is complete. The proof follows:

(1)	(~P ⊃ ~D) ⊃ ~(H ∨ B)	Premise
(2)	~B ⊃ (H · R)	Premise
(3)	(P ∨ D) ⊃ R	Premise
(4)	~R	Assumption
(5)	~(P ∨ D)	(3), (4), DC
(6)	~P · ~D	(5), DM
(7)	~D · ~P	(6), Comm
(8)	~D	Simp
(9)	~D ∨ P	(8), Add
(10)	P ∨ ~D	(9), Comm
(11)	~~P ∨ ~D	(10), DN
(12)	~P ⊃ ~D	(11), Imp
(13)	~(H ∨ B)	(1), (12), AA
(14)	~H · ~B	(13), DM
(15)	~H	(14), Simp
(16)	~B · ~H	(14), Comm
(17)	~B	(16), Simp
(18)	H · R	(2), (17), AA
(19)	H	(18), Simp
(20)	H · ~H	(19), (15), Conj
∴ (21)	R	(4) to (20), RAA

Notice that in the strategy for the above proof we simply used our assumption and whatever premises and rules of inference we could, to see what could be derived. We carried out this process until we found that 'H

· ~H' could be derived. As an exercise, you might try constructing a proof of the validity of argument 20 by deriving 'B · ~B'.

In this section we expanded our earlier discussion of indirect proof and looked at indirect proofs which involve the additional rules of inference developed earlier in this chapter. The essential feature of indirect proofs is assuming the negation of the conclusion we want to derive and then attempting to derive a contradiction by using this assumption. We also noted that there is no particular contradiction which must be derived; as a result, we are not provided with "direction" as we are with CP. As an aid in deriving the contradiction, we mentioned three sources: the assumption and its negation, one of the premises and its negation, or some statement and its negation which are both derived from the premises and the assumption.

EXERCISE 5-11

1. What is an indirect proof?

2. Is it necessary to have indirect proof as a procedure in our system of natural deduction? Explain your answer.

3. Explain the procedure used for constructing indirect proofs.

4. What are the three general forms that the derived contradiction in an indirect proof can have?

5. Explain the relationship of indirect proofs to conditional proofs and the argument form denying the consequent.

EXERCISE 5-12

1. Show the validity of each of the following arguments by providing an indirect proof.

a. $(B \lor C) \supset D$
   $\sim A$
   $D \supset A$
   $\therefore \sim B$

b. $(A \lor B) \supset C$
   $\sim(C \cdot \sim D)$
   $\sim D$
   $\sim A \supset E$
   $\therefore E$

c. $C \lor (A \cdot \sim B)$
   $A \supset (\sim B \cdot C)$
   $\therefore C$

d. $A \lor B$
   $A \lor \sim B$
   $\therefore A$

e. $\sim C \supset D$
   $A \supset (B \lor \sim(C \lor D))$
   $\therefore \sim B \supset \sim A$

f. A
   $\therefore B \supset (B \lor A)$

g. $P \lor Q$
   $Q \supset (R \cdot S)$
   $(R \lor P) \supset T$
   $\therefore T$

h. $(A \cdot \sim B) \supset (A \supset C)$
   $\sim(B \lor \sim A)$
   $C \supset D$
   $\therefore A \supset D$

i. $\sim C$
   $A \supset (B \supset C)$
   $\therefore \sim(A \cdot B)$

j. $A \supset ((B \cdot D) \supset (E \lor C))$
   $\sim E$
   $(D \cdot B) \cdot A$
   $\therefore C$

k. $A \supset (B \cdot C)$
   $B \supset \sim C$
   $\therefore \sim A$

2. Show the validity of the arguments in problem 2 of Exercise 5-8 by providing indirect proofs.

5:6 DERIVING TAUTOLOGIES

A tautology is a statement form which takes the value true for every possible assignment of truth values to the variables in the statement. Any argument whose conclusion is a tautology must be valid, since there is no way for the argument to have all true premises *and* a false conclusion. One consequence is that the premises of an argument whose conclusion is a tautology do not affect the validity of the argument. Perhaps the best way to see this is to consider the following two examples:

EXAMPLE 22   EXAMPLE 23

q $\sim q$
$\therefore p \supset p$ $\therefore p \supset p$

In examples 22 and 23, the conclusion is a tautology: If 'p' is assigned the value T, then '$p \supset p$' is true (this is the first line of the truth table for '$\supset$'); and if 'p' is assigned the value F, then '$p \supset p$' is again true (this is the fourth line of the truth table for '$\supset$'). Since '$p \supset p$' is always true, it is not possible for 'q' in example 22 to be true and the conclusion false; nor is it possible for '$\sim q$' in example 23 to be true and the conclusion false. In neither case, then, does the truth or falsity of the premise play a role in the validity of the argument.

Since the argument form in example 23 is valid, we should be able to construct a proof within our system to show this. With the addition of CP to the system, this is an easy task. One such proof follows:[4]

(1) $\sim q$	Premise
(2) p	Assumption
(3) $p \lor \sim p$	(2), Add
(4) $\sim p \lor p$	(3), Comm
(5) $\sim\sim p$	(2), DN
(6) p	(4), (5), DS
$\therefore$ (7) $p \supset p$	(2)–(6), CP

Notice that we made no use of the premise '$\sim q$'; the proof of the validity of the

[4] Steps (3) to (5) appear in the proof because there is no rule of inference which allows us to derive 'p' from 'p' in one step. An alternative way of deriving 'p' from step (1) would be to use DN twice, first deriving '$\sim\sim p$' and then deriving 'p'.

argument form in example 22 would be identical to the above with the exception of line (1), where we would have 'q'. In proofs such as these, where a statement is derived without using any premises, we derive the statement from the **empty set of premises.**

In constructing proofs for tautologies, the rule of thumb to follow is to use CP if the tautology is a conditional statement, and use RAA otherwise. Several examples follow.

EXAMPLE 24

Construct a proof for the following tautology:

$(p \cdot q) \supset (q \vee r)$

Step 1: Since this tautology is a conditional statement, we shall follow our rule of thumb and try to construct a proof using CP.

Step 2: For CP, we shall assume the antecedent '$p \cdot q$' and then try to derive the consequent '$q \vee r$'. This is straightforward, since with '$p \cdot q$' we can get 'q' and then, by Add, derive '$q \vee r$'. The proof follows:

(1) $p \cdot q$	Assumption
(2) $q \cdot p$	(1), Comm
(3) q	(2), Simp
(4) $q \vee r$	(3), Add
(5) $(p \cdot q) \supset (q \vee r)$	(1) to (4), CP

EXAMPLE 25

Construct a proof of the following tautology:

$(p \supset q) \vee (q \supset p)$

Step 1: Since the statement form we want to derive is not a conditional statement, we shall follow our rule of thumb and use RAA. For this, we assume '$\sim((p \supset q) \vee (q \supset p))$'.

Step 2: Since we have an outside negation sign on a disjunction, we shall appeal to another of our rules of thumb and eliminate the negation sign by using DM. This provides us with a conjunction, both of whose conjuncts have an outside negation sign.

Step 3: At this point we can use Simp and eliminate outside negation signs. With this done, the remainder of the proof will be obvious. The proof follows:

(1) $\sim((p \supset q) \vee (q \supset p))$	Assumption
(2) $\sim(p \supset q) \cdot \sim(q \supset p)$	(1), DM
(3) $\sim(p \supset q)$	(2), Simp
(4) $\sim(\sim p \vee q)$	(3), Imp

(5) $p \cdot \sim q$ (4), DM

(6) $\sim(q \supset p) \cdot \sim(p \supset q)$ (2), Comm

(7) $\sim(q \supset p)$ (6), Simp

(8) $\sim(\sim q \vee p)$ (7), Imp

(9) $q \cdot \sim p$ (8), DM

(10) p (5), Simp

(11) $\sim p \cdot q$ (9), Comm

(12) $\sim p$ (11), Simp

(13) $p \cdot \sim p$ (10), (12), Conj

$\therefore$ (14) $(p \supset q) \vee (q \supset p)$ (1) to (13), RAA

Having discussed how to derive tautologies within our system, we can now draw a few connections between the system developed in this chapter and the truth-table method discussed in the previous chapter. Recall that in checking the validity of an argument by the truth-table method, we rewrite the argument as a conditional statement whose antecedent is a conjunction of the premises and whose consequent is the conclusion. Schematically, we begin with

P_1

P_2

$\ldots$

P_n

$\therefore C$

and rewrite it as

$$((P_1 \cdot P_2) \cdot \ldots \cdot P_n) \supset C$$

For a valid argument, the instance of this conditional statement takes the value T for every line of the truth table; in other words, *the conditional statement associated with every valid argument is a tautology.* As a result, for every valid argument form which can be expressed in our system, we can derive as a tautology the conditional statement associated with that argument form; this we do by using CP. Schematically, the structure for this proof is

SCHEMA 1

(1) $((P_1 \cdot P_2) \cdot \ldots \cdot P_n)$ Assumption

$\ldots$

(m) C However C was derived

$\therefore$ (n) $((P_1 \cdot P_2) \cdot \ldots \cdot P_n) \supset C$ (1) to (m), CP

By using Assoc, Comm, and Simp on line (1), we would be able to get the following:

SCHEMA 2

(1) $((P_1 \cdot P_2) \cdot \ldots \cdot P_n)$ Assumption

. . .

(m) P_1 Simp

. . .

(n) P_2 Simp

. . .

(o) P_n Simp

The missing lines in schema 2 are lines where we would have used Comm and/ or Assoc in order to use Simp to get each premise of the original argument form on an independent line of our proof. Schema 2 can now be expanded so as to indicate that we have derived 'C' and can, therefore, by CP, derive '$((P_1 \cdot P_2) \cdot \ldots \cdot P_n) \supset C$'. This is shown in the next schema.

SCHEMA 3

(1) $((P_1 \cdot P_2) \cdot \ldots \cdot P_n)$ Assumption

. . .

(m) P_1 Simp

. . .

(n) P_2 Simp

. . .

(o) P_n Simp

. . .

(p) C However C is derived

(p + 1) $((P_1 \cdot P_2) \cdot \ldots \cdot P_n) \supset C$ (1) to (p), CP

The relationship between providing a proof of the validity of an argument by deriving the conclusion from the premises, and providing a proof by showing that the conditional statement associated with a valid argument is a tautology, should now be obvious. In particular, every line from line (o) through line (p) of the schematized proof in schema 3 will be exactly the same as the lines of the proof which would be given in the case where P_1 to P_n are taken as premises (as opposed to being assumed for CP). Lines (1) to (o) in schema 3 merely enable us to break down our conjunctive assumption.

The relationship developed here is made explicit by showing the validity of the following argument, first by deriving the conclusion from the premises and then by showing that the conditional statement associated with the argument is a tautology:

EXAMPLE 26

$(A \lor B) \supset C$

$\sim C \cdot D$

$\therefore D \cdot \sim A$

We first derive the conclusion from the premises:

(1)	$(A \lor B) \supset C$	Premise
(2)	$\sim C \cdot D$	Premise
(3)	$\sim C$	(2), Simp
(4)	$\sim(A \lor B)$	(1), (3), DC
(5)	$\sim A \cdot \sim B$	(4), DM
(6)	$\sim A$	(5), Simp
(7)	$D \cdot \sim C$	(2), Comm
(8)	D	(7), Simp
(9)	$\sim A \cdot D$	(6), (8), Conj
$\therefore$ (10)	$D \cdot \sim A$	(9), Comm

We now show that the conditional statement associated with the argument in example 26 is a tautology. The tautology we want to derive is '$(((A \lor B) \supset C) \cdot (\sim C \cdot D)) \supset (D \cdot \sim A)$'.

(1)	$((A \lor B) \supset C) \cdot (\sim C \cdot D)$	Assumption
(2)	$(A \lor B) \supset C$	(1), Simp
(3)	$(\sim C \cdot D) \cdot ((A \lor B) \supset C)$	(1), Comm
(4)	$\sim C \cdot D$	(3), Simp
(5)	$\sim C$	(4), Simp
(6)	$\sim(A \lor B)$	(2), (5), DC
(7)	$\sim A \cdot \sim B$	(6), DM
(8)	$\sim A$	(7), Simp
(9)	$D \cdot \sim C$	(4), Comm
(10)	D	(9), Simp
(11)	$\sim A \cdot D$	(8), (10), Conj
(12)	$D \cdot \sim A$	(11), Comm
$\therefore$ (13)	$(((A \lor B) \supset C) \cdot (\sim C \cdot D)) \supset (D \cdot \sim A)$	(1) to (12), CP

A little reflection on the relationship between these two proofs should enable you to appreciate more fully the relationship between our system of natural deduction and the techniques for showing validity as developed in the previous chapter.

EXERCISE 5-13

1. Provide a proof of each of the following tautologies.
   a. $(p \cdot q) \supset p$
   b. $(p \supset q) \supset (p \supset (p \cdot q))$
   c. $(p \cdot q) \supset q$
   d. $(p \cdot q) \supset (p \lor q)$
   e. $((p \supset q) \supset p) \supset p$
   f. $(p \supset q) \lor (q \supset p)$
   g. $((p \supset q) \cdot (q \supset p)) \equiv ((\sim p \lor q) \cdot (\sim q \lor p))$
   h. $(p \cdot q) \lor (\sim p \lor \sim q)$
   i. $(p \lor q) \lor (\sim p \cdot \sim q)$
   j. $\sim ((p \cdot q) \cdot (\sim p \lor \sim q))$

2. Construct the conditional statements associated with the arguments in problem 1 of Exercise 5-12, and show that they are tautologies.

3. Explain why arguments whose conclusions are tautologies are always valid. Give an example of an argument with a conclusion which is a tautology.

4. Explain the relationship that exists among the following: (a) showing an argument valid by truth tables, (b) providing a proof for that argument, and (c) proving the conditional statement associated with the argument to be a tautology.

STUDENT STUDY GUIDE

Chapter Summary

1. A **decision procedure** is a step-by step procedure for deciding, in each and every case, on the validity or invalidity of an argument form whose validity depends on the truth-functional relationships among the statement variables occurring in that argument form. (Introduction)

2. A logical system composed of a limited number of logical forms and equivalencies which is used to derive the conclusion of an argument from its premises in a step-by-step manner is a system of **natural deduction.** (Introduction)

3. Our system of natural deduction is *not* a decision procedure, for it does not provide us with a method of *determining* in a finite number of steps whether an argument is valid or invalid. However, for every valid argument expressible in the system, there is a way of showing that the argument is valid by showing that its conclusion can be derived from its premises by using instances of basic argument forms and some logical equivalencies. (Introduction)

4. **Rules of inference** are basic argument forms whose validity is established by constructing truth tables. By using these rules, formal proofs of validity can be given for arguments which are more complex than the rules themselves. The system of natural deduction discussed here consists of eight rules of inference.

These rules must be applied to a complete statement, and not to a statement which is itself part of a statement. (section 5:1)

5. A **proof** is a sequence of statements in which the premises occur first, the conclusion occurs as the last line, and every statement is either a premise or is inferred from previous statements in the sequence by one of the rules of inference. Each line of a proof includes a **justification** that explains how that line was derived. *Only one rule of inference can be used on each line of the proof.* (section 5:2)

6. The **Rule of Replacement** enables us to replace a statement, or part of a statement, with another statement which is *logically* equivalent to what is replaced. Since the Rule of Replacement will never take us from a statement which is true to one which is false, it is truth-preserving in the same way as all the other valid rules of inference. (section 5:3.1)

7. **Conditional proofs** are used to derive statements whose form is that of a conditional statement. Such proofs are constructed by assuming the antecedent of the conditional statement and then deriving the consequent. By adding conditional proof to our system, we make it easier to show the validity of some arguments. Of more importance, however, is the fact that, without the addition, the validity of some arguments could be shown by using truth tables but could not be shown with only the eight rules of inference and the ten instances of the Rule of Replacement. (section 5:4)

8. The **scope** of an assumption in a conditional proof is indicated by a vertical line to the left of the proof; the top of this line is at the line of the proof where the assumption is made, and the bottom is at the line where the consequent is derived. This line indicates those statements which were derived, at least in part, on the basis of the assumption. (section 5:4)

9. We **discharge the assumption** in a conditional proof by writing a conditional statement whose antecedent is the assumption in the proof and whose consequent is a statement derived from the assumption. The latter statement is marked by a horizontal line and is the last statement in the proof which falls within the scope of the assumption. (section 5:4)

10. **Indirect proofs** are a special case of conditional proofs. In such proofs we assume the *negation* of the statement we want to derive and then derive a *contradiction* from the assumption. There is no particular contradiction that has to be derived, and the contradiction can concern any of the following three pairs: the assumption and its negation; one of the premises and its negation; and some statement and its negation, both derived from the premises and the assumption. (section 5:5)

11. A **tautology** is a statement form which takes the value true for every possible assignment of truth values to the variables which occur in the statement form. Any argument whose conclusion is a tautology must be valid, since there is no way for such an argument to have all true premises and a false conclusion. (section 5:6)

12. When a statement is derived without using any premises, the statement is derived from the **empty set of premises**. All tautologies expressible in our system of natural deduction can be derived from the empty set of premises. Conditional proofs and indirect proofs are used for deriving such tautologies,

since these two forms of proof enable us to introduce an assumption with which to begin the proof. (section 5:6)

13. Every argument which can be shown to be valid by using truth tables can be rewritten as a conditional statement whose antecedent is a conjunction of the premises and whose consequent is the conclusion. All such statements are tautologies and can be derived in our system of natural deduction from the empty set of premises. (section 5:6)

Key Terms

Decision Procedure   Conditional Proof

Natural Deduction   Scope of an Assumption

Rules of Inference   Discharging an Assumption

Proof   Indirect Proofs

Justification   Tautology

Rule of Replacement   Empty Set of Premises

Self-Test/Exercises

1. Using the eight rules of inference without the Rule of Replacement, construct proofs to show the validity of the following argument forms. (section 5:2)

a. $(p \cdot q) \supset (p \supset (s \cdot t))$
   $(p \cdot q) \cdot r$
   $\therefore s \vee t$

b. $(p \vee q) \supset (r \supset (s \equiv t))$
   $r \cdot s$
   $(r \vee u) \supset p$
   $\therefore s \equiv t$

c. $p \vee (q \vee r)$
   $q \supset s$
   $r \supset t$
   $(s \vee t) \supset (p \vee r)$
   $\sim p$
   $\therefore r$

d. $(p \supset q) \cdot (r \supset s)$
   $t \vee \sim q$
   $\sim t \cdot s$
   $\therefore \sim p \vee r$

e. $(\sim p \vee \sim q) \supset (r \supset (s \cdot \sim t))$
   $(\sim p \cdot \sim u) \cdot (\sim v \vee r)$
   $(\sim p \cdot \sim u) \supset ((s \cdot \sim t) \supset v)$
   $\therefore r \supset v$

2. Show that each of the following arguments is valid by giving a proof. You may use the Rule of Replacement, but you may not use a conditional proof or an indirect proof. (sections 5:2 and 5:3)

a. $M \supset \sim R$
   $(R \vee V) \cdot M$
   $\therefore V$

b. $((A \cdot B) \supset C) \cdot ((A \cdot D) \supset E)$
   $(D \vee B) \cdot A$
   $\therefore C \vee E$

c. $P \supset R$
   $Q \supset S$
   $T \supset (\sim R \vee \sim S)$
   $T \cdot P$
   $\therefore \sim Q$

d. If all countries *guaranteed* the civil liberties of their citizens, people everywhere would have religious *freedom*. If people everywhere had religious freedom, there would be no religious *persecution*. But, since there is religious persecution, it's not the case that all countries guarantee the civil liberties of their citizens. (G, F, P)

e. If the employees do not *increase* productivity, then management is going to be *upset*, and if the new *product* line is not on the market in November, the *competition* will take over a larger share of the market. If the competition takes over a larger market share and management is upset, then a lot of people will *lose* their jobs. But a lot of people will not lose their jobs. Consequently, either the employees will increase productivity or the new product line will be on the market by November. (I, U, P, C, L)

f. If a teacher who has made a mistake in class does not *tell* her students, then she is *dishonest*; but if she does tell her students, some of them will think she is not very well *prepared* and she will be *embarrassed*. Obviously, she either has to tell them about the mistake or not tell them. Consequently, she is either dishonest or embarrassed. (T, D, P, E)

3. Show that each of the following arguments is valid by giving a proof. You may use the rules of inference, the Rule of Replacement, and both conditional and indirect proofs. (sections 5:2 through 5:5)

a. $\sim(Q \cdot \sim R)$
   $P \supset (Q \cdot S)$
   $\therefore P \supset R$

b. $P \supset (Q \cdot R)$
   $P \cdot S$
   $\therefore R$

c. $(F \supset R) \cdot (F \supset U)$
   $(R \cdot U) \supset D$
   $\therefore D \vee \sim F$

d. $(A \vee B) \supset ((C \vee D) \supset (E \cdot F))$
   $(E \vee G) \supset F$
   $\therefore A \supset (C \supset F)$

e. $(L \vee M) \supset N$
   $\sim O$
   $\sim(N \cdot \sim O)$
   $\sim L \supset P$
   $\therefore P$

f. $P \supset R$
   $Q \supset S$
   $T \supset (\sim R \vee \sim S)$
   $T \cdot P$
   $\therefore \sim Q$

g. $(T \supset C)$
   $(\sim T \cdot P) \supset F$
   $F \supset C$
   $\therefore \sim C \supset \sim P$

h. $A \supset ((B \cdot C) \vee E)$
   $(B \cdot C) \supset \sim A$
   $D \supset \sim E$
   $\therefore A \supset \sim D$

4. Provide proofs of the following tautologies. (section 5:6)

a. $\sim(((p \supset q) \cdot p) \cdot \sim q)$

b. $(\sim p \cdot q) \supset (p \supset (s \vee r))$

c. $(p \supset (q \supset r)) \supset (q \supset (p \supset r))$

d. $(p \supset q) \supset ((p \vee r) \supset (q \vee r))$

CHAPTER 6

CATEGORICAL

ARGUMENTS

Thus far, all the arguments we have dealt with have consisted solely of simple statements, or compound statements which are truth functions of simple statements. Our general analysis procedure has been to determine the logical form of the argument and then determine its validity using one of the methods discussed in Chapters 3 to 5. There are, however, other kinds of arguments whose validity cannot be determined using the methods outlined in the previous chapters. One such argument is the following:

ARGUMENT 1

All university presidents are educators.

Some Ivy League graduates are university presidents.

∴ Some Ivy League graduates are educators.

If we were to follow our earlier procedure and assign a statement variable to each statement in argument 1, we would get the following as its logical form:

FORM OF ARGUMENT 1

p

q

∴ r

The argument form exhibited above is obviously invalid. A little consideration of argument 1 will show, however, that if the premises are true, then the conclusion must be true as well; thus, there is some argument form by virtue of which argument 1 is valid, but it cannot be the one we just considered.

The purpose of this chapter is to develop methods for determining the validity of arguments like argument 1. What we shall find is that the validity of these kinds of arguments depends not on the relationships among whole statements, but rather on the relationships *among the terms occurring in the statements*. Our task, then, is first to characterize the kinds of arguments for which consideration of the relations among terms is relevant to determining validity, and second to provide a method for determining the validity of such arguments.

6:1 CATEGORICAL STATEMENTS

Each of the statements occurring in argument 1 is a[categorical statement. There are four forms of categorical statements, and any statement is a categorical statement if, and only if, it is an instance of one of the four forms.] In this section we shall examine the four forms of categorical statements and look at some statements which are logically equivalent to them.

6:1.1 Four Forms of Categorical Statements The following are the four forms of categorical statements:

FORMS OF CATEGORICAL STATEMENTS

A: All $\underline{S}$ are $\underline{P}$ E: No $\underline{S}$ are $\underline{P}$

I: Some $\underline{S}$ are $\underline{P}$ O: Some $\underline{S}$ are not $\underline{P}$

Some examples of statements having these forms follow.

A-STATEMENTS (All $\underline{S}$ are $\underline{P}$) **UP**

All people are mortal.

All mammals are warm-blooded.

All politicians are honest.

All snakes are reptiles.

E-STATEMENTS (No $\underline{S}$ are $\underline{P}$) **UN**

No people are mortal.

No mammals are warm-blooded.

No politicians are honest.

No snakes are reptiles.

I-STATEMENTS (Some $\underline{S}$ are $\underline{P}$) **PA**

Some people are mortal.

Some mammals are warm-blooded.

Some politicians are honest.

Some snakes are reptiles.

O-STATEMENTS (Some $\underline{S}$ are not $\underline{P}$) **PN**

Some people are not mortal.

Some mammals are not warm-blooded.

Some politicians are not honest.

Some snakes are not reptiles.

[Each categorical statement consists of two terms: a **subject term** indicated by '$\underline{S}$', and a **predicate term** indicated by '$\underline{P}$'.] In a categorical statement the subject and predicate terms refer to *classes*. For example, in the statement 'All people are mortal', 'people' refers to the class of all those things which are people, and 'mortal' refers to the class of all those things which are mortal. Similarly, in the statement 'No snakes are reptiles', 'snakes' refers to the class of all those things which are snakes, and 'reptiles' refers to the class of all those things which are reptiles.

In general, the name of the class identifies the property or characteristic by virtue of which a thing is a member of the class. For example, the class designated by the name 'reptile' includes all, and only, those things which have the characteristic of being a reptile; that is, the class includes all reptiles and only those things which are reptiles.

For every class, there is another class related to it and known as the **class complement.** The complement of a given class includes all those things which are *not* members of the given class. For example, the class complement of the class designated by the name 'reptiles' has as its members all those things which are *not* reptiles: Among the many members of this class are people, horses, cats, numbers, months of the year, and chairs.

One might ask what all these things have in common that makes them members of the class complement of the class of reptiles. The answer is, simply, that they have in common the characteristic of *not* being a reptile. More generally, we say that they are all *nonreptiles.* To designate the class complement of any given class, we shall adopt the convention of prefixing 'non' to the name of the given class. Then, the class complement of the class of people is the class of nonpeople; the class complement of the class of snakes is the class of nonsnakes, and so on for each and every class.

It should be clear that for any given class and any given thing or individual, the individual either is a member of the class or is not a member of the class. If the individual is a member of the class, then it is **included** in the class; if it is not a member, then it is **excluded** from the class. Moreover, if we consider any two classes, say the class designated by 'C_1' and the class designated by 'C_2', then each of the following is possible:[1]

(1) Every member of C_1 is also a member of C_2.

(2) No member of C_1 is a member of C_2.

(3) There is at least one member of C_1 which is also a member of C_2.

(4) There is at least one member of C_1 which is not a member of C_2.

In terms of class inclusion and class exclusion, each of (1) to (4) can be rephrased as follows:

(1)' Every individual which is included in class C_1 is included in class C_2.

---

[1] Depending on which classes 'C_1' and 'C_2' designate, more than one of these may be true. For example, if 'C_1' designates the class of those things which are dogs and 'C_2' designates the class of those things which have long tails, then both (3) and (4) are true. We shall return to this issue later in the chapter.

(2)′ Every individual which is included in class C_1 is excluded from class C_2.

(3)′ At least one individual which is included in class C_1 is included in class C_2.

(4)′ At least one individual which is included in class C_1 is excluded from class C_2.

With the above as background, we are now ready to examine what is asserted in each of the four forms of categorical statements introduced earlier in this section. Recall first that the subject terms and predicate terms of categorical statements refer to classes. Now, if we replace 'C_1' with '$\underline{S}$' and 'C_2' with '$\underline{P}$', where '$\underline{S}$' and '$\underline{P}$' are the subject and predicate terms, respectively, of the four forms of categorical statements, then (1)′ to (4)′ are what is asserted in the A-form, E-form, I-form, and O-form categorical statements, in order.

To see this, consider (1)′ and the related A-form categorical statement 'All $\underline{S}$ are $\underline{P}$'. What is asserted in 'All $\underline{S}$ are $\underline{P}$' is that every individual which is included in the class $\underline{S}$ is also included in the class $\underline{P}$. For example, 'All snakes are reptiles' asserts that every individual which is included in the class of snakes is also included in the class of reptiles. Similar remarks hold for the remaining categorical statements.

At this point we are ready to further classify the four forms and develop some relationships which hold among them. This we shall do in the remainder of this section and in sections 6:2 and 6:3.

EXERCISE 6-1

1. What are the four forms of categorical statements?

2. What is a subject term, and what is a predicate term?

3. Give an example of each form of categorical statement, and identify the subject term and the predicate term in each example.

4. To what do the subject term and predicate term of a categorical statement refer?

5. What is a class complement?

6. What does it mean to say that an individual is included in a class? What does it mean to say that an individual is excluded from a class?

7. Using the discussion of the relationship between (1)′ and the A-form categorical statement as a model, explain what is asserted in each of the other forms of categorical statements in terms of (2)′ to (4)′.

6:1.2 Classifying the Four Forms of Categorical Statements

Consideration of the four forms of categorical statements shows that each form shares some common features with some other forms. In this section we shall discuss these features.

In two of the forms (the *A*-form and the *I*-form) it is asserted that all members, or at least one member, of the class designated by the subject term are *included* in the class designated by the predicate term. In two other forms (the *E*-form and the *O*-form) it is asserted that all members, or at least one member, of the class designated by the subject term are *excluded* from the class designated by the predicate term.

In discussing class inclusion and class exclusion, we are discussing the **quality** of a categorical statement. When a statement asserts that all, or at least one member of, the subject class is *included* in the predicate class, the statement is an **affirmative** one. When a statement asserts that all, or at least one member of, the subject class is *excluded* from the predicate class, the statement is a **negative** one. As a result, *A*-form and *I*-form categorical statements are affirmative, and *E*-form and *O*-form categorical statements are negative.

In addition, in two of the forms (the *A*-form and the *E*-form) the statement is about *all* the members of the subject class; either they are included in (*A*-form) or excluded from (*E*-form) the predicate class. In two other forms (the *I*-form and the *O*-form) the statement is about at least one member of the subject class; either it is included in (*I*-form) or excluded from (*O*-form) the predicate class.

At this point, it may seem puzzling to you that the *E*-form statement is about *all* the members of the subject class. To see that this is a feature of *E*-form categorical statements, consider the statement 'No dogs are reptiles'. If this statement is true (and it is), then we know that there are no dogs which are also reptiles or, what is the same thing, that all dogs are nonreptiles.

In discussing whether all or just some members are included in the class designated by the subject term of a categorical statement, we are discussing the **quantity** of a categorical statement. When a statement is about all the members of the subject class, the statement is a **universal** one. When a statement is about some, but not all, members of the subject class, the statement is a **particular** one. As a result, *A*-form and *E*-form categorical statements are universal statements, and *I*-form and *O*-form categorical statements are particular statements.

If we consider *both* quality and quantity, then each of the four forms of categorical statements is uniquely characterized. In particular, *A*-form categorical statements are **universal affirmative** statements, *E*-form categorical statements are **universal negative** statements, *I*-form categorical statements are **particular affirmative** statements, and *O*-form categorical statements are **particular negative** statements. This is shown in Table 6-1.

	TABLE 6-1	
	Quality	
Quantity	Affirmative	Negative
Universal	*A*: All <u>S</u> are <u>P</u>	*E*: No <u>S</u> are <u>P</u>
Particular	*I*: Some <u>S</u> are <u>P</u>	*O*: Some <u>S</u> are not <u>P</u>

EXERCISE 6-2

1. What do we mean by the quality of a categorical statement?

2. What do we mean by the quantity of a categorical statement?

3. What does it mean to say that a categorical statement is affirmative?

4. What does it mean to say that a categorical statement is negative?

5. What does it mean to say that a categorical statement is universal?

6. What does it mean to say that a categorical statement is particular?

7. What are the names of the four standard-form categorical statements? Explain why each is called what it is.

6:1.3 Interpreting Categorical Statements Very often in the English language universal statements carry with them the suggestion that the class mentioned by the subject term has at least one member. For example, if someone says "All my friends are bores" or "None of my friends are bores," we would probably assume that the speaker has friends. Similarly, if someone said that all her record albums were stolen, one would assume that the speaker did, at one time, have some record albums, but now she does not. On the other hand, some universal statements do not carry with them the suggestion that there are members of the subject class. One such instance is a sign in a parking lot with the warning "Tenants only—all violators will be towed away." In saying that all violators will be towed away, the intent is *not* to suggest that there are violators and that they will be towed away; on the contrary, the intent is to try to bring about that there are *no violators*. "All trespassers will be prosecuted" functions is a similar way. An example of a universal negative statement of this type is "No student who cuts class will get an 'A'." An instructor who says this is not asserting that there are students who cut class; rather, the statement is usually made in the hope that, once it is made, no one will cut class.

For the purpose of analyzing arguments which consist of categorical statements, we shall treat all universal statements (A-form and E-form statements) as *not* suggesting that there are members of the subject class. In particular, the universal statement will be understood as a kind of conditional statement. 'All dogs are mammals', then, will be understood as 'If any thing is a dog, then that thing is a mammal', *without* the additional claim that there are dogs. Similarly, 'No snakes are mammals' will be understood as 'If any thing is a snake, then that thing is not a mammal', *without* the additional claim that there are snakes.

The sense in which universal statements are to be understood as a kind of conditional statement can be explained further by recalling our discussion of inclusion and exclusion in the previous section. We shall here discuss the A-form statement, though analogous remarks hold for the E-form.

We have noted that a statement of the form 'All $\underline{S}$ are $\underline{P}$' can be understood as, "Every individual which is included in the class designated by the subject term is also included in the class designated by the predicate term." In this, we leave open the question as to whether or not any individuals are included in the class designated by the subject term. In particular, we can, and shall, treat the universal affirmative statement as equivalent to the conditional statement, "*If* there are any individuals included in the class designated by the subject term, then each, and every, such individual is also included in the class designated by the predicate term."

The advantage in treating all universal categorical statements as conditional statements, without the suggestion that there are members of the subject class, is that we have one uniform way of treating *all* universal statements. Furthermore, if we determine that a particular argument which consists at least in part of a universal statement is valid, without the suggestion that there are members of the subject class, then the additional fact (if it is a fact) that there are members of that class will not affect the validity of the argument in question.[2] Another advantage of treating universal categorical statements in this way is that we can apply to categorical statements much of the knowledge that you have already acquired concerning conditional statements, and we can extend this to the arguments discussed in the next chapter.

The occurrence of 'some' in the particular statements is also given an interpretation for the purpose of determining the validity of categorical syllogisms: We shall understand 'some' to mean 'at least one.' For example, the particular affirmative statement 'Some politicians are honest' will be understood as 'At least one politician is honest'. Given this interpretation of 'some', particular affirmative and particular negative statements will be used when we want to state something about some members of a particular class but not about all of them, even when what we are stating about some is actually true of all the members. For example, if we want to assert that there is at least one snake which is a reptile, we shall use an *I*-form statement, even though it's true that all snakes are reptiles.

EXERCISE 6-3

1. Give three examples of universal categorical statements in which it is *not* suggested that there are members in the class designated by the subject term.

2. Explain the interpretation given to universal categorical statements and the advantages of such an interpretation.

3. Explain the interpretation given to particular categorical statements.

---

[2] The converse of this is *not* the case, since the assumption that there are members of the class designated by the subject term in a universal statement (called *existential import*) in effect functions as an additional premise. As a result, some arguments which are valid under the assumption of existential import are invalid without the assumption. One such argument is 'All snakes are reptiles; therefore some snakes are reptiles'. With the assumption of existential import, the conclusion follows from the premise. Without this assumption, we are not entitled to assume that there are snakes and, hence, are not entitled to infer that there is at least one thing which is *both* a snake *and* a reptile.

6:2 CATEGORICAL STATEMENTS IN ORDINARY LANGUAGE

So far each of the statements we have considered has been a standard-form categorical statement. That is, it has been written in one of the four forms exhibited in Table 6-1. It is easy to identify categorical statements written in standard form, and it is easy to identify their form. In particular, all *A*-form statements begin with 'All'; this is followed by a term designating a class, then a form of the verb "to be," and finally another term designating another class. The *E*-form statements are similar, except that they begin with 'No'. *I*-form and *O*-form statements both begin with 'Some'; they are differentiated by the occurrence of 'not' between the verb and the predicate term in the *O*-form.

Many sentences in English are not expressed as standard-form categorical statements but can be rewritten as such. Since the procedures for determining the validity of arguments will be explained for, and applied to, standard-form statements, we need to develop methods for working with English sentences which are not so expressed. This we shall do in this section.

6:2.1 Universal Affirmative Statements   Each of the following statements, though not a standard-form categorical statement, is equivalent to a universal affirmative statement.

(1) Students are industrious.

(2) Any person caught cheating will fail the course.

(3) Unless an animal is a mammal, it's not a giraffe.

(4) Anyone who pays his or her dues is eligible to vote for the new president.

(5) Every cloud has a silver lining.

(6) Ralph Nader is a consumer advocate.

None of (1) to (5) is a standard-form universal affirmative statement since none is of the form 'All $\underline{S}$ are $\underline{P}$'. The issue, then, is how to rewrite each of these statements so that it does have the appropriate form.

A helpful guide in rewriting ordinary sentences which are not in standard form is to recall that a universal categorical statement can be understood as a kind of conditional statement. A universal affirmative statement is roughly of the form 'If an individual is a member of some given class, then it is a member of another class'. So the question to ask of each of (1) to (5) is whether it "describes" such a situation and, if so, what are the subject class and the predicate class.

Let's look at (1). This statement can easily be understood in terms of class inclusion. In particular, it can be understood as the statement 'If an individual is included in the class of students, then that individual is also included in the class of those things which are industrious'. Now it should be clear that the term 'student' can be used to designate the subject class, and 'all those things which are industrious' is the predicate class. Using 'I' to represent this latter class, we see that (1) can be represented as follows:

(1)' All S are I

Just as we distinguished statement variables and statement constants in Chapters 4 and 5, we can make a similar distinction here. The 'S' and the 'I' which occur in (1)' are **predicate constants** since they represent *particular characteristics:* being a student and being industrious, respectively.[3] Instead of discussing particular characteristics, we can also discuss the structure, or form, of (1)'. In doing so, we note that it has the form 'All $\underline{S}$ are $\underline{P}$', where '$\underline{S}$' represents the place occupied by the subject term, and '$\underline{P}$' represents the place occupied by the predicate term. In expressing the *form* of universal affirmative categorical statements as 'All $\underline{S}$ are $\underline{P}$', we use '$\underline{S}$' and '$\underline{P}$' as **predicate variables,** since they are *placeholders* for terms which designate particular characteristics.

Since both predicate constants and predicate variables are written as uppercase letters, we need a way to differentiate between them. For this, we shall adopt the convention of indicating predicate *variables* by *underlining* the letter which indicates the place wherein a predicate constant can occur; predicate constants will be written simply as uppercase letters.

Now let's look at (2), which can be handled in much the same way as (1). Once we see that (2) amounts, roughly, to the claim that all persons who are members of the class of those who are caught cheating are also members of the class of those who will fail the course, it's clear that (2) has the form 'All $\underline{S}$ are $\underline{P}$'.[4] If we let 'C' represent the class of those who are caught cheating, and 'F' represent the class of those who will fail the course, (2) can be represented as

(2)' All C are F

Statement (3) is unlike (1) and (2), since it contains the word 'unless'. We noted in Chapter 3 that 'unless' translates as 'if not', so (3) can also be understood as 'If an animal is not a mammal, then it's not a giraffe'. If you consider what is asserted here in terms of class inclusion, you should see that (3) characterizes the same situation which is characterized by 'All nonmammals are nongiraffes'. Letting 'non-M' represent the class of nonmammals (the complement of the class of mammals), and 'non-G' represent the class of nongiraffes (the complement of the class of giraffes), we have the following:

(3)' All non-M are non-G

---

[3] The expression 'predicate constant' as it applies to 'S' in (1)' may be misleading since 'S' is the *subject* term in the statement and 'I' is the *predicate* term. In the next chapter you will see why both are called 'predicate constants'; our point here is to once again focus on the difference between a constant and a variable. Do not be misled by the word 'predicate'.

[4] Also notice that in the contexts where one might assert (2), one might equally well assert 'If you're caught cheating, then you will fail the course'. This latter way of looking at (2) brings out more forcefully the conditional-statement element of universal statements.

Notice that (3)' has the form 'All $\underline{S}$ are $\underline{P}$', where 'non-M' (a predicate constant) occupies the place indicated by '$\underline{S}$', and 'non-G' occupies the place indicated by '$\underline{P}$'.

Statement (4) is like (2) in that 'anyone' functions like 'any person'. As a result, what is expressed in (4) is that all those individuals who are members of the class of those who pay their dues are also members of the class of those who are eligible to vote for the new president. Letting 'D' represent the former class and 'E' the latter, we have

(4)' All D and E

Statement (4)' is, of course, of the form 'All $\underline{S}$ are $\underline{P}$'.

Statement (5) can be understood as 'Everything which is a cloud is also a thing which has a silver lining'. So understood, this amounts to the same thing as 'All clouds are things which have silver linings'. Using 'C' to represent the class of things which are clouds, and 'S' to represent the class of things which have silver linings, we have

(5)' All C are S

Statement (6) is different from any of (1) to (5), since in (6) we are saying something about a *particular individual*, Ralph Nader. It is not obvious, then, that (6) expresses an inclusive relation between two *classes*. To handle cases like (6), we shall adopt the convention that a particular proper name refers to the class of which the individual designated by that name is the only member.[5] With this convention, (6) asserts a relationship between the class of those things which are members of the class of which Ralph Nader is the only member and the class of all things which are included in the class of consumer advocates. Letting 'R' represent the former class and 'C' the latter, we have

(6)' All R are C

It should be emphasized that (1) to (6) are not the only ways in which sentences that are equivalent to universal affirmative statements are expressed in English. They are provided so that you can begin to develop some skill in recognizing such sentences and in rewriting them as standard-form categorical statements. In the next sections we shall look at some additional examples.

6:2.2 Universal Negative Statements

In the previous section we discussed statements in which it is asserted that all members of a given class are included

---

[5] The author is not particularly fond of this approach, since, among other things, more than one individual can have the same name. As a result, some additional defining characteristics for the class are needed to ensure that one, and only one, individual is a member of the class, and that it is the "right" individual—in the present case, that it is the "right" Ralph Nader. Such considerations go beyond the scope of an introductory logic text, however. The convention does have the benefit of providing a way to handle such sentences within the context of syllogistic logic. Moreover, since we shall consider in the next chapter a more acceptable way to display the form of such sentences, nothing is lost by adopting the convention in this chapter.

in another class. The only difference between those statements and the statements discussed here is that now we are considering statements in which it is asserted that all members of a given class are *excluded* from another class.

Among the statements which can be rewritten as universal negative statements are the following:

(1) None who attended the ceremony was happy.

(2) Anteaters aren't reptiles.

(3) Nothing the President does is liked by Congress.

(4) Laura is not one of the better competitors on the team.

None of (1) to (4) is a standard-form universal negative statement, since none is of the form 'No $\underline{S}$ are $\underline{P}$'. As we noted in the last section, however, each of these statements can be rewritten once we identify the subject class and the predicate class.

Statement (1) clearly expresses a relation between the class of those who attended the ceremony and the class of those who were happy. In particular, it is asserted that no member of the former class is a member of the latter class. Letting 'A' and 'H' represent these classes respectively, we see that (1) can be rewritten as

(1)′ No A are H

Statement (2) is about the class of things which are anteaters and the class of things which are reptiles. If (2) is true, one of the things which follows from it is that any individual which is an anteater is an individual which is not a reptile. This corresponds with the conditional-statement element of E-form categorical statements. More directly, what is asserted in (2) is that no member of the class of anteaters is a member of the class of reptiles. Letting 'A' and 'R' represent these classes, we have

(2)′ No A are R

In (3) something is asserted about the things the President does and the things which are liked by Congress. In particular, it is asserted that nothing which is included in the things the President does is a thing which is liked by Congress. Using 'P' and 'C' to represent these two classes, we have

(3)′ No P are C

Statement (4) is similar to (6) of the previous section, since we have to treat the proper name 'Laura' as designating a class of which she is the only member. If we let 'L' represent this class and let 'C' represent the class of better competitors on the team, we see that it is asserted in (4) that Laura is excluded from this class. As a result, we have

(4)′ No L are C

Each of (1)′ to (4)′ has the form 'No $\underline{S}$ are $\underline{P}$' and, as such, is a universal negative categorical statement.

6:2.3 Particular Affirmative Statements   Consider the following particular affirmative statement:

(1) Some students are industrious.

Since 'some' is understood to mean 'at least one,' what is asserted here is that at least one individual is included in the class of things which are students and in the class of things which are industrious. The key to recognizing those statements in English which can be rewritten as particular affirmative statements is to keep in mind that the condition which must be satisfied is that at least one individual be included in each of two different classes. Thus, each of the following is another way of expressing what is expressed by 'Some students are industrious':

(2) At least one student is industrious.

(3) Something is both a student and is industrious.

(4) There are industrious students.

(5) Many students are industrious.

(6) The vast majority of students are industrious.

(7) A few students are industrious.

Statement (2) is, of course, just the way we said that *I*-form statements would be understood. Statements (3) and (4) satisfy the "key": that it be asserted that at least one individual is included in each of two different classes. Statements (5) and (6), however, are "stronger" than (1), because when they are understood as 'at least one student is industrious,' some of their force is lost. That is, one who asserts either (5) or (6) is saying something more than just that there is at least one industrious student. With the techniques developed in this chapter there is no way to distinguish between (5) and (6) on the one hand, and (1) on the other, though more powerful logical systems have been developed which do enable logicians to more accurately reflect the differences in these statements.

Although we cannot here distinguish between words like 'few' and 'most', the procedures we shall develop are independent of such distinctions. In particular, both imply that there is *at least one* member of the class designated by the subject term; if there is more than one member, this does not affect the validity of the arguments considered in this chapter.

Now consider the following:

(8) Students are industrious.

Since (8) does not contain either 'all' or 'some', it is unclear whether this statement should be understood as a particular affirmative statement or as a universal affirmative statement. In such cases, we must ordinarily rely on the *context* in which the statement is made to determine which kind of statement it is.

Among the contextual clues are the terms which occur in the statement. In the case of (8), and given what we all know about students, it is likely that in almost all contexts (8) would be a particular statement. However, if (8) were asserted by the student-body president, responding to charges that *all* students are lazy and no good since they obviously are going to school to avoid having to work for a living, then it might be reasonable to regard (8) as a universal statement.

Statements similar to (8) would typically be understood as universal statements; as an example, consider

(9) Whales are mammals.

Since 'mammals' is a classificatory term, it is very likely that one who asserts (9) means that *all* whales are mammals, not that just some are.

The foregoing remarks underscore some of our discussion in Chapter 1. Arguments in "real life" are always given in some context, and the context in which something is asserted must often be relied upon to determine what, exactly, the speaker intended by what he or she said.

6:2.4 Particular Negative Statements   Consider the following particular negative statement:

(1) Some students are not industrious.

The key to recognizing those statements in English which can be rewritten as particular negative statements is to keep in mind that the condition which must be satisfied is that at least one individual be included in one class but excluded from another. Thus, each of the following is another way of expressing what is expressed by 'Some students are not industrious':

(2) At least one student is not industrious.

(3) There are students who are not industrious.

(4) Many students are not industrious.

(5) A few students are not industrious.

(6) The vast majority of students are not industrious.

The remarks concerning 'many', 'a few', and 'majority' in the previous section also apply in the case of particular negative statements; hence, they will not be repeated here.

It is, however, worth looking at another example which does not contain 'all', 'no', or 'some':

(7) Students are not industrious.

Statement (7), like (8) in the previous section, could be understood as either the particular negative statement '*Some* students are not industrious' or, depending on context, as the universal negative statement '*No* students are industrious'. To determine how (7) should be rewritten, we would have to rely on the context in which it was asserted.

6:2.5 Exclusive and Exceptive Statements   Very often in English we encounter sentences like 'None but the virtuous shall enter the Kingdom of

Heaven' or 'Almost all people like pizza.' These are examples of sentences which are used to make **exclusive statements** and **exceptive statements,** respectively. In this section we shall see how to rewrite such statements as standard-form categorical statements.

Exclusive statements can generally be recognized by the fact that the predicate expression is said to apply *exclusively* to the individual or individuals designated by the subject expression. For example, in saying 'None but the virtuous shall enter the Kingdom of Heaven', it is asserted that the characteristic of entering the Kingdom of Heaven applies exclusively to those who are virtuous.

If we ask, then, under what conditions such statements are true, our answer is they are true if all the individuals who are members of the class designated by the predicate expression are also members of the class designated by the subject expression. In the case under discussion, this is the same as saying:

(1) All who enter the Kingdom of Heaven are virtuous.

Another way of looking at exclusive statements is via the conditional-statement element of universal categorical statements. In 'None but the virtuous shall enter the Kingdom of Heaven,' it is *not* asserted that *every* virtuous person shall enter; in other words, it is not asserted that if an individual is virtuous then he or she shall enter the Kingdom of Heaven. We do know, however, that if an individual has entered the Kingdom of Heaven, then he or she is virtuous. This conditional element is partially reflected in (1).

Another word which is used to express exclusive statements is 'only', as in the statement 'Only sophomores can register for History 203'. Treating this statement in the same way as the last one, we have:

(2) All those who can register for History 203 are sophomores.

Exceptive statements can generally be recognized by the fact that a particular characteristic is said to apply to a certain group of individuals, with the *exception* of a few members in the group. Moreover, there is generally the additional assertion that the characteristic in question does *not* apply to those other few members. As a result, exceptive statements are typically understood as *conjunctions*. Let's see how this general characterization applies to the exceptive statement with which we began this section:

(3) Almost all people like pizza.

If (3) is true, then there is at least one person who likes pizza. However, the 'almost all' modifier would, in ordinary contexts, be taken to imply also that there are some people who do not like pizza. As a result, we rewrite (3) as the conjunction of two standard-form categorical statements, one having the *I*-form and the other the *O*-form. Our result follows:

(3)' Some people are people who like pizza *and* some people are people who do not like pizza.

Other expressions which indicate exceptive statements whose form is best represented as the conjunction of *I*-form and *O*-form categorical statements are 'not quite all' and 'almost everyone'. Examples showing statements containing these expressions and the way they are rewritten follow.

(4) Not quite all the cookies are chocolate chip cookies.

(4)' Some cookies are chocolate chip cookies *and* some cookies are not chocolate chip cookies.

(5) Almost everyone attended the funeral.

(5)' Some people are people who attended the funeral *and* some people are people who did not attend the funeral.

In addition to exceptive statements in which the rewritten statement is a conjunction of *I*-form and *O*-form categorical statements, there are some exceptive statements which are written as the conjunction of *A*-form and *E*-form categorical statements. Such exceptive statements contain the expressions 'all except', 'all but,' and 'alone'. Examples of these kinds of exceptive statements and their rewritten forms follow.

(6) All except those making less than $1800 a year must pay income tax.

(6)' All those who do not make less than $1800 a year must pay income tax *and* no person who makes less than $1800 a year must pay income tax.

(7) All but convicted felons are allowed to vote.

(7)' All those who are not convicted felons are allowed to vote *and* no convicted felon is allowed to vote.

(8) Faculty alone are eligible for a discount at the bookstore.

(8)' All faculty are people who are eligible for a discount at the bookstore *and* no nonfaculty are people who are eligible for a discount at the bookstore.

EXERCISE 6-4

1. What is the difference between a predicate constant and a predicate variable? How is each expressed in our notation?

2. How are sentences which contain proper names translated into a standard-form categorical statement?

3. When an English sentence does not contain 'all', 'no', or 'some', how do we determine which form of categorical statement the sentence expresses?

4. What is an exclusive statement? What is an exceptive statement? Explain how such statements are written as standard-form categorical statements. Give an example of each kind of statement, and rewrite each as a standard-form categorical statement.

5. Where necessary, rewrite each of the following as a standard-form categorical statement. Assign predicate constants to the statement and symbolize it. Indicate whether the statement is an *A*-form, *E*-form, *I*-form, or *O*-form categorical statement.

a. Some people can't be trusted.
b. All the pretzels were eaten last night.
c. Nobody likes to be embarrassed in public.
d. Some football players don't run very fast.
e. None but the brave deserve the fair.
f. Margaret Mead was a famous anthropologist.
g. Almost everyone likes good music.
h. Politicians are a strange breed.
i. Not quite all the books were destroyed by the fire.
j. Any person with self-respect also respects others.
k. None who like exercise watch television eight hours a day.
l. There are incompetent judges.
m. Many judges are not incompetent.
n. All except Murray were invited to the party.
o. Anyone who wants to ride to Miami should call 481-7900.
p. Aardvarks aren't nice animals.
q. A few people don't mind being laughed at.
r. The vast majority of Americans are patriotic.
s. Students alone will be admitted at half price.
t. Many people have incomes below the poverty level.
u. A day without prune juice is like a day without sunshine.
v. Many athletes are not injured while competing.
w. Hoot Gibson likes to ride horses.
x. Nothing Johnson says will make Gloria change her mind.
y. A few people have not been exposed to religion.

6:3 SOME RELATIONSHIPS AMONG CATEGORICAL STATEMENTS

Various relationships hold among the four forms of categorical statements. We shall not examine all these relationships, but shall focus our attention on those which are essential for determining the validity of arguments consisting of categorical statements. In section 6:4 these relationships will be used to put arguments into a logical form whose validity can then be determined by the methods developed in sections 6:5 and 6:6.

6:3.1 Relationships between Universal Categorical Statements To develop the relationships which hold between universal categorical statements, let's consider in a somewhat informal way the following statement:

(1) All graduates are people who receive diplomas.

Given the two characteristics of being a graduate and being a person who has received a diploma, any arbitrarily selected individual either has both these characteristics, has one but not the other, or has neither characteristic. If an individual has either (or both) characteristics, then the individual is *included* in the class of all those things having the characteristic(s). Similarly, if an individual does not have either (or both) characteristics, then the individual is *excluded* from the class of all those things having the characteristic(s).

Consider now the class of all those things which are graduates. If an individual is *not* a member of this class (is *excluded* from the class), then the individual is a member of the class of nongraduates (the class complement of the class designated by 'graduates'). Generalizing this point, we can say that, for every class, an individual is either a member of the class or a member of the class complement. Consequently, every individual is also a member either of the class of those people who have received diplomas or of the complement of this class.

Let's use 'G' to represent the class of graduates, 'non-G' to represent the class of nongraduates, 'R' to represent the class of those people who have received diplomas, and 'non-R' to represent the class of those people who have not received diplomas. If we limit our discussion to just these four classes, then every individual is a member of one of the following combinations of classes:

(A) $G \cdot R$ (B) $G \cdot \text{non-}R$

(C) $\text{non-}G \cdot R$ (D) $\text{non-}G \cdot \text{non-}R$

Now, let's suppose that (1) is true; that is, let's suppose that all graduates are people who receive diplomas. One thing that follows from this is that if an individual is a graduate, then he or she is also a person who has received a diploma. If we assume (correctly) that at least one individual is a graduate, then there is at least one member of the class designated in (A), the class of those things which are graduates and are people who have received diplomas. Moreover, on the assumption that (1) is true, all individuals who are graduates are members of the class designated in (A).

In addition to knowing that all graduates are members of the class designated in (A), we know something else if (1) is true: We know that there are *no* graduates who are people who did *not* receive a diploma [if there were at least one such person, (1) would be false]. In terms of our earlier discussion, we know that if (1) is true, that is, that all graduates receive diplomas, then *no* individual is a member of the class designated in (B).

Having made this point, we are ready to make explicit the relationship between universal categorical statements. If *all* individuals who are graduates are members of the class designated in (A), then *no* individuals are members of the class designated in (B). More specifically, if 'All G are R' is true, then 'No G are non-R' must also be true. By analogous reasoning, we could also explain why if 'No G are non-R' is true, then 'All G are R' is also true.

Generalizing the above case, we have

(All $\underline{S}$ are $\underline{P}$) ≡ (No $\underline{S}$ are non-$\underline{P}$)

Now consider the following universal negative statement:

(2) No multiple-choice exam is an exam which develops writing ability.

If we let 'M' represent the class of multiple-choice exams, 'non-M' represent the class of exams which are not multiple-choice exams, 'W' represent the class of exams which develop writing ability, and 'non-W' represent the class of exams which do not develop writing ability, every exam will be a member of one of the following combinations of classes:

(A) $M \cdot W$ (B) $M \cdot$ non-W

(C) non-$M \cdot W$ (D) non-$M \cdot$ non-W

On the assumption that (2) is true, it follows that if an exam is a multiple-choice exam, then it is also an exam which does not develop writing ability. As a result, *all* multiple-choice exams are exams which are included in the class designated in (B). As a result, if 'No M are W' is true, then 'All M are non-W' is also true. An argument similar to that given in the case of (1) will also show that if 'All M are non-W' is true, then 'No M is W' is also true. Generalizing this case, we have

(No $\underline{S}$ are $\underline{P}$) ≡ (All $\underline{S}$ are non-$\underline{P}$)

Combining our results from the discussions of (1) and (2), we see that we have established the following:

(All $\underline{S}$ are $\underline{P}$) ≡ (No $\underline{S}$ are non-$\underline{P}$)

(No $\underline{S}$ are $\underline{P}$) ≡ (All $\underline{S}$ are non-$\underline{P}$)

Since each of the above is written in terms of predicate variables, we can characterize what we have shown as follows: *Any universal affirmative statement can be rewritten as an equivalent universal negative statement, and any universal negative statement can be rewritten as an equivalent universal affirmative statement.* All that remains is to make explicit how this is done.

A little reflection on the above equivalencies shows that the right-hand member of each has the quality opposite that of the left-hand member (one form is affirmative, the other negative), and that the predicate term in the right-hand member designates the class complement of the class designated by the predicate term in the left-hand member. As a result, we can convert any A-form statement to an E-form statement, and vice versa, by doing the following:

TOP TRANSFORMATION[6]

(1) Change the quality of the original statement to its opposite.

(2) Replace the predicate term of the original statement with its class complement.

EXAMPLE 1

Apply the top transformation to

All M are non-S

---

[6] The reason for calling this the 'top transformation' will become apparent shortly. This equivalency is also known as *obversion*.

Step 1: Change the quality. Since the original statement is an *A*-form statement, we change the form to the *E*-form, obtaining

No _____ are _____

Step 2: Replace the predicate term with its complement. The predicate term in the original statement is 'non-*S*', so we replace this with '*S*'. Since the top transformation says nothing about the subject term, we leave that the same. Our result is:

No *M* are *S*

6:3.2 Relationships between Particular Categorical Statements   The kind of relationship which holds between the universal categorical statements also holds between the particular categorical statements. That is, *any particular affirmative statement can be rewritten as an equivalent particular negative statement, and any particular negative statement can be rewritten as an equivalent particular affirmative statement.* For reasons which will soon become apparent, this rewriting is called the *bottom transformation.*[7]

That the above relationship holds is most easily seen when particular negative statement are rewritten as particular affirmative statements. Consider the following:

(1) Some compounds are not acids.

Statement (1) has the form 'Some S̲ are not P̲', where 'S̲' represents the place occupied by the subject term 'compounds' and 'P̲' represents the place occupied by the predicate term 'acids'. Our discussion of particular negative statements tells us that what is asserted is that there is at least one individual which is *included* in the class designated by the subject term and *excluded* from the class designated by the predicate term. As a result, if (1) is true, then there is at least one thing which is included in the class of those things which are compounds and excluded from the class of those things which are acids. For the moment, let's designate this individual by '*X*'.

Since *X* is excluded from the class of things which are acids, *X* is included in the class of things which are nonacids. Since *X* is also included in the class of things which are compounds, it follows that *X* is included in the class of things which are compounds *and* in the class of things which are nonacids. This condition, however, is just the one which is satisfied in the case of particular affirmative statements; that is, that there is at least one individual which is included in each of two different classes. As a result, if 'Some compounds are not acids' is true, then, 'Some compounds are nonacids' is also true. A similar argument will establish that if 'Some compounds are nonacids' is true, then 'Some compounds are not acids' is also true. Letting '*C*' represent 'compounds', '*A*' represent 'acids', and 'non-*A*' represent 'nonacids', we have shown the following:

(Some *C* are not *A*) ≡ (Some *C* are non-*A*)

---

[7] This equivalency is also known as *obversion.*

Now let's consider a particular affirmative statement:

(2) Some compounds are bases.

We know that a particular negative statement has the form 'Some S̲ are not P̲'. In converting (2) into a particular negative statement, then, we must provide a statement equivalent to (2) in which we state that some compounds do *not* have a particular property. The question here is, "what property is this?"

In (2) it is asserted that at least one thing is *included* in the class of compounds and *included* in the class of bases. Once again, let's designate this individual by '*X*'. Since *X* is included in the class of bases, it follows that X is excluded from the class of nonbases. That is, *X* is both included in the class of compounds and excluded from the class of nonbases.[8] Since this condition is the one which obtains when a particular negative statement is true, it follows that if 'Some compounds are bases' is true, then 'Some compounds are not nonbases' is also true.[9] A similar argument will also establish that if 'Some compounds are not nonbases' is true, then 'Some compounds are bases' is also true. Letting '*C*', '*B*', and 'non-*B*' represent the obvious expressions, we have

(Some *C* are *B*) ≡ (Some *C* are not non-*B*)

This discussion can be generalized to any particular affirmative or particular negative categorical statement. The procedure to be followed in making such conversions is as follows:

BOTTOM TRANSFORMATION

(1) Change the quality of the original statement to its opposite.

(2) Replace the predicate term of the original statement with its class complement.

EXAMPLE 2

Apply the bottom transformation to

Some non-*M* are not *S*

Step 1: Change the quality. Since this statement is an *O*-form statement, we change the form to the *I*-form. This gives us

Some _____ are _____

Step 2: Replace the predicate term with its complement. Here we replace '*S*' with 'non-*S*'. Our subject term remains the same, so we have

Some non-*M* are non-*S*

Now, as to why the conversions we have discussed are called the 'top

---

[8] Of course, if *X* is included in the class of compounds, *X* is also excluded from the class of noncompounds. In the present case, however, we are looking for a statement equivalent to (2) in which *X* is correctly characterized as being excluded from the class designated by the *predicate* term. Hence, we focus on the complement of the class of bases.

[9] Notice the similarity to double negation.

transformation' and the 'bottom transformation': This is brought out in Figure 6-1.

Figure 6-1

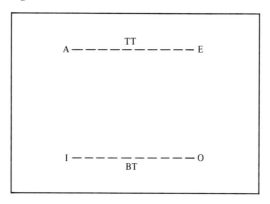

If we arrange the four forms of categorical statements in a square, universals at the top and particulars on the bottom, then we have the arrangement shown in Figure 6-1. The dashed lines between 'A' and 'E' and between 'I' and 'O' indicate statement forms that can be rewritten in terms of each other. 'TT' and 'BT' stand for 'top transformation' and 'bottom transformation', respectively. In the next two sections we shall add to Figure 6-1 as we look at some additional relationships which hold among categorical statements.

EXERCISE 6-5

Apply the top transformation or bottom transformation, as appropriate, to the symbolized statements you gave in answer to problem 5 of Exercise 6-4.

6:3.3 Contradictories   In addition to the equivalencies which are derivable by the top and bottom transformations, the relation *contradiction* holds between some pairs of categorical statements. If we add diagonals to Figure 6-1 as indicated in Figure 6-2, then the two statements connected by each diagonal line are contradictory. That is, universal affirmative and particular negative statements with the same subject and predicate terms are contradictory, and universal negative and particular affirmative statements with the same subject and predicate terms are contradictory. Recall that if two statement forms are contradictory, then they always have opposite truth values.

Consider the A-form and O-form statements. Statements of the form 'All S̲ are P̲' state that every individual which is included in the class designated by 'S̲' is also included in the class designated by 'P̲'. As a result, if a given A-form statement is true, it follows that there is no individual which is both a

Figure 6-2

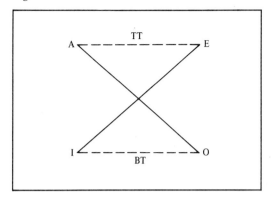

member of the class designated by 'S' and not a member of the class designated by 'P'. As a result, if (1) below is true, then (2) must be false.

(1) All S are P

(2) Some S are not P

Statement (2) states that at least one individual is included in the class designated by 'S' and excluded from the class designated by 'P', a situation which cannot obtain if (1) is true. On the other hand, suppose that (2) is true. If (2) is true, then at least one individual is both a member of S and not a member of P. Under these conditions, (1) would have to be false.

Now consider the E-form and I-form statements. Statements of the form 'No S are P' state that every individual which is included in the class designated by 'S' is excluded from the class designated by 'P'. As a result, if a given E-form statement is true, it follows that there is no individual which is both a member of the class designated by 'S' and a member of the class designated by 'P'. As a result, if (3) below is true, then (4) must be false.

(3) No S are P

(4) Some S are P

Statement (4) states that at least one individual is included in both the class designated by 'S' and the class designated by 'P', a situation which cannot obtain if (3) is true. Now suppose that (4) is true. Under this assumption, we do have an individual which is a member of both the class designated by 'S' and the class designated by 'P'. Under these conditions, (3) would have to be false.

The results of the above discussion are summarized in Table 6-2. Given the information presented in Table 6-2, it is easy to construct a set of equivalencies which hold between pairs of categorical statements. One such pair follows:

(5) 'It's not the case that all dogs are brown' is equivalent to 'Some dogs are not brown'.

TABLE 6-2							
A	O	E	I	I	E	O	A
T	F	T	F	T	F	T	F
F	T	F	T	F	T	F	T

Assigning predicate constants to (5), we obtain

(5)′ ~(All D are B) ≡ Some D are not B

To see that (5) and (5)′ are true, we need merely consider two cases—the first where 'All D are B' is true, and the second where it is false.

Case 1: 'All D are B' is true. If 'All D are B' = T, then '~(All D are B)' = F. We know from Table 6-2, however, that if 'All D are B' = T, then 'Some D are not B' = F. Hence, in this case '~(All D are B)' and 'Some D are not B' have the same truth value.

Case 2: 'All D are B' is false. If 'All D are B' = F, then '~(All D and B)' = T. From Table 6-2 we know that in this case 'Some D are not B' = T. Hence, in this case '~(All D are B)' and 'Some D are not B' have the same truth value.

Cases 1 and 2 show that (5)′ is true and, hence, that 'It's not the case that all dogs are brown' is equivalent to 'Some dogs are not brown'. Analogous arguments can be given for other pairs of categorical-statement equivalencies. For convenience, these equivalencies are summarized in Table 6-3.

We shall later use the equivalencies discussed here to eliminate negation signs preceding categorical statements. This will be referred to as the **diagonal transformation**; a description of the procedure follows.

DIAGONAL TRANSFORMATION

(1) Change the form of the original statement to the form opposite it on the diagonal.

(2) Remove the negation sign.

EXAMPLE 3

Apply the diagonal transformation to

~(Some non-L are not T)

TABLE 6-3		
~(All $\underline{S}$ are $\underline{P}$)	≡	Some $\underline{S}$ are not $\underline{P}$
~(No $\underline{S}$ are $\underline{P}$)	≡	Some $\underline{S}$ are $\underline{P}$
~(Some $\underline{S}$ are $\underline{P}$)	≡	No $\underline{S}$ are $\underline{P}$
~(Some $\underline{S}$ are not $\underline{P}$)	≡	All $\underline{S}$ are $\underline{P}$

Step 1: This is the negation of an *O*-form categorical statement. We change the form to the *A*-form.

Step 2: Remove the negation sign. Since the subject term and predicate term remain the same, our result is

All non-*L* are *T*

EXERCISE 6-6

Apply the diagonal transformation to each of the following statements.
a. ~(All *T* are *S*)   b. ~(No non-*S* are *R*)
c. ~(Some *L* are *T*)   d. ~(Some *M* are not *T*)
e. ~(All non-*T* are non-*R*)   f. ~(Some non-*L* are not *T*)
g. ~(No *R* are non-*S*)   h. ~(All *P* are non-*R*)
i. ~(Some non-*S* are non-*R*)   j. ~(No non-*L* are *S*)

6:3.4 Two Additional Equivalencies

Both universal negative and particular affirmative statements are such that interchanging the subject and predicate terms results in a statement equivalent to the original statement. That is, the following equivalencies hold:

(1) No $\underline{S}$ are $\underline{P}$ ≡ No $\underline{P}$ are $\underline{S}$

(2) Some $\underline{S}$ are $\underline{P}$ ≡ Some $\underline{P}$ are $\underline{S}$

Consider (1) first. If 'No $\underline{S}$ are $\underline{P}$' is true, then every individual which is included in the class designated by '$\underline{S}$' is *excluded* from the class designated by '$\underline{P}$'. That is, there is no individual which is included in both classes. But, if 'No $\underline{P}$ are $\underline{S}$' is true, it also follows that no individual is included in both classes. As a result, if one of the statements is true, the other is true as well. A similar argument will show that if one of the statements is false, the other is false as well. As a result, the two statements are equivalent.

Now consider (2). We have seen that statements of the form 'Some $\underline{S}$ are $\underline{P}$' are to be understood as 'At least one *S* is *P*'. That is, there is at least one thing which is *both* an *S* and a *P*. But if something is both an *S* and a *P*, it is both a *P* and an *S*. However, to say that there is at least one thing which is both a *P* and an *S*, we would write 'Some $\underline{P}$ are $\underline{S}$'. Similar remarks show that if a statement of the form 'Some $\underline{P}$ are $\underline{S}$' is true, then the statement of the form 'Some $\underline{S}$ are $\underline{P}$' is also true. As a result, the two statements are equivalent.

We shall make use of these equivalencies later, in providing the logical forms for arguments whose validity we shall determine with techniques to be developed in the following sections. Such equivalencies will be referred to as the **box transformations**.[10]

In this section we have examined various relationships which hold between categorical statements and have developed some equivalent ways of writing

---

[10] These equivalencies are also known as *converses*.

any given categorical statement. These will be used later, when we turn to the task of determining the validity of arguments. For convenience, all the transformations discussed in this section are displayed in Figure 6-3.

Figure 6-3

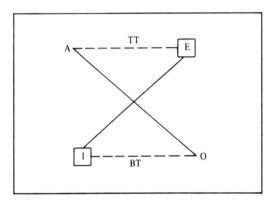

6:4 CATEGORICAL SYLLOGISMS

In this section we shall characterize a kind of argument composed solely of categorical statements, thereby laying the groundwork for handling arguments like argument 1, which introduces this chapter. We shall first look at the defining characteristics of categorical syllogisms, and then provide an explanation of these characteristics.

6:4.1 Characteristics of Categorical Syllogisms

Every argument which satisfies the following conditions, and only those arguments which do satisfy the conditions, is a categorical syllogism.

CHARACTERISTICS OF CATEGORICAL SYLLOGISMS

(1) The argument consists of two, and only two, premises and a conclusion.

(2) The two premises and the conclusion are categorical statements.

(3) The argument contains three terms, and each term occurs twice, once in each of two different statements.

Condition (1) should, at this point, require no explanation. You are already well acquainted with the notion of the conclusion and the premises of an argument. It is worth emphasizing, nonetheless, that a categorical syllogism *must* contain two premises. Hence, the following argument, though valid, is *not* a categorical syllogism.

ARGUMENT 2

No dogs are reptiles.

∴ No reptiles are dogs.

It is also worth noting here that the methods we shall later develop for determining the validity of categorical syllogisms will enable us to show as well that argument 2 is valid; it just happens that argument 2 is not a categorical syllogism, since it has only one premise.

Condition (2) needs little comment at this point. In sections 6:1 and 6:2 we discussed the four forms of categorical statements. Condition (2) is just the requirement that each of the statements in a categorical syllogism must be a standard-form categorical statement.

Condition (3) does need some comment. To facilitate discussion, let's take as our example the following argument:

ARGUMENT 3

All acids are hydrogenous.

All water is hydrogenous.

∴ All acid is water.

The *terms* in a categorical syllogism are the subject and predicate terms of each of the three categorical statements which compose the argument. Hence, the terms in argument 3 are 'acids', 'hydrogenous', and 'water'. The **end terms** of a categorical syllogism are *the subject term of the conclusion and the predicate term of the conclusion.* The end terms of argument 3, then, are 'acid' and 'water'. The **middle term** of a categorical syllogism is that term which does not occur in the conclusion but does occur in both the premises. The middle term of argument 3, then, is 'hydrogenous'. We can easily see that argument 3 satisfies condition (3) for categorical syllogisms: It has three terms—'acids', 'hydrogenous', and 'water'—and each term occurs twice, once in each of two different statements.

Consider, for a moment, the following argument:

ARGUMENT 4

All green plants contain chlorophyll.

Some things which contain chlorophyll need sunshine.

∴ Some things which need sunshine contain chlorophyll.

Argument 4 satisfies conditions (1) and (2) for categorical syllogisms, but it does not satisfy condition (3). Whereas it is true that argument 4 contains three terms—'green plants', 'things which contain chlorophyll', and 'things which need sunshine'—each of the terms does not occur twice. In particular, 'green plants' occurs only once, and 'things which contain chlorophyll occurs three times. Hence, argument 4 is *not* a categorical syllogism.

EXERCISE 6-7

1. Explain the conditions which an argument must fulfill to be a categorical syllogism. Give an example of a categorical syllogism.

2. Explain which terms are the end terms and the middle term of a categorical syllogism.

3. Give three examples of arguments which are not categorical syllogisms, such that each example fails to satisfy a different one of the conditions for being a categorical syllogism.

4. Determine whether each of the following arguments is a categorical syllogism. If an argument is not a categorical syllogism, explain why not.
   a. All carbohydrates are proteins.
      All proteins are energy producers.
      ∴ All carbohydrates are energy producers.
   b. Some proteins are energy producers.
      Some energy producers are not carbohydrates.
      ∴ Some energy producers are not proteins.
   c. No proteins are carbohydrates.
      ∴ No carbohydrates are proteins.
   d. If all carbohydrates are proteins, then all carbohydrates are energy producers.
      All carbohydrates are proteins.
      ∴ All carbohydrates are energy producers.
   e. Some vitamins are minerals.
      All minerals are found naturally in nature.
      ∴ Some things found naturally in nature are vitamins.
   f. Some vitamins are not minerals.
      Some minerals are found naturally in nature.
      All things found naturally in nature are health-producing.
      ∴ Some health-producing things are vitamins.
   g. All teddy bears are fuzzy things.
      Some fuzzy things are things which tickle.
      Some things which tickle are things which make people sneeze.
      ∴ Some teddy bears are things which make people sneeze.

6:4.2 Eliminating Extra Terms   In section 6:3 we discussed some relationships among categorical statements, developed several transformations, and noted that these transformations would be used to put arguments into a form from which we could determine the validity of the arguments. One argument which shows the need for the transformations is the following:

ARGUMENT 5

All who are condemned are nonbelievers.

All believers will be saved.

∴ None who are condemned are saved.

If we use 'non-*B*' to represent the class of nonbelievers, '*C*' to represent the class of those who are condemned, '*B*' to represent the class of believers, and '*S*' to represent the class of those who are saved, then we can symbolize argument 5 as follows:

FORM OF ARGUMENT 5

All *C* are non-*B*

All *B* are *S*

∴ No *C* are *S*

The difficulty we face with argument 5 is that it is *not* a categorical syllogism. Whereas the argument does have two premises and one conclusion, all of which are categorical statements, the argument does not have three terms, each of which occurs in two different statements. In particular, the argument has *four* terms, 'non-*B*', '*C*', '*B*', and '*S*'; and 'non-*B*' and '*B*' each occur only *once*. The issue before us, then, is whether argument 5 can be converted into a categorical syllogism and, if so, how this is to be done.

Given the earlier discussion in this chapter, it should be clear that argument 5 can be converted into a categorical syllogism if, and only if, the first premise can be rewritten as an equivalent categorical statement in which the term '*B*' replaces the term 'non-*B*', *or* the second premise can be rewritten as an equivalent categorical statement in which the term 'non-*B*' replaces '*B*'. Of course, in doing either of these two things we must maintain two occurrences of '*C*' and two of '*S*', or we would still not have a categorical syllogism.

Both premises of argument 5 are universal affirmative statements. In section 6:3.1 we saw that any such statement can be rewritten as an equivalent universal negative statement by using the *top transformation*. In applying that transformation, we replace the predicate term of the original statement with its complement. As a result, if we were to apply the top transformation to the first premise, our result would be a universal negative statement whose predicate term is '*B*'. Moreover, the subject term '*C*' of the original statement would remain the same. Consequently, we can eliminate the difficulty with argument 5 by using the top transformation to derive 'No *C* are *B*', thereby obtaining a categorical syllogism with three terms—'*C*', '*B*', and '*S*'—each of which occurs twice in two different premises. Our result is:

ARGUMENT 5'

No *C* are *B*

All *B* are *S*

∴ No *C* are *S*

We noted above that another way of converting argument 5 into a categorical syllogism would be to replace '*B*' in the second premise with 'non-*B*'. Let's consider this possibility. A little reflection on the transformations discussed in section 6:3 shows that *the only way to replace a term with its complement is by using either the top transformation or the bottom transformation*. Moreover, in either of these transformations, *a term can be replaced by its complement only if the term is in predicate position*.

We can, then, replace '*B*' in the second premise with 'non-*B*' only if we can first get '*B*' in predicate position. Again from our earlier discussions, the only way we can move a subject term into predicate position is by using the *box transformation;* that is, we must have either an *E*-form statement or an *I*-form statement.

Since premise two is an *A*-form statement, we must convert it into an *E*-form statement by using the top transformation before we can use the box transformation. Applying these two transformations would give us

(1) No *B* are non-*S*   (top transformation)

(2) No non-*S* are *B*   (box transformation)

Now we can replace '*B*' with its complement by using the top transformation. This gives us

(3) All non-*S* are non-*B*

Notice that in using the transformations necessary to replace '*B*' in the second premise with 'non-*B*', we also ended up by replacing '*S*' in that premise with 'non-*S*'. *Whenever we use the top transformation on an A-form statement so as to use the box transformation, and then replace the resultant predicate term with its complement by another use of the top transformation, the result is to replace both the original terms with their complements.* A similar remark applies in the case of *O*-form statements and the bottom transformation.

Having replaced '*S*' with 'non-*S*' in the process of replacing '*B*' with 'non-*B*', we have introduced another term into our argument. As a result, we must now either replace '*S*' with 'non-*S*' or 'non-*S*' with '*S*'. Since a term can be replaced with its complement only if the term is in predicate position, and since 'non-*S*' is now in subject position, we should check the occurrence of '*S*'. We see that in the conclusion '*S*' is in predicate position; as a result, by applying the top transformation, we can get

(4) All *C* are non-*S*

This leaves us with the first premise as given in the argument, (3) as the second premise, and (4) as the conclusion. Combining these results shows that argument 5 can also be rewritten as

ARGUMENT 5″

All *C* are non-*B*

All non-*S* are non-*B*   .

∴ All *C* are non-*S*

Notice that argument 5″ contains three terms—'*C*', 'non-*B*', and 'non-*S*'—and that each term occurs in two different statements. Since each statement is a categorical statement, we have a categorical syllogism.

It is important to realize that either argument 5′ or argument 5″ is an acceptable rewrite of argument 5. The former is simpler to derive, since it involves using only one transformation, though the latter is also a categorical syllogism.

Let us return to the fact that in replacing 'B' with 'non-B' in the second premise, we also ended up replacing 'S' with 'non-S'. This created more work for us in argument 5, but this is not always the case. To see this, consider the following argument:

ARGUMENT 6

All dogs are nonfelines.

Some felines are not Persians.

∴ Some nondogs are Persians.

Using 'D', 'F', and 'P' to represent the obvious terms, we have

FORM OF ARGUMENT 6

All D are non-F

Some F are not P

∴ Some non-D are P

In argument 6 we have two pairs of terms which do not match up: the 'D' and 'non-D' pair and the 'F' and 'non-F' pair. We must replace one member of each pair with its complement so that we have three terms, each of which occurs twice. We can do this in several ways, but the most straightforward way is to convert the first premise to an E-form statement by using the top transformation, use the box transformation to interchange the subject term and predicate term, and then use the top transformation again. This results in our replacing 'D' with its complement and 'non-F' with its complement, thereby taking care of both troublesome pairs by transforming only one premise. The results of applying these transformations to the first premise follow:

(1) No D are F (top transformation)

(2) No F are D (box transformation)

(3) All F are non-D (top transformation)

Combining this result with the second premise and the conclusion of argument 6, we obtain

ARGUMENT 6'

All F are non-D

Some F are not P

∴ Some non-D are P

This argument has three terms, each of which occurs in two different statements, so the argument is a categorical syllogism.

Another way to convert argument 6 into a categorical syllogism (that is, to eliminate the extra terms) would be to replace 'non-F' with 'F' in the first premise and replace 'non-D' with 'D' in the conclusion by first using the box transformation. This is left as an exercise.

By now it has probably occurred to you that there is no *one* correct way to eliminate extra terms. As a result, there is no specific procedure that must be followed in every case. However, there are some *general guidelines* and features of our transformations that you should keep in mind when eliminating extra terms:

(1) Once the argument has been symbolized, determine which pairs of terms are such that one member is the complement of the other. One member of each such pair must be replaced with the other member.

(2) The only way to replace a term with its complement is by using either the top transformation in the case of universal statements or the bottom transformation in the case of particular statements.

(3) A term that is to be replaced with its complement must be in predicate position.

(4) If both members of the mismatched pair are in subject position, check to see if the statements in which one or both terms occur are either *E*-form statements or *I*-form statements. If so, then the term can be moved into predicate position by the box transformation, and then the term can be eliminated by using either the top transformation or bottom transformation, as appropriate.

(5) When the top transformation is used on an *A*-form statement or the bottom transformation is used on an *O*-form statement prior to the use of the box transformation to get a subject term into predicate position, *both* terms will be replaced by their complements. This is an advantage when both terms in such statements must be eliminated, and a disadvantage when only one term is to be eliminated.

In section 6:3 we also discussed the contradictory relationship which holds between *A*-form and *O*-form statements and between *E*-form and *I*-form statements. Out of these relationships we developed the diagonal transformation. The need for this transformation is brought out in the following argument.

ARGUMENT 7

All matadors are brave. Consequently, it's not the case that some matadors are cowardly since none who are brave are cowardly.

Letting 'M', 'B', and 'C' represent the terms in argument 7, we have the following:

FORM OF ARGUMENT 7

All *M* are *B*

No *B* are *C*

∴ ~(Some *M* are *C*)

In this case we have a negation sign preceding the conclusion. To apply the techniques developed later in this chapter, we must eliminate this negation sign. The conclusion of argument 7 is the negation of an *I*-form statement whose terms are '*M*' and '*C*'. By the diagonal transformation we can derive an equivalent *E*-form statement having the same subject term and predicate term. Our result is

ARGUMENT 7′

All *M* are *B*

No *B* are *C*

∴ No *M* are *C*

This concludes our discussion of the elimination of extra terms. In the next section we shall develop the basis for one method of determining the validity of categorical syllogisms.

EXERCISE 6-8

1. What difficulty do the transformations enable us to handle?

2. Why must a term be in predicate position so that it can be eliminated by replacing it with its complement?

3. What transformation must be used if a term to be eliminated is not in predicate position?

4. What happens to the terms in an *A*-form categorical statement if one applies the following sequence of transformations: top transformation, box transformation, top transformation?

5. What happens to the terms in an *O*-form categorical statement if one applies the following sequence of transformations: bottom transformation, box transformation, bottom transformation?

6. Why is there always more than one way to eliminate extra terms?

7. What is the diagonal transformation used for?

8. Eliminate the outside negation signs in each of the following arguments, and rewrite the arguments as categorical syllogisms by eliminating extra terms where necessary.

a. ~(All non-*S* are *M*)
   Some *T* are *S*
   ∴ ~(No *M* are non-*T*)

b. Some non-*R* are not *T*
   ~(Some *T* are *M*)
   ∴ ~(No *R* are non-*M*)

c. Some *T* are non-*R*
   ~(No non-*S* are non-*T*)
   ∴ ~(Some *R* are *S*)

d. Some *R* are *S*
   ~(Some *S* are non-*T*)
   ∴ ~(All *T* are non-*R*)

e. ~(No *P* are non-*L*)
   No non-*L* are *S*
   ∴ Some *P* are *S*

f. ~(Some *L* are not *M*)
   All *M* are *R*
   ∴ No *L* are *R*

g. ~(Some *T* are not non-*S*)
   ~(Some *S* are not non-*R*)
   ∴ ~(Some *T* are *R*)

h. All non-*L* are *M*
   ~(Some *M* are non-*T*)
   ∴ ~(No *L* are *T*)

i. No non-*L* are *M*
   ~(All *M* are non-*T*)
   ∴ ~(All *L* are *T*)

j. ~(Some *T* are not non-*R*)
   ~(Some *R* are non-*S*)
   ∴ ~(Some non-*T* are not *S*)

6:5 VENN DIAGRAMS

The first method we shall use for determining the validity of categorical syllogisms is that of drawing **Venn diagrams.** We shall first discuss how to diagram each of the four forms of categorical statements, and then how to diagram whole arguments.

6:5.1 Diagramming the Categorical Statements We saw in section 6:1 that categorical syllogisms, if valid, are valid because of the relationships which hold among the various *terms* in the argument. The method we shall use to diagram categorical statements enables us to represent the various relations which hold between the terms in categorical statements. We shall represent each term in a categorical statement with a circle, so *the diagram for each categorical statement will consist of two circles;* one will represent the class designated by the subject term, and the other the class designated by the predicate term.

Figure 6-4

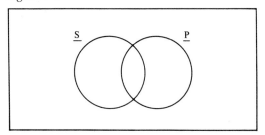

The basic diagram for any categorical statement is given in Figure 6-4. The left-most circle represents the class designated by the subject term 'S', and the right-most circle represents the class designated by the predicate term 'P'. Figure 6-4 is to be interpreted in the following way: *If* there are any members of the class designated by the term 'S', then they will be "located" within the S circle. Similarly, *if* there are any members of the class designated by 'P', then they will be located within the P circle. Note that in Figure 6-4 we have marked out three areas: that which is S but not P, that which is P but not S, and that which is *both* S and P (the intersection of the two circles). These areas are labeled in Figure 6-5.

Figure 6-5 is to be interpreted as follows: If anything is an S but not a P, then it will be located in area *a*; if anything is both an S and a P, then it will be located in area *b*; if anything is a P but not an S, then it will be located in area *c*. Anything which is neither an S nor a P will be located outside both circles, that is, in area *d*.

With this background, we are ready to provide diagrams for each of the categorical statements. Keep in mind, however, that the S circle and P circle of Figures 6-4 and 6-5 *can represent any subject term and any predicate term whatsoever.*

Universal Affirmative Statements We shall first diagram statements of the form 'All S are P'. In diagramming this statement form, we must remember

Figure 6-5

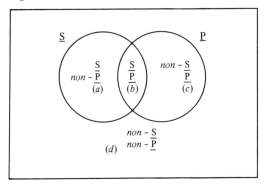

two things: First, the statement in effect says that all members included in the class designated by '$\underline{S}$' are also included in the class designated by '$\underline{P}$'; and, second, we cannot infer on the basis of the statement that there are or are not members of the subject class designated by the subject term—that is, we don't want to indicate on the diagram either that there are or that there are not any members of the class designated by '$\underline{S}$'.

What we want to show in our diagram, then, is that there are no $\underline{S}$'s which are not also $\underline{P}$'s, and we don't want to specify whether there are any $\underline{S}$'s. We could do this by indicating in Figure 6-5 that there is nothing in area a—the area which would contain all those things which are $\underline{S}$ but not $\underline{P}$. Hence we need some convention for showing that that part of our diagram contains no members. The method we shall adopt is that of *crosshatching*.

Figure 6-6

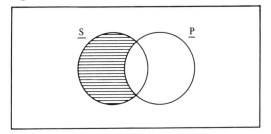

Figure 6-6 is the correct way to diagram universal affirmative statements of the form 'All $\underline{S}$ are $\underline{P}$'. Reading the crosshatch marks as 'there is nothing here', consider what must be the case *if* anything is an $\underline{S}$. We know from our earlier discussion of Figures 6-4 and 6-5 that anything which is an $\underline{S}$ must be located within the $\underline{S}$ circle. Since part of the $\underline{S}$ circle has effectively been erased (the effect of the crosshatching), anything which is an $\underline{S}$ must be located within that part of the $\underline{S}$ circle which remains—namely, that part which overlaps the $\underline{P}$ circle. The effect of this is that any $\underline{S}$ must also be a $\underline{P}$, since anything located in the remainder of the $\underline{S}$ circle will also be within the $\underline{P}$ circle.

Also notice that nothing about Figure 6-6 indicates whether or not there are any S̲'s; all we can determine from the figure is that if there are any S̲'s they will also be P̲'s. Note that this is just the interpretation we have given to statements of the form 'All S̲ are P̲'.

Before we move on to the other categorical statements, a quick word is in order concerning the crosshatching. There is a temptation on the part of some to read the crosshatch area as one which has members; *do not do this*. Keep in mind that *a crosshatched area is the same as an erased area*. In effect, what we have done in Figure 6-6 is to represent Figure 6-7. That is, there is no longer any area in which we could locate anything which is both an S̲ and not a P̲.

Figure 6-7

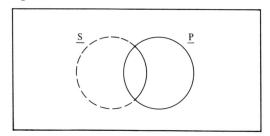

Universal Negative Statements Consider now statements of the form 'No S̲ are P̲'. Again we begin with our basic diagram, Figure 6-4. 'No S̲ are P̲' is to be understood as the claim that all members included in the class designated by 'S̲' are excluded from the class designated by 'P̲'. As in the case of universal affirmative statements, we cannot assume that there are any members of the class designated by 'S̲'. In our diagram, then, we must "erase" area *b* of Figure 6-4—that area wherein we would locate those things which are both S̲ and P̲. We erase this area since if 'No S̲ are P̲' is true, then nothing could be located in it.

Figure 6-8 is the correct way to diagram statements of the form 'No S̲ are P̲'. If there is anything which is an S̲, it must be located within the S̲ circle of Figure 6-8. Having "erased" part of the circle, however, we see that anything which is an S̲ will not be a P̲, since no one thing can be located in both the S̲ circle and the P̲ circle of Figure 6-8.

The effect of the crosshatching in Figure 6-8 is shown in Figure 6-9. That is, the S̲ circle and the P̲ circle are independent of one another.

Figure 6-8

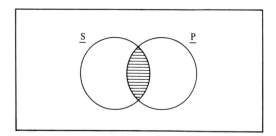

Figure 6-9

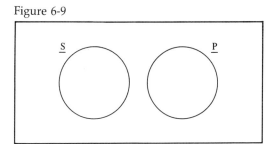

Particular Affirmative Statements When we say 'Some S̲ are P̲', what we are saying is that there is at least one thing which is both an S̲ and a P̲. We shall adopt the convention that an 'X' indicates that there is something located within the area of the diagram in which the 'X' is drawn. In the case of particular affirmative statements, we want to indicate on our diagram that there is something which is both an S̲ and a P̲. We can do this by placing an 'X' in the area where the S̲ circle and the P̲ circle overlap.

Figure 6-10 is the correct diagram for statements of the form 'Some S̲ are P̲'. The 'X' is within the S̲ circle, indicating that there is something which is an S̲; it is also within the P̲ circle, indicating that there is something which is a P̲. The result is that there is something which is both S̲ and P̲, just what we claim when we say 'Some S̲ are P̲'.

Figure 6-10

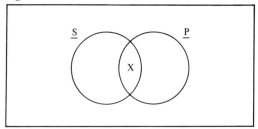

Particular Negative Statements Particular negative statements are like particular affirmative statements in that we *do* claim that there is at least one thing that is an S̲. In the case of particular negative statements, however, we say of this thing that it is not a P̲. What we must do in diagramming such statements, then, is place an 'X' in the S̲ circle but *not* within the P̲ circle. That is, we want an 'X' in area *a* of Figure 6-5. Our result is shown in Figure 6-11.

Figure 6-11

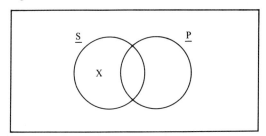

EXERCISE 6-9

1. Describe the basic diagram used for categorical statements by explaining what the circles represent and what each area of the diagram represents.

2. What does the crosshatching represent in a Venn diagram?

3. Explain how to diagram universal affirmative categorical statements.

4. Explain how to diagram universal negative categorical statements.

5. What does the 'X' represent in a Venn diagram?

6. Explain how to diagram particular affirmative categorical statements.

7. Explain how to diagram particular negative categorical statements.

8. Symbolize each of the following statements using the given symbols as constants, and provide a Venn diagram for each statement. In some cases it is necessary to first rewrite the statement as a standard-form categorical statement.

   a. All acids are bases. (A, B)
   b. All nonacids are nonbases. (A, B)
   c. No acids are bases. (A, B)
   d. No acids are nonbases. (A, B)
   e. Some vitamins are not minerals. (V, M)
   f. Some heretics were burned at the stake. (H, B)
   g. Some foods contain hydrogen and oxygen. (F, C)
   h. All abominable snowmen have hairy legs. (A, H)
   i. It's false that all monsters are handsome. (M, H)
   j. All problems have a solution. (P, S)
   k. Some good men are not needed. (M, N)
   l. It's not the case that some Lilliputians are not tiny. (L, T)
   m. All intelligent beings are mammals. (I, M)
   n. No drugs are illegal. (D, I)
   o. The majority of Americans are overweight. (A, O)
   p. It's not the case that none who eat right are unhealthy. (E, U)
   q. Only a few criminals are ever sentenced for their crimes. (C, S)
   r. None but those with talent will be a success. (T, S)
   s. No hefflelumps are woozles. (H, W)
   t. Some alien species are not very attractive to look at. (S, A)
   u. Almost everyone who was invited accepted the invitation. (I, A)
   v. Samantha did not accept the invitation. (S, A)
   w. It's false that no good will come from complaining. (G, C)
   x. All except Leonard enjoyed the movie. (L, M)
   y. All's well that ends well. (W, E)

6:5.2 Diagramming the Premises of Categorical Syllogisms Having diagrammed some individual categorical statements, we are now ready to diagram the premises of a categorical syllogism. In section 6:5.1 it was pointed out that we need two circles to represent each categorical statement, one for each term occurring in the statement. Moreover, only *three* terms occur in a categorical syllogism; as a result, we can diagram its premises using three circles—one for each term that occurs in the argument.

Consider the following argument form:

ARGUMENT 8

All S̲ are M̲

All M̲ are P̲

∴ All S̲ are P̲

If we were to diagram the two premises of the argument separately, we would have the diagrams shown in Figure 6-12.

Figure 6-12

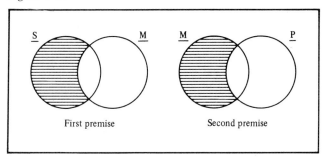

First premise   Second premise

In determining the validity of categorical syllogisms we are concerned with the relationships among the terms of the argument as they occur in each of the statements. We need, then, a diagram which enables us to show these relationships—relationships which are not brought out in the diagrams in Figure 6-12. Figure 6-13 is such a diagram. Following the convention used in Figure 6-5, the various areas wherein things might be located are shown in Figure 6-13.[11] For example, anything located in area *a* would be an S̲ but not an M̲ and not a P̲; anything located in area *b* would be an M̲ and a P̲ but not an S̲; anything located in area *c* would be a P̲ and an M̲ and an S̲; and so on.

Notice that the premises of argument 8 can *both* be diagrammed using the format of Figure 6-13. We could begin by diagramming the first premise, with the result shown in Figure 6-14.

In Figure 6-14 we do not specify whether, if there are any S̲'s, there are or are not P̲'s. That is, from Figure 6-14 all we know is that if there are any S̲'s they are in one or the other or both of areas *a* and *b*, but we don't know where.

Adding the second premise to Figure 6-14 gives us the result shown in Figure 6-15. The addition of the second premise to our diagram has the effect of "erasing" area *a* of Figure 6-14. Hence, we now know that if there are any

---

[11] Note that these eight areas correspond to the eight lines in a truth table constructed for three variables.

Figure 6-13

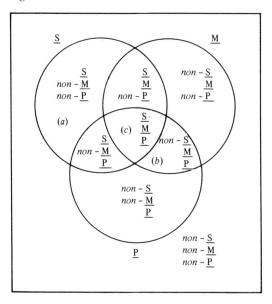

Figure 6-14

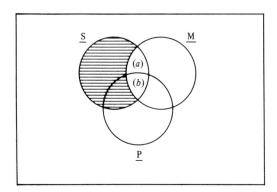

Figure 6-15

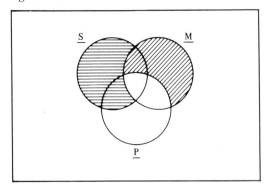

<u>S</u>'s they will also be <u>P</u>'s, since anything which is in the remainder of the <u>S</u> circle will also be in the <u>P</u> circle (actually in the area designated '*SMP*').

The procedure outlined for argument 8 is followed in diagramming the premises of any categorical syllogism. In particular, we first construct a figure like Figure 6-13, with one circle representing each of the terms which occurs in the argument. The next step is to diagram each of the premises, using the two circles applicable to that premise. This procedure is applied in the following example.

ARGUMENT 9

All *A* are *B*

Some *A* are *C*

∴ Some *B* are *C*

Step 1: Construct the appropriate diagram with three overlapping circles, one for each term in the argument. This is shown in Figure 6-16.

Figure 6-16

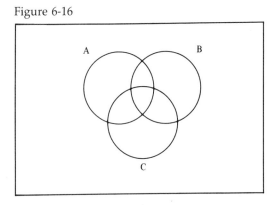

Step 2: Diagram the first premise. In diagramming 'All *A* are *B*', the only circles we are concerned with are the *A* circle and the *B* circle. We ignore the *C* circle, since it plays no role in the premise in question. The result is shown in Figure 6-17.

Figure 6-17

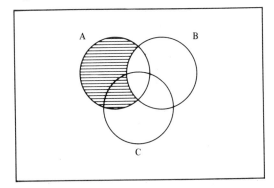

Step 3: Diagram the second premise. In diagramming the second premise, 'Some *A* are *C*', the two circles which need to be considered are the *A* circle and the *C* circle. In particular, we need to place an '*X*' in the overlap of the two circles. In Figure 6-17 we see, however, that in diagramming the first premise we have "erased" part of the overlap between the *A* circle and the *C* circle; since nothing can be in this "erased" area, we must place our '*X*' in the remaining part of the overlap between the *A* circle and the *C* circle. Our result is Figure 6-18.

Figure 6-18

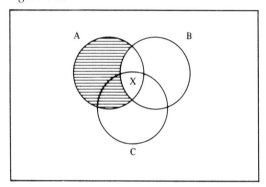

It should be noted here that we *diagram universal premises before diagramming particular premises.* If both premises are universal or both premises are particular, it does not matter in what order they are drawn.

6:5.3 Diagramming the Conclusions of Categorical Syllogisms   Since the conclusions of categorical syllogisms are categorical statements, you already know how they are diagrammed: in exactly the way in which we diagrammed categorical statements in section 6:5.1. To aid in determining the validity of categorical syllogisms, we shall make a slight change to the diagrams given in that section. To see the change, consider again argument 8:

ARGUMENT 8

All S̲ are M̲

All M̲ are P̲

∴ All S̲ are P̲

The premises diagram for argument 8 is given in Figure 6-19.

In drawing a diagram for the conclusion we are, strictly speaking, concerned only with the S̲ circle and the P̲ circle. We shall, however, follow the procedure of drawing three circles, but the circle which represents the term that does not occur in the conclusion will be drawn *dashed.* Furthermore, we shall orient the circles for the conclusion diagram in the same way as in the premises diagram.

Figure 6-19

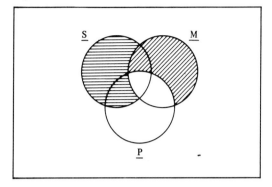

The conclusion diagram for argument 8, then, looks like Figure 6-20. The conclusion diagram for argument 9 is shown in Figure 6-21.

Figure 6-20

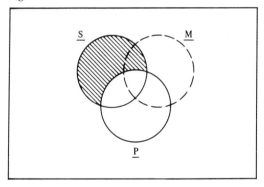

Figure 6-21

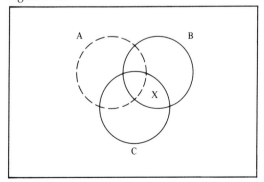

6:5.4 Using Venn Diagrams to Determine Validity We can now state how one determines the validity of categorical syllogisms. The principle is the following:

[A categorical syllogism is valid if, and only if, what is drawn in the conclusion diagram has also been drawn in the premises diagram.]

To determine the validity of a categorical syllogism, then, we first draw the premises diagram, then draw the conclusion diagram, and finally check to see if what is drawn in the conclusion diagram has also been drawn in the premises diagram.

There are three things worth noting here: First, this procedure for checking categorical syllogisms for validity is a pictorial representation of the definition of validity, since *if* the premises are true, then the premises diagram is a true representation of the facts; therefore, the conclusion must be true as well, since it represents at least some of these facts. Second, this procedure is also a pictorial representation of condition (2) of valid arguments—that the information or factual content of the conclusion is already contained in the premises. Third, it is not actually necessary to draw a conclusion diagram to check the validity of a categorical syllogism. All one need actually do is look at the premises diagram and see if the conclusion has been diagrammed. Nonetheless, even though conclusion diagrams are not necessary, we shall draw them. Drawing a conclusion diagram minimizes the chance of making careless errors in answering the question "Has the conclusion already been diagrammed in the premises diagram?" It is also to avoid careless errors that we adopted the convention of drawing the three circles for the conclusion diagram (one dashed) and orienting the conclusion diagram with the premises diagram.

In this and the preceding sections we have seen how to diagram the premises and conclusion of categorical syllogisms and how to determine the validity of categorical syllogisms. In the next section we shall apply these methods to some problems.

6:5.5 Some Examples   The purposes of this section are to provide further examples of how one determines the validity of categorical syllogisms and to point out some of the problems one can encounter in working with categorical syllogisms.

EXAMPLE 4

Since some politicians are dishonest and some politicians are Democrats, it follows that some Democrats are dishonest.

> *Step 1:* Rewrite the argument in standard form, separating the premises and the conclusion.
>
>> Some politicians are dishonest.
>>
>> Some politicians are Democrats.
>>
>> ∴ Some Democrats are dishonest.
>
> *Step 2:* Symbolize the argument. Here we let 'P' represent 'politicians', 'H' represent 'dishonest', and 'D' represent 'Democrats'. Then we have
>
>> Some P are H
>>
>> Some P are D
>>
>> ∴ Some D are H

Step 3: Draw the premises diagram, providing one circle for each of the terms in the argument. This is shown in Figure 6-22.

Figure 6-22

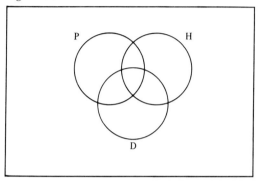

Step 4: Diagram the premises. First check to see if there are both universal and particular premises in the argument; if so, diagram the universal premise first. Since both premises of example 4 are particular, it does not matter which one is diagrammed first. We begin, then, with the first premise. The circles relevant to the first premise are the *P* circle and the *H* circle. We know that we are to draw an 'X' in the overlap of these two circles. We find, however, that there is a line running through the overlap. Since the thing which is both *P* and *H* might or might not be *D* as well, we must put the 'X' on the line, indicating that the thing could be in either area of the overlap between the *P* circle and the *H* circle. Our result is shown in Figure 6-23.

Figure 6-23

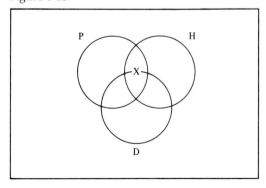

Step 5: Diagram the second premise. Again we must put an 'X' in the overlap between the *P* circle and the *D* circle. Since there is a line running through this overlap, we put the 'X' on the line. Our completed premises diagram is shown in Figure 6-24.

Step 6: We are now ready to draw the conclusion diagram. We begin by drawing two solid circles for the terms in the conclusion and a

Figure 6-24

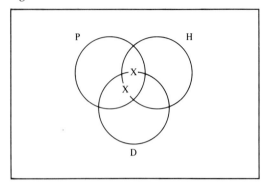

dashed circle for the term which does not occur in the conclusion; we orient the diagram in the same way as the premises diagram is oriented. This is shown in Figure 6-25.

Figure 6-25

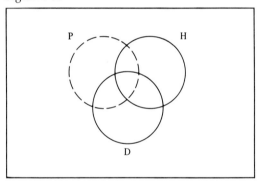

Step 7: Diagram the conclusion. This is shown in Figure 6-26.

Figure 6-26

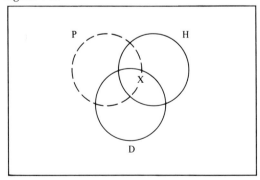

Step 8: Determine the validity of the argument. To do this, we find out whether the conclusion diagram has already been drawn in the

premises. For convenience, these two diagrams are reproduced together in Figure 6-27.

Figure 6-27

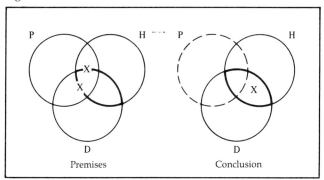

Premises   Conclusion

The area of the conclusion diagram relevant to the determination of validity is marked in heavy outline, as is the same area in the premises diagram. Looking at the conclusion diagram, we see that *there is an 'X' wholly in the outlined area.* In the premises diagram, however, *the two 'X's' are on the line.* Since the conclusion diagram has not been drawn in the premises diagram, the argument in question is *invalid.*

Before we proceed, a note on the interpretation of the premises diagram in step 8 is in order. We know from earlier chapters that any argument form can be shown to be invalid if we can find just one case in which all the premises are true and the conclusion is false. The diagrams in step 8 show us how to do this in the case of example 4. In particular, the two 'X's' on the lines in the premises diagram indicate that the thing which is P and H might or might not be D and the thing which is P and D might or might not be H. Hence, the following is one way of making the premises of example 4 true:

(1) The thing which is P and H is not D.

(2) The thing which is P and D is not H.

Statement (1) is sufficient for the truth of the first premise (there is something which is a politician and is dishonest), and (2) is sufficient for the truth of the second premise (there is something which is a politician and is a Democrat). Notice, however, that the individual which is dishonest is not a Democrat, from (1); and the Democrat is not dishonest, from (2). In this situation, and based solely on the premises, our conclusion (there is something which is a Democrat and is dishonest) is false.

EXAMPLE 5

Since it's not the case that no Whig is honest and it is the case that no Whigs are politicians, it follows that some honest people are not politicians.

Step 1: Rewrite the argument in standard form.

It's not the case that no Whig is honest.

No Whigs are politicians.

∴ Some honest people are not politicians.

Step 2: Symbolize the argument.

~(No *W* is *H*)

No *W* are *P*

∴ Some *H* are not *P*

Step 3: Eliminate the outside negation sign on the first premise. We can do this by making use of the equivalencies discussed earlier. In particular, the negation of a universal negative statement is a particular affirmative statement, by the diagonal transformation. Hence, we can rewrite the first premise as

Some *W* are *H*

Step 4: Draw the format for the premises diagram. This is given in Figure 6-28.

Figure 6-28

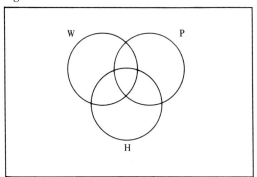

Step 5: Diagram one of the premises. Since one premise is universal and the other is particular, we begin with the universal premise: the second. The diagram is shown in Figure 6-29.

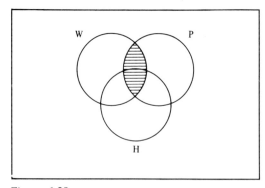

Figure 6-29

Step 6: Diagram the remaining premise. For the first premise we must place an 'X' in the overlap of the W circle and the H circle. Since part of that overlap was "erased" when we diagrammed the second premise, we must place the 'X' in the remainder of the overlap. This is shown in Figure 6-30.

Figure 6-30

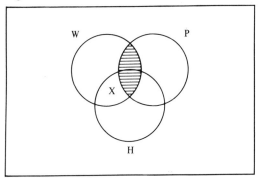

Step 7: Draw the conclusion diagram, and diagram the conclusion. The diagram is shown in Figure 6-31.

Figure 6-31

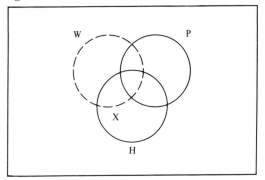

Step 8: Determine the validity of the argument. The premises diagram and the conclusion diagram are reproduced together in Figure 6-32, with the parts that are relevant to the determination of validity outlined heavily.

In the conclusion diagram in Figure 6-32, there is an 'X' in the H circle and outside the P circle. In the premises diagram we also find an 'X' in this area. Hence, the argument is *valid.*

A note about Figure 6-32 may help forestall a possible confusion. You might be inclined to say that the 'X' which appears in the premises diagram is not only an H and not a P, but is a W as well, whereas this does not seem to be the case in the conclusion diagram. On these grounds you might also be inclined to say that the argument in question is invalid. The reply here is that you would

Figure 6-32

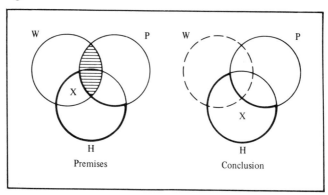

be correct in pointing out that the H which is not a P and is a W in the premises need not be a W in the conclusion; but you would be wrong in thinking that this shows that the argument is invalid. Let (1) below be a description of the thing which is signified by the 'X' in the premises diagram, and (2) be a description of the thing which is signified by the 'X' in the conclusion diagram.

(1) H and W and non-P

(2) H and non-P

We can readily see here that if there is a thing correctly described by (1) then there is also a thing correctly described by (2), since anything which is H, W, and non-P is also H and non-P. What we have in the above diagrams is an instance where *the premises give us more information than is contained in the conclusion*. That, however, does not make an argument invalid. What is needed to make an argument invalid is that the conclusion give us more information than is contained in the premises. In short, if (1) is true, then (2) must be true as well; but this is just the same as saying if the premises of example 5 are true then the conclusion of example 5 must be true. Hence, the argument is valid.

A general procedure for determining the validity of categorical syllogisms can be gleaned from the above examples:

Step 1: Rewrite the argument in standard form.

Step 2: Symbolize the argument.

Step 3: If necessary, convert those statements which are not categorical statements into categorical statements by using the diagonal transformation to eliminate any outside negation signs.

Step 4: If necessary, use the appropriate transformations to convert premises or conclusions so that the argument contains only three terms.

Step 5: Draw the premises diagram, drawing all universal premises before drawing particular ones.

Step 6: Draw the conclusion diagram.

Step 7: See if the conclusion diagram has already been drawn in the premises diagram. If so, the argument is valid; if not, the argument is invalid.

Also notice that in the example in which the argument was invalid, example 4, at least one of the particular statements was such that the 'X' had to be drawn on a line. *Any categorical syllogism in which a particular premise has the 'X' drawn on the line is invalid.* A word of warning here, however; this rule applies only to *categorical syllogisms* and not to other arguments composed of categorical statements. For example, the following *valid* argument has an 'X' on a line in the premises diagram.

ARGUMENT 10

All *A* are *B*

Some *B* are *C*

∴ Some *C* are *B*

Although argument 10 is valid, as can be seen from Figure 6-33, it is not a categorical syllogism since it does not satisfy the condition we placed on terms—that there be three terms and that each term occur in two different statements. Argument 10 has three terms, but they don't each occur twice; '*A*' occurs only once, and '*B*' occurs three times.

Figure 6-33

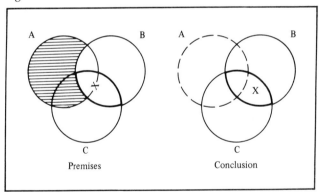

Premises   Conclusion

In this section we have developed the Venn-diagram method for determining the validity of categorical syllogisms. In the next section we shall examine another method for determining validity: that of using a set of rules which must be satisfied for a categorical syllogism to be valid.

EXERCISE 6-10

1. Give the basic Venn diagram for the premises of a categorical syllogism, and explain what each section of the diagram represents.

2. Explain why, in diagramming a categorical syllogism with one universal premise and one particular premise, the universal premise is diagrammed first.

3. Explain why, and in what cases, an 'X' is to be put on the line between two areas of a Venn diagram. What does an 'X' on a line represent?

4. Explain how one determines the validity or invalidity of a categorical syllogism once the premises diagram and the conclusion diagram have been drawn.

5. Use Venn diagrams to determine the validity or invalidity of the arguments in problem 8 of Exercise 6-8.

6. Put the following arguments into standard form, and symbolize the arguments by using the given symbols as constants. Determine the validity or invalidity of the arguments by using Venn diagrams.

   a. No *hefflelumps* are *woozles* because woozles have *little* ears, and no hefflelump has little ears. (H, W, L)

   b. All *wonderful* things are *tiggers*. Hence, tiggers have *stripes* because at least one thing which is wonderful has stripes. (W, T, S)

   c. We all know that every *successful* person is someone who was born with *talent*. Hence, it's not the case that all *unfortunate* people are born with talent, since many unfortunate people will not be a success in life. (S, T, U)

   d. There is no question but that all *good* things must come to an *end*. But, since it's false that no *bad* things come to an end, it must also be the case that some bad things are good things. (G, E, B)

   e. It must be the case that some *people* have *heart* trouble. After all, some people are *overweight*, and it's clearly not the case that no one who is overweight has heart trouble. (P, H, O)

   f. Everyone who doesn't eat *right* is unhealthy. Hence, it's simply not the case that all *people* are *healthy*, for it's false that all people eat right. (R, P, H)

   g. Since it's false that some *politicians* are *dishonest*, and since all who are dishonest *lie*, it follows that no politician lies. (P, D, L)

   h. All *satyrs* are *interested* in Sabine women. But since no satyr is *human*, it follows that some who are interested in Sabine women are not human. (S, I, H)

   i. We all know that some *criminals* are not *apprehended*. Hence, some who are *wanted* by the law are not apprehended, for all criminals are obviously wanted by the law. (C, A, W)

   j. Since it's false that some true *believers* were *heretics*, and since all heretics were *condemned*, it follows that no true believers were condemned. (B, H, C)

   k. Since some *foods* contain *hydrogen* and oxygen, and since it's not the case that some *carbohydrates* do not contain hydrogen and oxygen, it follows that some foods are carbohydrates. (F, H, C)

   l. Everything *worth* worrying about is also a *problem*. Hence, since a few things worth worrying about have *solutions*, all problems have solutions. (W, P, S)

m. Since all *abominable* snowmen have *hairy* legs, it must be the case that they also have *sweet* dispositions. After all, we know it's not the case that some who have hairy legs don't also have sweet dispositions. (*A, H, S*)

n. Since it's not the case that some *Lilliputians* are not *tiny*, and since it's also not the case that none who are tiny have *big* mouths, it follows that it's not the case that no Lilliputians have big mouths. (*L, T, B*)

o. All *good* men must come to the *aid* of their country. Hence, some good men are not needed since it's false that all who come to the aid of their country are *needed*. (*G, A, N*)

p. All *happy* people are also hard *workers*. As a result, not all *people* work hard, since some people are unhappy. (*H, W, P*)

q. There is no question but that all that *glitters* is not *gold*. But, since it's false that no *jewelry* is gold, it must also be the case that some jewelry glitters. (*Gl, G, J*)

r. Since all *Venuvians* are *mammals* and all *intelligent* beings are mammals, it follows that all Venuvians are intelligent beings. (*V, M, I*)

s. No *person* can *fail* to be affected by the current drug situation. But, since all who are affected by the situation should *work* for stricter drug laws, it follows that every person should work for stricter drug laws. (*P, F, W*)

t. Since all *medicines* are *drugs* and since it's not the case that no drugs are *illegal*, it follows that some medicines are illegal. (*M, D, I*)

6:6. USING RULES TO DETERMINE THE VALIDITY OF CATEGORICAL SYLLOGISMS

In the previous section we developed the Venn-diagram method for determining the validity or invalidity of categorical syllogisms. Strictly speaking, then, we do not need any other method for doing this. Nonetheless, we shall here discuss an additional method, that of using rules. One of the most obvious advantages of the rule method is that it does not require the drawing of diagrams. As a result, it can be applied when no pen or pencil is handy. Also, when an argument violates one or more of the rules, we are able to say *why* the argument is invalid. A third benefit, related to that just mentioned, is that knowing why an argument is invalid enables us to repair the argument. That is, by understanding what, in particular, is wrong with the argument, we can construct a new argument which does not have this defect. We can then go on to ask whether the premises of this new argument are true and, if so, whether we would be justified in accepting the conclusion.

To gain a general understanding of the way in which the rule method works, consider the following situation: There are 256 forms of categorical syllogisms. By using the Venn-diagram method, we could test all 256 forms for validity. Having found those forms which are valid, we could compile a list of those, and only those, forms. Then, to determine the validity of any given categorical syllogism, we would simply determine its form and then see if that form is on our list of valid forms. If so, the given syllogism would be valid; if not, it would be invalid.

This procedure will clearly work as a means of determining validity. What the procedure lacks, however, is a specification or explanation of *why* the argument forms included in the list are valid.[12] One way of providing this explanation is to find what characteristics are shared by the forms on the list and are lacking in those forms which do not appear on the list. Having established these characteristics, we could dispense with the list and simply ask of any given categorical syllogism whether it has all the characteristics needed to be valid.

The four rules to be discussed in this section specify the characteristics possessed by each and every valid categorical syllogism. Every invalid categorical syllogism lacks one or more of these characteristics. As a result, we can determine the validity of any given categorical syllogism by seeing whether it satisfies the rules. *Any categorical syllogism which satisfies all four rules is valid; any categorical syllogism which fails to satisfy all four rules is invalid.*

6:6.1 The First Two Rules   By considering the Venn diagrams for valid categorical syllogisms it is possible to establish the first two characteristics possessed by all valid syllogisms. A little reflection on Venn diagrams will show that each of the following is true:

(A) To be valid, a categorical syllogism with an affirmative conclusion must have two affirmative premises.

(B) To be valid, a categorical syllogism with a negative conclusion must have one, and only one, negative premise.

By combining (A) and (B), we obtain our first rule which applies to all instances of valid categorical syllogisms:

RULE 1

In a valid categorical syllogism, the number of negative premises must be the same as the number of negative conclusions.

A comment is in order concerning rule 1. Of course, a categorical syllogism will have just one conclusion. What rule 1 tells us is that if the conclusion is negative, then the syllogism must have one, and only one, negative premise. This aspect of rule 1 picks up the point made in (B) above. Where the conclusion is affirmative there are *no* negative conclusions, so rule 1 tells us that there can be no negative premises or, what comes to the same thing, that both premises must be affirmative. This aspect of rule 1 picks up the point made in (A) above.

By examining the Venn diagrams of valid categorical syllogisms, we can also find the following:

---

[12] Of course, one could say the forms are valid because they have been shown to be valid by drawing Venn diagrams. The "why" question raised above would then have to be pushed back one step: What characteristics are shared by all those categorical syllogisms which can be shown to be valid by the Venn-diagram method?

(C) To be valid, a categorical syllogism with a universal conclusion must have two universal premises.

(D) To be valid, a categorical syllogism with a particular conclusion must have one universal premise and one particular premise.

By combining (C) and (D), we obtain our second rule which applies to all instances of valid categorical syllogisms.

RULE 2

In a valid categorical syllogism, the number of universal premises must be exactly one more than the number of universal conclusions.

As noted in the case of rule 1, a categorical syllogism has just one conclusion. Rule 2 tells us that if the conclusion is a particular statement, then there must be one, and only one, particular premise (the other, of course, would be a universal premise). This aspect of rule 2 picks up the point made in (D) above. If, on the other hand, the conclusion is universal, then rule 2 tells us that there must be two universal premises. This aspect of rule 2 picks up the point made in (C) above.

This completes our discussion of the first two rules. In the next section we shall consider a relationship which holds among the terms of valid categorical syllogisms. Based on that relationship, we shall present the other two rules.

6:6.2 Distribution of Terms and the Second Two Rules To see why rules 1 and 2 alone are not adequate for picking out all, and only, valid categorical syllogisms, consider the following argument.

ARGUMENT 11

All poodles are mammals.

All Siamese cats are mammals.

∴ All Siamese cats are poodles.

Argument 11 clearly satisfies rules 1 and 2; just as clearly, the argument is invalid since it has all true premises and a false conclusion. What we want to determine, then, is what characteristic of valid categorical syllogisms is missing from argument 11. To do this, let's begin by diagramming the premises of argument 11, as shown in Figure 6-34.

However, if argument 11 were valid, we would have diagrammed at least what is shown in Figure 6-35 when we drew our premises diagram.

A careful comparison of Figures 6-34 and 6-35 shows that, whereas the truth of the conclusion *excludes* there being something which is an S but not a P, the premise *do not exclude* this possibility. In particular, in Figure 6-34 the S–M–non-P area of the diagram has not been shaded. This shows us that even if the premises are true, there could still be something which is a Siamese cat, is a mammal, and is *not* a poodle; any Siamese cat is obviously such a thing.

The difficulty here can perhaps best be brought out by considering the

Figure 6-34

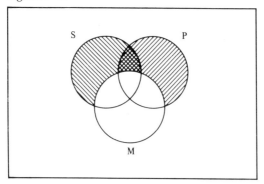

relationship which has to hold between the premises and the conclusion of a valid syllogism and then seeing why that relationship does not hold in the present case. In the conclusion of any valid syllogism, a relationship is asserted to hold between those things designated by the subject term and those things designated by the predicate term. Moreover, this relationship is asserted to hold *because* of the relationship which those things designated by the subject terms and the predicate term have to those things designated by the middle term. In a sense, the middle term in a valid syllogism ties the subject term and predicate term together in whatever way is specified in the conclusion.

As a result, if 'M' is to serve as a tie between 'S' and 'P', those things designated by 'S' and 'P' must bear a relationship to *all* the things which are designated by 'M'; if they do not bear such a relationship, then there is no "guarantee" that those things designated by 'S' and 'P' will be tied together by 'M'. Indeed, this is exactly what goes wrong in the argument under discussion. In particular, for a categorical syllogism to be valid, it is necessary that a statement be made in at least one premise about all those individuals designated by the middle term. The middle term in argument 11 is 'mammals', and in neither premise is a statement made about *all* mammals.

Logicians have an expression for characterizing a term in a categorical

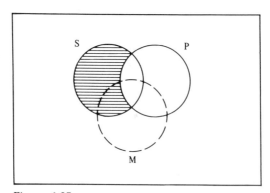

Figure 6-35

statement such that the statement is used to state something about all the individuals designated by the term; such a term is **distributed** in (or by) the statement. In particular:

A categorical statement *distributes* a term if the statement is used to state something about all the individuals designated by the term. In such a case, the term is said to be *distributed*.

With the above terminology, we can recharacterize the difficulty with argument 11: In neither premise is the middle term 'mammals' *distributed*. This gives rise to our third rule for determining the validity of categorical syllogisms.

RULE 3

In a valid categorical syllogism, the middle term must be distributed at least once.

Before we consider the fourth and final rule, let's expand our discussion of distributed terms. In the *A*-form categorical statement, the subject term is distributed, since the statement is used to say something about all the things designated by '$\underline{S}$', whereas the predicate term is *not* distributed because the statement is not used to say something about all the things designated by '$\underline{P}$'. We represent this schematically by circling the distributed term:

A: All Ⓢ are $\underline{P}$

Now consider the universal negative statement form 'No $\underline{S}$ are $\underline{P}$', and let's take as an example the statement 'No dogs are reptiles'. In this categorical statement we *do* assert something about those individuals (dogs) designated by the subject term, namely, that each and every dog is such that it is not a reptile. As a result, 'dogs' is distributed in (or by) the categorical statement 'No dogs are reptiles'.

What of the predicate term 'reptiles'? Given that the truth of the statement 'No dogs are reptiles' entails that each and every dog is not a reptile, we also know that each and every reptile is not a dog. (This is, perhaps, most easily seen by considering the Venn diagram for 'No $\underline{S}$ are $\underline{P}$' and realizing that it is the same diagram as would be drawn for 'No $\underline{P}$ are $\underline{S}$', where the latter asserts that for each and every $\underline{P}$, it is not an $\underline{S}$.) As a result, 'reptiles' is distributed in (or by) the categorical statement 'No dogs are reptiles'. The *E*-form case is summarized as follows:

E: No Ⓢ are Ⓟ

In the case of a particular affirmative categorical statement, of the form 'Some $\underline{S}$ are $\underline{P}$', *neither* term is distributed. To see this, take as an example 'Some business people are swindlers'. You know from our earlier discussion of categorical statements that this statement is to be understood as the claim that at least one business person is a swindler. Notice that we obviously are *not* making a statement about all business people. This is easily seen by considering the Venn diagram for 'Some $\underline{S}$ are $\underline{P}$' and realizing that this is not a statement about all those things designated by 'S'. In addition, since the diagram for 'Some S are P' is the same as the diagram for 'Some P are S', we are not making a statement about all those things designated by 'P' either. As a result, neither the subject term nor the predicate term is distributed in an I-form categorical statement. This is shown as

I: Some S̲ are P̲

Now for the O-form statements. Let's take as our example the statement 'Some federally funded projects are not worth the money'. It might initially be thought that the O-form statement is just like the I-form in that neither term is distributed; this is *not* the case, however. In claiming that some federally funded projects are not worth the money, we are not saying something about all such projects; as a result 'federally funded projects' is not distributed in the statement. We are, however, saying something about all the things which *are* worth the money—namely, of all the things which *are* worth the money, those particular federally funded projects mentioned in our statement are excluded from those things. In the case of an O-form statement, the particular individuals designated by the subject term are said to be excluded from those individuals designated by the predicate term; for this to be the case, those particular individuals have to be excluded from *all* those individuals designated by the predicate term. As a result, the predicate term in an O-form statement is distributed; this is shown as

O: Some S̲ are not Ⓟ

To summarize our discussion of the four forms of categorical statements, we have the following:

A: All Ⓢ are P̲   E: No Ⓢ are Ⓟ

I: Some S̲ are P̲   O: Some S̲ are not Ⓟ

The terms which are distributed in (or by) a categorical statement, then, are *the subject terms of universal statements and the predicate terms of negative statements.*

Having provided a characterization of distribution, we are now ready to take up the final rule for determining the validity of categorical syllogisms. To facilitate the discussion, consider the following argument:

ARGUMENT 12

All cats are mammals.

Some cats are not dogs.

∴ Some dogs are not mammals.

Since argument 12 has all true premises and a false conclusion, it is invalid. Let's symbolize it using 'S̲' for the subject term of the conclusion, 'P̲' for the predicate term of the conclusion, and 'M̲' for the middle term:

FORM OF ARGUMENT 12

All <u>M</u> are <u>P</u>

Some <u>M</u> are not <u>S</u>

∴ Some <u>S</u> are not <u>P</u>

Since argument 12 is invalid but satisfies rules 1 to 3, there must be some additional condition which categorical syllogisms must satisfy to be valid. To see what this condition might be, let's again consider the form of argument 12 and indicate which terms are distributed and which are not be circling the distributed terms. This gives us

All Ⓜ are <u>P</u>

Some <u>M</u> are not Ⓢ

∴ Some <u>S</u> are not Ⓟ

Given that the terms are so distributed, we see that in the first premise we are making a statement about all those things designated by '<u>M</u>', in the second premise we are making a statement about all those things designated by '<u>S</u>', and in the conclusion we are making a statement about all those things designated by '<u>P</u>'.

At this point it is useful to recall one of the conditions which must be satisfied for an argument to be valid, CD2:

CD2

In a valid argument, all the information or factual content of the conclusion is already contained in the premises.

What is wrong with argument 12 is that it violates CD2, and it does so for the following reason: In our conclusion, since '<u>P</u>' is distributed, we are asserting something about *all* those things designated by '<u>P</u>'—namely that the individuals designated by the subject term of the conclusion are excluded from the whole class of mammals. In our premises, however, we do *not* state anything about *all* mammals. The other occurrence of 'mammals' is as the predicate term in the first premise, a universal affirmative statement; as a result, 'mammals' is *not* distributed.

What has happened, then, is that we have brought into our conclusion information which is not contained in the premises: information about *all* mammals. To prevent this kind of case, we add a fourth and final rule to the conditions which must be satisfied for a categorical syllogism to be valid:

RULE 4

In a valid categorical syllogism, any term which is distributed in the conclusion must also be distributed in the premises.

Rule 4 ensures that if we make a statement about all the individuals designated by one of the terms in the conclusion, then we will also have a statement about all such individuals in our premises.

Rules 1 to 4 enable us to determine the validity or invalidity of any of the 256 possible forms a categorical syllogism might have. Any syllogism which violates one or more of the rules is invalid. Any syllogism which satisfies all four rules is valid, provided that if a given rule does not apply to the syllogism, it is considered to be satisfied. In the next section we shall apply the rules to some examples. The rules are presented together below.

RULES FOR THE VALIDITY OF CATEGORICAL SYLLOGISMS

Rule 1: In a valid categorical syllogism, the number of negative premises must be the same as the number of negative conclusions.

Rule 2: In a valid categorical syllogism, the number of universal premises must be exactly one more than the number of universal conclusions.

Rule 3: In a valid categorical syllogism, the middle term must be distributed at least once.

Rule 4: In a valid categorical syllogism, any term which is distributed in the conclusion must also be distributed in the premises.

6:6.3 Some Examples   In this section we shall look at several examples of categorical syllogisms and determine their validity by applying the four rules developed in the previous sections.

ARGUMENT 13

Some rulings by the Supreme Court are politically oppressive.

All politically oppressive actions are wrong.

∴ Some rulings by the Supreme Court are wrong.

Step 1: Symbolize the argument. In applying the rules for determining validity, it is helpful to symbolize the argument by using 'S' to represent the subject term of the conclusion, 'P' to represent the predicate term of the conclusion, and 'M' to represent the middle term. In argument 13, these terms are, respectively, 'Rulings by the Supreme Court', 'wrong actions', and 'politically oppressive actions'. This gives us the following:

Some S are M

All M are P

∴ Some S are P

Step 2: Determine which terms are distributed. Since universal subjects and negative predicates are distributed, the circled term in the following is distributed in the argument:

Some *S* are *M*

All Ⓜ are *P*

∴ Some *S* are *P*

Step 3: See if rule 1 is satisfied. For rule 1 to be satisfied, the number of negative premises must be the same as the number of negative conclusions. Since our conclusion is affirmative, there are no negative conclusions and, hence, there can be no negative premises. Since both premises are affirmative, rule 1 is satisfied.

Step 4: See if rule 2 is satisfied. For rule 2 to be satisfied, the number of universal premises must be exactly one more than the number of universal conclusions. Since the conclusion of the argument is particular, we must have one, and only one, universal premise. This we have with 'All *M* are *P*', so rule 2 is satisfied.

Step 5: See if rule 3 is satisfied. For rule 3 to be satisfied, the middle term must be distributed at least once. Checking the form given in step 2, we see that '*M*' is distributed in the second premise, so rule 3 is satisfied.

Step 6: See if rule 4 is satisfied. For rule 4 to be satisfied, any term distributed in the conclusion must also be distributed in the premises. Again checking the form given in step 2, we see that neither term in the conclusion is distributed. Since rule 4 does not apply to this argument, we consider it satisfied.

Step 7: Since rules 1 to 4 are all satisfied, and since any categorical syllogism which satisfies all the rules is valid, argument 13 is *valid*.

ARGUMENT 14

Some anthropologists prefer the cultures they study to their own.

Some who prefer the cultures they study to their own are not very smart.

∴ Some anthropologists are not very smart.

Step 1: Determine the form of the argument. Here the subject term is 'anthropologists', the predicate term is 'very smart', and the middle term is 'those who prefer the cultures they study to their own'. This gives us

Some *S* are *M*

Some *M* are not *P*

∴ Some *S* are not *P*

Step 2: Determine which terms are distributed. Again, universal subjects and negative predicates are distributed, so we have

Some S are M

Some M are not P

∴ Some S are not P

Step 3: See if rule 1 is satisfied. Rule 1 is satisfied if, and only if, the number of negative premises is the same as the number of negative conclusions. Since the conclusion is negative, we must have one, and only one, negative premise. The first premise is affirmative and the second negative, so rule 1 is satisfied.

Step 4: See if rule 2 is satisfied. Rule 2 is satisfied if, and only if, there is exactly one more universal premise than there are universal conclusions. Since the conclusion of the argument is a particular statement, we must have one, and only one, universal premise. Since both premises are particular statements, rule 2 is violated and, hence, the argument is invalid.

Having shown that argument 14 violates rule 2, we do not have to consider rules 3 and 4. However, we shall consider these rules to gain some practice in using them.

Step 5: See if rule 3 is satisfied. Rule 3 is satisfied if, and only if, the middle term is distributed at least once. Checking the form given in step 2, we see that neither occurrence of 'M' is distributed, so rule 3 is violated.

Step 6: See if rule 4 is satisfied. Rule 4 is satisfied if, and only if, every term which is distributed in the conclusion is also distributed in the premises. Again looking at the form given in step 2, we see that 'P' is distributed in the conclusion so 'P' must also be distributed in the premises to satisfy rule 4. Checking the premises, we see that 'P' is distributed in the second premise, so rule 4 is satisfied.

EXERCISE 6-11

1. What are the benefits of the rule method of determining the validity or invalidity of categorical syllogisms?

2. When rules are used to determine the validity or invalidity of a categorical syllogism, what general criterion must be satisfied for a syllogism to be valid?

3. Explain the first rule for the validity of categorical syllogisms. Give an example of a syllogism which violates this rule.

4. Explain the second rule for the validity of categorical syllogisms. Give an example of a syllogism which violates this rule.

5. Explain what it means to say that a term is distributed in a categorical statement.

6. Give an example of each of the following:
   a. A statement in which only the subject term is distributed
   b. A statement in which only the predicate term is distributed
   c. A statement in which both the subject term and the predicate term are distributed
   d. A statement in which neither the subject term nor the predicate term is distributed.
7. Explain the third rule for the validity of categorical syllogisms. Give an example of a syllogism which violates this rule.
8. Explain the fourth rule for the validity of categorical syllogisms. Give an example of a syllogism which violates this rule.
9. Circle each term which is distributed in the statements in problem 8 of Exercise 6-9.
10. Use the rules for the validity of categorical syllogisms to determine the validity or invalidity of the arguments in problem 8 of Exercise 6-8.
11. Use the rules for the validity of categorical syllogisms to determine the validity or invalidity of the arguments in problem 6 of Exercise 6-10.

STUDENT STUDY GUIDE

Chapter Summary

1. There are four forms of **categorical statements.** Each such statement consists of a **subject term** and a **predicate term,** and both terms refer to classes. In general each term in a categorical statement identifies that property or characteristic by virtue of which an individual is a member of the class designated by the term. (section 6:1.1)

2. The **class complement** of a class includes all those individuals which are not members of the given class. The class complement of a class is designated by prefixing 'non' to the term which designates the given class. (section 6:1.1)

3. If an individual is a member of a class, the individual is **included** in the class; if an individual is not a member of a class, the individual is **excluded** from the class. For every individual and every class, the individual is either included in the class or excluded from the class. (section 6:1.2)

4. In each of the four forms of categorical statements it is asserted that all, or some, individuals which are members of one class are either included in or excluded from another class. The **quantity** of a categorical statement is determined by whether all or some members of a given class are mentioned; the **quality** of a categorical statement is determined by whether these members are included in or excluded from another class. (section 6:1.2)

5. When a categorical statement is about some, but not all, members of the subject class, the statement is a **particular** statement. When a categorical statement is about all the members of the subject class, the statement is a **universal** statement. If it is asserted in a categorical statement that the members of the subject class

are also members of the predicate class, the statement is **affirmative.** If it is asserted in a categorical statement that the members of the subject class are excluded from the predicate class, the statement is **negative.** (section 6:1.2)

6. With regard to quantity and quality, every categorical statement is one of the following: a **universal affirmative** statement, a **universal negative** statement, a **particular affirmative** statement, or a **particular negative** statement. (section 6:1.2)

7. Universal categorical statements are interpreted as a kind of conditional statement. In particular, they are interpreted as the claim that if an individual is a member of the subject class, than that member is included in the predicate class (universal affirmative statement) or excluded from the predicate class (universal negative statement). In particular categorical statements, the word 'some' is understood as 'at least one'. (section 6:1.3)

8. In symbolizing categorical statements, uppercase letters are used to represent the subject term and the predicate term. Such letters are **predicate constants,** and they represent the particular characteristic by virtue of which an individual is a member of the given class. In symbolizing the form of a categorical statement, **predicate variables** are used. These are uppercase letters which have been underlined, and they represent the place wherein a predicate or a predicate constant can occur. (section 6:2.1)

9. **Exclusive statements** are those in which it is asserted that the predicate expression applies only to the individual or individuals designated by the subject expression. The words that typically are used to indicate this are 'only' and 'none but'. **Exceptive statements** are those in which it is asserted that a particular characteristic applies to a certain group of individuals, with the exception of a few members in the group. Exceptive statements are best translated as conjunctions of *I*-form and *O*-form statements or of *A*-form and *E*-form statements. The expressions that typically are used in exceptive statements are 'almost all', 'not quite all', 'almost everyone', 'all except', 'all but', and 'alone'. (section 6:2.5)

10. Any universal affirmative statement can be rewritten as a universal negative statement, and any universal negative statement can be rewritten as a universal affirmative statement. To do this, one uses the **top transformation.** To apply this transformation, the quality of the original statement is changed, and the predicate term of the original statement is replaced by its complement. (section 6:3.1)

11. Any particular affirmative statement can be rewritten as a particular negative statement, and any particular negative statement can be rewritten as a particular affirmative statement. To do this, one uses the **bottom transformation.** To apply this transformation, the quality of the original statement is changed, and the predicate term of the original statement is replaced by its complement. (section 6:3.2)

12. *A*-form and *O*-form categorical statements are contradictory, and *E*-form and *I*-form categorical statements are contradictory. As a result, we can eliminate a negation sign preceding a categorical statement by using the **diagonal transformation.** To apply this transformation, the form of the original statement is changed to the form of its contradictory, and the negation sign is removed from the original statement. (section 6:3.3)

13. Both universal negative and particular affirmative categorical statements are such that interchanging the subject term and the predicate term results in a statement equivalent to the original statement. This is the **box transformation.** (section 6:3.4)

14. A **categorical syllogism** is an argument which consists of two, and only two, premises and a conclusion. The premises and the conclusion are categorical statements, and the argument contains three terms, each of which occurs twice and occurs in two different statements. (section 6:4.1)

15. The **terms** in a categorical syllogism are the subject and predicate terms of the three categorical statements which compose the argument. The subject term and predicate term of the conclusion are the **end terms,** and the term which does not occur in the conclusion but does occur in both premises is the **middle term.** (section 6:4.1)

16. Some arguments in ordinary language are equivalent to categorical syllogisms but are not themselves categorical syllogisms since they contain more than three terms. To rewrite such arguments as categorical syllogisms, one must **eliminate extra terms.** The way to do this is to replace a term with its complement by using either the top or bottom transformation, as appropriate. (section 6:4.2)

17. The validity or invalidity of a categorical syllogism can be determined by using **Venn diagrams.** To diagram a categorical statement using Venn diagrams, two overlapping circles are drawn; one circle represents the class of all those individuals designated by the subject term, and the other circle represents the class of all those individuals designated by the predicate term. (section 6:5.1)

18. To diagram universal statements, one crosshatches that area of the Venn diagram which contains no members; the crosshatching is like erasing. To diagram particular statements, one places an 'X' in the area of the diagram which contains the individual designated in the statement. (section 6:5.1)

19. Since the premises of a categorical syllogism contain three terms, the **premises diagram** of a categorical syllogism consists of three overlapping circles. In diagramming each premise, only the circles representing the terms which occur in the premise are considered. When a syllogism has both a universal premise and a particular premise, the universal premise is diagrammed first. (section 6:5.2)

20. To determine the validity of a categorical syllogism by using Venn diagrams, one first draws the premises diagram and then the conclusion diagram. A categorical syllogism is valid if, and only if, what is drawn in the conclusion diagram has also been drawn in the premises diagram. (section 6:5.4)

21. The validity or invalidity of a categorical syllogism can also be determined by using a set of four rules. Any categorical syllogism which satisfies all four rules is valid; any categorical syllogism which fails to satisfy all four rules is invalid. (section 6:6)

22. The first two rules can be established by considering Venn diagrams for valid categorical syllogisms. These rules are, first, that in a valid categorical syllogism the number of negative premises must be the same as the number of negative conclusions and, second, that in a valid categorical syllogism the number of universal premises must be exactly one more than the number of negative conclusions. (section 6:6.1)

23. A term is **distributed** in a categorical statement if the statement is about all the individuals designated by the term. As a result, the subject terms of universal categorical statements and the predicate terms of negative categorical statements are distributed. (section 6:6.2)

24. The third and fourth rules for establishing the validity of categorical syllogisms concern the distribution of terms. These rules are, first, that in a valid categorical syllogism the middle term must be distributed at least once and, second, that in a valid categorical syllogism any term which is distributed in the conclusion must also be distributed in the premises. (section 6:6.2)

Key Terms

Categorical Statement	Predicate Variables
Subject Term	Exclusive Statements
Predicate Term	Exceptive Statements
Class Complement	Top Transformation
Class Inclusion	Bottom Transformation
Class Exclusion	Diagonal Transformation
Quantity of a Categorical Statement	Box Transformation
Quality of a Categorical Statement	Categorical Syllogism
Particular Statement	End Term
Universal Statement	Middle Term
Affirmative Statement	Venn Diagram
Negative Statement	Distributed Term
Predicate Constants	

Self-Test/Exercises

1. What does one mean by the quality of a categorical syllogism? The quantity? (section 6:1.2)

2. What are the names of the four standard-form categorical statements? Explain why each is called what it is. (section 6:1.2)

3. How are sentences which contain proper names translated into standard-form categorical statements? (section 6:1.3)

4. What is an exclusive statement? What is an exceptive statement? Explain how such statements are written as standard-form categorical statements. (section 6:2.5)

5. Where necessary, rewrite each of the following as a standard-form categorical statement. Symbolize each statement using the given symbols, and circle those terms which are distributed in the statement. (section 6:2)
   a. All but a few of the *plants* died in last night's *frost*. (P, F)
   b. *Aristotle* was a famous *philosopher*. (A, P)
   c. Many *people* don't like to be *awakened* in the middle of the night by a phone call. (P, A)

    d. Only *students* will be *admitted* on Green and Gold night. (*S, A*)

    e. Nobody who has *studied* the subject *thinks* that mental telepathy really happens. (*S, T*)

    f. Anyone who likes *baseball loves* the World Series. (*B, L*)

6. Explain the conditions which an argument must satisfy to be a categorical syllogism. (section 6:4.1)

7. Explain which terms are the end terms and the middle term of a categorical syllogism. (section 6:4.1)

8. Explain the top transformation, the bottom transformation, and the box transformation. For what purpose are these transformations used? (section 6:3)

9. What is the diagonal transformation used for? (section 6:3.3)

10. Rewrite each of the following as a categorical syllogism. (section 6:4.2)

    a. ~(All non-*S* are *N*)
      Some *T* are *S*
    ∴ ~(No *N* are non-*T*)

    b. ~(Some *R* are not non-*S*)
      ~(Some *S* are non-*T*)
    ∴ ~(Some non-*R* are not non-*T*)

    c. No non-*L* are *M*
      Some non-*M* are not *R*
    ∴ Some *L* are not non-*R*

11. Explain the basic diagram used for diagramming categorical statements by explaining what the circles represent and what each area of the diagram represents. (section 6:5.1)

12. Symbolize each of the following statements using the given symbols as constants, and provide a Venn diagram for each statement. In some cases it is first necessary to rewrite the statement as a standard-form categorical statement. (section 6:5.1)

    a. The vast majority of *Americans* have ancestors from *Europe*. (*A, E*)

    b. None but licensed *lawyers* are able to practice in *Arizona*. (*L, A*)

    c. *Santa* Claus *works* hard on Christmas Eve. (*S, W*)

    d. Some *alien* species are not *very* attractive. (*A, V*)

    e. Nobody who *tried* to enroll late was *admitted* to the course. (*T, A*)

13. Explain why, and in what cases, an '*X*' is placed on the line between two areas of a Venn diagram. What does an '*X*' on a line represent? (section 6:5.2)

14. Explain how one determines the validity or invalidity of a categorical syllogism once the premises diagram and the conclusion diagram have been drawn. (section 6:5.4)

15. Put each of the following arguments into standard form and symbolize the arguments by using the given symbols as constants. Determine whether the arguments are valid or invalid, first by drawing a Venn diagram and then by using the rules for the validity of categorical syllogisms. (sections 6:5.5 and 6:6.3)

    a. Some *people* do not like the pressures they *find* from others. Those who find pressure from others are often *neurotic*. Hence, some people are neurotic. (*P, F, N*)

b. Some of the *best* things in life are *free*. All *coupons* cut from the newspaper are free. It must be the case, then, that some of the best things in life are coupons cut from the newspaper. (*B, F, C*)

c. Nobody who really *understands* people *envies* everyone else. As a result, some who envy everyone else have not read much *psychology*, for some who understand people have read a lot of psychology. (*U, E, P*)

d. Every so often an *opportunity* comes along that is *passed* up. Since most of the things which are passed up are later *regretted*, some opportunities are regretted. (*O, P, R*)

e. Since none but those who were *selected* were eventually *initiated*, and since those who were initiated were *worthy* of the honor, it follows that none but those who were worthy were selected. (*S, I, W*)

f. Since it's not the case that nobody who likes *classical* music also likes *harpsicord* music, and since all who like harpsicord music are people who like music that *sounds* strange, it follows that some who like classical music like music that sounds strange. (*C, H, S*)

CHAPTER 7

PREDICATE

LOGIC

With this chapter we conclude our discussion of deductive arguments. When we are done, we shall have developed a much more powerful logic system than those thus far discussed. As in earlier chapters, one of our goals will be to build upon what you already have learned so as to provide the ability to analyze arguments of even greater complexity.

At the present time our bag of logical tools consists of the truth-table method of determining validity and a system of natural deduction which we can use to construct proofs for arguments whose validity is a function of truth-functional relationships among whole statements. We also have the Venn-diagram method (or rules) which we can use to determine the validity of categorical syllogisms. But what are we to do with the following?

ARGUMENT 1

The Statue of Liberty is over 150 feet high.

∴ Something is over 150 feet high.

ARGUMENT 2

Brown University is an Ivy League school and is in the east.

∴ Something is in the east.

If we attempt to analyze these arguments by using truth tables or our system of natural deduction, argument 1 would have to be symbolized as

p

∴ q

Argument 2 would have to be symbolized either in the same way or, if we read the premise as 'Brown University is an Ivy League school *and* Brown University is in the east', as

$p \cdot q$

∴ r

That is, our system of natural deduction is applicable when we deal with *whole statements* or truth-functional compounds consisting of whole statements. As a result, the premises and conclusions of the above arguments must be symbolized with *statement variables* if we are to use either truth tables or the system of natural deduction to show their validity. The difficulty we face here is, of course, that what is required by the system in terms of symbolism results in an invalid argument form; but it is clear that each of the above arguments is *valid*.

This situation is analogous to the situation we encountered in Chapter 6 when we first discussed categorical statements and syllogisms. That is, we are confronted with arguments which are obviously valid but whose validity cannot be shown if the argument forms are expressed in the system we are working with. We might consider using the ideas developed in the last chapter on categorical statements. The difficulty here is that the conclusions in the above arguments are not categorical statements. Moreover, though the premise in argument 1 can be treated as an *A*-form statement whose subject term denotes a class with only one member, the premise in argument 2 cannot be so treated. So we still have two arguments which are obviously valid but whose validity cannot be shown with the methods thus far discussed.

It may have occurred to you that what is needed to analyze arguments 1 and 2 is some system or method which *combines* the rules of inference from statement logic with what we have already found about the expressions 'all' and 'some'. This is exactly what we shall discuss in this chapter. Our general goal will be to develop a system which will enable us to use all the rules of inference from Chapter 5, including the Rule of Replacement, by combining them with a way of dealing with 'all' and 'some' from the previous chapter.

It should be noted from the outset that we shall not be discussing a decision procedure for handling arguments like those above. Instead, we shall develop the means for constructing proofs of validity for such arguments. For reasons which will soon become obvious, the system we shall be discussing is a system of **predicate logic** or, as it is sometimes called, **quantificational logic.**

7:1 SOME BASIC CONCEPTS

As mentioned above, our goal in this chapter is to develop a system whereby we can use the rules of inference from statement logic to construct proofs of the validity of arguments more complex than those of statement logic or of the syllogism. At the outset, it should be noted that our difficulty with arguments 1 and 2 is *not* simply the occurrence of the expression 'something' in the arguments. To see this, consider the following argument:

ARGUMENT 3

If something is in New York, then something is east of the Mississippi River.

Something is in New York.

∴ Something is east of the Mississippi River.

If we assign the statement variable '*p*' to the place occupied by the sentence 'Something is in New York' and the statement variable '*q*' to the place occupied by the sentence 'Something is east of the Mississippi River', then we have the following as the form of argument 3.

FORM OF ARGUMENT 3

$p \supset q$

p

$\therefore q$

This is, of course, a valid argument form, namely, affirming the antecedent.

To prove the validity of arguments 1 and 2, then, what is needed is a way to represent the form of the statements which occur in the arguments, along with some additional rules of inference which will enable us to work with those forms. This we develop in the next few sections.

7:1.1 Singular Statements   It is clear that the premises and conclusions of arguments 1 and 2 are statements. It is also clear that the arguments are valid but cannot be shown to be so by assigning statement variables to the statements which occur in the arguments. Following the strategy of the previous chapter, let's focus on the internal structure of each of the statements.

To see what this internal structure is, consider the premise from argument 1, 'The Statue of Liberty is over 150 feet high'. In asserting this statement, we say of some particular object, the Statue of Liberty, that it has a particular characteristic, that of being over 150 feet high. Statements like this one are **singular statements,** as are some other kinds of statements.[1]

In general, we can say that a singular statement is one in which something is asserted about some *particular individual.* The simplest kind of singular statements are those in which it is asserted that some particular individual has a particular characteristic.[2] All the following are singular statements of this kind:

(1) The Statue of Liberty is in New York.

(2) The Statue of Liberty was a gift from France.

(3) The Washington Monument is over 150 feet high.

(4) The Empire State Building is over 150 feet high.

A little reflection shows that (1) and (2) have something in common, and (3) and (4) have something else in common. In the first pair the same expression, 'The Statue of Liberty', is used to pick out a particular individual, and in the second pair the same expression, 'is over 150 feet high', is used as a predicate.

---

[1] These other singular statements are discussed later in this section.

[2] In English, 'individual' often has the connotation of *being human.* Here, 'individual' is used as a general expression, applicable to anything which can be named, described, or otherwise "picked out" by using language.

One way, then, of more fully exhibiting the logical structure of these singular statements is to differentiate the term which picks out the individual from the predicate term of the statement. Adopting the convention that uppercase letters will represent predicate terms and lowercase letters will represent terms for individuals, we can construct the following "dictionary":

s: the Statue of Liberty	*N*: is New York
w: the Washington Monument	*G*: is a gift from France
e: the Empire State Building	*O*: is over 150 feet high

It is customary in predicate logic to write the letter which represents the predicate term first, followed by the letter which represents the individual. Therefore, the premise in argument 1 would be written as '*Os*', and statements to (1) to (4) would be written as follows:

(1)' *Ns*

(2)' *Gs*

(3)' *Ow*

(4)' *Oe*

The important point about representing these singular statements in the form predicate term–individual term, as opposed to using a statement constant or a statement variable, is that we are thereby able to show that some of the statements have something in common—either the same individual term or the same predicate term. As for categorical syllogisms, this feature will be used to show the relationships which hold between the premises and conclusions of valid arguments in predicate logic. First, several points must be made.

We noted above that a singular statement is one in which something is asserted about some particular individual, and that the simplest statement of this kind is an affirmative subject-predicate statement. That is not the only kind of singular statement however. In addition to the kinds of statements already discussed, we can also have negative subject-predicate statements and statements which contain the logical connectives 'and', 'or', 'if-then', and 'if, and only if'. For example, all the following are singular statements because something is asserted about one particular individual.

John is not hungry.

Marie is going sailing and to a picnic.

Audrey is going to enroll in a chemistry class or in a biology class.

If Sandra is accepted, then she will go to medical school.

Tom will pass the test tomorrow if, and only if, he crams tonight.

Although we shall discuss how to symbolize such statements in more detail in a later section, their symbolization is provided here so that you may begin getting familiar with the new notation. In the symbolized expressions which follow, the first letter of the individual's name has been used to represent the individual term, and the first letter of a major word occurring in the predicate expression has been used to represent the predicate term:

$\sim Hj$

$Sm \cdot Pm$

$Ca \lor Ba$

$As \supset Gs$

$Tt \equiv Ct$

Notice that in each of the above expressions, the same individual term occurs throughout the expression; that is, each of the statements symbolized is about only one individual. Also notice that each of the statements is truth-functional; that is, the truth value of each statement depends on the truth value of its component statements and the truth table for the appropriate logical connective.

In addition to truth-functional statements such as these, there are truth-functional compound statements which are composed of singular statements but which are not themselves singular statements. As an example, consider the following:

Marie is going sailing and Tom is going to cram tonight.

Using 'm' to represent 'Marie', 'S' to represent 'is going sailing', 't' to represent 'Tom', and 'C' to represent 'is going to cram tonight', we have

$Sm \cdot Ct$

This statement is truth-functional, since its truth value depends on the truth values of the left conjunct 'Sm' and the right conjunct 'Ct'. Each conjunct is a singular statement because it is a statement about a particular individual—Marie in one case and Tom in the other. The statement as a whole is *not*, however, a singular statement, since it is *not* about a particular individual but rather about two individuals.

7:1.2 Constants and Variables We have already noted the distinction between constants and variables in our discussion of statement logic. Here we shall extend the concept to apply to different kinds of cases. In (1)' to (4)' in the previous section, we used two letters to represent the statements in (1) to (4): an uppercase letter to represent the predicate term, and a lowercase letter to represent the individual term. Each of these letters is a *constant*, since each represents a particular characteristic or a particular individual. More specifically, the uppercase letters are **predicate constants,** and the lowercase letters are **individual constants.** We shall adopt the convention of using the letters 'a' through 'w' for individual constants and, where possible, the first letter of an individual's name as the individual constant representing that individual.[3] Once we have chosen an individual constant to represent an individual—a different constant for each individual—that constant will represent that individual throughout the particular argument and its discussion.

In addition to individual constants, we shall also make use of **individual variables.** To see fully what we mean by an individual variable, consider (3) and (4) again.

(3) The Washington Monument is over 150 feet high.

(4) The Empire State Building is over 150 feet high.

Recall that we symbolize these as

(3)′ *Ow*

(4)′ *Oe*

Clearly (3) and (4), and therefore (3)′ and (4)′, have something in common, namely the same predicate term. In each statement we say of some particular individual, first the Washington Monument and then the Empire State Building, that it possesses the characteristic of being over 150 feet high. The *structure* of both (3)′ and (4)′, then, can be represented as '*O*_____', where the '_____' indicates that there is another symbol which occurs to the right of the predicate expression.

Instead of using '_____' to represent the structure of (3)′ and (4)′, we can use a letter. For this we shall use '*x*', since '*a*' through '*w*' are reserved for individual constants. The structure of (3)′ and (4)′ can now be represented as '*Ox*', where '*x*' is an *individual variable*. That is, '*x*' functions as a placeholder, indicating that one, and only one, individual constant can be written in its place to produce a singular statement. To represent the structures of statements with more than one individual variable, we can use '*y*' and '*z*' in addition to '*x*'.

One important point to be made here is that '*Ox*' *is not a statement*. A literal reading of '*Ox*' is '*x* is over 150 feet high', so in asserting '*Ox*' we have not said that a particular individual has the characteristics of being over 150 feet high. As a result, '*Ox*' *does not have a truth value*.

Expressions like '*Ox*', containing only predicate constants and individual variables (and perhaps one or more logical connectives), are **open sentences.**[4] Putting the point made in the preceding paragraph in another way, we can say that *open sentences do not express statements and do not have truth values*. On the other hand, were we to replace the '*x*' in '*Ox*' with an individual constant, and thereby assert of some particular individual that it is over 150 feet high, the result would be a singular statement with a truth value.

---

[3] It would not be possible to do this if, for example, an argument concerned the two individuals Mark and Mary. Here only one of the individuals could be assigned the individual constant '*m*'; another letter would have to be chosen to represent the other individual.

[4] Open sentences are further characterized in section 7:1.4.

EXERCISE 7-1

1. Why can't the validity of the following argument be shown by using only the rules of inference from statement logic?

   Suzi is going to the movies and Marnie is going to the opera.
   ∴ Someone is going to the opera.

2. What is a singular statement?

3. What is the difference between individual constants and individual variables?

4. What is an open sentence?

5. Which of the following are singular statements?
   a. John hit a home run.
   b. Cake is better than bread. **A b**
   c. Everyone loves a lover. **N0**
   d. He did it.
   e. Someone is coming to dinner. **A0**
   f. Sharon is very articulate.
   g. Time passes quickly.
   h. No one is home. **No**
   i. Sam and Louis are both going. **N0**
   j. Someone does not like the taste of licorice. **No**

6. For each of the singular statements in problem 5, identify the subject term and the predicate, assign constants to the expressions, and write the statement in correct logical form.

7. Convert each of the following open sentences to a singular statement by choosing an appropriate subject term.
   a. *x* is the capital of the United States.
   b. *x* is famous for fried chicken.
   c. *x* is a city on the west coast.
   d. *x* is fun.
   e. *x* is my favorite book.

8. Assign a predicate constant and an individual constant to each of the singular statements you constructed in problem 7, and write the statement in correct logical form.

9. Given that '*M*', '*S*', '*T*', and '*H*' represent the predicate expressions 'going to the movies', 'studying for an exam', 'throwing a party', and 'going home for the weekend', respectively, and given that '*a*', '*b*', '*c*', '*d*' and '*e*' represent 'Allan', 'Barbara', 'Carlisle', 'Donna', and 'Edward', rewrite each of the following expressions in words.
   a. *Mb*
   b. ~*Hc*
   c. *Te* ⊃ *Ma*
   d. *Td* ∨ *Hd*
   e. (*Sd* · ~*Te*) ⊃ *Hc*
   f. (*Mb* ∨ *Sd*) ⊃ (*He* · *Te*)
   g. *Td* ≡ ~*Hb*
   h. (~*He* · ~*Sc*) ⊃ *Td*
   i. ((*Md* · *Sb*) ∨ ~*Tc*) ⊃ *Ha*
   j. *Ha* ⊃ ((*Md* · *Sd*) ∨ *Td*)

7:1.3 Quantifiers   The previous section introduced individual constants and individual variables. We noted there that an expression consisting of just predicate constants and individual variables is an open sentence. One feature of open sentences is that they do not express a statement and, therefore, do not have a truth value.

Since the individual variable which occurs in the expression of an open sentence is a placeholder for individual constants, we can replace the variable with a constant. For example, from the open sentence 'Gx', read 'x is a gift from France', we can get a singular statement by replacing 'x' with an individual constant. Replacing 'x' with 's', we get 'Gs', which is read 'The Statue of Liberty is a gift from France'. Similarly, if we were to replace 'x' in 'Gx' with 'e', we would get 'Ge', read 'The Empire State Building is a gift from France'.

Notice that when we replace the individual variable in an open sentence with an individual constant, the result is a statement which does have a truth value. When we replaced 'x' with 's', the resultant statement was true; and when we replaced 'x' with 'e', the resultant statement was false.

Replacing an individual variable in an open sentence with an individual constant is called **instantiation.** We can say, therefore, that when we replaced the 'x' in 'Gx' with 's', we instantiated 'Gx' with 's'; and a similar remark applies in the case of 'e'. When an open sentence is instantiated, the result is a **substitution instance** of the open sentence; both 'Gs' and 'Ge' are substitution instances of the open sentence 'Gx'.

Thus far our discussion has been limited primarily to singular statements. Predicate terms do not occur only in singular statements, however. For example, we often have expressions like the following:

(5) Everything has a color.

(6) Something is heavy.

Since these statements are not about some particular individual, they are not singular statements. That they are not about a particular individual can be seen from the fact that no thing has been named or uniquely described by the subject term. We shall say that statements like (5) and (6) are **general statements,** subject-predicate statements which are not about a particular individual.[5]

Although (5) and (6) are not singular statements, it should be clear that they are nonetheless statements and that they both have truth values. Since they do have truth values, it is also the case that neither of them is an open sentence. (If you do not see this, reread the remarks on open sentences in the previous section.) What is needed, then, is a way to represent the form of general statements; it is also to this that we now turn.

Let's begin by considering (5). We can express this in a slightly different way as

All things have a color.

---

[5] General statements are further characterized in section 7:1.4.

Furthermore, if all things have a color, then we can further generalize and say

For any individual thing whatever, that thing has a color.

Now, notice that the above statement is not about any particular individual, but if the statement is true, it is true of all individuals. To see the distinction here, suppose that the world consists of only three individuals and that we represent these individuals with the individual constants '*a*', '*b*', and '*c*'. Statement (5) is not about *a*, *b*, or *c* in particular, but if (5) is true, then it is true that *a* has a color, that *b* has a color, and that *c* has a color. Since (5) is not about *a*, *b*, or *c* in particular, we cannot use '*a*', '*b*', and '*c*' to represent the logical form of (5). What we can do, however, is to use an *individual variable* to do this. Recall that an individual variable merely marks the place in the structure of a sentence where one may substitute individual constants. We can therefore say, using an individual variable:

For any *x*, *x* has a color.

The expression '*x* has a color' can further be symbolized by using the convention adopted earlier of using uppercase letters to represent predicate terms. Using '*C*' for 'has a color', we have

For any *x*, *Cx*

Our final step in symbolizing (5) is to deal with the expression 'for any *x*'. We shall adopt the convention of using the symbol '(*x*)' to represent this expression. The symbol '(*x*)' is a **universal quantifier,** and its use gives us

(5)' (*x*)*Cx*

Before we move on to deal with (6), one important point must be made. To see the point, consider the expression '*Cx*', read '*x* has a color'. As we noted earlier, '*Cx*' is an open sentence and does not, therefore, have a truth value. On the other hand, '(*x*)*Cx*' does express a statement (the statement that all things have a color) and does have a truth value; it is *not* an open sentence. What follows from this, then, is that we now have an additional way of converting open sentences into statements; namely, to **universally quantify** them.

Let's now turn our attention to (6). Following the methods of Chapter 6 and our discussion of 'some', we may express (6) as

There is at least one thing which is heavy.

As in the case of (5), this statement is not about any particular individual, with the result that we cannot symbolize it with individual constants. We can, however, symbolize the statement by using an individual variable. Doing so, we have

There is at least one *x* such that *x* is heavy.

Using '*H*' to represent the predicate 'is heavy', we have

There is at least one *x* such that *Hx*.

The final step in symbolizing (6) is to deal with the expression 'there is at least one x such that'. We shall use the expression '$(\exists x)$' for this purpose. This expression is an **existential quantifier,** and (6) now becomes

(6)′ $(\exists x)Hx$

The same kind of remarks we made about the relationship between '$(x)Cx$' and 'Cx' applies to '$(\exists x)Hx$' and 'Hx'. That is, 'Hx' is an open sentence and does not, therefore, have a truth value. On the other hand, '$(\exists x)Hx$' does express a statement and does have a truth value. An additional way, then, of converting open sentences into statements is to **existentially quantify** them. Combining this result with earlier ones, we can more generally say that *a statement may be formed from an open sentence either by instantiation* (replacing individual variables with individual constants) *or by generalization* (placing a universal quantifier or an existantial quantifier in front of the open sentence).

EXERCISE 7-2

1. Provide an English translation for each of the following general statements, using the indicated predicate term.

   Example: $(\exists x)Gx$ (G: is good)
   Answer: Something is good.

   a. $(\exists x)Lx$ (L: is lonely)
   b. $(x)Bx$ (B: is blue)
   c. $(x)Cx$ (C: is cold)
   d. $(\exists x)Cx$ (C: is cold)
   e. $(x)Mx$ (M: is mutilated)

2. In what ways can an open sentence be converted to a statement?

3. Symbolize the following statements, using the given symbol as the predicate term.
   a. Something is foul. (F)
   b. Everything is extended. (E)
   c. Someone lied. (L)
   d. Everyone went home early. (H)
   e. Someone went home early. (H)

7:1.4 Free and Bound Variables   So far, our discussions in this chapter have been relatively informal. We are now in a position to expand those discussions and provide a more rigorous characterization of some of the concepts. The major points we have so far discussed include the following:

1. An expression which consists only of predicate terms and individual variables is an open sentence.

2. Open sentences may be converted into statements either by instantiation or generalization.

3. To instantiate an open sentence, we replace all occurrences of individual variables with individual constants.

4. To generalize an open sentence, we place either an existential quantifier or a universal quantifier in front of it.

Let's see how the above four points apply to a particular example. We say that 'Nx' is an open sentence and can be converted into a statement either by instantiation or generalization. One instantiation of this open sentence is 'Ns', where 's' represents 'Syracuse' and 'N' represent 'is in New York'. Generalizing this same open sentence by placing an existential quantifier in front of it, we have '(∃x)Nx', which is read as 'Something is in New York'; generalizing with the universal quantifier, we have '(x)Nx', read as 'Everything is in New York'.

The individual variable 'x' as it occurs in the open sentence 'Nx' is a **free variable.** A free variable is one which has not been quantified; that is, it is one which is not preceded by either an existential or universal quantifier containing the same variable. On the other hand, the second occurrence of 'x' in '(∃x)Nx' and in '(x)Nx' are **bound variables** since they are preceded by a quantifier containing the same variable.

Now consider the expression '(∃x)Fx · Gx'. This expression is a conjunction of two expressions, '(∃x)Fx' and 'Gx'. In the left conjunct, the variable (the 'x' following the 'F') is *bound* because the expression is preceded by a quantifier containing the same variable. In the right conjunct 'Gx', the variable is *free* because the expression is *not* preceded by a quantifier containing the same variable; it's not preceded by a quantifier at all. Also notice that the left conjunct of the conjunction expresses a statement, the statement that something is *F*, whereas the right conjunct is an open sentence.

Now consider the expression '(∃x)(Fx · Gx)'. In this case, the 'x' following the 'G' and the 'x' following the 'F' are *both* bound. Both occurrences of the 'x' are bound because they fall under the **scope** of the existential quantifier. That is, the existential quantifier applies both to 'Fx' and to 'Gx'. In this case, the scope of the quantifier is indicated by the parentheses following the quantifier. Similarly, in the expression '(x)(Gx ⊃ Mx)', the second and third occurrences of 'x' are bound by the universal quantifier.

Let's consider some more examples. First, take the expression '(∃x)(Fx · Gx) · Lx'. In this expression, the 'x' following the 'F' and the 'x' following the 'G' are both *bound,* whereas the 'x' following the 'L' is *free.* The two variables which are bound fall under the scope of the quantifier, as indicated by the parentheses around 'Fx · Gx', whereas the 'x' following the 'L' does not fall under the scope of the quantifier. We can represent this graphically as follows:

$$(\exists x)\underbrace{(Fx \cdot Gx)} \cdot Lx$$

What we have done here is pick out the left parenthesis immediately following the quantifier and then identify the right parenthesis with which it is paired. Every variable 'x' falling within these parentheses is under the scope of the quantifier.

As another example, consider the expression '$(\exists x)((Fx \cdot Gx) \cdot Lx)$'. In this case, all the variables are bound because they all fall under the scope of the existential quantifier. This is represented graphically as follows:

$$(\exists x)((Fx \cdot Gx) \cdot Lx)$$

That all the variables fall under the scope of the quantifier can be determined by finding the right parenthesis that is paired with the left parenthesis immediately following the quantifier; this is the one following 'Lx'.

So far we have limited our discussion to expressions which contain only one variable 'x'. Now, however, we shall extend our discussion of free and bound variables to include expressions containing more than one variable. For our purposes here, and following our earlier convention, we shall also take 'y' to be an individual variable.

Consider, then, the expression '$(\exists x)(Fx \cdot Gy)$'. The best logical reading of this expression would be 'There is at least one thing x such that x is F, and y is G'. The point here is that *the y which is G is not expressed as having any relationship to the x which is F*. In particular, our expression might better be symbolized as '$(\exists x)(Fx) \cdot Gy$', which clearly indicates the structure of the expression. Though the distinction is subtle, we might read this latter expression as 'There is at least one x such that x is F and (moreover) y is G'.

This point might better be made by considering actual predicates. Suppose 'F' represents the expression 'is far away' and 'G' represents the expression 'is made of gold'. Then '$(\exists x)(Fx \cdot Gy)$' might be read as 'There is at least one thing x such that x is far away and y is made of gold' or, in a different form, 'Something is far away and y is made of gold'. Here, there is no temptation to treat the thing (whatever it is) which is made of gold as in any way related to the thing (whatever it is) which is far away. What has to be brought out here, then, is that whereas the 'x' following 'F' falls under the scope of the quantifier, the 'y' does not, even though 'Gy' is within the pair of parentheses following the quantifier. The variable 'y' does *not* fall under the scope of the quantifier because the variable quantified *by* the quantifier is 'x', not 'y': This is represented by the 'x' following the '$\exists$' in '$\exists x$'.

Given the above, we can say that *a variable is bound by a quantifier if, and only if, the variable is the same letter as occurs in the quantifier and the variable falls under the scope of the quantifier*. Any variable which is not bound is, therefore, *free*. In addition, we can say that *an open sentence is any expression containing a free variable*.

In this section we have developed a more rigorous characterization of open sentences, variables, and quantification. We did this by distinguishing two types of variables, free and bound, and characterizing these in terms of the scope of a quantifier. In the next two sections, we shall further examine quantifiers and develop some relationships which hold between the existential quantifier and the universal quantifier.

EXERCISE 7-3

For each of the following, indicate which of the occurrences of the variables are free and which are bound.

a. $(\exists x)(Ax \cdot Bx) \cdot Cx$

b. $(y)((Cy \supset Dy) \vee Fy)$

c. $(\exists x)(Lx \cdot Ab)$

d. $(Ab \cdot (\exists x)(Lx)) \cdot By$

e. $Ab \cdot (\exists x)(Lx)$

f. $(\exists x)(Ax \vee By)$

g. $(y)(Gy \equiv Fx)$

h. $(\exists x)(y)(By \supset Lx)$

i. $(y)(\exists x)(By \supset Lx)$

j. $(y)((Lx \cdot By) \vee Cb)$

k. $(\exists x)(Mx) \supset (y)(my \cdot Gx)$

l. $(Ma \cdot Bc) \equiv (y)(My \vee By)$

m. $(y)(My \vee Bx) \equiv (Mc \cdot Ba)$

n. $(y)(My \vee Bx) \equiv (Mc \cdot By)$

o. $(Gx \cdot Bx) \supset (Ga \cdot Ba)$

p. $(Gx \cdot Bx) \supset (\exists y)(Gy \cdot By)$

q. $(\exists x)(y)(Rx \supset (Ly \cdot Gx))$

r. $(y)(\exists x)(Rx \supset (Ly \cdot Gx))$

s. $(\exists x)(y)((Rx \supset Ly) \cdot Gx)$

t. $(y)(\exists x)((Rx \vee Ly) \cdot Gx)$

7:1.5 The Universe of Discourse The focus of our attention in this section will be on the universal quantifier. To begin, let's consider the expression '$(x)Hx$' and let 'H' represent the predicate 'is hungry'.

As we have noted, the expression '(x)' is to be read 'for any x', where 'x' represents anything at all in the universe. As a result, 'x' might be a house, you, me, a number between 12 and 23, and so on. In short, 'for any x' really means *for any x*. Our quantified expression '$(x)Hx$' is then obviously *false*, for what is asserted is that *everything* in the universe is hungry; houses, planets, and numbers between 12 and 23 are just some of the many falsifying instances of this statement.

Suppose, however, that we want to symbolize the statement '*Everyone* is hungry'. What is typically intended in saying that everyone is hungry is that the predicate applies to people and, more often, to a small group of people; say, the group getting ready to sit down for Thanksgiving dinner. We need, then, some way of dealing with universal statements like the one we are considering so that they are not false simply because the predicate is not applicable to all things.

There are several possibilities. First, since we intend the predicate 'is hungry' to apply to people, we might rewrite our statement that everyone is hungry as '$(x)(Px \supset Hx)$', where 'P' represents 'is a person'. We then have 'For any x, if x is a person, then x is hungry'. It may well be, of course, that this is a false statement; but when 'is a person' is specified as the antecedent, the statement about being hungry cannot become false simply because there are some things in the universe to which 'is hungry' does not apply. We could, of course, specify in even greater detail the intended objects which are said to be hungry. If we are discussing all those people who are at Grandma Nellie's for Thanksgiving dinner, we could, for example, express our statement as follows (where 'G' represents 'is at Grandma Nellie's for Thanksgiving dinner'):

$(x)((Px \cdot Gx) \supset Hx)$

The important thing to notice in these two examples is that we have used the conditional statement to *limit* the range of individuals to which we intend the predicate 'is hungry' to apply. This procedure—limiting the range by using a conditional statement—while acceptable, has the drawback of introducing additional predicates and more complex statements into our eventual deductions. And the simpler we keep our statements, the easier it typically is to do deductions. As a result, it would be preferable to find another means for limiting the range of individuals. Fortunately, there is a straightforward, easy way to do this.

Unless otherwise specified, the universal and existential quantifiers range over all the individuals in the universe. We say, then, that the **universe of discourse** is everything in the universe, where the expression 'universe of discourse' means all those individuals we are discussing. But instead of taking everything in the universe as our universe of discourse, we can specify a subset of these individuals. For example, in the first case discussed in this section, we can agree to let the universe of discourse be persons, and then assert of this group of individuals that everyone of them is hungry.[6]

We can specify our universe of discourse in any way we please, and how we specify it will depend on the particular subject matter with which we are dealing. For example, if we were working with deductions in mathematics, we might specify the universe of discourse as the whole numbers; if we were concerned with political parties, we might choose countries for the universe of discourse; and so on. For convenience, we shall take the expressions 'someone' and 'everyone' as indicating that the universe of discourse has been limited to human beings.

EXERCISE 7-4

1. For each of the following statements, indicate a universe of discourse appropriate to the statement.

Example: Everything is either odd or even.
Answer: The whole numbers

Example: Someone was shot at Bill's Bar last night.
Answer: People at Bill's Bar last night

---

[6] In the Venn diagrams of the previous chapter, each circle can be said to have established a universe of discourse which was a subset of all the individuals in the universe.

a. Someone failed Professor Dudley's logic class.
b. Everyone chose French toast instead of scrambled eggs for breakfast.
c. Everything that goes up must come down.
d. Someone is born every thirteen seconds.
e. Nothing is easy in life.
f. Everyone at the convention voted for Rasmusson.
g. No one wanted to stay up and watch the late movie.
h. None of the elevators work.
i. Someone borrowed my favorite record.
j. Everyone applauded Joan's performance last night.

2. Having specified the universe of discourse for each statement in problem 1, assign a predicate constant to the predicate expressions and symbolize the statement.

Example: Everything is either odd or even.
Answer: Universe of discourse: the whole numbers
Predicate constants: O: is odd
E: is even
Symbolization: $(x)(Ox \lor Ex)$

Example: Someone was shot at Bill's Bar last night.
Answer: Universe of discourse: people at Bill's Bar last night
Predicate constant: S: was shot
Symbolization: $(\exists x)(Sx)$

7:1.6 Quantifier Exchange

Now that we have discussed singular and general statements, and you are familiar with the existential quantifier and the universal quantifier, we are ready to develop some relationships among quantified statements. The relationships will later be summarized as a new rule of inference that we can use in constructing proofs which contain quantified statements.

Consider the general statement 'Everything is composed of matter' or, in our earlier language, 'For any x, x is composed of matter'. This statement is symbolized as '$(x)Cx$'. If this statement is true, then there is *not* a single individual in the universe which is *not* composed of matter. We can put this in a slightly different way as follows:

It is not the case that there is at least one thing x such that x is not composed of matter.

We know that the expression 'there is at least one thing x such that' is the verbal equivalent of the existential quantifier and that 'x is not composed of matter' is symbolized as '$\sim Cx$'. The above statement can therefore be symbolized by '$\sim(\exists x)\sim Cx$'.

Similarly, we can argue the opposite way and say that *if* it is the case that there is not a single individual in the universe which is not composed of matter, symbolized as '~(∃x)~Cx', then everything in the universe is composed of matter, symbolized by '(x)Cx'.[7]

The above discussion establishes the following conditional statements:

$$(x)Cx \supset \sim(\exists x)\sim Cx$$

$$\sim(\exists x)\sim Cx \supset (x)Cx$$

Moreover, given these two conditional statements, we can write

$$(x)Cx \equiv \sim(\exists x)\sim Cx$$

Although our discussion above dealt with a particular predicate, 'is composed of matter', it clearly holds for any predicate whatsoever. Hence, we can generalize the above case to say that any statement of the form '(x)ϕx', where 'ϕ' represents any predicate whatsoever, is equivalent to a statement of the form '~(∃x)~ϕx'.[8] That is,

(1) $(x)\phi x \equiv \sim(\exists x)\sim\phi x$[9]

Now suppose that it's *not* the case that everything is composed of matter. Since the statement 'Everything is composed of matter' is symbolized '(x)Cx', this new statement is symbolized as '~(x)Cx'. If it's not the case that everything is composed of matter, then it is also the case that there is at least one thing which is not composed of matter. That is,

$$\sim(x)Cx \supset (\exists x)\sim Cx$$

Similarly, if it's the case that at least one individual is not composed of matter, then it's not the case that everything is composed of matter, or

$$(\exists x)\sim Cx \supset \sim(x)Cx$$

The above results enable us to write

$$\sim(x)Cx \equiv (\exists x)\sim Cx$$

As in our previous discussion, the result may be applied to any predicate whatsoever, so we can generalize it as follows:

(2) $\sim(x)\phi x \equiv (\exists x)\sim\phi x$

---

[7] Notice the similarity to our discussion of the contradictories of categorical statements in section 6:3.3. '(x)(Cx)' is similar to, though not itself, an *A*-form categorical statement; and '~(∃x)~Cx' is similar to, though not itself, a negated *O*-form categorical statement. As we have already noted, an *A*-form categorical statement is equivalent to a negated *O*-form categorical statement having the same subject term and predicate term.

[8] To say that 'ϕ' represents any predicate whatsoever is to say that 'ϕ' is a *predicate variable*. 'ϕ' is, therefore, much like an individual variable, but whereas individual variables function as placeholders for individual constants, 'ϕ' functions as a placeholder for predicate expressions.

[9] Although this expression is given in terms of the quantifiers '(x)' and '(∃x)', the equivalency would obviously hold for quantifiers which contained variables other than 'x'. For example, '(y)ϕy ≡ ~(∃y)~ϕy' is an instance of (1).

Now consider the following two statements:

Something is composed of matter.

It's not the case that something is composed of matter.

For the first statement, arguments similar to those presented above show that

$(\exists x)Cx \supset \sim(x)\sim Cx$

$\sim(x)\sim Cx \supset (\exists x)Cx$

This gives us

(3) $(\exists x)\phi x \equiv \sim(x)\sim\phi x$

In the case of the second statement, arguments similar to those presented above show that

$\sim(\exists x)Cx \supset (x)\sim Cx$

$(x)\sim Cx \supset \sim(\exists x)Cx$

This gives us

(4) $\sim(\exists x)\phi x \equiv (x)\sim\phi x$

Summarizing the results of our four cases, we have:

(1) $(x)\phi x \equiv \sim(\exists x)\sim\phi x$

(2) $\sim(x)\phi x \equiv (\exists x)\sim\phi x$

(3) $(\exists x)\phi x \equiv \sim(x)\sim\phi x$

(4) $\sim(\exists x)\phi x \equiv (x) \sim\phi x$

We are now ready to develop the rule **quantifier exchange,** which we shall annotate in the later proofs as 'QE'. A little reflection leads to the realization that every quantified expression begins with either a universal or an existential quantifier, and either there is no negation sign before or after the quantifier, or there is a negation sign before the quantifier but not after it, or there is a negation sign after the quantifier but not before it, or there are negation signs both before and after the quantifier. These possiblities are represented as follows:[10]

(A) (x) (B) $\sim(x)$

(C) $(x)\sim$ (D) $\sim(x)\sim$

(E) $(\exists x)$ (F) $\sim(\exists x)$

(G) $(\exists x)\sim$ (H) $\sim(\exists x)\sim$

In (A) to (D) the universal quantifier is shown in the four possible ways it

---

[10] To focus on the quantifier expressions themselves, the predicate expression and the following variable have been omitted. None of (A) to (H) is a statement or a statement form.

might occur, and in (E) to (H) the existential quantifier is shown in the four possible ways it might occur. Equivalencies (1) to (4) above enable us to *replace* each possible occurrence of the universal quantifier with an equivalent existential quantifier and each possible occurrence of the existential quantifier with an equivalent universal quantifier. To do this, we select the appropriate biconditional expressed in (1) to (4). For example, for case (A), the biconditional in (1) allows us to say:

(A)′ '(x)' can be replaced with '$\sim(\exists x)\sim$'

For case (B), the biconditional in (2) allows us to say:

(B)′ '$\sim(x)$' can be replaced with '$(\exists x)\sim$'

For case (C), the biconditional in (4) allows us to say:

(C)′ '$(x)\sim$' can be replaced with '$\sim(\exists x)$'

In a similar way, we can get:

(D)′ '$\sim(x)\sim$' can be replaced with '$(\exists x)$'

(E)′ '$(\exists x)$' can be replaced with '$\sim(x)\sim$'

(F)′ '$\sim(\exists x)$' can be replaced with '$(x)\sim$'

(G)′ '$(\exists x)\sim$' can be replaced with '$\sim(x)$'

(H)′ '$\sim(\exists x)\sim$' can be replaced with '(x)'

Now, examine the structure of each of (A)′ to (H)′. They indicate that we can replace the occurrence of a universal quantifier with an existential quantifier and the occurrence of an existential quantifier with a universal quantifier, if we change the sign before and after the quantifier. That is, if there is a negation sign before the quantifier, remove it; and if there is no negation sign before it, place one there. The same holds for a negation sign after the quantifier.[11] This gives us a new rule:

QUANTIFIER EXCHANGE (QE)

From a universally or existentially quantified statement, or from the negation of a universally or existentially quantified statement, one may infer a statement having the opposite quantifier and having the opposite sign before and after the quantifier.

EXERCISE 7-5

In the following, convert each universally quantified statement to an existentially quantified statement and each existentially quantified statement to a universally quantified statement.

---

[11] What we are doing here, of course, is changing the quantifier and adding a negation sign before and after it. Double negation then allows us to drop both negation signs in those cases where we end up with a double negation.

a. $(x)Fx$ b. $\sim(\exists x)Gx$

c. $\sim(\exists x)\sim(Gx \lor Lx)$ d. $(x)\sim(Cx \cdot Mx)$

e. $\sim(x)(Cx \cdot Mx)$ f. $(\exists x)\sim(Lx \lor \sim Mx)$

g. $(\exists x)(Lx \cdot Cx)$ h. $\sim(x)\sim(Gx \supset Mx)$

i. $\sim(x)Gx$ j. $\sim(\exists x)(\sim Cx \supset Lx)$

7:2 SYMBOLIZING QUANTIFIED STATEMENTS

Thus far our discussion of quantified statements has, for the most part, been limited to the generalization of open sentences consisting of one predicate term and a single occurrence of an individual variable. In this section we shall cover more complex statements, including the categorical statements discussed in the previous chapter.

7:2.1 Symbolizing Categorical Statements

Recall from the previous chapter that there are four forms of categorical statements, A, E, I, and O, and that these forms have the following structure:

A: All <u>S</u> are <u>P</u> E: No <u>S</u> are <u>P</u>

I: Some <u>S</u> are <u>P</u> O: Some <u>S</u> are not <u>P</u>

The following are instances of the four forms, in order:

(1) All mice are furry.   (2) No mice are furry.

(3) Some mice are furry.   (4) Some mice are not furry.

Statements (1) to (4) are all general statements and, therefore, must be symbolized by using predicate terms, individual variables, and the appropriate quantifier. Let's begin by considering (1) and (2). We noted in Chapter 6 that universal catregorical statements could be understood as a kind of *conditional statement:* The A-form statement 'All <u>S</u> are <u>P</u>' was understood as 'If a thing is an <u>S</u>, then it's a <u>P</u>', and the E-form statement 'No <u>S</u> are <u>P</u>' was understood as 'If a thing is an <u>S</u>, then it's not a <u>P</u>'. Given the material already developed in this chapter, we can more generally rewrite (1) and (2) as follows:

(1)' For any x, if x is a mouse then x is furry.

(2)' For any x, if x is a mouse then x is not furry.

The 'x' in (1)' and (2)' is an individual variable, indicating anything at all. Using 'M' to represent the predicate expression 'is a mouse', 'F' to represent the predicate 'is furry', and the universal quantifier to represent the expression 'for any x', we get the following:

(1)'' $(x)(Mx \supset Fx)$

(2)'' $(x)(Mx \supset \sim Fx)$

Consider now (3) and (4). These are also general statements that must similarly be symbolized by using predicate terms, individual variables, and the appropriate quantifier. Again, in Chapter 6 we determined that 'some' as it occurs in categorical statements would mean 'at least one' and that particular categorical statements could be understood as a kind of *conjunction*. We can, therefore, rewrite (3) and (4) as follows:

(3)' There is at least one thing x such that x is a mouse and x is furry.

(4)' There is at least one thing x such that x is a mouse and x is not furry.

Using the same predicates as we did in (1) and (2), and using the existential quantifier to represent the expression 'there is at least one thing x such that', we get the following:

(3)'' $(\exists x)(Mx \cdot Fx)$

(4)'' $(\exists x)(Mx \cdot {\sim}Fx)$

One of the points made in Chapter 6 was that A-form and O-form categorical statements with the same subject term and predicate term are contradictory, and similarly for E-form and I-form statements. We can now demonstrate this using our present symbolism.

In the case of the A-O pair, consider the following:

All mice are furry.

Some mice are not furry.

The first of these is symbolized as '$(x)(Mx \supset Fx)$', and the other as '$(\exists x)(Mx \cdot {\sim}Fx)$'. To say that the A-O pair is contradictory is to say that the A-form is equivalent to the *negation* of the O-form and that the O-form is equivalent to the *negation* of the A-form. For our present example, this is to say the following:

$(x)(Mx \supset Fx) \equiv {\sim}(\exists x)(Mx \cdot {\sim}Fx)$

$(\exists x)(Mx \cdot {\sim}Fx) \equiv {\sim}(x)(Mx \supset Fx)$

Consider the first statement. Given '$(x)(Mx \supset Fx)$', we can use QE to get '${\sim}(\exists x) {\sim}(Mx \supset Fx)$'. We can eliminate the outside negation on '$(Mx \supset Fx)$' by rules analogous to implication and DM, thereby getting '${\sim}(\exists x)(Mx \cdot {\sim}Fx)$'. This gives us the left-to-right conditional of our first statement. Now for the right-to-left conditional: Given '${\sim}(\exists x)(Mx \cdot {\sim}Fx)$', we can use QE to get '$(x){\sim}(Mx \cdot {\sim}Fx)$'. Eliminating the outside negation on '$(Mx \cdot {\sim}Fx)$', we have '$({\sim}Mx \lor Fx)$'. Following a procedure analogous to that for the rule *implication,* we can rewrite '$({\sim}Mx \lor Fx)$' as '$(Mx \supset Fx)$', obtaining '$(x)(Mx \supset Fx)$'. This takes care of the right-to-left reading of the biconditional, so we have established

$(x)(Mx \supset Fx) \equiv {\sim}(\exists x)(Mx \cdot {\sim}Fx)$

Now consider the second statement. Given '$(\exists x)(Mx \cdot {\sim}Fx)$', we can use QE to get '${\sim}(x){\sim}(Mx \cdot {\sim}Fx)$'. Eliminating the outside negation on '$(Mx \cdot {\sim}Fx)$', we obtain '$(\sim Mx \lor Fx)$'. Again following a procedure analogous to implication, we can convert this to '$(Mx \supset Fx)$'. This gives us '$\sim(x)(Mx \supset Fx)$' and takes care of the left-to-right conditional.

For the right-to-left conditional we begin with '$\sim(x)(Mx \supset Fx)$'. Once again using QE, we obtain '$(\exists x)\sim(Mx \supset Fx)$'. Removing the outside negation, we then get '$(\exists x)(Mx \cdot \sim Fx)$', which gives us the right-to-left conditional. With these two cases we have established

$$(\exists x)(Mx \cdot \sim Fx) \equiv \sim(x)(Mx \supset Fx)$$

and have shown that the *A-O* pair of categorical statements is contradictory. The *E-I* pair can be shown to be contradictory in a similar way, and this is left as an exercise.

In this section we have symbolized categorical statements by using the quantifiers '(x)' and '$(\exists x)$'. In the next section we shall consider other kinds of statements which can be symbolized with the notation thus far developed.

EXERCISE 7-6

1. Show that the *E-I* pair of categorical statements are contradictories.

2. Symbolize each of the following statements using the given symbols.
   a. All Martians are green. (*M, G*)
   b. Some Martians like blue cheese. (*M, L*)
   c. No one who likes good chicken buys chicken at a fast-food place. (*L, B*)
   d. Some friends are not worth having. (*F, W*)
   e. Not everyone who was invited went to the party. (*I, W*)
   f. It's not the case that all unicorns are friendly. (*U, F*)
   g. It's not the case that some people are not to be trusted. (*P, T*)
   h. Some calamity is about to happen. (*C, H*)
   i. No one who likes good wine buys cheap wine. (*L, B*)
   j. Not everything is as easy as it looks. (*E, L*)
   k. It's not the case that all who are shy don't go on dates. (*S, D*)
   l. People are interesting creatures. (*P, C*)
   m. Some jobs take a long time to complete. (*J, T*)

7:2.2 Symbolizing Other Statements   One of the more frustrating experiences people have when introduced to predicate logic is learning how to symbolize statements. The reason is that there is no single approach which, if followed, will always result in a correct translation. And this comes about because many sentences in English simply do not have *one* correct translation. The difficulty is compounded by the fact that many idiomatic expressions look like they have one form but actually have another.

Our purpose in this section, then, is to provide some *guidelines* and examples to familiarize you with some of the ways in which statements can be symbolized. In logic, as in many endeavors, one does better with practice; the translation of English into symbolic notation is typical in this regard. The exercises at the conclusion of this section will enable you to begin to develop your skill at translation.

In the translation of English sentences into symbolic notation, the symbolized expression will either be a singular statement, for example, '*Pa*'; or a generalized statement with a simple predicate, for example, '$(\exists x)Px$'; or a truth-functional compound of such statements, for example, '*Pa* · *Lb*' and '$(\exists x)(Px \lor Lx)$'. The first guideline we can offer for translating, then, is:

> Determine whether the statement to be symbolized is a singular statement or a general statement. It it is a general statement, determine whether it is an existential statement or a universal statement.

The second guideline is:

> Determine whether the statement to be symbolized is a simple statement or a truth-functional compound statement.

If the statement is a truth-functional compound statement, then:

> Identify the main connective.

If you keep the above in mind, the task of symbolizing statements will be much easier.

Let's consider a couple of examples.

EXAMPLE 1

Symbolize the statement 'Horace likes to read'.

Since this statement is about a particular individual, Horace, it is a *singular statement*. Moreover, we say only one thing about Horace, that he likes to read, so the statement is not a truth-functional compound statement. All we have to do, then, is assign an individual constant to 'Horace' (let this be '*h*'), and a predicate constant to 'likes to read' (let this be '*L*'). Our result then is '*Lh*'.

EXAMPLE 2

Symbolize the statement 'Mary likes classical music and Nigel likes rock.'

This is a truth-functional compound statement, as indicated by the connective 'and'. Moreover, each of the conjuncts is a singular statement mentioning a particular individual: Mary on the one hand and Nigel on the other. Assigning '*m*' to 'Mary', '*n*' to 'Nigel', '*C*' to 'likes classical music', and '*R*' to 'likes rock', we obtain '(*Cm* · *Rn*)'.

EXAMPLE 3

Symbolize the statement 'Everyone likes good music'.

This statement is not about a particular individual, but rather is a general statement about everyone. Since it's about everyone, it is a universally quantified statement. We also see that it is not a truth-functional compound statement, since only one predicate, 'likes good music', appears in the statement. Assigning the predicate constant '*L*' to 'likes good music', we obtain '(*x*)*Lx*'.

EXAMPLE 4

Symbolize the statement 'If Maureen passes the exam then everyone will pass'.

In this truth-functional compound statement whose main connective is 'if-then', we have the two component statements 'Maureen passes the exam' and 'Everyone will pass'. The former is a singular statement about Maureen, and the latter is a general statement. Letting '*m*' represent 'Maureen' and '*P*' represent 'passing the exam', we can symbolize the singular statement as '*Pm*' and the general statement as '(*x*)*Px*'. Using '⊃' to represent 'if-then', we obtain, for the whole statement, '*Pm* ⊃ (*x*)*Px*'.

EXAMPLE 5

Symbolize the statement 'Some animals are brown and other are gray.'

This too is a truth-functional compound statement: One of its component statements is 'Some animals are brown', and the other is 'Some animals are gray'; the main connective is 'and'. Each component statement is a general *I*-form statement. Letting '*A*' represent 'is an animal', '*B*' represent 'is brown', and '*G*' represent 'is gray' we obtain for the left conjunct '(∃*x*)(*Ax* · *Bx*)' and for the right conjunct '(∃*x*)(*Ax* · *Gx*)'. As a result, we have '(∃*x*)(*Ax* · *Bx*) · (∃*x*)(*Ax* · *Gx*)' as the symbolization for the whole statement.

A couple of comments are in order regarding example 5. Notice that in symbolizing both conjuncts we used the quantifier '(∃*x*)'. Also notice that '*Ax* · *Bx*' falls under the scope of the first occurrence of '(∃*x*)' but not the second, and that '*Ax* · *Gx*' falls under the scope of the second occurrence of '(∃*x*)' but not the first. One consequence is that the animal which is brown may not be the animal which is gray. In particular, the symbolized statement in example 5 is *not* equivalent to '(∃*x*)(*Ax* · (*Bx* · *Gx*))', read 'Some animals are (both) brown and gray'. We shall return to this topic in section 7:3, but it is important that you realize here that the above conjunction does *not* require that our assertion is about one individual, even though '(∃*x*)' occurs in both conjuncts.

In section 6:2.5 we examined some of the ways in which statements equivalent to categorical statements are often expressed in ordinary language. Among the kinds of statements discussed there are the following:

(1) Only those who are registered can vote.

(2) Not every person invited attended the party.

(3) Almost all the peanuts are gone.

(4) All but minors are allowed to drink.

Each of (1) to (4) can be rewritten as a standard-form categorical statement. Following the guidelines discussed in Chapter 6, we have:

(1)′ All those who can vote are those who are registered.

(2)′ Some who were invited to the party are not people who attended the party.

(3)′ Some peanuts are things which are gone and some peanuts are things which are not gone.

(4)′ All nonminors are people who are allowed to drink, and no minors are people who are allowed to drink.

Since every categorical statement can be written in the notation developed in this chapter, each of (1)′ to (4)′ can be written in that notation. By doing so, we obtain the following:

(1)″ $(x)(Vx \supset Rx)$

(2)″ $(\exists x)(Ix \cdot \sim Ax)$

(3)″ $(\exists x)(Px \cdot Gx) \cdot (\exists x)(Px \cdot \sim Gx)$

(4)″ $(x)(\sim Mx \supset Dx) \cdot (x)(Mx \supset \sim Dx)$

The above cases do not, of course, include all the ordinary-language statements which are equivalent to categorical statements. They are provided as a reminder that there are a great many such statements and that, once they have been translated into standard categorical-statement form, they can be symbolized using our new notation.

The examples discussed above should help you become familiar with the translation of English sentences into symbolic notation. As further help, the symbolic notation for some English sentences is listed below, along with a literal, logical reading of the notation and an ordinary English reading of the notation. The list includes both the existential and universal quantifiers, their negations, and the ways in which they might occur in truth-functional statements. To aid you in reading the expressions, I have arbitrarily chosen 'B' to represent 'is a bird' and 'F' to represent 'flies'.

(1) $(\exists x)Bx$

Logical reading: There is at least one thing x such that x is a bird.

Ordinary reading: Something is a bird.

(2) $\sim(\exists x)Bx$

Logical reading: It's not the case that there is at least one thing x such that x is a bird.

Ordinary reading: There are no birds.   *or*   Nothing is a bird.

(3) $(\exists x)\sim Bx$

Logical reading: There is at least one thing x such that x is not a bird.

Ordinary reading: Something is not a bird.

(4) $(\exists x)(Bx \cdot Fx)$

Logical reading: There is at least one thing x such that x is a bird and x flies.

Ordinary reading: Some birds fly.

(5) $(\exists x)(Bx \lor Fx)$

Logical reading: There is at least one thing x such that x is a bird or x flies.

Ordinary reading: Something is either a bird or flies.

(6) $(\exists x)(Bx \supset Fx)$

Logical reading: There is at least one thing x such that if x is a bird then x flies.

Ordinary reading: Something is either not a bird or flies.

(7) $(\exists x)(Bx \equiv Fx)$

Logical reading: There is at least one thing x such that x is a bird if, and only if, x flies.

Ordinary reading: Something is either a bird and flies or is not a bird and doesn't fly.

(8) $(x)Bx$

Logical reading: For any x, x is a bird.

Ordinary reading: Everything is a bird.

(9) $\sim(x)Bx$

Logical reading: It's not the case that for any x, x is a bird.

Ordinary reading: Not everything is a bird. *or* Something is not a bird.

(10) $(x)\sim Bx$

Logical reading: For any x, it's not the case that x is a bird.

Ordinary reading: Nothing is a bird.

(11) $(x)(Bx \cdot Fx)$

Logical reading: For any x, x is a bird and x flies.

Ordinary reading: Everything is both a bird and flies.

(12) $(x)(Bx \lor Fx)$

Logical reading: For any x, either x is a bird or x flies.

Ordinary reading: Everything is either a bird or flies.

(13) $(x)(Bx \supset Fx)$

Logical reading: For any x, if x is a bird then x flies.

Ordinary reading: All birds fly.

(14) $\sim(x)(Bx \supset Fx)$

Logical reading: It's not the case that for any x, if x is a bird then x flies.

Ordinary reading: Not everything that is a bird flies.

(15) $(x)(Bx \equiv Fx)$

    Logical reading: For any x, x is a bird if, and only if, x flies.

    Ordinary reading: Everything is either a bird and flies or is not a bird and doesn't fly.

EXERCISE 7-7

Translate each of the following statements into symbolic notation using the given symbols as predicate constants and individual constants.

a. Birds fly. (B, F)

b. Only birds fly. (B, F)

c. Some birds don't fly. (B, F)

d. All birds don't fly. (B, F)

e. Leo went home and everyone stayed on campus. (l, H, S)

f. There are cows. (C)

g. There are no cows. (C)

h. Nothing matters. (M)

i. Something is not right. (R)

j. Everything is both wonderful and pleasant. (W, P)

k. Something awful is going to happen. (A, H)

l. Something is either an exam in logic and is hard or is not an exam in logic and is not hard. (E, H)

m. Everything is fun. (F)

n. Something will get better or Leon will be angry. (B, l, A)

o. Something is either pleasant or not worth doing. (P, W)

p. Everything is either work or fun. (W, F)

q. Dana stayed in bed and everyone went to class. (d, B, C)

r. Not everyone is beautiful. (B)

s. Something is either not worth doing or brings great reward. (W, R)

t. All who enter here are blessed. (E, B)

u. John hit a home run and everyone cheered. (j, H, C)

v. Not everything which is pleasant is easy. (P, E)

w. Only if someone tries will we all succeed. (T, S)

x. Everyone is worth knowing, or no one is. (W)

y. Some people are greedy and others are kind. (G, K)

7:3 SOME ADDITIONAL RULES

Our purpose in this section is to present and explain four additional rules which we shall use in constructing proofs of validity for some arguments that contain general statements. Each of the four rules will be presented, an informal explanation of why they are truth-preserving will be given, and then they will be applied to some simple cases. In section 7:5 we shall expand our discussion to apply them in even more complex cases.

7:3.1 Universal Instantiation   To develop this rule, let's consider a particular example:

ARGUMENT 4

All matadors are brave.

Everyone either is not brave or is careful.

Jose is a matador.

∴ Jose is careful.

Using 'M' to represent 'is a matador', 'B' to represent 'is brave', 'C' to represent 'is careful', and 'j' to represent 'Jose', we obtain the following form for the argument:

FORM OF ARGUMENT 4

$(x)(Mx \supset Bx)$

$(x)(\sim Bx \vee Cx)$

Mj

∴ Cj

Given that all matadors are brave and that Jose is a matador, we can determine that Jose is brave. Moreover, given that everyone is either not brave or careful, and having determined that Jose is brave, we can therefore determine that he is careful. As a result, we see that argument 4 is valid; what is needed is a way to show this. For this purpose we shall introduce a new rule, but before doing that let's consider the kind of rule we need.

Recall that in section 7:1.3 we noted that the universal quantifier is to be understood as 'for any x', and that any universally generalized statement is true if, and only if, every instantiation of that statement is true. As a result, we need a rule which is truth-preserving in that if a universally quantified statement is true, then no matter which individual constant is chosen for the instantiation, the resultant statement will also be true. In terms of the example under discussion, if it's true that all matadors are brave, then it's also true that if Jose is a matador, then Jose is brave; and it's also true that if Ferdinand is a matador, then Ferdinand is brave; and so on for each and every individual in the universe of discourse. The rule which serves our purpose here is **universal instantiation.**

UNIVERSAL INSTANTIATION (UI)

From a universally quantified statement one may infer another statement not containing the quantifier by deleting the quantifier and replacing all occurrences of its variable with the same individual constant.

If we let 'ϕx' stand for any open sentence containing at least one free occurrence of 'x', and let '$\phi \alpha$' be the same expression with 'α' replacing every occurrence of 'x', then we can represent UI schematically as follows:[12]

UI: $(x)\phi x$

∴ $\phi \alpha$

It should be noted that UI is applicable only when the expression represented by 'ϕx' falls entirely within the scope of the universal quantifier '(x)'. For example, it is a legitimate use of UI to derive '$Fa \supset P$' from '$(x)(Fx \supset P)$' since '$Fx \supset P$' falls entirely within the scope of the quantifier. However, UI cannot be used to derive '$Fa \supset P$' from '$(x)Fx \supset P$', since '$Fx \supset P$' does *not* fall entirely within the scope of the quantifier; 'Fx' is within the scope, but 'P' is not.

Before returning to argument 4, let's examine a few examples of UI.

EXAMPLE 6

Universally instantiate the following statement:

$(x)(Gx \supset Lx)$

Here the open sentence '$Gx \supset Lx$' is the 'ϕx' in our schematic representation of UI.

Step 1: Our rule tells us to delete the quantifier from the quantified statement, so our new statement will not contain '(x)'.

Step 2: The rule further tells us to replace all occurrences of the quantifier's variable with the same individual constant. There are two occurrences of 'x', the one following 'G' and the one following 'L'. Since we can use any individual constant for the instantiation, let's use 'a'. Our result is

  $Ga \supset La$

Here 'a' is the 'α' in our schematic representation of U.I.

EXAMPLE 7

Universally instantiate 'y' in the following statement:

$(y)(\exists x)(Lx \lor \sim My)$

Here the open sentence '$(\exists x)(Lx \lor \sim My)$' is the '$\phi x$' in our schematic representation of UI. This is an open sentence since the 'y' following 'M' is a free variable; that is, 'y' is not bound by a quantifier.

---

[12] Although UI is given in terms of the variable 'x', the rule is applicable to expressions containing variables other than 'x'.

Step 1: To instantiate 'y', we are going to delete the quantifier '(y)' from the original statement.

Step 2: We must now replace all occurrences of 'y' with the same individual constant; there is one such occurrence: after the 'M'. Once again using 'a', we obtain

$(\exists x)(Lx \lor \sim Ma)$

Here 'a' is the 'α' in our schematic representation of UI.

EXAMPLE 8

Universally instantiate the following statement:[13]

$(x)(\sim Cax \equiv Dbx)$

Step 1: Once again we are to delete the quantifier '(x)'.

Step 2: Now we must replace all occurrences of 'x' with the same individual constant: These occurrences are the 'x' following 'a' in '~Cax' and the 'x' following 'b' in 'Dbx'. Our rule allows us to replace 'x' with any individual constant so long as all occurrences are replaced with the *same* constant. So we may, if we wish, replace 'x' with either 'a' or 'b', or we may use a new constant.[14] All the following, then, are acceptable instantiations:

$\sim Caa \equiv Dba$

$\sim Cab \equiv Dbb$

$\sim Cac \equiv Dbc$

Returning now to argument 4, we are ready to use UI in showing validity. Let's consider the two universal premises, '(x)(Mx ⊃ Bx)' and '(x)(~Bx ∨ Cx)'. Both these statements can be universally instantiated to any individual constant we choose. However, they both occur in the context of an argument in which a particular individual, Jose, is mentioned. Since we want to derive 'Cj' from the premises, we should instantiate both premises to 'j'.

If we chose some constant other than 'j', we would not be able to show how the relationships between being a matador, being brave, and being careful held in Jose's case. For example, if we let 'f' represent 'Ferdinand' and instantiated the first premise to 'f', we would have 'If Ferdinand is a matador then Ferdinand is brave'. This statement, even if true, is of no use to us in the context of Jose's being a matador.

---

[13] '~Cax' and 'Dbx' are *relational expressions,* and 'C' and 'D' as they occur in these expressions are two-place predicates. Although we shall not discuss relational expressions, they are used here so that you can see how UI applies in such cases. An example of such a predicate is 'more careful than', as in 'a is more careful than b', symbolized as 'Cab'.

[14] Which constant we actually choose for the instantiation is a function of the overall context in which the statement to be instantiated occurs. Typically this is in an argument, and, for reasons we shall discuss later, the constant chosen is one which facilitates constructing a proof. It should be recognized, however, that UI allows us to instantiate to *any* individual constant.

The decision to instantiate the two universal premises to 'j' allows us to show that Jose is careful as follows, given the premises of argument 4:

(1)	$(x)(Mx \supset Bx)$	Premise
(2)	$(x)(\sim Bx \lor Cx)$	Premise
(3)	Mj	Premise
(4)	$Mj \supset Bj$	(1), UI
(5)	$\sim Bj \lor Cj$	(2), UI
(6)	$Bj \supset Cj$	(5), Imp
(7)	$Mj \supset Cj$	(4), (6), HS
∴ (8)	Cj	(3), (7), AA

7:3.2 Existential Generalization You may recall that we began this chapter with two valid arguments, neither of which could be shown to be valid with the procedure we had thus far developed. One of those arguments was the following:

ARGUMENT 1

The Statue of Liberty is over 150 feet high.

∴ Something is over 150 feet high.

Using the symbolism developed in this chapter and letting 's' represent 'the Statue of Liberty' and 'O' represent 'is over 150 feet high', we see that argument 1 has the following form:

Os

∴ $(\exists x)Ox$

By now it should be clear to you why this is a valid argument; in particular, given that the Statue of Liberty is over 150 feet high, it follows that there is at least one thing x such that x is over 150 feet high. What is needed, then, is some rule which captures the obviously valid relationship between the statement that a particular thing has some characteristic and the statement that something has that characteristic. The rule **existential generalization** is such a rule. Its formulation is as follows:

EXISTENTIAL GENERALIZATION (EG)

From a statement containing an individual constant, one may infer an existentially quantified statement whose form is derived by prefixing to the statement an existential quantifier whose variable does not already occur in the statement and replacing all occurrences of the constant being generalized with the variable of the new quantifier.

If we let '$\phi\alpha$' stand for an expression containing at least one individual constant 'α', and let 'ϕx' be an open sentence with 'x' replacing every occurrence of 'α', then we can represent EG schematically as follows:

EG: ϕα   (where 'x' does not occur in 'ϕα')

∴ (∃x)ϕx

Before explicitly showing that argument 1 is valid by EG, let's examine a few applications of the rule.

EXAMPLE 9

Existentially generalize 'a' in the statement

Ga

Here 'Ga' is the 'ϕα' in our schematic representation of EG; 'a' is the individual constant represented by 'α', and 'G' is 'ϕ'.

Step 1: Our rule tells us to form a new statement by prefixing to the statement an existential quantifier whose variable does not already occur in the statement. Since no variable occurs in the statement, we can use any existential quantifier at all; let us use '(∃x)'.

Step 2: The rule further tells us to replace all occurrences of the constant being generalized with the variable of the new quantifier. We are generalizing 'a', which has only one occurrence, so we shall replace 'a' with 'x'. Our result is

(∃x)Gx

Here 'Gx' is the open sentence derived by replacing every occurrence of 'a' with 'x'.

EXAMPLE 10

Existentially generalize 'b' in the statement

Gb ⊃ Fb

Here 'Gb ⊃ Fb' is the 'ϕα' is our schematic representation of EG, and 'b' is the individual constant represented by 'α'.

Step 1: As in our previous example, no variable occurs in this statement so we can use any existential quantifier; we shall, therefore, prefix '(∃x)' to 'Gb ⊃ Fb'.

Step 2: In this case there are two occurrences of the constant we are generalizing, so both must be replaced with 'x'. The result is

(∃x)(Gx ⊃ Fx)

Here 'Gx ⊃ Fx' is the open sentence derived by replacing every occurrence of 'b' with 'x'.

EXAMPLE 11

Existentially generalize 'b' in the statement

Gb ⊃ (∃x)Fx

Here, unlike our previous two cases, the constant to be generalized occurs as part of a singular statement '*Gb*' which is itself a component statement in the compound statement '*Gb* ⊃ (∃*x*)*Fx*'. In this case the compound statement is the 'ϕα' in our schematic representation, and '*b*' is the individual constant represented by 'α'.

Step 1: We already have one occurrence of the variable '*x*' in '(∃*x*)*Fx*'. In accordance with our rule, we must, therefore, choose a quantifier with a variable other than '*x*' for our generalization. Let us use '(∃*y*)'.

Step 2: Since we are generalizing '*b*', we must replace '*b*' with '*y*' and prefix '(∃*y*)' to '*Gb* ⊃ (∃*x*)*Fx*'. Our result is

$$(∃y)(Gy ⊃ (∃x)Fx)$$

Notice that the scope of the quantifier '(∃*y*)' is the *whole expression* '*Gy* ⊃ (∃*x*)*Fx*'. Remember that when you apply EG, the scope of the quantifier that is introduced must be the whole expression with which you began. This situation is analogous to that of UI, wherein UI is applicable only when 'ϕ*x*' is entirely within the scope of the universal qualifier.

Having seen how to apply EG, we are now ready to show the validity of argument 1. This is a very simple, straightforward case:

(1) *Os*   Premise

∴ (2) (∃*x*)*Ox*   (1), EG

To examine a slightly more complex case, let's return to the second argument introduced in this chapter:

ARGUMENT 2

Brown University is an Ivy League School and is in the east.

∴ Something is in the east.

Using obvious letters to symbolize this argument, we obtain

Ib · *Eb*

∴ (∃*x*)*Ex*

The strategy here should be quite obvious: Given that Brown is in the east, we can derive that something is in the east by EG. What we must do, then, is derive '*Eb*' from the premise and then use EG to get our desired result. Applying the rules for statement logic developed in Chapter 5, we obtain

(1) *Ib* · *Eb*   Premise

(2) *Eb* · *Ib*   (1), Comm

(3) *Eb*   (2), Simp

∴ (4) (∃*x*)*Ex*   (3), EG

This completes our discussion of existential generalization. In the next section we shall examine a companion rule.

7:3.3 Existential Instantiation   The rule we shall develop in this section is typically employed along with existential generalization in constructing proofs to show validity. The usefulness of the rule will be brought out through consideration of the following argument:

ARGUMENT 5

All matadors are brave.

Some matadors are injured.

∴ Some who are brave are injured.

Argument 5 can easily be shown to be valid by the procedures developed in the previous chapter. Our purpose here is to develop a rule which will, when combined with the rules already discussed in this chapter and those of statement logic, enable us to show the validity of the argument by providing a proof.

Let's begin by symbolizing the argument. Using the letters 'M', 'B', and 'I' to represent the predicate terms, we obtain

$(x)(Mx \supset Bx)$

$(\exists x)(Mx \cdot Ix)$

∴ $(\exists x)(Bx \cdot Ix)$

Consider the second premise: '$(\exists x)(Mx \cdot Ix)$'. In this premise it is asserted that there is at least one thing x such that x is a matador and x is injured. Moreover, this is a general statement in that no particular individual is mentioned in the statement. Although no particular individual is mentioned, however, we do know that *if* the second premise is true, then there is at least one particular individual who is both a matador and is injured. For reasons that will soon become clear, it is convenient to be able to refer to this individual and to say things about the individual, even though the individual has not been designated by an individual constant.

The situation we face here is analogous to that of police departments and newspaper editors when they are confronted by a series of crimes, all apparently committed by the same individual. It's obvious that *someone* is committing the crimes, but it is not known which particular individual this is. In one such case, personnel at Scotland Yard chose to designate the individual as 'Jack the Ripper'. The important point here is that the name 'Jack' was used to designate an individual who was committing a series of crimes, although this may not have been the individual's real name and, moreover, some other individuals were named 'Jack'.

The procedure followed by Scotland Yard is the one that we are going to use to represent an individual about whom some existential statement is made; that is, we are just going to pick some individual constant to represent that individual. So as not to confuse that individual with some other individual which might also be designated by the same constant, we shall also introduce a restriction on the choice of constant.

Given the above, the new rule may be stated as follows:

EXISTENTIAL INSTANTIATION (EI)

From an existentially quantified statement one may infer another statement not containing the quantifier by deleting the quantifier and replacing all occurrences of its variable with the same individual constant, *provided that* the chosen constant does not occur in the statement to be instantiated, nor in any other statement occurring earlier in a proof in which the statement to be instantiated occurs.

If we let 'ϕx' stand for any open sentence containing at least one free occurrence of 'x', and let '$\phi\alpha$' be the same expression with 'α' replacing every occurrence of 'x', then we can represent EI schematically as follows:

EI: $(\exists x)\phi x$ [where 'α' does not occur in '$(\exists x)\phi x$' nor in any statement
$\therefore\ \phi\alpha$ occurring earlier in a proof in which '$(\exists x)\phi x$' occurs]

Let's consider several examples of EI.

EXAMPLE 12

Existentially instantiate the statement

$(\exists x)(Px \cdot Rx)$

Step 1: Our rule tells us first to delete the existential quantifier. We must then replace all occurrences of its variable with the same individual constant.

Step 2: We must now select an individual constant. Any constant will do so long as the 'provided that' clause of the rule is not violated. Since '$(\exists x)(Px \cdot Rx)$' does not contain a constant, we need not worry about the first part of the restriction, and since the statement does not occur in the context of a proof, we need not worry about the second part of the restriction.

Step 3: Since we are now free to choose any constant without violating the restriction, let's choose 'a'. Our result is

$Pa \cdot Ra$

EXAMPLE 13

Existentially instantiate the statement

$Pa \cdot (\exists x)Rx$

Step 1: Delete the quantifier.

Step 2: Choose an individual constant to replace all occurrences of the variable of the deleted quantifier. Checking our 'provided that' clause, we see that we are *not* free to pick 'a' as the constant since 'a' occurs in '$Pa \cdot (\exists x)Rx$'. Since this statement does not occur in the context of a proof, the second part of the restriction does not apply.

Step 3: Given step 2, we are free to choose any individual constant except 'a'; choosing 'b', then, we obtain

Pa · Rb

Before looking at another example, let's consider the need for the first part of the restriction in EI. One statement which could be symbolized as 'Pa · (∃x)Bx' is the following:

Allan is proud and someone brags.

This statement is, of course, true if Allan is not only proud but also brags, for then the right conjunct is also satisfied. But notice that the statement is also true if Allan is proud and someone *other than Allan* brags. The point is that, given that someone brags, we cannot simply assume that that individual is Allan; hence, the restriction that the constant chosen for the instantiation not already occur in the line instantiated. Another way of looking at the need for the restriction is to recall that the validity of an argument is a formal property that holds for any possible instance of the argument. As a result, whereas Allan *may* be a person who brags, it is also possible that he is not, but that someone else, say Ralph, is. Under these conditions Ralph's bragging makes '(∃x)Bx' true, and the statement 'Pa · (∃x)Bx' is *true*, whereas the statement 'Pa · Ba' is false.

The second part of the restriction functions in a similar way, for a similar purpose. If, in the context of a proof, we have a statement about some particular individual, this statement will include an individual constant. If further along in the proof there is an existentially generalized statement that is to be instantiated we must keep in mind that this statement merely says that something or someone has some characteristic. Since this individual may not be an individual already singled out by an individual constant, we must choose some other constant to instantiate the existential statement. Such a restriction serves, therefore, to avoid invalid inferences like the following:

Frankenstein is a monster.

Someone is handsome.

∴ Frankenstein is handsome and is a monster.

With the obvious symbolism, the "proof" for the above argument might go as follows:

(1)	Mf	Premise
(2)	(∃x)Hx	Premise
(3)	Hf	(2), EI (*error*)
∴ (4)	Hf · Mf	(3), (1), Conj

The error at step (3) occurs because we have instantiated (2) to 'f', but 'f' already occurs in a previous line—line (1). It is more important, however, to realize why we cannot instantiate (2) to '*f*': Even though it may be true that someone is handsome, this is not sufficient for saying that the someone in question is Frankenstein; we therefore must instantiate by using some other individual constant.

We shall now use the new rule EI to show the validity of argument 5. In doing so, you will see that there is a guideline to be followed in using EI in constructing proofs.

(1) $(x)(Mx \supset Bx)$	Premise
(2) $(\exists x)(Mx \cdot Ix)$	Premise
(3) $Ma \cdot Ia$	(2), EI
(4) $Ma \supset Ba$	(1), UI
(5) Ma	(3), Simp
(6) Ba	(5), (4), AA
(7) $Ia \cdot Ma$	(3), Comm
(8) Ia	(7), Simp
(9) $Ba \cdot Ia$	(6), (8), Conj
∴ (10) $(\exists x)(Bx \cdot Ix)$	(9), EG

Notice that at line (3) of the above proof we had two choices: Either we could have applied EI to line (2)—the choice we made—or we could have applied UI to line (1). It is no accident that we chose the former, for if we had chosen the latter the first three lines of our proof would have been

(1) $(x)(Mx \supset Bx)$	Premise
(2) $(\exists x)(Mx \cdot Ix)$	Premise
(3) $Ma \supset Ba$	(1), UI

Now, when we were ready, on line (4) to apply EI to line (2), we would have had to instantiate with some constant *other than* '*a*'. This is so because '*a*' already occurs in the proof so that the second part of the restriction on the use of EI would have ruled out our using '*a*'. Instantiated with some constant other than '*a*', say '*b*', line (4) would have been

(4) $Mb \cdot Ib$	(2), EI

This line, combined with line (3), would not enable us to derive the singular statement needed to get '$(\exists x)(Bx \cdot Ix)$' by EG. Before reading on, you should attempt to see why.

Lines (3) and (4) would not enable us to get the desired singular statement because line (3) is about one individual and line (4) is about another. What is needed is a statement about *one* individual, stating that that individual is both brave and injured.

At this point you might think that all would have been lost, but such is not the case. Just as we did in the actual proof, we could still have derived a conditional statement about some individual that could have been used to complete the proof. In particular, we could have *once again applied UI to line* (1), only this time instantiating with '*b*'. The result would have been

(5) $Mb \supset Bb$ (1), UI

From this point on, our proof would have continued in the same way as the earlier one, but for '*b*' instead of for '*a*'.

There are two points to be made here: First, you can apply UI at any time and instantiate to any constant, for to say that something holds *for any x* is to say that it holds no matter what individual constant you instantiate to. Second, *when using both EI and UI in a proof, you should apply EI first.* This will avoid your having to use UI again so that the statements end up containing the appropriate constants for the proof. Notice that this second point is a "rule of thumb" that makes it easier to construct proofs. We have already seen that logically we need not always apply EI before UI; failure to do so, however, results in longer proofs with unnecessary steps.

This completes our discussion of existential instantiation. Notice that EI was used with EG to derive an existentially generalized statement. In the next section we shall discuss our final rule, universal generalization. This is the companion to UI with which it functions in much the same way as EG and EI do.

7:3.4 Universal Generalization   In this section we shall discuss the final rule needed for constructing proofs in predicate logic. Our procedure here will be first to introduce an argument wherein the rule is needed for constructing a proof and then to present the rule and explain it by applying it in a proof of the validity of the argument. Let's begin, then, with the following argument:

ARGUMENT 6

All award-winning movies either have an exciting plot or have been poorly judged and, furthermore, no award-winning movie has been poorly judged. As a result, all movies directed by Artis have an exciting plot since all Artis' movies are award-winning movies.

We begin by putting the argument into standard form:

All award-winning movies either have an exciting plot or have been poorly judged.

No award-winning movie has been poorly judged.

All movies directed by Artis are award-winning movies.

∴ All movies directed by Artis have an exciting plot.

Taking movies as our universe of discourse and using '*A*' to represent 'is award-winning', '*E*' to represent 'has an exciting plot', '*P*' to represent 'has poor judging', and '*D*' to represent 'is directed by Artis', we have the following as the form of argument 6:

$(x)(Ax \supset (Ex \lor Px))$

$(x)(Ax \supset {\sim}Px)$

$(x)(Dx \supset Ax)$

$\therefore (x)(Dx \supset Ex)$

A careful look at the logical structure of this argument shows that the open sentences 'Ax', 'Ex', 'Px', and 'Dx' occur in a pattern which, if the open sentences were statements, could easily be shown to be valid by the rules for statement logic. The analogous pattern they represent is the following:

$p \supset (q \lor r)$

$p \supset {\sim}r$

$s \supset p$

$\therefore s \supset q$

For this argument, a conditional proof could be used in a relatively straightforward manner to derive 'q' once 's' had been assumed.

The difficulty we face in the argument at hand, however, is that the open sentences occur as parts of general statements and are not themselves statements. We can, of course, use UI on the premises to derive *statements* which are truthfunctional statements and on that basis derive a truth-functional statement which is a *substitution instance* of the open sentence '$Dx \supset Ex$'. The conclusion of our argument, however, is *not* a substitution instance of the open sentence '$Dx \supset Ex$'; it is, rather, the **universal generalization** of that open sentence. Some means is needed, then, for deriving universal generalizations of open sentences. The following rule provides that means:

UNIVERSAL GENERALIZATION (UG)

From a statement containing an individual constant, one may infer a universally quantified statement whose form is derived by prefixing to the statement a universal quantifier whose variable does not already occur in the statement and replacing all occurrences of the constant being generalized with the variable of the new quantifier, *provided that* the constant generalized represents an individual which has been chosen arbitrarily.

If we let '$\phi\alpha$' stand for an expression containing at least one individual constant 'α', and let 'ϕx' be an open sentence with 'x' replacing every occurrence of 'α', then we can represent UG schematically as follows:

UG: $\phi\alpha$ (where 'α' represents an individual which has been arbitrarily

$\therefore (x)\phi x$ chosen, and 'x' does not occur in '$\phi\alpha$')

An understanding of UG, like an understanding of EI, requires an understanding of the 'provided that' clause in the formulation of the rule. For this purpose, we shall show the validity of argument 6 with a proof in which the individual constant which is generalized is chosen arbitrarily. We shall then discuss the 'provided that' clause with reference to the proof.

Returning to argument 6, we begin with the following:

(1) $(x)(Ax \supset (Ex \lor Px))$ Premise

(2) $(x)(Ax \supset \sim Px))$ Premise

(3) $(x)(Dx \supset Ax)$ Premise

(4) $Aa \supset (Ea \lor Pa)$ (1), UI

(5) $Aa \supset \sim Pa$ (2), UI

(6) $Da \supset Aa$ (3), UI

To this point we have merely listed the premises and applied UI to them. Notice that each of the premises has been instantiated to 'a'. This we can do since each premise is a universally generalized statement and, if true, is true for all substitution instances of the open sentence following the quantifier. Moreover, we instantiated to the same constant to be able to show the relationships holding among the predicates.

The next thing to notice is that each of lines (4) to (6) is a statement and each is a truth-functional compound of singular statements. For example '$Aa \supset (Ea \lor Pa)$' is a conditional statement having the form '$p \supset (q \lor r)$'; similar remarks apply to lines (5) and (6). We can, therefore, use the rules of statement logic to work with these lines in the proof. The conclusion of argument 6 is a conditional statement in which the predicate 'D' occurs in the antecedent and the predicate 'E' occurs in the consequent. Recalling some of the strategy developed in Chapter 5 for constructing proofs, we note that if we assumed 'Da', we would be able to derive 'Ea' from lines (4) to (6). This would give us a conditional statement similar to, though not the same as, the conclusion of the argument. The conditional proof part of the proof is as follows:

(7) Da Assumption

(8) Aa (6), (7), AA

(9) $Ea \lor Pa$ (4), (8), AA

(10) $\sim Pa$ (5), (8), AA

(11) $Pa \lor Ea$ (9), Comm

(12) Ea (10), (11), DS

(13) $Da \supset Ea$ (7) to (12), CP

We have now derived a conditional statement which reads 'If a is D then a is E' or, given the way we have assigned predicate constants, 'If a is directed by Artis then a has an exciting plot'. The conclusion of the original argument is 'All movies directed by Artis have an exciting plot', so we have not yet derived the required statement. However, we can use the rule UG to do this, obtaining

(14) $(x)(Dx \supset Ex)$ (13), UG

Let's now look at the justification for line (14) of the proof. It says that we have derived this line by universally generalizing on line (13). Our rule tells us that we can derive a universally generalized statement from one containing a constant by prefixing the universal guantifier and replacing all occurrences of the constant being generalized with the variable of the new quantifier. Comparison of '*Da* ⊃ *Ea*' with '(*x*)(*Dx* ⊃ *Ex*)' indicates that we have done just this.

The rule also has a restriction, however. It tells us, in effect, that line (14) can be derived from line (13) *only if* '*a*' *represents an individual which has been chosen arbitrarily.* The issue before us, then, is whether '*a*' represents such an individual. The answer here is yes. The constant '*a*' was introduced in lines (4) to (6) of our proof by universal instantiation. Of course, '*a*' does represent a particular individual, but *this individual was arbitrarily chosen.* This can be seen by realizing that, whereas we chose '*a*' to represent one of all the individuals about whom (1) to (3) are true, we could have chosen another constant to represent one of all the other individuals about whom (1) to (3) are true. In short, what we have found to be the case about *a* (namely, that if *a* was directed by Artis, then *a* has an exciting plot) we would have found to be true about any other arbitrarily chosen individual in our universe of discourse.

It is also worth noting that we introduced '*Da*' into our proof in line (7) as the assumption for CP, and we discharged this assumption on line (13). This shows that line (13) validly follows from the premises alone. Therefore, the fact that we assumed '*Da*' does *not* mean that '*a*' was not arbitrarily chosen in lines (4) to (6).

We can generalize these comments about "an arbitrarily chosen individual" by saying that whenever UG is applied to an individual constant which has been introduced by UI, the individual represented by that constant will have been arbitrarily chosen. Therefore, *UG can always be applied to an individual constant introduced by UI.*

We have yet to consider those cases in which an individual is *not* arbitrarily chosen. The most straightforward way of doing this is to note that UG must be applied to an individual constant; moreover, other than by universal instantiation, a constant can occur in a line of a proof only in the following ways:

Case 1: The constant appears in a premise.

Case 2: The constant appears in a line of a proof which was derived from a premise which contains the constant.

Case 3: The constant appears as the result of applying existential instantiation to some line in a proof.

An example of case 1 is the statement 'John is a basketball player', symbolized as '*Bj*'. This is a statement about a particular individual, John, and not a statement about an arbitrarily chosen individual. Hence, UG cannot be applied to a constant which appears in a premise. Such a restriction rules out invalid arguments of the following kind:

John is a basketball player.

∴ Everyone is a basketball player.

An example of case 2, related to case 1, is provided by the following argument:

All basketball players are coordinated.

John is a basketball player.

∴ Everyone is coordinated.

Symbolizing this argument, we have

$(x)(Bx \supset Cx)$

Bj

∴ $(x)Cx$

The only reasonable "proof" that might be provided for this invalid argument is the following:

(1) $(x)(Bx \supset Cx)$ Premise
(2) Bj Premise
(3) $Bj \supset Cj$ (1), UI
(4) Cj (2), (3), AA
∴ (5) $(x)Cx$ (4), UG (*error*)

The error noted in line (5) occurs because the line that is generalized, line (4), contains a constant '*j*' which appears in a premise, line (2), from which the line was derived. [That is, line (4) was derived from lines (2) and (3) by AA, and line (2) is a premise in which '*j*' occurs.] Hence, UG may not be applied in case 2.

An example of case 3 is provided by the following invalid argument:

Someone is intelligent.

∴ Everyone is intelligent.

Again, the only reasonable "proof" that might be provided here is the following:

(1) $(\exists x)Ix$ Premise
(2) Ia (1), EI
∴ (3) $(x)Ix$ (2), UG (*error*)

It should be perfectly clear that one cannot validly derive the statement that everyone is intelligent from the statement that someone is intelligent. Nonetheless, it might be thought that the individual represented by '*a*' in line (2) of the "proof" was arbitrarily chosen, since '*a*' itself was arbitrarily chosen (recall our discussion of EI), and, therefore, that the restriction for using UG does not apply in this case.

While this might be thought to be the case, it is still *not* the case. It is true that '*a*' in line (2) was arbitrarily chosen, but it is false that '*a*' represents an arbitrarily chosen individual. Recall that, in using EI, we select an *arbitrary constant* (subject to the restriction for using EI) to represent a *particular individual*—

the individual of whom the existentially generalized statement is true. As a result, *the individual represented by the constant is not arbitrarily chosen,* even though the constant used to represent that individual is.

The discussion of case 3 shows, therefore, that we may not use UG on a constant introduced by EI. To do so would lead us to accept as valid arguments which are obviously invalid.

EXERCISE 7-8

1. Explain why, when using EI, one may not instantiate to a constant which occurs in the statement to be instantiated.

2. Explain why, when using EI, one may not instantiate to a constant which occurs earlier in the proof than the statement to be instantiated.

3. Explain why, when using UG, one may not generalize on an individual constant which is not arbitrarily chosen.

4. Existentially instantiate each of the following statements.
   a. $(\exists y)(La \supset By)$ b. $(\exists x)(Mx \cdot {\sim}Lx)$
   c. $(\exists y)(My \cdot Pa)$ d. $(\exists x)({\sim}Lx \lor (y)My)$
   e. $(\exists x)({\sim}Lx \lor {\sim}(y)My)$ f. $(\exists x)(Mbx \cdot (y)Cy)$
   g. $(\exists x)(Cabx \cdot Mbx)$ h. $(\exists x)Cxa$
   i. $(\exists x)(Lx \cdot Mxb)$ j. $(\exists x)((Pa \lor Lb) \cdot Gx)$

5. Existentially generalize 'b' in each of the following statements.
   a. $(y)(Lb \supset By)$ b. $Mb \cdot {\sim}Lba$
   c. $(\exists y)My \cdot Pb$ d. $(\exists x) {\sim}Lx \lor Mb$
   e. $(\exists x) {\sim}Lx \cdot Mb$ f. $(y)Cy \cdot (\exists x)Mxb$
   g. $(\exists x)(Cbx \cdot Mbx)$ h. $(\exists y)Cby$
   i. $(y)(Ly \cdot Mb)$ j. $(\exists x)((Pa \lor Lb) \cdot Gx)$

6. Universally instantiate each of the following statements.
   a. $(x)((Pa \lor Lb) \cdot Gx)$ b. $(y)(La \supset By)$
   c. $(x)(Lx \cdot Mxb)$ d. $(x)(Mx \cdot {\sim}Lx)$
   e. $(y)Cya$ f. $(y)(My \cdot Pa)$
   g. $(x)(Cabx \cdot Mbx)$ h. $(y)((\exists x) {\sim}Lx \lor My)$
   i. $(y)(Cy \cdot (\exists x)Mbx)$ j. $(y)((\exists x) {\sim}Lx \cdot {\sim}My)$

7. Universally generalize 'b' in each of the following statements.
   a. $(\exists x)(Lb \supset By)$ b. $(\exists x)((Pa \lor Lb) \cdot Gx)$
   c. $Mb \cdot {\sim}Lba$ d. $(\exists y)(Ly \cdot Mb)$
   e. $(y)(My \cdot Pb)$ f. $(\exists x)(Cbx \cdot Mbx)$
   g. $(\exists x)({\sim}Lx \lor Mb)$ h. $(y)Cy \cdot (\exists x)Mxb$
   i. $(\exists x)({\sim}Lx \cdot {\sim}Mb)$ j. $(\exists y)Cby$

7:4 SHOWING INVALIDITY

In section 4:6 we discussed the short truth-table method and saw that an argument can be shown to be invalid if there is an assignment of truth values to the statements in the argument such that all the premises are true and the conclusion is false. Recall that our procedure was the following:

(1) Assign truth values to the statements in the conclusion so as to make the conclusion *false*. In some cases there is more than one way to do this; in these cases consider all possible ways in which the conclusion might be made false.

(2) Having assigned a truth value to each of the statements occurring in the conclusion, assign the same truth value to every other occurrence of the statements in the premises.

(3) Attempt to assign truth values to the remaining statements in the premises in such a way as to make all the premises true.

A method that is analogous to this short truth-table method can be used to show the invalidity of arguments in predicate logic. The method is developed in this section.

7:4.1 How the Method Works   Let's begin by recalling our definitions of the universal and existential quantifiers. A universally quantified statement of the form $'(x)\phi x'$ is true if, and only if, everything in the universe of discourse is ϕ. For example, if the universe of discourse consists of three members a, b, and c, then the statement $'(x)\phi x'$ is equivalent to the following:

$$\phi a \cdot \phi b \cdot \phi c$$

In general, we can say that if the universe of discourse consists of n members, then the statement $'(x)\phi x'$ is equivalent to the *conjunction* of all the singular statements derived from this general statement by instantiating to every individual in the universe of discourse. Schematically, then, we have the following:

$$(x)\phi x \equiv \phi a \cdot \phi b \cdot \cdots \cdot \phi n$$

In the case of the existential quantifier we saw that a statement of the form $'(\exists x)\phi x'$ is true if there is at least one individual which is ϕ. If we again suppose that there are three individuals a, b, and c in the universe of discourse, then the statement $'(\exists x)\phi x'$ is equivalent to the following:

$$\phi a \vee \phi b \vee \phi c$$

In general, we can say that if the universe of discourse consists of n members, then the statement $'(\exists x)\phi x'$ is equivalent to the *disjunction* of all the singular statements derived from this general statement by instantiating to every individual in the universe of discourse. As a result, we have the following:

$$(\exists x)\phi x \equiv \phi a \vee \phi b \vee \cdots \vee \phi n$$

One difference between the short truth-table method and the method we are about to develop is that when we are dealing with arguments in predicate logic, we have to consider universes of discourse containing different numbers of members. In particular, whereas *an argument in predicate logic is valid only if it is valid no matter how many members there are in the universe of discourse*, some arguments can be *shown* to be invalid only if the universe of discourse contains at least a certain number of individuals. This point will be expanded below, after we have applied the method to a particular argument.

ARGUMENT 7

$(x)(Lx \supset Mx)$

$(x)(Rx \supset Mx)$

$\therefore (x)(Lx \supset Rx)$

Let us begin by supposing that the universe of discourse consists of only one member *a*. Argument 7 is then equivalent to the following:

$La \supset Ma$

$Ra \supset Ma$

$\therefore La \supset Ra$

Now, to make the conclusion false, we must assign the truth value T to '*La*' and F to '*Ra*'. Having made this assignment in the conclusion, we must make the same assignment to these singular statements as they occur in the premises. This gives us

$La \supset Ma$
T

$Ra \supset Ma$
F

$\therefore La \supset Ra$
  T F F

Now we consider whether we can assign a truth value to '*Ma*' which will make both premises true. The value T will do this. As a result, when '*La*' is true, '*Ma*' is true, and '*Ra*' is false, argument 7 is invalid. Since we have shown that the argument is invalid in a universe of discourse containing only one member, the argument is invalid in every universe of discourse, regardless of how many members are contained in each such universe.

Let's consider another example.

ARGUMENT 8

$(x)(Lx \supset Mx)$

$(\exists x)(Rx \cdot \sim Mx)$

$\therefore (x)(Rx \supset \sim Lx)$

If we consider a universe of discourse containing only one member, we have the following:

$La \supset Ma$

$Ra \cdot \sim Ma$

$\therefore Ra \supset \sim La$

To assign truth values to the statements which occur in the conclusion in such a way as to make the conclusion false, we assign T to 'Ra' and T to 'La'. This gives us a conditional statement with a true antecedent and a false consequent. Making the same assignment of truth values to 'Ra' and 'La' as they occur in the premises, we obtain the following:

$La \supset Ma$
T

$Ra \cdot \sim Ma$
T

$\therefore Ra \supset \sim La$
  T F F T

Now, to make all the premises true, we have to assign the value T to 'Ma' in the first premise. (If we assigned the value F, we would have a conditional statement with a true antecedent and a false consequent; hence, the premise would be false.) Having assigned T to 'Ma' in the first premise, we must also assign T to 'Ma' in the second premise. The result, however, is that '$\sim Ma$' is false and, therefore, the second premise is also false.

Thus, in a universe of discourse consisting of only one member, there is no way to show that argument 8 is invalid. Does this show that the argument is valid? The answer here is that it *does not,* for there may be a universe of discourse containing more than one member in which we can find an invalidating case. Indeed, this can be done for argument 8 in a universe of discourse containing two members.

Recall that universally quantified statements are expanded by the conjunction of the singular statements one derives by instantiating to all the members of the universe of discourse, and existentially quantified statements are similarly expanded as disjunctions. Then the following is equivalent to argument 8 in a universe of discourse containing two members:

$(La \supset Ma) \cdot (Lb \supset Mb)$

$(Ra \cdot \sim Ma) \vee (Ra \cdot \sim Mb)$

$\therefore (Ra \supset \sim La) \cdot (Rb \supset \sim Lb)$

Since the conclusion of this argument will be false if one or the other or both conjuncts is false, there are three possible cases that must be considered in testing for validity. Consider the case in which the left conjunct '$Ra \supset \sim La$' is to be false; for this we must assign T to 'Ra' and T to 'La'. With these assignments, we have the following:

$(La \supset Ma) \cdot (Lb \supset Mb)$
 T

$(Ra \cdot \sim Ma) \vee (Rb \cdot \sim Mb)$
 T

$\therefore (Ra \supset \sim La) \cdot (Rb \supset \sim Lb)$
  T F FT F

We now try to make all the premises true. Since the first premise is a conjunction, it will be true only if both conjuncts are true. As a result, we must assign T to 'Ma' in 'La ⊃ Ma'. We must then assign T to 'Ma' in the second premise. We then have

$$(La \supset Ma) \cdot (Lb \supset Mb)$$
$$\text{T} \quad \text{T} \quad \text{T}$$

$$(Ra \cdot \sim Ma) \lor (Rb \cdot \sim Mb)$$
$$\text{T} \quad \text{FF} \quad \text{T}$$

$$\therefore (Ra \supset \sim La) \cdot (Rb \supset \sim Lb)$$
$$\text{T} \quad \text{F F T} \quad \text{F}$$

Since the second premise is a disjunction, and since the left disjunct is false, we must make the right disjunct true if the premise is to be true. Since the right disjunct is a conjunction, we must assign T to 'Rb' and F to 'Mb' (the latter makes '∼Mb' true). Making the same assignments to 'Rb' and 'Mb' as they occur elsewhere in the argument, we obtain

$$(La \supset Ma) \cdot (Lb \supset Mb)$$
$$\text{T} \quad \text{T} \quad \text{T} \qquad\qquad \text{F}$$

$$(Ra \cdot \sim Ma) \lor (Rb \cdot \sim Mb)$$
$$\text{T} \quad \text{F F T} \quad \text{T} \quad \text{T} \text{ T T F}$$

$$\therefore (Ra \supset \sim La) \cdot (Rb \supset \sim Lb)$$
$$\text{T} \quad \text{F F T} \quad \text{F T}$$

All that remains is to see if we can assign a truth value to 'Lb' which will make the first premise true. Since the first premise is a conjunction, we must make 'Lb ⊃ Mb' true. This we can do by assigning F to 'Lb'. As a result, under the following interpretation, argument 8 is shown to be invalid:

La	Lb	Ma	Mb	Ra	Rb
T	F	T	F	T	T

If we had begun by making the right conjunct of the conclusion false, we would have obtained another interpretation which shows the invalidity of the argument; this is left as an exercise.

We are now able to expand the earlier remark that some invalid arguments in predicate logic can be shown to be invalid only if the universe of discourse contains at least a certain number of individuals. Argument 8 is one such argument in that although it is invalid, it could not be shown to be invalid in a universe of discourse containing only one member; instead, we had to consider a universe containing two members.

If we had not been able to show that argument 8 is invalid in a universe of discourse containing two members, we would have considered a universe with three members; if this did not provide an invalidating case, we would have considered a universe with four members; and so on. This naturally raises the question of how large a universe has to be considered before one knows that no invalidating case can be found. The answer is that when an argument in predicate logic consists only of monadic (or one-place) predicates of the kind we have been discussing, one must at most consider universes of discourse containing 2^n members, where n represents the number of predicates in the argument. (For example, in argument 8 there are three predicates 'L', 'M', and 'R', so theoretically one would consider universes of discourse containing up to eight members.) If no invalidating instance can be constructed for the universe of discourse containing 2^n members, then the argument is valid no matter how large (or small) the universe of discourse is.

In summary, our procedure for showing the invalidity of arguments which contain only one-place predicates is the following:

(1) Count the number of distinct predicates, and calculate the largest universe of discourse that must be considered as 2^n, where n represents the number of predicates in the argument.

(2) Beginning with a universe of discourse of one member, instantiate all the statements in the argument to the same individual constant.

(3) Assign truth values to the singular statements in the conclusion and the premises in such a way as to try to make the conclusion false and all the premises true. If this can be done, the argument is invalid.

(4) If an invalidating instance cannot be found with a universe of discourse containing only one member, consider a universe of discourse which contains two members. Expand all universally quantified statements as conjunctions, and all existentially quantified statements as disjunctions.

(5) Once again attempt to construct an invalidating case. If no case is found, continue the above procedure until the largest universe of discourse has been considered. If no invalidating case is found, the argument is valid.

It should be clear that, for arguments containing very many predicates, the above procedure can be extremely time-consuming. In the exercise which follows, invalidating instances can be found by considering universes of discourse no larger than three members. In the next section we shall develop a way of showing that arguments in predicate logic are valid: constructing proofs.

EXERCISE 7-9

1. Explain why universally quantified statements are expanded as conjunctions of the singular statements derivable from instantiation to every individual in the universe of discourse.

2. Explain why existentially quantified statements are expanded as disjunctions of the singular statements derivable from instantiation to every individual in the universe of discourse.

3. Explain why the failure to find an invalidating instance in a universe of discourse containing only one individual does not show that an argument in predicate logic is valid.

4. Show that argument 8 is invalid by describing an assignment of truth values in which the right conjunct of the expanded conclusion is false and all the premises are true.

5. Show that each of the following arguments is invalid by describing an invalidating interpretation. (None of the problems requires a universe of discourse of more than three members.)

a. $(x)(Mx \supset Lx)$
   $(x)(Nx \supset Lx)$
   $\therefore (x)(Mx \supset Nx)$

b. $(x)(Rx \supset \sim Lx)$
   $(x)(Rx \supset \sim Mx)$
   $\therefore (x)(Lx \supset \sim Mx)$

c. $(x)(Mx \supset Lx)$
   $(\exists x)(Rx \cdot Lx)$
   $\therefore (\exists x)(Rx \cdot \sim Mx)$

d. $(\exists x)(Rx \cdot \sim Mx)$
   $(\exists x)(Rx \cdot Lx)$
   $\therefore (x)(Lx \supset \sim Mx)$

e. $(x)(Mx \supset Lx)$
   $\sim Ma$
   $\therefore \sim La$

f. $(\exists x)(Mx \cdot Lx)$
   $(\exists x)(Rx \cdot Sx)$
   $\therefore (\exists x)(Mx \cdot Rx)$

g. $(x)(Mx \supset Lx)$
   $(\exists x)(Lx \cdot Rx)$
   $(\exists x)(Rx \cdot \sim Lx)$
   $\therefore (x)(Mx \supset Rx)$

h. $(\exists x)(Mx \cdot Lx)$
   $(\exists x)(Rx \cdot Lx)$
   $\therefore (\exists x)(Mx \cdot \sim Rx)$

i. $(x)(Mx \supset Lx)$
   Lb
   $\therefore Mb$

j. $(x)(Mx \supset \sim Lx)$
   $(\exists x)(Rx \cdot \sim Lx)$
   $\therefore (x)(Mx \supset Rx)$

k. $(x)(Lx \supset Mx)$
   $(x)(Lx \supset \sim Rx)$
   $\therefore (x)(Rx \supset \sim Mx)$

l. $(x)(Rx \supset \sim Mx)$
   $(x)(Mx \supset Lx)$
   $\therefore (\exists x)(Lx \cdot \sim Mx)$

m. $(\exists x)(Lx \cdot Mx)$
   $\therefore (x)(Lx \cdot Mx)$

n. $(\exists x)(Rx \cdot \sim Lx)$
   $(x)(Mx \supset Rx)$
   $\therefore (x)(Mx \supset \sim Lx)$

o. $(\exists x)(\sim Mx \cdot Rx)$
   $(\exists x)(\sim Rx \cdot Lx)$
   $\therefore (\exists x)(\sim Lx \cdot Mx)$

7:5 CONSTRUCTING PROOFS

In the previous sections of this chapter we used proofs to explain some of the material that was presented and discussed. In addition, our work with statement logic in Chapter 5 provided an extensive discussion of how to annotate proofs and the various strategies which can be employed in constructing them. Since predicate logic consists only of the rules developed in Chapter 5, augmented by the five new rules developed earlier in this chapter, our discussion of proofs here will not be as extensive as that in Chapter 5.

Our major purpose is to develop some familiarity with the use of the rules developed in this chapter in combination with those discussed earlier. This we shall do by first offering some suggestions regarding the use of the new rules and second by working through several examples. The exercise that follows this section will give you the opportunity to apply and practice what you have learned about deduction in this and earlier chapters.

7:5.1 Some Suggestions
This section contains seven suggestions designed to facilitate the construction of proofs in predicate logic with a minimum amount

of aggravation. As shown in Chapter 5 and mentioned earlier in this chapter, there is no single correct proof which can be used to show the validity of most valid arguments. As a result, it is not possible to find and follow a "recipe" which will always result in an acceptable proof. What we can do, however, is follow some guidelines that are of help in constructing an acceptable proof. The first, and perhaps most important, of these is:

SUGGESTION 1

Do not make things harder than they are.

It might strike you as strange that this is offered as a suggestion for proof construction. Nonetheless, one of the things those new to predicate logic often assume is that constructing proofs in the system is hard and, therefore, that every argument must require a difficult proof. This is simply not the case. For example, consider the following:

If all parrots are birds, then all parrots have feathers. As a result, all parrots have feathers, since all parrots are birds.

The above argument *can* be symbolized in the notation of predicate logic and shown to be valid by using, among other rules, UI and UG to drive the conclusion. It is much easier, however, simply to treat the argument as one in statement logic, since this is just an instance of affirming the antecedent; this can readily be seen once 'p' is assigned to the place occupied by 'All parrots are birds' and 'q' is assigned to the place occupied by 'All parrots have feathers'.

SUGGESTION 2

In developing a proof strategy for arguments symbolized in predicate logic, look for a related structure from statement logic.

We have already discussed one example of this suggestion, relative to argument 6 above. There, once we instantiated the general statements, we found that we could use conditional proof and the rules of statement logic to derive a singular statement which, when generalized, produced the desired result. Another example is provided by the following.

ARGUMENT 9

All drugs are such that if they are abused, then they kill. Moreover, some drugs are medicines. But, since no medicine kills, something is not abused.

Using 'D' to represent 'is a drug', 'A' to represent 'is abused', 'K' to represent 'kills', and 'M' to represent 'is a medicine', we obtain the following form for argument 9:

$(x)(Dx \supset (Ax \supset Kx))$

$(\exists x)(Dx \cdot Mx)$

$(x)(Mx \supset {\sim}Kx)$

$\therefore (\exists x) {\sim}Ax$

This form is analogous to the following form from statement logic:

$p \supset (q \supset r)$

$p \cdot s$

$s \supset \sim r$

$\therefore \sim q$

In the above form, '$\sim q$' has to be derived from '$q \supset r$', which can be derived from '$p \supset (q \supset r)$' and 'p'; and the latter comes from '$p \cdot s$'. Also, 's' can be used with '$s \supset \sim r$' to derive '$\sim r$' which, with '$q \supset r$', gives '$\sim q$', the desired result. All that is needed, then, is to instantiate argument 9 to an appropriate constant, do the steps of the proof involving the rules from statement logic, and then generalize the result. The actual proof of the validity of argument 9 is left as an exercise.

SUGGESTION 3

If the conclusion of the argument at hand is an existentially generalized statement, consider deriving a substitution instance of the open sentence following the quantifier by using EI, and then using EG to derive the general statement.

Argument 9 is just one instance in which suggestion 3 is applicable. That is, by instantiating the premises of argument 9, one is able to derive '$\sim Aa$' (or a similar statement with a different individual constant). Since '$\sim Aa$' is a substitution instance of the open sentence '$\sim Ax$', one can then existentially generalize '$\sim Aa$' to obtain '$(\exists x)\sim Ax$'.

SUGGESTION 4

If the conclusion of the argument at hand is a universally generalized statement, consider deriving a substitution instance of the open sentence following the quantifier by using UI, and then using UG to derive the general statement.

One simple instance of the use of suggestion 4 is provided by the following argument.

ARGUMENT 10

All who commit crimes ultimately pay, and all who are honest are rewarded. But, since everyone either commits crimes or is honest, everyone ultimately pays. This is so because no one is rewarded.

Using 'C' to represent 'commits crimes', 'U' to represent 'ultimately pays', 'H' to represent 'is honest', and 'R' to represent 'is rewarded', we obtain the following form for argument 10:

$(x)(Cx \supset Ux)$

$(x)(Hx \supset Rx)$

$(x)(Cx \lor Hx)$

$(x)\sim Rx$

$\therefore (x)Ux$

Since the conclusion of this argument is a universally generalized statement, we should consider deriving a substitution instance of 'Ux' that we can universally generalize. Moreover, since the conclusion and the premises are all universal statements, we can instantiate all the variables to the same constant. If we can then derive 'Ua', an instantiation of the open sentence 'Ux', from the premises, and if 'a' designates an arbitrarily chosen individual, we can then use UG to derive the conclusion. This can easily be done, and it is left as an exercise (recall suggestion 2).

SUGGESTION 5

Since the open sentences following a universal quantifier often are conditional statements, consider using a conditional proof to derive such statements.

The following argument provides an example to which this suggestion and the previous one are both applicable.

ARGUMENT 11

Everyone who is free is lucky. This is so because everyone who is free is born that way, and everyone is either wealthy or is not born free. Moreover, everyone is either lucky or is not wealthy.

Using 'F' to represent 'is free', 'L' to represent 'is lucky', 'B' to represent 'is born free', and 'W' to represent 'is wealthy', we obtain the following form for argument 11:

$(x)(Fx \supset Bx)$

$(x)(Wx \lor \sim Bx)$

$(x)(Lx \lor \sim Wx)$

$\therefore (x)(Fx \supset Lx)$

By following suggestions 5 and 2, a proof of the validity of this argument can quite easily be given. The proof follows.

(1)	$(x)(Fx \supset Bx)$	Premise
(2)	$(x)(Wx \lor \sim Bx)$	Premise
(3)	$(x)(Lx \lor \sim Wx)$	Premise
(4)	$Fa \supset Ba$	(1), UI
(5)	$Wa \lor \sim Ba$	(2), UI
(6)	$La \lor \sim Wa$	(3), UI
(7)	Fa	Assumption
(8)	Ba	(4), (7), AA
(9)	$\sim Ba \lor Wa$	(5), Comm
(10)	$Ba \supset Wa$	(9), Imp
(11)	Wa	(8), (10), AA
(12)	$\sim Wa \lor La$	(6), Comm

(13) $Wa \supset La$ (12), Imp

(14) La (11), (13), AA

(15) $Fa \supset La$ (7) to (14), CP

∴ (16) $(x)(Fx \supset Lx)$ (15), UG

SUGGESTION 6

Eliminate the negation signs before quantifiers by using QE.

This is less a suggestion than a procedure to be followed in applying the rules developed in this chapter. In particular, none of the rules except QE tells us how to handle quantifiers which are preceded by a negation sign. As a result, at the beginning of any proof, QE is the rule to use to eliminate negation signs preceding quantifiers. Using QE is analogous to the procedures developed in the previous chapter for eliminating outside negation signs on categorical statements.

SUGGESTION 7

Use the strategy rules developed in Chapter 5.

There is little to be said about this suggestion except to remind you that various features of statement logic "point" in the right direction for finding a proof strategy. If you do not recall these pointers, it would be a good idea to review briefly some of the examples and arguments discussed in Chapter 5.

In this section we have looked at several suggestions that are useful in developing a strategy for constructing proofs. In the next section we shall apply some of these suggestions to the proofs of additional arguments in predicate logic.

7:5.2 Some Examples   Our purpose in this section is to work through several examples so as to increase your familiarity with proofs in predicate logic. Once again, you are reminded that much that is essential in constructing proofs has already been covered in Chapter 5. In this section, then, we shall emphasize the five rules presented earlier in this chapter. To begin, consider the following argument:

ARGUMENT 12

All animals that have not received a rabies shot will be quarantined. Moreover, all squirrels are animals. As a result, something received a rabies shot since some squirrels are not quarantined.

Step 1. Assign variables to the argument, and put it into standard form. Letting 'A' represent 'is an animal', 'R' represent 'received a rabies shot', 'Q' represent 'is quarantined', and 'S' represent 'is a squirrel', we have the following:

$(x)((Ax \cdot \sim Rx) \supset Qx)$

$(x)(Sx \supset Ax)$

$(\exists x)(Sx \cdot \sim Qx)$

∴ $(\exists x)Rx$

Step 2: Develop a strategy for the proof. Since the conclusion of the argument is an existentially quantified statement, we should follow suggestion 3 and consider deriving a substitution instance of the open sentence '*Rx*' by existential instantiation. We could then use EG to derive the desired result.

Step 3: Examining our premises, we see that any substitution instance of '*Rx*' is likely to come from '*Ax* · ~*Rx*' of the first premise. What is needed, then, is a way to derive a substitution instance of '*Rx*' from the occurrence of '~*Rx*' in '*Ax* · ~*Rx*' of this premise.

Step 4: Following suggestion 2, we see that the structure of the argument is analogous to the following argument form in statement logic:

$$(p \cdot \sim q) \supset r$$
$$s \supset p$$
$$s \cdot \sim r$$
$$\therefore q$$

If, from the first premise, we could get a truth-functional statement consisting only of the variables '*p*' and '*q*', then we might be able to derive '*q*'. This we can do by commutation and simplification on the third premise to get '~*r*', which can be used with DC on the first premise. From this point on, the strategy is straightforward, since, given '*s*' in '*s* · *r*', we can also derive '*p*'.

Step 5: We must now consider the appropriate instantiations of our premises. Since there is only one existential premise, we shall follow our earlier guideline and instantiate this premise first. We shall then instantiate the universal premises to the same constant. This gives us

$$(Aa \cdot \sim Ra) \supset Qa$$
$$Sa \supset Aa$$
$$Sa \cdot \sim Qa$$

where we want to derive '*Ra*'.

With the above, we can now construct a proof of the validity of argument 12:

(1)	$(x)((Ax \cdot \sim Rx) \supset Qx)$	Premise
(2)	$(x)(Sx \supset Ax)$	Premise
(3)	$(\exists x)(Sx \cdot \sim Qx)$	Premise
(4)	$Sa \cdot \sim Qa$	(3), EI
(5)	$(Aa \cdot \sim Ra) \supset Qa$	(1), UI
(6)	$Sa \supset Aa$	(2), UI
(7)	$\sim Qa \cdot Sa$	(4), Comm
(8)	$\sim Qa$	(7), Simp
(9)	$\sim(Aa \cdot \sim Ra)$	(5), (8), DC

(10) $\sim Aa \lor Ra$	(9), DM
(11) Sa	(4), Simp
(12) Aa	(6), (11), AA
(13) $Aa \supset Ra$	(10), Imp
(14) Ra	(12), (13), AA
$\therefore$ (15) $(\exists x)Rx$	(14), EG

This proof could be shortened a bit by using exportation on line (5); constructing such a proof is left as an exercise.

As in the case of statement logic, some arguments in predicate logic have only one premise. The following is one such argument.

ARGUMENT 13

Everyone who pokes along will be left behind. Therefore, if everyone pokes along, everyone will be left behind.

By using the obvious predicate terms, this argument can be symbolized as

$(x)(Px \supset Lx)$

$\therefore (x)Px \supset (x)Lx$

The conclusion of this argument is a conditional statement, so, following suggestion 5, we consider using a conditional proof. Doing so provides a simple proof of validity:

(1) $(x)(Px \supset Lx)$	Premise
(2) $Pa \supset La$	(1), UI
(3) $(x)Px$	Assumption
(4) Pa	(3), UI
(5) La	(2), (4), AA
(6) $(x)Lx$	(5), UG
$\therefore$ (7) $(x)Px \supset (x)Lx$	(3) to (6), CP

EXERCISE 7-10

1. Show that argument 9 in section 7:5.1 is valid.

2. Show that argument 10 in section 7:5.1 is valid.

3. Use exportation to show that argument 12 in section 7:5.2 is valid.

4. Provide the justification for each line in the following proofs.
   a. (1) $(x)(Mx \supset \sim Mx)$ Premise
       (2) $Ma \supset \sim Ma$

    (3) $\sim Ma \lor \sim Ma$
∴ (4) $\sim Ma$
b. (1) $(x)((Lx \lor Mx) \supset (Rx \cdot Sx))$ Premise
    (2) $(La \lor Ma) \supset (Ra \cdot Sa)$
    (3) $\sim(La \lor Ma) \lor (Ra \cdot Sa)$
    (4) $(\sim(La \lor Ma) \lor Ra) \cdot (\sim(La \lor Ma) \lor Sa)$
    (5) $\sim(La \lor Ma) \lor Ra$
    (6) $Ra \lor \sim(La \lor Ma)$
    (7) $Ra \lor (\sim La \cdot \sim Ma)$
    (8) $(Ra \lor \sim La) \cdot (Ra \lor \sim Ma)$
    (9) $(Ra \lor \sim Ma) \cdot (Ra \lor \sim La)$
   (10) $Ra \lor \sim Ma$
   (11) $\sim Ma \lor Ra$
   (12) $Ma \supset Ra$
∴ (13) $(x)(Mx \supset Rx)$
c. (1) $\sim(\exists x) \sim (Ax \supset Bx)$ Premise
    (2) $(x)((Bx \lor Cx) \supset Mx)$ Premise
    (3) $(x)(Ax \supset Bx)$
    (4) $(Ba \lor Ca) \supset Ma$
    (5) $Aa \supset Ba$
    (6) $\sim Aa \lor Ba$
    (7) $(\sim Aa \lor Ba) \lor Ca$
    (8) $\sim Aa \lor (Ba \lor Ca)$
    (9) $Aa \supset (Ba \lor Ca)$
   (10) $Aa \supset Ma$
∴ (11) $(x)(Ax \supset Mx)$
d. (1) $\sim(\exists x) \sim (Mx \supset Lx)$ Premise
    (2) $\sim(x) \sim Mx$ Premise
    (3) $\sim(\exists x) \sim (Lx \supset Nx)$ Premise
    (4) $(x)(Mx \supset Lx)$
    (5) $(\exists x)Mx$
    (6) $(x)(Lx \supset Nx)$
    (7) Ma
    (8) $Ma \supset La$
    (9) La
   (10) $La \supset Na$
   (11) Na
∴ (12) $(\exists x)Nx$
e. (1) $(x)(Ax \supset Cx)$ Premise
    (2) $(x)((Cx \cdot \sim Bx) \supset \sim Dx)$ Premise
    (3) $Ab \cdot \sim Bd$ Premise
    (4) $Ab \supset Cb$
    (5) $(Cb \cdot \sim Bb) \supset \sim Db$
    (6) Ab
    (7) Cb
    (8) $\sim Bb \cdot Ab$
    (9) $\sim Bb$

(10) $Cb \cdot \sim Bb$
(11) $\sim Db$
∴ (12) $(\exists x) \sim Dx$
f. (1) $(\exists x)(Rx \cdot \sim Mx)$ Premise
   (2) $(x)(Rx \supset (Sx \lor Tx))$ Premise
   (3) $(x)(Tx \supset Mx)$ Premise
   (4) $Ra \cdot \sim Ma$
   (5) $Ra \supset (Sa \lor Ta)$
   (6) $Ta \supset Ma$
   (7) Ra
   (8) $Sa \lor Ta$
   (9) $\sim Ma \cdot Ra$
   (10) $\sim Ma$
   (11) $\sim Ta$
   (12) $Ta \lor Sa$
   (13) Sa
   (14) $Ra \cdot Sa$
∴ (15) $(\exists x)(Rx \cdot Sx)$

5. Construct a proof of validity for each of the following arguments.
   a. $(\exists x)((Lx \lor Nx) \cdot Mx)$
      $(x) \sim (Mx \cdot Lx)$
      ∴ $(\exists x)(Nx \cdot \sim Lx)$
   b. $(x)(Lx \supset Gx)$
      $\sim(x)Gx$
      ∴ $(\exists x) \sim Lx$
   c. $(x)((Bx \cdot Ax) \supset Cx)$
      $(x)(Ax \supset Bx)$
      ∴ $(x)(Ax \supset (Ax \cdot Cx))$
   d. $(x)((Lx \lor Mx) \supset Nx)$
      $(\exists x)(Lx \cdot Ox)$
      ∴ $(\exists x)Nx \cdot (\exists x)Ox$
   e. $(x)(Sx \supset Lx)$
      $(x)(\sim Sx \supset \sim Fx)$
      $(x)(Dx \supset \sim Lx)$
      ∴ $(x)(Dx \supset \sim Fx)$
   f. $(\exists x)(Cx \cdot Wx)$
      $(x)(Wx \supset Nx)$
      ∴ $\sim(x) \sim (Cx \cdot Nx)$
   g. $(x)(Mx \supset Nx)$
      ∴ $(x)Mx \supset (x)Nx$
   h. $(x) \sim (Lx \cdot \sim Mx)$
      ∴ $\sim(Lb \cdot \sim Mb)$
   i. $(x)(Cx \supset (Bx \lor Px))$
      $(x)((Cx \cdot Wx) \supset \sim Bx)$
      ∴ $(x)((Cx \cdot Wx) \supset Px)$
   j. $Rd \supset (x)(\sim Cx \supset \sim Kx)$
      $(x)(Cx \supset Ax)$
      $(\exists x) \sim Ax$
      ∴ $\sim Rd \lor (\exists x)\sim Kx$

6. Symbolize each of the following arguments using the given symbols as predicate terms, and construct a proof of the validity of each argument.
   a. Everything made in *heaven* has a happy *ending*. But, since some *marriages* don't have happy endings, some marriages are not make in heaven. (H, E, M)
   b. Every *good* athlete *exercises* a lot. Moreover, no one who is *healthy smokes*. Hence, it's not the case that everyone is a good athlete or smokes, since some who are healthy do not exercise a lot. (G, E, H, S)
   c. Everyone who is *up-to-date* with world happenings either *reads* a newspaper or watches the *news*. Since some people who are up-to-date and

informed don't watch the news, it follows that it's false that no one who reads a newspaper is informed. (*U, R, N, I*)

d. Some cars, in addition to being *expensive* to run, are both *ugly* and uncomfortable. Every car which is expensive to run is either *noisy* or *comfortable.* Hence, some cars are both noisy and ugly. (*Note:* Assume a universe of discourse of cars.) (*E, U, N, C*)

e. No one who *loves* another and is *jealous* or *possessive* is *envied.* Hence, no one who loves another and is envied is jealous and possessive. (*L, J, P, E*)

f. Everything which is both *costly* and not *time*-consuming is available to the *rich.* All *friendships* are costly. Therefore, something is time-consuming since some friendships are not available to the rich. (*C, T, R, F*)

g. Some *wars* are just *political* actions. Moreover, every war is *unjust.* Since everything which is unjust is *immoral,* it follows that some political actions are immoral. (*W, P, U, I*)

h. Everything has a *purpose.* But a thing has a purpose if, and only if, it is *willed* by God. Since some things are either not willed by God or are mere *happenstance,* it follows that something that has a purpose is mere happenstance. (*P, W, H*)

i. Everyone who *enters* is either *blessed* or *cursed.* Moreover, everyone who is cursed either does not *repent* or does feel *sorrow.* Hence, since it's not the case that someone is blessed or does not repent, it follows that all who enter feel sorrow. (*E, B, C, R, S*)

j. None but the most *deserving* receive *honorary* degrees. Since only those who have made *significant* contributions to society are most deserving, it follows that those who receive honorary degrees have made significant contributions. (*D, H, S*)

STUDENT STUDY GUIDE

Chapter Summary

1. A **singular statement** is a statement in which something is asserted about some particular individual. The simplest statement of this kind is an affirmative subject-predicate statement, although some singular statements also contain truth-functional logical connectives. (section 7:1.1)

2. Singular statements are written in symbolic notation by assigning an uppercase letter to the **predicate term** and a lowercase letter to the **individual term.** These letters are written in the order predicate term–individual term in symbolizing a statement. (section 7:1.1)

3. The uppercase letters which represent particular predicate terms are **predicate constants,** and the lowercase letters which represent particular individual terms are **individual constants.** We adopt the convention of using the letters '*a*' through '*w*' for individual constants and, where possible, the first letter of an

individual's name as the individual constant representing that individual. (section 7:1.2)

4. An **individual variable** is a placeholder for individual constants and indicates that one, and only one, individual constant can replace the variable. We adopt the convention of using 'x', 'y', and 'z' as individual variables. (section 7:1.2)

5. Any expression containing only predicate constants and individual variables, and perhaps one or more logical connectives, is an **open sentence.** Since open sentences do not express statements, they do not have truth values. (section 7:1.2)

6. **Instantiation** is the replacing of an individual variable in an open sentence with an individual constant. When we instantiate an open sentence, the result is a **substitution instance** of the open sentence. (section 7:1.3)

7. The symbol '(x)' is the **universal quantifier** and is read 'for any x'. The symbol '$(\exists x)$' is the **existential quantifier** and is read 'There is at least one x such that'. To place a universal quantifier before an open sentence containing the same variable as the quantifier is to **universally quantify** the open sentence. To place an existential quantifier before such an open sentence is to **existentially quantify** the open sentence. (section 7:1.3)

8. A **free variable** in an open sentence is one which is not preceded by either an existential or a universal quantifier containing that variable. A **bound variable** is one which is preceded by a quantifier containing that variable and under whose **scope** the variable occurs. The scope of a quantifier is indicated by a pair of parentheses following the quantifier. (section 7:1.4)

9. A variable is bound by a quantifier if, and only if, the variable is the same letter as occurs in the quantifier and the variable falls under the scope of the quantifier. Any variable which is not bound is free. Hence, an open sentence is any expression containing a free variable. (section 7:1.4)

10. In a particular context, usually an argument, the **universe of discourse** is that group of individuals over which the existential and universal quantifiers range. The universe of discourse can be specified in any way we choose; for convenience we take the expressions 'someone' and 'everyone' as indicating that the universe of discourse has been limited to human beings. (section 7:1.5)

11. The rule **quantifier exchange** (QE) enables us to replace an occurrence of an existential quantifier with a universal quantifier, and the occurrence of a universal quantifier with an existential quantifier. To do this, we must also add a negation sign before and after the new quantifier, where double negation signs are then eliminated. (section 7:1.6)

12. Categorical statements are symbolized in predicate logic by writing the universal statements as conditional statements preceded by the universal quantifier, and the particular statements as conjunctions preceded by the existential quantifier. We must also place a negation sign before the consequent of a universal negative statement and before the right conjunct of a particular negative statement. (section 7:2.1)

13. **Universal instantiation** (UI) enables us to infer from a universally quantified statement another statement not containing the quantifier by deleting the

quantifier and replacing all occurrences of its variable with the same individual constant. (section 7:3.1)

14. **Existential generalization** (EG) enables us to infer from a statement containing an individual constant an existentially quantified statement. This latter statement is derived by prefixing to the former statement an existential quantifier whose variable does not already occur in the statement, and replacing all occurrences of the constant being generalized with the variable of the new quantifier. (section 7:3.2)

15. **Existential instantiation** (EI) enables us to infer from an existentially quantified statement another statement not containing the quantifier by deleting the quantifier and replacing all occurrences of its variable with the same individual constant, provided that that constant does not occur in the statement being instantiated or in any earlier statement of a proof that contains the statement to be instantiated. (section 7:3.3)

16. **Universal generalization** (UG) enables us to infer from a statement containing an individual constant a universally quantified statement whose form is derived by prefixing to the statement a universal quantifier whose variable does not already occur in the statement and replacing all occurrences of the constant being generalized with the variable of the new quantifier, provided that the constant being generalized represents an individual which has been chosen arbitrarily. (section 7:3.4)

17. A universally quantified statement can be expanded as the *conjunction* of all the singular statements derived from the general statement by instantiating to every individual in the universe of discourse. An existentially quantified statement can be expanded as the *disjunction* of all the singular statements derived from the general statement by instantiating to every individual in the universe of discourse. (section 7:4.1)

18. To show that an argument in predicate logic is *invalid*, we follow a procedure analogous to the short truth-table method. Beginning with a universe of discourse containing only one member, we instantiate the statements in the argument and then assign truth values in such a way as to make the conclusion false; we then try to assign truth values so as to make all the premises true. If we cannot find an invalidating assignment, we then consider a universe of discourse containing two members. This procedure is carried out until we find an invalidating assignment or until we have considered universes of discourse containing up to 2^n members. (section 7:4.1)

Key Terms

Singular Statement	Existential Quantifier
Predicate Term	Free Variable
Individual Term	Bound Variable
Predicate Constant	Scope of a Quantifier
Individual Constant	Universe of Discourse
Individual Variable	Quantifier Exchange

Open Sentence	Universal Instantiation
Instantiation	Existential Generalization
Substitution Instance	Existential Instantiation
Universal Quantifier	Universal Generalization

Self-Test/Exercises

1. In what ways can an open sentence be converted into a statement? (section 7:1.2)

2. In each of the following, indicate which variables are free and which are bound. (section 7:1.4)
   a. $(y)(Gy \equiv Fx)$
   b. $(\exists x)(Mx) \supset (y)(My \cdot Gx)$
   c. $(y)(\exists x)(Rx \supset (Ly \cdot Gx))$
   d. $(Gx \cdot Bx) \supset (Ga \cdot Ba)$
   e. $(Ab \cdot (\exists x)(Lx)) \cdot By$

3. Convert each of the following universally quantified statements into existentially quantified statements, and each of the existentially quantified statements into universally quantified statements. (section 7:1.6)
   a. $\sim(\exists x) \sim(Gx \lor Lx)$
   b. $\sim(x) \sim(Lx \supset Mx)$
   c. $\sim(\exists x)(\sim Cx \supset Lx)$
   d. $\sim(x)(Cx \cdot Mx)$
   e. $(x)(Lx \equiv Mx)$

4. Translate each of the following statements into symbolic notation using the given symbols as constants. (section 7:2)
   a. Everything is both wonderful and pleasant. (W, P)
   b. Someone will come up with an answer or Professor Dudley will be furious. (A, F, d)
   c. None but juniors can register on Wednesday. (J, R)
   d. Almost everyone who was invited to the party came. (I, C)
   e. Dana studied, and Laura went to a movie. (S, M, d, l)

5. Explain why, when using EI, one may not instantiate to a constant which occurs in the statement to be instantiated. (section 7:3.3)

6. Explain why, when using UG, one may not generalize on an individual constant which is not arbitrarily chosen. (section 7:3.4)

7. Explain why universally quantified statements are expanded as conjunctions of the singular statements derivable from instantiation to every individual in the universe of discourse. (section 7:3.4)

8. Show that each of the following arguments is invalid by describing an invalidating interpretation. (section 7:4.1)
   a. $(x)(Rx \supset \sim Lx)$
      $(x)(Rx \supset \sim Mx)$
      $\therefore (x)(Lx \supset \sim Mx)$
   b. $(\exists x)(Rx \cdot \sim Mx)$
      $(\exists x)(Rx \cdot Lx)$
      $\therefore (x)(Lx \supset \sim Mx)$
   c. $(x)(Mx \supset \sim Lx)$
      $(\exists x)(Rx \cdot \sim Lx)$
      $\therefore (x)(Mx \supset Rx)$
   d. $(\exists x)(Lx \cdot Mx)$
      $\therefore (x)(Lx \cdot Mx)$
   e. $(\exists x)(\sim Mx \cdot Rx)$
      $(\exists x)(\sim Rx \cdot Lx)$
      $\therefore (\exists x)(\sim Lx \cdot Mx)$

9. Construct a proof of validity for each of the following arguments. (section 7:5)

a. $(x)(Lx \supset Gx)$
   $\sim(x)Gx$
   $\therefore (\exists x) \sim Lx$

b. $(x)((Lx \lor Mx) \supset Qx)$
   $(\exists x)(Ox \cdot Lx)$
   $\therefore (\exists x)Qx \cdot (\exists x)Ox$

c. $\sim(x) \sim (Cx \cdot Rx)$
   $(x)(Rx \supset Nx)$
   $\therefore (\exists x)(Cx \cdot Nx)$

d. $\sim(\exists x) \sim (Cx \supset (Bx \lor Px))$
   $(x)((Cx \cdot Wx) \supset \sim Bx)$
   $\therefore \sim(\exists x) \sim ((Cx \cdot Wx) \supset Px)$

e. $(x)(Lx \supset \sim Mx)$
   $\therefore (x)Lx \supset (x) \sim Mx$

CHAPTER 8

INDUCTIVE

ARGUMENTS

In this chapter and the next we shall be discussing inductive arguments. We shall examine several forms of inductive arguments and discuss some things that one must guard against before accepting the conclusion of an inductive argument.

8:1 THE NATURE OF INDUCTION

Let us begin our discussion of argument forms by reviewing the characteristics of both deductive and inductive support.

CHARACTERISTICS OF DEDUCTIVE SUPPORT

(DC1) If all the premises are true, then the conclusion must be true.

(DC2) All the information in the conclusion is contained in the premises.

(DC3) The conclusions of different valid arguments always follow from their premises with the same degree of strength.

CHARACTERISTICS OF INDUCTIVE SUPPORT

(C1) If all the premises of the argument are true, then the conclusion is probably true, although it might be false.

(C2) The conclusion contains information which is not contained in the premises.

(C3) The conclusions of different inductive arguments follow from their premises with different degrees of probability.

In our discussions in previous chapters we noted that there is an air of finality to deductive arguments—the conclusion follows from the premises in clearly specifiable ways, nothing is left up in the air, and, if the premises of such arguments are true, we are fully justified in accepting the conclusion. Just a cursory look at the characteristics of inductive arguments is enough to show that inductive arguments do not have all these characteristics; even in the best of circumstances it just might turn out that the conclusion of a particular argument is false.

Additionally, inductive logic is not as fully developed as is deductive logic. As one can see from conditions (1) and (3), much of what constitutes a good inductive argument depends, ultimately, upon one's analysis of probability. It would be misleading, and indeed false, to suggest that there are no problems with probability theory, or to suggest that inductive logic is as clearly understood as deductive logic. These points notwithstanding, we can still make a fair amount of headway in a discussion of inductive logic, without ever raising issues of probability theory. In fact, most of what we shall discuss here is independent of any particular view of probability theory or any particular analysis of justification.

The above considerations might lead one to think that there is something bogus about inductive arguments—that somehow one ought not to accept their conclusions. It is important *not* to draw this inference. Even though a number of important foundational or theoretical problems concerning induction remain, it is nonetheless indispensible that we accept the conclusions of some inductive arguments and, moreover, that we realize we are justified in doing so. A couple of cases should make this clear.

One of the first things to note about arguments in general is that only inductive arguments provide grounds for accepting, *on the basis of reasons*, new information. If we were limited to accepting only that which could be established by deductive means, we would never go beyond that which we already have available in the premises of an argument; this is a consequence of (DC2). A second thing to note is that a large amount of work in the sciences, both natural and social, is inductive in character. For example, conclusions are often made on the basis of observations in a number of cases and then generalized to cover as yet unobserved cases.

Before we look at some inductive argument forms, it is worth reemphasizing that the support relation in an argument can be evaluated independently of the actual truth or falsity of the premises. Paralleling the case of deductive support, the issue we are concerned with in the case of inductive support is whether it is likely, or probable, that the conclusion is true given that, or under the assumption that, all the premises are true.

8:2 INDUCTIVE ARGUMENT FORMS

In this section we shall examine various inductive argument forms, see what conditions have to be met for an argument to be one of the forms, and look at several examples of the argument forms.

8:2.1 Induction by Enumeration   Consider the following argument:

ARGUMENT 1

Since 90 percent of the eggs sampled from Farmer Brown's chicken farm have been grade A, 90 percent of all the eggs on Farmer Brown's chicken farm are grade A.

If we let 'E' represent 'eggs from Farmer Brown's chicken farm', and let 'A' represent 'eggs which are grade A', we obtain the following form for argument 1:

FORM OF ARGUMENT 1

90 percent of sampled E are A

∴ 90 percent of all E are A

Notice that argument 1 (and, hence, its form) satisfied the three conditions for inductive arguments. If the premise is true, then the conclusion is probably true, though it might be false: For example, the sample might have come from just one hen house where Brown keeps the better hens. The conclusion contains information not contained in the premises: In particular, the conclusion is about *all* the eggs from Farmer Brown's chicken farm, whereas the premise gives us information only about *those eggs which were sampled.* Other inductive arguments are stronger, and some weaker, then argument 1. The degree to which the conclusion is probably true depends on the size of the sample chosen, whether the sample was representative of all the eggs, and so on. We shall discuss such considerations further in section 8:4.

Let's look at another example.

ARGUMENT 2

81 percent of all Americans favor the President's position on an increase in the federal tax on gasoline. We know this because a recent poll showed that 81 percent of those Americans polled favored his position.

If we let 'A' represent 'Americans' and 'F' represent 'people who favor the President's position', then argument 2 has the following form:

FORM OF ARGUMENT 2

81 percent of polled A are F

∴ 81 percent of all A are F

As in the case of argument 1, argument 2 satisfies the three conditions for inductive arguments. Arguments like argument 2 are probably the inductive arguments most people are familiar with—arguments whose conclusion is a generalization based on some sample class. Other instances are the ratings of television programs and political polls establishing front-runners in primary elections. All such arguments are instances of **induction by enumeration,** which is characterized by the fact that the conclusion of the argument is about *all* the members of the class but is based on premises which are about some *observed* members of that class.

Consider now a slightly different instance of induction by enumeration:

ARGUMENT 3

Bethany has gotten an 'A' in every course she has so far taken; therefore, she will get an 'A' in all her remaining courses.

Letting 'C' represent 'courses Bethany takes' and 'A' represent 'courses in which Bethany gets an 'A' ', we get the following:

FORM OF ARGUMENT 3

100 percent of past C have been A

∴ 100 percent of future C will be A

Even if we suppose that the premise is true, it could still be the case that the conclusion is false.

What argument 3 points out is that even when *every* member of a sample has a particular property, the conclusion that all the other members of that class have the property is still the result of an inductive argument: induction by enumeration. Argument 3 is different from arguments 1 and 2 in that, in the latter two all members of the sampled class were available. That is, all the eggs from Farmer Brown's chicken farm and all the Americans were available at the time the sample or poll was taken, whereas in argument 3 all the courses Bethany will take were not available. This is not a crucial difference, for we may construe the courses which she has so far taken as a subset of all the courses she will take. Argument 3, then, is an instance of an argument which predicts future occurrences on the basis of past occurrences. Arguments 1 and 2 do not have this characteristic.

Besides arguments in which every member of the sample class has a particular property, there are instances of induction by enumeration in which *no* member of the sample class has a particular property. The following argument is one such instance.

ARGUMENT 4

None of the students interviewed thought that final exams were very well scheduled. Hence, no student thinks that final exams are very well scheduled.

Letting 'S' represent 'students' and 'E' represent 'people who think that final exams are very well scheduled', we obtain the following as the form of argument 4:

FORM OF ARGUMENT 4

0 percent of interviewed S are E

∴ 0 percent of all S are E

Argument 4, like the preceding three arguments, has a conclusion which is a generalization about all the members of a particular class based on a sample of the class. This is the general feature of all instances of induction by enumeration.

If we used 'observed' to represent adjectives like 'sampled', 'polled', and 'interviewed,' then we can generalize the above four argument forms as follows:

ARGUMENT FORM OF INDUCTION BY ENUMERATION

Y percent of observed A are B   (where Y is equal to or greater than 0

∴ Y percent of all A are B   and equal to or less than 100)

8:2.2 Statistical Syllogisms   In the preceding section we saw that we could draw certain conclusions about all members of a class, based on a sample from that class. In this section we shall look at an argument form which enables us to draw conclusions about *a particular member of a class,* based on information about all members of the class. Such arguments are **statistical syllogisms.** One such argument follows:

ARGUMENT 5

80 percent of the chickens on Farmer Brown's chicken farm are grade A. Since Mortimer is a chicken on Farmer Brown's chicken farm, Mortimer is grade A.

Letting 'C' represent 'chickens on Farmer Brown's chicken farm', 'A' represent 'chickens which are grade A', and 'M' represent 'Mortimer', we get the following as the form of argument 5:

FORM OF ARGUMENT 5

80 percent of all C are A

M is C

∴ M is A

In some statistical syllogisms, the percentage is not made explicit in the argument. The next two arguments are of this type.

ARGUMENT 6

Most of the remarks made by Sarah are insulting. The next remark made will be insulting because Sarah will make the remark.

ARGUMENT 7

60,000 of the tickets in the drum were purchased by people from Michigan, 15,000 of the tickets were purchased by people from Canada, and 5000 of the tickets were purchased by people from Ohio. The million-dollar ticket will be drawn from the drum. Hence the million-dollar ticket was purchased by someone from Michigan.

In argument 6 'most' is understood as 'more than half'. As a result, it is more likely than not that the next remark will be insulting. Letting 'S' represent 'remarks by Sarah', 'I' represent 'remarks which are insulting', and 'N' represent 'the next remark to be made', we obtain for argument 6 the following form:

FORM OF ARGUMENT 6

More than half of all S are I

N is S

∴ N is I

To determine the form of argument 7, we must first determine what percentage of the tickets in the drum were purchased by people from Michigan.

This is 75 percent. Now if we let '*T*' represent 'tickets in the drum', '*M*' represent 'tickets purchased by people from Michigan', and '*D*' represent 'the million-dollar ticket', we get the following argument form:

FORM OF ARGUMENT 7

75 percent of all *T* are *M*

D is *T*

∴ *D* is *M*

Consider two final arguments.

ARGUMENT 8

15 percent of the people who enter the Ohio lottery win money in the lottery. Hence, Ebenezer will win money in the lottery since he entered the Ohio lottery.

The following is the form of argument 8:

FORM OF ARGUMENT 8

15 percent of *O* are *W*

E is *O*

∴ *E* is *W*

Notice that even if the premises of argument 8 are true, it is not the case that it is more likely than not that Ebenezer will win money in the Ohio lottery. On the contrary, it is more likely than not that Ebenezer *will not* win money in the lottery. As this example indicates, in a good inductive argument of the form of a statistical syllogism, *more than 50 percent of the class in question must have the property in question.*

ARGUMENT 9

We know that Mark is concerned about his grade in the logic course because all students of logic are concerned with their grade in logic courses.

Letting '*S*' represent 'students who are in logic courses', '*C*' represent 'students who are concerned about their grade in logic courses', and '*M*' represent 'Mark', we have

FORM OF ARGUMENT 9

100 percent of all *S* are *C*

M is *S*

∴ *M* is *C*

The important point concerning argument 9 is that if the premises are all true, then *the conclusion must be true;* that is, argument 9 is *valid.* Since statistical syllogisms are inductive arguments, argument 9 cannot be a statistical syllogism. This example shows that, in a good inductive argument of the form of a statistical syllogism, *less than 100 percent of the class in question must have the property in question.*

The above cases can be generalized as follows:

ARGUMENT FORM OF STATISTICAL SYLLOGISMS

Y percent of all A are B (where Y is greater than 50 and less than 100)

x is A

$\therefore$ x is B

8:2.3 Modified Induction by Enumeration   In the argument forms discussed above, we drew certain inferences about all the members of a class based on the results of sampling some of the members of the class (induction by enumeration), and we drew certain inferences about a particular member of a class given information about all the members of a class (statistical syllogism). In this section we shall examine an argument form which enables us to draw certain inferences about a *particular* member of a class given the results of sampling *some* of the members of the class. Such arguments are instances of **modified induction by enumeration.** The next argument is typical.

ARGUMENT 10

87 percent of the students polled were dissatisfied with the scheduling of final exams. Since Rotund is a student, he is dissatisfied with the scheduling of final exams.

If we let 'S' represent 'students', 'D' represent 'people who are dissatisfied with the scheduling of final exams', and 'R' represent 'Rotund', we get the following as the form of argument 10.

FORM OF ARGUMENT 10

87 percent of polled S are D

R is S

$\therefore$ R is D

To see why argument 10 (and, hence, its form) is a good inductive argument, consider the following two arguments:

ARGUMENT 11	ARGUMENT 12
87 percent of polled S are D	87 percent of all S are D
$\therefore$ 87 percent of all S are D	R is S
	$\therefore$ R is D

In argument 11 we have a standard case of induction by enumeration: That is, based on a sample in which 87 percent of the S's were D, we conclude that 87 percent of all S's are D. In argument 12 we have a standard case of a statistical syllogism. The relationship between argument 10 and arguments 11 and 12 is that arguments 10 and 11 have the same first premise. As a result, we can conclude that 87 percent of all S are D in *both* arguments, though we don't do this explicitly in argument 10. Instead, in argument 10 we implicitly use as evidence the statement which occurs as the conclusion of argument 11, and this information, along with the premise 'R is S', is used as a statistical syllogism of the form shown in argument 12. In other words, argument 10 functions much like a statistical syllogism whose first premise is derived on the basis of induction by enumeration.[1]

Since the conclusion in the argument form modified induction by enumeration depends, in part, on a statistical syllogism, the percentage of the sample that has the property in question must be greater than 50. For an example of this, consider the following argument:

ARGUMENT 13

10 percent of the voters polled favored proposal B. Edwards is a voter, and therefore Edwards favors proposal B.

The form of argument 13 is

FORM OF ARGUMENT 13

10 percent of observed V are F

E is V

$\therefore E$ is F

As with argument 10, argument 13 can be understood on the basis of induction by enumeration and a statistical syllogism. The relevant instances of these argument forms are the following:

ARGUMENT 14	ARGUMENT 15
10 percent of observed V are F	10 percent of all V are F
$\therefore$ 10 percent of all V are F	E is V
	$\therefore E$ is F

Now, whereas argument 14 satisfies all the conditions necessary for an acceptable instance of induction by enumeration (correct form and correct percentages), argument 15 is not an acceptable instance of a statistical syllogism since the percentage of V's which are F is not greater that 50 percent. Since the acceptability of argument 13 rests on both argument 14 and argument 15, and since argument 15 is unacceptable, argument 13 is also unacceptable. You might compare this case to that of complex arguments discussed in Chapter 3, wherein a whole argument was rejected because of the unacceptability of a part of the argument.

Consider one last case:

ARGUMENT 16

100 percent of the Americans polled favored a reduction in national defense spending. Braganaw favors a reduction in national defense spending since Braganaw is an American.

---

[1] This situation is analogous to the deductions of Chapters 3 and 5, where we make explicit what is only implicit in the premises of an argument.

Argument 16 has the following form:

FORM OF ARGUMENT 16

100 percent of observed A are F

B is A

∴ B is F

The two arguments relevant to understanding and assessing argument 16 are these:

ARGUMENT 17	ARGUMENT 18
100 percent of observed A are F	100 percent of all A are F
∴ 100 percent of all A are F	B is A
	∴ B is F

Argument 17 is clearly an acceptable instance of induction by enumeration, whereas argument 18 is *not* an acceptable instance of a statistical syllogism. In argument 18, if the premises are true then the conclusion must also be true; in other words argument 18 is *valid*. The issue that confronts us, then, is whether argument 16 is an acceptable instance of modified induction by enumeration.

The answer here is yes. If the premises of argument 16 are true, then the conclusion is probably true. Additionally, since the conclusion rests, in part, on a sample of all A's, it might be false: Braganaw may be an American who does not favor a reduction in national defense spending. Understood in terms of arguments 17 and 18, argument 16 is acceptable, since induction by enumeration is an acceptable argument form and argument 18 is an acceptable deductive argument.

Consideration of the above cases gives the following as the argument form of modified induction by enumeration:

ARGUMENT FORM OF MODIFIED INDUCTION BY ENUMERATION

Y percent of observed A are B (where Y is greater than 50 and less

x is A than or equal to 100)

∴ x is B

Before we move on, it should be noted that in general the argument form modified induction by enumeration is weaker than the argument form statistical syllogism. This is so because the statistical syllogism part of modified induction by enumeration depends on an argument of the form induction by enumeration. As a result, in the case of modified induction by enumeration, the x which is said to be B depends upon the strength of the induction by enumeration argument. That is, modified induction by enumeration, understood in terms of two inductive arguments—statistical syllogism and induction by enumeration— is likely to lead to false conclusions more often than is statistical syllogism, since the possibility of error is greater when two inductive arguments, rather than only one, are considered.

EXERCISE 8-1

1. Briefly explain the three conditions which are satisfied whenever the premises of an argument inductively support the conclusion.

2. Give the argument forms for a statistical syllogism, induction by enumeration, and modified induction by enumeration. Explain the percentage range of 'Y' for each of these forms.

3. Explain the relationship that modified induction by enumeration has to induction by enumeration and statistical syllogism.

4. Explain why argument a below is an acceptable inductive argument whereas argument b is not.

    a. 100 percent of observed F are G   b. 100 percent of all F are G
       x is F   x is F
       ∴ x is G   ∴ x is G

5. Put each of the following arguments into standard form, and give the form of the argument. If the form has a name, give the name of the form.

    a. Of the 10 marbles Smith sampled from an urn containing 100 marbles, he found that 7 were green. He returned the sample to the urn and mixed up the marbles, and he is about to draw one marble from the urn. Smith predicts that the marble will be green.

    b. In a recent survey taken in the suburbs of Los Angeles it was found that 83 percent of those polled favor a high tax on the use of gasoline as opposed to rationing. Therefore, 83 percent of all Americans prefer a high gas tax to rationing.

    c. McNivey, the racing driver, has won 80 percent of her races, all of which were run by at least twenty-three drivers of top caliber. The weather forecast for today's race, in which McNivey will be racing against twenty-five drivers, is for a slippery track due to freezing rains. McNivey will win the race.

    d. In each day of the trial, new and exciting information has been brought out about the role some congressmen played in bringing about legalized gambling. Hence, tomorrow's testimony will be such that more new information about some congressmen and legalized gambling will be brought out.

    e. In a recent survey conducted by the *News* among shoppers on Main Street, it was found that six of the ten people interviewed favored preferential voting, and four did not. As a result, 60 percent of the people in Metropolis favor preferential voting.

    f. Less than half the eligible voters have voted in the last three elections on the school bond issue. It is likely, therefore, that less than half of them will vote on the school bond issue tomorrow.

    g. The latest survey showed that more people watched the news on channel 4 than on the other two stations combined. It's clear, then, that the majority of people in Our Town watch the news on channel 4.

    h. Of the ten faculty members polled by the student newspaper, seven felt that students should have a greater role in governing the university than they presently have. This clearly establishes that the majority of the faculty feel the same way.

i. Almost everyone I've talked with has been dissatisfied with the service he or she has received at Neptune's. In spite of my telling them this, Jon and Martha are going there for dinner tonight. I'll bet they'll be dissatisfied too.

j. Eighty percent of the people who have cancer which is diagnosed in its early stages live for at least five more years with proper treatment. Until I found this out, I was really scared because my father just found out he has cancer. Fortunately, they found it in its early stages.

k. Of course we're going to beat Western on Saturday! They've only beaten us once in the past twenty-three years, and that was only because we had one of our touchdowns called back.

l. There must still be a lot of resistance to reestablishing diplomatic relations with Cuba. A recent survey showed that of those Americans polled, 78 percent were opposed to our doing this.

m. Foreman to workers: Last week our quality control department found that out of every 100 Whazzits they sampled, 7 were defective. Whereas we expect some problems in production, our pricing is based on there being only 2 percent defects. We are all going to have to be more careful in the future and be sure that we each do our part of the job carefully.

n. This is clearly not a good year to be seeking public office as a Democrat; over 60 percent of the people polled in a national survey indicate that they will vote for Republican candidates in next week's election. I realize that Danielson is a fairly well-known, popular candidate around here, but with the results of the poll, there's a good chance that even she will not be elected.

o. Senator, we are just going to have to step up our campaign in the rural areas. You know we can't win without carrying those districts, and our latest survey shows that you are trailing by a 2-to-1 margin in those areas.

p. You may find this surprising—I know I did—but more than half the students who graduate from our high school can't read beyond the eighth-grade level. Grayson's son just graduated from our high school, so it's a good bet that he can't read very well either.

q. A random sample of state income-tax returns for this year shows that almost 8 percent of the returns contain one or more errors. Whenever the error percentage for all returns goes higher than 4 percent, it's usually the result of a form that is too complex, so we should make next year's form simpler.

6. Suppose that the softball team sponsored by R&D has won eleven of eighteen games this season. Construct a good inductive argument whose conclusion is that the team will win their game this weekend. Give the name of the argument form.

7. Suppose that Governor Rensen is up for reelection and is running as the Republican candidate. Suppose further that the governor has never been defeated in any election he has entered, but that seven out of ten Republican

governors who recently sought reelection in other states were defeated. Construct a good inductive argument whose conclusion is that Rensen will win the election and another good inductive argument whose conclusion is that he will lose. Which of the arguments is stronger, and why?

8. Willy Wunda, champion race-car driver, has won 93 percent of all his races. He is racing again today. Unfortunately, Riley Ridum, Willy's old nemesis, is also in the race; and every time Wunda and Ridum have raced, Ridum has won. Construct an argument which shows that Wunda will win the race and another which concludes that he will lose. Which argument is stronger, and why?

8:3 SOME THOUGHTS ON 'PROBABLY' AS A RELATIONAL EXPRESSION

The thought may have occurred to you that in the three argument forms discussed in the previous sections, we might have overstated the conclusion. In particular, you may have thought that instead of saying either that Y percent of all A are B or that x is B, we should have said that Y percent of all A are *probably B* or that x is *probably B*. In this section you will see why, in the three argument forms already discussed and in the argument forms to be discussed in later sections, we should *not* put 'probably' in the conclusion. Our remarks will be limited to the argument form induction by enumeration, but the ideas are applicable in obvious ways to the other inductive forms.

To facilitate our discussion, let us compare induction by enumeration and the argument form affirming the antecedent. We know that affirming the antecedent is a valid argument form and, as a result, is such that if all the premises are true then the conclusion must also be true. Now notice when we say in the case of a valid argument that the conclusion *must be true* we are commenting on *the support relationship which holds between the premises and the conclusion.* We are *not* saying that the conclusion must be true all by itself, in the way we claimed this in Chapter 4 about statements which are tautologies. This distinction is schematized in Figure 8-1.[2]

Suppose that 'Q' represents the statement 'John will study' and 'P' represents the statement 'John will stay home'. What we would say, then, about A of Figure 8-1 is that *if* both 'If John stays home then he will study' and 'John stays home' are true, *then* it must be (or necessarily is) the case that 'John studies' is true. What we do not mean is that John must study, independently of the two premises. For example, John might go to the movies, or he might do any number of other things, thereby showing that 'Q' (and, hence, at least one of the premises of A) is false. If we were to assert 'Necessarily John studies' or 'It must be the case that John studies', we would have the conclusion to B of

---

[2] Notice that B in Figure 8-1 is an accurate representation of an argument only if 'Q' is a tautology.

Figure 8-1

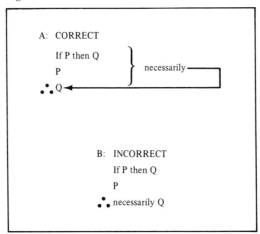

Figure 8-1. We have just seen, however, that we are not claiming of John that necessarily he studies. In short, the 'must' or 'necessarily' in the case of deduction is a comment on the relationship which holds between the premises and the conclusion of the argument (A of Figure 8-1) and *not* part of the conclusion (B of Figure 8-1).

Analogous remarks hold in the case of 'probably' and inductive arguments. Recall our discussion of condition (C3) of induction, where we pointed out that different premises can confer different probabilities on one and the same conclusion. For example, 'John will survive' is probable with respect to 'John is a patient in General Hospital, and 98 percent of General Hospital patients survive', but it is improbable with respect to 'John is two years old and a patient in General Hospital, and 60 percent of child patients in this hospital do not survive'. As a result, it is wrong to say simply 'John will probably survive'. This error is illustrated in Figure 8-2.

When we say of inductive arguments that if the premises are true then the

Figure 8-2

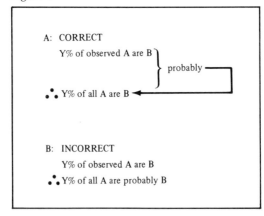

conclusion is probably true [(C1) of induction], it is A of Figure 8-2 that we are claiming. That is, 'probably' is used to characterize the relationship which holds between the premises and the conclusion of an inductive argument. Were we to understand 'probably' as B of Figure 8-2, then we would no longer be treating it as a characterization of the relationship which holds between the premises and the conclusion but, rather, as *part of the conclusion.*

8:4 WHEN NOT TO ACCEPT THE CONCLUSION OF AN INDUCTIVE ARGUMENT

If we distinguish the form and content of inductive arguments, just as we drew this distinction in the case of deductive arguments, there are certain conditions under which, though the inductive argument in question has an acceptable form, we are not justified in accepting the conclusion of the argument. In the case of deduction there is only one condition under which we can reject the conclusion of a valid argument: that at least one of the premises is false. This case is also relevant when we are examining inductive arguments, but other things must be taken into account as well.

Since the acceptability of an inductive argument rests on a probabilistic relationship between the premises and the conclusion, the higher the probability that the conclusion is true, given the premises, the more likely it is that the conclusion is true. Similarly, if the probability that the conclusion is true, given the premises, is low, the more likely is it that the conclusion is false. In this section we shall examine several kinds of cases in which arguments have an acceptable inductive argument form but are such that the conclusion ought not to be accepted. This does not mean, of course, that there are no good inductive argument forms, any more than the falsity of a premise in the case of deduction means that there are no valid argument forms.

Before considering these cases, we shall introduce a fourth characteristic of deductive and inductive arguments:

ADDITIONAL CHARACTERISTIC OF DEDUCTIVE ARGUMENTS

(DC4) Adding additional premises to the argument does not require a change in the original conclusion, although additional conclusions may be drawn.

ADDITIONAL CHARACTERISTIC OF INDUCTIVE ARGUMENTS

(C4) Adding additional premises to the argument *may* require a change in the original conclusion.

To see how (DC4) applies in the case of deduction, consider the following argument:

ARGUMENT 19

(1) All men are mortal.

(2) Jodivi is a man.

∴ Jodivi is mortal.

Since argument 19 is valid, we know that if the premises are true then the conclusion must also be true. In the strongest possible sense, the conclusion of argument 19 *follows from* the premises. Since the conclusion does follow from the premises, no additional premises could be such that we would have to retract the conclusion, given the truth of the original premises. One way of clearly seeing this is to consider (DC2) of deductive support: that all the information in the conclusion is already contained in the premises. Since argument 19 is valid, all the information in 'Jodivi is mortal' is contained in premises (1) and (2). Surely, adding additional premises to argument 19 and retaining premises (1) and (2) is not going to change the information contained in the two original premises. But, then, adding additional premises will not change the conclusion of the argument either, since it just is part of the information or factual content of the two original premises.

The above discussion shows that we do not (cannot) change the conclusion of a deductive argument simply by adding more premises. Characteristic (DC4) tells us more than this, however—in particular, that the addition of more premises to a deductive argument *may* enable us to draw additional conclusions. To see how this part of the condition works, consider the following argument, which is argument 19 with an additional premise.

ARGUMENT 20

(1) All men are mortal.

(2) Jodivi is a man.

(3) All men are chauvinists.

∴ Jodivi is mortal.

The addition of premise (3) to argument 19 (giving us argument 20) enables us to conclude, from premises (2) and (3), that

(4) Jodivi is a chauvinist.

Let's now consider (C4) of inductive arguments. To facilitate our discussion, we shall examine the following argument:

ARGUMENT 21

80 percent of the nonconference games played by Big Eight teams in the past have been won by Big Eight teams. It follows that next season Big Eight teams will win 80 percent of their nonconference games.

Argument 21 is just a simple case of induction by enumeration. Suppose, however, that we are provided with the following new information:

(1) All 20 percent of the nonconference games that Big Eight teams have lost have been played against Alabama, Notre Dame, Ohio State, and Michigan.

(2) Next season, all nonconference games played by Big Eight teams will be against Alabama, Notre Dame, Ohio State, and Michigan.

Given the information in (1) and (2), it is easy to see that we must reevaluate the conclusion of argument 21. In particular, our new information supports the claim that the Big Eight teams will *lose all their nonconference games*. Argument 21, along with (1) and (2), provides a clear case in which the addition of new premises to an inductive argument changes the conclusion of the argument.

It is because additional information may sometimes lead to a change in the conclusion of an inductive argument that we must, when deciding whether to accept the conclusion of an inductive argument on the basis of the premises, be on guard against certain general cases which typically exhibit this feature. In the remainder of this section we shall examine several of these cases.

8:4.1 Insufficient Evidence   To see what the problem of insufficient evidence is, consider the following instance of induction by enumeration.

ARGUMENT 22

72 percent of the voters polled favored the conservative candidate over the liberal candidate. Therefore, 72 percent of all voters favor the conservative candidate over the liberal.

Suppose that there are 10,000 voters who will choose between the conservative and liberal candidates on election day. Suppose further that the evidence that gave rise to the premise of argument 22 is that fifty people were called on the telephone and thirty-six preferred the conservative candidate. If we assume that no special efforts have been made to sample members from the divergent groups of voters, then we have a case of **insufficient evidence** in that the number of people in the survey was just a very small percentage of the whole class from which the sample was chosen.[3]

The general feature, then, of insufficient evidence is that *the sample examined is not large enough to justify the inference about the whole class from which the sample was chosen.* the obvious question that arises in this regard is how large the sample must be before it is big enough. Unfortunately, there is no clear answer to this question; It is fairly easy to tell when the sample is *much* too small and, as in the next argument, it is fairly easy to tell when the sample is clearly large enough.

ARGUMENT 23

28 percent of the voters polled favored the conservative candidate over the liberal candidate. Hence, 28 percent of all voters favor the conservative candidate over the liberal candidate.

Suppose, as in the previous case, that there are 10,000 voters who will choose between the two candidates, but in this case the evidence that gave rise to the premise is that 2520 people out of 9000 polled favored the conservative candidate. In this case we have sampled 90 percent of the voters—a very large sample and

---

[3] In the next section we shall discuss some of the problems associated with not having a representative sample.

one which practically guarantees that the sample was representative of the divergent groups of voters.

Although the question of how much is enough cannot be decisively answered, there are some guidelines that can be followed. Two of the most important things to keep in mind when considering whether enough members of the class in question have been sampled are (1) the purpose for taking the sample and (2) how important it is that the results of the induction be correct. Clearly, the more there is at stake in accepting a given hypothesis, the more careful one should be in gathering as much relevant information as possible. For an example of this kind of situation, consider the following argument:

ARGUMENT 24

53 percent of the voters polled in the Twelfth Precinct said they were going to vote for Abax for mayor. Therefore, 53 percent of all the voters in the Twelfth Precinct will vote for Abax.

Suppose Abax and his political strategists decide that to win the election he must win in the Twelfth Precinct, which contains 1000 voters. As a result, Abax has his workers conduct a random telephone poll of the people in that precinct to determine whether he should do more campaigning in the precinct or direct his efforts elsewhere. The campaign workers call 100 voters and find that 53 of them are going to vote for Abax (hence, the premise in argument 24). Now suppose that, in the same situation, 87 of the 100 voters called say they will vote for Abax. This give us

ARGUMENT 25

87 percent of the voters polled in the Twelfth Precinct said they were going to vote for Abax for mayor. Therefore, 87 percent of all the voters in the Twelfth precinct are going to vote for Abax.

What is important here is that in both argument 24 and argument 25 exactly the same number of voters were called (100, or 10 percent of the voters). As a result, it might seem reasonable that if a sufficient number of voters were polled in the case of argument 25, then a sufficient number would also have been polled in the case of argument 24. But in the case of argument 24, and with Abax needing to win the Twelfth Precinct to win the election, he would probably have his workers call more people in that precinct before he decided that he need not campaign there any more.

In the case of argument 24 there is, at least from Abax's point of view, a lot which depends on his acceptance of the conclusion of that argument. As a result, if he has not polled enough of the voters to get a sample large enough to reflect accurately the attitude of all the voters in the Twelfth Precinct, he just might lose the precinct; the percentage of polled voters who favor him is not much more than is needed to carry the Twelfth Precinct. In argument 25, on the other hand, there is a very strong indication that the voters in the Twelfth Precinct favor Abax over his opponent. In this case it is much more unlikely, even if the poll does not reflect with a very high degree of accuracy the attitude of all the voters in the precinct, that Abax will lose the precinct in the election.

Of course, it may well be that the poll taken in argument 24 does accurately reflect the attitudes of all the voters in the Twelfth Precinct and that the result of 100 calls is sufficient evidence for supporting the conclusion. The point, however, is whether it is reasonable to accept the conclusion to argument 24 on the basis of the evidence and, given what is at stake and the nature of inductive arguments, it seems reasonable to sample more voters before deciding whether to campaign further in the Twelfth Precinct.

An additional feature that is often considered in determining how large a sample is needed to support an induction is the relationship between what is asserted in the argument and currently accepted theory.[4] For example, a few trials are sufficient to determine the boiling point of a newly discovered substance, since the currently accepted theory is that the boiling point is a constant which is independent of all but a few easily controllable factors. In contrast, if the acceptance of some inductive argument would entail rejecting one or more highly confirmed theories, then many instances would have to be considered before accepting the argument.

Another general consideration in attempting to determine whether a given sample is sufficiently large to support an induction is the diversity of the members of the class from which the sample is taken. We must take this into account, for if there are many different kinds of individuals in the class we are sampling, then it will typically take a larger sample to ensure that we get an accurate representation of the class as a whole. This leads us to the second kind of case in which the conclusion of an inductive argument should not be accepted.

8:4.2 Unrepresentative Sample

An **unrepresentative sample** is a sample which, for whatever reason, turns out not to be an accurate "picture" of the whole class from which it was chosen. Let's consider a relatively simple example.

ARGUMENT 26

70 percent of the marbles we have sampled from the urn have been blue; hence, 70 percent of all the marbles in the urn are blue.

Suppose our evidence for argument 26 is as follows: We have an urn containing fifty marbles, and, of these, thirty are red and twenty are blue. We choose twenty marbles from the urn and find that fourteen of these are blue and six are red. In this case our sample contains 70 percent blue marbles and 30 percent red ones, whereas it is actually the case that 60 percent of the marbles in the urn are red and 40 percent are blue. In other words, our sample is not representative of the distribution of red and blue marbles in the urn.

There are two things to note about this case: First, we do *not* have a case of insufficient evidence; on the contrary, our sample consisted of 40 percent of all the marbles and it is reasonable to suppose that this is a sufficiently large sample, especially if we know that the marbles have been well mixed in the urn. Second, if we didn't know that the sample was unrepresentative, after we had ensured that the marbles had been well mixed in the urn, then it would

---

[4] This feature is discussed in more detail in the next chapter.

be reasonable to accept the conclusion of argument 26. In other words, if there are no grounds that we are aware of which make the conclusion of an inductive argument more likely false than true, then it is reasonable to accept the conclusion of the argument. In the case of argument 25 we shall end up accepting something which is false. We know, however, that in all inductive arguments the conclusion *might* be false; the best we can do is take all reasonable precautions to ensure that we get a large enough sample and that the sample is representative of the whole class. In argument 26 we have done this.

It is important to realize that in argument 26 our sample was *typically* large enough to justify the induction to all the marbles in the urn; we would not typically expect an error as large as 30 percent when we have sampled 40 percent of the class in question. In most cases of the kind described in argument 26, a sample of 40 percent of a well-mixed collection of marbles would approximate very closely the color distribution of all the marbles. Argument 26, then, is a case in which we do end up with an unrepresentative sample, but not on the basis of our sample's being too small or our not making an effort to get a representative sample.

In contrast to argument 26, consider the following case: Suppose there are two urns, each containing 100 marbles. In urn A there are marbles of eight different colors, whereas in urn B there are marbles of only two colors. We mix up the marbles in each urn and then draw ten marbles from each. Our results are:

Urn A	Urn B
3 red	6 red
3 blue	4 blue
2 yellow	
1 orange	
1 green	

It is more likely that our sample of six red and four blue marbles from urn B closely approximates the distribution of all the marbles in urn B than it is that our sample from urn A represents the distribution of all the marbles in urn A. Indeed, our sample from urn A consists of marbles of only five colors, whereas we know that there are marbles of eight colors in the urn. If we were to draw inferences about all the marbles in urn A on the basis of our sample, our results would be:

30 percent of all the marbles are red.

30 percent of all the marbles are blue.

20 percent of all the marbles are yellow.

10 percent of all the marbles are orange.

10 percent of all the marbles are green.

We know, of course, that at least one of these conclusions must be false because there is no mention of the other three colors. Since there is no mention of the other three colors, we have here an obvious case of an unrepresentative sample; as a result, we would not be justified in accepting the conclusion.

If, then, we wanted to determine the distribution of all the marbles in urn A, we would have to take a larger sample than we did. Cases like these are not difficult to find. For example, in a primary election in which four candidates are running, as opposed to, say, two candidates, one would need to poll more voters to determine which candidate is likely to be the winner; one would need to poll even more in a race in which the top seven candidates out of a slate of twelve were to be elected to the city council; and so on. In general, then, *the more diverse the members of the sampled class, the larger the sample has to be to ensure that it is representative.*

In the case just discussed we have focused on the fact that we sometimes have an unrepresentative sample because the sample is not large enough for the range of possible responses. Other instances of unrepresentative sample often occur when the methods used to gather the information bias the results in one way or another. For example, suppose a television station decides to conduct a poll to determine the attitudes of local residents toward legalizing prostitution, and this poll is conducted on the street with a television camera; the fact that the respondents may be on television will obviously affect what they say. In a similar way, phone-in polls conducted by television and radio stations often produce unrepresentative samples because those who choose to call in are often just those who have very strong feelings on *one* side of the issue.

What all this points to is the need to ensure as fair a sample as possible when conducting polls or surveys. Depending on the issue in question, one should strive to elicit responses from groups of people as diverse as possible, in such a way that the number of people in each group is proportional to their number in the overall population from which the sample is taken.

Perhaps the best way of seeing what constitutes a fair sample is to realize that if we *knew*, for a particular survey, that the sample was fair and then added this as a premise in our argument, the resultant argument would be *valid* instead of inductive. It would be valid because if the sample accurately reflects the class as a whole, then what is true of the sample would also be true of the class.

In this section we have noted that it is possible to have an unrepresentative sample even when the size of the sample is sufficiently large to support the induction; that if the members of a class are very diverse, it may be necessary to increase the size of the sample to ensure that the sample is representative of the whole class; and that the method one uses to collect data from the sample can often result in the sample's not being representative.

8:4.3 Suppressed Evidence

In this section we shall examine a set of circumstances which leads to the unacceptability of the conclusion of any given inductive argument. To see what these circumstances are, consider the following situation: Suppose that Farmer Brown is going to be visited by the state chicken inspector for the purpose of grading Farmer Brown's chickens for possible government purchase. Brown knows that well over half his 1000 chickens are grade B and, if the chicken inspector finds out, he will not be able to sell his chickens to the government. Having dealt with the chicken inspector before, and knowing that she usually examines only the chickens from hen house 1, Brown does the following: He gathers up all his grade A chickens, 180 in number, and puts them in hen house 1 along with 20 of his grade B chickens. When the inspector arrives, Brown "steers" her toward hen house 1. At the conclusion of the inspection, Brown presents the following argument to the inspector:

ARGUMENT 27

90 percent of the chickens you have examined have been grade A. Hence, 90 percent of all my chickens are grade A.

The chicken inspector agrees with this, and, having duped the inspector, Brown gets yet another year's contract to supply chickens to the government.

Three essential features of this case make it a case of **suppressed evidence.** First of all, not only is there *general* information available which would lead to the rejection of the conclusion to argument 27, there is also *particular* information of this kind; namely, that the inspector has examined an unrepresentative sample of Brown's chickens. Second, Brown, who has placed the best chickens in hen house 1, is aware of this fact (which is why he did what he did). Finally, Brown knows that if he were to tell the chicken inspector that the sample examined was not representative of all the chickens, the inspector would not agree that 90 percent of all Brown's chickens are grade A. As a result, Brown withholds the information about the unrepresentative sample. These three features are given in general terms below:

※CONDITIONS FOR SUPPRESSED EVIDENCE

(1) There is particular information which, if made known, would change the conclusion of the argument.

(2) The person presenting the argument is aware of the information in (1) and knows that the information would change the conclusion of the argument.

(3) As a result of (1) and (2), the person presenting the argument withholds the information.

It is important to realize that if any of the above three conditions is not met, then there is no case of suppressed evidence. For example, in argument 26 we had an unrepresentative sample, but this was *not* a case of suppressed evidence on the part of the speaker for he or she was not aware of the information. Another kind of case which is not a case of suppressed evidence is that in which condition (1) is satisfied, the person presenting the argument is aware of the information, but the arguer *does not realize that the information would change the conclusions of the argument.* Even if he or she fails to mention the information in the argument, we do not have a case of suppressed evidence.

The one salient feature about all cases of suppressed evidence is that there is an element of *deceit* on the part of the speaker, to get someone to accept the conclusion to an argument. In the evaluation of inductive arguments, as soon as you notice this element of deceit, you should ask yourself, "Are the three conditions for suppressed evidence present here?" If so, the argument should be rejected.

Instances of suppressed evidence are not so much a logical constraint on the acceptability of arguments as a moral constraint. That is, since one of the purposes in offering arguments is to extend our knowledge by finding out what is *true*, one who knowingly misrepresents the facts in a case sabotages this effort.

EXERCISE 8-2

1. What is the difference between '70 percent of observed F are G, so probably 70 percent of all F are G' and '70 percent of observed F are G, so 70 percent of all F are probably G'?

2. Explain the fourth condition of deductive and inductive arguments. Give two example arguments, one valid and one inductive, which illustrate these conditions.

3. Explain the notion of insufficient evidence. Give an example of an inductive argument which would not be acceptable because of insufficient evidence. What steps can one take to avoid this problem?

4. Explain the notion of an unrepresentative sample. Give an inductive argument which would not be acceptable because of this problem.

5. What are the conditions under which one is guilty of suppressed evidence? Construct an example in which one would be guilty of suppressing evidence, and explain the example.

6. Evaluate each of the arguments in problem 5 of Exercise 8:1. State whether or not the argument is acceptable, and identify any errors in the argument.

7. Construct the argument which is implicit in the following dialogue, and evaluate it:

   A: I just found out that only 12 percent of the people who apply to law school are accepted.

   B: Aren't you going to apply to law school?

   C: Yes.

   B: I guess you won't be accepted.

8. Suppose that A knows that C received a 750 on the LSAT and that 95 percent of the people who receive 750 or better on the LSAT are accepted into law school. Construct the argument which is implicit in the following dialogue, and evaluate it:

A: I just found out that only 12 percent of the people who apply to law school are accepted.

B: Isn't C going to apply to law school?

A: Yes.

B: I guess he won't be accepted then.

A: Right.

9. Suppose that B knows that C received a 750 on the LSAT and that 95 percent of the people who receive 750 or better on the LSAT are accepted into law school. Suppose further that B knows that 70 percent of the applicants to law school from C's college are accepted. Construct the argument which is implicit in the following dialogue, and evaluate it:

A: I just found out that only 12 percent of the people who apply to law school are accepted.

B: Yes, but 70 percent of the people who apply from our college are accepted.

A: C is applying to law school, isn't he?

B: Yes.

A: I guess he'll be accepted then.

B: Right.

10. Suppose the situation is the same as described in problem 9, and consider the following dialogue:

A: I just found out that only 12 percent of the people who apply to law school are accepted.

B: Yes, but 70 percent of the people who apply from our college are accepted, so since C applied he will be accepted.

A: It doesn't matter that he's from our college, since only 12 percent of the people who apply are accepted; that's sufficient evidence for the claim that C will not be accepted.

B: But he also got a 750 on the LSAT, and almost everyone who scores that high is accepted.

A: That doesn't matter either; the following is a perfectly good inductive argument, so C will not be accepted:

> 12 percent of all those who apply to law school are accepted. C applied to law school.
> Therefore, C will not be accepted.

B: Well, it can't be a good inductive argument since its conclusion is probably false; you're getting carried away with all that stuff they teach you in your intro logic course.

What is wrong with A's position in the above dialogue? What should B tell him about the acceptability of the argument proposed by A, and what might B offer as an argument for the alternative position? How would you respond to B's last remark about the argument not being any good because the conclusion is probably false?

11. Identify the form of each of the following arguments. Then, in each case, explain whether and why the additional information given would or would not change the acceptability of the argument. Treat each item of information separately.

a. 73 percent of the students surveyed indicated that they liked the food served at the Student Union.
∴ 73 percent of all students like the food served at the Student Union.

    (1) The survey was conducted throughout the day at the Student Union.
    (2) The survey was conducted at breakfast time at the Student Union.
    (3) The survey was the result of a student newspaper poll in which respondents were asked to return the questionnaire by campus mail.
    (4) The survey was conducted by the manager at the Student Union.

b. An analysis of selected transcripts shows that 68 percent of students choose a philosophy course instead of a religion course to satisfy their distribution requirements. Since Sheila is a student, it is likely that she will take a philosophy course instead of a religion course.

    (1) Of the 10,000 transcripts, 200 were examined for the survey.
    (2) All the transcripts examined were of students whose last name begins with 'A', 'M', or 'S'.
    (3) All the transcripts examined were those of students who had just completed their sophomore year.
    (4) Sheila is a freshman.
    (5) Sheila attended parochial school from the third grade until she graduated from high school.
    (6) Sheila is a junior majoring in political science.
    (7) Sheila is a senior majoring in comparative religion.
    (8) Sheila is a junior majoring in physics.
    (9) Sheila is an atheist.
    (10) Sheila's mother teaches philosophy at a small liberal arts college.

c. A recent analysis of those who receive social security benefits shows that a little more than half of all eligible males retire before age 65. I would expect, then, that Mr. Winkleman will retire before age 65.

    (1) Winkleman is 57 and just suffered a massive heart attack.
    (2) Winkleman is 59 and is the sole owner of a small, family-run shoe store.
    (3) Winkleman is 63 and is self-employed as a consultant to organizations that are setting up new retirement programs for their employees.
    (4) Winkleman, who is now 62, was just appointed president of the company he works for.
    (5) Winkleman is 48 and finds his job to be the most enjoyable part of his life.
    (6) Winkleman is 48 and hates his job.
    (7) Winkleman is 61 and hates his job.

8:5 ARGUMENT FROM AUTHORITY

We have all, at one time or another, been in the position of asking "But why should I believe that?" or "How do you know that?" and have been given responses like "Because so-and-so said so." For example, I might ask, "Why should I believe that it is going to snow tomorrow?" and receive the response, "Because Joanne Weatherby said so."

Whereas there are often good reasons for not accepting a statement as true simply because someone tells us that it is true, there are also cases in which we are justified in accepting statements as true because someone asserts the statement. In this section we shall discuss when such statements should be accepted and when they should not.

8:5.1 The Form of the Argument As an initial step in developing the **argument from authority,** let's consider the argument implicit in the short dialogue mentioned above:

ARGUMENT 28

Joanne Weatherby said that it's going to snow tomorrow.

Therefore, it's going to snow tomorrow.

Symbolizing the statement 'It's going to snow tomorrow' with 'P', we obtain the following as the form of argument 28:

FORM OF ARGUMENT 28

Joanne Weatherby said that P

$\therefore P$

We can further symbolize the argument by using 'j' to indicate 'Joanne'. This gives us

j said that P

$\therefore P$

The first thing to notice about this very general form of argument 28 is that basically it claims that what is asserted in the conclusion is the case on the grounds that someone—Joanne—asserted the conclusion. The second thing to notice, and of utmost importance, is that someone's asserting some statement is not, in and of itself, a good reason for accepting that the statement is true.

If, then, it is ever reasonable to accept the conclusion of an argument because someone asserted it, we must find some grounds, in addition to the conclusion's being claimed to be true, to justify our acceptance of the conclusion. What might these grounds be? You know from our earlier discussion that in an acceptable argument the conclusion must be related to the premises. Since the only premise we have in the argument under discussion is that Joanne said that it is going to snow, we can begin by asking what relationship holds between *Joanne's* saying that it is going to snow and the truth of the statement that it is going to snow. More generally, we can begin by considering the issue of which conditions, if any, justify us in accepting a statement as true on the grounds that someone asserted the statement?

For example, in argument 28 we were given as evidence for the claim that it is going to snow tomorrow that Joanne Weatherby said so; an obvious question to ask is, "Who is Joanne Weatherby?" Suppose that Joanne is one of the reporters from Channel 3 News. With this information, we can make argument 28 more explicit as follows:

> Joanne Weatherby, a reporter from Channel 3 News, said that it's going to snow tomorrow.
>
> Therefore, it's going to snow tomorrow.

If this expansion of the argument makes the conclusion more acceptable, given the premises, than in the original argument, it does so because Joanne's being a reporter for Channel 3 News is relevant to the truth of the conclusion. There are several reasons why this could be so, but her being a reporter is not, in and of itself, sufficiently good reason to accept that it is going to snow tomorrow; lots of people in lots of professions make predictions about the weather, and lots of times they are wrong.

What is needed, then, is some additional information which shows that Joanne's saying that it is going to snow is good evidence that it will snow. Let's suppose, then, that Joanne happens to be the weather forecaster on Channel 3 and that she said during the eleven o'clock news broadcast that it was going to snow. With this information, we can once again expand the original argument:

> Joanne Weatherby, the weather forecaster on Channel 3 News, said on the 11 o'clock broadcast that it's going to snow tomorrow.
>
> Therefore, it's going to snow tomorrow.

This expansion is much stronger than the original argument since Joanne's being the weather forecaster is relevant to the truth of the statement that it is going to snow tomorrow. It is relevant, of course, because weather forecasters are people who are trained to forecast the weather—they are the authorities on just such phenomena.

With this in mind, we can now generalize the last formulation of our argument in the following way:

> Joanne Weatherby, an authority on weather, said that it's going to snow tomorrow.
>
> Therefore, it's going to snow tomorrow.

Using 'j' to represent 'Joanne', 'S' to indicate the subject upon which she is an authority, and 'P' to represent the claim that it is going to snow tomorrow, we get the following general form of the above argument:

> j, an authority on S, said that P
>
> $\therefore P$

What is not yet explicit in the above general form is the fact that the statement Joanne made is also one upon which she is an authority; that is, 'P' is a statement within the subject area about which Joanne is an authority. Making this explicit, we have:

j, an authority on *S*, said that *P*

P is a statement about *S*

∴ *P*

This formulation provides us with an argument form which is such that if the premises are true then the conclusion is probably true. The conclusion need not be true, of course, since even authorities make false statements about the field in which they are authorities.

To round out our argument form, building on the material developed in earlier sections, we should consider what it is for someone to be an authority on a given subject. Many things are relevant to one's being an authority—for example, having received training or education in the subject in question, being a member of trade or professional societies, writing books or articles on the subject or doing creative work which receives favorable acceptance from others in the field, or being a recognized spokesperson for others in the profession.

One thing related to all the above is the fact that authorities are not only looked to by others in their own and other fields as the people most likely to know what is true about their subject, *authorities are more often than not correct in their assertions about the field in which they are authorities.* All the training in the world, all the writing one might do in a field, all the professional societies to which one belonged would not make one an authority if most of the claims one made about the subject area were false.

The fact that authorities are more often than not correct (say things which are true) when speaking about their field can be used to expand the last formulation of the argument from authority, giving us the form of the argument from authority:

✴FORM OF THE ARGUMENT FROM AUTHORITY

Most of what *x* says about *S* is true

x says *P* (a statement about *S*)

∴ *P*

Notice that the above argument form is like that of statistical syllogism or modified induction by enumeration. Perhaps the easiest way to see that this is so is to read the second premise as " '*P*' is something that *x* said about *S*." One cannot say, without working with a particular argument, whether an instance of the argument from authority is a statistical syllogism or a modified induction by enumeration. You should try to determine why this is so, although as we look at some examples in the next section, the reason will be brought out.

8:5.2 Some Examples Consider the following argument:

ARGUMENT 29

The Director of the American Cancer Society announced in his last press conference that recent research findings make it likely that there will be a cure for many forms of cancer within the next ten years.

As always, the first thing we must do is determine the form of the argument. Letting 'x' represent 'the Director', 'S' represent 'cancer', and 'P' represent 'There will be a cure for most forms of cancer within the next ten years', we obtain the following:

x said P (a statement about S)

∴ P

Notice that the argument thus far represented does not fit the form of the argument from authority. What is missing is the crucial premise that the Director of the American Cancer Society is an authority on cancer: that more often than not what she says about cancer is true. What we must then ask is whether this information is given in argument 29. It seems reasonable to suppose that whereas the information is not explicitly given, it is implicit in that we are told the comment was made by the director. That is, we would expect her to be right more often than not when she makes statements about the subject. With this understanding, we have

FORM OF ARGUMENT 29

Most of what x says about S is true

x said P (a statement about S)

∴ P

The next thing we must do is evaluate the argument: ask whether the argument has an acceptable form, whether the premises are true, and, since it is an inductive argument, whether there are any reasons for not accepting the conclusion even if the argument has an acceptable form and all true premises.

As to the form of the argument, it is the form argument from authority, an acceptable inductive form (with the understanding that the Director of the American Cancer Society is an authority on cancer). Since the premises are true, we need only ask if anything else might be wrong with the argument. In previous sections we saw that we should concern ourselves about the size of the sample, whether it was representative, and whether there might be a case of suppressed evidence. In the argument under discussion, there is no evidence that any of the things which must be guarded against have occurred; hence, the conclusion of the argument is acceptable, given the premises.

The last thing we should do is ask ourselves whether the argument is a statistical syllogism or a modified induction by enumeration. Recall that what differentiates these two argument forms is that in a modified induction by enumeration the percentage of instances which is observed to have a particular characteristic can be equal to 100, whereas in a statistical syllogism the percentage must be less than 100 (see sections 8:2.2 and 8:2.3 if you do not recall this difference). We also noted that whenever the particular individual or thing mentioned in the argument could *not* have been one of the individuals or things in the sample class which was used to establish the percentage of instances which had the particular characteristic, the argument has to be a modified induction by enumeration.

With the above in mind, we see that argument 29 is a *modified induction by enumeration* since the statement that there will be a cure for most forms of cancer within the next ten years could not have been used to help establish that the director is an authority on cancer. Why not? Because the truth value of this statement is as yet unknown. As a result, this statement could not be used to determine the percentage of true (or false) statements the director has made about cancer.

Before moving on to the next section, let's consider another example:

ARGUMENT 30

Affirming the antecedent is a valid argument form. The reason I know that it is valid is that Amy just told me so, and she got an 'A' in logic last semester.

Having already looked at two examples of the argument from authority, we can dispense with some of the intermediate stages. We shall proceed directly to rewriting argument 30 in the form of an argument from authority, where the first premise is a result of Amy's having gotten an 'A' in logic last semester:

Most of what Amy says about logic is true.

Amy says that affirming the antecedent is a valid argument form.

∴ Affirming the antecedent is a valid argument form.

Letting 'x' represent 'Amy', 'S' represent 'logic', and 'P' represent the statement that affirming the antecedent is a valid argument form, we obtain

FORM OF ARGUMENT 30

Most of what x says about S is true

x says P (a statement about S)

∴ P

There are several things to note about this argument. First, given that Amy did get an 'A' in logic, the first premise of the argument would be true, but one would ordinarily *not* take the truth of that premise as establishing that Amy is an authority in logic; most students who get 'A's' in introductory courses are not authorities on the subject taught in the course. As a result, saying that Amy is an authority on logic seems to be misleading.

It is this kind of case which makes it useful to treat arguments from authority as statistical syllogisms or modified inductions by enumeration, since what we are primarily concerned with is the likelihood of the conclusion's being true. The most relevant information here is how often 'x' has been right about things like 'P' in the past. This brings us to our second point: Granting that Amy is not an authority on logic in the standard sense of being an authority in some field, we should be especially careful about the relationship between the kinds of statements she has made about logic in the past and her statement that affirming the antecedent is a valid argument form (and so too for any other instance of the argument from authority, where x is not an authority on S in the standard sense).

In argument 30 there is a very good relationship between the evidence presented in the premises and the claim asserted in the conclusion; knowing or not knowing whether affirming the antecedent is valid is one of the (many) things one would expect of a student who had gotten an 'A' in logic. As a result, the premises provide good support for the conclusion of the argument.

On the other hand, suppose Amy had made some statement about logic which was not supported by her experience in the course she took; then there would be much less reason, and perhaps none at all, to accept the statement on the basis that most of what she had so far said about logic had been true. An authority in a given field knows more about the field than most other people and is, as well, more likely to be right about more advanced or tentative claims made in the field; we shall return to this point in the next section.

The third thing to note about argument 30 is that it, unlike the previous arguments, is a *statistical syllogism* and not a modified induction by enumeration. Before reading on, you should attempt to determine why this is so. Argument 30 is a statistical syllogism since the statement that affirming the antecedent is a valid argument form is included among those statements which Amy should have affirmed or denied in the process of getting an 'A' in the logic course. Perhaps the easiest way to see this is to suppose that Amy responded correctly to true-false questions 93 percent of the time, among which was included the statement that affirming the antecedent is a valid argument form.

This completes our discussion of the form argument from authority. In the next section we shall look at some circumstances under which one should *not* accept the conclusion on the basis of the evidence presented in the premises of such arguments.

8:5.3 Some Things to Guard Against   The purpose of this section is to point out some typical kinds of things which, if they occur, provide reasonable grounds for not accepting the conclusion of an argument from authority, given the evidence presented in the premises. We shall look at three cases; in two of them, putting the argument into the form argument from authority leads to one of the premises being false, and, in the other, even when the premises are true, we are not justified in accepting the conclusion. First, though, a general word of caution is in order. We have already noted that there are clear cases in which it is appropriate to appeal to a legitimate authority. However, even appeals to legitimate authority are often inadequately grounded, so we must be particularly careful when assessing such arguments. Since one of the benefits of studying logic is that it frees us from undue dependence on what others say, it is often better, where possible, to present direct arguments in support of a conclusion than to rely on an indirect appeal to what someone else says.

The first instance we shall look at is that of *misquoting or misrepresenting an authority.* To see what is involved here, consider the following case:

> Suppose that at a press conference prior to the Rose Bowl the Commissioner of the Big Ten remarks, "This is the best Big Ten football team ever to play in the Rose Bowl." In reporting on the press conference, a sportswriter from the hometown newspaper of the Big Ten representative writes the following:
>
> > At long last the Big Ten is going to bring home the Rose Bowl Trophy. Just this morning the Commissioner predicted that the Big Ten would win.

Implicit in the reporter's story is the following argument:

ARGUMENT 31

Most of what the Commissioner says about Big Ten football is true.

The Commissioner says that the Big Ten team will win the Rose Bowl.

∴ The Big Ten team will win the Rose Bowl.

It's clear enough that argument 32 has the form of an argument from authority. The problem with the argument, however, is that the sportswriter has *misrepresented* what the commissioner said: The Commissioner said that the Big Ten team was the best ever to play in the Rose Bowl, *not* that it would win—and, of course, these are two different statements. There are many cases in which the best team in a particular conference loses to a team from another conference.

In our analysis of the argument it should be noted that the premises, if true, *would* provide support for the conclusion. The second premise, however, is not true, and as a result we should reject the conclusion on the basis of the evidence presented in the premises. *Further, in any instance in which an authority has been misquoted or misrepresented, the premise concerning what the authority said will be false.*

Since arguments from authority are special instances of statistical syllogisms or modified inductions by enumeration, it should be clear that such arguments are subject to instances of insufficient statistics, unrepresentative sample, and suppressed evidence. It is well worth asking whether the present argument is a case of suppressed evidence. In argument 32 we do have an instance of evidence which would change the conclusion, namely, that the commissioner did not say what the sportswriter alleges he said. The issue, then, is whether or not the sportswriter withheld this evidence and misrepresented the commissioner intentionally so that readers would accept the statement that the Big Ten team would win. If so, we have a case of suppressed evidence; if not, we have just a sloppy reporter, one who does not know the difference between being best in a conference and winning a nonconference game.

When analyzing arguments from authority, it is always a good idea to keep in mind the problem of suppressed evidence, for one of the ways to commit this error is to misrepresent or misquote someone else.

We have already looked at some of the characteristics of one's being an authority in some field or subject. It often happens, however, that someone who is *an authority in one field will make statements which are outside her or his field of expertise.* When this is done, we also have a case in which the conclusion of the argument advanced should not be accepted on the basis of the evidence presented. As an example of this, consider the following case:

> When the referendum in Michigan to ban throw-away bottles and cans was on the ballot, spokespeople for the beverage industry (among the chief opponents of the ban) argued against the referendum on the grounds that it would result neither in saving large amounts of energy nor in contributing to a cleaner environment.

Implicit in this campaign against the referendum was the following argument:

ARGUMENT 32

Spokespeople for the beverage industry say that banning throw-away bottles and cans will not result in saving large amounts of energy or result in a cleaner environment.

∴ Banning throw-away bottles will not result in saving large amounts of energy or result in a cleaner environment.

If this is the only argument advanced, then the only grounds for accepting the conclusion on the basis of the premise must be that some group has said that the conclusion is true; in other words, if the argument is any good, it is so because it is an argument from authority. Making this point explicit, we have the following:

> Most of what the spokespeople for the beverage industry say about energy and the environment is true.

> The spokespeople say that banning throw-away bottles and cans will not result in saving large amounts of energy or result in a cleaner environment.

∴ Banning throw-away bottles and cans will not result in saving large amounts of energy or result in a cleaner environment.

Once argument 32 is presented in this way, it is clear that the conclusion should not be accepted on the basis of the evidence presented in the premises, since the first premise is false. It may well be the case that the spokespeople for the beverage industry are authorities in many fields—for example, in efficient manufacturing, advertising, and industrial economics. It does not follow from this, however, that they are authorities in other fields and, in particular, it does not follow that they are authorities on energy and environmental matters.

In instances of this kind, it is important to ask, before accepting some assertion on the grounds that it was affirmed by an authority, whether what is affirmed falls within the authority's field of expertise. By putting such assertions (particularly the first premise) into the form of an argument from authority, it is often easy to see that the authority has made a pronouncement outside his or her field.

In the above two instances we were justified in not accepting the conclusion of the arguments on the basis of the evidence presented in the premises, since at least one of the premises was false. The next kind of case is one in which the premises are true, but nonetheless the conclusion of the argument should not be accepted on the basis of those premises.

> Suppose that Bruto is on trial for allegedly killing Cero and the defense attorney calls Frodo, an authority in the field of psychology, as one of the witnesses on behalf of her client. Suppose further that Frodo testifies that Bruto is insane. In addressing the jury the defense attorney says, "Ladies and gentlemen of the jury, you have heard Frodo testify that my client is insane. Therefore, on the basis of the testimony of this noted psychologist you have no choice but to bring in a verdict of 'not guilty'."

Here the defense attorney is attempting to get her client acquitted on the grounds of insanity. Implicit here is the following argument for her client's being insane:

ARGUMENT 33

Frodo is an authority in the field of psychology.

Frodo said that Bruto is insane (a statement about psychology).

∴ Bruto is insane.

We can suppose that in this hypothetical case both premises of the argument are true. It is easy enough to imagine, however, what a prosecuting attorney would do when confronted with the above line of defense: have Bruto examined by an equally competent psychologist who (the prosecutor hopes) would come to the conclusion that Bruto is not insane.

Were this to happen, we would have a case in which *authorities in the same field disagree with each other*. In this instance the reasonable thing to do would be to *suspend judgment* on what the authorities have said. The reason for suspending judgment here is that the basis for accepting the conclusion of an argument from authority is that the authority has knowledge and training in his or her field and has been right a great many times in what he or she has said about the field. When equally competent authorities disagree, however, their respective arguments "offset" one another; neither argument is stronger than the other. This is not to say, of course, that neither authority is correct. It is rather, to say that we need more evidence before we accept the view of either authority.

The kind of evidence we would like to have should include the *reasons* each of the authorities has for his or her position, since knowing the reasons for an authority's opinion will sometimes enable us to decide which of two conflicting opinions is more likely true. For example, in the present case, the jurors would surely want to know the reasons each psychologist has for his or her view, as a way of helping to determine which is more likely correct regarding the sanity of Bruto.

Another kind of case is similar to that just discussed—the case in which two authorities are, by ordinary standards, competent, but one of them is vastly more respected than the other. Should these authorities disagree over some issue within their field of expertise, the reasonable thing to do is to accept that which is asserted by the more respected authority. Here, the premise which corresponds with one's being an authority in an argument from authority is best understood in terms of the percentage of times the authority has been right when making claims about his or her field. If the more respected authority has a deserved reputation, the probability that this authority is correct will be higher than the probability that the other authority is correct.

8:6 ARGUMENT FROM ANALOGY

In this section we shall examine one final inductive argument form, argument from analogy, consider several guides in assessing the strength of such arguments, and work through several examples.

8:6.1 The Form of the Argument The central idea behind arguments from analogy is that if two things, or two kinds of things, have certain characteristics in common, then if one of these things has an additional particular characteristic, it is likely that the other also has this additional characteristic. As an example, consider the following argument.

ARGUMENT 34

Joe and Ann both had the same six math courses, through advanced algebra, while in high school, and both got an 'A' in Professor Demetri's Calculus 120 class last year. Last semester Joe took Calc 121 from Professor Demetri and got an 'A', and this semester Ann is taking Calc 121 from Professor Demetri. It's likely that Ann will get an 'A' too.

Putting the argument into standard form and breaking it down so we can see its structure, we get the following:

Joe had six math courses in high school, through advanced algebra, and got an 'A' in Professor Demetri's Calculus 120 class last year.

Ann had six math courses in high school, through advanced algebra, and got an 'A' in Professor Demetri's Calculus 120 class last year.

Joe got an 'A' in Professor Demetri's Calc 121 class last semester.

This semester Ann is taking Calc 121 from Professor Demetri.

∴ Ann will get an 'A'.

If we use 'J' to represent 'Joe', 'A' to represent 'Ann', and 'C_1', 'C_2', and 'C_3' to represent the characteristics of taking six math courses in high school through advanced algebra, getting an 'A' in Professor Demetri's Calculus 120 class, and getting an 'A' in Professor Demetri's Calculus 121 class, respectively, we have the following as the form of argument 34:

J has characteristics C_1 and C_2

A has characteristics C_1 and C_2

J also has characteristic C_3

$\therefore A$ will have characteristic C_3

The above form represents the central idea, mentioned earlier, behind arguments from analogy: Two things have certain characteristics in common (J and A share C_1 and C_2), one of them has an additional characteristic (J had C_3), and so it is likely that the other has or will have this additional characteristic (A will have C_3). We can further generalize the form of argument from analogy by discussing not Joe and Ann, but any two objects or kinds of objects, and by leaving open the number of characteristics the objects have in common. Doing this, we obtain:

FORM OF THE ARGUMENT FROM ANALOGY

Objects of type x have characteristics C_1 to C_n

Objects of type y have characteristics C_1 to C_n

Objects of type x have characteristic C_{n+1}

$\therefore$ Objects of type y have characteristic C_{n+1}

8:6.2 Some Comments on the Argument Form   In the previous section we looked at one argument and developed from it the form of the argument from analogy. We have not yet, however, discussed the relationship which holds between the premises and the conclusion in an argument from analogy. In the argument we did examine there is a relationship between the truth of the premises and the likely truth of the conclusion, since there is a relationship between the math courses one has taken (and how well he or she has done) and one's likely performance in subsequent math courses.

But this is just one example. It would be helpful if we had a more generalized account of the relationship between the characteristics mentioned in the premises and the characteristic mentioned in the conclusion. It is to that task which we now turn.

The first general point is that *all things being equal, the more characteristics the two objects have in common, the stronger the analogy.* We can show this by comparing argument 34 with the following argument.

ARGUMENT 35

Joe and Ann both had the same six math courses, through advanced algebra, while in high school. They went to the same high school and took their math courses from the same teachers and both of them got 'A's' in all the courses. They both competed in a statewide math competition and scored in the top 1 percent of all contestants. Last year they both took Calculus 120 from Professor Demetri and got an 'A'. Last semester Joe took Calc 121 from Professor Demetri and got an 'A', and this semester Ann is taking Calc 121 from Professor Demetri. Like Joe, Ann has received an 'A' on the first two exams. It follows that Ann will probably get an 'A' too.

In argument 35 the characteristics shared by Joe and Ann have been expanded to include going to the same high school and taking the same math courses from the same teachers while there, scoring very high on a statewide math competition, and getting an 'A' in the first two exams in Calc 121. This additional information clearly makes argument 35 stronger than argument 34.

The obvious question here is whether it is always the case that the more characteristics two objects share, the stronger the analogy; the answer here is no. To see why this is so, consider the following two arguments.

ARGUMENT 36

Last month Stan bought a new Chevy van with an eight-cylinder engine and a four-speed manual transmission. The only optional equipment he purchased was an AM-FM stereo radio with a cassette player and factory air conditioning. While on trips, Stan has been getting 18 miles per gallon. On the basis of Stan's recommendation, Helen just bought a new Chevy van with the same engine and transmission as Stan's. She too bought only the radio–cassette player and air conditioning as an option. She will probably get 18 miles per gallon when she takes her van on trips.

ARGUMENT 37

Last month Audrey bought a new Chevy van, painted silver with black leather interior and gray carpeting. The van has an eight-cylinder engine and a four-speed manual transmission. Audrey also purchased air conditioning, an AM-FM stereo radio with a cassette player, a sun roof, steel-belted radial tires, a CB unit, reclining swivel seats, and the optional interior decor package. When Neal saw Audrey's van, he liked it so much that he went out and bought one exactly like it. Unfortunately, after Audrey had her van for just two weeks, she had a flat tire; so Neal will probably have a flat tire within two weeks, too.

In both argument 36 and argument 37 an analogy is drawn between two vans, first in terms of getting 18 miles per gallon while on trips and then in terms of having a flat tire. In the first argument five similar characteristics are cited, whereas in the latter thirteen are cited. Nonetheless, most of us would be inclined—correctly—to say that argument 36 is stronger than argument 37, in spite of the additional characteristics in the latter argument (indeed, argument 37 is very weak).

Argument 36 is the stronger mainly because, with the exception of the radio, the characteristics in which Stan's and Helen's vans are similar are all related to the gas mileage one might expect to get on a trip: make of the van, engine size, type of transmission, and the air conditioner. In argument 37, on the other hand, even though Audrey's and Neal's vans are similar in many respects, the similarities do not have much to do with getting or not getting a flat tire. The most relevant characteristic in this case is the type of tire on the van, steel-belted radials, and, if anything, it is likely that Neal would not get a flat with such tires. This brings us to our second point: Not only is the number of characteristics that the two objects have in common important, but *the more relevant the similar characteristics are to the characteristic mentioned in the conclusion, the stronger the analogy.*

Although we cannot give a precise account of relevance, there are two general ways in which the similar characteristics in an argument from analogy might be related to the characteristic mentioned in the conclusion, and being aware of these may aid you in determining whether some characteristic is relevant or not. The two ways in which the characteristics might be relevant are **causal relevance** and **statistical relevance.**

We shall discuss causality in more detail in the next chapter and shall here rely on our common understanding of 'cause', after using an example to show the idea of causal relevance:

ARGUMENT 38

Lenny and George each bought a jade plant at the nursery across the street from the campus. Lenny placed his plant in a spot where it received six hours of sun a day, watered it whenever the soil dried out, and fertilized it every other month. In the summer he moved the plant outside, and it bloomed. George has been taking care of his jade plant in the same way, so his plant should bloom soon too.

Here the characteristic we are concerned about in the conclusion is the jade plant's blooming. The characteristics of Lenny's jade plant include the right amount of sunshine, proper watering, fertilizing on a regular basis, and a move outside in the summer. The conclusion of the argument is that George's plant will also bloom under similar circumstances. In this case the characteristics the two plants share are *causally* related to the plants' blooming; they are the conditions which, if met, cause the plant to bloom and if not met prevent the plant from blooming.

We also had an instance of causal relevance in argument 36: the type of van, engine size, and type of transmission are all causally relevant to the mileage one gets when driving the van on a trip. Other instances of causal relevance include taking aspirin as related to relieving a headache; body size, the amount of alcohol consumed over a given time, and metabolism rate as related to getting drunk; and the amount one smokes as related to lung cancer.

As was pointed out earlier, the characteristics mentioned in an argument from analogy can also be statistically related. One example is the following:

ARGUMENT 39

Ted and his brother Lon are alike in that both grew up in a fatherless home in a poor section of a large city, both were poor students who often got into trouble in school, neither was interested in athletics or any other school activities, both started smoking pot at the age of 12, and both were arrested for auto theft at the age of 14. Ted was convicted of a felony, armed robbery, at the age of 22. It is likely, therefore, that Lon will also be convicted of a felony at an early age.

The characteristic we are focusing on here is that of being convicted of a felony at an early age. The characteristics Ted and Lon share which are offered as relevant to Lon's being convicted are the kind of environment they grew up in, their performance in school, and their record with the police while they were young. These characteristics do not *cause* one to commit felonies, but there is a good deal of evidence that people with this kind of background are more likely to commit felonies than those of a different background. In other words, there is a statistical correlation between being arrested at an early age, and so on, and committing a felony at a later age. In such cases, we say that the similar characteristics are *statistically relevant* to the characteristic mentioned in the conclusion.

Other instances of statistical relevance include one's high school grade-point average and likely success in college, one's socioeconomic position and which political party one is likely to vote for, and one's income level and the type of residence one is likely to live in. In none of these cases does the former cause the latter, though the two items in each pair are statistically correlated.

In discussing arguments from authority, we noted that whereas there are legitimate appeals to authority, we must be cautious about accepting something on the basis of such arguments, since there are also illegitimate appeals to authority. Similar remarks hold in the case of arguments from analogy. That is, although there are acceptable instances of this argument, there are also many unacceptable instances. One such case follows.[5]

ARGUMENT 40

Correctly believing that Lewis is lazy and shiftless, Peter concludes that it is probable that Calvin is also lazy and shiftless since Calvin, like Lewis, is black.

The difficulty with this argument is that Peter has incorrectly concluded that being black is relevant to being lazy and shiftless. However, Peter has no good reason to believe that these characteristics are either causally or statistically related.

Another kind of error which often occurs in arguments from analogy results when one or more of the characteristics cited in the analogy is relevant to one of the object's having the additional property, but is *not* relevant to the other object's having this property. Consider the following argument:

ARGUMENT 41

Few people would deny that parents have the obligation to protect their children from harm, to provide them with adequate food, clothing, and

---

[5] This example is also an instance of a hasty generalization. Such errors are discussed in more detail in section 10:7.

shelter and to see that they receive an education. Parents also have the obligation to keep filthy, pornographic literature away from their children. Few people would deny that the government has an obligation to protect its citizens from harm, to ensure that they have adequate food, clothing, and shelter, and to see that they receive an education. By the same reasoning, it's clear that the government has an obligation to keep filthy, pornographic literature away from its citizens.

In this case the speaker has argued that parents and governments are similar in some respects in that the former have obligations to their children and the latter to its citizens. The argument is defective, however, in its comparison of children with the citizens of a country, because the characteristic concerning pornographic literature is not relevant to the other characteristics cited about citizens, even though it may be relevant to the other characteristics as applied to children. What is overlooked in the argument is that the relationship between parents and children is very different from the relationship between a government and its citizens.

EXERCISE 8-3

1. What is the form of an argument from authority? Give an example of an acceptable argument from authority and an example of one which is not acceptable.

2. Explain the various grounds on which one should reject an argument from authority. Give an instance of each kind of case.

3. What is the form of an argument from analogy? Give an example of an argument which has this form.

4. What does it mean to say that the characteristics mentioned in an argument from analogy must be relevant to the characteristic mentioned in the conclusion? In what two ways might a characteristic be relevant? Give an example of each.

5. Put each of the following arguments into standard form, and give the name of the argument if it has one. State whether each argument is acceptable or unacceptable and, if it is unacceptable, explain why.
    a. What do you mean, am I sure that Raydac is coming out with a new tape deck? My father is in charge of production for Raydac and he told me last night that a new deck will be on the market in time for Christmas.
    b. Every time the chairperson of the English Department talks about one of his articles he makes me sick; you would think that he's the greatest critic alive. I just read a critique of his latest article, and was it ever panned.
    c. Two years ago when Central, a medium-sized state university, faced a severe budget shortage and declining enrollments, they balanced the budget by laying off fifteen faculty members and cutting back the student services budget. Now that Western is facing exactly the same situation, and since the president at Western was president at Central two years

ago, it's likely that we will lose some faculty members and that there will be a reduction in student services.

d. Advertisement: As a former running back who had to be quick on his feet, believe me when I tell you that Lyte beer is the only beer to drink.

e. There's an old saying to the effect that you reap what you sow. I simply cannot understand the president's foreign policy: On the one hand he talks about world peace, and on the other he has raised defense spending to its highest level in history. It escapes me how one can reap peace by sowing the machines of mass destruction.

f. I was really impressed by the debate on nuclear energy last night. The spokesperson from Neutronics really knew what she was talking about, but the fellow from the Environmental Protection Agency kept pushing the issue of disposing of nuclear waste. I really don't know what to think about this issue, but I'm inclined to think that the woman from Neutronics was right when she said that nuclear waste can be disposed of safely. After all, she's an expert in the field, and all the other guy really knows about are environmental issues.

g. I really wouldn't go out with Ron if I were you. He's a member of Delta house, and I went out with one of those guys last semester. My date was a real animal, and you know how it goes: Houses always attract the same kind of person.

h. A report released just recently showed that long periods of unemployment often lead to domestic violence, an increase in drinking, and tension between spouses. One of my friends was unemployed for a long time, and his marriage also ended in a divorce. My next-door neighbor has also been unemployed for a long time, and I've noticed that he's been hitting the bottle pretty heavy recently. I also noticed the other day that his wife had bruises all over her arms. She said she got them by slipping on the stairs, but I don't believe that story. Given all that's been going on, it's likely that my neighbor's marriage will end in divorce too.

i. A: The mayor decided to run for reelection next term.

   B: Where did you get that idea?

   A: The reporter who covers City Hall said so on last night's news.

   B: I watched last night's news too, and what the reporter said is that the mayor had not ruled out running for another term.

   A: Don't quibble. It all means the same thing.

j. Mayor at press conference: We don't want to raise any false hopes, but we believe that after nineteen months we have apprehended the Carnaby Killer. As you know, we have had a special task force working on this case for over a year, and the leader of that task force just reported to me that they're almost positive that the person in custody is the killer.

k. When I tell you that Lincoln wrote the Gettysburg Address while riding on a train, believe me: He wrote it on a train. With all the history courses I've taken, I ought at least to know that.

l. I don't care what all those scientists say. Cardinal Bodinski has said the

Shroud of Turin was used to wrap Jesus' body after the crucifixion. He ought to know; after all, you don't get to be a cardinal without being an authority on religion.

m. It's no wonder that so many men are up at arms about their wives wanting to get out of the house and have a career of their own. The husband-wife relationship in many homes is no different from the master-slave relationship of years gone by. The stronger enforces his will on the weaker and attempts to control how she thinks, what she does, and who she does it with. And when the slave finally can stand it no longer and seeks to escape, the master drags her back, kicking and screaming, to enforce his will upon the innocent victim. All because she wanted to be free to make her own choices and be the master of her own life.

n. Vice-president for marketing to chief executive officer: The last three product lines we introduced were all spectacular successes, and I think we can attribute this to Grant down at the Wonder Sales advertising agency. Each time he worked out a program which maximized our advertising punch by coordinating our radio, television, and print advertising, tested the advertising on a sample market, and was extremely helpful in identifying potential customers for our products. He's done all that for our newest line, and I fully expect that it will be a great success as well.

STUDENT STUDY GUIDE

Chapter Summary

1. Even though a number of important foundational or theoretical problems concerning induction remain, it is nonetheless indispensable that we accept the conclusions to some inductive arguments and realize that we are justified in doing so. One important reason is that only inductive arguments provide grounds for accepting, on the basis of the premises, new information. (section 8:1)

2. In **induction by enumeration** we draw a conclusion about all the members of a class on the basis of premises about some observed members of that class. (section 8:2.1)

3. In a **statistical syllogism** we draw a conclusion about a particular member of a class on the basis of premises which provide information about all members of that class. (section 8:2.2)

4. In a **modified induction by enumeration** we draw a conclusion about a particular member of a class on the basis of premises about some observed members of that class. Modified induction by enumeration can be understood in terms of the two argument forms induction by enumeration and statistical syllogism. (section 8:2.3)

5. The word 'probably' as it occurs in some inductive arguments refers to the relationship between the premises of an argument and the conclusion, just as

'necessarily' as it occurs in some valid arguments refers to the relationship between the premises and the conclusion. It is a mistake to include 'probably' in the conclusion itself, since different premises can confer different probabilities on one and the same conclusion. (section 8:3)

6. Although adding premises to a valid argument does not require a change in the conclusion of the argument, adding premises to an inductive argument *may* require that the conclusion be changed. That is, adding premises to a valid argument does not affect the support relation, though it sometimes affects this relation in inductive arguments. (section 8:4)

7. We have a case of **insufficient evidence** when the sample size is too small to support a generalization about all members of the class from which the sample was taken. Among the things which affect the adequacy of the sample size are considerations of how important it is that the induction be accurate and the diversity of the members in the class from which the sample was taken. (section 8:4.1)

8. We have a case of an **unrepresentative sample** when the sample, for whatever reason, turns out not to be an accurate picture of the whole class from which the sample was taken. Often unrepresentative samples occur because the sample is too small; in other cases it can occur even when the sample class is quite large. This latter situation often occurs when the methods used to gather information on the sample class bias the results in one way or another. (section 8:4.2)

9. We have a case of **suppressed evidence** when the following conditions are all satisfied: (1) There is particular information which, if made known, would change the conclusion of the argument; (2) the person presenting the argument is aware of this information and knows that the information would change the conclusion; and (3) as a result of (1) and (2), the person presenting the argument withholds the information. (section 8:4.3)

10. **Arguments from authority** are a special instance of either a statistical syllogism or a modified induction by enumeration. In such arguments it is asserted that someone has been more often right than wrong when making claims within a particular subject area and, therefore, that it is likely that the present claim is true. (section 8:5.1)

11. Not all arguments from authority are acceptable arguments. Among the things which make a given instance of this kind of argument unacceptable are the following: misquoting or misrepresenting an authority (such cases result in the argument's having a false premise); an authority in one field making statements which are outside his or her field of expertise (this also results in the argument having a false premise); and authorities in the same field disagreeing with each other. (section 8:5.3)

12. In **arguments from analogy** it is argued that because two things, or two kinds of things, have certain characteristics in common, and because one of them has an additional particular characteristic, it is likely that the other also has this characteristic. (section 8:6.1)

13. In assessing a given instance of an argument from analogy, two main points should be kept in mind: (1) All things being equal, the more characteristics the two objects have in common, the stronger is the analogy, and (2) the more

relevant the similar characteristics are to the characteristic mentioned in the conclusion, the stronger is the analogy. (section 8:6.2)

14. The two ways in which the characteristics in an argument from analogy might be relevant are via **causal relevance** and **statistical relevance.** In the former there is a causal relationship such that whenever the set of characteristics is present, the characteristic in the conclusion is also present. In the latter there is a high correlation between the presence of the set of characteristics and the characteristic mentioned in the conclusion. (section 8:6.2)

Key Terms

Induction by Enumeration	Suppressed Evidence
Statistical Syllogism	Argument from Authority
Modified Induction by Enumeration	Argument from Analogy
Insufficient Evidence	Causal Relevance
Unrepresentative Sample	Statistical Relevance

Self-Test/Exercise

1. Explain the relationship that modified induction by enumeration has to induction by enumeration and statistical syllogism. (section 8:2.3)

2. Explain why a below is an acceptable inductive argument whereas b is not. (section 8:3.1)
   a. 70 percent of observed F are G b. 70 percent of observed F are G
   ∴ 70 percent of all F are G ∴ 70 percent of all F are probably G

3. Give the fourth characteristic of inductive arguments, and explain its relationship to insufficient evidence and unrepresentative sample.(section 8:4)

4. What are the conditions under which one is guilty of suppressed evidence? (section 8:4.3)

5. Explain the various grounds on which one should reject an argument from authority, and give an instance of each kind of case. (section 8:5.3)

6. Put each of the following arguments into standard form. Then give the form of the argument and the name of the form, if it has a name. State whether each argument is acceptable or unacceptable and, if it is unacceptable, explain why. (sections 8:2, 8:5, and 8:6)
   a. A recent survey taken in Miami, Florida, showed that the average age of the people who live there is 57.6 years. I conclude, therefore, that the average age of all people living in Florida is more than 57 years.
   b. The President of Sonic Boom, a large aircraft manufacturing company, recently announced that the company is going to begin production on a new fighter plane. Whenever they have begun production of a new plane in the past, it has been as a result of a soon-to-be-announced increase in spending by the Department of Defense. I expect that we will soon hear that defense spending is going to be increased.
   c. Trish Abramson recently told reporters that there has been a significant rise in the number of complaints her office has received about unscrupulous

contractors. Since she heads the local Better Business Bureau, I guess more unscrupulous contractors are in business now than in the past.

d. I have noticed that whenever I keep current with reading assignments and study well before an exam, I do well on the exam. I have every reason to believe, then, that I will do well on this afternoon's chemistry exam since I have kept up and have studied well for the exam.

e. Advertisement: I'm Monster Mulligan, defensive tackle for the Hornets. It gets really hot on that playing field, let me tell you that. But I've got my protection, and I don't mean a helmet and pads. I mean Pit Stop deodorant. Take it from one who knows, nothing stops pits like Pit Stop deodorant. Try some today.

f. Many people find it surprising that many small colleges are currently facing grave financial difficulties, and some are even closing. I don't find this surprising, however. After all, a college is just like any other business, and small businesses always have trouble competing with the large ones. Like any business, colleges are trying to sell a commodity, only it's packaged in courses instead of boxes. When the cost of making the commodity goes up, so does the selling price; and when the price gets too high, people just don't buy what is being offered. And, as anyone who has studied even a little bit about manufacturing knows, the fewer items manufactured, the higher the cost for each individual item. Small colleges have small courses, so each one costs more than at larger schools. It should be clear, then, that small colleges will soon be a thing of the past, just like cottage industries have become.

g. I recently read that Skip Hullston is entering a new boat in the Hattaras-to-Newport Race. Since he's won this race each of the three times he's competed, it's likely that he will win this year's race as well. Of course, the new boat might make a difference, but it was designed by C. Gull, and, as every fan of sailboat racing knows, Gull is one of the very best designers in the business.

h. Athletic director to media: I don't understand all the fuss about our hiring of Dudorf as head football coach. We have a strong tradition of winning at Pater Nostre and, as you all know, this tradition has been earned by consistently beating the very best teams from some of the largest universities in the country. Coach Dudorf has shown that he is a winner with his .908 career average. The fact that he has only coached at high schools is beside the point. A winner is a winner, and we fully expect his career here to be every bit as good as it has already been.

i. It's easy to understand why Toland is down in the dumps. He just totaled his car and is going to have to buy a new one. Whenever anyone loses a close friend, someone who has gone places with him, been reliable, and been part of a great many happy experiences, he's naturally sad. That's the way it is with Toland; he has just lost a good friend, and he's very sad about that.

j. Recent statistics have shown that the average wage of female employees is only 60 percent that of male employees. Moreover, many of these female employees are also single parents who must spend a significant portion of their income on child care—an expense which makes the gap in real income even larger. Since my next-door neighbor to the east, Brenda, is a single parent, and my next-door neighbor to the west, Bob, is a bachelor, it should be obvious that Brenda is making significantly less real income than Bob. At the very best, she's making only 60 percent of what he makes, and she has additional expenses that he doesn't have.

CHAPTER 9

HYPOTHESES AND

MILL'S METHODS

In this chapter we shall extend the discussion of inductive arguments begun in Chapter 8. The early sections of the chapter are devoted to a discussion of hypotheses and their relationship to inductive arguments, as well as to a discussion of the hypothetico-deductive method for confirming hypotheses. In later sections of the chapter we shall extend the discussion of causal and statistical relevance from the preceding chapter and examine five methods, known as Mill's methods, which are useful in establishing causal and statistical relationships.

9:1 INDUCTIVE ARGUMENTS AND HYPOTHESES

In the previous chapter we examined a variety of inductive argument forms and some of the conditions under which these argument forms are or are not acceptable. One of these forms, induction by enumeration, is often used to support statements of the form 'All A are B'. As you know, such statements can be understood as conditional statements of the form '$(x)(Ax \supset Bx)$', read as 'For any x, if x is A then x is B'. For the time being, let's say that such statements are **hypotheses;** we shall say more about hypotheses below.

One of the features of hypotheses is that they enable us to make *predictions*. In the statement form just discussed, we are able to make predictions about instances of A which we have *not yet observed*, predictions that these individuals will also be B. Such predictions are **observational predictions,** and they are such that if the hypothesis upon which the prediction is based is true, then what is asserted in the prediction is also true.

The following is an instance of the kind of case we have been discussing:

EXAMPLE 1

Suppose that Sharon has visited eight different zoos and has noticed that all the tigers are yellow and have black stripes.

On the basis of this observation, Sharon formulates the following argument:

All of the tigers thus far observed have been yellow and have had black stripes.

∴ All tigers are yellow and have black stripes.

The conclusion of this argument is a hypothesis which enables Sharon to make predictions about other tigers which she has not yet observed. Suppose she has never been to the Bronx Zoo, but is going to visit it the following week. On the basis of her hypothesis, she formulates the following argument:

All tigers are yellow and have black stripes.

∴ The tigers at the Bronx Zoo are yellow and have black stripes.

The conclusion of this argument is an observational prediction. If Sharon goes to the zoo and finds out that the tigers are yellow and have black stripes, then she has a **confirming instance** of her hypothesis. On the other hand, if she finds there is a tiger which is not both yellow and has black stripes, she has a **disconfirming instance** of her hypothesis. Notice that the confirming instance does *not* conclusively establish the truth of the hypothesis, even though it does provide support for it. Also notice that a disconfirming instance *does* conclusively establish that the hypothesis is false.

The support provided by the confirming instance is *inductive* support. Perhaps the easiest way to see this is to realize that prior to her visit to the Bronx Zoo, Sharon had eight instances which she used as the basis for the induction by enumeration argument that she gave in support of the hypothesis. Having visited the Bronx Zoo, she now has nine instances to use as the basis of the hypothesis. This additional instance does not, however, conclusively confirm the hypothesis any more than did the original eight instances.

A little reflection on the above will show that whereas the observational prediction was *deductively* derived from the hypothesis, the prediction's being true provides *inductive* support for the hypothesis. As a result, when testing hypotheses we use deduction to make observational predictions; but if a prediction is true, it provides inductive support for the hypothesis. If the prediction is false, it shows that the hypothesis is false because a valid argument with a false conclusion must have at least one false premise. In the case under discussion there is only one premise, the hypothesis, so the hypothesis must be false. In section 9:2 we shall examine arguments having more than one premise and see what we can and cannot conclude about the truth value of the hypothesis on the basis of an observational prediction's being false.

If we simplify the above case into its barest essentials, we see that the argument has the following structure:

SCHEMA 1

Hypothesis

∴ Observational prediction

In section 9:2 we shall fill out this schema in more detail, showing the other things which must be considered, besides the hypothesis itself, to derive an observational prediction.

Note that, in example 1, the hypothesis was formulated on the basis of prior *observational* evidence. In many cases, however, a hypothesis is not formulated on this basis. It may, for example, be formulated on the basis of other hypotheses which have already been accepted, or it may be an "educated guess" based upon what an experimenter already knows. There are no rules or guidelines for forming hypotheses; indeed, this is one area of the sciences where creativity plays a prominent role. In the discussion which follows, we shall not be concerned with how hypotheses come to be formulated. Instead, we shall focus on the way in which hypotheses are confirmed or disconfirmed once they have been formulated.

9:1.1 The Meaning of 'Hypothesis'   In the previous section we saw that some statements of the form 'All *A* are *B*' are called *hypotheses*. In the sciences, hypotheses are often distinguished from laws and theories. The distinctions will not concern us here, and we shall adopt the position that laws and theories are also hypotheses. In this regard, Newton's laws of motion and the special theory of relativity would be hypotheses. In general, we can say that a **hypothesis** is a statement which is offered as the explanation of certain phenomena, or a statement which is offered as the basis for further investigation of certain phenomena. More important, a hypothesis is any statement from which we can derive observational predictions.

Thus far, the only instance of hypotheses which we have examined has been a universal generalization—that is, a statement of the form 'All *A* are *B*'. Some hypotheses, however, are *statistical* generalizations, statements of the form '*Y* percent of *A* are *B*'. One such example is the statement '71 percent of the students who enroll at Midwestern University eventually receive a degree'. Although statistical generalizations can also be used to make observational predictions, we shall focus our discussion on hypotheses which are universal generalizations. One of the important differences between these two kinds of statements is that whereas universal generalizations enable us to *validly* deduce observational predictions, statistical generalizations enable us only to *inductively* infer observational predictions.

9:2 THE HYPOTHETICO-DEDUCTIVE METHOD

In this section we shall examine a method which is used in the sciences to confirm or disconfirm hypotheses. This method, the **hypothetico-deductive method,** is the one we discussed somewhat informally in section 9:1. The essential structure of the method is this: Observational predictions are first validly deduced from a hypothesis. These predictions are then tested; if the predictions are correct, the hypothesis is inductively confirmed, and if the predictions are incorrect, the hypothesis is disconfirmed. We shall fill out this outline of the method in the remainder of this section.

9:2.1 Initial Conditions   In schema 1 an observational prediction is deduced from a hypothesis. Although this is a part of the hypothetico-deductive method, schema 1 does not sufficiently characterize everything which must be considered in making an observational prediction. To see why this is so, consider the hypothesis that the time required for an object dropped from any height to reach the ground is equal to the square root of twice the height from the ground divided by the acceleration due to gravity. Symbolically we have

$$t = \sqrt{\frac{2h}{g}}$$

To make observational predictions, we must be able to measure the height from the ground of a particular object, as well as the amount of time it takes this object to reach the ground (this assumes that we know the acceleration due to gravity). We could test this hypothesis by dropping objects from some known height and then measuring the time that it took for these objects to reach the ground. For each of the experiments, the height of the object is an **initial condition.** More generally, initial conditions specify the circumstances under which a hypothesis is being tested. In deriving our observational predictions, these initial conditions are given as premises in the argument from which we deduce these predictions.

With this in mind, we can expand schema 1 in the following way:

SCHEMA 2

Hypothesis

Initial conditions

∴ Observational prediction

In schema 2 we begin with a hypothesis that we wish to test and then specify the conditions under which the hypothesis is being tested. Based on these two things, we make an observational prediction of what we expect to occur. If the prediction is correct, then we have a confirming instance of the hypothesis.

Suppose, however, that the observational prediction is incorrect. Since this prediction was validly deduced from the premises in schema 2, and since the prediction is false, it follows that at least one of the premises in schema 2 is false. In schema 1, when the prediction is false we can conclude that the hypothesis is false, since it is the only premise in the argument. In schema 2, in contrast, the best we can say is that *either* the hypothesis is false *or* the statement of initial conditions is false. We cannot reject the hypothesis on the basis of the observational prediction unless we can show that the statement of initial conditions is true.

9:2.2 Auxiliary Hypotheses   In the example discussed in the preceding section, one of our simplifying assumptions was that we already know the acceleration of gravity when we test our hypothesis. That the acceleration of gravity is a fixed, known value is an **auxiliary hypothesis.** More generally, an auxiliary hypothesis is one whose truth has been independently established, typically by an inductive argument of the form of schema 2, and which is used in deducing observational predictions for testing other hypotheses. With this consideration we can expand schema 2 in the following way:

SCHEMA 3

Hypothesis

Initial conditions

Auxiliary hypotheses

∴ Observational prediction

It may have occurred to you that insofar as auxiliary hypotheses are themselves hypotheses, some of them are confirmed in the way shown in schema 2, and others in the way shown in schema 3. Moreover, it begins to look like no one hypothesis is independent of any other since, eventually, each is relied on as an auxiliary hypothesis to establish other hypotheses. For this reason some philosophers of science have characterized hypotheses as being individual parts of a whole "net," where each of them supports other hypotheses and is, in turn, supported by these other hypotheses. This accounts in large measure for the fact that when new hypotheses are advanced which are counter to previously accepted hypotheses that are part of the net, these new hypotheses are not given very much consideration. This is our topic in the next section.

9:2.3 Prior Probabilites   Considerations raised in the previous section naturally lead to the issue of how seriously any particular hypothesis should be considered, given everything that we know. To address this issue we shall here consider the notion of **prior probability.** In general, the prior probability of a given hypothesis is the likelihood that the hypothesis is true, independent of any efforts to confirm the hypothesis. In almost all cases this probability is assessed via considerations of background knowledge and the hypotheses already accepted by the person who frames the hypothesis. Prior probabilities play a significant role in the confirmation of hypotheses, since those which are assigned a relatively low prior probability typically are not considered, and those which are assigned a relatively high prior probability are the ones which are singled out for further testing.

This last comment is, in part, a pragmatic one based on the fact that people do not want to expend a lot of effort trying to show that a given statement is true when all the antecedent facts point to the likelihood that it is false. More important, hypotheses with very low prior probabilities more often than not *are false.*

To see what is meant by prior probabilities, suppose that someone has come down with the chicken pox. Further suppose that the following hypotheses are offered as an explanation of this:

(1) The person had chicken for dinner three nights ago.

(2) The person's great-grandmother died of chicken pox when she was eight years old.

(3) The person just returned from a skiing vacation in Aspen.

(4) The person worked as a baby sitter for a child who has since been diagnosed as having chicken pox.

Based upon what we know about contacting any disease, (1) and (3) have a very low prior probability. Even independently of any effort to confirm these two hypotheses, we can say that there is little likelihood that either of these is the explanation for the disease. In contrast, (4) has a very high prior probability, mostly because it is compatible with what we already know about how many diseases are contracted. The prior probability of (2) is lower than that of (4) but higher than either of (1) or (3). Hypothesis (2) might be supported by background knowledge about some disease being hereditary, for example.

On this basis we are ready to discuss one additional consideration before formalizing the hypothetico-deductive method.

9:2.4 Alternative Hypotheses   There are literally an infinite number of hypotheses from which any observational prediction might validly be derived. As a result, any true observational prediction which is a result of schema 3 is a confirming instance of all these hypotheses. Different hypotheses which are offered as an explanation of a given observational prediction are known as **alternative hypotheses.**

Whereas theoretically an infinite number of alternative hypotheses can be confirmed by a given observational prediction, in practice typically only a very small number of hypotheses are taken as potentially viable explanations. These are the hypotheses which are given a relatively high prior probability based on other things which are known or assumed to be true. Although the following list is not exhaustive, it will give you some idea of why certain hypotheses are considered as potential explanations while others are rejected out of hand.

(1) In general, when there are two or more alternative hypotheses, the one which is simpler is given a higher prior probability than those which are more complex. The notion of simplicity is itself a complex matter in the philosophy of science, but we need not go into this matter here. Suffice it to say that one of the characteristics of an acceptable hypothesis, especially in the physical sciences, is **simplicity.**

(2) **Compatibility** with hypotheses which have already been confirmed and accepted is another mark of an acceptable hypothesis. We have already noted the netlike nature of hypotheses, and hypotheses which are incompatible with those that have already been confirmed are given low prior probabilities.

(3) Hypotheses function in part as a means by which to make observational predictions. As a result, when there are two or more alternative hypotheses, the one with the greatest **predictive power** is given the highest prior probability.

(4) Related to predictive power is the scope of the hypothesis and its **explanatory power.** When there are two or more alternative hypotheses,

the one which explains the most phenomena is given the highest probability. We might put this another way by noting that if two alternative hypotheses explain the same observational prediction, but one of them explains additional observational predictions not explained by the other, then the former is the stronger hypothesis.

Given the above, we are ready to discuss just how the hypothetico-deductive method provides confirmation for hypotheses.

9:2.5 Formalizing the Method   Schema 3 is the "backbone" of the hypo-thetico-deductive method. What remains to be seen is how the truth of the observational prediction confirms the hypotheses. For convenience, schema 3 is reproduced below.

SCHEMA 3

Hypothesis

Initial conditions

Auxiliary hypotheses

∴ Observational prediction

Assuming that the observational prediction is true, one might conclude that the hypothesis is confirmed on the basis of the following argument:

If the hypothesis is true, then the observational prediction is true.

The observational prediction is true.

∴ The hypothesis is true.

This is, however, an instance of the invalid argument form affirming the consequent. As a result, if the truth of the observational prediction is to serve as a reason for accepting the hypothesis, some additional premises must be added to this argument. What these premises are can be explained in terms of the ideas discussed above.

The first thing we require is that the hypothesis be plausible in the sense that it has a relatively high prior probability. The second thing we require is that if there are alternative hypotheses which also explain the observational prediction, these other hypotheses are not as strongly confirmed as the given hypothesis. In short, we require that all other alternative hypotheses have a *lower* prior probability than the given hypothesis. Putting these together with our earlier argument, we have the following as the general form of confirming hypotheses by the hypothetico-deductive method:

SCHEMA 4

If the hypothesis is true, then the observational prediction is true.

The observational prediction is true.

The hypothesis has a relatively high prior probability.

All alternative hypotheses have a lower prior probability.

∴ The hypothesis is true.

Notice that schema 4 is an inductive argument whose premises support the conclusion in that if they are true, then it is probable that the hypothesis is also true. The argument represented by schema 4 occurs frequently in the sciences, in support of many hypotheses.

9:2.6 Crucial Experiments An important premise in schema 4 is that no alternative hypotheses have a higher prior probability than the hypothesis which we claim is confirmed by the observational prediction. The importance of this premise derives from the fact that if it were not true, we would not be justified in singling out the hypothesis at hand as the one which is confirmed by the prediction.

In many situations one hypothesis does have a higher prior probability than all alternative hypotheses. Sometimes, however, *two* hypotheses have equal prior probabilities. When this happens, there is no way, on the basis of schema 4, to pick one hypothesis over the other. In such cases we turn our efforts toward trying to *disconfirm* one of the two hypotheses.

Let 'H_1' and 'H_2' represent the two hypotheses which have equal prior probability. Since these two hypotheses are different, there is at least one case in which the observational predictions derived from these hypotheses are different. Let 'O_1' represent the observational prediction which follows from H_1, and 'O_2' represent the observational prediction which follows from H_2. We can represent the situation as follows:

If H_1 is true, then O_1 is true.

If H_2 is true, then O_2 is true.

What we now do is set up, or find, a situation to which both H_1 and H_2 are applicable and see which of O_1 or O_2 is true. Such a situation is a **crucial experiment.** Suppose that it is O_2 which is true. In this case, then, O_1 is false, with the result that H_1 is disconfirmed. (That H_1 is false follows from both our first statement above and the fact that O_1 is false by the argument form denying the consequent.) Since H_1 is disconfirmed, we can now return to schema 4 and inductively argue that H_2 is true.

EXERCISE 9-1

1. Explain why the truth of an observational prediction is not by itself sufficient to confirm the hypothesis from which the prediction was derived.

2. Explain what it means to say that observational predictions are validly derived from hypotheses, but that the truth of the predictions inductively confirms the hypotheses.

3. Why is a statement of initial conditions needed to derive an observational prediction?

4. Explain the role that prior probabilities play in the confirmation of hypotheses.

5. Why must alternative hypotheses be considered in attempting to confirm a given hypothesis?

6. What are some of the general characteristics of hypotheses which have a relatively high prior probability?

7. What is a crucial experiment? Explain how such experiments are used to confirm a hypothesis.

8. When an observational prediction is false, it disconfirms the hypothesis from which the prediction was derived. In some cases, however, the observational prediction is rejected instead of the hypothesis. Give three cases in which it would be reasonable to reject an observational prediction and retain the hypothesis.

9. Given below are several hypotheses, each with an observational prediction. Construct an inductive argument showing that each prediction is a confirming instance of the hypothesis. Be sure to include any auxiliary hypotheses or initial conditions that might be needed.
   a. All the students enrolled in Professor Wilson's logic class passed the course. John was enrolled in Professor Wilson's logic class and passed the course.
   b. All new tape decks sold by Ultra Sound are troublefree for at least six months. Sandra bought a tape deck from Ultra Sound seven months ago and hasn't had any trouble with it.
   c. The amount of time it takes to drive from one town to another is given by the equation $D/\bar{v}$, where 'D' is the distance between the towns and '$\bar{v}$' is the average speed. It took Fran 30 minutes to drive from Bordentown to Webster, a distance of 20 miles, and she was driving at an average speed of 40 miles per hour.
   d. All Scandinavians have blonde hair. Ingrid is from Norway, and she has blonde hair.
   e. The electric company had a power outage between 8:30 and 10:00 PM last Tuesday. The Murdocks were without electricity between 8:30 and 10:00 PM last Tuesday.
   f. Freemont High School has the best swimming team in the state. Freemont won the state championship in swimming last week.
   g. No one with less than 20/20 vision is able to enroll for flight school. Fred has 20/30 vision and was not able to enroll in flight school.
   h. Animals feel pain just as people do. I stepped on my dog's tail by accident and he yelped.
   i. Everyone in the congregation gives 10 percent of his or her income to the church. Beth is in the congregation, and she gave 10 percent of her income to the church last year.
   j. The earth is shaped like a sphere. When watching tall-masted ships sail

toward the horizon, one loses sight of the hull before losing sight of the mast.

10. Where possible, for each part of problem 9, describe a situation which would show that the given hypothesis is false.

11. Identify those parts of problem 9 for which there are reasonable alternative hypotheses which could explain the observational prediction. What are these alternative hypotheses? Are any of them more highly confirmed than the given hypothesis?

12. For each of the hypotheses you proposed in problem 11, indicate any changes which have to be made in the auxiliary hypotheses you used in your arguments in problem 9.

13. Identify those parts of problem 9 for which there is at least one alternative hypothesis which is just as likely to be correct as the given hypothesis. Describe a crucial experiment which would enable you to determine which of the two hypotheses is more likely to be the correct one.

9:3 CAUSALITY

In our discussion of the argument from analogy in the previous chapter we noted that the strength of the analogy rests in part on the relationship between the characteristics mentioned in the premises and the characteristic mentioned in the conclusion. We further noted that this relationship is such that an object's having the set of characteristics mentioned in the premises is either statistically or causally relevant to the object's having the additional characteristic mentioned in the conclusion.

Although we looked at several examples of causal relevance (for example, argument 38), we did not provide any account of what it is for one characteristic to be causally relevant to another. In the remainder of this chapter we shall discuss one way of characterizing causal relevance, extending this characterization in ways which will enable you to apply what you have learned about induction to additional situations. We shall also discuss statistical relevance.

One of the main reasons why people study causal relationships is to gain an understanding of what causes what, so as to be able either to bring about desired events (by causing them) or to prevent undesired events by preventing their causes from occurring. It is within this context that the discussions in sections 9:5 through 9:8 will take place. In those sections we shall discuss a set of methods that are often used to determine the conditions which, if they occur, will bring about a given state of affairs (these are called *sufficient conditions*) and those which, if they do not occur, will prevent a given state of affairs from occurring (these are called *necessary conditions*). The methods were proposed by John Stuart Mill in his *System of Logic*, published in 1843 (hence the name 'Mill's Methods'), and have been modified by other logicians since then. Our discussion will be based on some of the modified principles. Finally, we shall apply each of the methods discussed to several examples so as to develop a clear understanding of how and why the methods work and what their limitations are.

9:3.1 Proximate and Remote Causes

When discussing what caused some event, we often find that a series of events has taken place, such that each event in the series is the cause of the event following it. For example, in explaining why a car crashed into a tree, we might find the following:

(1) The driver slammed on his brakes.

(2) The wheels locked up.

(3) The car skidded sideways.

(4) The car hit the tree.

It would be natural to say that the driver's slamming on the brakes caused the wheels to lock up, the locked wheels caused the car to skid sideways, and the skidding caused the car to hit the tree. In a series such as this, a *causal chain*, the event which immediately precedes the last event is the **proximate cause,** and all the other events in the chain are the **remote causes.**

In explaining what caused something else, we sometimes refer to one of the remote causes and very often to the proximate cause. Which of the causes we refer to often depends on our particular interest in the event in question. For example, someone who is concerned about the design of the brakes on a car would be most interested in the fact that the wheels locked up on the car, would want to determine why this happened, and would try to change the design to prevent this from happening in the future. From this point of view, the "cause" of the accident would likely be taken as the locked wheels and not the skidding. On the other hand, the State Division of Motor Vehicles might be interested in driver error and its relationship to accidents. Here, the "cause" might well be taken as the driver's slamming on the brakes.

Causal chains can extend indefinitely far back. If we were investigating the accident for insurance purposes, we might very well want to know why the driver slammed on the brakes. Here we might find that it was to avoid hitting a dog which ran into the street, that the dog ran into the street to get away from a master who was beating it, that the master was beating the dog because he was angry, that the master was angry about the flower bed the dog had dug up, and so on. As insurance investigators, we would likely conclude that the accident was caused by the driver's attempt to avoid hitting the dog and, hence, that the driver was not at fault.

Just how far back one goes in a causal chain depends on the event being explained and whether one wants to be able to prevent or cause similar events. If the dog had not dug up the flower bed, the driver would not have slammed on the brakes, and there would not have been an accident. It is unlikely, however, that anyone would say that the dog's digging in the flower bed caused the accident. One reason for not focusing on the dog as the cause of the accident is that there is little, if anything, that one can do in that regard to prevent similar accidents from occurring in the future; but one can, for example, find that the design of the brakes could be modified to prevent the wheels from locking up and the car from going into a skid.

9:3.2 Cause as Necessary and Sufficient Conditions   Given the diverse ways of describing many causal situations, philosophers and others have found it useful to discuss not causes, but the **conditions** under which some event or kind of event occurs. For the remainder of this chapter, then, we shall focus on conditions instead of causes. As can be seen in the discussion and examples which follow, and in our earlier discussion of the hypothetico-deductive method, the conditions under which an event occurs are often just what is meant by the cause of an event.

The conditions under which an event takes place include all the situational *characteristics* which are present or absent when the event takes place. For example, if we are discussing why a ship sank and are trying to explain the sinking in terms of the prevalent conditions, we might characterize the situation in terms of its being a foggy night, there being no radio aboard to summon help, there being a large hole below the waterline, the ship's having hit a reef, and so on. All these characteristics give us a description of the conditions under which the sinking took place.

Before proceeding, we should note that some of the characteristics that describe the conditions under which an event takes place may not be causes of the event. For example, one of the characteristics of burning leaves is the presence of smoke, but the smoke does not cause the burning. Moreover, some of the characteristics we find might be jointly produced by the event in question and another event. For example, one of the characteristics present when interest rates rise is a slowdown in new home building. This slowdown is a result not only of the high interest rates but also of the unwillingness of investors to make money available for new home building. The characteristics might also be merely accidental; for example, it might happen that just as the pot on the stove begins to boil over, the phone rings.[1]

Realizing that all the characteristics that describe the conditions under which an event takes place are not necessarily causes of the event, we are now in a position to characterize two kinds of conditions: necessary conditions and sufficient conditions. A **necessary condition** for the occurrence of an event is one such that *if the condition were not present, the event would not occur*. As examples, a necessary condition for a car's crashing into a tree is that the car be moving; a necessary condition for a person's dying is that his or her heart stops functioning; and a necessary condition for graduating from college is to complete satisfactorily a required number of courses. We can make our characterization of necessary conditions explicit in the following way:

B IS A NECESSARY CONDITION FOR A

A is not present unless B is present.

---

[1] Such cases are discussed in more detail in section 10:7.

A **sufficient condition** for the occurrence of an event is one such that *if the condition is present, the event will occur*. As examples, a sufficient condition for being dead is being run over by a steamroller; a sufficient condition for graduating with honors is to accumulate a 4.0 grade-point average; and a sufficient condition for making a salary of at least $50,000 per year is to be elected President of the United States. We can make our characterization of sufficient conditions explicit in the following way:

A IS A SUFFICIENT CONDITION FOR *B*

If *A* is present, then *B* is present.

Some conditions are both *necessary and sufficient* for the occurrence of some events. For example, scoring more points than the opponent in a basketball game is both necessary and sufficient for winning the game. That is, it is necessary to score more points to win *and* scoring more points is sufficient for winning.

Although some conditions are both necessary and sufficient, we must be careful not to make the mistake of treating necessary conditions as sufficient or of treating sufficient conditions as necessary. For example, it is necessary for a car to be moving in order that the car crash into a tree. A car's moving is not, however, a sufficient condition for crashing into a tree; if it were, then all people who drive would crash into trees, and they don't. As another example, a sufficient condition for making a salary of at least $50,000 a year is to be President of the United States. It is not necessary, however, to be President to make such a salary; any number of other occupations enable one to earn that much.

We can summarize some of the above and develop further relationships between necessary and sufficient conditions by recalling our discussions of conditional statements in Chapter 3. We have noted that if *B* is a necessary condition for *A*, then *A* is not present unless *B* is present; that is,

(1) *A* is not present unless *B* is present.

By changing 'unless' to 'if–not' and inverting, we obtain

(2) If *B* is not present, then *A* is not present.

Next, by using contraposition on (2), we obtain

(3) If *A* is present, then *B* is present.

Statement (3) can be shortened to 'if *A* then *B*'. In other words, the statement that one condition is necessary for another can be written as a conditional statement in which the condition which is necessary is the *consequent* and the other condition is the *antecedent*.

Now consider the case of sufficient conditions. We have said that *A* being a sufficient condition for *B* means that if *A* is present then *B* is present; this, too, we can shorten to 'If *A* then *B*'. It follows, then, that the statement that one condition is sufficient for another can be written as a conditional statement in which the condition which is sufficient is the *antecedent* and the other condition is the *consequent*.

We have just shown that the statement '*B* is a necessary condition for *A*' and the statement '*A* is a sufficient condition for *B*' can both be written as 'If *A* then *B*'; in short, the two statements are equivalent. This is shown in Figure 9-1.

Figure 9-1

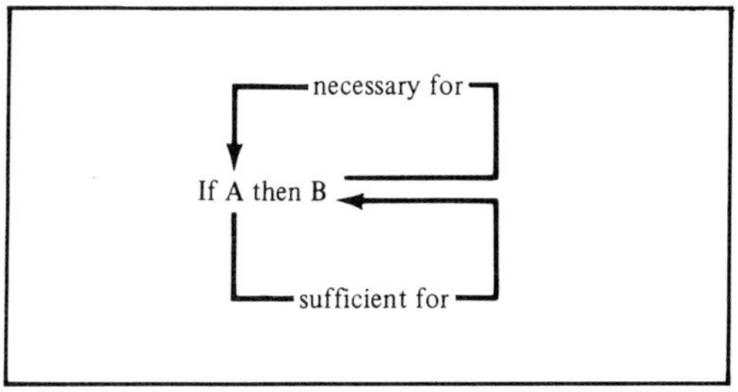

By using conditional statements to express the relationship between necessary and sufficient conditions, we can also show that being a necessary condition and being a sufficient condition are *not the same thing:* Consider the statement '*A* is a necessary condition for *B*' and the statement '*A* is a sufficient condition for *B*'. The former can be written as 'If *B* then *A*', whereas the latter is written as 'If *A* then *B*'. Since these conditional statements are not equivalent (they are converses), neither are the two statements from which they were derived.

9:3.3 Some Relationships Using conditional statements and some of their equivalent forms, we can develop a set of relationships which hold between necessary and sufficient conditions. The first of these was shown in the previous section:

P1: If *A* is a sufficient condition for *B*, then *B* is a necessary condition for *A*.

Corresponding to P1, we have the following:

P2: If *C* is a necessary condition for *D*, then *D* is a sufficient condition for *C*.

P2 can easily be shown to be true by rewriting its antecedent and consequent as conditional statements. '*C* is a necessary condition for *D*' is written as 'If *D* then *C*', and '*D* is a sufficient condition for *C*' is written as 'If *D* then *C*'. This gives us

P2': If (if *D* then *C*) then (if *D* then *C*)

P2' can easily be shown to be true by using truth tables.

By making use of contraposition, we can develop four additional relationships. These relationships are important because they show how a condition's being present in one situation is related to its being absent in another. For the first two of these relationships, consider the case in which A is a sufficient condition for B; this we write as

If A then B

Contraposition then gives us

If $\sim B$ then $\sim A$

Combining these results, we obtain

If (if A then B) then (if $\sim B$ then $\sim A$)

This result can now be written as two additional principies:

P3: If A is a sufficient condition for B, then $\sim B$ is a sufficient condition for $\sim A$.

P5: If A is a sufficient condition for B, then $\sim A$ is a necessary condition for $\sim B$.

You should satisfy yourself that the antecedent and consequent of P3 and P5 are indeed equivalent to the conditional statement 'If A then B' and 'If $\sim B$ then $\sim A$', respectively.

The next pair of relationships are developed by considering the statement that C is a necessary condition for D, written as

If D then C

Contraposition gives us

If $\sim C$ then $\sim D$

Combining these results, we obtain

If (if D then C) then (if $\sim C$ then $\sim D$)

This result can be written as two additional principles:

P4: If C is a necessary condition for D, then $\sim D$ is a necessary condition for $\sim C$.

P6: If C is a necessary condition for D, then $\sim C$ is a sufficient condition for $\sim D$.

As in the case of P3 and P5, you should satisfy yourself that the antecedent and consequent of P4 and P6 are equivalent to the conditional statements 'If D then C' and 'If $\sim C$ then $\sim D$', respectively.

The usefulness of P3 to P6 is that they enable us to specify the same relationships between conditions, either in terms of the conditions being present or in terms of their being absent. For example, P3 tells us that "whenever A is present, B is present" is the same thing as "whenever B is absent, A is absent" (we shall make use of this fact in a later section, when we discuss a method for testing for sufficient conditions). The relationships in P4 to P6 can similarly be specified in terms of present and absent characteristics, and this is left as an exercise.

EXERCISE 9-2

1. Explain why in some causal chains different remote causes are selected as the cause of some particular event.

2. In each of the following, a situation is described and a list is given of people who have an interest in what happened. From the point of view of each of these people, pick out the cause of the event in question and explain why that person would be likely to call this the "cause" of the event.

   a. Donald just recently bought a new power saw to use in building some bookcases for the living room. While Don was cutting the wood for the bookcases, his wife Eleanor came downstairs to tell him that his boss wanted to speak with him on the phone. When Don looked up to speak with Eleanor, his attention shifted to her, and he cut off the first third of the index finger on one hand.

      (1) Don
      (2) Eleanor
      (3) Don's boss
      (4) The company that sold Don the saw
      (5) The insurance company with which Don has medical coverage

   b. Gwen and Steve had been dating each other for five years, ever since they were in high school. During the latter part of their junior year in college, Gwen broke up with Steve because she felt he was not very considerate of her feelings. Part of the basis of Gwen's decision was that Steve often was late in picking her up for dates, and he often called to say that he was still with the guys and would it be all right to cancel out on their date. After several weeks of being without Gwen, Steve decided that he really had been inconsiderate, and he called her up to apologize and to ask her to go out on Saturday night. Gwen agreed to go out with him again. While Steve was getting ready to go out, one of his best friends came over and asked to borrow Steve's car so that he could run over to the auto parts store and get what he needed to fix his own car. Steve loaned him the car. While driving to the parts store, Steve's friend had a flat tire and found that there was no jack in the car. He tried to call Steve, but the phone was busy (actually the phone company was having trouble with the lines). Steve's friend returned the car an hour and a half late, and Steve was half an hour late when he went to pick up Gwen. When he arrived, Gwen told him she never wanted to see him again and that he was just as inconsiderate as he always had been.

      (1) Gwen
      (2) Steve
      (3) Steve's friend

EXERCISE 9-3

1. What does it mean to say that A is a necessary condition for B?

2. What does it mean to say that A is a sufficient condition for B?

3. Explain the relationship between necessary and sufficient conditions.

4. If A is a necessary condition for B, then
   a. If A then B.
   b. If B then $\sim A$.
   c. If B then A.
   d. If $\sim B$ then $\sim A$.
   e. B cannot occur without A.
   f. A cannot occur without B.
   g. You cannot have A without B.
   h. You cannot have B without A.

5. If B is a sufficient condition for C, then
   a. If $\sim B$ then C.
   b. If $\sim C$ then $\sim B$.
   c. If C then B.
   d. B cannot occur without C.
   e. If B then C.
   f. You cannot have C without B.
   g. C cannot occur without B.
   h. B is the only way to get C.

6. Which of the following are logically equivalent to: $\sim Q$ is a necessary condition for P?
   a. $\sim Q$ is a sufficient condition for P.
   b. P is a sufficient condition for $\sim Q$.
   c. $\sim Q$ is a necessary condition for P.
   d. $\sim P$ is a sufficient condition for Q.
   e. $\sim P$ is a necessary condition for Q.
   f. Q will fail to occur when P occurs.
   g. Only if Q occurs will P fail to occur.
   h. Only if P occurs will Q fail to occur.
   i. Unless Q occurs, P cannot occur.
   j. Unless P occurs, Q cannot occur.

7. Show that the following is true: If $\sim A$ is a sufficient condition for $\sim D$, then A is a necessary condition for D.

9:4   COMPLEX CHARACTERISTICS

Thus far our discussion has been in the context of a single, or **simple characteristic,** being present as either a necessary or a sufficient condition for the occurrence of an event. Sometimes, however, a characteristic not being the case may be necessary for an event to occur; or any one of several characteristics might be necessary for an event to occur, with no one particular characteristic being necessary; or several conditions together might be sufficient for an event to occur, with no one characteristic by itself being sufficient. In such cases we say that a **complex characteristic** is necessary, or sufficient, or both for an event to occur. Our purpose in this section is to explore these possibilities and to develop a method for working with them.

9:4.1 The Negation of Simple Characteristics Sometimes, a characteristic *not* being present or *not* being absent may be a necessary or sufficient condition for the occurrence of an event. For example, not being run over by a steamroller is a necessary condition for being alive; in many states, not having been convicted of a felony is a necessary condition for being able to teach in the public schools; or a jury's not being able to reach a verdict is a sufficient condition for the judge to declare a mistrial. We can show these, and related, characteristics with **presence tables.** A presence table merely displays whether a given characteristic is present or absent when a particular event occurs.

As an example, consider the trials of two people, Judson and Moore. Let us take as our simple characteristic that the jury reaches a decision, and as our event that a mistrial is declared. Our *complex characteristic* is that the jury does *not* reach a decision. Suppose that in the case of Judson the jury does reach a decision and a mistrial is not declared, but in the case of Moore the jury does not reach a decision and a mistrial is declared. We can show this by using 'P' to show that the characteristic in question is *present* and 'A' to indicate that it is *absent*. Moreover, a characteristic which is present is *not* absent, and one which is absent is *not* present. This gives us Table 9-1.

The relationship between the two characteristics, the jury reaching a decision and the jury not reaching a decision, in the two cases can be generalized to cover **negative characteristics** by applying the following rule:

R1: RULE FOR NEGATIVE CHARACTERISTICS

If a characteristic is present, then the negation of that characteristic is absent, and if a characteristic is absent, then the negation of that characteristic is present.

You will no doubt notice that a presence table for negative characteristics would resemble the truth table for 'not' discussed in Chapter 4. The difference is that we are now talking about the presence or absence of characteristics, not the truth or falsity of statements, but the use of 'P' to indicate 'present' corresponds with the use of 'T' to indicate 'true', and the use of 'A' to indicate 'absent' corresponds with the use of 'F' to indicate 'false'.

	TABLE 9-1		
	Characteristics		
Cases	Jury Reaches Decision	Jury Does Not Reach Decision	Event: Mistrial Declared
Judson	P	A	A
Moore	A	P	P

9:4.2 The Conjunction of Simple Characteristics
For some events, no single characteristic is sufficient for the event to occur, although several characteristics being present at the same time is sufficient. In such cases we say that a **conjunctive characteristic** is sufficient for the event to occur. As an example of this kind of situation, consider the degree requirements at your school. Most schools require a student to do several things to receive a degree: complete a certain number of hours of coursework, do that work at a sufficiently high academic level, complete a specified number of hours in a particular subject area, etc. It is not sufficient for receiving a degree that a student do just some of these things; what is sufficient is that a student do all of them.

As in the case of negative characteristics, we can also construct a presence table for conjunctive characteristics. The rule which is appropriate for doing this is the following.

R2: RULE FOR CONJUNCTIVE CHARACTERISTICS

For any two characteristics A and B, the conjunctive characteristic $A \cdot B$ is present when, and only when, *both A is present and B is present*.

Since each of the two characteristics A and B could be either present or absent, there are *four* possible cases in constructing a presence table for such characteristics: A and B are both present, A is present and B is absent, A is absent and B is present, and A and B are both absent. This table is similar to that for conjunction, discussed in Chapter 4. As in the case of the presence table for negative characteristics, the occurrences of 'P' and 'A' correspond with the occurrences of 'T' and 'F' in the truth table for conjunction.

9:4.3 The Disjunction of Simple Characteristics
For some events, no one particular characteristic is necessary for the event to occur, although it is necessary that one or the other of several characteristics be present. In such cases we say that a **disjunctive characteristic** is necessary for the event to occur. Using the example of the degree requirements again, we might find that to receive a degree a student must complete a major of 30 hours and a minor of 20 hours *or* the student must complete an interdisciplinary curriculum of 54 hours. In such a case, neither requirement by itself is a necessary condition for receiving a degree, although *one or the other* is.

Using the following rule, we could construct a presence table for disjunctive characteristics:

R3: RULE FOR DISJUNCTIVE CHARACTERISTICS

For any two characteristics A and B, the disjunctive characteristic $A \lor B$ is absent when, and only when, *both A is absent and B is absent*.

As in the case of conjunctive characteristics, there are four cases to consider, since A could be either present or absent and B could be either present or absent. The presence table for disjunctive characteristics corresponds with the truth table for disjunction discussed in Chapter 4.

9:5 TESTING FOR NECESSARY CONDITIONS

As noted above, a major reason for trying to determine which conditions are necessary or sufficient for a particular event to occur is to be able either to prevent some undesirable event from occurring or to bring about a desired one. If we are interested in *preventing* some event, then we want to find out which characteristics have to be present for the event to occur—that is, which characteristics are necessary. Knowing that, we can attempt to structure things so that at least one of the characteristics is not present and, thereby, prevent the event from occurring. In this section we shall develop a method for identifying necessary conditions.

9:5.1 The Direct Method of Agreement In section 9:3.2 we determined that a characteristic C is a necessary condition for an event E if E cannot occur unless C is present. We then wrote this as a conditional statement:

If E is present, then C is present.

Since the conditional statement above is just another way of expressing what we mean by saying that C is a necessary condition for E, any time the conditional statement is *false* it will also be the case that C is *not* a necessary condition for E. You know from our earlier discussion of conditional statements that they are false only when the antecedent is true and the consequent is false. Hence, *any case in which E is present and C is absent is a case which shows that C is not a necessary condition for E.*

This last point can be used to find which characteristics are necessary conditions for E by first considering which characteristics might be necessary and then, by a process of elimination, searching for instances in which E is present and a characteristic is *absent*; any such case would eliminate the characteristic as a necessary condition for E.

This procedure is applied in the following example. Let's suppose that investigators are attempting to determine the cause of malaria. 'Having malaria' will be represented by 'E' in our presence table. Let us also suppose that the investigators have good reason to believe that one or more of the following conditions is a necessary condition for contracting malaria:[2]

C_1: Having a vitamin deficiency

C_2: Being bitten by a mosquito

C_3: Drinking contaminated water

C_4: Living in unsanitary conditions

Finally, let's suppose that the investigators examine four different groups of people, indicated as cases 1 to 4 in our presence table, and obtain the following information:

---

[2] In terms of our discussion earlier in this chapter, the investigators have assigned a fairly high prior probability to each of these hypotheses.

EXAMPLE 2

Cases	Characteristics				Event: E
	C_1	C_2	C_3	C_4	
1	A	P	P	A	P
2	P	P	P	A	P
3	A	P	A	A	P
4	A	P	A	A	P

In the presence table of example 2, case 1 is read as follows: E was present while characteristics C_1 and C_4 were absent and characteristics C_2 and C_3 were present. Cases 2 through 4 are read similarly. On the basis of case 1, we know that C_1 is not a necessary condition for E and C_4 is not a necessary condition for E. The reason is that *a characteristic which is a necessary condition for E must be present whenever E is present*; since E is present in case 1, C_1 and C_4 can be eliminated. Another way of looking at this is in terms of our conditional-statement characterization of necessary conditions. If C_1 were a necessary condition for E, then (1) below would be true; and if C_4 were a necessary condition for E, then (2) below would be true:

(1) If E then C_1

(2) If E then C_4

Statement (1) is false, however, since, in case 1, E is present and C_1 is absent. Similarly, in case 1, E is present and C_4 is absent. This corresponds to a conditional statement with a true antecedent and a false consequent; in this case the conditional statement is false.

Looking at case 2, we find that E is present while C_4 is absent and C_1 to C_3 are present. For the reasons noted in our discussion of case 1, C_4 is again eliminated as a necessary condition for E since C_4 is absent while E is present. Note that C_1 is also present in case 2. This does *not* show that C_1 is a necessary condition for E; that possibility was eliminated in case 1. Once again, keep in mind that for a characteristic to be a necessary condition for E, *the characteristic must be present whenever E is present,* and this did not happen for C_1 in case 1.

After examining two cases we see that if any of C_1 to C_4 is a necessary condition for E, it is either C_2 or C_3 since these are the only characteristics which have been present whenever E has been present. Turning to case 3, we see that C_3 is eliminated as a necessary condition for E, since in this case C_3 is absent while E is present.

Finally, turning to case 4, we find a situation in which C_1, C_3, and C_4 are eliminated. This case tells us nothing new about these characteristics, since all of them had been eliminated in earlier cases. We do find, however, that once again C_2 is present while E is present.

Having looked at the four cases, we can now say that if any of C_1 to C_4 is a necessary condition for E, then C_2, being bitten by a mosquito, is such a condition, since it is the only characteristic which is present whenever E is present. Before we proceed this point needs to be emphasized. We have *not* unequivocally shown that C_2 *is* a necessary condition for E; what we have shown is that C_2 is a necessary condition for E if any of C_1 to C_4 are. Given that we have carefully chosen C_1 to C_4, it is *probable* that C_2 is a necessary condition for E, but it need not be. This is the feature of Mill's methods which makes them inductive: Given all the evidence in the presence table (corresponding to the premises of an argument), if we can eliminate all but one of the characteristics by using the direct method of agreement, then it is probable that the remaining characteristic is a necessary condition for E. If more than one characteristic remains, then it is probable that all these characteristics are necessary conditions for E.

That the conclusions we reach by using the direct method of agreement are, at best, probable and conditional in character can also be seen by making the conditional aspect more obvious; this we do in the following argument:[3]

(1) C_1 or C_2 or C_3 or C_4 is a necessary condition for E.   Assumption[4]

(2) C_1 is not a necessary condition for E.   Cases 1 and 4

(3) C_3 is not a necessary condition for E.   Cases 3 and 4

(4) C_4 is not a necessary condition for E.   Cases 1 to 4

∴ (5) If C_1 or C_2 or C_3 or C_4 is a necessary condition for E,
       then C_2 is.   (1) to (5), CP

In example 2 you may have noted that C_4 is *absent* whenever E is present. This might lead us to suspect that perhaps $\sim C_4$ is a necessary condition for E. And, indeed, this suggestion is borne out by noting that in all four cases $\sim C_4$ is present whenever E is present. What effect does this have on our earlier claim that if any of the characteristics is necessary for E it is C_2? None at all. What we have done by introducing the negative characteristic $\sim C_4$ is show that it too could be a necessary condition for E, given all the evidence we have in the presence table.

Before proceeding to a more detailed example, let's summarize the steps involved in using the direct method of agreement.

(1) We are interested in determining which characteristics are necessary for some event E.

(2) Based on background knowledge (what we know about E or events like

---

[3] To be rigorous, one would have to fill in some of the steps in this argument by making use of the rules of inference presented in Chapter 5. Since the argument is obviously valid, this has not been done here, but it is left as an exercise.

[4] This line of the argument is labeled 'Assumption' in following our procedure for constructing conditional proofs. In actuality, this premise of the argument is most often a justified belief based on background knowledge and the prior probabilities of C_1 to C_4.

E), we hypothesize that any of the characteristics from the set C_1 to C_n might be a necessary condition for *E*.

(3) We construct a presence table listing C_1 to C_n and *E*.

(4) We then attempt to find cases, either by observing them or by creating them (as in an experiment), in which each of the characteristics C_1 to C_n is absent when *E* is present.

(5) Those characteristics which are absent when *E* is present are then eliminated as necessary conditions for *E*.

(6) The characteristic (or characteristics) which is present whenever *E* is present is a necessary condition for *E* if *any* of the characteristics with which we started is such a condition.

9:5.2 An Example   Let's suppose that we have been enrolled in a sociology class for six weeks and have been given as an assignment the task of trying to determine the necessary conditions for receiving financial aid at our school. All we are told is that this is to be done by interviewing students that we choose randomly.

The first thing we must do, then, is determine what questions we shall ask during our interview. The first one which comes to mind is, of course, "Do you receive financial aid?" We must also formulate hypotheses concerning the characteristics we think might be necessary for receiving aid. How do we choose such hypotheses? We do it based on what we know about the kinds of students who are likely to receive financial aid; that is, we rely on our background knowledge to formulate the hypotheses and pick those which we have reason to believe have a high prior probability. Notice here that the more we know about students and about financial aid, the more likely it is that we shall select characteristics which are necessary conditions, and the less likely it is that we shall pick characteristics which are not necessary conditions. Also notice that there is no mechanical way of formulating these hypotheses—no way of guaranteeing that any of the characteristics we choose is a necessary condition for receiving aid.

These two points are applicable to all cases in which Mill's methods are used, including the case of a scientist who may be working with very sophisticated phenomena and very sophisticated hypotheses about the necessary conditions for these phenomena. These facts indicate that the success we have in using Mill's methods, in terms of both finding necessary conditions and the amount of time this takes, is directly related to our ability to pick characteristics which are likely related to the event we wish to explain.

Returning to our example, let us further suppose that we think there are five characteristics which might be necessary conditions for receiving financial aid. These are

C_1: Participates in a varsity sport

C_2: Graduated in top 20 percent of high-school class

C_3: Had College Board scores of more than 1000

C_4: Comes from a family whose annual income is less than $9000 per year

C_5: Has a parent who teaches at the school

Then, having interviewed our subjects, asking whether they receive financial aid and whether C_1 to C_5 apply to them, suppose we find that even though we interviewed many people, all the responses fall into just five different patterns. These patterns are designated as cases in the following presence table:

	Characteristics					
Case	C_1	C_2	C_3	C_4	C_5	Event: E
1	P	P	P	P	A	P
2	A	A	A	P	A	P
3	P	A	A	A	P	A
4	A	P	P	A	A	A
5	A	P	A	A	A	P

In case 1, all the characteristics except C_5 were present while E was present. As a result, having a parent who teaches at the school is not a necessary condition for receiving financial aid, since people with the first pattern received financial aid but were not children of instructors at the school.

Proceeding to case 2, we see that all the characteristics are absent except C_4. It follows, then, based on cases 1 and 2, that if any of our characteristics is a necessary condition for receiving aid, it is the characteristic of coming from a family whose annual income is less than $9000 per year.

Now for case 3: Here we notice that the people responding in this pattern *did not* receive financial aid. What does this case tell us about the necessary conditions for receiving financial aid? The answer is that it tells us nothing; *when the direct method of agreement is used, those cases in which E is absent are of no use.*

The reason why case 3 (and case 4) tells us nothing about the necessary conditions for receiving aid can best be brought out by returning to the conditional-statement form of the claim that some characteristic is necessary for E. That form, recall, is 'If E then C'. Now, if E is absent, which corresponds to the antecedent of the conditional statement being false, *nothing follows from the conditional statement* (compare this to the discussion of denying the antecedent in Chapter 3). That is, we know nothing about C when we are given the two statements 'If E then C' and '$\sim E$'. In short, the absence of E neither confirms nor disconfirms the statement that C is necessary for E.

Let's turn, then, to case 5, a case where E is present. Here we find that all the characteristics except C_2 are absent; hence, C_1 and C_3 to C_5 are *not* necessary conditions for E. Cases 1 and 2 showed that if any of the characteristics is a necessary condition for E, it is C_4. Now, however, we see in case 5 that C_4 is *not* a necessary condition for E, since C_4 is absent while E is present. What can we conclude then? *That none of the simple characteristics is a necessary condition for E.*

At this point, if we were actually attempting to determine the necessary conditions for receiving financial aid, we would have two choices: First, *we could expand our list of simple characteristics* and, second, *we could consider whether some complex characteristic,* built on the simple characteristics, *is a necessary condition.* We shall not expand our list of simple characteristics, but rather consider complex characteristics.

When we work with necessary conditions, the complex characteristics we are interested in are negated characteristics and disjunctive characteristics; we are not interested in conjunctive characteristics, since if we knew all the individual necessary conditions we could construct all the necessary conjunctive characteristics. Let's begin, then, with negation.

If the negation of any of the simple characteristics is a necessary condition for E, then the negative characteristic must be present whenever E is present. Hence, the simple characteristic itself must be absent whenever E is present. Since E is present in cases 1, 2, and 5, we must ask if any of the simple characteristics is absent in all those cases. Checking the presence table, we find that one of them is—C_5. Hence, given our assumptions, it is probable that $\sim C_5$ is a necessary condition for E.

Now we consider the case of disjunctive characteristics. Our rule for disjunction states that a disjunctive characteristic is present whenever one or the other or both disjuncts is present. Our goal, then, is to check the presence table to see if any disjunctive characteristics are present whenever E is present.

To do this we turn to cases 2 and 5 first, since in each of these cases only one characteristic is present when E is present; these are C_4 in case 2 and C_2 in case 5. As a hypothesis, let's suppose that the disjunctive characteristic $C_2 \vee C_4$ is a necessary condition for E. Checking the other case in which E is present, case 1, we see that this disjunctive characteristic is present there. Hence, given our assumptions, it is probable that $C_2 \vee C_4$ is a necessary condition for E.

This procedure can be used to find necessary conditions in any situation, but the success of the procedure depends upon the ability to pick relevant simple characteristics, based on background knowledge, and to determine which compound characteristics might be necessary if none of the simple ones are.

EXERCISE 9-4

1. Using a presence table, construct two cases which show, when taken together, that $A \vee B$ is necessary for E, but that neither A by itself nor B by itself is necessary for E.

2. Given the presence table below and the responses which follow it, circle the responses which are true on the basis of the presence table.

| | Characteristics | | | | |
Case	A	B	C	D	Event: E
1	P	A	A	A	P
2	A	P	A	A	A
3	A	P	P	A	P
4	A	A	P	A	A
5	P	P	P	A	P

a. A is necessary for E.
c. C is necessary for E.
e. A ∨ B is necessary for E.
g. B ∨ C is necessary for E.
i. B · C is necessary for E.

b. B is necessary for E.
d. D is necessary for E.
f. A ∨ C is necessary for E.
h. A · C is necessary for E.
j. (A ∨ B) ∨ (C ∨ D) is necessary for E.

9:6 TESTING FOR SUFFICIENT CONDITIONS

One reason for attempting to determine the sufficient conditions for the occurrence of an event is to be able to bring that event about, since whenever a sufficient condition is present the event will occur. In this section we shall develop a method for identifying sufficient conditions.

9:6.1 The Inverse Method of Agreement
In section 9:3.2 we noted that a characteristic C is a sufficient condition for an event E if E occurs whenever C is present. We then wrote this as the statement

If C is present then E is present.

Since the conditional statement above is just another way of expressing what we mean by saying that C is a sufficient condition for E, any time the conditional statement is *false*, it will be the case that C is *not* a sufficient statement for E. Since a conditional statement is false only when its antecedent is true and its consequent is false, *any case in which C is present and E is absent is a case which shows that C is not a sufficient condition for E.* For example, striking a match is not a sufficient condition for its igniting because there are cases in which C is present (the match is struck) but E is absent (no ignition)—as when the match is damp.

This last point can be used to find those characteristics which are sufficient conditions for E. We first consider which characteristics might be sufficient and then, as in the direct method of agreement, use a process of elimination to search for cases in which a *characteristic is present and E is absent*; any such case eliminates the characteristic as a sufficient condition for E.

Let's work through an example: Suppose that C_1, C_2, C_3, and C_4 are suspected to be sufficient conditions for E and that, through observation or experimentation, we get the following results:

EXAMPLE 3

	Characteristics				
Case	C_1	C_2	C_3	C_4	Event: E
1	P	A	A	P	A
2	A	A	A	A	A
3	P	P	A	A	A
4	P	A	A	A	A

On the basis of case 1, C_1 is *not* a sufficient condition for E and C_4 is *not* a sufficient condition for E. This is so since *a characteristic which is a sufficient condition for E must be absent every time E is absent.* Since E is absent in case 1 but both C_1 and C_4 are present, C_1 and C_4 can both be eliminated.

Looking at case 2, we see that all the characteristics are absent while E is absent. This case, *all by itself,* does not enable us to eliminate any of the characteristics. Nonetheless, even though C_1 and C_4 are absent in case 2, we cannot conclude that they are sufficient conditions for E. In fact, C_1 and C_4 have been ruled out in case 1. Thus far, we have found that if any of C_1 to C_4 *is sufficient for E*, it is C_2 or C_3, since these are the only characteristics which are absent whenever E is absent. Turning to case 3, we see that C_2 is eliminated as a sufficient condition for E, since in this case C_2 is present while E is absent.

Finally, case 4 again eliminates C_1, but C_3 is again absent while E is absent. Now, having examined all four cases, we can say that, given our assumptions, C_3 is a sufficient condition for E since it is the only characteristic which is absent whenever E is absent.

As when we dealt with necessary conditions, it should be emphasized that we have *not* unequivocally shown that C_3 is a sufficient condition for E; we have shown the weaker claim that *if* any of the characteristics is sufficient, then C_3 is that characteristic. No matter how many cases we might examine, it is always possible that in the inverse method of agreement a new case will be found in which the characteristic thought to be sufficient for E is shown not to be sufficient (compare this to an induction by enumeration where, *so far,* all observed A's have been B's).

Having just noted that the inverse method of agreement might sometimes lead us to accept a hypothesis which is false, let us recall the positive aspect of this method: In the method we first select those conditions which we have good reason to believe have a high prior probability as a sufficient condition for E. Then, insofar as the cases we examine support one of these conditions, *we have confirming evidence* that the condition is a sufficient condition for E.

The inverse method of agreement can also be seen as an instance of the direct method of agreement applied to *negative characteristics*. This we shall show by first establishing the truth of the conditional statement 'If $\sim C$ is a necessary condition for $\sim E$, then C is a sufficient condition for E' and then applying this to the first four cases in the presence table just discussed.

PROOF: If ($\sim C$ is a necessary condition for $\sim E$), then (C is a sufficient condition for E)

(1) $\sim C$ is a necessary condition for $\sim E$	Assumption
(2) $\sim E \supset \sim C$	Rewrite of (1)
(3) $C \supset E$	(2), Contra
(4) C is a sufficient condition for E	Rewrite of (3)
$\therefore$ (5) ($\sim C$ is a necessary condition for $\sim E$) $\supset$ (C is a sufficient condition for E)	(1) to (4), CP

Having established the truth of the conditional statement, we may construct an abbreviated presence table considering the characteristic C_3, E, and the negations of both. This gives us the following:

Case	Characteristics		Events	
	C_3	$\sim C_3$	E	$\sim E$
1	A	P	A	P
2	A	P	A	P
3	A	P	A	P
4	A	P	A	P

By applying the direct method of agreement to the above table, we see that $\sim C_3$ is a necessary condition for $\sim E$, since whenever $\sim E$ is present, $\sim C_3$ is present. This situation corresponds with the situation in which C_3 is absent every time E is absent (and which establishes that C_3 is a sufficient condition for E). As a result, if $\sim C_3$ is a necessary condition for $\sim E$, then C_3 is a sufficient condition for E.

The steps involved in the inverse method of agreement are as follows:

(1) We are interested in determining which characteristics are sufficient for some event E.

(2) Based on our background knowledge (what we know about E or events like E), we hypothesize that any of the characteristics of the set C_1 to C_n might be a sufficient condition for E.

(3) We construct a presence table listing C_1 to C_n and E.

(4) We then attempt to find cases, either by observation or experimentation, in which E is absent and each of the characteristics C_1 to C_n is present.

(5) Those characteristics which are present when E is absent can be eliminated as sufficient conditions for E.

(6) The characteristic (or characteristics) which is absent whenever E is absent is a sufficient condition for E if *any* of the characteristics with which we started is such a condition.

9:6.2 An Example   In this section we shall apply the method of the previous section to a particular example.

In researching the cause of tooth decay in an effort to prevent cavities, a group of researchers experimented with eight groups of rats, one group assigned to each researcher. The hypothesis that they were testing was that the presence of bacteria in the mouth or the presence of food is the cause of tooth decay. To test the hypothesis concerning food, half the groups were fed intravenously and half in the usual manner. Additionally, the researchers brushed the teeth of half the animals in each of these groups. To test the hypothesis concerning bacteria, half the groups fed intravenously and half the groups fed in the usual manner were also administered a mouthwash. The results of the tests are shown below, where E is tooth decay and C_1 to C_5 are the following characteristics:

C_1: Fed intravenously

C_2: Brushed teeth

C_3: Food particles in mouth

C_4: Administered mouthwash

C_5: Bacteria in mouth

On the basis of the experiment, the researchers found that the presence of food particles *or* the presence of bacteria is not sufficient for tooth decay. This is shown in case 1 and cases 6 to 8 below, where tooth decay is *absent* while food or bacteria is *present*. Moreover, none of the other simple characteristics is sufficient for E, since in at least one case each of the characteristics is present while E is absent.

Case	C_1	C_2	C_3	C_4	C_5	$C_3 \lor C_5$	Event: E
	Characteristics						
1	A	A	P	P	A	P	A
2	A	A	P	P	P	P	P
3	A	P	P	A	P	P	P
4	A	P	P	A	P	P	P
5	P	A	A	P	A	A	A
6	P	A	A	P	P	P	A
7	P	P	A	A	P	P	A
8	P	P	A	A	P	P	A

Believing that the presence of bacteria in the mouth at least contributes to tooth decay but finding that it is not itself sufficient, the researchers decided that perhaps bacteria *and* the presence of food might be sufficient. The next step in the research, then, was to test the complex characteristic $C_3 \cdot C_5$ as a possible sufficient condition for E. Since conjunctive characteristics are present only when both characteristics are present, we find that the complex characteristic $C_3 \cdot C_5$ is present in cases 2 to 4 and absent in all the others. We further see that every time E is absent, $C_3 \cdot C_5$ is also absent. Hence, on the basis of the information contained in the above table, we can say that the presence of food particles *and* bacteria in the mouth is a sufficient condition for tooth decay.

EXERCISE 9-5

1. By using a presence table, construct *two* cases which show, when taken together, that $A \cdot B$ is a sufficient condition for E, but that neither A by itself nor B by itself is a sufficient condition for E.

2. Given the presence table below and the responses which follow it, circle all the responses which are true on the basis of the table.

Case	\multicolumn{4}{c}{Characteristics}	Event: E
	A	B	C	D	
1	P	P	P	A	P
2	P	P	A	P	A
3	P	A	P	A	P
4	P	A	A	P	A
5	P	P	P	A	P
6	P	P	A	P	A

  a. $\sim D$ is a sufficient condition for E.
  b. $\sim B$ is a sufficient condition for E.
  c. $\sim A$ is a sufficient condition for E.
  d. $\sim C$ is a sufficient condition for E.
  e. $B \lor C$ is a sufficient condition for E.
  f. $C \cdot D$ is a sufficient condition for E.
  g. $A \lor D$ is a sufficient condition for E.
  h. $B \cdot C$ is a sufficient condition for E.
  i. $(B \lor C) \lor (C \cdot D)$ is a sufficient condition for E.
  j. $(A \lor D) \cdot (B \cdot C)$ is a sufficient condition for E.

3. Given the presence table below and the responses which follow it, circle all the responses which are true on the basis of the table.

Case	\multicolumn{4}{c}{Characteristics}	Event: E
	A	B	C	D	
1	P	A	A	A	A
2	A	P	A	A	A
3	A	P	P	A	A
4	A	A	P	A	A
5	P	P	P	A	P

a. $A \lor C$ might still be a sufficient condition for E.
b. $A \lor B$ might still be a sufficient condition for E.
c. $A \cdot B$ might still be a sufficient condition for E.
d. $B \cdot C$ might still be a sufficient condition for E.
e. D may still be a necessary condition for E.

4. Based on the presence table in section 9:6.2, what conclusions can be drawn about the effectiveness of tooth brushing to remove food particles? What conclusions can be drawn about the effectiveness of mouthwash as a means of killing bacteria in the mouth?

5. Using presence tables, show that each of the following is true.
   a. If A is a sufficient condition for B, then $\sim A$ is a necessary condition for $\sim B$.
   b. If C is a necessary condition for D, then $\sim C$ is a sufficient condition for $\sim D$.

6. On the basis of the presence table below, answer the questions which follow it.

Case	Characteristics					Event: E
	C_1	C_2	C_3	C_4	C_5	
1	A	P	P	P	A	P
2	A	A	A	A	A	A
3	P	P	A	P	A	P
4	P	P	P	P	P	P
5	A	A	A	P	A	A
6	A	A	A	P	A	A

a. If you wanted to make E occur in another case, what could you do?
b. If you wanted to prevent E from occurring in another case, what could you do?
c. Suppose we have an additional case, case 7, as follows:

	C_1	C_2	C_3	C_4	C_5	E
7	A	A	A	P	P	A

If you wanted to make E occur now, what could you do?
d. Suppose we have an additional case, case 8, as follows:

	C_1	C_2	C_3	C_4	C_5	E
8	P	A	A	P	A	A

If you wanted E to occur now, what could you do?

9:7 TESTING FOR A PARTICULAR SUFFICIENT CONDITION

We now have the means for determining the conditions which are necessary and those which are sufficient for an event to occur. Recall that *all* the conditions which are necessary for an event to occur have to be present or the event will not occur, and that *just one* of the conditions which are sufficient has to be present for the event to occur.

In the case of sufficient conditions, where sometimes more than one condition is sufficient for an event's occurring, the inverse method of agreement can be used to find those conditions. This method is used to find the conditions which, if present, would bring about the event in question. Such cases are analogous to the case of someone who wants to travel from Boston to New York City and reasons that she can get there by car, by plane, by bus, or by hitchhiking, where all of these are sufficient for making the trip.

Suppose, however, that our interest is not in developing a list of the various conditions which are sufficient for an event to occur but is, rather, more limited. Considering the last example, we might grant that all the ways mentioned are sufficient for getting from Boston to New York, but we may be interested in how some *particular* person, say Patsy, made the trip. That is, granted that it is sufficient for Patsy's getting from Boston to New York that she drive, fly, take a bus, or hitchhike, we might want to know which *particular* way she made the trip—which of all the ways that are sufficient for getting to New York actually occurred in her case.

In this section we shall develop a method for determining the answers to such questions. That is, we shall develop a method for determining the sufficient conditions for a *particular* occurrence of an event. This method is the method of difference.

9:7.1 The Method of Difference   Even though any number of characteristics might be sufficient for an event to occur, none of those characteristics would be *the* sufficient condition for a particular occurrence of an event unless that characteristic were present when the event occurred. Suppose, for example, that one of the sufficient conditions for a person's being admitted to Hobbit University is that he or she be less than 3 feet tall; this could not be the condition which was sufficient for Wilt's being admitted if he is 7 feet tall. Whatever was *the* sufficient condition for his admission, it was not his size.

Before we proceed, it is important that you grasp the following point: If being less than 3 feet tall is a sufficient condition for being admitted to Hobbit University, then it is sufficient in all cases, all the time. In particular, the condition applies to Wilt as much as it does to anyone else, where we mean by this that *if* Wilt is less than 3 feet tall, then he can be admitted to Hobbit University. It just turns out to be the case that Wilt is not less than 3 feet tall, with the result that this could not have been the basis for *his* admission.

Another example might help to bring out this point. A sufficient condition for death is decapitation; what we mean by this is that if someone is decapitated, then that person is dead. Moreover, decapitation is a sufficient condition for anyone's death. This need not, and does not, mean that everyone who is dead has been decapitated (to argue so is to use the invalid argument form affirming the consequent); many people have died in ways other than decapitation.

The next point that must be grasped is that if a characteristic is *not* a sufficient condition for some event occurring, then it cannot be the sufficient condition for a particular occurrence of the event. For example, if being hit on the head with a sparrow feather is not a sufficient condition for death, then it cannot be the condition which was sufficient for some particular death.

This point can be brought out in the following way: Suppose that someone has died and the coroner is asked to determine the cause of death. Following an autopsy, the coroner reports that the deceased died from a blow to the head with a sparrow feather. Being skeptical of this finding, someone asks the coroner to explain it. The coroner then offers the following explanation:

> If anyone is hit on the head with a sparrow feather, then the person will die from the blow.
>
> The deceased was hit on the head with a sparrow feather.
>
> ∴ The deceased died from the blow.

The above "explanation" is satisfactory only in the sense that the argument presented is valid. The first premise of this argument is, however, false. As a result, the argument does not provide an acceptable reason for the cause of death. Moreover, the falsity of the claim that being hit on the head with a sparrow feather is a sufficient condition for death is also established by the falsity of the first premise, since this premise is just the conditional-statement equivalent of the sufficient-condition claim.

We can make these two points more explicit as follows:

(A) If some characteristic C is the sufficient condition for the occurrence of some particular event E, then C must be present when E is present.

(B) If some characteristic C is the sufficient condition for the occurrence of some particular event E, then C must be absent every time events like E are absent.

What (A) and (B) come to is this: For some characteristic to be sufficient for the occurrence of some particular event, the characteristic has to be sufficient for these kinds of events and has to be present when the particular event occurred. These two points serve as the basis for the method of difference.

9:7.2 How the Method Works

In using this method, we shall begin by identifying the particular case with which we are concerned with an asterisk (*) in the presence table. All other cases will be treated as they have been thus far. Let us suppose, then, that we are interested in determining the sufficient condition for the occurrence of some particular event E, and that we have reason to believe that one or more of the characteristics C_1 to C_5 might be sufficient. Let us further suppose that upon examining E we come up with the following information:

Cases	Characteristics					Event: E
	C_1	C_2	C_3	C_4	C_5	
*	P	A	P	P	A	P

On the basis of the above information, we know that neither C_2 nor C_5 could be the sufficient condition for E in case *. The reason for this comes from (A) in the previous section: If some characteristic C is the sufficient condition for the occurrence of some particular event E, then C must be present when E is present. In case *, E is present but neither C_2 nor C_5 is present. As a result, even if C_2 or C_5 were a sufficient condition for events like E, they could not have been the sufficient condition for this occurrence of E because E occurred without the presence of either of these characteristics.

The point can be brought out by an example. Suppose the E is some particular death, C_2 is decapitation, and C_5 is being hit in the head with a sparrow feather. Since in case * the person is dead but was neither decapitated nor hit in the head with a sparrow feather, neither of these was the cause of death; and neither of them is the sufficient condition for E in this case. Moreover, even though decapitation is a sufficient condition for death, it was not the sufficient condition in this case since decapitation did not occur.

At this point, then, we know that if any of C_1 to C_5 is the sufficient condition for E in case *, then it is C_1, C_3, or C_4; these are the only characteristics which are present when E is present.

Before we discuss the remainder of the method of difference, let's recap what we have done up to this point and what we have not done. You may be feeling confused about a method in which the *presence* of characteristics and events is used as part of a test for sufficient conditions; after all, we used this criterion in the direct method of agreement to determine necessary conditions.

It must be emphasized here that *we are not using case * to test for necessary conditions*. All that we are doing is trying to find those characteristics which are present when E is present, since a characteristic which is absent in a case when E is present could not be the sufficient condition for E in that case. Nonetheless, it is *possible* that C_1, C_3, or C_4 is a necessary condition for E, since each of these characteristics is present while E is present. If we were trying to determine necessary conditions, however, we would look at more cases in which E is present and attempt to eliminate characteristics by using the direct method of agreement.

We know the following three things as a result of case *:

(1) C_2 and C_5 could not be sufficient conditions for E in case *, since E occurred but neither C_2 nor C_5 was present [this is a result of (A) above].

(2) C_1, C_3, and C_4 could be necessary conditions for E, since they are present

while E is present (this is a result of the direct method of agreement). If we were interested in necessary conditions, we would want to look at more cases in which E is present and see if any, or all, of C_1, C_3, and C_4 could be eliminated.

(3) Any of C_1 to C_5 *could* be sufficient conditions for E given the information in case *. Since E is present in this case, we can't eliminate any of the characteristics (this is a result of the inverse method of agreement).

We are now ready to develop the remainder of the method of difference. This we do by considering (B) above: To be a sufficient condition for the occurrence of a particular event E, a characteristic must be absent every time events like E are absent. In other words, we now want to determine which, if any, of C_1, C_3, and C_4 is a sufficient condition for E. How do we do this? By using the inverse method of agreement—the method for finding sufficient conditions.

Let us suppose that in examining additional instances of events like E in case *, we come up with the following information

Case	Characteristics					Event: E
	C_1	C_2	C_3	C_4	C_5	
1	A	A	A	A	P	A
2	A	A	A	A	A	A
3	P	A	A	A	A	A
4	P	P	A	A	P	P
5	P	A	P	A	A	A

We know from our discussion in section 9:6 that to be a sufficient condition for E a characteristic must be absent every time E is absent. Looking at the presence table, we see that E is absent in cases 1, 2, 3, and 5. Therefore, we need to determine if any of C_1 to C_5 is absent in each of these cases. Again checking the presence table, we see that C_2 and C_4 are, indeed, absent in these cases. It follows, then, that *if* any of C_1 to C_5 is a sufficient condition for E, then C_2 and/ or C_4 is.

This completes the second part of the method of difference. Combining what we know from case *—that C_1, C_3, and C_4 are present when E is present— and what we just learned from the last presence table—that C_2 and/or C_4 is sufficient for E if any of C_1 to C_5 is—we can now say that *if any of C_1 to C_5 is sufficient for E in case *, then C_4 is that characteristic*. This is so because C_4 is the only possible sufficient condition for E which also happens to be present when E is present in case *.

By way of summary, we can break the method of difference into three steps.

(1) For the occurrence of E in which we are interested, identify all those characteristics which are present when E is present.

(2) Use the inverse method of agreement to determine which characteristics are sufficient conditions for E.

(3) See if any characteristics were identified in *both* the first step and the second step; if so, then if any of the characteristics are sufficient for the particular occurrence of E, then the characteristic or characteristics identified in this step are.

9:7.3 An Example   Suppose that there has been a serious accident at a nuclear power plant and that radioactive water has become combined with the nonradioactive water in the cooling system, with the result that nuclear contaminants are now being released into the atmosphere. In an attempt to determine the cause of the accident, a team of physicists visits the accident site as well as four other nuclear power plants. After their investigation, they come up with the results shown in the table below, where case * is the plant where the accident happened, cases 1 to 4 are the other plants visited, E is the type of accident just described, and C_1 to C_5 are the following characteristics:

C_1: Plant built by Speedy Construction Company

C_2: Faulty valve installed in primary loop

C_3: Employees not adequately trained in emergency shutdown procedures

C_4: Final site inspection inadequately performed

C_5: Walls of reactor not built to specification

Case	Characteristics					Event: E
	C_1	C_2	C_3	C_4	C_5	
*	P	P	A	P	A	P
1	P	A	A	A	A	A
2	A	A	A	A	A	A
3	A	A	P	A	A	A
4	P	A	A	P	A	A

Applying the method of difference to the presence table, we see that at the site of the accident the plant was built by the Speedy Construction Company, a faulty valve was installed in the primary loop, and the final site inspection was inadequately performed. Hence, if any of C_1 to C_5 is a sufficient condition for the accident, then it is one of the three characteristics just mentioned, for they are the only ones present while E is present.

Now we must determine which, is any, of C_1 to C_5 is sufficient for E by using the inverse method of agreement. In the presence table, we see that E is *absent* in cases 1 to 4. We also see the C_2, the installation of a faulty valve in the primary loop, and C_5, the reactor walls not built to specifications, are also absent in each of these four cases. On the basis of our information we can say that both these characteristics are sufficient for an accident of the type described.

We have identified *two* characteristics which are sufficient for the accident.

However, one of them, the walls not built to specifications, could not have been the cause of the accident in case *, for at that plant the walls *were* built to specification. The other characteristic which has been identified as sufficient for E, the installation of a faulty valve, is, however, present in case *. Hence, if any of C_1 to C_5 are sufficient for the accident, it is the faulty valve; this is the only characteristic which is both present in the cases of the accident and sufficient for the accident.

EXERCISE 9-6

1. Explain why, when we use the method of difference, checking for instances where a characteristic is present in case * is not checking for necessary conditions.

2. Explain why a condition which is not sufficient in general cannot be sufficient in a particular case.

3. Given the presence table below, answer the questions which follow it.

Case	C_1	C_2	C_3	C_4	$C_1 \vee C_2$	$C_3 \cdot C_4$	Event: E
1	P	P	P	A	P	A	P
2	A	P	A	P	P	A	A
3	A	A	P	A	A	A	A
4	A	P	P	P	P	P	P

(column group header: Characteristics)

a. Which, if any, of the characteristics is necessary for E?
b. Which, if any, of the characteristics is sufficient for E is we use the inverse method of agreement?
c. Which, if any, of the characteristics is sufficient for E in case 1?
d. Explain why none of the characteristics is sufficient for E in case 2.
e. Which, if any, of the characteristics is sufficient for E in case 4?

9:8 TESTING FOR NECESSARY AND SUFFICIENT CONDITIONS

In section 9:3.3 we saw that some characteristics are both necessary and sufficient for an event to occur. For example, it is both necessary and sufficient that one score more points than the opponent to win a basketball game. In this section we shall discuss a method for determining which characteristics are *both* necessary and sufficient conditions for some event E.

Not surprisingly, we already have the concepts we need for finding these conditions. In particular, we have a method for finding necessary conditions (the direct method of agreement) and two methods for finding sufficient conditions (the inverse method of agreement and the method of difference). Since there are two methods for finding sufficient conditions, one applicable in general and the other in a particular case, there are two methods for finding characteristics which are both necessary and sufficient. The first of these, the double method of agreement, is used to find conditions which are necessary and sufficient in general. The second, the joint method of agreement and difference, is used to find conditions which are necessary and sufficient in a particular case. These two methods are schematized as follows:

$$\frac{Necessary}{conditions} + \frac{sufficient}{conditions} = \frac{necessary\ and}{sufficient\ conditions}$$

$$\frac{Direct\ method}{of\ agreement} + \frac{inverse\ method}{of\ agreement} = \frac{double\ method}{of\ agreement}$$

$$\frac{Direct\ method}{of\ agreement} + \frac{method\ of}{difference} = \frac{joint\ method\ of}{agreement\ and\ difference}$$

In using either of the two methods, our procedure is first to use the direct method of agreement to determine which characteristics are necessary for some event E. Next, depending on whether we are interested in sufficient conditions in general or sufficient conditions in a particular case, we use either the inverse method of agreement or the method of difference to determine the sufficient conditions. Finally, we select as the conditions which are both necessary and sufficient those which were selected by *both* methods we used. The two combined methods are discussed in the following sections.

9:8.1 The Double Method of Agreement
Our purpose in using this method is to determine those characteristics which are both necessary and sufficient for the occurrence of E. To see how this method works, let's suppose that we have good reason to believe that one or more of C_1 to C_6 are both necessary and sufficient for E. Let's further suppose that after examining six cases we find the following:

Case	Characteristics						Event: E
	C_1	C_2	C_3	C_4	C_5	C_6	
1	P	P	P	P	P	A	P
2	A	P	A	A	A	A	A
3	P	A	A	A	A	A	A
4	A	P	P	P	P	P	P
5	P	P	P	A	P	A	P
6	A	A	A	A	P	P	A

Our first step is to determine which conditions, if any, are necessary for E by using the direct method of agreement. To do this, we first find all those cases in which E is *present* and then eliminate any characteristic which was *absent* in at least one of those cases. This is the same thing, of course, as requiring that, to be a necessary condition for E, a characteristic must be present every time E is present.

Checking the column under E, we see that E is present in cases 1, 4, and

5. Now, checking the columns under the chracteristics, we see that C_2, C_3, and C_5 are also present in each of these cases. Hence, if any of C_1 to C_6 is necessary for E, then it is C_2 and/or C_3 and/or C_5. On the other hand, neither C_1, C_4, nor C_6 is a necessary condition for E, since these characteristics are absent when E is present. These characteristics are eliminated in the following cases:

C_1: Case 4 C_4: Case 5

C_6: Cases 1 and 5

Having found those conditions which are necessary for E, we are now ready to test for sufficient conditions; to do this, we use the inverse method of agreement. In applying this method, we want to find all those cases in which E is *absent* and then eliminate any characteristic which is *present* in at least one of those cases, or, what comes to the same thing, identify those characteristics which are absent every time E is absent.

Checking the column under E, we see that E is absent in cases 2, 3, and 6. Checking the columns under each of the characteristics, we see that C_3 and C_4 are also absent in each of these cases. Hence, if any of C_1 to C_6 is sufficient for E, then it is C_3 and/or C_4. The other characteristics are eliminated as sufficient conditions because they are each present in at least one case when E is absent; in particular, they are eliminated in the following cases:

C_1: Case 3 C_2: Case 2

C_5: Case 6 C_6: Case 6

Having found those conditions which are sufficient for E, we are now ready to identify the condition or conditions which are both necessary and sufficient for E. Summarizing the results of the two methods, we have:

Necessary conditions: C_2, C_3, and C_5

Sufficient conditions: C_3 and C_4

Hence, if any of C_1 to C_6 is both necessary and sufficient for E, then it is characteristic C_3, since this is the only characteristic which was found to be necessary for E by the direct method of agreement and sufficient for E by the inverse method of agreement.

In summary, then, the double method of agreement is used to find those characteristics which are both necessary and sufficient for E. The method involves three steps:

✳ (1) Using the direct method of agreement, find all those characteristics which are necessary conditions for E.

(2) Using the inverse method of agreement, find all those characteristics which are sufficient conditions for E.

(3) Identify those characteristics which were picked out in both (1) and (2).

9:8.2 The Joint Method of Agreement and Difference

This method is similar to that just discussed, only here we are interested in finding those characteristics which are both necessary and sufficient for a *particular* occurrence of E. As before, we use the direct method of agreement to identify the necessary conditions, but since we are interested in a particular occurrence of E, we use the method of difference to find the sufficient conditions.

To illustrate this method, let's suppose that we wish to find those characteristics which are both necessary and sufficient for E in case 3 below:

Case	Characteristics C_1	C_2	C_3	C_4	C_5	C_6	Event: E
1	P	A	A	P	A	A	A
2	A	P	P	P	P	P	P
3	A	P	A	P	P	A	P
4	P	P	A	P	A	A	A
5	A	P	P	P	P	A	P
6	P	A	A	A	A	A	A

Our first step is to determine those characteristics, if any, which are necessary for E by using the direct method of agreement. Checking the table, we see that E is present in cases 2, 3, and 5. Checking the columns under the characteristics, we see that C_2, C_4, and C_5 are present in each of these cases. Hence, if any of C_1 to C_6 is necessary for E, then it is C_2 and/or C_4 and/or C_5.

We are now ready to see which, if any, of C_1 to C_6 is sufficient for E in case 3 by using the method of difference. Recall that this method involves three steps: First, identify those characteristics which are present for the particular occurrence of E in which we are interested; second, use the inverse method of agreement to determine which characteristics are sufficient conditions for E; and third, identify those characteristics, if any, which were identified in both the preceding steps.

Applying the first step, we see that C_2, C_4, and C_5 are all present in case 3. So far, all these characteristics might be sufficient for E in case 3. C_1, C_3, and C_6 can be eliminated because they are absent in case 3 while E is present.

For the second step, we see that E is absent in cases 1, 4, and 6. Checking the columns under the characteristics, we also see that C_3, C_5, and C_6 are absent in these cases.

Combining the results of these two steps, we see that whereas C_3, C_5, and C_6 might all be sufficient for E, only C_5 happens to be present in case 3 when E is present. Hence, if any of C_1 to C_6 is sufficient for E in case 3, it is C_5.

We are now ready to combine the results of the direct method of agreement and the method of difference. Summarizing the results of the two methods, we have:

Necessary conditions: C_2, C_4, and C_5

Sufficient conditions, case 3: C_5

Hence, if any of C_1 to C_6 is both necessary and sufficient for E in case 3, it is characteristic C_5 since this is the only characteristic which was found to be necessary for E by the direct method of agreement and sufficient for E by the method of difference.

In summary, the joint method of agreement and difference is used to find those characteristics which are both necessary for E and sufficient for a particular occurrence of E. The method involves three steps:

(1) Using the direct method of agreement, find all those characteristics which are necessary conditions for E.

(2) Using the method of difference, find all those characteristics which are sufficient conditions for E in the particular case of interest.

(3) Identify those characteristics which were picked out in *both* (1) and (2).

EXERCISE 9-7

1. Explain how the double method of agreement works.

2. Explain how the joint method of agreement and difference works.

3. On the basis of the presence table below, answer the questions which follow it.

Case	C_1	C_2	C_3	C_4	C_5	Event: E
1	P	P	A	A	P	P
2	A	A	P	A	A	A
3	A	A	P	A	A	A
4	A	A	P	P	P	P
5	A	A	P	A	A	A
6	A	P	P	P	P	P
7	A	A	P	A	A	A
8	A	A	P	A	A	A

(Characteristics)

a. Which, if any, of the characteristics is necessary for E?
b. Which, if any, of the characteristics is sufficient for E?
c. Which, if any, of the characteristics is both necessary and sufficient for E?
d. Which, if any, of the characteristics is sufficient for E in case 1?
e. Which, if any, of the characteristics is sufficient for E in case 2?
f. Which, if any, of the characteristics is sufficient for E in case 3?
g. Which, if any, of the characteristics is sufficient for E in case 4?
h. Which, if any, of the characteristics is sufficient for E in case 5?

i.   Which, if any, of the characteristics is sufficient for E in case 6?

j.   Which, if any, of the characteristics is sufficient for E in case 7?

k.   Which, if any, of the characteristics is sufficient for E in case 8?

l.   Which, if any, of the characteristics is both necessary and sufficient for E in case 1?

m.   Which, if any, of the characteristics is both necessary and sufficient for E in case 2?

n.   Which, if any, of the characteristics is both necessary and sufficient for E in case 3?

o.   Which, if any, of the characteristics is both necessary and sufficient for E in case 4?

p.   Which, if any, of the characteristics is both necessary and sufficient for E in case 5?

q.   Which, if any, of the characteristics is both necessary and sufficient for E in case 6?

r.   Which, if any, of the characteristics is both necessary and sufficient for E in case 7?

s.   Which, if any, of the characteristics is both necessary and sufficient for E in case 8?

STUDENT STUDY GUIDE

Chapter Summary

1. Predictions based on hypotheses are **observational predictions.** These predictions are such that if the hypothesis from which they have been validly derived is true, then what is asserted in the predictions is also true. (section 9:1)

2. When an observational prediction is derived from a hypothesis, the prediction is derived deductively, although the truth of the prediction provides inductive support for the hypothesis from which it was derived. Cases in which the prediction is true are **confirming instances** of the hypothesis. When the observational prediction is false, this shows that the hypothesis is false as well. Such a case constitutes a **disconfirming instance** of the hypothesis. (section 9:1)

3. A **hypothesis** is a statement which is offered as the explanation of certain phenomena or as the basis for further investigation of certain phenomena. The primary role of hypotheses is to serve as statements from which observational predictions can be derived. (section 9:1.1)

4. The **hypothetico-deductive method** is a method which is often used in science to confirm or disconfirm hypotheses. In this method observational predictions are validly derived from a hypothesis. These predictions are then tested; insofar as they are true they provide confirming instances of the hypothesis, and insofar as they are false they provide disconfirming instances. (section 9:2)

5. **Initial conditions** specify the circumstances under which a hypothesis is being tested. In deriving observational predictions, initial conditions are given as premises in the argument from which we deduce these predictions. (section 9:2.1)

6. An **auxiliary hypothesis** is one which is used in the derivation of observational predictions but whose truth has been established independently of the hypothesis being tested. (section 9:2.2)

7. The **prior probability** of a given hypothesis is the likelihood that the hypothesis is true, independently of any efforts to confirm the hypothesis. The prior probability of a hypothesis is usually determined on the basis of the background knowledge of the person who frames the hypothesis and on the basis of those hypotheses already accepted by this person. (section 9:2.3)

8. An **alternative hypothesis** is any hypothesis from which a given observational prediction can be derived. Although theoretically there are an infinite number of alternative hypotheses for any given hypothesis, in practice alternative hypotheses are limited to those which are given a relatively high prior probability as an explanation for the phenomenon in question. (section 9:2.4)

9. Among the things which are considered in determining the prior probability of a hypothesis are its **simplicity,** its **compatibility** with hypotheses which have already been confirmed and accepted, its **predictive power,** and its **explanatory power.** (section 9:2.4)

10. A **crucial experiment** is used to determine which of two competing hypotheses is true when both have been assigned equal prior probabilities. In such an experiment we either observe or set up a situation in which the observational predictions of the two hypotheses cannot both be true. The hypothesis which yields the false observational prediction is therefore *disconfirmed.* (section 9:2.6)

11. Often, in a series of events, each event is the cause of the event following it. In such **causal chains,** the event which immediately precedes the last event is the **proximate cause,** and all the other events in the chain are **remote causes.** (section 9:3.1)

12. Given the diverse meanings of 'cause', it is useful to talk instead about the **conditions** under which some event occurs. The conditions are those characteristics of the situation which are present or absent when the event takes place. A **necessary condition** is such that if it is not present, then the event will not occur. A **sufficient condition** is such that if it is present, then the event will occur. (section 9:3.2)

13. Necessary and sufficient conditions can be understood in terms of conditional statements. The statement that one condition is necessary for another can be written as a conditional statement in which the necessary condition is the consequent and the other condition is the antecedent. The statement that one condition is sufficient for another can be written as a conditional statement in which the sufficient condition is the antecedent and the other condition is the consequent. In any conditional statement, the consequent is a necessary condition for the antecedent, and the antecedent is a sufficient condition for the consequent. (section 9:3.2)

14. It sometimes happens that a characteristic's *not* being the case may be a necessary or a sufficient condition for an event to occur. Similarly, any one of several characteristics might be necessary for one event to occur, with no one characteristic in particular being necessary; or, several characteristics together may be sufficient for an event to occur, with no one characteristic by itself being sufficient. Such characteristics are **complex characteristics.** (section 9:4)

15. A **presence table** is used to indicate, in a display, whether given characteristics are present or absent when a particular event occurs. By use of rules similar to those for the truth table for 'not', 'or', and 'and', presence tables can also be used to show which complex characteristics are present or absent. (section 9:4)

16. The **direct method of agreement** is used to test for *necessary* conditions. Since an event will not occur unless all the necessary conditions are present, any characteristic which is absent when an event is present cannot be a necessary condition for that event. To test for necessary conditions, we construct a presence table which lists all the characteristics which are likely to be necessary for events of the kind in which we are interested, along with the event. We then examine cases of this kind and eliminate any characteristic which is absent in at least one case in which the event is present. (section 9:5.1)

17. The **inverse method of agreement** is used to test for *sufficient* conditions. Since an event will occur any time a sufficient condition for that event is present, any characteristic which is present when an event is absent cannot be a sufficient condition for that event. To test for sufficient conditions, we construct a presence table which lists all the characteristics which are likely to be sufficient for events of the kind in which we are interested, along with the event. We then examine cases of this kind and eliminate any characteristic which is present in at least one case in which the event is absent. (section 9:6.1)

18. The **method of difference** is used to test for sufficient conditions in a particular occurrence of some event. Since any characteristic which is the sufficient condition for a particular occurrence of an event must be both a sufficient condition for events of this kind and present when the particular event occurs, the method of difference is a two-step procedure. We first determine which characteristics are present when the particular event occurs, and then we use the inverse method of agreement to determine which, if any, of these characteristics is a sufficient condition for events of the kind in question. The characteristic which satisfies both parts of this test is a sufficient condition for the particular occurrence of the event. (section 9:7.1)

19. The **double method of agreement** is used to test for conditions which are both necessary and sufficient. To find such conditions, we first use the direct method of agreement to find those conditions which are necessary and then use the inverse method of agreement to find those which are sufficient. (section 9:8.1)

20. The **joint method of agreement and difference** is used to test for conditions which are both necessary and sufficient in a particular case. To find such conditions, we first use the direct method of agreement to find those conditions which are necessary and then use the method of difference to find those conditions which are sufficient in the particular case we are examining. (section 9:8.2)

Key Terms

Hypothesis	Sufficient Condition
Observational Prediction	Simple Characteristic
Hypothetico-Deductive Method	Complex Characteristic
Initial Conditions	Negative Characteristic

Auxiliary Hypothesis	Conjunctive Characteristic
Prior Probability	Disjunctive characteristic
Alternative Hypotheses	Presence Table
Crucial Experiment	Direct Method of Agreement
Causal Chain	Inverse Method of Agreement
Proximate Cause	Method of Difference
Remote Cause	Double Method of Agreement
Necessary Condition	Joint Method of Agreement and Difference

Self-Test/Exercises

1. Explain what it means to say that in the hypothetico-deductive method an observational prediction is deductively derived from a hypothesis, but if the observational prediction is true it inductively supports the hypothesis. (section 9:2)

2. What role do alternative hypotheses and prior probabilities play in confirming a hypothesis? (sections 9:2.3 and 9:2.4)

3. What is a crucial experiment? Give an example of a crucial experiment, and explain what the experiment shows and why. (section 9:2.6)

4. Explain the difference between proximate and remote causes. Give an example of a causal chain, and explain which causes are proximate and which are remote. (section 9:3.1)

5. Explain what it means to say that A is a necessary condition for B. (section 9:3.2)

6. Explain what it means to say that A is a sufficient condition for B. (section 9:3.2)

7. Show that each of the following is true. (section 9:3.3)
   a. If A is sufficient for B, then B is necessary for A.
   b. If $\sim A$ is necessary for B, then A is sufficient for $\sim B$.
   c. If $\sim A$ is sufficient for B, then A is necessary for $\sim B$.
   d. If A is necessary for $\sim B$, then B is necessary for $\sim A$.

8. Explain how to determine the presence or absence of the negations, conjunctions, and disjunctions of simple characteristics. (sections 9:4.1 through 9:4.3)

9. State what each of the following methods shows, and explain how each works.
   a. The direct method of agreement (section 9:5.1)
   b. The inverse method of agreement (section 9:6.1)
   c. The method of difference (section 9:7.2)
   d. The double method of agreement (section 9:8.1)
   e. The joint method of agreement and difference (section 9:8.2)

10. Complete the presence table below, and answer the questions which follow it. (sections 9:5 through 9:8)

	Characteristics							
Case	C_1	C_2	C_3	C_4	$\sim C_4$	$C_3 \cdot C_2$	$C_1 \vee \sim C_4$	Event: E
1	A	P	P	A				P
2	A	A	A	P				A
3	P	P	P	A				P
4	A	A	P	P				A
5	A	P	P	A				P
6	A	A	A	A				A

a. Which, if any, of the characteristics is necessary for E?
b. Which, if any, of the characteristics is sufficient for E?
c. Which, if any, of the characteristics is both necessary and sufficient for E?
d. Which, if any, of the characteristics is sufficient for E in case 1?
e. Which, if any, of the characteristics is sufficient for E in case 2?
f. Which, if any, of the characteristics is sufficient for E in case 3?
g. Which, if any, of the characteristics is sufficient for E in case 4?
h. Which, if any, of the characteristics is sufficient for E in case 5?
i. Which, if any, of the characteristics is sufficient for E in case 6?
j. Which, if any, of the characteristics is both necessary and sufficient for E in case 1?
k. Which, if any, of the characteristics is both necessary and sufficient for E in case 2?
l. Which, if any, of the characteristics is both necessary and sufficient for E in case 3?
m. Which, if any, of the characteristics is both necessary and sufficient for E in case 4?
n. Which, if any, of the characteristics is both necessary and sufficient for E in case 5?
o. Which, if any, of the characteristics is both necessary and sufficient for E in case 6?

CHAPTER 10

INFORMAL

FALLACIES

Our topic throughout this book has been the analysis of arguments. With this chapter we conclude our analysis by examining some kinds of arguments which traditionally have been singled out for discussion by logicians. What all these arguments have in common is that, whereas they may seem plausible, the fact is that their premises do *not* support their conclusions. In short, we shall be examining a group of arguments which, though they may appear to be acceptable, really are unacceptable.

10:1 AN OVERVIEW

When someone offers an argument for some position, he or she also offers evidence for the position. We call the position being argued for the *conclusion* of the argument, and the evidence that is offered is the *premises* of the argument. One of the conditions which must be satisfied in a good argument is that the premises support the conclusion. This support relation can be satisfied in either of two ways: deductive support (or validity), in which the truth of the premises necessitates the truth of the conclusion, or inductive support, in which the truth of the premises makes the conclusion more likely true than not.

Since the support relation between the premises and the conclusion is satisfied only if the conclusion follows either validly or probably from the premises, we ask two questions regarding the support relation of any argument: First we ask "Is it valid?" and, if the answer to this question is no, we ask "Do the premises inductively support the conclusion?" A negative answer to *both* questions entitles us to say that the premises do not support the conclusion and, therefore, that the conclusion ought not to be accepted on the basis of the argument.

You already possess the information and skills needed to ask and answer these questions, so in an important respect this chapter will not require anything new. In particular, no new techniques will be developed, nor will any new concepts be introduced.

An obvious question, then, is "Why have some arguments been singled out for discussion in this chapter?" The answer to this question rests on the fact that many different arguments may nonetheless have something in common: their form. As a result, if there is something wrong with that form, or structure, every argument having that form will suffer the same defect. The more specific answer to the question, based on this feature of form, is that of all the possible bad arguments, a certain group is more or less frequently offered in support of various positions. Singling out some of these arguments provides the opportunity to use what you have learned about analyzing arguments, and to become aware that these arguments are bad by showing them to be so.

10:2   ANALYZING ARGUMENTS

Our purpose in the remainder of the chapter is to apply what you have already learned about analyzing arguments to some additional ones. Again we note that in every good argument the premises support the conclusion and the premises are true. As a result, two basic reasons can be offered for rejecting any argument: that the premises neither deductively nor inductively support the conclusion, or that at least one of the premises is false. In each of the arguments we shall discuss, our primary concern will be with the question of support. First, however, a few remarks are in order concerning the unacceptability of arguments; this is the topic of the next section.

10:2.1 Unacceptable Arguments   Ever since logicians first began examining the support relation between the premises and the conclusions of arguments, attempts have been made to classify the various ways in which the premises of an argument can fail to support the conclusion. Given the multitude of errors that can be made in arguments, it is not surprising that no one adequate classification of these errors has ever been given; indeed, it is unlikely that one can be given.

Nonetheless, it is possible to point out certain similarities among arguments, and this is the procedure we shall follow here. It is important to remember, however, that some of the things we shall note about a group of arguments may apply to other arguments in another group, and there may be yet other arguments which, though not discussed, are similar to those which are discussed. In short, our groupings are not particularly strict, nor are they all-inclusive. Rather, the groupings are offered as indicating very *general* ways in which the premises may fail to support the conclusion.[1] Further, the groupings should assist you in your analysis of other arguments by serving as a reminder of some of the kinds of mistakes that are made in giving arguments.

Some logicians use the word 'fallacy' when talking about unacceptable

---

[1] These groupings are general in the sense in which we used the expression 'insufficient evidence' in Chapter 8. There are many ways in which the evidence cited in the premises of an argument may be insufficient for establishing the truth of the conclusion. It is not reasonable, nor important, to establish all these ways. What is reasonable and important is to realize that there is a *kind* of error which prevents an argument from being acceptable, and to be able to recognize when an error of this kind has occurred.

arguments. Strictly speaking, a **fallacy** is an invalid form of argument, though the use of 'fallacy' is often limited to just those invalid forms of argument which seem plausible and which people often mistake for good arguments. Fallacies in this latter sense are often divided into two types: **formal fallacies** and **informal fallacies.**

Among the arguments which are sometimes called 'formal fallacies' are the two argument forms denying the antecedent and affirming the consequent. As shown in Chapter 3 and elsewhere in this text, these two argument forms are invalid, although they can be confused with the two valid argument forms denying the consequent and affirming the antecedent.

In spite of the lack of any single classification of arguments as fallacies, some argument forms have traditionally been identified by logicians as informal fallacies. We shall examine some of these arguments in the remainder of the chapter. What is important about the arguments we shall discuss is not how they fit into any particular system of classification; the important point is that we can use the methods developed in the previous chapters to analyze these arguments. As a result, we shall continue our procedure of identifying an argument's form to assess whether the support relation is satisfied. It is this task to which we now turn.

10:3 ARGUING AGAINST PEOPLE, NOT POSITIONS

When someone presents an argument, he or she also presents reasons (offers premises) in support of the conclusion. In criticizing an argument, one must show that either the form of the argument is in some way deficient or, even if the form is good, that at least one of the premises is false. This most basic feature of arguments, that it is the *premises* of an argument which establish or fail to establish the conclusion, is often overlooked by those who attempt to show that some particular conclusion is false or to get others to believe that it is false.

In general, this type of argument, an **argument against the person,**[2] involves the criticism of some person's beliefs or the position that person holds by criticizing the person rather than the beliefs or position. Of course, the defect in such criticism is that it is not the person who offers the argument which makes the argument a good one or a bad one; it is the evidence presented in the premises which determine this.

So-called 'arguments against the person' occur in many contexts and in many forms. In the following sections we shall look at three such forms.

10:3.1 Abusive Arguments   Our first instance of an argument against the person is **abusive arguments.** Such arguments get their name from the fact that

---

[2] The traditional name for such arguments is *'argumentum ad hominem'* or *'argument directed to the man'*. Where the arguments we discuss have a traditional name, I shall provide that name in a footnote.

they typically involve a direct attack on the *character* of some person and often involve *insults*. For example, suppose in a political debate that one candidate has just argued that the federal government should provide funds to the elderly to offset the high cost of heating oil, since inflation has outpaced their fixed incomes. In response, the candidate's opponent replies, "I would have expected my opponent to favor giving away money; he's always been soft-headed."

Implicit in the above remark is the following argument:

ARGUMENT 1

My opponent has always been soft-headed.

My opponent favors giving federal money to the elderly.

∴ We should not give federal money to the elderly.

Argument 1 is an instance of an abusive use of the argument against the person, since the crucial premise, 'My opponent has always been soft-headed', is no more than an attack on the character of the opponent; moreover, the remark is an insult.

The more important thing to note is that even though premise (1) may well be true, the person who gave argument 1 simply has not offered any support for the claim that federal money should not be given to the elderly to pay for heating oil. This can readily be seen by noting that argument 1 is not valid and, as it is formulated, is not an acceptable inductive argument.

We could, of course, add additional premises to the argument to give it a correct form; we could justify this by appealing to the principle of charity discussed earlier in the text. One such reformulation follows:

My opponent has always been soft-headed.

Everything that soft-headed people favor should not be done.

My opponent favors giving federal money to the elderly.

∴ We should not give federal money to the elderly.

The above argument does have a valid form, as can easily be shown with the procedures discussed earlier in the text. Notice, however, that the additional premise needed to make the argument valid is very likely *false*; even a soft-headed person might sometimes, if for no reason other than "by accident," favor something which should be done. As a result, the addition of the premise satisfies the support relation required of a valid argument; but, since the needed premise is false, the argument still does not provide good reason for accepting the conclusion.

Instead of adding those premises needed to make the argument valid, we might consider whether there is some inductive form appropriate to the argument. One such reformulation is:

My opponent has always been soft-headed.

Almost everything that soft-headed people favor should not be done.

My opponent favors giving federal money to the elderly.

∴ We should not give federal money to the elderly.

Changing 'everything' in the second premise to 'almost everything' changes the previous formulation to one that is not valid but *is* inductive. The crucial premise is still the added one, however. This is so since it too is likely false, or at least would need to be established by additional argumentation. Moreover, it would also have to be established that the opponent actually *is* soft-headed in the sense that everything he has always favored should not be done. Needless to say, the original argument, and hence the reformulation, does not address itself to these issues. We might also note at this point that it would probably be easier to establish the truth of the conclusion by offering *another, different,* argument than to establish the 'almost everything' premise. That this is so points to the diversionary nature of abusive arguments; they rest on attacking a person instead of arguing for the issue.

An additional reformulation of the argument can be given, a reformulation analogous to the arguments from authority discussed in Chapter 8:

Most of what my opponent favors are things which should not be done.

My opponent favors giving federal money to the elderly.

∴ We should not give federal money to the elderly.

This reformulation of the argument *is* an *inductive* argument—an instance of the form modified induction by enumeration. Therefore the support relation is satisfied, so the remaining relevant issue is that of the truth of the premises. The second premise is true; the opponent has asserted that he does favor giving federal money to the elderly.

The first premise, however, has not been established as true; no evidence has been given in support of it unless we take 'My opponent has always been soft-headed' as the "evidence." In short, we can say that abusive arguments against the person can be converted into inductive arguments having the form of a modified induction by enumeration, but the crucial premise is likely *not* to be supported by the insulting or abusive remark given in the original argument.[3]

We earlier noted that many informal fallacies appear to be plausible and persuasive. In abusive arguments the speaker typically attempts to evoke negative feelings or attitudes on the part of the audience in the hope that these will lead to their rejecting what someone else has asserted. For example, in the case just discussed, there is likely to be some emotional effect on those who are listening to the debate, and the effect on at least some of them will likely be to accept the view that federal money should not be given to the elderly. Keep in mind, however, that a negative feeling which leads to the rejection of a position is a psychological, not a logical, connection, and that no one should accept the conclusion of an argument for which no evidence has been given.

---

[3] As we have noted, they can also be converted into valid arguments, but again at the cost of introducing a premise which is likely to be false.

Our discussion of abusive arguments has been somewhat lengthier than the discussions of the other forms of argument against the person will be. The point, however, was to use this initial discussion as a model for the analysis of other forms. Moreover, we can use the following procedure when analyzing abusive arguments and the others that we shall consider:

1. Determine the logical form of the argument.

2. Determine if the argument is valid or inductive.

3. If the argument is either valid or inductive, determine whether the premises are true.

4. If the argument is neither valid nor inductive, consider reconstructing the argument by adding one or more additional premises. Often it will be clear what the suppressed premise is, and often that premise will clearly be implausible.

5. If the reconstructed argument has a false or highly improbable premise, then the original argument was not a good one.

10:3.2 Circumstantial Arguments   A second form in which arguments against the person occur has to do with citing circumstances about the person in such a way as to suggest, or imply, that these circumstances are sufficient for discrediting some position the person holds. Such arguments are **circumstantial arguments.** One instance of such an argument is the following claim:

(1) Of course she thinks the drinking age should be lowered; she owns a lot of stock in a liquor company.

Implicit in this remark is the view that the drinking age should *not* be lowered. If we suppose that the remark has been made in response to an argument whose conclusion was that it *should* be lowered, the effect of (1) is to suggest that the argument and position be discounted because the person who offered the argument has a vested interest in the drinking age. Notice that in this case the person who asserted (1) is citing some circumstance, that the opponent owns a lot of stock in a liquor company, as evidence that the opponent's position is wrong. Since this circumstance has no logical relationship to the issue of whether or not the drinking age should be lowered, citing it does nothing to support the position one way or the other.

Another instance of a circumstantial argument is provided in the following example.

EXAMPLE 1

Almost every year at every institution, the administration considers raising the tuition and often ends up doing so. Suppose that the student government at one of these schools forms a committee, examines the tuition levels at other schools, finds areas in the institution's budget where significant amounts of money could be saved, and then presents all this evidence in support of the position that tuition should *not* be raised. Suppose that the administration then responds to all of this with, "Why wouldn't the students say that tuition should not be raised? They're the ones who pay it."

This is a clear case of a circumstantial argument since, instead of arguing that tuition should be raised or showing what is wrong with the arguments put forth by the student government, the administration has simply cited the fact that students are the ones who pay tuition.

Before we look at another example, it is worth noting that the students, since they do pay tuition, would not want tuition to go up. As a result, it is not surprising that they hold this view and that they offer arguments in support of it. We can generalize this by saying that people very often defend their own views or offer arguments in support of issues which affect their lives. There is nothing wrong with this; the difficulty in example 1 is that the administration has simply cited this fact about the students and has not given any evidence at all to show that the students' position is wrong.

Situations like that in example 1 abound in the areas of government and business. For example, we often hear comments like the following:

(2) It's not surprising that Congressman Davidson voted for an increase in the defense budget; Grumman Aviation employs more people than any other corporation in his district.

(3) Of course Senator Roberts is opposed to gun-control legislation. The National Rifle Association was the single largest contributor in her last campaign.

(4) One would expect the automobile industry to favor protective tariffs. After all, their profits have declined immensely with the increase in foreign imports.

(5) It came as no surprise to me that savings and loans favor deregulating savings accounts. People have been withdrawing money and investing where they can get a higher rate of interest.

In (2) to (5), circumstances are cited as a way of discrediting the position held by some person or group. As a result, all are instances of circumstantial arguments, and they do not, therefore, show that the position being attacked is wrong.

Once again a word of caution is in order here. Consider (2): It may well be the case that Congressman Davidson does *not* really believe that an increase in the defense budget is necessary and that he voted for an increase only because Grumman is in his district. In this case we have someone who is acting contrary to his beliefs. Nonetheless, this is *not* sufficient to establish that there should *not* be an increase in the defense budget. To resolve this issue, other considerations and arguments would have to be raised, addressing such issues as national security, foreign policy, and the overall state of the economy.

Similar remarks apply to (3) through (5). The important point to be grasped here is that in assessing a position and the arguments for or against it, we want premises which are logically related to the conclusion; instances of circumstantial arguments do not meet this requirement.

In addition to citing circumstances about persons (that they own a lot of stock, have to pay for certain things, belong to a particular political party, attend a certain church, and so on), circumstantial arguments may cite facts about the way people live, to suggest or imply that they are really not sincere in what they are saying and, therefore, that what they are saying is false.[4] Two examples of this kind are provided by the following:

(6) Just listen to that. She sits there telling us abortion is not morally wrong. I guess that's what you'd expect from someone who had two of them in high school.

(7) He tells everyone that vegetarianism is the only healthy way to eat, but I saw him eating a hamburger at Dot's last Saturday night.

The real issues here are whether abortion is morally right and whether vegetarianism is the only healthy way to eat. Neither issue is resolved by pointing out that someone has had an abortion or someone has eaten a hamburger.

Each of the examples discussed above can be converted into a valid argument in much the same way as we did for abusive arguments. What one finds in doing this, however, is that the premise necessary for validity is obviously false. For example, the crucial premise in (6) and (7) would be something like 'Everything that an insincere person says is false'. It should also be noted that in many cases of circumstantial arguments, the information presented *is true*. The problem is that this information does not supply any support for the conclusion.

We earlier noted that there is no way of neatly classifying types of bad arguments. This is equally true of our use of the expressions 'abusive argument' and 'circumstantial argument' as a means of referring to some *general* features of some bad arguments. This is brought out by the following example:

(8) No wonder my opponent is opposed to rent-control legislation; she's been a slum landlord in this city for the past fifteen years.

In this case it is reasonable to say that circumstances have been invoked to question the sincerity of the individual and that calling her a slum landlord is also abusive. Whether one says that this is an abusive argument, a circumstantial argument, or both does not really matter. What is important is that the evidence presented in the premise, that someone has been a slum landlord for over fifteen years, supports neither the position that there should be rent-control

---

[4] It should be reiterated here that the purpose of presenting an argument is to provide support for the truth of the conclusion, and, hence, it is the truth of the conclusion which is at issue. Arguments against the person, as well as other arguments to be discussed in this chapter, skirt this issue of truth by focusing attention elsewhere. Implicit in circumstantial arguments is the idea that because of certain facts about a person, what the person says is not true. It is because these facts are typically irrelevant to the truth of the issue being discussed that such arguments are bad.

legislation nor the position that there should not. Moreover, this is shown by the fact that the original argument is neither valid nor inductive, and the premises necessary for it to have a good form are false or highly improbable.

10:3.3 "You, too" Arguments   Our final instance of arguments against the person is a favorite of children. Perhaps the psychological force of all such arguments can be appreciated when one realizes how much discomfort a child can cause a parent by saying, "You do it; why can't I?" We shall call this kind of argument the **"you, too" argument,** since it typically occurs as a response to a certain charge, and the response has the form "You do it, too."[5]

For example, when an eight-year-old child is found smoking a cigarette in the basement, a parent might say "You should not smoke" and receive the reply "You do."[6] The child's argument is of the following form:

ARGUMENT 2

You smoke.

∴ I should be allowed to smoke too.

As this argument stands, it is clearly invalid. What is needed is a premise to the effect that if a parent smokes then his or her eight-year-old child should be allowed to smoke. However, no evidence is provided for this premise, and it would be difficult to provide such evidence.

One reason for the difficulty of providing evidence in support of the needed premise is that one would have to establish the truth of 'At least some people should be allowed to smoke'. Having done that, one would also have to establish that the parent is one of these people and that the child is similar to the parent in those respects relevant to being allowed to smoke. We are *not* saying that such an argument cannot be given; what we are saying is that it has not been given and, therefore, the fact that the parent smokes does not provide support for the position that the child should be allowed to smoke.

Another way of viewing the difficulty with "you, too" arguments is to "turn them on their heads." Even if one could establish the truth of the statement 'If the parent is allowed to smoke, then the child should be allowed to smoke', it does *not* follow from this that either of them should be allowed to smoke. On the contrary, if the conditional statement could be established, then one of its consequences is 'If the child is not to be allowed to smoke, then the parent should not be allowed to smoke'. The two conditional statements leave open the question of whether the parent *and* the child should be allowed to smoke or whether neither of them should be allowed to smoke. A general feature of "you, too" arguments is a reliance on some principle to the effect that if

---

[5] Such arguments are traditionally called '*tu quoque* arguments'.

[6] As noted above, our characterization of certain kinds of arguments in this section is not intended to be strict. This is brought out in the present example by noting the suggestion of insincerity or hypocrisy on the part of the parent—a feature found in some circumstantial arguments.

something is appropriate for one person or thing, it is appropriate for another; but even if the needed instance of this principle can be established, one still must show that the thing at issue is appropriate for both, as opposed to being inappropriate for both.

10:3.4 Some Other Considerations   So far our discussion of arguments against the person has focused on cases in which either something *negative* has been said about a person or an argument or remark has been offered to *discredit* some position. Sometimes, however, such arguments consist of someone's saying something *positive* about a person or offering a remark in *favor* of a position. If we wanted a name for such cases, we might call them 'arguments for the person'. The important point is that these arguments go wrong in the same way as those we have already examined: Information is cited which is irrelevant to the truth or falsity of the issue under consideration. One example is the following:

EXAMPLE 2

Sandra received both her undergraduate and graduate law degrees from the most prestigious university in the state and has been a resident of our community for the past eight years. I urge you to support her antibusing position.

In this case quite flattering things have been said about Sandra, but they do not provide much, if any, support for the position that an antibusing position is correct. Here, by focusing on some positive aspects of Sandra, the speaker hopes to convince the audience to also think favorably about the position she holds. This example parallels argument 1, except that the present case focuses on the positive, not the negative.

As in the circumstantial arguments already discussed, we often find positive circumstances being offered as reasons for accepting some position. We shall not discuss any of these examples, since the comments in section 10:3.2 are also applicable to them. Instead, a few instances are listed below:

(9) Joe Simon has been a long-time member of our church and is a good family man. If he says Swenson is the one to vote for, that's good enough for me.

(10) Lauren is the friendliest person in our office, and she always has time to help out anyone with a personal problem. I think she should have been promoted to chief accountant instead of Brenda.

(11) Senator Mumphrey has always been a defender of the rights of us ordinary citizens. I urge you to support her efforts to secure passage of the animal welfare bill.

In each case of abusive or circumstantial arguments we have discussed, we have noted that the argument is a bad one because the characteristics of the individual, or the circumstances noted, were irrelevant to the issue under discussion. This does *not* mean that the character and circumstances of an individual are *always* irrelevant to the issue under discussion; in a great many cases they are relevant.

For example, the fact that someone had been convicted of income-tax evasion and perjury in the past may well be relevant to assessing his or her testimony during a tax audit. Or, we often cite circumstances in good arguments from authority; for example, graduating from a prestigious law school and being a senior partner in a highly regarded law firm *are* relevant to many issues regarding the law. However, in these kinds of cases we can construct deductive or inductive arguments concerning the point at issue, and these arguments typically have premises which are true or are very likely true. Neither of these conditions prevails in the examples we have discussed.

The fact that characteristics and/or circumstances are sometimes relevant and sometimes are irrelevant to an issue points to the need to examine each case on its own merits. It also points to the value of the procedures we have developed throughout this text, for these procedures are the ones which enable us to determine when something is relevant and when it is not.

EXERCISE 10-1

1. What are the two general things which can justify not accepting the conclusion of an argument on the basis of the evidence presented in the premises?

2. What is a fallacy? How is this word typically used?

3. Give an example of an argument against the person which is *both* abusive and circumstantial.

4. Give an example of an argument against the person which is *both* abusive and has the form of a "you, too" argument.

5. Give an example of an argument against the person which is *both* circumstantial and has the form of a "you, too" argument.

6. Are all arguments which cite the characteristics and/or circumstances of an individual bad arguments? Explain your answer.

7. Explain the error, or errors, which occur in each of the following examples by naming the error and explaining its occurrence in the example. Where possible, reconstruct the examples as arguments and then show that (1) if the premises are true, then the argument does not have an acceptable form and (2) if the argument has an acceptable form, then at least one of the premises is false.

    a. Don't pay any attention to what Robertson says about Professor Cline's math class. Robertson's nothing but a dumb jock anyway.

    b. What do you mean I'm being fired for using the company computer for my own consulting work? Murphy and a lot of others do the same thing and they haven't been fired.

    c. You have heard our colleague argue that in spite of the recent business slump the people in the secretarial pool deserve a substantial raise this year. But ever since Williams took over that area, she has pampered those women; I guess it's all part of her Women's Lib trip. The secretaries make plenty of money as it is. They don't need a raise.

d. Ladies and gentlemen, you can vote for me and bring responsible fiscal management to this city, or you can vote for my opponent.

circ. e. I was in Joe Riley's platoon when we were in the Army together, and he was the best leader I ever saw. Of course, he's the one to lead us out of our present financial difficulties and get this city back on its feet. I urge you to go to the polls and vote for Joe.

f. I would suggest that you pay no attention to Professor Donaldson's view that without increasing salaries the university will lose some of its best scholars. He, of course, would also gain personally from an increase.

g. I realize it's difficult for a southern Republican to get decent coverage for his campaign from the northeastern papers. But, then, what would you expect from lunatic liberals who are always pushing radical causes.

h. You have all heard the chairman of Motown Motors testify that unless an import tariff is levied, the balance-of-payments deficit will increase greatly over the next few years. Far be it from me to disagree with such an analysis; I will merely point out that sales for Motown Motors are down 23 percent this year, and most of that can be attributed to the rise in sales of imports.

i. For my opponent to call me soft on welfare legislation is surely a case of the pot calling the kettle black. His own voting record on these issues isn't one to brag about.

j. For almost a week now I have sat through these hearings while each of you senators has badgered me about the sources of my campaign funds. Yet, none of you has made public the source of your funds.

abus. circ. k. You have all heard Ms. Pemberton claim that women and men are equal in all things. She has told us that women are denied equal pay for equal work and are denied the opportunity for advancement, among other things. We have all politely sat here and listened to this while her children are in a day-care center somewhere and no one is taking care of her house and husband. Now I ask you, can we reasonably be expected to pay any attention to the testimony of such a person?

l. Whereas the mayor has made a wonderful presentation regarding the benefits the city will receive if the new convention center is approved by city council, I think it's only fair to point out that the mayor's brother owns the land on which the proposed center would be built.

m. Dean Aaron, when you asked me to come to your office to discuss a serious matter, I thought you had something important on your mind. You really shouldn't take seriously the talk of sexual harrassment in my class by someone as bubble-headed as Ms. Brighton. After all, she's one of the poorest students I've ever had.

n. If you're looking for someone to add a new family room onto your house, I strongly recommend Martin. He added a garage to my house, and before I hired him I checked with others he had built garages for.

> They were all as satisfied as I am.
>
> *you, too* o. We certainly would not deny that when the new president came to the university, almost $85,000 was spent on refurbishing the president's house. We also agree that with the recent rise in tuition, our timing may have been a little bad. Nonetheless, we would like to remind you members of the board that we also raised tuition last year. You may also recall that we made that decision at the meeting at which you approved the redecoration of the Board Room and the funds to have three of you members spend two weeks in Africa studying our A.I.D. project. In case you don't remember, those two items alone cost the university almost $35,000.

10:4 ARGUING FOR (OR AGAINST) THE WRONG POSITION

In the previous section we discussed one kind of bad argument, the attempt to discredit some position by discrediting the person who argues for it. We characterized such attempts as arguing against people, not positions. That is, the speaker shifts the focus from the argument which has been given to the person who is giving the argument. A related kind of bad argument occurs when the speaker shifts the focus from the initial issue to a different issue, or purports to be arguing for one position but actually offers an argument in support of a different position. Such arguments are the topic of this section.

10:4.1 Irrelevant Conclusion   Whenever a speaker offers an argument which is supposedly for (or against) one issue but is actually directed toward a different issue, the argument is an instance of an **irrelevant conclusion**.[7] Before looking at some examples, let's consider the two general ways in which irrelevant conclusion occurs.

SITUATION 1

The speaker wants to establish position A, but offers an argument which actually establishes B.

SITUATION 2

In response to someone else's argument for position C, the speaker offers an argument which shows that D is wrong.

The important thing to note about these cases, in contrast to those we discussed in the previous section, is that arguments which are instances of irrelevant conclusion can themselves be *good* arguments. For example, in situation 1 the speaker may well succeed in establishing that B is the case. In criticizing arguments of irrelevant conclusion, however, we do not directly criticize the argument which was offered. Rather, we show that *even if the argument which*

---

[7] Such arguments are traditionally called *'ignoratio elenchi'*.

was offered is a good one, it has nothing to do with the acceptability of the issue under consideration. Of course, the speaker may mistakenly believe that he or she has established that B is the case (situation 1) or that D is wrong (situation 2). In these cases the argument which is offered is not even acceptable itself, and it certainly cannot count for or against the issue under consideration.

Instances of irrelevant conclusion often occur in student term papers. One such instance follows.

EXAMPLE 3

Suppose that Muriel has decided to write a term paper in support of the position that the country should switch to solar energy as a means of meeting the country's energy needs. She then writes a nice ten-page paper pointing out, among other things, that fossil fuels are the major contributor to pollution of the environment as well as being nonrenewable. She then points out some of the dangers of nuclear energy, including problems like those at Three Mile Island and the problems associated with disposing of nuclear waste. "In conclusion," she writes, "it is clear that we should switch to solar energy."

The difficulty here is not with the claims made about fossil fuels and nuclear energy. Muriel may well have established that there are immense problems associated with both these forms of energy. The difficulty is that this conclusion does not establish what she set out to show: that we should switch to solar energy. To establish this conclusion, considerations such as technological feasibility and economic practicality would have to be treated. In summary, Muriel's term paper is an instance of irrelevant conclusion because the position actually supported by her paper is different from the one under consideration. As an instance of situation 2, consider the following dialogue:

EXAMPLE 4

Neighbor: (To student home from college) What are you majoring in at school?

Student: (Somewhat shyly) Well, since I like the subject, it's interesting, and the skills that I'm learning can be used no matter what career I might ultimately pick, I've decided to major in philosophy.

Neighbor: (Somewhat aghast) That's a strange choice. I have a nephew who majored in history and he still hasn't decided what he wants to do for a living.

In this example, the respondent has offered a claim which is irrelevant to the issue under discussion. Here the issue is whether one should major in a field which is interesting, which one likes, and which provides valuable skills regardless of career choice. The fact that someone who was in a different field has not decided what he wants to do does not address this central issue.

One may well wonder how anyone can be taken in by arguments which are instances of an irrelevant conclusion. Part of the answer to this was pointed out in our discussion of arguments against the person: There is often an emotional transference (positively or negatively) from one issue to another. Also, many uses of language tend to arouse emotions, with the result that we are sometimes less critical than we should be in analyzing the arguments presented for some conclusion. The following case is an example of this kind.

EXAMPLE 5

Prosecuting attorney to jury: Ladies and gentlemen of the jury: You have heard the testimony of over fifteen witnesses in this case. You have heard several noted psychologists testify that even sane people can become so enraged as to brutally attack and disfigure other human beings before killing them. To inflict such pain and suffering on other persons, and then to wantonly kill them, is behavior which no civilized society should tolerate. We should do everything in our power, then, to prevent such heinous behavior, and take strong, forceful measures to ensure that someone who has behaved that way will no longer be able to commit such mayhem on the members of our society. Thank you.

There is no doubt that the prosecuting attorney has painted a gruesome picture for the jury—a picture no doubt designed to persuade them to reach a verdict of "guilty." But, whereas the prosecutor wants the jury to conclude that the defendant is guilty, none of the evidence presented in his speech to the jury is relevant to this conclusion. At best, the evidence establishes a *different* conclusion: that society should attempt to prevent such brutal actions and punish those who commit them. Additional evidence and argumentation is needed to establish that the defendant is guilty of such behavior and should, therefore, be punished. In short, the prosecutor has argued for an irrelevant conclusion.

Instances of this kind of argument occur much more frequently than might be supposed. In general, they consist in arguing for some *overall principle* and then supposing, or hoping the audience will suppose, that what has been established is that some *particular action* is an instance of that principle. Examples of this are rampant in politics, where, for example, a mayor may attempt to convince his constituency that a particular mass-transit proposal should be funded by arguing, instead, that the city needs a mass-transit system. Similarly, a school board may attempt to convince people to support a bond issue for a particular remedial program by arguing that every student has the right to a good education. In such cases, everyone may agree that some mass-transit system or other is required or that every student has a right to a good education. The real issue, however, is whether the particular mass-transit system and the particular remedial program are the best way to achieve these goals; a different kind of evidence and argument is needed to establish that they are.

There is another large class of arguments which often are instances of an irrelevant conclusion: advertisements. We are all aware that the purpose of advertisements is to get the public to buy the manufacturer's product. If we were to reconstruct advertisements as arguments, most would have as their conclusion something like "You should buy our product." As arguments, we would expect advertisements to provide reasons in support of this position, reasons that are relevant to the kind of product being advertised.

For example, it would be reasonable to suppose that a car manufacturer would advertise such features as manufacturing quality, good mileage, reasonable price, low maintenance costs, and reliability. Often, however, the real "message" is more like, "If you buy our car you will get a product that allows you to escape" or "You will get a product that will attract members of the opposite sex." Or, cigarette manufacturers tell us that some of us have come a long way, or that by smoking their cigarettes we'll get more out of life. In a great many cases what is offered in the advertisement, if it is evidence for anything, is evidence for something other than the fact that the product is a good one. My favorite example of this kind is the long-time chain of muffler installers which, after starting to do brake work as well, advertised that it had more than twenty years experience under the car; this claim was, of course, part of an ad for brakes. Having that amount of experience is relevant, but it is relevant to claims about mufflers, not brakes, and is therefore an instance of irrelevant conclusion.

10:5 TRYING TO HAVE IT BOTH WAYS

In this section we shall look at argument forms whose plausibility rests on an ambiguity in the argument. There are two ways in which an argument, or a statement, might be ambiguous: Some word or expression in the argument may have more than one meaning, or the grammatical form of one of the sentences in the argument may be such that the statement as a whole may have more than one meaning. We shall discuss both cases.

10:5.1 Equivocation   When some word or expression is used with more than one meaning in an argument, the argument is a case of **equivocation.** We are all accustomed to the fact that many words in our language have more than one meaning. For example, 'pupil' is used sometimes to refer to someone who is a student and at other times to refer to a part of the eye. In a great many cases, the fact that some word or expression has more than one meaning causes no difficulty, since the context usually makes clear the sense in which the word is used.

In other cases, however, the meaning which is intended is not always clear, and using a word or expression in both its senses in the same context often leads to a bad argument. The following rather whimsical case is an example.

ARGUMENT 3

The end of everyone's life is his or her ultimate success.

Having a wooden stake pounded through his heart was the end of Dracula's life.

∴ Having a wooden stake pounded through his heart was Dracula's ultimate success.

At first glance the structure of this argument seems correct and, therefore, it seems that if the premises are true the conclusion is also true. But, obviously, the conclusion of argument 3 is false.

What we find on examining the premises is that the second one is true, but it is true in the sense that having a wooden stake pounded through his heart *caused* Dracula's death or brought his life to an end. Now, if we read 'The end of everyone's life' in the first premise in this sense, the premise is obviously false; death, or being killed, is hardly the ultimate success in everyone's life.

The sense in which the first premise is plausible is that in which 'end' is understood as 'goal'. If, however, we read 'end' in the second premise in this way, the second premise is obviously false. Having a wooden stake pounded through his heart was certainly not Dracula's goal; on the contrary, it was the one thing he wanted to avoid.

The two meanings of 'end', which make each of the premises true, involve an *equivocation* in argument 3. We can display the fact that argument 3 is a bad argument by rewriting it so that the appropriate meaning of 'end' occurs in each premise.

ARGUMENT 4

The goal of everyone's life is his or her ultimate success.

Having a wooden stake pounded through his heart killed Dracula.

∴ Having a wooden stake pounded through his heart was Dracula's ultimate success.

In argument 4 it is obvious that the premises, even if true, do not provide any support for the conclusion.

Many arguments which are instances of equivocation are ones which, at first glance, seem valid and seem to have all true premises. What we find, however, is that for all the premises to be true, at least one word or expression which occurs in the argument must be used with different meanings in its several occurrences. As a result, we can show that the argument is bad by pointing out that if we read the premises and the conclusion in such a way as to make the argument valid (that is, assign the ambiguous word or expression the same meaning throughout the argument), then at least one of the premises will be false or we will not have the intended conclusion of the argument. On the other hand, if the ambiguous word or expression is given the meaning which makes the premises and conclusions true, then the argument will be invalid. Since both support and true premises are required for the conclusion of an argument to be acceptable on the basis of the evidence presented in the premises, we are justified in rejecting the argument.

There are other ways in which equivocation leads to an unacceptable argument. We shall briefly discuss two of these.

There is a class of expressions whose meanings seems to change depending on the context in which they are used. One example is 'big' as it is used in:

(1) A tarantula is a big spider.

(2) Los Angeles is a big city.

The occurrences of 'big' in (1) and (2) are perfectly acceptable and involve no ambiguity in either use. However, the truth of the statements in which 'big' occur is in part a function of the kind of thing which is said to be big, as opposed to the idea that there is some certain fixed size such that anything larger is called 'big'.

For example, although Williamsburg, Virginia, is bigger than a tarantula, it is false that Williamsburg is a big city. Other instances of this type of expression are 'tall', 'heavy', and 'light'. Such expressions are **relative terms.**

The reason for introducing relative terms is that some arguments are valid when relative terms *do not* occur in them, and some related arguments are invalid because relative terms *do* occur in them. One example of such a valid argument is

ARGUMENT 5

Saint Bernards are dogs.

∴ A brown Saint Bernard is a brown dog.

An instance of a related but invalid argument is

ARGUMENT 6

Saint Bernards are dogs.

∴ A small Saint Bernard is a small dog.

We can explain the apparent difficulty with arguments which contain relative terms, and thereby avoid accepting an argument which should be rejected, by noting that these terms are *comparative*. By this we mean that the expressions in which they occur are best understood as implying some standard appropriate to the kind of things being talked about. For example, the statement that some dog is a small Saint Bernard should be understood as the claim that the dog is a small Saint Bernard *as Saint Bernards go*. Similarly, the statement that some dog is small should be understood as the claim that the dog is small *as dogs go*.

Given the above, the falsity of the conclusion of argument 6 is easily brought out by reading the conclusion as

A small Saint Bernard (as Saint Bernards go) is a small dog (as dogs go).

By reading relative terms in this comparative way, you are likely to avoid accepting arguments like argument 6. The error just noted often occurs with the use of evaluative terms such as 'good', 'great', 'superior', and 'bad'. An example of this error follows.

ARGUMENT 7

Henry is a good employee, and all employees are human beings. Therefore, Henry is a good human being.

10:5.2 Amphiboly   When the grammatical form of one of the sentences in an argument is such that the sentence has more than one meaning in the argument, we have a case of **amphiboly.** The problem here is that the statement expressed by the sentence as understood in one of its meanings may be true, while the statement expressed by the sentence as understood in its other meaning may be false. An example follows.

EXAMPLE 6

Suppose that while testifying in an arson case, one of the witnesses makes the following remark:

> Having started by someone's tossing a match on a pile of rubbish, the fire department then brought the blaze under control.

In this example the witness's remark has two significantly different interpretations:

(1) The blaze, which was started by someone's tossing a match on a pile of rubbish, was later brought under control by the fire department.

(2) After starting a fire by tossing a match on a pile of rubbish, the fire department later brought the blaze under control.

The difficulty here is that (1) and (2) are such that one could be true and the other false. In the trial, it is surely necessary to determine whether the witness's statement is to be understood as the claim that someone from the fire department started the fire or that it was started by someone else.

A similar case is provided by the following example. If you were the judge, would you be pleased or fine the lawyer for contempt of court?

EXAMPLE 7

Having badgered one witness after the other, and having angrily responded to the judge on several occasions, a famous lawyer was finally ordered by the judge to apologize in open court. With the greatest dignity, the lawyer approached the bench, bowed to the judge, and said, "I apologize. Your honor is right and I am wrong, as your honor generally is."

EXERCISE 10–2

1. Explain why, even in a good argument, we can have a case of irrelevant conclusion.

2. What are the two ways in which an argument can be ambiguous? Explain these, and give an example of each.

3. Each of the following words or expressions has at least two meanings. For each, provide two meanings and construct sentences in which each meaning is appropriate.
   a. Eye   b. The end of   c. Prime

d. Rare   e. Party   f. Plastic
g. Joint   h. Bent   i. Single
j. Swing

4. For each word or expression in problem 3, construct an argument in which there is an equivocation on the word in question.

5. What is a relative term?

6. We are sometimes accused of making mountains out of molehills. Suppose someone says, "A big molehill is just a little mountain." Is this person committed to saying that one and the same thing is both big and little? Explain.

7. Explain the error or errors which occur in each of the following examples by naming the error and explaining its occurrence in the example. Where possible, reconstruct the argument to show that if the premises are true then the argument does not have an acceptable form, or that if the argument has an acceptable form then at least one of the premises is false.

a. A: Tom was the rage of the party.

   B: What made him so angry?

b. Manager to employees: I realize that your salaries over the past two years have not kept up with inflation, and I honestly am glad that you also brought up the fact that you have three fewer holidays this year than last. These are, of course, important considerations in your request for a 12 percent raise, but I'm sure you also realize that a 12 percent raise would necessitate our raising the prices on our products, and we pride ourselves as having the lowest-priced Whazzit on the market.

c. What do you mean that Cecil and Gloria are still not getting along? Of course their marriage is well. After all, all's well that ends well and their marriage ended well.

d. A: I don't care what you say; I know that Benson promised to give his son Israel.

   B: What are you talking about?

   A: I witnessed Benson's will, and in the will he said that upon his death his son could have the promised land, and Israel is the promised land.

e. Lawyer to jury: I realize that the prosecutor has argued that my client is guilty of throwing the television set out the dorm window. But we all know that when people have a little too much to drink, they sometimes do things that they wouldn't ordinarily do; my client is just like everyone else in this regard.

f. A: Every age has its heroes.

   B: Who's the hero for forty-six-year-olds?

g. It's too bad that Mortimer's success didn't last very long. Only yesterday I heard that he spent years fighting against overwhelming odds, but he persevered until one day he succeeded.

h. There is no question that we ought to expand our present facilities. After all, the Board of Directors has approved the expansion and it's only a matter of time before they will urge us to open a branch location.

i. Cop: (To student driver) Say buddy, don't you know this is a one-way street?

Driver: Yes I do, officer.

Cop: They why are you driving the wrong way?

Driver: Well, after I turned right at the last block, my instructor said, "That was a good turn." My mom always told me that one good turn deserves another—so I turned here too.

j. Office staff to boss: We don't understand why you require us to spend so much time preparing annual reports and goals and objectives for next year. No one ever looks at all that stuff.

k. The awful movie *Blood and Guts* obviously made a lot of money. After all, the reviewers all said that *Blood and Guts* was the end of the producer, and every movie buff knows that the end of every producer is to make money.

l. A: Pam just told me she had a heavy date last night.

B: That's strange; I always thought she preferred smaller guys.

m. A: Last week my sociology class visited the county prison, and I was appalled at the conditions there: dirty cells, unsanitary plumbing, twelve people crowded in a cell built for six, and ghastly looking food. No human being should be treated that way.

B: Those bums should have thought about that before they broke the law. Maybe next time they'll think twice before doing it again.

n. A: The hostess must have been awfully embarrassed last night.

B: Why?

C: I just heard that everyone at the party cheered when, wrapped in cellophane, Brad arrived with his famous avocado dip.

o. Mother to child: I don't care if you don't like asparagus; eat it anyway. Just think of all those starving children in Asia who don't have enough food to eat.

p. Don't worry, Grandma; Leon won't break your antique chair by sitting in it. He's a lightweight boxer; not a heavyweight.

10:6 MAKING THINGS EASY—MAKING THINGS HARD

In this section we shall examine two forms of arguments which are often employed in public debate to obscure the central issue being discussed. In the first of these arguments the speaker presents a case in such a way as to suggest that there are only two satisfactory approaches or solutions to a given issue. Such arguments are instances of a **false dilemma**. Since there are more than two possible courses of action in almost all situations, we say that one who presents a false dilemma is making things easy—in the sense that the full complexity of the situation is not acknowledged. In the second form of argument, **complex question,** the speaker makes things hard for the audience by acting or speaking as though there is only one issue involved when in fact there are several, and then "forcing" the audience to respond in such a way that it appears that the audience has the same attitude toward the several issues.

10:6.1 False Dilemma   Our first example of a false dilemma is as follows:

ARGUMENT 8

If the operation of the proposed arena is subsidized by local funds, then property taxes will go up. If it is subsidized by funds presently provided by the state, then some presently offered services will have to be eliminated. Since the operation must be subsidized either by local funds or by state funds, either property taxes will go up or some services will be eliminated.

In discussing arguments of irrelevant conclusion, we noted that there are cases in which the argument presented by a speaker is unacceptable even if it happens to satisfy the support relation. Our present example of false dilemma is a case of this kind: Even though the argument is valid, it is unacceptable. The reason for its unacceptability is a result of the truth value of the premises; it is there that we shall direct our criticism.

Imagine the argument as being presented during a public debate by a person who is arguing against building the arena. The central issue is the effect that certain kinds of funding would have on the residents of the community, and the speaker suggests that, regardless of how the arena's operation is funded, the effects will be negative.

Now, in suggesting that the effects will be negative regardless of the manner of funding the arena, the speaker mentions only two funding alternatives: local funds and funds presently provided by the state. The speaker, in an attempt to get the audience to focus on the alleged negative effects of building the arena, has made things easy by not acknowledging the full complexity of funding possibilities for the operation of the arena.

For example, it might be possible to acquire *additional* state funds to subsidize the operation, or the community might sell bonds for this purpose. Or, perhaps the operation would not need to be subsidized at all. Again, it might be possible to scale down the project so as to avoid subsidizing.

The point which emerges is that the person who presented the argument has presented the audience with a *false dilemma*, since the 'either-or' premise is false. As a result, one need not accept the conclusion of the argument, since alternatives other than those offered by the speaker are available. In general, an argument of the above form, which depends on the truth of some 'either-or' statement, should be examined carefully; in most situations several alternatives are available, yet speakers often employ such arguments to direct attention to just two of them.

There are, of course, instances of 'either-or' statements which are all-inclusive in the sense that one of the disjuncts must be true: statements of the form 'p or not p'. An instance of this kind of statement occurs in the following argument.

ARGUMENT 9

If Myra has an abortion, then she will be doing something she considers immoral. If she doesn't have an abortion, then her child will be raised in an environment where it is neither wanted nor loved. Since she will either have an abortion or she won't, Myra will either do something she considers immoral or the child will be raised in an unhealthy environment.

This argument has the same form as the previous one and, like the previous one, is valid. Hence, if one is to reject the conclusion of the argument, at least one of the premises must also be rejected. Since the disjunctive statement is true, 'Myra will either have an abortion or she won't', we must look at the two conditional statements.

Let us suppose that Myra considers abortions to be immoral. In this case we have to consider the other conditional statement. Implicit in the statement is the assumption that the child will be raised in an unhealthy environment *because* Myra, though she does not want the child, will raise it. But this assumption is surely open to challenge, since Myra could bear the child and then put it up for adoption. There is no reason to suppose that in this situation the child will be unwanted or unloved, and good reason to suppose just the opposite.

In summary, when presented with arguments like the two just discussed, and especially the first of these, we should ask whether the two options cited in the 'either-or' statement are really the only two available. We should also ask whether the two conditional statements are true or whether they rest on some unwarranted assumption. This is, of course, just the procedure we used earlier in the book in assessing arguments: Having determined that the support relationship was satisfied, we then asked whether the premises were true.

10:6.2 Complex Question   The other instance of a logical error that we shall examine is brought out in the following example:

EXAMPLE 8

Suppose that Jason has been busted for drug possession and is on the witness stand in his own behalf. During the examination, the prosecutor asks, "Do you still associate with that group of degenerate pushers who hang out at Pinball Heaven?"

Although the prosecutor has asked what is verbally a single question, with the expectation of a single 'yes' or 'no' answer, the question actually involves at least three issues:

(1) That a group of degenerate pushers does hang out at Pinball Heaven

(2) That Jason used to associate with these people

(3) That Jason still does associate with these people

By asking the question in this way, the prosecutor wants to take the answer to one question as the answer to more than one, thereby establishing that even if Jason no longer associates with a certain group, he at least once did.

The proper response in situations like this, in which what looks like a single question is actually several questions, is to be certain to identify each of the questions and answer them individually. By doing so, one can avoid having the answer to one of the questions taken as the answer to the others as well.

Other cases, though not themselves instances of a complex question, are sufficiently similar to them to warrant attention here. One example follows.

EXAMPLE 9

In arguing that prayer should be allowed in public schools, an irate citizen says, "Would any right-thinking, patriotic American be opposed to these little children saying a prayer in school?"

The two issues raised in this example are what it is to be a right-thinking, patriotic American and whether prayer should be allowed in school.

Implicit in the speaker's remark is the view that anyone who is right-thinking and patriotic favors prayer in the schools, and anyone who opposes such prayer is neither right-thinking nor patriotic. In other words, the speaker is trying to disallow the possibility that one might be right-thinking and patriotic and yet be opposed to prayer in the schools.[8] This is not the case. It may be, for example, that a patriotic person who has carefully studied the Constitution has come to the conclusion that prayer should not be allowed in the public schools because it impinges on the separation of church and state that the framers of the Constitution intended to establish.[9]

In summary, we can say that one who asks a complex question makes things hard on the responder, since there is no way to answer what looks like a single question without answering others as well—others for which one is likely to want to give a different answer. We have also noted that a speaker may sometimes ask a question in such a way as to suggest that two or more issues are related in specific ways, whereas they need not be related in the way suggested by the speaker.

10:7 CAUSALITY

In this section we shall examine five kinds of logical errors, each related at least partially to some misconceptions about causal relationships. It is beyond the

---

[8] Notice the similarity here to abusive arguments against the person. Such phrases as 'simple-minded liberal' and 'closed-minded conservative' are designed to suggest that every liberal is simple-minded and that every conservative is closed-minded. We know, of course, that such generalizations are false. Yet such phrases, skillfully employed, carry a "guilt-by-association" aspect, one we should guard against.

[9] It is because the speaker's question can be answered with a simple 'yes' that example 9 is not an instance of a complex question.

scope of this text to treat such relationships in any detail, and, therefore, we shall rely on our common understanding of causality, supplemented by the discussion in the chapter on hypotheses and Mill's methods.

Grouping these five errors under the heading 'causality' does not mean that this is the only grouping possible, nor that each instance of the five errors always involves some misconstrued cause-effect relationship. As pointed out earlier in this chapter, our groupings are more or less arbitrary and are designed primarily to assist you in learning and remembering some of the more common logical errors that people make.

10:7.1 False Cause The first of the errors we shall discuss is that of **false cause.** This error is committed when one supposes that just because two events are found together, or happen at the same time, one is the cause of the other. For example, the nation's first major problem with a nuclear power plant occurred at the Three Mile Island plant. The plant also happens to be built on an island. One who argues that we can avoid any future accidents in nuclear power plants by not building them on islands, on the grounds that being built on an island caused the accident at Three Mile Island, has argued from a false cause. It was not being built on an island that caused the accident but, rather, the construction of the plant and certain procedures which were not followed; these things could happen again, regardless of where a plant is built.

Another, more serious, instance of this error occurs in the following example:

EXAMPLE 10

Person arguing against Gay Rights: Ever since the Women's Liberation movement began, we've had nothing but an erosion in the values this country was built on. It was bad when they started saying such stupid things as that a woman's place is not in the home or that a woman should be paid for raising kids and making sure that her husband was happy. As if it weren't enough to attack the sanctity of marriage, and to destroy many a good one, they're also bringing an end to healthy sexual relationships. Why, do you know that since the Women's Lib movement began, the number of gays has more than doubled?

The point the speaker is apparently attempting to make here is that concurrent with the Women's Liberation movement has been an increase in the number of gays; therefore, the movement has caused this increase. Now, even if there has been an increase in the number of gays, it is not sufficient to explain this by ("blame" it on) the Women's Lib movement; further argumentation is needed to establish this point.

More important, however, is the fact that the speaker has *not* established that there has been an increase in the number of gays. A more plausible explanation is that the number of gays has remained relatively constant, though more people are willing to openly express their sexual preference now than in the past. The argument does not succeed in establishing that the number of gays has more than doubled, let alone that the Women's Liberation movement has caused this.

Both these examples involve someone's thinking that one thing was the cause of something, whereas it was actually something else which was the cause. There is another instance of false cause which is more specific than this. This error is called *'post hoc ergo propter hoc'*, meaning 'after this, therefore because of this'; sometimes the error is just called the *'post hoc* fallacy'. The error consists in concluding that an event E_1 was caused by another event E_2 simply because E_1 followed E_2.

EXAMPLE 11

Ed, sitting with his roommate, comments that he really misses his girlfriend Diane and wishes that she would call. Just then the phone rings, and it is Diane.

If Ed should conclude that his wishing Diane would call was the cause of her calling, this would be an instance of the *post hoc* fallacy.

Of course, not may people would be likely to call example 11 an instance of a causal connection; more likely, it would be regarded as a coincidence. Nonetheless, people sometimes do mistake a coincidence for a causal connection simply because one event preceded another. Someone who has had a sore back and hangs a clove of garlic around her neck may argue that the garlic cured the sore back; or someone who wins a raffle drawing on the day the newspaper astrology section says he will be lucky may argue that the position of the planets caused him to win the raffle.

As we noted in Chapter 9, causal relationships, causal laws, and the ways they are established are complex matters. We also noted that one event's following another is relevant to determining whether there is a causal relationship between the two events. However, a causal relationship between two events is typically reinforced by a statement of the form 'Whenever events of kind E_1 occur under conditions C, events of kind E_2 occur'. As a result, we can often test an alleged causal relationship between two events by seeing if the relationship holds in *another case*. For example, if wearing a clove of garlic is causally related to curing sore backs, then wearing garlic should work more than once, and it should work for more than one person.

Before concluding this section, let us show the error involved in instances of false cause by displaying the argument form of these arguments. The form is as follows:

FORM OF FALSE CAUSE

A occurred at the same time as (or immediately following) *B*.

∴ *A* was caused by *B*.

This form is obviously invalid, as can be shown with many counterexamples (example 11 is one). We can, of course, reconstruct the argument to make it valid by applying the principle of charity, supposing that one who argues in the above way has simply left out an "obvious" premise. The most reasonable reconstruction of the above argument form is

Any thing E_1 which occurs at the same time as (or immediately following) another thing E_2 is caused by E_2.

A occurred at the same time as (or immediately following) B.

∴ A was caused by B.

This argument form can easily be shown to be valid by the methods developed in Chapter 7.[10] Whereas the argument is valid, it nonetheless fails to be acceptable since the additional criterion of truth is not satisfied. In particular, the added premise is false. Once again, we have an example in which we can show that an argument is unacceptable by showing, first, that its form is unacceptable and, second, that when it is put in an acceptable form, we end up with a premise whose truth is highly questionable or obviously false.

10:7.2 Common cause   An error related to false cause is that of **common cause.** This error occurs when one mistakenly concludes that A was caused by B, when in fact both A and B were caused by some other thing C. An example follows.

EXAMPLE 12

Alexis, a new salesperson recently hired by the High Pressure Sales Company, notices that three of his colleagues were recently promoted and then each received a bonus. Wishing to earn a bonus, Alexis reasons that all he has to do is get promoted.

In this example Alexis has mistakenly argued in the following way:

Three salespersons received a bonus immediately following a promotion.

∴ The promotion was the cause of the bonus.

Suppose that the actual explanation is that the three people who were promoted and received a bonus did so because they each had exceptionally high sales. In other words, suppose that *because* they had high sales, they were promoted *and* they received a bonus.

Given that this is the explanation, there are two points to note about example 12. The first is that this example does not rest on just one instance of some event being followed by another. Were Alexis to observe still more instances of people receiving a promotion and then a bonus, he would gather an increasing amount of evidence for the hypothesis that the promotion results in a bonus. In such a case, it is reasonable to treat the resultant argument as an inductive one and to assess it in terms of the discussion of Chapter 8.

---

[10] We need merely instantiate E_1 and E_2 in the first premise to A and B, respectively, and the conclusion follows by affirming the antecedent.

The second point is that whereas Alexis may gather more and more evidence in support of the hypothesis that being promoted results in a bonus, this hypothesis is nonetheless *false*. What we end up with in such a case is an inductive argument with all true premises and a false conclusion. It should be noted, therefore, that even when it may be reasonable to accept the conclusion of an inductive argument of the kind presented in example 12, such an argument may still be an instance of the error of common cause.[11]

10:7.3 Hasty Generalization

In our discussion of inductive arguments in Chapter 8, we noted that even if an inductive argument has all true premises, we must nonetheless make sure that some additional features are not present before we accept the conclusion on the basis of the premises. Two of these features singled out for discussion were *insufficient evidence* and *unrepresentative sample*. Although the two errors we are about to discuss do not go beyond anything you have already learned in prior chapters on induction, they occur frequently enough to warrant their being mentioned again here.

The first of these errors is that of making a **hasty generalization.** This error often occurs when, on the basis of a single case or a few cases, someone argues that all individuals have some property. For example, the owner of a drugstore who is robbed by a Chicano may conclude on this basis that all Chicanos are thieves, or a student who takes one exam in a course and does well on it may conclude that she will do well on all the exams.

This error also occurs in causal contexts, which is why it is in this section. In such contexts one typically concludes, on the basis of one case or a limited number of cases, that one kind of event is the cause of another kind of event. For example, someone may erroneously conclude that eating raw oysters makes people sick on the basis that he ate raw oysters once and got sick.

Instances of a hasty generalization are typically those which indicate that someone has *jumped to a conclusion.* We can avoid this error by remembering that, for any inductive generalization to be an acceptable one, the sample size must be large enough and must be representative of the total class of objects about which the generalization is made.

Another error, which is almost the mirror image of hasty generalization, is that of **accident.** This error occurs when one mistakenly concludes that some generalization is applicable to a particular case, either on the basis of some accidental features of the case or because the generalization has been applied to a case for which it was not intended. This error is committed in the following argument:

---

[11] In addition to common-cause arguments, other false-cause arguments may contain premises which show that there is a well-established correlation between events of kind E_1 and events of kind E_2. In such cases the correlation is not sufficient for establishing that there is a causal relationship between the kinds of events, or instances of these kinds. For example, there is a very high correlation between those events described as getting up in the morning and those described as getting dressed; yet my getting up this morning was not the cause of my getting dressed.

ARGUMENT 10

Anyone in possession of stolen goods is guilty of a crime.

Officer McDougal, having just arrested Benny the Fence, is in possession of a stolen diamond necklace.

∴ Officer McDougal is guilty of a crime.

In argument 10, the generalization that those who are in possession of stolen goods are guilty of a crime has been mistakenly applied to Officer McDougal. Moreover, it has been mistakenly applied because the generalization is not intended to apply to police officers who recover stolen objects in the line of duty. As a result, even though McDougal may be in possession of the necklace, it does not follow that he is guilty of a crime.

It should be noted here that since McDougal is not guilty of a crime, the first premise of the argument as stated is not true; McDougal provides an instance in which someone does possess a stolen object but is not guilty of a crime. The intent of the generalization may be made clear by saying, for example, that someone who steals an object and has it in his or her possession is guilty of a crime; then it becomes clear that the mere fact that McDougal now has the necklace in his possession does not mean that he is a criminal.

Perhaps the most important point here is that generalizations are often expressed by citing only one or two characteristics, whereas additional ones are also intended to apply. By making these additional characteristics explicit, we can show that the original argument is either invalid or has at least one false premise, and we can thereby avoid making the error of accident.

10:7.4 Appeal to Ignorance   Whenever someone argues that a statement is false because it has not been proved to be true, or is true because it has not been proved to be false, we have an instance of an **appeal to ignorance.**[12] Although such arguments are not specifically limited to causal cases, they are included in this section because a great many instances of this error do occur when people attempt to show that certain hypotheses or causal explanations are right or wrong. One such example follows.

ARGUMENT 11

With all the effort people have spent trying to show that people do not communicate with one another through mental telepathy, no one has succeeded in showing that telepathy does not occur. As a result, people do communicate with one another through mental telepathy.

The structure of this argument is straightforward:

No one has shown that people do not communicate through mental telepathy.

∴ People do communicate through mental telepathy.

---

[12] Such arguments are traditionally called 'argumentum ad ignorantiam'.

Schematically, we have:

Claim C has not been shown to be false.

∴ Claim C is true.

This structure is clearly invalid, as can be shown with dozens of counterexamples. Consider one case: No one has shown that it is false that a major war will break out on August 14, 1991. It surely does not follow from this that a major war *will* break out on that date!

Although in many instances such arguments are obviously bad, it is somewhat surprising how often one finds them being used. For example, one often hears comments like "No one has shown that God doesn't exist; therefore He does"; and we often hear people say things like "We don't know everything there is to know," as though this fact alone establishes the truth of their position. And consider the example with which we began this section. Perhaps none of us would accept argument 11 as a good one, but how many times have you heard someone say something like "No one has shown that psychic phenomena occur; therefore they don't"? This is just another appeal to ignorance in its other form.

In the appeal to ignorance exemplified in argument 11, the fact that there is no evidence against a claim has been taken to be evidence for the claim. As we have just shown, this is clearly wrong. In the other version of the appeal to ignorance (that since a statement has not been shown to be true, it is false) the lack of evidence for a claim has been taken as evidence against the claim. In most cases this is equally wrong. I use the words 'in most cases' here because there are situations in which the failure to find evidence for a claim *is* evidence against the claim. These are cases in which the following conditions are met:

(1) If the claim were true, evidence of its truth could be found.

(2) Sincere efforts have been made to secure this evidence.

(3) The evidence has not been found.

One instance of this kind is the following:

EXAMPLE 13

Joan Reynolds has just applied for a mortgage to buy a new home. After a careful examination of her employment record, income, and credit history, the bank finds no evidence to suggest that she is a bad credit risk.

In example 13, the failure to find any evidence that Joan Reynolds is a bad credit risk *is evidence* that she is not a bad credit risk. Indeed, it is just the evidence lending institutions look for before making a loan.

If we ask what the difference is between example 13 and some appeals to ignorance, the answer can be found in (1) to (3) above. Notice that these three conditions could be written as an argument having the form denying the consequent, a valid argument form, and that in the case of example 13 the premises are true. In contrast, in those instances in which we do have an appeal to ignorance, no such argument can be constructed.

10:8 PLAYING ON EMOTIONS

In this section we shall examine methods which are often employed to get a person or a group of people to accept a position. In each case the speaker attempts to secure agreement not by offering evidence in support of the position, but rather by appealing to the audience's emotions.

10:8.1 Appeal to the People
The first method we shall discuss can be recognized by the fact that the speaker attempts to get some group to agree to a particular position by appealing solely to their bigotry, biases, and prejudices or, in some cases, merely to their desire to hear what they already believe. Any such case is an **appeal to the people**.[13] The persuasiveness of such appeals probably is due to the fact that people generally like to have their own beliefs and feelings reinforced, and the fact that such appeals make it easy to avoid the often hard work involved in critically evaluating a position.

The next two examples are instances of appeal to the people.

EXAMPLE 14

Owner of a small store to other store owners: I've heard that Sanchez and that greasy group of his are trying to buy the old drugstore on the corner and are planning on starting a business there. Well if they do, you can be certain that before long the place will be crawling with dope pushers and junkies, and not long after that our nice quiet neighborhood will be the target of roving street gangs. Hell, besides ruining our businesses, it won't even be safe to walk the streets anymore. I urge you to join with me to prevent those outsiders from moving into this neighborhood.[14]

EXAMPLE 15

Football coach to alumni after a 2–9 season: I know you're disappointed about this year's record. Heck, we're all disappointed—no one more than me. And I know you want a winning team. We all do, and no one wants it more than me. Well, we've got a group of kids who are hungry for winning. And I'm hungry for winning. So you can bet that come this time next year, I'll be standing in this very same spot but glorying with you about the success of our season.

In the first of these examples, the store owner has attempted to get the other store owners to assist him in preventing a group of people from a different ethnic group from buying property in the neighborhood. Notice, however, that no good evidence has been presented for the claim that this group should not

---

[13] Such arguments are traditionally called 'argumentum ad populum'.

[14] This example also has elements of an abusive argument against the people.

buy the property. Instead, the speaker has appealed to the group's prejudices and fears by using such expressions as 'that greasy group of his', 'dope pushers and junkies', 'outsiders', and 'roving street gangs'. In short, the speaker has attempted to arouse the group's emotions and then, on the basis of these emotions, get them to accept his position.

It should be clear that this is an unacceptable argument since what has been presented as evidence for the conclusion simply does not support the conclusion. The fact (if it is a fact) that a group has a certain emotional attitude toward something in no way establishes the accuracy of that attitude.

In example 15 the coach has not appealed to fears, prejudices, etc., but has instead appealed to the hope and desire of the alumni that the school have a winning football team. As in the previous case, the coach has simply talked about attitudes: being disappointed, wanting a winning team, etc. By arousing such feelings, the coach is attempting to get the alumni group to accept the view that next year's team will have a winning record. As in example 14, however, having these desires in no way provides evidence for the conclusion that the team will have a winning season. We can put this quite succinctly by saying that wanting something does not mean that one will get what one wants.

One more important point needs to be made in this section: when people are engaged in a discussion about significant social issues, it is nearly impossible to avoid using some expressions which will arouse emotions or to avoid appealing to these emotions. For example, not even a reasoned debate on the issue of reinstituting capital punishment can proceed very far without raising issues of justice, individual rights, the rights of society, and fairness. The fact that such issues are discussed and people have divergent attitudes toward them does not mean that all such discussions should be labeled appeals to the people. Appeals to the people occur when the speaker's case rests *entirely* on an appeal to the prejudices, biases, or attitudes of the audience. When other evidence is given in support of a position, we can evaluate the resultant argument by using the procedures developed throughout this book.

10:8.2 Appeal to Pity   The second kind of argument which trades on appeals to people's emotions is an **appeal to pity**.[15] Such arguments are characterized by the speaker's citing circumstances which are designed to arouse feelings of pity in the audience, to get them to accept the speaker's position. A more or less "classic" instance of this argument is the following example:

EXAMPLE 16

Suppose that a student has failed all the exams in a course and expects, therefore, to receive a failing grade in the course. As a result, the student goes to the professor and says: "I know that I have not done very well in this course, but all my other grades are very good. I wouldn't even have taken this course except that it's required; after all, it isn't at all connected

---

[15] Such arguments are traditionally called *'argumentum ad misericordiam'*.

with what I'm going to do after I graduate. I have a terrific job offer in another city waiting for me as soon as I get my degree. Surely you don't want to destroy my future, so why don't you give me a 'C' in the course?"

The student's argument here is a clear case of appeal to pity, one which ignores the fact that he has failed all the exams in the course. It is this latter fact, of course, which is relevant to determining the grade the student should receive in the course. Instead of addressing this issue, the student attempts to get the professor to take pity on him and give him a better grade by talking about a ruined future, and so on. In short, the student has argued that owing to his original circumstances (about which he hopes the professor will have some pity), he should receive a 'C' in the course. These circumstances are irrelevant to the determination of the grade the student should receive, so they do not satisfy the support relation between the premises and conclusion of the argument.

Arguments involving an appeal to pity are not limited to individuals; many organizations and groups also resort to this tactic. With the passage of legislation to improve working conditions, to increase safety, and to decrease pollution, many corporations have resorted to an appeal to pity in an attempt to convince the government that they should be exempt from such legislation. An example follows.

EXAMPLE 17

While testifying before a congressional committee, the spokesman for a large coal-mining company says the following: "We realize that at the present time we are in violation of several regulations regarding safety in our mines. Nonetheless, we would like to point out to you that with the recently negotiated contract with the union our operating costs have gone up drastically. Moreover, our profits have declined greatly during the past two quarters. We would also like to mention that with the present energy situation in this country we are doing all that we can to increase productivity and lessen our dependence on foreign imports. Even in these hard times, we have spent almost a quarter of a million dollars on safety improvements in our mines. To ask us to do more at this time is simply not to realize how hard things are for us."

In this example the speaker has focused on the "hard times" the company is having, with the hope that the members of the committee will take pity on the company and exempt it from some of the safety requirements.

Thus far we have focused on illegitimate appeals to pity. There are some situations, however, in which personal circumstances may be relevant in assessing someone's position. For example, suppose that to buy some food for her hungry children and to get some money for rent so she won't be evicted, a mother who has been unable to find a job attempts to rob a small corner store but is apprehended. Her circumstances do not in any way change the fact that she is guilty of a robbery (to argue that she should not be found guilty because of her circumstances would be to make the error of appealing to pity); however, they may well be relevant in determining the sentence that she should receive as a result of the robbery.

The point of this case is that personal circumstances are sometimes relevant in assessing a position. Their relevancy is not, however, a function of the feelings of pity they arouse but, rather, a function of the relationship these circumstances have to the issue. In the above case, the woman's circumstances are not relevant to the issue of guilt, though they are relevant to the issue of her sentence.

In the previous section we noted that in some cases the fact that some arguments arouse feelings on the part of the audience does not automatically indicate an appeal to the people. A similar situation holds for some arguments in which the audience has feelings of pity for the speaker or for those whom the speaker represents. For example, if someone argued that a company's retirement program was inadequate because the retirees were unable to maintain a reasonable standard of living and many of them had to sell their homes to make ends meet, the fact that most people would feel pity toward the retirees does not mean that this is an appeal to pity. Not being able to maintain a reasonable standard of living and having to sell one's home upon retirement *are* relevant to the issue of the adequacy of a retirement program. To determine whether we do have an appeal to pity, we must ask whether the argument appeals only to our feelings of pity or whether the speaker also offers premises which are relevant to the issue under discussion.

10:8.3 Appeal to Force   Our final instance of arguments which turn on people's emotions is the **appeal to force**.[16] It is perhaps misleading to call such instances 'arguments', since typically appeals to force are used to get people to *do* certain things by threatening harm, not to get them to accept the conclusion of an argument. For example, suppose a prisoner of war is told that unless he signs a confession, he will be tortured. If the prisoner has not done what he is supposed to "confess" to, the threat of being tortured is unlikely to make him accept as true the claims in the "confession." Nonetheless, the threat of force is used to get him to do something—namely, sign the confession.

Another instance of the appeal to force is given in the following example:

EXAMPLE 18

Parents to daughter: We simply cannot stand that guy you have been dating, and we want you to stop seeing him. Unless you tell him you're not going to go out with him any more, we're not going to give you the money for next semester's tuition.

In this example the parents are attempting to get the daughter to stop seeing her boyfriend. No good reasons are given to support the claim that she should do this, but, instead, the threat of not paying next semester's tuition is used to try to force her to do what her parents want.

---

[16] Such arguments are traditionally called '*argumentum ad baculum*'.

EXERCISE 10-3

1. What do the arguments which commit the errors of appeal to the people, appeal to force, and appeal to pity have in common?

2. In what ways can one respond to arguments which commit the error of false dilemma?

3. Explain what it means to say that someone has asked a complex question. Provide three examples of such questions.

4. Does the defense attorney who says to the jury "No evidence has been presented which shows that my client is guilty; therefore he is innocent" commit the error of argument from ignorance? Explain.

5. Could we ever discover instances of a common cause by using Mill's methods? Explain.

6. What kinds of things should we do to avoid making the error of hasty generalization?

7. Identify any errors in each of the following, and explain why they are errors.
   a. Do you really believe that God, in all His infinite goodness, would actually inflict needless suffering on His people?
   b. I've noticed that every time I stumble around, I'm drunk. Therefore, stumbling causes drunkenness.
   c. If I study this material, then it won't be on the exam, so my studying won't do any good. If I don't study the material, then it will be on the exam, but since I didn't study it, it still won't do me any good. Therefore, since what I do study won't be on the exam and what I don't study will be on the exam, there is no point in studying.
   d. Yes, your honor, I know that when my client drove his car through the store window he was going 45 in a 25-mile-an-hour zone. But if you suspend his license, he'll no longer be able to commute from school to work so he will be unable to continue to support himself and get an education.
   e. Yesterday I bought my first lottery ticket, and it was a $100 winner. I'm going to go buy another $100 winner today.
   f. In spite of all the talk about it, no one has shown that X-rated movies cause an increase in sex-related crimes. Therefore, these movies don't cause an increase in such crimes.
   g. Why, even after we've told you that we don't approve, are you going to continue to see that sleazy, good-for-nothing bum?
   h. Congressman A: Is it true that the bill you're trying to get passed still needs more supporters?

      Congressman B: Yes, that's true.

      Congressman A: Well, if you don't vote to keep Grinstead Air Force Base open, I'll vote against your bill.
   i. Mr. President, no one has shown that if we intervene in the Mideast, the Soviet Union will also send in troops. Therefore, they won't send in troops.

j. Senator, a great many auto workers are from your state. If you don't vote to subsidize Crestler Motors, you can be sure that we will remind the workers of that the next time you are up for reelection.

k. If you want to sail, you'd better not buy a catamaran. Johnson got one, and the first time out he fell overboard and drowned.

l. Memo from university president to faculty: Commencement is next week, and I'm sure that you all want to attend. Of course, you're also aware that those who are worthy of promotion support our university's activities.

m. Why are all Democrats flaming liberals and all Republicans backward-thinking conservatives?

n. Your honor, if I am going to be found guilty and punished for driving 90 miles an hour, then you must certainly also do the same to Officer Dunhill. After all, he had to be driving at least 90 miles an hour to catch me.

o. I don't care what those other parents let their kids do. I'm the boss in this family and as long as you live in this house you'll do what I say.

p. It's wrong to hurt another person. So when McGoon sacked the quarterback and hurt him, McGoon did something wrong. As a result, it's wrong to sack a quarterback.

STUDENT STUDY GUIDE

Chapter Summary

1. A good argument is one in which the premises support the conclusion and in which the premises are true. (section 10:1)

2. Arguments should be rejected if either the premises do not support the conclusion or at least one premise is false. (section 10:2)

3. A **fallacy** is an invalid form of argument. This term is often limited to those invalid forms of arguments which seem plausible and which people often mistake for good arguments. (section 10:2.1)

4. In an **argument against the person,** one criticizes someone's beliefs or the position someone holds by criticizing the person rather than the belief or position. Such arguments are unacceptable because it is not the person who offers the argument which makes the argument good or bad; it is the evidence presented in the premises which does this. (section 10:3)

5. **Abusive arguments** are a type of argument against the person and typically involve a direct attack on the character of some person. Such arguments also often involve insults. (section 10:3.1)

6. **Circumstantial arguments** are a type of argument against the person and typically involve citing circumstances about a person in such a way as to suggest that these circumstances are sufficient for discrediting some position the person holds. (section 10:3.2)

7. In **"you, too"** arguments, one responds to a charge or criticism by replying that the critic is also guilty of the charge or criticism. (section 10:3.3)

8. One way to show the problem with "you, too" arguments is to note that they rely on some principle to the effect that if something is appropriate for one person or thing, it is appropriate for another. One may either show that there are relevant differences in the two cases or, if there are no relevant differences, it may be argued that the issue in dispute is inappropriate for both parties. (section 10:3.3)

9. An argument which is supposedly for (or against) one issue but is actually directed toward a different issue is an instance of an **irrelevant conclusion.** (section 10:4.1)

10. In criticizing arguments of irrelevant conclusion, we show that even if the argument which was offered is a good one, it has nothing to do with the acceptability of the issue under consideration. (section 10:4.1)

11. The plausibility of some bad arguments rests on the fact that the arguments are ambiguous. Arguments may be ambiguous because some word or expression in the argument has more than one meaning or because the grammatical form of one of the sentences used in giving the argument is such that the sentence has more than one meaning. (section 10:5)

12. When some word or expression is used with more than one meaning in an argument, the argument is a case of **equivocation.** (section 10:5.1)

13. **Relative terms** are words or expressions whose meaning seems to change, depending on the context. Relative terms are comparative in the sense that they imply some standard appropriate to the kind of things being discussed. (section 10:5.1)

14. When the grammatical form of one of the sentences in an argument is such that the sentence has more than one meaning in the argument, the argument is an **amphiboly.** (section 10:5.2)

15. A **false dilemma** occurs when a speaker presents a case in such a way as to suggest that there are only two satisfactory approaches or solutions to a given case, whereas in fact there are more than two. (section 10:6.1)

16. A **complex question** occurs when a speaker asks one question which involves more than one issue and then expects to take the answer to the one question as a response to all the issues. (section 10:6.2)

17. In general, the error of **false cause** is committed when one supposes that just because two events occur at the same time, one is the cause of the other. (section 10:7.1)

18. If one concludes that E_1 is the cause of E_2 simply because E_2 followed E_1, we have a case of *post hoc ergo propter hoc,* or the *post hoc* fallacy. Such errors result in taking a correlation between two events, or two kinds of events, as sufficient evidence to establish a causal relationship. (section 10:7.1)

19. The error of concluding that one thing was caused by another when in fact both were caused by yet a third is an instance of **common cause.** Many common-cause and false-cause arguments are based on well-established correlations. The problem is that these correlations are not causal relationships. (section 10:7.2)

20. When one concludes on the basis of a single case or a limited number of cases that one kind of event is the cause of another kind of event, or concludes that

all individuals in a given group have a characteristic possessed by one or a few individuals, one makes the error of **hasty generalization.** Such errors can often be detected by noting that the person jumped to a conclusion. (section 10:7.3)

21. When one mistakenly concludes that some generalization is applicable to a particular case, either on the basis of some accidental features of the case or because the generalization has been applied to a case for which it was not intended, we have an instance of the error of **accident.** (section 10:7.3)

22. When someone argues that a statement is false because it has not been proved to be true, or is true because it has not been proved to be false, we have an instance of an **appeal to ignorance.** (section 10:7.4)

23. In some cases the failure to show that a statement is true is evidence that the statement is false. In such cases, three conditions have to be satisfied: (1) If the claim were true, evidence of its truth could be found; (2) sincere efforts have been made to secure this evidence; and (3) the evidence has not been found. (section 10:7.4)

24. When a speaker attempts to get some group to agree to a particular position by appealing solely to their bigotry, biases, and prejudices or, in some cases, merely to their desire to hear what they already believe, we have an instance of **appeal to the people.** (section 10:8.1)

25. In an **appeal to pity,** the speaker cites circumstances which are designed to arouse feelings of pity in the audience, to get the audience to accept the speaker's position. Sometimes appeals to pity are legitimate, but when they are they are relevant to the conclusion of the speaker's argument. (section 10:8.2)

26. An **appeal to force** is an attempt to get people to do certain things by threatening to harm them. Such "arguments" differ from others we have discussed, since they are not an attempt to get the audience to accept the conclusion of an argument. (section 10:8.3)

Key Terms

Fallacy	Complex Question
Argument against the Person	False Cause
Abusive Argument	Common Cause
Circumstantial Argument	Hasty Generalization
"You, Too" Argument	Accident
Irrelevant Conclusion	Appeal to Ignorance
Equivocation	Appeal to the People
Relative Terms	Appeal to Pity
Amphiboly	Appeal to Force
False Dilemma	

Self-Test/Exercises

1. What two general things would justify not accepting the conclusion of an argument on the basis of the evidence presented in the premises? (section 10:2)

2. What is a fallacy? How is this word typically used? (section 10:2.1)

3. Give an argument against the person which is both abusive and circumstantial. (sections 10:3.1 and 10:3.2)

4. Give an abusive argument which is also an instance of an irrelevant conclusion. (sections 10:3.1 and 10:4.1)

5. Explain why even a good argument can be a case of irrelevant conclusion. (section 10:4.1)

6. Give an example of each of the following kinds of arguments: (sections 10:3.1 through 10:8.3)
   a. False dilemma
   b. Equivocation
   c. False cause
   d. Abusive argument
   e. Hasty generalization
   f. Appeal to pity

7. Identify the error or errors which occur in each of the following examples, and explain why they are errors. (sections 10:3 through 10:8.3)
   a. If Jackson signs with the Penguins, then he won't be able to complete his education. On the other hand, if he doesn't sign, he won't get the bonus and will not be able to help his parents out of their financial difficulty. Therefore, either he won't get his degree or he won't be able to help his parents.
   b. What do you mean that praying is useless? Last night I prayed for snow so that I could go skiing today, and sure enough it snowed.
   c. It's hardly surprising that McIntock would claim that the government should not subsidize Motown Motors and then go on to say that the company is very badly mismanaged. What would you expect from someone who was passed over for president in favor of a younger person?
   d. I just don't understand how my opponent can stand up here and tell me I don't know anything about the educational needs of our children. That's a strange claim from someone who never even finished high school.
   e. Everyone has an obligation to prevent needless suffering. Since most terminally ill patients are suffering needlessly, it is our obligation to kill them and thereby prevent their suffering.
   f. Sunday-school teacher to child: Who is God?
      Child: Gibralter is God.

      Teacher: What do you mean Gibralter is God?

      Child: I learned in school that Gibralter is a mighty fortress and just today in church we sang that a mighty fortress is our God.
   g. Mother to small child: Don't you want to eat your dinner and have Mommy read you a nice story before bed?
   h. The mean age of the children in Burrion Elementary School is 9.0 years. Hence, Tom, the sixth-grade class bully, must be nine years old, since he's at an age where he's mean.
   i. Why wouldn't she cry about losing her job? It's just what you would expect, since all women are emotional.
   j. I've listened to enough of her garbage. First she comes in here and tells us she's an atheist and then she tells us our loving children shouldn't be allowed to pray in school. We might expect that from someone like her; what do atheists care about the values that gave this country its greatness?

k. We are surely justified in taking any steps necessary to defend ourselves against foreign aggression. We are therefore justified in increasing our expenditures to improve our strike capability.

l. Don't ever buy a sports car. I had one and it was in the shop more than it was on the road. And I hate to tell you how expensive those repairs were!

m. Dear Addy:

I'm responding to your suggestion to "Can't Wait" that she postpone intercourse until she is married. My husband and I just celebrated our thirty-fifth anniversary, and even though I couldn't wait, these have been thirty-five wonderful years and I'm still a lady. Sign me "Impatient."

Dear Impatient:

You may have been impatient, but what I said still goes. A lady doesn't go to bed with someone before she's married.

n. I am proud of the contributions you have all made to the company this year. As a result, if you really want us to start a retirement plan, we shall do so. You should know, however, that the cost of such a plan will necessitate that some of you be laid off. Now, do you want us to lay some of you off and implement the plan?

o. Company director to shareholders: I don't know why you chide us for providing Corvettes to our younger executives. You all drive expensive cars.

p. I applied for a job at Acme and they turned me down. I applied for a job at Zender's and they turned me down. I'll never get a job, so what good was it to waste four years of my life going to school?

q. When you think about all the crime, pollution, poverty, and overcrowded conditions in our major cities, it's clear that our cities have grown too big too fast. We need to return to simpler times.

r. Dear Professor Conrad:

I know that your policy is that no makeup exams will be given without first getting approval before the missed exam. I'm sorry that I missed last week's exam, but I had been partying the night before and had a horrible hangover. I'm sure you realize that no one can do very well on an exam at 8:00 in the morning when she has a hangover. Therefore, I think you will agree that in this situation it is appropriate for me to take a makeup exam.

s. A: I'm absolutely convinced that this planet was visited by beings from another planet many years ago.

B: Why do you say that?

A: Because many things that happened years ago could be explained by this hypothesis.

B: But has anyone shown that the hypothesis is true?

A: Of course not. But no one has shown that it's false, and you know how those so-called "open-minded" people are these days: They never accept anything they don't already believe.

t. Surveys have shown that those of high intelligence tend to be more liberal sexually than those with less intelligence. Therefore, if you want to be smarter, you too should be sexually more liberal.

SOLUTIONS

CHAPTER 1

EXERCISE 1-1

1. A group of at least two statements, of which one is the conclusion and the others are the premises, which are offered as support for the conclusion

EXERCISE 1-3

2. That the speaker asserts in the conclusion something which is either true or false, and that what is offered as premises is either true or false

4. An incomplete argument, or one which has one or more missing premises or an unstated conclusion

EXERCISE 1-4

1. Make sure that the speaker is using language to make statements and that something has been put forward as a conclusion with reasons given in support of the conclusion

4. No; 'Go see it' is an imperative, not a statement.

7. A word or an expression which points out the conclusion or a premise in an argument

9. a. Conclusion indicator
   g. Conclusion indicator
   m. Premise indicator
   d. Conclusion indicator
   j. Conclusion indicator

EXERCISE 1-5

1. a. Argument
   g. Argument
   m. Argument
   d. Argument
   j. Argument

2. a. Premise: Slippery Soap costs 23 cents a bar and Grime Remover costs 28 cents a bar.
      Conclusion: Slippery Soap is the better buy.

   f. Premises: Everyone has either read or been told that Pluto is the planet most distant from the sun.
                   From now until 1999 Neptune will be farther from the sun than Pluto.
      Conclusion: You can't always trust what you have read or what you have been told.

   j. Premise: The situation in the Middle East is much more serious than it looks.
      Conclusion: Only a fool would consider going to Jerusalem for a Christmas vacation.

EXERCISE 1-6

a. Unstated conclusion: We can service your tape deck.

d. Unstated conclusion: You should eat at Better Burger.

g. Unstated conclusion: We should nominate Brian Burmeister.

j. Missing premise: If grain is being stored to subsidize farmers while people in the world are starving, we should stop the subsidies and feed the people.

EXERCISE 1-7

1. a. (Most people in middle-management positions feel that their chances for advancement will be jeopardized by supporting their subordinates in controversial situations.) As a result, middle-level managers are natural allies of their superiors, regardless of how inane some of their decisions may be.
   d. Since (mathematics is one of the few disciplines which fosters intellectual rigor,) it can, when taught correctly, lead to startling improvements in any student's ability to comprehend other disciplines.
   g. (Only members and their guests are allowed to swim here.) Since (every member has a membership card and every guest has a guest pass,) I cannot admit you, for (you obviously have neither.)
   j. It's very likely that no day this year will be a day on which the temperature reaches over 70 degrees, owing to the fact that (the year is already one-quarter gone and we have yet to have a day in the 70s.)
   m. (If all would treat their neighbor as they themselves wish to be treated, then there would be no need for laws.) As, however, (it is our fate that some think so little of themselves that we too be thought as worthless,) so then is it necessary that laws be made.
   p. I've had all I can stand 'cause (I can't stands no more.)
   s. (If the sky is falling and Foxy Loxy doesn't catch her, then Chicken Little will run to see the king.) But (the sky is not falling.) Consequently, Chicken Little won't be running to see the king, for (Foxy Loxy broke his leg playing kick-the-can and he can't catch anyone,) not even a plump chicken.

2. a. Most people in middle-management positions feel that their chances for advancement will be jeopardized by supporting their subordinates in controversial situations.
      When people feel their chances for advancement might be jeopardized, they side with their superiors. (missing premise)
      ∴ Middle-level managers are natural allies of their superiors, regardless of how inane some of their decisions may be.

   d. Mathematics is one of the few disciplines which fosters intellectual rigor.
      If a discipline fosters intellectual rigor, it can lead to improvements in one's understanding of other disciplines. (missing premise)
      ∴ Mathematics can, when taught properly, lead to startling improvements in any student's ability to comprehend other disciplines.

   g. Only members and their guests are allowed to swim here
      Every member has a membership card and every guest has a guest pass.
      You do not have a membership card nor a guest pass.
      I can only admit people who are allowed to swim here. (missing premise)
      ∴ I cannot admit you.

   j. The year is already one-quarter gone and we have yet to have a day in the 70s.
      ∴ No day this year will be a day on which the temperature reaches over 70 degrees.

   m. If all would treat their neighbor as they themselves wish to be treated, then there would be no need for laws.

Some think so little of themselves that others are also thought of as worthless.
∴ It is necessary that laws be made.

p. I can't stands no more.
∴ I've had all I can stand.

s. If the sky is falling and Foxy Loxy doesn't catch her, then Chicken Little will run to see the king.
The sky is not falling.
Foxy Loxy broke his leg playing kick-the-can and he can't catch anyone.
∴ Chicken Little won't be running to see the king.

EXERCISE 1-8

1. a. Used
   g. Mentioned; mentioned
   m. Mentioned

   d. Mentioned
   j. Used

2. a. If I've told you once, I've told you a thousand times: don't shout "wolf" when you're not in trouble.
   d. A lot of people misspell 'misspell'.
   g. The numeral for the word 'eight' is '8'.
   j. More words in the English language begin with 'e' than with 'j'.
   m. One generally can change an adjective into an adverb by adding 'ly' to the end of the word. For example, if one adds 'ly' to the adjective 'slow', the result is the adverb 'slowly'.

EXERCISE 1-9

(There can be more than one correct answer to some of the problems.)

a. Make a statement

g. Give a warning

m. Make a statement

s. Mixed use

y. Mixed use

d. Make a request

j. Mixed use

p. Make a statement

v. Make a statement (rhetorical question)

EXERCISE 1-10

a. Verbal and factual

g. Taste

d. Verbal

j. Verbal and factual

SELF-TEST/EXERCISES

1. a. False; logicians are primarily concerned with the support relationship between the premises and the conclusion.
   b. True
   c. False; an argument is presented only when one offers both a position and support for that position.
   d. True
   e. True
   f. False; sometimes it is very difficult to identify an unstated conclusion.
   g. False; no conditional statement is an argument.
   h. True
   i. False; it is used as a conclusion indicator.
   j. False; it is used as a premise indicator.
   k. False; in giving an argument one must also give the support for the conclusion.

l. False; single quotation marks are used to indicate that a word or expression is being mentioned instead of used.

m. False; this principle tells us to construct the strongest argument we can by relying on context and background knowledge.

n. True

o. False; they are used in other ways as well.

p. True

q. False; some uses of language involve making a statement and doing something else as well.

r. False; sometimes the information is subject to interpretation.

s. True

t. True

u. False; we can sometimes get someone to see the facts in a new way.

v. True

w. False; for example, some disagreements in taste may not be resolved in this way.

x. False; some verbal disagreements may be disagreements in taste or appraisal.

y. False; there are a lot of disagreeable people in the world.

2. a. There's no fool like an old fool.
My grandfather is an old fool.
∴ My grandfather is no fool.

b. Every abortion results in the taking of a human life.
Whenever one takes a human life, one does something immoral.
Providing funds for abortions is the taking of a human life. (missing premise)
∴ If the Federal Government continues to provide funds for abortions, it will be doing something immoral.

c. Everyone wants to be able to relax.
Lay-z-chair is the chair that redefined 'relaxation'.
∴ Everyone should want a Lay-z-chair. (unstated conclusion)

d. The price of gold continues to go down, and the cost of living continues to go up.
A wise investment is one which keeps up with, or moves ahead of, the cost of living.
∴ I didn't make a wise investment when I decided to buy gold.

e. To play baseball, and to be good at it, you need at least four months of warm, dry weather.
Schools in the deep south or the southwest have at least four months of warm, dry weather. (missing premise)
∴ It's no wonder that most of the schools which have won the College World Series in the past two decades have come from the deep south or the southwest.

f. It's a rare occasion when I meet someone and then develop a lasting friendship.
In the last ten parties I've gone to, of all the people I've met, Sharon is the only one with whom I'm now friends.
∴ I will not meet anyone at tonight's party with whom I'll form a lasting friendship.

4. a. Factual
c. Verbal
e. Appraisal or verbal and taste

b. Verbal
d. Taste and/or appraisal
f. Taste

CHAPTER 2

EXERCISE 2-1

1. The premises, if true, support the conclusion, and the premises are true.

6. True and false

EXERCISE 2-2

1. Deductively and inductively

7. Because the conclusion contains information not contained in the premises

13. One whose conclusion must be true if its premises are true

EXERCISE 2-3

1. a. Inductive support   d. No support; looks inductive
   g. Inductive support   j. Inductive support
   m. No support; looks inductive

EXERCISE 2-4

1. To represent a particular statement; with uppercase letters

4. Because the form has no content

9. Yes; see section 2:3.2.

EXERCISE 2-5

1. a. If I then R d. If R then S
   g. S or T j. B and S

2. a. If I then R d. M
       W $\therefore$ E, if S
       If W then I
       $\therefore R$

   g. If T then S j. If P then M
       If F then Q If G then R
       Either T or F P and G
       $\therefore$ Either S or Q $\therefore$ M and R

EXERCISE 2-6

2. A valid form is one in which there can be no substitution instance which has all true premises and a false conclusion; an invalid form is one in which such a substitution instance is possible.

5. Yes; if it's an instance of a valid form

7. An argument which is valid and has all true premises

9. No; the premises might not support the conclusion.

EXERCISE 2-7

1. To show that a particular argument is invalid

4. b. If Daffy Duck is a cow, then Daffy is a mammal.
       Daffy is a cow or Daffy is a duck.
       $\therefore$ Daffy is a mammal.

SELF-TEST/EXERCISES

1. a. False; every statement is either true or false.
   b. True
   c. True
   d. False; the premises may be irrelevant to the conclusion.
   e. False; support does not depend on the actual truth value of the conclusion.
   f. False; although this is a characteristic of inductive support, all the characteristics must be satisfied if we are to have inductive support.

g. False; we have deductive support only when the conclusion must be true whenever all the premises are true.
h. True
i. False; they are used to indicate the form of an argument.
j. True
k. True
l. True
m. True
n. True
o. False; to be valid, the argument must have a valid argument form.
p. False; some arguments with true conclusions are not valid—for example, inductive arguments.
q. False; an argument is invalid only if there is no valid form of which it is an instance.
r. False; an argument is invalid only if there is no valid form of which it is an instance.
s. False; the argument could have all false premises, or some which are false.
t. True
u. False; it must have at least one false premise but they need not all be false.
v. False; some valid arguments with all false premises also have a true conclusion.
w. True
x. False; the argument could have a true conclusion.
y. False; if the argument is an instance of a valid argument form, then the argument is valid.
z. False; if the argument is not an instance of a valid argument form, then the argument is invalid.
aa. True
bb. False; the argument might have one or more false premises.
cc. True
dd. False; the person may have failed to find a counterexample which shows that the argument is invalid.

2. a. No support; looks deductive   b. Inductive support
    c. No argument   d. No argument
    e. Inductive support or no support   f. No support; looks deductive

3. a. If R then L b. If S then not R
       Not L If L then C
    $\therefore$ Not R S or L (enthymeme)
       If p then q $\therefore$ Not R or C
       Not q If p then not q
    $\therefore$ Not p If r then s
                                                   p or r
                                                $\therefore$ Not q or s

    c. If W then E d. If E then W
       Not E If T then not W
    $\therefore$ Not W (enthymeme) $\therefore$ If T then not E
       If p then q If p then q
       Not q If r then not q
    $\therefore$ Not p $\therefore$ If r then not p

    e. L or C
       If C then D
       If L then B
       If (D or B) then not H
    $\therefore$ Not H
       p or q
       If q then r

If p then s
If (r or s) then not t
∴ Not t

CHAPTER 3

EXERCISE 3-1

1. A statement of the form 'if p then q'

3. a. If the price of oil goes up, then the price of food will come down.
   d. The price of oil will come down if either more people use less oil or they stop buying plastic toys.

4. a. Either the price of oil will come down or the federal government will subsidize its cost if either more people use less oil or if new sources of domestic oil are found.
   d. There's no hope of beating the Diamonds if Murdock can't pitch by next Saturday.

EXERCISE 3-2

1. That the consequent grammatically precedes the antecedent; by rewriting the sentence so that the antecedent precedes the consequent

4. a. Henry did not leave this morning on flight 342.
   d. Socialism and Marxism are the same form of government.
   g. It's safe to walk down Broad Street after dark.
   j. There is not a high correlation between family income level and health.

EXERCISE 3-3

1. It functions like the expression 'if not.'

6. By negating the antecedent and consequent of the original statement and then interchanging the two resultant statements

EXERCISE 3-4

1. a. If we can stem the tide of inner-city crime, then we curb the flow of illegal drugs into this country.
   d. If we don't spend money, then we can't win the war on poverty.
   g. If the U.S. does not contribute to the world food program, then many people will starve.
   j. If the President does not appeal the executive privilege, then the truth will be made public.
   m. If the day is not sunny, then we won't frolic in the park.
   p. If I don't get busted, then I'll have the stuff at your place tomorrow morning.
   s. If he does not get caught in Spiderman's web, then the Green Hornet will come to the rescue.

2. a. If we don't curb the flow of illegal drugs into this country, then we can't stem the tide of inner-city crime.
   d. If we can win the war on poverty, then we spend money.
   g. If many people will not starve, then the U.S. did contribute to the world food program.
   j. If the truth is not made public, then the President did appeal to executive privilege.
   m. If we frolic in the park, then the day is sunny.
   p. If I don't have the stuff at your place tomorrow morning, then I got busted.
   s. If the Green Hornet does not come to the rescue, then he got caught in Spiderman's web.

EXERCISE 3-5

1. See section 3:4.1.

2. See section 3:4.2.

3. See section 3:4.3.

4. See Section 3:4.4.

EXERCISE 3-6

1. a. The economy will decline unless there is a rise in wages.
       The economy will decline.
       ∴ There must not have been a rise in wages.

    If ~R then D   If ~p then q
    D   q
    ∴ ~R   ∴ ~p
    Affirming the consequent; *invalid*

   d. If capital punishment deterred crime, then it would be justified.
       Capital punishment does not deter crime.
       ∴ Capital punishment is not justified.

    If D then J   If p then q
    ~D   ~p
    ∴ ~J   ∴ ~q
    Denying the antecedent; *invalid*

   g. Only if cities receive enough federal funds can they carry out good service programs.
       Cities aren't carrying out good service programs.
       ∴ Cities don't receive enough federal funds.

    If G then R   If p then q
    ~G   ~p
    ∴ ~R   ∴ ~q
    Denying the antecedent; *invalid*

   j. Only if the castle was in the deep woods would a beautiful princess live in it.
       A beautiful princess lived in a magnificent castle.
       ∴ The castle was in the deep woods.

    If L then D   If p then q
    L   p
    ∴ D   ∴ q
    Affirming the antecedent; *valid*

   m. That stuff growing over there is edible only if it's asparagus.
       The stuff growing over there is not asparagus.
       ∴ The stuff growing over there is not edible. (enthymeme)

    If E then A   If p then q
    ~A   ~q
    ∴ ~E   ∴ ~p
    Denying the consequent; *valid*

EXERCISE 3-7

1. An argument which contains more than one simple conditional argument

4. a. Unless something drastic happens, this country will find itself in the throes of a depression in a few short years.

Unless Congress acts to limit government spending, something drastic will happen.
Congress will not act to limit government spending.
∴ This country will find itself in the throes of a depression.

If ~H then D	If ~p then q
If ~L then H	If ~r then p
~L	~r
∴ D	∴ q

This argument is invalid. 'q' could only be derived from the first premise, and to do this we need '~p'. What follows from the second and third premises, however, is 'p'. Construct a counterexample to show that the argument is invalid.

d. Unless the Soviet Union is to be in the dark ages of the twentieth century, they must stop exiling their dissidents.
Only if they retain their present policies will they be in the dark ages.
They won't retain their policies.
∴ The Soviet Union will stop exiling dissidents.

If ~D then E	If ~p then q
If D then R	If p then r
~R	~r
∴ E	∴ q

(1) If ~p then q	Premise
(2) If p then r	Premise
(3) ~r	Premise
(4) ~p	(2), (3), DC; *valid*
∴ (5) q	(1), (4), AA; *valid*

g. If the price of cars is reduced, then more cars will be sold.
If the price of cars is reduced, the economy will improve.
More cars will not be sold.
∴ The economy will not improve.

If P then S	If p then q
If P then I	If p then r
~S	~q
∴ ~I	∴ ~r

This argument is invalid. '~r' cannot be derived from the second premise, and since this is the only premise in which '~r' or its negation occurs, there is no way to derive '~r'. Construct a counterexample to show that the argument is invalid.

j. Unless Congress approves the President's energy proposals, no action on energy will be taken.
If no action on energy is taken, then there will never be a gas tax.
Congress will not approve the President's proposals.
∴ There will never be a gas tax.

If ~C then A	If ~p then q
If A then G	If q then r
~C	~p
∴ G	∴ r

(1) If ~p then q	Premise
(2) If q then r	Premise
(3) ~p	Premise
(4) q	(1), (3), AA; *valid*
∴ (5) r	(2), (4), AA; *valid*

m. If the Steelers win the AFC playoff, then they'll go to the Super Bowl.
If the Steelers win the AFC playoff, they'll make a lot of extra cash.

If the Steelers do go to the Super Bowl, then the Raiders won't.
If the Raiders don't go to the Super Bowl, their fans will be unhappy.
The Steelers will win the AFC playoff.
∴ The Raider fans will be unhappy.

If W then G	If p then q
If W then M	If p then r
If G then ~R	If q then ~s
If ~R then U	If ~s then t
W	p
∴ U	∴ t

(1)	If p then q	Premise
(2)	If p then r	Premise
(3)	If q then ~s	Premise
(4)	If ~s then t	Premise
(5)	p	Premise
(6)	q	(1), (5), AA; *valid*
(7)	~s	(3), (6), AA: *valid*
∴ (8)	t	(4), (7), AA; *valid*

Note that premise 2 was not used in the proof.

EXERCISE 3-8

4. a. If the Middle East is to cease being a potential crisis area, many western nations must find another source of energy.
   Only if the western nations spend much money on research, will they find another source of energy.
   ∴ Unless the western nations spend much money on research, the Middle East will remain a potential crisis area.

If M then F	If p then q
If F then S	If q then r
∴ If ~S then ~M	∴ If ~r then ~p

(1)	If p then q	Premise
(2)	If q then r	Premise
*(3)	~r	Assumption
*(4)	~q	(2), (3), DC
*(5)	~p	(1), (4), DC
∴ (6)	If ~r then ~p	CP

d. Only if the public will spend tax-rebate money on new purchases, as opposed to debts, should a tax rebate be offered.
   The economic situation will improve if the public does spend tax-rebate money on new purchases.
   ∴ A tax rebate should be offered only if the economic situation will improve.

If O then S	If p then q
If S then I	If q then r
∴ If O then I	∴ If p then r

(1)	If p then q	Premise
(2)	If q then r	Premise
*(3)	p	Assumption
*(4)	q	(1), (3), AA
*(5)	r	(2), (4), AA
∴ (6)	If p then r	CP

g. Unless we continue to have bad weather, the air conditioner will be installed this week.
The air conditioner will be installed only if the new building opens on time.
∴ If there is no more bad weather, the building will open on time.

If ~B then I	If ~p then q
If I then O	If q then r
∴ If ~B then O	∴ If ~p then r

	(1) If ~p then q	Premise
	(2) If q then r	Premise
*(3)	~p	Assumption
*(4)	q	(1), (3), AA
*(5)	r	(2), (4), AA
∴ (6)	If ~p then r	CP

j. A Raydac is worth buying only if it performs better than a Landon.
You should spend your money on a Raydac only if it is worth buying.
∴ Unless a Raydac performs better than a Landon, you should not spend your money on
a Raydac.

If W then P	If p then q
If S then W	If r then p
∴ If ~P then ~S	∴ If ~q then ~r

	(1) If p then q	Premise
	(2) If r then p	Premise
*(3)	~q	Assumption
*(4)	~p	(1), (3), DC
*(5)	~r	(2), (4), DC
∴ (6)	If ~q then ~r	CP

EXERCISE 3-10

1. b.
(1)	If ~p then q	Premise
(2)	If p then r	Premise
(3)	~r	Premise
*(4)	~q	Assumption
*(5)	~~p	(1), (4), DC
*(6)	p	(5), double negation
(7)	~p	(2), (3), DC
*(8)	p and ~p	(6), (7), conjunction
∴ (9)	q	RAA

f.
(1)	If ~p then ~q	Premise
(2)	If r then q	Premise
(3)	r	Premise
*(4)	~p	Assumption
*(5)	~q	(1), (4), AA
(6)	q	(2), (3), AA
*(7)	q and ~q	(6), (5), conjunction
∴ (8)	p	RAA

j.
(1)	If ~p then q	Premise
(2)	If q then r	Premise
(3)	~p	Premise
*(4)	~r	Assumption
*(5)	~q	(2), (4), DC
(6)	q	(1), (3), AA
*(7)	q and ~q	(6), (5), conjunction
∴ (8)	r	RAA

n. (1) If $\sim p$ then $\sim q$ Premise
   (2) If $\sim q$ then r Premise
   (3) $\sim p$ Premise
  *(4) $\sim r$ Assumption
  *(5) $\sim\sim q$ (2), (4), DC
   (6) $\sim q$ (1), (3), AA
  *(7) $\sim q$ and $\sim\sim q$ (6), (5), conjunction
∴ (8) r RAA

2. a. We won't win the game unless we have the support of the fans.
Only if we improve our image will we have the support of the fans.
We shall win.
∴ We shall improve our image.

If $\sim S$ then $\sim W$ If $\sim p$ then $\sim q$
If S then I If p then r
W q
∴ I ∴ r

   (1) If $\sim p$ then $\sim q$ Premise
   (2) If p then r Premise
   (3) q Premise
  *(4) $\sim r$ Assumption
  *(5) $\sim p$ (2), (4), DC
  *(6) $\sim q$ (1), (5), AA
  *(7) q and $\sim q$ (3), (6), conjunction
∴ (8) r RAA

d. If the mideast nations reduce the price of oil, then gasoline prices will not go higher.
If the mideast nations don't reduce the price of oil, sales of large automobiles will continue to decline.
Sales of large automobiles will not continue to decline unless the federal government does not provide tax relief to the automakers.
The government will provide tax relief.

∴ The price of gasoline will not go higher.

If R then $\sim H$ If p then $\sim q$
If $\sim R$ then C If $\sim p$ then r
If P then $\sim C$ If s then $\sim r$
P s
∴ $\sim H$ ∴ $\sim q$

   (1) If p then $\sim q$ Premise
   (2) If $\sim p$ then r Premise
   (3) If s then $\sim r$ Premise
   (4) s Premise
  *(5) $\sim\sim q$ Assumption
  *(6) $\sim p$ (1), (5), DC
  *(7) r (2), (6), AA
   (8) $\sim r$ (3), (4), AA
  *(9) r and $\sim r$ (7), (8), conjunction
∴ (10) $\sim q$ RAA

g. If Alexandra has a history of high blood pressure, she should not take the new vaccine.
If Alexandra does not have a history of high blood pressure, then the vaccine will protect her from the flu that is going around.
Alexandra should take the new vaccine.
∴ The vaccine will protect Alexandra from the flu.

If H then $\sim T$ 　　　　　　　If p then $\sim q$
If $\sim H$ then P 　　　　　　　If $\sim p$ then r
T 　　　　　　　　　　　　　　q
$\therefore P$ 　　　　　　　　　　　　$\therefore r$

(1) If p then $\sim q$	Premise
(2) If $\sim p$ then r	Premise
(3) q	Premise
*(4) $\sim r$	Assumption
*(5) $\sim\sim p$	(2), (4), DC
*(6) p	(5), double negation
*(7) $\sim q$	(1), (6), AA
*(8) q and $\sim q$	(3), (7), conjunction
$\therefore$ (9) r	RAA

   j. We'll make a profit only if it rains.
      We can afford to pay a pilot to seed the clouds only if we make a profit.
      This year's crop would be worth what it cost to plant only if we can afford a pilot.
      It is not going to rain soon.
   $\therefore$ This year's crop is not going to be worth what it cost to plant.

If P then R 　　　　　　　If p then q
If A then P 　　　　　　　If r then p
If W then A 　　　　　　　If s then r
$\sim R$ 　　　　　　　　　　　$\sim q$
$\therefore \sim W$ 　　　　　　　　　$\therefore \sim s$

(1) If p then q	Premise
(2) If r then p	Premise
(3) If s then r	Premise
(4) $\sim q$	Premise
*(5) $\sim\sim s$	Assumption
*(6) s	(5), double negation
*(7) r	(3), (6), AA
*(8) p	(2), (7), AA
*(9) q	(1), (8), AA
*(10) q and $\sim q$	(9), (4), conjunction
$\therefore$ (11) $\sim s$	RAA

SELF-TEST/EXERCISES

1. a. If Linda goes to Sweden, then June goes to France.
      If June does not go to France, then Linda does not go to Sweden.
  b. If no action is taken, then there will never be a gas tax.
      If there will be a gas tax, then some action is taken.
  c. If it hadn't been for the Dutch Elm disease, then this would still be a beautiful neighborhood.
      If this is not still a beautiful neighborhood, then it's because of the Dutch Elm disease.
  d. If we do not lose next Saturday's game, then we will be conference champs.
      If we are not conference champs, then it's because we lose next Saturday's game.
  e. If we have enough money to support our projects in the coming year, then the Phon-a-thon will be successful.
      If the Phon-a-thon is not successful, then we will not have enough money to support our projects in the coming year.

2. a. Unless the U.S. contributed to the world food program, many people would have starved.
      Many people didn't starve.
   $\therefore$ The U.S. contributed to the world food program.

If ~C then S	If ~p then q
~S	~q
∴ C	∴ p

Denying the consequent and double negation; *valid*

b. Books are worth reading only if they're either educational or entertaining.
This book was neither educational nor entertaining.
∴ This book was not worth reading.

If W then E	If p then q
~E	~q
∴ ~W	∴ ~p

Denying the consequent; *valid*

c. If you don't know the difference between socialism and Marxism, then I recommend that you take a course in political science.
∴ I recommend that you not take a course in political science only if you do know the difference between socialism and Marxism.

If ~D then R	If ~p then q
∴ If ~R then D	∴ If ~q then p

Contraposition; *valid*

d. Your portable mushroom is not working.
Unless your portable mushroom has batteries, it won't work.
∴ Your portable mushroom does not have batteries in it.

W	~p
If ~B then ~W	If ~q then ~p
∴ ~B	∴ ~q

Affirming the consequent; *invalid*

e. The Green Hornet came to the rescue.
The Green Hornet would have come to the rescue only if he did not get caught in Spiderman's web.
∴ The Green Hornet did not get caught in Spiderman's web.

R	p
If R then ~C	If p then ~q
∴ ~C	∴ ~q

Affirming the antecedent; *valid*

3. a. There is reason to think that UFOs are spaceships only if there is reason to think that there is life on other planets.
The Air Force has been unable to prove that there is life on other planets.
If there is life on other planets, the Air Force would have been able to prove it.
∴ There is no reason to think that UFOs are spaceships.

If S then L	If p then q
~P	~r
If L then P	If q then r
∴ ~S	∴ ~p

(1) If p then q	Premise
(2) ~r	Premise
(3) If q then r	Premise
(4) ~q	(3), (2), DC; *valid*
∴ (5) ~p	(1), (4), DC; *valid*

b. Unless the governor decides to run for the Senate, he will again run for governor.
The governor will decide to run for the Senate only if he has been seriously harmed by the PDQ controversy.

The governor has not been seriously harmed by the PDQ controversy.
∴ The governor will again run for governor.

If ~D then R	If ~p then q
If D then H	If p then r
~H	~r
∴ R	∴ q

	(1) If ~p then q	Premise
	(2) If p then r	Premise
	(3) ~r	Premise
	(4) ~p	(2), (3), DC; *valid*
∴	(5) q	(1), (4), AA; *valid*

c. Only if the stores are open late will I get my Christmas shopping done.
Only if I get my Christmas shopping done will I remain out of the doghouse on Christmas day.
Unless I remain out of the doghouse on Christmas day, I won't be out by New Year's day.
The stores will be open late.
∴ I won't be in the doghouse on New Year's day.

If D then L	If p then q
If R then D	If r then p
If ~R then ~O	If ~r then ~s
L	q
∴ O	∴ s

This argument is invalid. 's' cannot be derived from the third premise, and since this is the only premise in which 's' or its negation occurs, there is no way to derive 's'. Construct a counterexample to show that the argument is invalid.

4. a. Unless we play better this half, we're going to lose the game.
The alumni will continue to support us only if we win.
∴ Unless we play better this half, the alumni will no longer support us.

If ~P then L	If ~p then q
If C then ~L	If r then ~q
∴ If ~P then ~C	∴ If ~p then ~r

	(1) If ~p then q	Premise
	(2) If r then ~q	Premise
*(3)	~p	Assumption
*(4)	q	(1), (3), AA
*(5)	~~q	(4), double negation
*(6)	~r	(2), (6) DC
∴ (7)	If ~p then ~r	CP

b. Unless the property tax is lowered, many people on fixed incomes will be forced to sell their homes.
If the present city council remains in office, the property taxes will not be lowered.
If the citizens unite, people on fixed incomes will not have to sell their homes.
∴ If the citizens unite, the city council will not remain in office.

If ~P then H	If ~p then q
If R then ~P	If r then ~p
If U then ~H	If s then ~q
∴ If U then ~R	∴ If s then ~r

	(1) If ~p then q	Premise
	(2) If r then ~p	Premise

(3) If s then $\sim q$ Premise
*(4) s Assumption
*(5) $\sim q$ (3), (4), AA
*(6) $\sim\sim p$ (1), (5), DC
*(7) $\sim r$ (2), (6), DC
∴ (8) If s then $\sim r$ CP

c. Plato can be understood only if one has read Aristotle.
   If one understands neo-Platonism, then one understands Plato.
   ∴ Unless one has read Aristotle, one will not understand neo-Platonism.

If P then A	If p then q
If N then P	If r then p
∴ If $\sim A$ then $\sim N$	∴ If $\sim q$ then $\sim r$

(1) If p then q Premise
(2) If r then p Premise
*(3) $\sim q$ Assumption
*(4) $\sim p$ (1), (3), DC
*(5) $\sim r$ (2), (4), DC
∴ (6) If $\sim q$ then $\sim r$ CP

5. a. If Dierdre votes in favor of proposal A, then she must believe that passage of the proposal will help alleviate the problem of can and bottle litter on the highways.
   Dierdre would believe that passage of the proposal would help alleviate the problem of litter on the highways only if she had good evidence that this is true.
   Unless such proposals worked in other states, Dierdre would not have good evidence that proposal A would work.
   Such proposals did not work in other states.
   ∴ Dierdre will vote against proposal A.

If V then P	If p then q
If P then E	If q then r
If $\sim W$ then $\sim E$	If $\sim s$ then $\sim r$
$\sim W$	$\sim s$
∴ $\sim V$	∴ $\sim p$

(1) If p then q Premise
(2) If q then r Premise
(3) If $\sim s$ then $\sim r$ Premise
(4) $\sim s$ Premise
*(5) $\sim\sim p$ Assumption
*(6) p (5), double negation
*(7) q (1), (6), AA
*(8) r (2), (7), AA
*(9) $\sim\sim r$ (8), double negation
*(10) $\sim\sim s$ (3), (9),DC
*(11) $\sim s$ and $\sim\sim s$ (4), (10), conjunction
∴ (12) $\sim p$ RAA

b. Unless the property tax is lowered, many people on fixed incomes will be forced to sell their homes.
   If the present city council remains in office, property taxes will not be lowered.
   The citizens will unite.
   If the citizens unite, people on fixed incomes will not have to sell their homes.
   ∴ The present city council will not remain in office.

If $\sim P$ then H	If $\sim p$ then q
If R then $\sim P$	If r then $\sim p$

U
If U then $\sim H$
$\therefore \sim R$

(1) If $\sim p$ then q	Premise
(2) If r then $\sim p$	Premise
(3) s	Premise
(4) If s then $\sim q$	Premise
*(5) $\sim\sim r$	Assumption
*(6) r	(5), double negation
*(7) $\sim p$	(2), (6), AA
*(8) q	(1), (7), AA
*(9) $\sim\sim q$	(8), double negation
*(10) $\sim s$	(4), (9), DC
*(11) s and $\sim s$	(3), (10), conjunction
$\therefore$ (12) $\sim r$	RAA

s
If s then $\sim q$
$\therefore \sim r$

c. Unless he is able to catch a standby flight, Brad will not be able to get home for the funeral.
  Unless Brad is lucky, he will not get a flight.
  Brad is not lucky.
$\therefore$ Brad will not be able to get home for the funeral.

If $\sim C$ then $\sim F$
If $\sim L$ then $\sim C$
$\sim L$
$\therefore \sim F$

If $\sim p$ then $\sim q$
If $\sim r$ then $\sim p$
$\sim r$
$\therefore \sim q$

(1) If $\sim p$ then $\sim q$	Premise
(2) If $\sim r$ then $\sim p$	Premise
(3) $\sim r$	Premise
*(4) $\sim\sim q$	Assumption
*(5) $\sim\sim p$	(1), (4), DC
*(6) $\sim\sim r$	(2), (5), DC
*(7) $\sim r$ and $\sim\sim r$	(3), (6), conjunction
$\therefore$ (8) $\sim q$	RAA

CHAPTER 4

EXERCISE 4-1

1. The truth value of the statement is a function of the truth values of its component statements, along with the meanings of the other expressions which occur in the compound statement.

6. In the inclusive 'or', the disjunction is true when both disjuncts are true. In the exclusive 'or', the disjunction is false when both disjuncts are true. The inclusive sense.

8. $(p \vee q) \cdot \sim(p \cdot q)$

12. That they have the same truth value; that they always have the same truth value when the variables are uniformly replaced with the same statements.

EXERCISE 4-2

1. a. $\overset{*}{\sim}(S \supset T)$ d. $S \overset{*}{\supset} \sim T$

   g. $S \overset{*}{\cdot} (T \vee C)$ j. $S \overset{*}{\vee} \sim(T \cdot C)$

   m. $\overset{*}{\sim}(S \vee (T \cdot C))$ p. $(S \cdot T) \overset{*}{\supset} C$

2. a. $(C \supset W) \overset{*}{\lor} (\sim C \supset S)$

   g. $(L \cdot V) \overset{*}{\supset} (P \lor B)$

   m. $A \overset{*}{\equiv} (J \lor (F \cdot P))$

   d. $R \overset{*}{\supset} (\sim E \lor A)$

   j. $C \overset{*}{\supset} ((E \lor (\sim I \cdot D))$

EXERCISE 4-3

1. a. False

   g. True

   m. False

   d. False

   j. True

   p. False

2. a. $(A \cdot \sim X) \overset{*}{\equiv} (Y \lor B)$
   T T T F T F T T

   g. $(A \equiv \sim B) \overset{*}{\cdot} \sim (Y \cdot Z)$
   T F F T F T F F F

   m. $((A \supset Z) \cdot (X \supset C)) \overset{*}{\supset} (A \supset C)$
   T F F F F T T T T T T

   d. $(Y \lor \sim X) \overset{*}{\supset} (B \cdot \sim A)$
   F T T F F T F F T

   j. $((A \supset B) \cdot Y) \overset{*}{\lor} (((C \supset X) \cdot Z) \lor A)$
   T T T FF T   T F F FF TT

EXERCISE 4-4

1. A list of all the possible assignments of truth values to the variables which occur in a compound statement, along with the truth value the compound statement takes with these assignments to the variables

5. In the former we determine the truth value of the statement for one particular assignment of truth values to the component statements. In the latter we determine the truth value of the statements for all possible assignments of truth values to the component statements.

EXERCISE 4-5

1. a.

p	q	r	$(p \supset q) \cdot \sim r$
T	T	T	T F F
T	T	F	T T T
T	F	T	F F F
T	F	F	F F T
F	T	T	T F F
F	T	F	T T T
F	F	T	T F F
F	F	F	T T T

d.

p	q	r	$(\sim p \equiv q) \lor r$
T	T	T	F F T
T	T	F	F F F
T	F	T	F T T
T	F	F	F T T
F	T	T	T T T
F	T	F	T T T
F	F	T	T F T
F	F	F	T F F

g.

p	q	r	s	$(((p \supset q) \cdot (r \supset s)) \cdot (\sim s \lor \sim q)) \supset (\sim p \lor \sim r)$
T	T	T	T	T T T FF FF T F F F
T	T	T	F	T F F FT TF T F F F
T	T	F	T	T T T FF FF T F T T
T	T	F	F	T T T· TT TF T F T T
T	F	T	T	F F T FF TT T F F F
T	F	T	F	F F F FT TT T F F F
T	F	F	T	F ₋·F T FF TT T F T T
T	F	F	F	F F T FT TT T F T T
F	T	T	T	T T T FF FF T T T F
F	T	T	F	T F F FT TF T T T F
F	T	F	T	T T T FF FF T T T T
F	T	F	F	T T T TT TF T T T T
F	F	T	T	T T T TF TT T T T F
F	F	T	F	T F F FT TT T T T F
F	F	F	T	T T T TF TT T T T T
F	F	F	F	T T T TT TT T T T T

j.

p	q	r	s	(((p · q) · (r · s)) · (p · r)) ⊃ (q · s)
T	T	T	T	T T T T T T T
T	T	T	F	T F F F T T F
T	T	F	T	T F F F F T T
T	T	F	F	T F F F F T F
T	F	T	T	F F T F T T F
T	F	T	F	F F F F T T F
T	F	F	T	F F F F F T F
T	F	F	F	F F F F F T F
F	T	T	T	F F T F F T T
F	T	T	F	F F F F F T F
F	T	F	T	F F F F F T T
F	T	F	F	F F F F F T F
F	F	T	T	F F T F F T F
F	F	T	F	F F F F F T F
F	F	F	T	F F F F F T F
F	F	F	F	F F F F F T F

EXERCISE 4-6

1. One which sometimes takes the value true and sometimes takes the value false

5. That the statement that they are materially equivalent is a tautology; that is, that they always have the same truth value

EXERCISE 4-7

1. a. Contingent
   g. Tautology

   d. Tautology
   j. Contingent

2. a. Logically equivalent
   g. Not logically equivalent

   d. Logically equivalent
   j. Logically equivalent

EXERCISE 4-8

4. a.

p	q	r	(((p ⊃ (q ∨ r)) · ~r) · q) ⊃ p
T	T	T	T T F F F T
T	T	F	T T T T T T
T	F	T	T T F F F T
T	F	F	F F F T F T
F	T	T	T T F F F T
F	T	F	T T T T T F
F	F	T	T T F F F T
F	F	F	T F T T F T

Invalid (shown by the sixth line)

d.

p	q	r	(((p ⊃ q) · (p ∨ r)) · (r ⊃ q)) ⊃ q
T	T	T	T T T T T T
T	T	F	T T T T T T
T	F	T	F F T F F T
T	F	F	F F T F T T
F	T	T	T T T T T T
F	T	F	T T T T T T
F	F	T	T F F F F T
F	F	F	T F F F T T

Valid

g.

p	q	r	(((p ≡ q) · (r ⊃ (q · p))) · ~q) ⊃ ~r
T	T	T	T T T T F F T F
T	T	F	T T T T F F T T
T	F	T	F F F F F T T F
T	F	F	F F T F F T T T
F	T	T	F F F F F F T F
F	T	F	F F T F F F T T
F	F	T	T F F F F T T F
F	F	F	T T T F T T T T

Valid

j.

p	q	r	((~(p ∨ q) · (q ∨ ~r)) · (q ⊃ p)) ⊃ (r ≡ p)
T	T	T	F T F T F F T T T
T	T	F	F T F T T F T T F
T	F	T	F T F F F F T T T
T	F	F	F T F T T F T T F
F	T	T	F T F T F F F T F
F	T	F	F T F T T F F T T
F	F	T	T F F F F F T T F
F	F	F	T F T T T T T T T

Valid

5. a.

p	q	(~p ∨ q) ⊃ (p ⊃ q)
T	T	F T T T
T	F	F F T F
F	T	T T T T
F	F	T T T T

Valid

d.

p	q	((p ⊃ q) · p) ⊃ q
T	T	T T T
T	F	F F T
F	T	T F T
F	F	T F T

Valid

g.

p	q	((p ⊃ q) · ~p) ⊃ ~q
T	T	T F F T F
T	F	F F F T T
F	T	T T T F F
F	F	T T T T T

Invalid (shown by the third line)

j.

p	q	(p ⊃ q) ⊃ (~q ⊃ ~p)
T	T	T T F T F
T	F	F T T F F
F	T	T T F T T
F	F	T T T T T

Valid

m.

p	q	r	(((p ⊃ q) · (~p ⊃ r)) · ~r) ⊃ q
T	T	T	T T F T F F T
T	T	F	T T F T T T T
T	F	T	F F F T F F T
T	F	F	F F F T F T T
F	T	T	T T T T F F T
F	T	F	T F T F F T T
F	F	T	T T T T F F T
F	F	F	T F T F F T T

Valid

p.

p	q	r	$((p \lor q) \cdot (q \supset r)) \supset r$
T	T	T	T T T T
T	T	F	T F F T
T	F	T	T T T T
T	F	F	T T T F
F	T	T	T T T T
F	T	F	T F F T
F	F	T	F F T T
F	F	F	F F T T

Invalid (shown by the fourth line)

EXERCISE 4-9

2. a. $(((p \supset (q \lor r)) \cdot \sim r) \cdot q) \supset p$
       F T T F F T F   T   F
       Invalid

   d. $(((p \supset q) \cdot (p \lor r)) \cdot (r \supset q)) \supset q$
       T F F   T T F   F T F   F
       Valid

   g. $(((p \equiv q) \cdot (r \supset (q \cdot p))) \cdot \sim q) \supset \sim r$
       T T T   T T TTT   F T   F T
       Valid

   j. $((\sim(p \lor q) \cdot (q \lor \sim r)) \cdot (q \supset p)) \supset (r \equiv p)$
       T F F F   F F FT   F T F   T F F
       F T T T   T F   T   F F T
       F T T F
       Valid

3. a. $(\sim p \lor q) \supset (p \supset q)$
       FT F F   T F F
       Valid

   d. $((p \supset q) \cdot p) \supset q$
       T F F   T   F
       Valid

   g. $((p \supset q) \cdot \sim p) \supset \sim q$
       F T T   TF   FT
       Invalid

   j. $(p \supset q) \supset (\sim q \supset \sim p)$
       T F F   TF F FT
       Valid

   m. $((p \supset q) \cdot (\sim p \supset r)) \cdot \sim r) \supset q$
       F T F   T F F F   TF   F
       Valid

   p. $((p \lor q) \cdot (q \supset r)) \supset r$
       T T F   F T F   F
       Invalid

4. a. $(((p \equiv q) \cdot (r \supset (q \cdot p))) \cdot \sim q) \supset \sim r$
       F T F   T F F F F TF   F T
       Valid

   d. $(((r \supset \sim(\sim p \cdot \sim q)) \cdot (\sim r \lor s)) \cdot \sim s) \supset (p \lor q)$
       F T F TFTT F   TFT F   TF   F F F
       Invalid

   g. $((((p \cdot q) \lor (\sim r \cdot s)) \cdot \sim(\sim p \lor \sim q)) \cdot (s \supset \sim(\sim r \cdot q))) \supset (r \lor \sim q)$
       TTT T TFFF   T FT F FT   FT F FTFTT   F F FT
       Invalid

   j. $(((t \cdot q) \supset (r \lor s)) \cdot ((r \supset t) \equiv \sim(s \supset q))) \supset (t \supset s)$
       T   F   TT FFFT   TFF
       Valid

SELF-TEST/EXERCISE

1. a. Not truth-functional
   c. Truth-functional; 'and'
   e. Truth-functional; 'and'

   b. Truth-functional; 'and'
   d. Not truth-functional

2. a. $(S \lor T) \overset{*}{\supset} {\sim}C$

   b. $S \overset{*}{\supset} (T \cdot C)$

   c. $S \overset{*}{\supset} (T \lor C)$

   d. $S \overset{*}{\supset} (T \supset {\sim}C)$

   e. $(S \supset {\sim}C) \overset{*}{\supset} T$

3. a. True
   c. True
   e. True

   b. False
   d. True

4. a. $((A \lor {\sim}B) \cdot (X \cdot {\sim}C)) \overset{*}{\supset} ((X \lor {\sim}B) \lor ({\sim}A \cdot C))$
      T T F T F F F F T T F F F T F F T F T

   b. $({\sim}(A \lor {\sim}Z) \cdot ((B \cdot C) \lor Y)) \overset{*}{\supset} {\sim}(({\sim}Z \cdot {\sim}A) \supset {\sim}(B \lor C))$
      F T T T F F T T T T F T F T F F F T T F T T T

   c. $(((A \cdot {\sim}X) \lor {\sim}(B \lor {\sim}Z)) \cdot ({\sim}A \supset C) \cdot ({\sim}Y \lor B))) \overset{*}{\supset} (A \cdot {\sim}C)$
      T T T F T F T T T F T F T T T T T F T T   F T F F T

5. a. Tautology
   c. Contingent
   e. Contingent

   b. Tautology
   d. Contingent

6. a.

p	q	r	s	(((p ⊃ q) · (r ⊃ s)) · (p ∨ r)) ⊃ (q ∨ s)
T	T	T	T	T T T T T T T
T	T	T	F	T F F F T T T
T	T	F	T	T T T T T T T
T	T	F	F	T T T T T T T
T	F	T	T	F F T T T T T
T	F	T	F	F F F F T T F
T	F	F	T	F F T T T T T
T	F	F	F	F F T F T T F
F	T	T	T	T T T T T T T
F	T	T	F	T F F F T T T
F	T	F	T	T T T F F T T
F	T	F	F	T T T F F T T
F	F	T	T	T T T T T T T
F	F	T	F	T F F F T T F
F	F	F	T	T T T F F T T
F	F	F	F	T T T F F T F

Valid

   b.

p	q	r	((p ⊃ q) · (r ⊃ ~q)) ⊃ (p ⊃ ~r)
T	T	T	T F F F T F F
T	T	F	T F F F T T T
T	F	T	F F T T T F F
T	F	F	F F T T T T T
F	T	T	F F T F T T F
F	T	F	T T T F T T T
F	F	T	T T T T T T F
F	F	F	T T T T T T T

Valid

c.

p	q	r	s	(((p ∨ q) · (~p · ~r)) · (q ⊃ (r ∨ s))) ⊃ s
T	T	T	T	T F F FF F T T T
T	T	T	F	T F F FF F T T T
T	T	F	T	T F F FT F T T T
T	T	F	F	T F F FT F F F T
T	F	T	T	T F F FF F T T T
T	F	T	F	T F F FF F T T T
T	F	F	T	T F F FT F T T T
T	F	F	F	T F F FT F F F T
F	T	T	T	T F T FF F T T T
F	T	T	F	T F T FF F T T T
F	T	F	T	T T T TT T T T T
F	T	F	F	T T T TT F F F T
F	F	T	T	F F T FF F T T T
F	F	T	F	F F T FF F T T T
F	F	F	T	F F T TT F T T T
F	F	F	F	F F T TT F T F T

Valid

d.

p	q	r	(p ∨ (q · r)) ⊃ ((p ∨ q) · (p ∨ r))
T	T	T	T T T T T T
T	T	F	T F T T T T
T	F	T	T F T T T T
T	F	F	T F T T T T
F	T	T	T T T T T T
F	T	F	F F T T F F
F	F	T	F F T F F T
F	F	F	F F T F F F

Valid

e.

p	q	r	((p · (q ∨ r)) · ~q) ⊃ (p · r)
T	T	T	T T FF T T
T	T	F	T T FF T F
T	F	T	T T TT T T
T	F	F	F F FT T F
F	T	T	F T FF T F
F	T	F	F T FF T F
F	F	T	F T FT T F
F	F	F	F F FT T F

Valid

7. a. (((p ⊃ q) · (r ⊃ s)) · (p ∨ r)) ⊃ (q ∨ s)
   F T F   F T F   F F F   F F F
   Valid

b. ((p ⊃ q) · (r ⊃ ~q)) ⊃ (p ⊃ ~r)
   T T T   T FF T   T FF T
   Valid

c. (((p ∨ q) · (~p · ~r)) · (q ⊃ (r ∨ s))) ⊃ s
   F F F   TFT   TF   FTFFF   F
   Valid

d. (p ∨ (q · r)) ⊃ ((p ∨ q) · (p ∨ r))
   F F TFF   F T T   F F F
   F F FFT   F F F   F T T
   F F FFF   F F F   F F F
   Valid

e. ((p · (q ∨ r)) · ~q) ⊃ (p · r)
   T F F TF   TFF
   F F T TF   FFT
   F F F TF   FFF
   Valid

CHAPTER 5

EXERCISE 5-1

1. A step-by-step procedure for determining the validity of an argument form whose validity depends on the truth-functional relationships among the statement variables occurring in the argument form.

12. The rules must be applied to a complete statement, and not to a statement which is itself part of a statement.

EXERCISE 5-2

1. a. Affirming the antecedent
   g. None
   m. None

   d. None
   j. None

2. a. $q \lor s$; constructive dilemma
   g. $\sim(p \supset q) \cdot (r \supset s)$; conjunction

   d. $p \lor q$; simplification
   j. $\sim(p \supset \sim q)$; denying the consequent

EXERCISE 5-3

1. A sequence of statements in which the premises occur first, the conclusion occurs as the last line, and in which every statement is either a premise or is inferred from previous statements in the sequence by one of the given rules of inference

4. Affirming the antecedent and denying the consequent

EXERCISE 5-4

1. a. (4): (1), (3), DS
      (5): (2), (4), AA

   d. (5): (3), Simp
      (6): (2), (5), DC
      (7): (1), (6), DS
      (8): (4), (7), AA
      (9): (8), (5), DS

   g. (6): (3), Simp
      (7): (1), (5), HS
      (8): (7), (6), DC
      (9): (4), (8), DS
      (10): (9), Add
      (11): (2), (10), AA
      (12): (7), (11), HS

   j. (5): (1), (2), (3), CD
      (6): (5), (4), DS
      (7): (6), Add

2. a. (1) $\sim C \supset (D \supset E)$ Premise
      (2) $A \supset B$ Premise
      (3) $\sim C$ Premise
      (4) $C \lor (A \lor D)$ Premise
      (5) $D \supset E$ (1), (3), AA
      (6) $A \lor D$ (4), (3), DS
   ∴ (7) $B \lor E$ (2), (5), (6), CD

   d. (1) $(R \lor C) \supset (P \supset (S \equiv T))$ Premise
      (2) $P \cdot S$ Premise
      (3) $(P \lor Q) \supset R$ Premise
      (4) P (2), Simp
      (5) $P \lor Q$ (4), Add
      (6) R (3), (5), AA
      (7) $R \lor C$ (6), Add
      (8) $P \supset (S \equiv T)$ (1), (7), AA
   ∴ (9) $S \equiv T$ (8), (4), AA

g. (1) $\sim A \supset E$ Premise
   (2) $A \supset \sim C$ Premise
   (3) $\sim\sim C \cdot B$ Premise
   (4) $\sim\sim C$ (3), Simp
   (5) $\sim A$ (2), (4), DC
$\therefore$ (6) E (1), (5), AA

j. (1) $\sim\sim R$ Premise
   (2) $((P \vee Q) \vee (\sim R \vee \sim S)) \cdot T$ Premise
   (3) $\sim(P \vee Q)$ Premise
   (4) $(P \vee Q) \vee (\sim R \vee \sim S)$ (2), Simp
   (5) $\sim R \vee \sim S$ (4), (3), DS
$\therefore$ (6) $\sim S$ (5), (1), DS

EXERCISE 5-5

1. a. $(E \supset C) \vee I$
   $(E \supset C) \supset R$
   $I \supset (R \vee C)$
   $\sim R$
  $\therefore C$

   (1) $(E \supset C) \vee I$ Premise
   (2) $(E \supset C) \supset R$ Premise
   (3) $I \supset (R \vee C)$ Premise
   (4) $\sim R$ Premise
   (5) $\sim(E \supset C)$ (2), (4), DC
   (6) I (1), (5), DS
   (7) $R \vee C$ (3), (6), AA
  $\therefore$ (8) C (7), (4), DS

  d. $(P \supset C) \cdot (W \supset A)$
    P
  $\therefore C \vee W$

   (1) $(P \supset C) \cdot (W \supset A)$ Premise
   (2) P Premise
   (3) $P \supset C$ (1), Simp
   (4) C (3), (2), AA
  $\therefore$ (5) $C \vee W$ (4), Add

  g. $T \supset \sim A$
    $T \vee (S \cdot A)$
    $\sim\sim A$
  $\therefore S$

   (1) $T \supset \sim A$ Premise
   (2) $T \vee (S \cdot A)$ Premise
   (3) $\sim\sim A$ Premise
   (4) $\sim T$ (1), (3), DC
   (5) $S \cdot A$ (2), (4), DS
  $\therefore$ (6) S (5), Simp

  j. $(E \vee \sim R) \supset V$
    $H \supset V$
    $\sim R \supset (\sim E \supset \sim J)$
    $\sim R$
    $\sim E \vee H$
  $\therefore \sim J \vee V$

(1) $(E \lor \sim R) \supset V$ Premise
(2) $H \supset V$ Premise
(3) $\sim R \supset (\sim E \supset \sim J)$ Premise
(4) $\sim R$ Premise
(5) $\sim E \lor H$ Premise
(6) $\sim E \supset \sim J$ (3), (4), AA
$\therefore (7)$ $\sim J \lor V$ (6), (2), (5), CD

EXERCISE 5-6

2. Since logically equivalent statement forms have the same truth value given the same assignment of truth values to the variables which occur in the statement forms, truth values will not be changed by replacing some statement form with one which is logically equivalent to it.

EXERCISE 5-7

1. a. Double negation
   g. None
   m. None
   s. Implication
   y. None

   d. Contraposition
   j. Repetition
   p. None
   v. Implication

2. a. (3): (2), distribution
       (4): (3), commutation
       (5): (4), Simp
       (6): (5), Rep
       (7): (1), Assoc
       (8): (7), (6), DS
       (9): (8), Imp

   d. (4): (3), DN
       (5): (4), Imp
       (6): (2), Contra
       (7): (6), DN
       (8): (7), (5), HS
       (9): (1), Dist
       (10): (9), Comm
       (11): (10), Simp
       (12): (11), Comm
       (13): (12), DN
       (14): (13), Imp
       (15): (14), (8), HS
       (16): (15), Imp
       (17): (16), DN
       (18): (17), Rep

   g. (3): (2), Add
       (4): (3), DM
       (5): (1), (4), DC
       (6): (5), DM
       (7): (6), Simp

   j. (4): (1), Exp
       (5): (3), Comm
       (6): (5), Comm
       (7): (4), (6), AA
       (8): (7), DN
       (9): (8), Imp
       (10): (9), (2), AA

EXERCISE 5-8

1. a. (1) $P \supset (Q \cdot R)$ Premise
       (2) $P \cdot S$ Premise
       (3) P (2), Simp
       (4) $Q \cdot R$ (1), (3), AA
       (5) $R \cdot Q$ (4), Comm
       $\therefore (6)$ R (5), Simp

d. (1) ~O   Premise
   (2) (L ∨ M) ⊃ N   Premise
   (3) ~(N · ~O)   Premise
   (4) ~L ⊃ P   Premise
   (5) ~N ∨ O   (3), DM
   (6) O ∨ ~N   (5), Comm
   (7) ~N   (6), (1), DS
   (8) ~(L ∨ M)   (2), (7), DC
   (9) ~L · ~M   (8), DM
   (10) ~L   (9), Simp
   ∴ (11) P   (4), (10), AA

g. (1) ~A   Premise
   (2) ~B   Premise
   (3) (A ∨ B) ≡ C   Premise
   (4) ((A ∨ B) ⊃ C) · (C ⊃ (A ∨ B))   (3), Eq
   (5) (C ⊃ (A ∨ B)) · ((A ∨ B) ⊃ C)   (4), Comm
   (6) C ⊃ (A ∨ B)   (5), Simp
   (7) ~A · ~B   (1), (2), Conj
   (8) ~(A ∨ B)   (7), DM
   (9) ~C   (6), (8), DC
   (10) ~C ∨ ~D   (9), Add
   ∴ (11) ~(C · D)   (10), DM

j. (1) ~C ∨ ((B ⊃ D) · (E ⊃ D))   Premise
   (2) C · (B ∨ E)   Premise
   (3) C   (2), Simp
   (4) ~~C   (3), DN
   (5) (B ⊃ D) · (E ⊃ D)   (1), (4), DS
   (6) B ⊃ D   (5), Simp
   (7) (E ⊃ D) · (B ⊃ D)   (5), Comm
   (8) E ⊃ D   (7), Simp
   (9) (B ∨ E) · C   (2), Comm
   (10) B ∨ E   (9), Simp
   (11) D ∨ D   (6), (8), (9), CD
   ∴ (12) D   (11), Rep

2. a. (B ∨ M) ⊃ H
   ∴ ~H ⊃ ~B

   (1) (B ∨ M) ⊃ H   Premise
   (2) ~H ⊃ ~(B ∨ M)   (1), Contra
   (3) ~~H ∨ ~(B ∨ M)   (2), Imp
   (4) ~~H ∨ (~B · ~M)   (3), DM
   (5) (~~H ∨ ~B) · (~~H ∨ ~M)   (4), Dist
   (6) ~~H ∨ ~B   (5), Simp
   ∴ (7) ~H ⊃ ~B   (6), Imp

d. A ⊃ T
   R ∨ A
   ~R
   ∴ T

   (1) A ⊃ T   Premise
   (2) R ∨ A   Premise
   (3) ~R   Premise
   (4) A   (2), (3), DS
   ∴ (5) T   (1), (4), AA

g. $O \supset S$
   $D \supset H$
   $O \lor D$
   $O \supset {\sim}H$
   $D \supset {\sim}S$
   $\therefore S \equiv {\sim}H$

(1) $O \supset S$	Premise
(2) $D \supset H$	Premise
(3) $O \lor D$	Premise
(4) $O \supset {\sim}H$	Premise
(5) $D \supset {\sim}S$	Premise
(6) ${\sim}{\sim}S \supset {\sim}D$	(5), Contra
(7) $S \supset {\sim}D$	(6), DN
(8) $D \lor O$	(3), Comm
(9) ${\sim}{\sim}D \lor O$	(8), DN
(10) ${\sim}D \supset O$	(9), Imp
(11) $S \supset O$	(7), (10), HS
(12) $S \supset {\sim}H$	(11), (4), HS
(13) ${\sim}H \supset {\sim}D$	(2), Contra
(14) ${\sim}H \supset O$	(13), (10), HS
(15) ${\sim}H \supset S$	(14), (1), HS
(16) $(S \supset {\sim}H) \cdot ({\sim}H \supset S)$	(12), (15), Conj
$\therefore$ (17) $S \equiv {\sim}H$	(16), Eq

j. $E \supset ({\sim}W \lor {\sim}A)$
   $(P \supset A) \cdot (B \supset W)$
   $G \supset (P \cdot B)$
   E
   $\therefore {\sim}G$

(1) $E \supset ({\sim}W \lor {\sim}A)$	Premise
(2) $(P \supset A) \cdot (B \supset W)$	Premise
(3) $G \supset (P \cdot B)$	Premise
(4) E	Premise
(5) ${\sim}W \lor {\sim}A$	(1), (4), AA
(6) $P \supset A$	(2), Simp
(7) ${\sim}A \supset {\sim}P$	(6), Contra
(8) $(B \supset W) \cdot (P \supset A)$	(2), Comm
(9) $B \supset W$	(8), Simp
(10) ${\sim}W \supset {\sim}B$	(9), Contra
(11) ${\sim}B \lor {\sim}P$	(10), (7), (5), CD
(12) ${\sim}P \lor {\sim}B$	(11), Comm
(13) ${\sim}(P \cdot B)$	(12), DM
$\therefore$ (14) ${\sim}G$	(3), (13), DC

3. a. Here we want to show that each of the following argument forms is valid:

   $p \supset q$ $\qquad {\sim}q \supset {\sim}p$
   $\therefore {\sim}q \supset {\sim}p$ $\qquad \therefore p \supset q$

(1) $p \supset q$	Premise
(2) ${\sim}p \lor q$	(1), Imp
(3) $q \lor {\sim}p$	(2), Comm
(4) ${\sim}{\sim}q \lor {\sim}p$	(3), DN
$\therefore$ (5) ${\sim}q \supset {\sim}p$	(4), Imp
(1) ${\sim}q \supset {\sim}p$	Premise

$$(2) \sim\sim q \vee \sim p \qquad (1), \text{Imp}$$
$$(3) \sim p \vee \sim\sim q \qquad (2), \text{Comm}$$
$$(4) \ p \supset \sim\sim q \qquad (3), \text{Imp}$$
$$\therefore (5) \ p \supset q \qquad (4), \text{DN}$$

EXERCISE 5-9

1. Conditional proofs are used to derive conditional statements. Such proofs are constructed by assuming the antecedent of the conditional statement and then deriving the consequent.

4. Make the assumptions from left to right, and discharge them from right to left.

EXERCISE 5-10

1. a. (1) $P \vee \sim Q$ Premise
   (2) $\sim R \supset \sim P$ Premise
   ⌐(3) Q Assumption
   | (4) $\sim\sim Q$ (3), DN
   | (5) $\sim Q \vee P$ (1), Comm
   | (6) P (5), (3), DS
   | (7) $P \supset R$ (2), Contra
   ⌊(8) R (7), (6), AA
   ∴ (9) $Q \supset R$ (3 to 8), CP

   d. (1) $(P \vee Q) \supset (R \cdot S)$ Premise
   ⌐(2) P Assumption
   | (3) $P \vee Q$ (2), Add
   | (4) $R \cdot S$ (1), (3), AA
   ⌊(5) R (4), Simp
   (6) $P \supset R$ (2) to (5), CP
   ∴ (7) $\sim P \vee R$ (6), Imp

   g. (1) $(A \vee B) \supset C$ Premise
   ⌐(2) $(C \vee D) \supset E$ Assumption
   |⌐(3) A Assumption
   || (4) $A \vee B$ (3), Add
   || (5) C (1), (4), AA
   || (6) $C \vee D$ (5), Add
   || (7) E (2), (6), AA
   |⌊(8) $A \supset E$ (3) to (7), CP
   ∴ (9) $((C \vee D) \supset E) \supset (A \supset E)$ (2) to (8), CP

   j. (1) $(P \vee Q) \supset R$ Premise
   ⌐(2) P Assumption
   | (3) $P \vee Q$ (2), Add
   ⌊(4) R (1), (3), AA
   ∴ (5) $P \supset R$ (2) to (4), CP

2. a. (1) $(B \vee M) \supset H$ Premise
   ⌐(2) $\sim H$ Assumption
   | (3) $\sim(B \vee M)$ (1), (2), DC
   | (4) $\sim B \cdot \sim M$ (3), DM
   ⌊(5) $\sim B$ (4), Simp
   ∴ (6) $\sim H \supset \sim B$ (2) to (5), CP

   d. (1) $F \supset \sim C$ Premise
   (2) $F \supset (\sim C \supset \sim P)$ Premise
   (3) $\sim C \supset (\sim P \supset \sim R)$ Premise
   (4) $V \supset R$ Premise

```
 ┌(5)  F                    Assumption
 │ (6)  ~C ⊃ ~P             (2), (5), AA
 │ (7)  ~C                  (1), (5), AA
 │ (8)  ~P ⊃ ~R             (3), (7), AA
 │ (9)  ~P                  (6), (7), AA
 │(10)  ~R                  (8), (9), AA
 └(11)  ~V                  (4), (10), DC
∴(12)  F ⊃ ~V              (5) to (11), CP
```

EXERCISE 5-11

1. A special kind of conditional proof in which we assume the negation of the statement we want to derive, and then derive a contradiction from the assumption

4. The assumption and its negation; one of the premises and its negation; and some statement derived from the premises and the assumption and the negation of this statement

EXERCISE 5-12

```
1. a.   (1) (B ∨ C) ⊃ D         Premise
        (2) ~A                  Premise
        (3) D ⊃ A               Premise
      ┌(4) ~~B                  Assumption
      │(5) B                    (4), DN
      │(6) B ∨ C                (5), Add
      │(7) D                    (1), (6), AA
      │(8) A                    (3), (7), AA
      └(9) A · ~A               (8), (2), Cong
    ∴(10) ~B                    (4) to (9), RAA

   d.  (1) A ∨ B                Premise
       (2) A ∨ ~B               Premise
     ┌(3) ~A                    Assumption
     │(4) B                     (1), (3), DS
     │(5) ~B                    (2), (3), DS
     └(6) B · ~B                (4), (5), Conj
    ∴(7) A                      (3) to (6), RAA

   g.  (1) P ∨ Q                Premise
       (2) Q ⊃ (R · S)          Premise
       (3) (R ∨ P) ⊃ T          Premise
     ┌(4) ~T                    Assumption
     │(5) ~(R ∨ P)              (3), (4), DC
     │(6) ~R · ~P               (5), DM
     │(7) ~P · ~R               (6), Comm
     │(8) ~P                    (7), Simp
     │(9) Q                     (1), (8), DS
     │(10) R · S                (2), (9), AA
     │(11) R                    (10), Simp
     │(12) ~R                   (6), Simp
     └(13) R · ~R               (11), (12), Conj
    ∴(14) T                     (4) to (13), RAA

   j.  (1) A ⊃ ((B · D) ⊃ (E ∨ C))     Premise
       (2) ~E                          Premise
       (3) (D · B) · A                 Premise
```

```
  ┌(4)  ~C                        Assumption
  │(5)  A · (D · B)               (3), Comm
  │(6)  A                         (5), Simp
  │(7)  (B · D) ⊃ (E ∨ C)         (1), (6), AA
  │(8)  D · B                     (3), Simp
  │(9)  B · D                     (8), Comm
  │(10) E ∨ C                     (7), (9), AA
  │(11) C ∨ E                     (10), Comm
  │(12) E                         (11), (4), DS
  └(13) E · ~E                    (12), (2), Conj
∴ (14) C                          (4) to (13), RAA
```

2. a.
```
   (1)  (B ∨ M) ⊃ H               Premise
  ┌(2)  ~(~H ⊃ ~B)                Assumption
  │(3)  ~(~~H ∨ ~B)               (2), Imp
  │(4)  ~H · B                    (3), DM
  │(5)  ~H                        (4), Simp
  │(6)  ~(B ∨ M)                  (1), (5), DC
  │(7)  ~B · ~M                   (6), DM
  │(8)  ~B                        (7), Simp
  │(9)  B · ~H                    (4), Comm
  │(10) B                         (9), Simp
  └(11) B · ~B                    (10), (8), Conj
∴ (12) ~H ⊃ ~B                    (2) to (11), RAA
```

d.
```
   (1)  A ⊃ T                     Premise
   (2)  R ∨ A                     Premise
   (3)  ~R                        Premise
  ┌(4)  ~T                        Assumption
  │(5)  ~A                        (1), (4), DC
  │(6)  A                         (2), (3), DS
  └(7)  A · ~A                    (6), (5), Conj
∴ (8)  T                          (4) to (7), RAA
```

g.
```
   (1)  O ⊃ S                     Premise
   (2)  D ⊃ H                     Premise
   (3)  O ∨ D                     Premise
   (4)  O ⊃ ~H                    Premise
   (5)  D ⊃ ~S                    Premise
  ┌(6)  ~(S ≡ ~H)                 Assumption
  │(7)  ~((S ⊃ ~H) · (~H ⊃ S))    (6), Eq
  │(8)  ~(S ⊃ ~H) ∨ ~(~H ⊃ S)     (7), DM
  │(9)  (S ⊃ ~H) ⊃ ~(~H ⊃ S)      (8), Imp
  │(10) ~~S ⊃ ~D                  (5), Contra
  │(11) S ⊃ ~D                    (10), DN
  │(12) D ∨ O                     (3), Comm
  │(13) ~~D ∨ O                   (12), DN
  │(14) ~D ⊃ O                    (13), Imp
  │(15) S ⊃ O                     (9), (14), HS
  │(16) S ⊃ ~H                    (15), (4), HS
  │(17) ~(~H ⊃ S)                 (9), (16), AA
  │(18) ~H ⊃ ~D                   (2), Contra
  │(19) ~H ⊃ O                    (18), (14), HS
  │(20) ~H ⊃ S                    (19), (1), HS
  └(21) (~H ⊃ S) · ~(~H ⊃ S)      (20), (17), Conj
∴ (22) S ≡ ~H                     (6) to (21), RAA
```

j. (1) $E \supset (\sim W \vee \sim A)$ Premise
   (2) $(P \supset A) \cdot (B \supset W)$ Premise
   (3) $G \supset (P \cdot B)$ Premise
   (4) E Premise
   (5) $\sim\sim G$ Assumption
   (6) G (5), DN
   (7) $P \cdot B$ (3), (6), AA
   (8) P (7), Simp
   (9) $P \supset A$ (2), Simp
   (10) A (9), (8), AA
   (11) $\sim W \vee \sim A$ (1), (4), AA
   (12) $\sim A \vee \sim W$ (11), Comm
   (13) $\sim\sim A$ (10), DN
   (14) $\sim W$ (12), (13), DS
   (15) $B \cdot P$ (7), Comm
   (16) B (15), Simp
   (17) $(B \supset W) \cdot (P \supset A)$ (2), Comm
   (18) $B \supset W$ (17), Simp
   (19) W (18), (16), AA
   (20) $W \cdot \sim W$ (19), (14), Conj
∴ (21) $\sim G$ (5) to (20), RAA

EXERCISE 5-13

1. a. (1) $p \cdot q$ Assumption
   (2) P (1), Simp
∴ (3) $(p \cdot q) \supset p$ (1) to (2), CP

d. (1) $p \cdot q$ Assumption
   (2) p (1), Simp
   (3) $p \vee q$ (2), Add
∴ (4) $(p \cdot q) \supset (p \vee q)$ (1) to (3), CP

g. (1) $(p \supset q) \cdot (q \supset p)$ Assumption
   (2) $(\sim p \vee q) \cdot (q \supset p)$ (1), Imp
   (3) $(\sim p \vee q) \cdot (\sim q \vee p)$ (2), Imp
   (4) $((p \supset q) \cdot (q \supset p)) \supset ((\sim p \vee q) \cdot (\sim q \vee p))$ (1) to (3), CP
   (5) $(\sim p \vee q) \cdot (\sim q \vee p)$ Assumption
   (6) $(p \supset q) \cdot (\sim q \vee p)$ (5), Imp
   (7) $(p \supset q) \cdot (q \supset p)$ (6), Imp
   (8) $((\sim p \vee q) \cdot (\sim q \vee p)) \supset ((p \supset q) \cdot (q \supset p))$ (5) to (7), CP
   (9) $(((p \supset q) \cdot (q \supset p)) \supset ((\sim p \vee q) \cdot (\sim q \vee p)))$
     $\cdot (((\sim p \vee q) \cdot (\sim q \vee p)) \supset ((p \supset q) \cdot (q \supset p)))$ (4), (8), Conj
∴ (10) $((p \supset q) \cdot (q \supset p)) \equiv ((\sim p \vee q) \cdot (\sim q \vee p))$ (9), Eq

j. (1) $\sim\sim((p \cdot q) \cdot (\sim p \vee \sim q))$ Assumption
   (2) $(p \cdot q) \cdot (\sim p \vee \sim q)$ (1), DN
   (3) $(p \cdot q) \cdot \sim(p \cdot q)$ (2), DM
∴ (4) $\sim(p \cdot q) \cdot (\sim p \vee \sim q)$ (1) to (3), RAA

2. In each case, use the conjunction of the premises as an assumption for CP and then use Comm and Simp to get each premise on a line by itself. Then construct a direct proof showing that the conclusion follows from the assumption, and close out the proof by CP. Part (a) is done below as an example.

    ⌐(1) $(((B \lor C) \supset D) \cdot \sim A) \cdot (D \supset A)$ Assumption
      (2) $((B \lor C) \supset D) \cdot \sim A$ (1), Simp
      (3) $(B \lor C) \supset D$ (2), Simp
      (4) $(D \supset A) \cdot (((B \lor C) \supset D) \cdot \sim A)$ (1), Comm
      (5) $D \supset A$ (4), Simp
      (6) $\sim A \cdot ((B \lor C) \supset D)$ (2), Comm
      (7) $\sim A$ (6), Simp
      (8) $\sim D$ (5), (7), DC
      (9) $\sim (B \lor C)$ (3), (8), DC
   (10) $\sim B \cdot \sim C$ (9), DM
   ⌊(11) $\sim B$ (10), Simp
$\therefore$ (12) $((((B \lor C) \supset D) \cdot \sim A) \cdot (D \supset A)) \supset \sim B$ (1) to (11), CP

SELF-TEST/EXERCISES

1. a. (1) $(p \cdot q) \supset (p \supset (s \cdot t))$ Premise
    (2) $(p \cdot q) \cdot r$ Premise
    (3) $p \cdot q$ (2), Simp
    (4) p (3), Simp
    (5) $p \supset (s \cdot t)$ (1), (3), AA
    (6) $s \cdot t$ (5), (4), AA
    (7) s (6), Simp
 $\therefore$ (8) $s \lor t$ (7), Add

  b. (1) $(p \lor q) \supset (r \supset (s \equiv t))$ Premise
    (2) $r \cdot s$ Premise
    (3) $(r \lor u) \supset p$ Premise
    (4) r (2), Simp
    (5) $r \lor u$ (4), Add
    (6) p (3), (5), AA
    (7) $p \lor q$ (6), Add
    (8) $r \supset (s \equiv t)$ (1), (7), AA
 $\therefore$ (9) $s \equiv t$ (8), (4), AA

  c. (1) $p \lor (q \lor r)$ Premise
    (2) $q \supset s$ Premise
    (3) $r \supset t$ Premise
    (4) $(s \lor t) \supset (p \lor r)$ Premise
    (5) $\sim p$ Premise
    (6) $q \lor r$ (1), (5), DS
    (7) $s \lor t$ (2), (3), (6), CD
    (8) $p \lor r$ (4), (7), AA
 $\therefore$ (9) r (8), (5), DS

  d. (1) $(p \supset q) \cdot (r \supset s)$ Premise
    (2) $t \lor \sim q$ Premise
    (3) $\sim t \cdot s$ Premise
    (4) $\sim t$ (2), Simp
    (5) $\sim q$ (2), (4), DS
    (6) $p \supset q$ (1), Simp
    (7) $\sim p$ (6), (5), DC
 $\therefore$ (8) $\sim p \lor r$ (7), Add

  e. (1) $(\sim p \lor \sim q) \supset (r \supset (s \cdot \sim t))$ Premise
    (2) $(\sim p \cdot \sim u) \cdot (\sim v \lor r)$ Premise
    (3) $(\sim p \cdot \sim u) \supset ((s \cdot \sim t) \supset v)$ Premise
    (4) $\sim p \cdot \sim u$ (2), Simp

(5) $\sim p$	(4), Simp
(6) $\sim p \lor \sim q$	(5), Add
(7) $r \supset (s \cdot \sim t)$	(1), (6), AA
(8) $(s \cdot \sim t) \supset v$	(3), (4), AA
$\therefore$ (9) $r \supset v$	(7), (8), HS

2. a.

(1) $M \supset \sim R$	Premise
(2) $(R \lor V) \cdot M$	Premise
(3) $M \cdot (R \lor V)$	(2), Comm
(4) M	(3), Simp
(5) $\sim R$	(1), (4), AA
(6) $R \lor V$	(2), Simp
$\therefore$ (7) V	(6), (5), DS

b.

(1) $((A \cdot B) \supset C) \cdot ((A \cdot D) \supset E)$	Premise
(2) $(D \lor B) \cdot A$	Premise
(3) $A \cdot (D \lor B)$	(2), Comm
(4) $(A \cdot D) \lor (A \cdot B)$	(3), Dist
(5) $(A \cdot B) \lor (A \cdot D)$	(4), Comm
(6) $(A \cdot B) \supset C$	(1), Simp
(7) $((A \cdot D) \supset E) \cdot ((A \cdot B) \supset C)$	(1), Comm
(8) $(A \cdot D) \supset E$	(7), Simp
$\therefore$ (9) $C \lor E$	(6), (8), (5), CD

c.

(1) $P \supset R$	Premise
(2) $Q \supset S$	Premise
(3) $T \supset (\sim R \lor \sim S)$	Premise
(4) $T \cdot P$	Premise
(5) T	(4), Simp
(6) $P \cdot T$	(4), Comm
(7) P	(6), Simp
(8) R	(1), (7), AA
(9) $\sim R \lor \sim S$	(3), (5), AA
(10) $\sim\sim R$	(8), DN
(11) $\sim S$	(9), (10), DS
$\therefore$ (12) $\sim Q$	(2), (11), DC

d.

(1) $G \supset F$	Premise
(2) $F \supset \sim P$	Premise
(3) P	Premise
(4) $\sim\sim P$	(3), DN
(5) $\sim F$	(2), (4), DC
$\therefore$ (6) $\sim G$	(1), (5), DC

e.

(1) $(\sim I \supset U) \cdot (\sim P \supset C)$	Premise
(2) $(C \cdot U) \supset L$	Premise
(3) $\sim L$	Premise
(4) $\sim (C \cdot U)$	(2), (3), DC
(5) $\sim C \lor \sim U$	(4), DM
(6) $\sim I \supset U$	(1), Simp
(7) $(\sim P \supset C) \cdot (\sim I \supset U)$	(1), Comm
(8) $\sim P \supset C$	(7), Simp
(9) $\sim U \supset \sim\sim I$	(6), Contra
(10) $\sim U \supset I$	(9), DN
(11) $\sim C \supset \sim\sim P$	(8), Contra
(12) $\sim C \supset P$	(11), DN
(13) $\sim U \lor \sim C$	(5), Comm
$\therefore$ (14) $I \lor P$	(10), (11), (12), CD

f. (1) $\sim T \supset D$ Premise
  (2) $T \supset (\sim P \cdot E)$ Premise
  (3) $T \lor \sim T$ Premise
  (4) $(\sim P \cdot E) \lor D$ (2), (1), (3), CD
  (5) $D \lor (\sim P \cdot E)$ (4), Comm
  (6) $(D \lor \sim P) \cdot (D \lor E)$ (5), Dist
  (7) $(D \lor E) \cdot (D \lor \sim P)$ (6), Comm
∴ (8) $D \lor E$ (7), Simp

3. a. (1) $\sim(Q \cdot \sim R)$ Premise
  (2) $P \supset (Q \cdot S)$ Premise
  (3) P Assumption
  (4) $Q \cdot S$ (2), (3), AA
  (5) $\sim Q \lor R$ (1), DM
  (6) Q (4), Simp
  (7) $\sim\sim Q$ (6), DN
  (8) R (5), (7), DS
∴ (9) $P \supset R$ (3) to (8), CP

b. (1) $P \supset (Q \cdot R)$ Premise
  (2) $P \cdot S$ Premise
  (3) P (2), Simp
  (4) $Q \cdot R$ (1), (3), AA
  (5) $R \cdot Q$ (4), Comm
∴ (6) R (5), Simp

c. (1) $(F \supset R) \cdot (F \supset U)$ Premise
  (2) $(R \cdot U) \supset D$ Premise
  (3) $\sim(D \lor \sim F)$ Assumption
  (4) $\sim D \cdot F$ (3), DM
  (5) $\sim D$ (4), Simp
  (6) $\sim(R \cdot U)$ (2), (5), DC
  (7) $\sim R \lor \sim U$ (6), DM
  (8) $F \supset R$ (1), Simp
  (9) $F \cdot \sim D$ (4), Comm
  (10) F (9), Simp
  (11) R (8), (11), AA
  (12) $\sim\sim R$ (11), DN
  (13) $\sim U$ (7), (12), DS
  (14) $(F \supset U) \cdot (F \supset R)$ (1), Comm
  (15) $F \supset U$ (14), Simp
  (16) U (15), (10), AA
  (17) $U \cdot \sim U$ (16), (13), Conj
∴ (18) $D \lor \sim F$ (3) to (17), RAA

d. (1) $(A \lor B) \supset ((C \lor D) \supset (E \cdot F))$ Premise
  (2) $(E \lor G) \supset F$ Premise
  (3) A Assumption
  (4) C Assumption
  (5) $A \lor B$ (3), Add
  (6) $(C \lor D) \supset (E \cdot F)$ (1), (5), AA
  (7) $C \lor D$ (4), Add
  (8) $E \cdot F$ (6), (7), AA
  (9) $F \cdot E$ (8), Comm
  (10) F (9), Simp
  (11) $C \supset F$ (4) to (10), CP
∴ (12) $A \supset (C \supset F)$ (3) to (11), CP

e. (1) $(L \lor M) \supset N$ Premise
   (2) $\sim O$ Premise
   (3) $\sim(N \cdot \sim O)$ Premise
   (4) $\sim L \supset P$ Premise
   (5) $\sim N \lor O$ (3), DM
   (6) $O \lor \sim N$ (5), Comm
   (7) $\sim N$ (6), (2), DS
   (8) $\sim(L \lor M)$ (1), (7), DC
   (9) $\sim L \cdot \sim M$ (8), DM
  (10) $\sim L$ (9), Simp
∴ (11) P (4), (10), AA

f. (1) $P \supset R$ Premise
   (2) $Q \supset S$ Premise
   (3) $T \supset (\sim R \lor \sim S)$ Premise
   (4) $T \cdot P$ Premise
   (5) T (4), Simp
   (6) $\sim R \lor \sim S$ (3), (5), AA
   (7) $P \cdot T$ (4), Comm
   (8) P (7), Simp
   (9) R (1), (8), AA
  (10) $\sim\sim R$ (9), DN
  (11) $\sim S$ (6), (10), DS
∴ (12) $\sim Q$ (2), (11), DC

g. (1) $T \supset C$ Premise
   (2) $(\sim T \cdot P) \supset F$ Premise
   (3) $F \supset C$ Premise
   (4) $\sim C$ Assumption
   (5) $\sim F$ (3), (4), DC
   (6) $\sim(\sim T \cdot P)$ (2), (5), DC
   (7) $T \lor \sim P$ (6), DM
   (8) $\sim\sim T \lor \sim P$ (7), DN
   (9) $\sim T \supset \sim P$ (8), Imp
  (10) $\sim C \supset \sim T$ (1), Contra
  (11) $\sim C \supset \sim P$ (10), (9), HS
  (12) $\sim C \supset (\sim C \supset \sim P)$ (4) to (11), CP
  (13) $(\sim C \cdot \sim C) \supset \sim P$ (12), Exp
∴ (14) $\sim C \supset \sim P$ (13), Rep

h. (1) $A \supset ((B \cdot C) \lor E)$ Premise
   (2) $(B \cdot C) \supset \sim A$ Premise
   (3) $D \supset \sim E$ Premise
   (4) A Assumption
   (5) $(B \cdot C) \lor E$ (1), (4), AA
   (6) $\sim\sim A$ (4), DN
   (7) $\sim(B \cdot C)$ (2), (6), DC
   (8) E (5), (7), DS
   (9) $\sim\sim E$ (8), DN
  (10) $\sim D$ (3), (9), DC
∴ (11) $A \supset \sim D$ (4) to (10), CP

3. a. (1) $\sim\sim(((p \supset q) \cdot p) \cdot \sim q)$ Assumption
   (2) $(((p \supset q) \cdot p) \cdot \sim q)$ (1), DN
   (3) $(p \supset q) \cdot p$ (2), Simp
   (4) $p \cdot (p \supset q)$ (3), Comm
   (5) p (4), Simp

(6) $(p \supset q)$	(3), Simp
(7) q	(6), (5), AA
(8) $\sim q \cdot ((p \supset q) \cdot p)$	(2), Comm
(9) $\sim q$	(8), Simp
(10) $q \cdot \sim q$	(7), (9), Conj
$\therefore$ (11) $\sim(((p \supset q) \cdot p) \cdot \sim q)$	(1) to (10), RAA

b.
(1) $\sim p \cdot q$	Assumption
(2) $\sim p$	(1), Simp
(3) $\sim p \vee (s \vee r)$	(2), Add
(4) $p \supset (s \vee r)$	(3), Imp
$\therefore$ (5) $(\sim p \cdot q) \supset (p \supset (s \vee r))$	(1) to (4), CP

c.
(1) $p \supset (q \supset r)$	Assumption
(2) $\sim p \vee (q \supset r)$	(1), Imp
(3) $\sim p \vee (\sim q \vee r)$	(2), Imp
(4) $(\sim p \vee \sim q) \vee r$	(3), Assoc
(5) $(\sim q \vee \sim p) \vee r$	(4), Comm
(6) $\sim q \vee (\sim p \vee r)$	(5) Assoc
(7) $q \supset (\sim p \vee r)$	(6), Imp
(8) $q \supset (p \supset r)$	(7), Imp
$\therefore$ (9) $(p \supset (q \supset r)) \supset (q \supset (p \supset r))$	(1) to (8), CP

d.
(1) $p \supset q$	Assumption
(2) $p \vee r$	Assumption
(3) $\sim(p \vee \sim p)$	Assumption
(4) $\sim p \cdot p$	(3), DM
(5) $p \vee \sim p$	(3) to (4), RAA
(6) $\sim\sim p \vee r$	(2), DN
(7) $\sim p \supset r$	(6), Imp
(8) $q \vee r$	(1), (7), (5), CD
(9) $(p \vee r) \supset (q \vee r)$	(2) to (8), CP
$\therefore$ (10) $(p \supset q) \supset ((p \vee r) \supset (q \vee r))$	(1) to (9), CP

CHAPTER 6

EXERCISE 6-1

1. All $\underline{S}$ are $\underline{P}$; no $\underline{S}$ are $\underline{P}$; some $\underline{S}$ are $\underline{P}$; some $\underline{S}$ are not $\underline{P}$.

5. A class complement includes all those individuals which are not members of the given class.

EXERCISE 6-2

1. Whether the statement is affirmative or negative

4. That all or some of the members of the subject class are excluded from the predicate class

7. Universal affirmative; universal negative; particular affirmative; particular negative

EXERCISE 6-3

2. They are understood as a kind of conditional statement in which it is asserted that if an individual is included in the subject class then that individual is included in (affirmative) or excluded from (negative) the predicate class.

EXERCISE 6-4

1. Predicate constants represent particular classes, and predicate variables are placeholders for class names. The former are represented with uppercase letters, and the latter with underlined uppercase letters.

4. A statement in which the predicate term applies exclusively to those individuals mentioned in the subject term. A statement in which it is asserted that a characteristic applies to a certain group of individuals with the exception of a few members in the group. The former are like 'only if' statements, and the latter are treated as conjunctions.

5. a. Some people are people who cannot be trusted.
   Some *P* are not *T*; *O*-form

   d. Some football players are people who don't run very fast.
   Some *P* are not *F*; *O*-form

   g. Some people like good music, and some people don't like good music.
   Some *P* are *L*, and some *P* are not *L*; *I*-form and *O*-form

   j. All people who respect themselves are people who respect others.
   All *R* are *O*; *A*-form

   m. Some judges are not incompetent.
   Some *J* are not *I*; *O*-form

   p. All aardvarks are non-nice animals. (*or* No aardvark is a nice animal.)
   All *A* are non-*N* (*or* No *A* are *N*); *A*-form (*or* *E*-form)

   s. All students will be admitted at half-price, and no nonstudent will be admitted at half-price.
   All *S* are *A*, and no non-*S* are *A*; *A*-form and *E*-form

   v. Some athletes are not injured while competing.
   Some *A* are not *I*; *O*-form

EXERCISE 6-5

a. Some *P* are non-*T*

d. Some *P* are not non-*F*

g. Some *P* are not non-*L* and some *P* are non-*L*

j. No *R* are non-*O*

m. Some *J* are non-*I*

p. No *A* are *N* (*or* All *A* are non-*N*)

s. No *S* are non-*A* and all non-*S* are non-*A*

v. Some *A* are non-*I*

y. Some *P* are non-*R*

EXERCISE 6-6

a. Some *T* are not *S*

d. All *M* are *T*

g. Some *R* are non-*S*

j. Some non-*L* are *S*

EXERCISE 6-7

4. a. Categorical syllogism
   d. Not a categorical syllogism; first premise is not a categorical statement.
   g. Not a categorical syllogism; it has three premises and four terms.

EXERCISE 6-8

1. To eliminate extra terms

4. Both terms are replaced by their complements, and the complement of the subject term

becomes the predicate term and the complement of the predicate term becomes the subject term.

7. To eliminate outside negation signs

8. a. Some non-S are not M
   Some T are not non-S
   ∴ Some M are not T

   g. All T are non-S
   All R are non-S
   ∴ No T are R

   d. Some R are S
   No S are non-T
   ∴ Some R are not non-T

   j. No T are R
   No R are non-S
   ∴ All non-S are T

EXERCISE 6-9

2. An empty class

5. That there is at least one member of the class represented by the circle in which the 'X' is located

8. a. All A are B

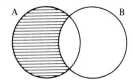

   d. No A are non-B

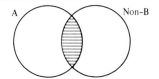

   g. Some F are C

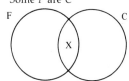

   j. All P are S

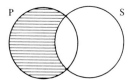

   m. All I are M

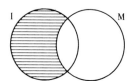

   p. Some E are U

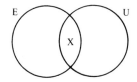

   s. No H are W

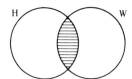

   v. All S are non-A

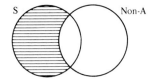

   y. All W are E

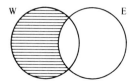

EXERCISE 6-10

5. a.

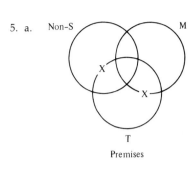
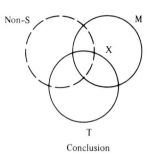

Premises   Conclusion

Invalid

d.

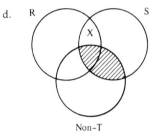
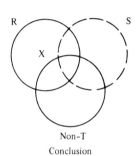

Non-T   Non-T
Premises   Conclusion

Valid

g.

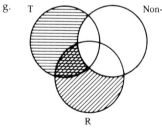
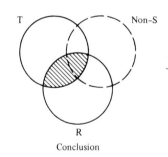

R   R
Premises   Conclusion

Invalid

j.

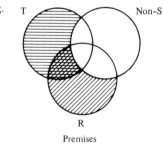
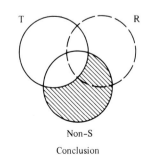

Non-S   Non-S
Premises   Conclusion

Invalid

6. a. All *W* are *L*
    No *H* are *L*
    ∴ No *H* are *W*

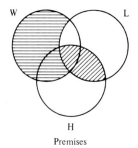

Premises   Conclusion

Valid

d. All *G* are *E*
    Some *B* are *E*
    ∴ Some *B* are *G*

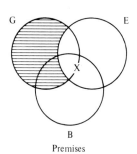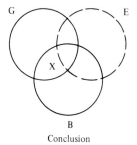

Premises   Conclusion

Invalid

g. No *P* are *D*
    All *D* are *L*
    ∴ No *P* are *L*

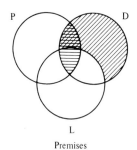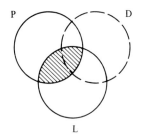

Premises   Conclusion

Invalid

j. No *B* are *H*
   All *H* are *C*
   ∴ No *B* are *C*

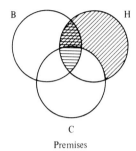

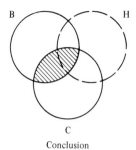

C   C
Premises   Conclusion
            Invalid

m. All *A* are *H*
   All *H* are *S*
   ∴ All *A* are *S*

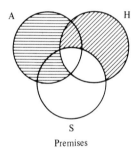

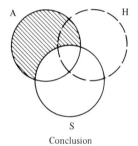

S   S
Premises   Conclusion
            Valid

p. All *H* are *W*
   Some *P* are not *H*
   ∴ Some *P* are not *W*

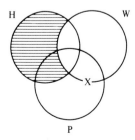

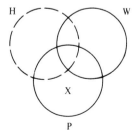

P   P
Premises   Conclusion
            Invalid

s. All *P* are non-*F*
    All non-*F* are *W*
    ∴ All *P* are *W*

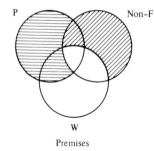

Premises	Conclusion

Valid

EXERCISE 6-11

9. a. All Ⓐ are *B*
    g. Some *F* are *C*
    m. All Ⓘ are *M*
    s. No Ⓗ are Ⓦ
    y. All Ⓦ are *E*

    d. No Ⓐ are ⓝon-*B*
    j. All Ⓟ are *S*
    p. Some *E* are *U*
    v. All Ⓢ are non-*A*

10. a. Invalid; violates R1, R2, and R4
    g. Invalid; violates R1 and R3

    d. Valid
    j. Invalid; violates R1

11. a. Valid
    g. Invalid; violates R4
    m. Valid
    s. Valid

    d. Invalid; violates R3
    j. Invalid; violates R4
    p. Invalid; violates R4

SELF-TEST/EXERCISES

1. Whether the statement is affirmative or negative; whether it's universal or particular

2. Universal affirmative; universal negative; particular affirmative; particular negative. The name gives the quantity and quality of the statement, in that order.

3. The proper name is treated as the name of the class whose only member is the individual named by the name.

4. An exceptive statement is one in which the predicate term is said to apply exclusively to the individual(s) designated by the subject term. Exceptive statements are those in which it is asserted that a characteristic applies to a certain group of individuals, with the exception of a few members in the group; such statements are translated as the conjunction of *I*-form and *O*-form statements, or of *A*-form and *E*-form statements.

5. a. Some *P* are *L* and some *P* are not Ⓛ
    c. Some *P* are not Ⓐ
    e. No Ⓢ are Ⓣ

    b. All Ⓐ are *P*
    d. All Ⓐ are *S*
    f. All Ⓑ are *L*

6. See section 6:4.1.

7. The end terms are the subject term and the predicate term of the conclusion. The middle term is the term which occurs in both premises.

8. See section 6:3. These transformations are used to eliminate extra terms.

9. To eliminate outside negation signs before categorical statements

10. a. Some non-*S* are not *N*
Some *T* are not non-*S*
∴ Some *N* are not *T*

b. All *S* are non-*R*
No *S* are non-*T*
∴ All non-*R* are non-*T*

c. All non-*L* are non-*M*
Some non-*M* are not *R*
∴ Some *R* are not non-*L*

11. See section 6:5.1

12. a. Some *A* are *E*

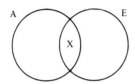

b. All *A* are *L*

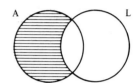

c. All *S* are *W*

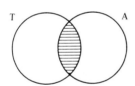

d. Some *A* are not *V*

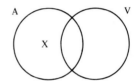

e. No *T* are *A*

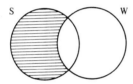

13. The 'X' represents the fact that the individual could be in either area that is bordered on the line the 'X' is on.

14. If the conclusion has been drawn in the premises diagram, the argument is valid. If it has not been drawn in the premises diagram, the argument is invalid.

15. a. Some *P* are not *F*
Some *F* are *N*
∴ Some *P* are *N*

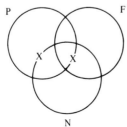

Premises

Invalid; violates R1

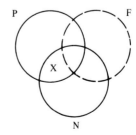

Conclusion

Invalid

b. Some *B* are *F*
   All *C* are *F*
   ∴ Some *B* are *C*

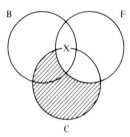

Premises   Conclusion

Invalid

Invalid; violates R3

c. No *U* are *E*
   Some *U* are *P*
   ∴ Some *E* are not *P*

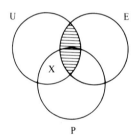 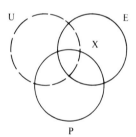

Premises   Conclusion

Invalid

Invalid; violates R4

d. Some *O* are *P*
   Some *P* are *R*
   ∴ Some *O* are *R*

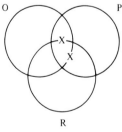 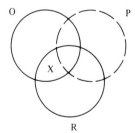

Premises   Conclusion

Invalid

Invalid; violates R2 and R3

e. All *I* are *S*
 All *I* are *W*
 ∴ All *S* are *W*

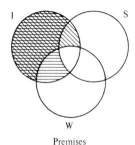

Premises   Conclusion

Invalid

Invalid; violates R4

f. Some *C* are *H*
 All *H* are *S*
 ∴ Some *C* are *S*

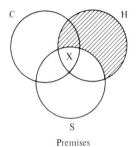

Premises   Conclusion

Valid

Valid

CHAPTER 7

EXERCISE 7-1

2. A statement in which something is asserted about a particular individual

5. a. Singular statement   d. Singular statement
 g. Singular statement   j. Not a singular statement

6. a. Subject term: John (*j*)   g. Subject term: time (*t*)
 Predicate term: hit a home run (*H*)   Predicate term: passes quickly (*P*)
 Hj   *Pt*

7. a. Washington, D.C.   d. Life

8. a. *Uw*   d. *Fl*

9. a. Barbara is going to the movies.
 d. Donna is throwing a party or going home for the weekend.
 g. Donna will throw a party if, and only if, Barbara does not go home for the weekend.
 j. If Allan goes home for the weekend, then either both Donna goes home for the weekend
 and studies for an exam or she throws a party.

EXERCISE 7-2

1. a. Someone is lonely

3. a. $(\exists x)Fx$ d. $(x)Hx$

EXERCISE 7-3

(In each of the following cases, the bound variables are underlined and the free variables are not underlined.)

a. $(\exists x)(A\underline{x} \cdot B\underline{x}) \cdot Cx$ d. $(Ab \cdot (\exists x)(L\underline{x})) \cdot By$

g. $(\underline{y})(G\underline{y} \equiv Fx)$ j. $(\underline{y})((Lx \cdot B\underline{y}) \vee Cb)$

m. $(\underline{y})(M\underline{y} \vee Bx) \equiv (Mc \cdot Ba)$ p. $(Gx \cdot Bx) \supset (\exists y)(G\underline{y} \cdot B\underline{y})$

s. $(\exists \underline{x})(\underline{y})((R\underline{x} \supset L\underline{y}) \cdot G\underline{x})$

EXERCISE 7-4

1. a. Students in Professor Dudley's logic class   d. People
   g. People watching television   j. People at Joan's performance

2. a. $(\exists x)(Sx)$ d. $(\exists x)(Bx)$
   g. $(x) \sim(Wx)$ j. $(x)(Ax)$

EXERCISE 7-5

a. $\sim(\exists x) \sim Fx$ d. $\sim(\exists x)(Cx \cdot Mx)$

g. $\sim(x) \sim(Lx \cdot Cx)$ j. $(x) \sim(\sim Cx \supset Lx)$

EXERCISE 7-6

1. Show that:

   $(x)(Mx \supset \sim Lx) \equiv \sim(\exists x)(Mx \cdot Lx)$
   $(\exists x)(Mx \cdot Lx) \equiv \sim(x)(Mx \supset \sim Lx)$

   (1) $(x)(Mx \supset \sim Lx)$ Premise
   (2) $\sim(\exists x) \sim(Mx \supset \sim Lx)$ (1), QE
   (3) $\sim(\exists x) \sim(\sim Mx \vee \sim Lx)$ (2), Imp
   (4) $\sim(\exists x)(Mx \cdot Lx)$ (3), DM

   (1) $\sim(\exists x)(Mx \cdot Lx)$ Premise
   (2) $(x) \sim(Mx \cdot Lx)$ (1), QE
   (3) $(x)(\sim Mx \vee \sim Lx)$ (2), DM
   (4) $(x)(Mx \supset \sim Lx)$ (3), Imp

   (1) $(\exists x)(Mx \cdot Lx)$ Premise
   (2) $\sim(x) \sim(Mx \cdot Lx)$ (1), QE
   (3) $\sim(x)(\sim Mx \vee \sim Lx)$ (2), DM
   (4) $\sim(x)(Mx \supset \sim Lx)$ (3), Imp

   (1) $\sim(x)(Mx \supset \sim Lx)$ Premise
   (2) $(\exists x) \sim(Mx \supset \sim Lx)$ (1), QE
   (3) $(\exists x) \sim(\sim Mx \vee Lx)$ (2), Imp
   (4) $(\exists x)(Mx \cdot Lx)$ (3), DM

2. a. $(x)(Mx \supset Gx)$ d. $(\exists x)(Fx \cdot \sim Wx)$
   g. $\sim(\exists x)(Px \cdot \sim Tx)$ j. $\sim(x)(Lx \supset Ex)$
   m. $(\exists x)(Jx \cdot Tx)$

EXERCISE 7-7

a. $(x)(Bx \supset Fx)$ d. $\sim(x)(Bx) \supset Fx)$

g. $\sim(\exists x)Cx$ j. $(x)(Wx \cdot Px)$

m. $(x)Fx$

p. $(x)(Wx \lor Fx)$

s. $(\exists x)(\sim Wx \lor Rx)$

v. $\sim(x)(Px \supset Ex)$

y. $(\exists x)Gx \cdot (\exists y)Ky$

EXERCISE 7-8

1. Because the individual may not be the same individual already mentioned

4. a. $La \supset Bb$

   g. $Cabc \cdot Mbc$

   d. $\sim La \lor (y)My$

   j. $(Pa \lor Lb) \cdot Gc$

5. a. $(\exists x)(y)(Lx \supset By)$

   g. $(\exists y)(\exists x)(Cyx \cdot Myx)$

   d. $(\exists y)((\exists x)(\sim Lx \lor My))$

   j. $(\exists y)(\exists x)((Pa \lor Ly) \cdot Gx)$

6. a. $(Pa \lor Lb) \cdot Ga$

   g. $Caba \cdot Mba$

   d. $Ma \cdot \sim La$

   j. $(\exists x) \sim Lx \cdot \sim Ma$

7. a. $(y)(\exists x)(Ly \supset By)$

   g. $(y)(\exists x)(\sim Lx \lor My)$

   d. $(x)(\exists y)(Ly \cdot Mx)$

   j. $(x)(\exists y)Cxy$

EXERCISE 7-9

1. Because the statement applies to all individuals in the universe of discourse

4.

La	Lb	Ma	Mb	Ra	Rb
T	T	F	T	T	T

5. (Sometimes there are additional invalidating interpretations which are not given here.)

   a.

La	Ma	Na
T	T	F

   d.

La	Lb	Ma	Mb	Ra	Rb
T	T	T	F	T	T

   g.

La	Lb	Lc	Ma	Mb	Mc	Ra	Rb	Rc
T	T	F	T	T	F	T	F	T

   j.

La	Lb	Ma	Mb	Ra	Rb
F	F	T	T	F	T

   m.

La	Lb	Ma	Mb
F	T	F	T

EXERCISE 7-10

1.

(1) $(x)(Dx \supset (Ax \supset Kx))$	Premise
(2) $(\exists x)(Dx \cdot Mx)$	Premise
(3) $(x)(Mx \supset \sim Kx)$	Premise
(4) $Da \cdot Ma$	(2), EI
(5) $Da \supset (Aa \supset Ka)$	(1), UI
(6) $Ma \supset \sim Ka$	(3), UI
(7) Da	(4), Simp
(8) $Aa \supset Ka$	(5), (7), AA
(9) $Ma \cdot Da$	(4), Comm
(10) Ma	(9), Simp
(11) $\sim Ka$	(6), (10), AA
(12) $\sim Aa$	(8), (11), DC
$\therefore$ (13) $(\exists x)\sim Ax$	(12), EG

4. a. (2): (1), UI

   (3): (2), Imp

   (4): (3), Rep

   d. (4): (1), QE

   (5): (2), QE

   (6): (3), QE

   (7): (5), EI

   (8): (4), UI

(9): (8), (7), AA
(10): (6), UI
(11): (10), (9), AA
(12): (11), EG

5. a. (1) $(\exists x)((Lx \lor Nx) \cdot Mx)$ Premise
       (2) $(x) \sim(Mx \cdot Lx)$ Premise
       (3) $(La \lor Na) \cdot Ma$ (1), EI
       (4) $\sim(Ma \cdot La)$ (2), UI
       (5) $\sim Ma \lor \sim La$ (4), DM
       (6) $Ma \cdot (La \lor Na)$ (3), Comm
       (7) Ma (6), Simp
       (8) $\sim\sim Ma$ (7), DN
       (9) $\sim La$ (5), (8), DS
       (10) $La \lor Na$ (3), Simp
       (11) Na (10), (9), DS
       (12) $Na \cdot \sim La$ (11), (9), Conj
    ∴ (13) $(\exists x)(Nx \cdot \sim Lx)$ (13), EG

   d. (1) $(x)((Lx \lor Mx) \supset Nx)$ Premise
       (2) $(\exists x)(Lx \cdot Ox)$ Premise
       (3) $La \cdot Oa$ (2), EI
       (4) $(La \lor Ma) \supset Na$ (1), UI
       (5) $Oa \cdot La$ (3), Comm
       (6) Oa (5), Simp
       (7) $(\exists x)Ox$ (6), EG
       (8) La (3), Simp
       (9) $La \lor Ma$ (8), Add
       (10) Na (4), (9), AA
       (11) $(\exists x)Nx$ (10), EG
    ∴ (12) $(\exists x)Nx \cdot (\exists x)Ox$ (11), (7), Conj

   g. (1) $(x)(Mx \supset Nx)$ Premise
       (2) $Ma \supset Na$ (1), UI
      ┌(3) $(x)Mx$ Assumption
      │(4) Ma (3), UI
      │(5) Na (2), (4), AA
      └(6) $(x)Nx$ (5), UG
    ∴ (7) $(x)Mx \supset (x)Nx$ (3) to (6), CP

   j. (1) $Rd \supset (x)(\sim Cx \supset \sim Kx)$ Premise
       (2) $(x)(Cx \supset Ax)$ Premise
       (3) $(\exists x)\sim Ax$ Premise
       (4) $\sim Aa$ (3), EI
      ┌(5) Rd Assumption
      │(6) $(x)(\sim Cx \supset \sim Kx)$ (1), (5), AA
      │(7) $\sim Ca \supset \sim Ka$ (6) UI
      │(8) $Ka \supset Ca$ (7), Contra
      │(9) $Ca \supset Aa$ (2) UI
      │(10) $Ka \supset Aa$ (9), (6), HS
      │(11) $\sim Ka$ (10), (4), DC
      └(12) $(\exists x)\sim Kx$ (11), EG
       (13) $Rd \supset (\exists x)\sim Kx$ (5) to (12), CP
    ∴ (14) $\sim Rd \lor (\exists x)\sim Kx$ (13), Imp

6. a. $(x)(Hx \supset Ex)$
       $(\exists x)(Mx \cdot \sim Ex)$
    ∴ $(\exists x)(Mx \cdot \sim Hx)$

(1) $(x)(Hx \supset Ex)$ Premise
(2) $(\exists x)(Mx \cdot \sim Ex)$ Premise
(3) $Ma \cdot \sim Ea$ (2), EI
(4) $Ha \supset Ea$ (1), UI
(5) Ma (3), Simp
(6) $\sim Ea \cdot Ma$ (3), Comm
(7) $\sim Ea$ (6), Simp
(8) $\sim Ha$ (4), (7), DC
(9) $Ma \cdot \sim Ha$ (5), (8), Conj
∴ (10) $(\exists x)(Mx \cdot \sim Hx)$ (9), EG

d. $(\exists x)(Ex \cdot (Ux \cdot \sim Cx))$
    $(x)(Ex \supset (Nx \lor Cx))$
∴ $(\exists x)(Nx \cdot Ux)$

(1) $(\exists x)(Ex \cdot (Ux \cdot \sim Cx))$ Premise
(2) $(x)(Ex \supset (Nx \lor Cx))$ Premise
(3) $Ea \cdot (Ua \cdot \sim Ca)$ (1), EI
(4) $Ea \supset (Na \lor Ca)$ (2), UI
(5) Ea (3), Simp
(6) $Na \lor Ca$ (4), (5), AA
(7) $(Ua \cdot \sim Ca) \cdot Ea$ (3), Comm
(8) $Ua \cdot \sim Ca$ (7), Simp
(9) Ua (8), Simp
(10) $\sim Ca \cdot Ua$ (8), Comm
(11) $\sim Ca$ (10), Simp
(12) $Ca \lor Na$ (6), Comm
(13) Na (12), (11), DS
(14) $Na \cdot Ua$ (13), (9), Conj
∴ (15) $(\exists x)(Nx \cdot Ux)$ (14), EG

g. $(\exists x)(Wx \cdot Px)$
    $(x)(Wx \supset Ux)$
    $(x)(Ux \supset Ix)$
∴ $(\exists x)(Px \cdot Ix)$

(1) $(\exists x)(Wx \cdot Px)$ Premise
(2) $(x)(Wx \supset Ux)$ Premise
(3) $(x)(Ux \supset Ix)$ Premise
(4) $Wa \cdot Pa$ (1), EI
(5) $Wa \supset Ua$ (2), UI
(6) $Ua \supset Ia$ (3), UI
(7) $Wa \supset Ia$ (5), (6), HS
(8) Wa (4), Simp
(9) Ia (7), (8), AA
(10) $Pa \cdot Wa$ (4), Comm
(11) Pa (10), Simp
(12) $Pa \cdot Ia$ (11), (9), Conj
∴ (13) $(\exists x)(Px \cdot Ix)$ (12), EG

j. $(x)(Hx \supset Dx)$
    $(x)(Dx \supset Sx)$
∴ $(x)(Hx \supset (Sx)$

(1) $(x)(Hx \supset Dx)$ Premise
(2) $(x)(Dx \supset Sx)$ Premise
(3) $Ha \supset Da$ (1), UI
(4) $Da \supset Sa$ (2), UI

$\quad$ (5) $Ha \supset Sa$ $\qquad$ (3), (4), HS

$\therefore$ (6) $(x)(Hx \supset Sx)$ $\qquad$ (5), UG

SELF-TEST/EXERCISES

1. By instantiation or by generalization

2. The bound variables are underlined below:
   a. $(y)(G\underline{y} \equiv Fx)$
   b. $(\exists x)(Mx \supset (y)(M\underline{y} \cdot Gx))$
   c. $(y)(\exists \underline{x})(Rx \supset (L\underline{y} \cdot Gx))$
   d. $(Gx \cdot B\underline{x}) \supset (Ga \cdot Ba)$
   e. $(Ab \cdot (\exists x)(L\underline{x})) \cdot By$

3. a. $(x)(Gx \lor Lx)$
   b. $(\exists x)(Lx \supset Mx)$
   c. $(x)\sim(\sim Cx \supset Lx)$
   d. $(\exists x)\sim(Cx \cdot Mx)$
   e. $\sim(\exists x)\sim(Lx \equiv Mx)$

4. a. $(x)(\sim Gx \cdot Px)$
   b. $(x)(Lx \cdot Px)$
   c. $(x)(Lx \cdot \sim Gx)$
   d. $(\exists x)(Lx \cdot Gx)$
   e. $(\exists x)((\sim Mx \cdot Px) \lor (Mx \cdot \sim Px))$

5. a. $(x)(Wx \cdot Px)$
   b. $(\exists x)Ax \lor Fd$
   c. $(x)(Jx \supset Rx) \cdot (x)(\sim Jx \supset \sim Rx)$
   d. $(\exists x)(Ix \cdot Cx) \cdot (\exists x)(Ix \cdot \sim Cx)$
   e. $Sd \cdot Ml$

6. Because the individual picked out by the constant instantiated to may not be the same individual picked out by the constant which occurs in the statement

7. Because an individual which is not arbitrarily chosen may not have the property attributed to it in the generalized statement.

8. Because every individual in the universe of discourse has the property attributed to all individuals by the universally quantified statement

9. a.
LA	Ma	Ra
T	T	F

   b.
La	Lb	Ma	Mb	Ra	Rb
T	T	T	F	T	T

   c.
La	Lb	Ma	Mb	Ra	Rb
F	F	T	T	F	T

   d.
La	Lb	Ma	Mb
F	T	T	T

   e.
La	Lb	Ma	Mb	Ra	Rb
T	T	F	T	T	F

10. a.
(1) $(x)(Lx \supset Gx)$	Premise
(2) $\sim(x)Gx$	Premise
(3) $(\exists x)\sim Gx$	(2), QE
(4) $\sim Ga$	(3), EI
(5) $La \supset Ga$	(1), UI
(6) $\sim La$	(5), (4), DC
$\therefore$ (7) $(\exists x)\sim Lx$	(6), EG

    b.
(1) $(x)((Lx \lor Mx) \supset Qx)$	Premise
(2) $(\exists x)(Ox \cdot Lx)$	Premise
(3) $Oa \cdot La$	(2), EI
(4) $(La \lor Ma) \supset Qa$	(1), UI
(5) Oa	(3), Simp
(6) $(\exists x)Ox$	(5), EG
(7) $La \cdot Oa$	(3), Comm
(8) La	(7), Simp

(9) $La \lor Ma$	(8), Add	
(10) Qa	(4), (9), AA	
(11) $(\exists x)Qx$	(10), EG	
$\therefore$ (12) $(\exists x)Qx \cdot (\exists x)Ox$	(11), (6), Conj	

c.
(1) $\sim(x)\sim(Cx \cdot Rx)$	Premise
(2) $(x)(Rx \supset Nx)$	Premise
(3) $(\exists x)(Cx \cdot Rx)$	(1), QE
(4) $Ca \cdot Ra$	(3), EG
(5) $Ra \supset Na$	(2), UG
(6) Ca	(4), Simp
(7) $Ra \cdot Ca$	(4), Comm
(8) Ra	(7), Simp
(9) Na	(5), (8), AA
(10) $Ca \cdot Na$	(6), (9), Conj
$\therefore$ (11) $(\exists x)(Ca \cdot Na)$	(10), EG

d.
(1) $\sim(\exists x)\sim(Cx \supset (Bx \lor Px))$	Premise
(2) $(x)((Cx \cdot Wx) \supset \sim Bx)$	Premise
(3) $(x)(Cx \supset (Bx \lor Px))$	(1), QE
(4) $Ca \supset (Ba \lor Pa)$	(3), UI
(5) $(Ca \cdot Wa) \supset \sim Ba$	(2), UI
(6) $Ca \cdot Wa$	Assumption
(7) $\sim Ba$	(5), (6), AA
(8) Ca	(6), Simp
(9) $Ba \lor Pa$	(4), (8), AA
(10) Pa	(9), (7), DS
(11) $(Ca \cdot Wa) \supset Pa$	(6) to (10), CP
(12) $(x)((Cx \cdot Wx) \supset Px)$	(11), UG
$\therefore$ (13) $\sim(\exists x)\sim((Cx \cdot Wx) \supset Px)$	(12), QE

e.
(1) $(x)(Lx \supset \sim Mx)$	Premise
(2) $(x)Lx$	Assumption
(3) $La \supset \sim Ma$	(1), UI
(4) La	(2), UI
(5) $\sim Ma$	(3), (4), AA
(6) $(x)\sim Mx$	(5), UG
$\therefore$ (7) $(x)Lx \supset (x)\sim Mx$	(2) to (6), CP

CHAPTER 8

EXERCISE 8-1

2. Statistical syllogism:

> Y percent of all A are B (where Y is greater than 50 and less than 100)
> x is A
> $\therefore$ x is B

Induction by enumeration:

> Y percent of observed A are B (where Y is equal to or greater than 0 and equal to
> $\therefore$ Y percent of all A are B or less than 100)

Modified induction by enumeration:

> Y percent of observed A are B (where Y is greater than 50 and less than or equal
> x is A to 100)
> $\therefore$ x is B

4. Argument a is the inductive argument form modified induction by enumeration. Argument b is an acceptable argument because it is *valid*. However, since b is valid, it is not inductive.

5. a. 70 percent of observed marbles in the urn are green
    x is a marble in the urn
    ∴ *x* is green

    70 percent of observed *M* are *G*
    x is *M*
    ∴ *x* is *G*

    Modified induction by enumeration

  d. In each day of the trial, new and exciting information has been brought out about the role some congressmen played in bringing about legalized gambling.
    Tomorrow is another day in the trial.
    ∴ Tomorrow new information about some congressmen and legalized gambling will be brought out.

    100 percent of observed *D* are *I*
    x is *D*
    ∴ *x* is *I*

    Modified induction by enumeration

  g. The majority of people surveyed in Our Town watched the news on channel 4.
    ∴ The majority of people in Our Town watch the news on channel 4.

    More than 50 percent of observed *P* are *W*
    ∴ More than 50 percent of all *P* are *W*

    Induction by enumeration

  j. 80 percent of the people who have cancer diagnosed in its early stages live at least five more years with proper treatment.
    My father had cancer diagnosed in its early stages.
    ∴ My father will live at least five more years with proper treatment.

    80 percent of observed *C* are *L*
    x is *C*
    ∴ *x* is *L*

    Modified induction by enumeration

  m. 7 percent of the Whazzits sampled were defective.
    ∴ 7 percent of all Whazzits are defective.

    7 percent of observed *W* are *D*
    ∴ 7 percent of all *W* are *D*

    Induction by enumeration, which gives:

    If more than 2 percent of the Whazzits are defective, the workers are going to have to do their jobs more carefully.
    More than 2 percent of the Whazzits are defective.
    ∴ The workers are going to have to do their jobs more carefully.

  p. More than half the students who graduate from our high school can't read beyond the eighth-grade level.
    Grayson's son just graduated from our high school.
    ∴ Grayson's son can't read beyond the eighth-grade level.

    More than 50 percent of all *G* are *R*
    x is *G*
    ∴ *x* is *R*
    Statistical syllogism

8. Willy Wunda has won 93 percent of all his races.
   Wunda is racing today.
   ∴ Wunda will win today's race.

   Whenever Wunda and Ridum have raced in the past, Wunda has lost.
   Wunda and Ridum are racing today.
   ∴ Wunda will lose.

EXERCISE 8-2

1. The first expresses an inductive argument, and the second expresses a deductive argument.

4. We have a case of an unrepresentative sample when the sample class turns out not to be an accurate picture of the whole class from which the sample was chosen.

6. a. Acceptable argument
   g. Acceptable argument
   m. Acceptable argument

   d. Acceptable argument
   j. Acceptable argument
   p. Acceptable argument

9. 70 percent of the people who apply to law school from C's college are accepted.
   C applied to law school.
   ∴ C will be accepted.

   The argument is acceptable, though it would have been even stronger if the information about the LSAT had been included.

11. a. Induction by enumeration
    (1) No effect
    (3) Weaken the argument

    (2) Weaken the argument
    (4) No effect

EXERCISE 8-3

1. Most of what x says about S is true
   x said P (a statement about S)
   ∴ P

4. That having the characteristics mentioned in the premises affects the likelihood that the object will also have the characteristic mentioned in the conclusion; causally relevant and statistically relevant

5. a. Most of what my father says about Raydac production schedules is true.
   My father said that a new Raydac tape deck will be on the market in time for Christmas.
   ∴ A new Raydac tape deck will be on the market in time for Christmas.

   Argument from authority; acceptable argument

   d. Lyte beer is the only beer to drink.
   ∴ You should drink Lyte beer.

   Argument from authority; unacceptable argument because the authority is making a statement outside his field of expertise

   g. One of my dates last year was from Delta house.
   Ron is from Delta house.
   My date was a real animal.
   ∴ Ron is a real animal.

   Argument from analogy; unacceptable analogy based on an insufficient number of relevant characteristics

   j. Most of what the leader of the task force investigating the Carnaby Killer says about the killer is true.
   The leader of the task force said that he is almost positive that the person in custody is the killer.
   ∴ The person in custody is the killer.

   Argument from authority; acceptable argument

m. If there is an argument here, it is an attempt at an argument from analogy and is unacceptable owing to the irrelevant analogy between slavery and marriage.

SELF-TEST/EXERCISES

1. Modified induction by enumeration is like a complex argument in which the induction by enumeration part supports the claim that Y percent of all A are B and the statistical syllogism part supports the claim that x is B.

2. Argument a is the inductive argument form induction by enumeration. Argument b is an acceptable argument because it is valid. However, since b is valid, it is not inductive.

3. See section 8:4.

4. (1) There is particular information which, if made known, would change the conclusion of the argument; (2) the person presenting the argument is aware of the information in (1) and knows that the information would change the conclusion of the argument; and (3), as a result of (1) and (2), the person presenting the argument withholds the information.

5. Misquoting or misrepresenting an authority; an authority in one field may make statements which are outside his or her field of expertise; and authorities in the same field sometimes disagree with one another.

6. a. A recent survey taken in Miami, Florida showed that the average age of the people who live there is 57.6 years.
   ∴ The average age of all people living in Florida is more than 57 years.

   Induction by enumeration; unacceptable argument, owing to an unrepresentative sample

   b. Whenever Sonic Boom has begun production of a new plane, there has been an increase in spending by the Department of Defense.
   Sonic Boom is going to begin production on a new fighter plane.
   ∴ There will be an increase in spending by the Department of Defense.

   Modified induction by enumeration; acceptable argument

   c. Most of what Trish Abramson says about business practice is true.
   Trish Abramson said that there has been a significant rise in the number of complaints her office has received about unscrupulous contractors.
   ∴ More unscrupulous contractors are in business now than in the past.

   Unacceptable argument; it would be an argument from authority if the conclusion was 'There has been a significant rise in the number of complaints her office has received about unscrupulous contractors'.

   d. Every exam for which I have kept current with reading assignments and have studied well has been an exam in which I have done well.
   This afternoon's chemistry exam is one for which I have kept current with reading assignments and have studied well.
   ∴ I will do well on this afternoon's chemistry exam.

   Modified induction by enumeration; acceptable argument

   e. Most of what Monster Mulligan says about deodorant is true.
   Monster Mulligan says that nothing stops pits like Pit Stop deodorant.
   ∴ Nothing stops pits like Pit Stop deodorant.

   Argument from authority; if Mulligan really has tried various deodorants (with the result that the first premise is true), then this is an acceptable argument.

   f. Small colleges and small businesses are similar in that they are always competing with larger businesses, trying to sell a commodity; when the cost of the commodity goes up so does the selling price; and the fewer items that are manufactured, the higher the cost for each individual item.

Small businesses are a thing of the past.
∴ Small colleges will soon be a thing of the past.

Argument from analogy; unacceptable argument due to irrelevant analogy between small businesses and small colleges

g. Each of the three times Skip Hullston has entered the Hattaras-to-Newport Race, he has won.
Hullston has entered this year's race.
∴ Hullston will win this year's race.

Modified induction by Enumeration; acceptable argument, though it would be helpful to know more about the new boat. That Gull is one of the very best designers in the business strengthens the argument by at least as much as it might be weakened by the fact that Hullston is entering a new boat.

h. Coach Dudorf has had a .908 winning record in his career as a coach.
Dudorf has just become coach at Pater Nostre.
∴ Dudorf will have as good a record at Pater Nostre.

Modified induction by enumeration; unacceptable argument due to biased statistics. The information about Dudorf is gathered from high-school football, not from football at a large university.

i. A close friend is someone who goes places with you, is reliable, and has been part of a great many happy experiences.
A good car is something that goes places with you, is reliable, and has been part of a great many happy experiences.
Whenever anyone loses a close friend, he's naturally sad.
Toland just totaled his car.
∴ Toland is sad.

Argument from analogy; unacceptable argument due to irrelevant analogy between friends and cars

j. Recent statistics have shown that the average wage of female employees is only 60% that of male employees.
My neighbor, Brenda is a female employee, and my neighbor Bob is a male employee.
∴ Brenda makes significantly less income than Bob.

Modified induction by Enumeration; this is likely an instance of biased statistics, since the incomes of people who live in the same neighborhood, and especially next door to each other, are typically fairly close.

CHAPTER 9

EXERCISE 9-1

1. Because the observational prediction is only one more instance of the generalization from which it was derived. To conclusively confirm the hypothesis, one would have to show that there were no instances which violate the hypothesis; no number of confirming instances will establish this.

4. Those hypotheses which are assigned a relatively low prior probability typically are not considered, and those which are assigned a relatively high prior probability are the ones which are singled out for further testing. The reason is that hypotheses with a very low probability are false more often then not.

7. An experiment in which we attempt to disconfirm one of two hypotheses which have equal prior probabilities. When one of the hypotheses is disconfirmed, the other is confirmed in accordance with schema 4 in section 9:2.6.

9. (In each of the following answers, the basic form of the argument is presented but no auxiliary hypotheses are given.)

   a. If it is true that all the students enrolled in Professor Wilson's logic class passed the course, then it's also true that John passed the course.
   John was enrolled in Professor Wilson's logic class.
   John passed the course.
   ∴ All the students enrolled in Professor Wilson's logic class passed the course.

   d. If it's true that all Scandinavians have blond hair, then it's also true that Ingrid has blond hair.
   Ingrid is from Norway.
   Norwegians are Scandinavians.
   Ingrid has blond hair.
   ∴ All Scandinavians have blond hair.

   g. If it's true no one with less than 20/20 vision is able to enroll in flight school, then it's also true that Fred is not able to enroll in flight school.
   Fred has 20/30 vision.
   Fred was not able to enroll in flight school.
   ∴ No one with less than 20/20 vision is able to enroll in flight school.

   j. If it's true that the earth is shaped like a sphere, then it's also true that one will lose sight of the hull before losing sight of the mast when tall-masted ships sail toward the horizon.
   When watching tall-masted ships sail toward the horizon, one loses sight of the hull before losing sight of the mast.
   ∴ The earth is shaped like a sphere.

10. a. Some student was enrolled in Professor Wilson's logic class and failed the course.
    e. The Murdocks were without electricity from 8:30 to 10:00 P.M. last Tuesday, but it was because of a faulty transformer in their service area.
    i. Brad is a member of the congregation and gave less than 10 percent of his income to the church.

11. (The following are among the alternative hypotheses which might be given.)
    a. Everyone who does passing work in Professor Wilson's class passes the course.
    e. The power line to the Murdock's house was broken during a storm.
    i. Everyone who works for the church gives 10 percent of his or her income to the church.

EXERCISE 9-2

1. Because different people sometimes have different interests in the same event, and because people want to be able to bring about or prevent a given kind of event in different ways

2. (There is more than one explanation for each case. One explanation for each case is given.)
   a. (1) The interruption by Eleanor
      (4) Don's carelessness
   b. (1) Steve's being inconsiderate

EXERCISE 9-3

1. If A is not present, then B will not occur.

4. The correct answers are c, e, and h.

5. The correct answers are b, d, and e.

6. The correct answers are b, c, e, and f.

7. (1) $\sim A$ is sufficient for $\sim D$
   (2) $\sim A \supset \sim D$
   (3) $D \supset A$
   (4) A is necessary for D

EXERCISE 9-4

1.

Case	Characteristics			Event: E
	A	B	$A \lor B$	
1	A	P	P	P
2	P	A	P	P

2. The correct answers are e, f, and j.

EXERCISE 9-5

1.

Case	Characteristics			Event: E
	A	B	$A \cdot B$	
1	A	P	A	A
2	P	A	A	A

2. The correct answers are a, c, f, h, and j.

3. The correct answer is c.

6. a. Make C_1, C_2, C_3, or C_5 occur.
   b. Prevent C_2 or C_4 from occurring.
   c. Make C_1, C_2, or C_3 occur.
   d. Make C_2 or C_3 occur.

EXERCISE 9-6

1. Because in this case we only want to know which charateristics were present when E occurred.

3. a. C_2, C_3, and $C_1 \lor C_2$
   b. C_1 and $C_3 \cdot C_4$
   c. C_1
   d. Because E did not occur in case 2
   e. $C_3 \cdot C_4$

EXERCISE 9-7

3. a. The correct answer is C_5.
   d. The correct answers are C_1, C_2, and C_5.
   g. The correct answers are C_4 and C_5.
   j. None
   m. None
   p. None
   s. None

SELF-TEST/EXERCISES

1. See section 9:2.

2. See sections 9:2.3 and 9:2.4.

3. See section 9:2.6.

4. See section 9:3.2

5. If A is not present, then B will not occur.

6. If A is present, then B will occur.

7. a. (1) A is sufficient for B
   (2) $A \supset B$
   (3) B is necessary for A

   b. (1) $\sim A$ is necessary for B
   (2) $B \supset \sim A$
   (3) $A \supset \sim B$
   (4) A is sufficient for B

   c. (1) $\sim A$ is sufficient for B
   (2) $\sim A \supset B$
   (3) $\sim B \supset A$
   (4) A is necessary for $\sim B$

   d. (1) A is necessary for $\sim B$
   (2) $\sim B \supset A$
   (3) $\sim A \supset B$
   (4) B is necessary for $\sim A$

8. See sections 9:4.1 through 9:4.3.

9. a. See section 9:5.1
   b. See section 9:6.1.
   c. See section 9:7.2.
   d. See section 9:8.1.
   e. See section 9:8.2.

10. a. The correct answers are C_2, C_3, $\sim C_4$, $C_3 \cdot C_2$, and $C_1 \vee \sim C_4$.
    b. The correct answers are C_1, C_2, and $C_3 \cdot C_2$.
    c. The correct answers are C_2 and $C_3 \cdot C_2$.
    d. The correct answers are C_2 and $C_3 \cdot C_2$.
    e. None.
    f. The correct answers are C_1, C_2, and $C_3 \cdot C_2$.
    g. None.
    h. The correct answers are C_2 and $C_3 \cdot C_2$.
    i. None
    j. The correct answers are C_2 and $C_3 \cdot C_2$.
    k. None
    l. The correct answers are C_2 and $C_3 \cdot C_2$.
    m. None
    n. The correct answers are C_2 and $C_3 \cdot C_2$.
    o. None

CHAPTER 10

EXERCISE 10-1

1. That the premises neither deductively nor inductively support the conclusion, or that at least one premise is false

7. a. Abusive argument; 'dumb jock' is abusive language.
   d. Abusive argument; it is suggested that the opponent is irresponsible.
   g. Abusive argument; 'lunatic liberals' is abusive language.
   j. "You, too" argument; the fact that the other senators have not made public the source

of their funds does not establish that the witness should not make public the source of his or her funds.

m. Circumstantial argument; the fact that Brighton may be one of the poorest students does not establish that there was no case of sexual harrassmant. Abusive argument; calling Brighton 'bubble-headed' is abusive.

EXERCISE 10-2

1. Because the argument may support a position which is irrelevant to the one under consideration

6. 'Big' and 'little' are relative terms here. What is big as a molehill can be small as a mountain; hence the speaker is not committed to saying that one and the same thing is both big and little

7. a. Equivocation; 'rage' is being used or understood in more than one way.
   d. Equivocation; 'the promised land' is being used in more than one way.
   g. Equivocation; 'one day' is being used in more than one way.
   j. Irrelevant conclusion; the boss has given reasons why an annual report is needed, and the staff has responded by saying that no one looks at the reports.
   m. Irrelevant conclusion; A has offered an argument in support of the claim that prison conditions should be improved, and B has responded by making a claim about thinking twice before one breaks the law.
   p. Equivocation; 'lightweight' and 'heavyweight' are being used in more than one way.

EXERCISE 10-3

1. They focus attention on people's attitudes or feelings and do not provide any evidence for or against the issue in question.

4. No. Our criminal justice system operates under the principle that a person is innocent until proved guilty. The attorney's remarks do not, however, prove that the client did not commit the crime he or she is charged with; rather, they are in support of the position that the client should not be *judged to be guilty* given our system of justice.

7. a. Complex question; the two issues are God's goodness and the suffering of people.
   d. Appeal to pity; the fact that the client will be unable to drive to school if his license is suspended does not show that the client is innocent of the charge against him.
   g. Complex question; the two issues are why someone is going to continue to see someone and whether the person is a sleazy, good-for-nothing bum.
   j. Appeal to force; the speaker is attempting to get the senator to vote in one way by threatening to work against him or her during the next election.
   m. Complex question; not all liberals are "flaming" and not all conservatives are "backward-thinking."
   p. Accident; in the game of football (and many other games), people sometimes get hurt. The claim that it's wrong to hurt another person applies to moral contexts, not cases in which someone happens to be injured by accident.

SELF-TEST/EXERCISES

1. That the premises neither deductively nor inductively support the conclusion, and that at least one premise is false

2. A fallacy is an invalid form of argument, but 'fallacy' is typically applied to those invalid forms of argument which seem plausible and which people often mistake for good arguments.

5. Because the argument which is given addresses an issue which is different from that under consideration

7. a. False dilemma; the first conditional premise is false.

b. Hasty generalization; the one case of something happening after one has prayed is insufficient evidence for the claim that "prayer is useful."

c. Circumstantial argument; the fact that McIntock was passed over for president does not establish that the government should subsidize Motown Motors.

d. Circumstantial argument; the fact that someone did not finish high school does not establish that someone else knows anything about the educational needs of children.

e. Accident; that we have an obligation to prevent needless suffering does not mean that we should kill people so that they won't suffer.

f. Equivocation; 'a mighty fortress' is being used in more than one way.

g. Complex question; the two issues are whether the child wants to eat dinner and whether the child wants a bedtime story. (There is also an appeal to force here.)

h. Equivocation; 'mean age' is being used in more than one way.

i. Complex question; the two issues are crying about losing a job and women being emotional. (There may also be a hasty generalization here about women being emotional.)

j. Circumstantial argument, abusive argument, and complex question; the fact that the woman is an atheist does not establish that there should be prayer in the schools, "someone like her" is probably meant to be abusive, and the two issues are religious ones and the values of the country.

k. Equivocation; 'defending ourselves' and 'improving our strike capability' are treated as being the same.

l. Hasty generalization; the one case of a sports car that needed a lot of repairs is insufficient evidence for the claim that no one should buy a sports car.

m. Equivocation; 'lady' is being used in more than one way. (There may also be a hasty generalization here that waiting worked in one case, so it will generally work.)

n. Appeal to force and complex question; the speaker has responded to the request for a retirement plan by threatening to lay off some of the employees. The two issues are a retirement plan and layoffs.

o. "You, too" argument; the fact that the shareholders drive expensive cars does not establish that the company should provide Corvettes to the younger executives.

p. Hasty generalization and complex question; the fact that two companies have not hired the person is insufficient evidence for the claim that he or she will not get a job. The two issues are whether the person will get a job and the value of an education.

q. Common cause; crime, pollution, poverty, and overcrowded conditions along with a city's being big are the result of some other common cause. Bigness does not cause these other conditions.

r. Appeal to pity; the fact that the student had a hangover does not support the position that the student should not have to take the exam. (There is also an element of a complex question, confusing the issues of being hungover and being allowed to take a makeup exam.)

s. Appeal to ignorance; the fact that no one has shown that the planet was not visited by beings from another planet does not show that it was.

t. False cause; being sexually liberal does not cause high intelligence.

INDEX

Abusive arguments, **466**–469, 499
Accident, fallacy of, **491,** 501
Addition, 184–185
Affirming the antecedent, 98–**99,** 130, 180
Affirming the consequent, 100–**101,** 130
Alternative hypotheses, **423**–424, 460
Ambiguity:
  and amphiboly, **482,** 500
  and equivocation, **479**–481, 500
  and parentheses, 142–143
  and punctuation, 141–143
Amphiboly, **482,** 500
"And":
  rule for, 136
  truth table for, 136, 147
Antecedent, **90,** 130, 175
  affirming the, 98–99, 130, 180
  denying the, **101**–102, 130
Appeal:
  to force, **497,** 501
  to ignorance, **492**–494, 501
  to the people, **494**–497, 501
  to pity, **495**–497, 501
Argument:
  abusive, **466**–469, 499
  from analogy, **407**–412, 415
    form of the argument, 408
    and relevant characteristics, 410, 416–417
  from authority, **398**–407, 415
    form of the argument, 400
  circumstantial, **469**–472, 499
  complex, **106**–111, 130, 178
  conclusion of an, **4,** 11, 43
  conditional, 98
  deductive, 54, 62, 84
  definition, 1, 3–**4,** 5, 43
  form (*see* Logical form)

Argument (*Cont.*):
  inductive, 54, 84
  invalid, **75**
  against the person, **466**–**474,** 499
  for the person, 473
  premises of an, **4,** 11, 43
  sound, 77–**79,** 86
  valid, 58, **73**–77, 85
  "you too," **472**–474, 499
Arguments:
  analysis of, 83–84, 86, 162
  and context, 6
  evaluating, 50
  good and bad, 48–50, 84
  identifying the conclusion of, 14–16
  identifying the premises of, 16–17
  recognizing, 5–10
  standard form of, 20–22, 44
  symbolizing, 64–71
  unacceptable, 465–466
Argumentum ad baculum, 497*n.*
Argumentum ad hominem, 466*n.*
Argumentum ad ignorantiam, 492*n.*
Argumentum ad misericordiam, 495*n.*
Argumentum ad populum, 494*n.*
Association, 209–211, 217
Assumptions:
  conditional proof, 114, 130
    discharging, **223**–229
  indirect proof, 122, 130, 231
    discharging, **232**
  scope of, **223**–229, 243
Auxiliary hypotheses, 421–**422,** 460

Biconditional, **139,** 175
Bottom transformation, **264**–266, 308

Bound variable, **322–324,** 370
Box transformation, **269–270,** 309

Categorical statements:
  affirmative, **250,** 308
  contradictions and, 266–269, 308
  forms of, **247–250,** 308
  interpreting, 251–252, 308
  negative, **250,** 308
  in ordinary language, 253–260
  particular, **250,** 307
    affirmative, **250,** 257–258
    negative, **250,** 258
  quality of, **250,** 307
  quantity of, **250,** 307
  relationships among, 261–270
  symbolizing in predicate logic, 331–333, 370
  term in, 246–247, 271, 309
  universal, **250,** 307
    affirmative, **250,** 253–255
    negative, **250,** 255–256
  Venn diagrams of, **278–**281, 309
Categorical syllogisms:
  characteristics of, **270–**271, 309
  determining validity using rules, 297–304, 309–310
    using Venn diagrams, 287–295, 309
  eliminating extra terms, 272–277, 309
Causal chain, **428,** 460
Causal implication, 138
Causal relationship, 17, 44
Causal relevance, **410,** 416, 427
Causality, 487–494
Cause:
  proximate, **428,** 460
  remote, **428,** 460
Characteristics, 429, 460
  complex, **434–**436, 460
  conjunctive, **436,** 442
  disjunctive, **436,** 442
  negative, **435,** 442, 445
  simple, **434–**437
Circumstantial arguments, **469–**472, 499
Claim, unsupported, **11,** 43
Class, 248
  complement of a, **248,** 262, 307
  exclusion from a, **248,** 307
  inclusion in a, **248,** 307
Common cause, fallacy of, **490–**491, 500
Commutation, 201–202, 217
Compatibility of hypotheses, 423, 460
Complement of a class, **248,** 262, 307
Complex arguments, **106–**111, 130, 178

Complex characteristics, **434–**436, 460
Complex questions, **485–**487, 500
Compound statements, **67–**69, 85
  with more than one connective, 141–143
  symbolizing, 144
  truth-functional, 134
  truth value of, 146–150
Conclusion:
  of arguments, **4,** 11, 43
  indicators for a, 15–16, 43
  irrelevant, **476–**479, 500
Conditional arguments, 98
Conditional proof, **113–119,** 130, 222–229, 243
  assumptions, 114, 130
  general form of, 115–117
  as part of indirect proof, 125
Conditional statements, 12, 43, **89,** 129, 175
  standard form of, 90, **93,** 130
Conditions:
  and causes, 429, 460
  initial, **421,** 459
  necessary, 95*n.,* 427, **429,** 460
    testing for, 437–442
  necessary and sufficient, **430,** 454
    testing for, 454–458
  sufficient, 427–**430,** 460
    testing for, 443–447, 449–454
Conjunct, 136, 175
Conjunction, **136,** 175, 182–183
Conjunctive characteristics, **436,** 442
Connective, 91
  main, **142–**143, 149, 162, 175
  truth-functional, **135,** 175
Consequent, **90,** 130, 175
  affirming the, 100–**101,** 130
  denying the, 99–**100,** 125, 130, 180
Constants:
  individual, **317–**318, 369
  predicate, **254,** 308
  statement, **65–**66, 74, 85
Constructive dilemma, 183–184
Context of arguments, 6
Contingent statements, **156–157,** 176
Contradictions, 121, 131, **156,** 176
  and categorical statements, 266–269, 308
  and indirect proof, 120–123, 230–231
Contraposition, 95–96, 207, 217
Contrapositive, **95,** 130, 157
Converse, **96–**97, 130, 269*n.*
Counterexamples, **80–82,** 86
  and logical form, 81
Crosshatching, 279, 309
Crucial experiments, **425,** 460

Decision making, 2
Decision procedure, **178**–179, 242, 314
Declarative sentences, 29
Deduction, natural, 179, 242
Deductive argument, 54, 62, 84
Deductive logic, **54**, 84
Deductive support, 53, **58**–**62**, 85, 162
   characteristics of, 374, 387
De Morgan's Law, 203–207, 217
Denying the antecedent, **101**–**102**, 130
Denying the consequent, 99–**100**, 125, 130, 180
   as part of indirect proof, 125
Diagonal transformation, **268**–269, 308
Direct method of agreement, **437**–**442**, 461
Disagreements, 33–41
   in appraisal, **38**–39, 44
   factual, **34**–36, 44
   resolving, 40–41, 45
   in taste, **39**–40, 44
   verbal, **36**–37, 44
Disjunct, 137, 175
Disjunction, **137**, 175
Disjunctive characteristics, **436**, 442
Disjunctive syllogism, 180–182
Distribution:
   and Rule of Replacement, 211–212, 217
   of terms, **301**, 310
Dot, 136
Double method of agreement, **455**–**456**, 461
Double negation, 92, 130, 157, **202**–203, 217

Emotions, 32
Empty set of premises, **238**, 243
End term, **271**, 309
Enthymeme, **8**, 13, 43
Equivalency:
   logical, 92, 130, 140, **157**–159, 175
   material, **139**–140, 157, 175
   and the Rule of Replacement, 214–217
Equivocation, **479**–481, 500
Evidence, suppressed, 393–395, 415
Exceptive statements, **258**–260, 308
Exclamatory sentences, 30
Exclusion from a class, **248**, 307
Exclusive statements, 258–**259**, 308
Existential generalization, **342**–**344**, 371
   statement of the rule, 342
Existential import, 252*n.*
Existential instantiation, **345**–349, 371
   statement of the rule, 346
Existential quantifier, **322**, 353, 370–371
Explanatory power of hypotheses, 423–424,
   460
Exportation, 212–214, 217

Fallacy, 465–**466**, 499
   formal, 466
   informal, 466
False cause, **488**–490, 500
False dilemma, **484**–486, 500
Form (*see* Logical form)
Free variable, **322**–**324**, 370

General statement, 320
Generalization:
   existential, **342**–**344**, 371
   hasty, **491**–492, 501
   universal, **349**–354, 371
Generalizations:
   statistical, 420
   universal, 420

Hasty generalization, **491**–492, 501
Hypotheses, 418, **420**, 459
   alternative, **423**–424, 460
   auxiliary, **421**–**422**, 460
   compatibility of, 423, 460
   explanatory power of, 423–424, 460
   predictive power of, 423, 460
   and simplicity, 423, 460
Hypothetical syllogism, 183
Hypothetico-deductive method, 420–425, 459

"If, and only if":
   rule for, 130
   truth table for, 140, 147
"If-then":
   rule for, 137
   truth table for, 138, 147
Ignoratio elenchi, 476*n.*
Imperative sentences, 30
Implication:
   causal, 138
   material, **138**, 157, 175
   as a rule of inference, 207–208, 217
Inclusion in a class, **248**, 307
Indicator words, **15**, 43
   for conclusions, 15–16, 43
   for premises, 16, 43
Indirect proof, **121**–**127**, 130, 230–236, 243
   assumptions, 122, 130, 231
   and contradictions, 120–123, 230–231
   and denying the consequent, 99–100, 125,
      130, 180
   structure of, 122–125
Individual constants, **317**–318, 369
Individual term, **316**–317, 369

Individual variables, **318,** 321, 370
Induction by enumeration, 375−**377,** 414, 418
 form of the argument, 377
Inductive argument, 54, 84
Inductive logic, **54,** 84
Inductive support, **53−58,** 62, 85, 374, 387
Inference (*see* Rules of inference)
Initial conditions, **421,** 459
Instantiation, **320,** 370
 existential, **345−349,** 371
 universal, **339−342,** 370−371
Insufficient evidence, **389−391,** 415
Interrogative sentences, 29
Invalidity, **75−76,** 85
 of arguments in predicate logic, 354−359,
  371
 showing by counterexamples, 80−82
Inverse method of agreement, **443−447,** 461
Inverted form, **90,** 130
Irrelevant conclusion, **476−479,** 500

Joint method of agreement and difference,
 457−458, 461
Justification in a proof, **188,** 243

Logic, **1,** 43
 deductive, **54,** 84
 inductive, **54,** 84
 predicate, 314
 quantificational, 314
Logic equivalency, 92, 130, 140, **157−159,** 175
 and the Rule of Replacement, 199
Logical form:
 of arguments, 74, 76, 85
 counterexamples and, 81
 valid, **75,** 85, 162
Logically false statements, **121−125,** 131
Logically true statements (*see* Tautology)

Main connective, **142−**143, 149, 162, 175
Material equivalency, **139−140,** 157, 175
Material implication, **138,** 157, 175
Mention of words or expressions, **26−28,** 44
Method of difference, **449−454,** 461
Middle term, **271,** 300, 309
Modified induction by enumeration, 380−**382,**
 414
 form of the argument, 382

Narrative, **14,** 43
Natural deduction, **179,** 242

Necessary conditions, 95*n.*, 427, **429,** 460
 testing for, 437−442
Necessary and sufficient conditions, **430,** 454
 testing for, 454−458
Negation, **91,** 130
 double, 92, 130, 157, **202−203,** 217
Negative characteristics, **435,** 442, 445
"Neither-nor," 203
"Not":
 as a connective, 91−93
 rule for, 135
 truth table for, 136, 147

Observational predictions, **418−419,** 459
Obversion, 263*n.*, 264*n.*
"Only if," 94−95, 130
Open sentences, **318,** 320, 322−324, 370
"Or":
 exclusive, 137
 inclusive, 137, 203
 rule for, 137
 truth table for, 137, 147

Parentheses, 142−143, 175
Particular affirmative statements, **250,**
 257−258, 281
Particular negative statements, **250,** 258, 281
Post hoc fallacy, 489, 500
Predicate constants, **254,** 308
Predicate logic, 314
 proof in, 360−366
Predicate term, **247,** 271, 316, 369
Predicate variables, **254,** 308
Prediction, 418
 confirming instance of, 419, 459
 disconfirming instance of, 419, 459
 observational, **418−419,** 459
Predictive power of hypotheses, 423, 460
Premise:
 of an argument, **4,** 11, 43
 indicators for a, 16, 43
Presence table, **435,** 461
Principle of charity, **9,** 43, 467
Prior probability, **422−423,** 460
"Probably" as a relational expression,
 385−387, 414−415
Problem solving, 2
Proof, 105, **188,** 243
 conditional, **113−119,** 125, 130, 222−229, 243
 indirect, **121−127,** 130, 230−236, 243
 in predicate logic, 360−366
 rules of inference and, 188−194
 strategy, 194

Proper names, 255
Proximate cause, **428,** 460
Punctuation, ambiguity and, 141–143

Quality of categorical statements, **250,** 307
Quantificational logic, 314
Quantifier:
    existential, **322,** 353, 370–371
    scope of a, **323,** 370
    universal, **321,** 355, 370–371
Quantifier exchange, 327–**330,** 370
    statement of rule, 330
Quantity of categorical statements, **250,** 307
Question, complex, **485**–487, 500
Quotation marks, 26–28
    double, 28
    single, 26

Reasoning, 2–3
Reductio ad absurdum (*see* Indirect proof)
Relational expression, 341*n.*
Relationship:
    causal, 17, 44
    support, 49, **53**–**62,** 75, **83**–**84,** 159
    temporal, 17, 44
Relative terms, **481,** 500
Relevance, statistical, 410–**411,** 416, 427
Remote cause, **428,** 460
Repetition, 208–209, 217
Rule of Replacement, **198**–**201,** 243
    distribution and, 211–212, 217
    limiting the rule, 201
    and logical equivalency, 214–217
    redundancy, 213–214
    statement of the rule, 199
Rules of inference, **179**–180, 242–243
    application of, 185–186
    implication as a rule, 207–208, 217
    and proofs, 188–194
Rules for validity of categorical syllogisms,
    297–304, 309–310

Scare quotes, **28**
Scope:
    of an assumption, **223**–229, 243
    of a quantifier, **323,** 370
Sentences:
    declarative, 29
    exclamatory, 30
    imperative, 30
    interrogative, 29
    open, **318,** 320, 322–324, 370

Short truth tables, 167–174, 176
Simple characteristics, **434**
    conjunction of, 436
    disjunction of, 437
    negation of, 435
Simple statements, **67**–69, 85, 134
Simplicity of hypotheses, 423, 460
Simplification, 182
Singular statements, **315**–317, 369
Sound arguments, 77–**79,** 86
    compared with valid, 77–79
Standard conditional-statement form, 90, **93,**
    130
Standard form:
    of arguments, **20**–22, 44
    of conditional statements, 9, **93,** 130
Statement constants, **65**–66, 74, 85
Statement variables, **66**–67, 74, 85, 314
Statements, 4, **6,** 29–32, 43, 44
    categorical (*see* Categorical statements)
    compound, **67**–69, 85, 134, 141–144
    conditional, 12, 43, **89,** 90, **93,** 129, 130,
        175
    contingent, **156**–**157,** 176
    contradictory, 121, 131, **156,** 176
    exceptive, **258**–**260,** 308
    exclusive, 258–**259,** 308
    logically equivalent, 92, 130, 140, **157**–159,
        175
    logically false, **121**–125, 131
    logically true (*see* Tautology)
    particular affirmative, **250,** 257–258
    particular negative, **250,** 258
    simple, **67**–69, 85, 134
    singular, **315**–317, 369
    truth-functional, 89, **134,** 317
    universal affirmative, **250,** 253, 255
    universal negative, **250,** 255–256
Statistical generalizations, 420
Statistical relevance, 410–**411,** 416, 427
Statistical syllogism, 378–**380,** 414
    form of the argument, 380
Strength of inductive support, 57–58
Subject term, **247,** 271
Substitution instance, **320,** 350, 370
Sufficient conditions, 427–**430,** 460
    testing for: in general, 443–447
        in a particular case, 449–454
Support:
    deductive, 53, **58**–**62,** 85, 162, 374, 387
    inductive, **53**–**58,** 62, 85, 374, 387
    between premises and conclusion, 50–53,
        83
Support relationship, 49, 75, **83**–**84,** 159
    deductive, **58**–**62**

Support relationship *(Cont.)*:
inductive, **53**−58
Suppressed evidence, 393−395, 415
conditions for, **394**, 415
Syllogisms:
disjunctive, 180−182
hypothetical, 183
statistical, 378−**380**, 414
(See also Categorical syllogisms)
Symbolizing arguments, 64−71

Tautology, **156**−157, 176, 237, 243
and associated conditional statement, 239
deriving, 237−242
valid arguments and, 160−163
Temporal relationship, 17, 44
Term:
in a categorical statement, 246−247, 271,
309
distributed, **301**, 310
end, **271**, 309
individual, **316**−317, 369
middle, **271**, 300, 309
predicate, **247**, 271, 316, 369
relative, **481**, 500
subject, **247**, 271
Tilde, 91
Top transformation, **263**−264, 308
Transformations:
bottom, **264**−266, 308
box, **269**−270, 309
diagonal, **268**−269, 308
top, **263**−264, 308
Triple bar, 140
Truth of premises and conclusion, 50−53, 83
Truth-functional connective, **135**, 175
Truth-functional statement, 89, **134**, 317
Truth table test for validity, 163−166
Truth tables, **135**, 150−155, 175
assigning truth values to variables, 151−152
number of lines, 151, 175
short, 167−174, 176
Truth value, **10**, 43, 50−53, 84
of compound statements, 146−150
Tu quoque argument, 472n.

Universal affirmative statements, **250**,
253−255, 278−280
Universal generalizations, 349−354, 371, 420
statement of rule, 350
Universal instantiation, **339**−342, 370−371
statement of rule, 340
Universal negative statements, **250**, 255−256,
280−281
Universal quantifier, **321**, 355, 370−371
Universe of discourse, 325−**326**, 370
"Unless," 93−94, 130
Unrepresentative sample, **391**−393, 415
Unsupported claim, **11**, 43
Use of words or expressions, **26**−28, 44

Valid arguments, 58, **73**−77, 85
compared with sound, 77−79
and tautologies, 160−163
Validity, 159
and form, 162
truth table test for, 163−166
Venn diagrams to determine, 287−295, 309
Variables, 146
free and bound, **322**−324, 370
individual, **318**, 321, 370
predicate, **254**, 308
statement, **66**−67, 74, 85, 314
Venn diagrams:
of categorical statements, 278−**281**, 309
conclusion diagram, 286−287
to determine validity, 287−295, 309
particular affirmative statements, 281
particular negative statements, 281
premises diagram, 282−286, 309
universal affirmative statements, 278−280
universal negative statements, 280−281

Wedge, 137
Words:
mention of, 26−28, 44
use of, 26−28, 44

"You, too" arguments, **472**−474, 499

Forms of Categorical Statements and their Venn Diagrams

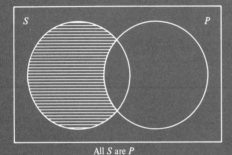

All *S* are *P*

No *S* are *P*

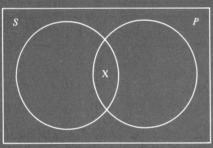

Some *S* are *P*

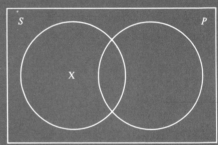

Some *S* are not *P*

Term Elimination

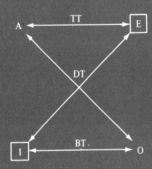

Top and Bottom Transformations:
  (1) Change the quality of the original statement to its opposite.
  (2) Replace the predicate term of the original statement with its class complement.

Box Transformation (*E*-Form and *I*-Form Statements Only):
  Interchange the subject term and the predicate term.

Diagonal Transformation:
  (1) Change the form of the original statement to the form opposite it on the diagonal.
  (2) Remove the negation sign.